KT-527-687

'[Dimbleby] skilfully tracks the shifts and turns of the campaign . . . a riveting account' Tony Rennell, *Daily Mail*, Book of the Week

'[An] encyclopedic new account . . . a vivid, meticulous tapestry, densely weaving the threads of German and Soviet military strategy, political calculation from Washington and London to Moscow, and war's pitiless human cost' Julian Evans, *Daily Telegraph*

'Brings to life the sheer staggering scale of these events with great skill, care and attention to detail' Keith Lowe, *Sunday Times*

'Dimbleby tells the story of strategic miscalculation and (self-)deception on all sides, and then of Hitler's "war of extermination", magnificently' Allan Mallinson, *Spectator*

'Jonathan Dimbleby's masterly account of the most monumental conflict in human history is an impressive achievement. This is a fast-paced, gripping read, but it is the wealth of eyewitness evidence detailing the unspeakable horror and hardship, the apocalyptic scenes and sheer savagery of Barbarossa that leaves the most lasting impression' Julia Boyd, author of *Travellers in the Third Reich*

'A masterful account of maybe the biggest event ever . . . essential' Lee Child

'Like a fast-moving juggernaut of horror, Dimbleby's *Barbarossa* is a page-turning descent into Hell and back . . . This fresh and compelling account of Hitler's failed invasion of the Soviet Union should be on everyone's reading list for 2021' Amanda Foreman, author of *A World on Fire*

'A brilliant account of the decisive land battle of the decisive land campaign of the Second World War, an epic in the story of industrialized land warfare . . . This is a wonderful piece of history, fresh with up-to-date details, new sources and novel insights' Robert Fox

'A chilling account of war at its worst' Bear Grylls

'Superb. Jonathan Dimbleby has produced an epic, compelling and powerfully written account of what was unquestionably the defining campaign of the Second World War. Full of fresh insights and vivid details, *Barbarossa* is a book of huge importance, and one that stays with you long after you have finished' Henry Hemming, bestselling author of *Our Man in New York*

'Jonathan Dimbleby's thought-provoking and elegantly written study of Operation Barbarossa describes in compelling detail how Nazi Germany, despite its earlier military triumphs, had lost this war already by the end of 1941. This book is a captivating eye-opener' Gerhard Hirschfeld, University of Stuttgart, former President of the International Committee for the Study of the Second World War

'Jonathan Dimbleby's analysis of this monumental struggle is masterly, not least by his use of unpublished Russian sources' General Sir Mike Jackson

'A great read. Dimbleby gives an excellent account of the relationships between the leaders and, thanks to a wide range of sources, an authentic sense of the military experience . . . he brings Barbarossa very vividly to life, as if you were there' Robert Kershaw, author of *War Without Garlands: Operation Barbarossa 1941–1942* and *Borodino Field 1812 and 1941*

'Jonathan Dimbleby rightly identifies the last six months of 1941 – following Hitler's invasion of the Soviet Union – as the fulcrum on which the history of twentieth-century Europe turns. It's a vital story, one everyone should know, and Dimbleby tells it with verve and elan' Laurence Rees, author of *Hitler and Stalin*

'With his customary literary flair and capacity to master and mobilize very many and varied sources, Jonathan Dimbleby gives us the best single-volume account of the Barbarossa campaign to date' Andrew Roberts, author of *Churchill: Walking with Destiny*

'After *The Battle of the Atlantic* comes another vivid and engrossing tableau from a master of military and high-political narrative' Brendan Simms, author of *Hitler: Only the World Was Enough*

'Jonathan Dimbleby's epic account captures all the drama and magnitude of an event that determined not just the outcome of the War, but the future of the world' Martin Sixsmith

'Expertly narrated and written with piercing (and often horrifying) clarity, this monumental work of popular history leaves no doubt that the holocaust of the Jews and the deliberate starvation and slaughter of many millions of Russian civilians were part of the Nazi plan from the outset' Frederick Taylor, author of *1939: A People's History*

ABOUT THE AUTHOR

Jonathan Dimbleby's previous books include the highly acclaimed Second World War histories *The Battle of the Atlantic* and *Destiny in the Desert: The Road to El Alamein*, which was shortlisted for the Hessell-Tiltman Prize and was followed by his BBC Two programme *Churchill's Desert War*. His other books include *Russia: A Journey to the Heart of a Land and Its People*, *Richard Dimbleby: A Biography*, *The Palestinians*, *The Prince of Wales: A Biography* and *The Last Governor: Chris Patten and the Handover of Hong Kong*.

Barbarossa

How Hitler Lost the War

JONATHAN DIMBLEBY

PENGUIN BOOKS

PENGUIN BOOKS

UK | USA | Canada | Ireland | Australia
India | New Zealand | South Africa

Penguin Books is part of the Penguin Random House group of companies
whose addresses can be found at global.penguinrandomhouse.com.

First published by Viking 2021
Published in Penguin Books 2022
003

Copyright © Jonathan Dimbleby, 2021

The moral right of the author has been asserted

The List of Illustrations on pp. ix–xi constitutes an extension of this copyright page

Typeset by Jouve (UK), Milton Keynes
Printed and bound in Great Britain by Clays Ltd, Elcograf S.p.A.

The authorized representative in the EEA is Penguin Random House Ireland,
Morrison Chambers, 32 Nassau Street, Dublin D02 YH68

A CIP catalogue record for this book is available from the British Library

ISBN: 978–0–241–97919–8

For my grandchildren
Barnaby, Chloe, Max and Arthur

Contents

Illustrations

Maps

Europe, June 1941

Norwegian Sea

ICELAND
• Reykjavík

North Sea

Atlantic
Ocean

NORWAY
Oslo •

SWEDEN
Stockholm •

DENMARK
Copenhagen •

Belfast •
Dublin •
IRELAND

UNITED
KINGDOM

London •

NETHERLANDS
Amsterdam •
Brussels •
BELGIUM
LUXEMBOURG

Danzig •

Berlin •

GERMANY

Prague •
CZECHOSLOVAKIA
Bratislava •

Paris •

Bern •
SWITZERLAND

Vienna •
AUSTRIA

YUGOSLAVIA

FRANCE

ITALY

PORTUGAL
Lisbon •

Madrid •
SPAIN

Rome •

Salerno •

SICILY

Algiers •

Mediterranean Sea

Tunis •

MOROCCO
(SP.)
Rabat •

TUNISIA
(FR.)

Tripoli •

MOROCCO
(FR.)

ALGERIA
(FR.)

LIBYA (IT.)

Axis-controlled
Soviet-controlled
Molotov–Ribbentrop Line

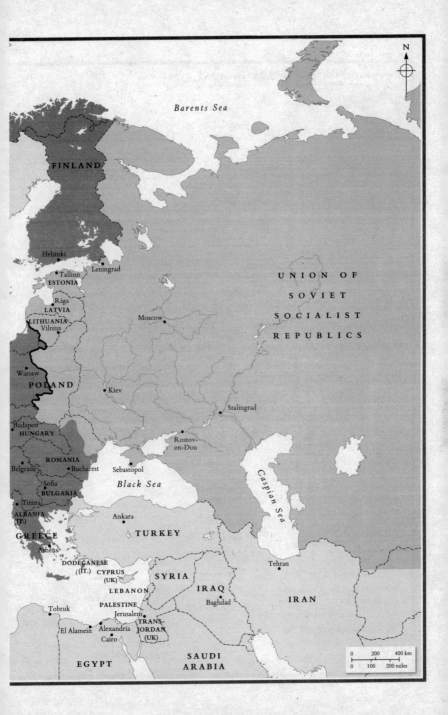

Europe after the Molotov–Ribbentrop Pact, 1939

Norwegian Sea

ICELAND
• Reykjavík

NORWAY
• Oslo

North Sea

DENMARK
Copenhagen •

Atlantic Ocean

Belfast •
Dublin •
IRELAND

UNITED KINGDOM

London •

NETHERLANDS

Amsterdam •

Brussels •
BELGIUM

Paris •   LUXEMBOURG

FRANCE

Berlin •

GERMANY

Prague •

AUSTRIA

Bern •
SWITZERLAND

ITALY

• Rome

Salerno •

PORTUGAL

Lisbon •

Madrid •

SPAIN

SICILY

Algiers •

Tunis •
TUNISIA
(FR.)

• Tripoli

MOROCCO
(SP.)

Rabat •

MOROCCO
(FR.)

ALGERIA
(FR.)

FRENCH
WEST AFRICA

German and Axis-controlled before Pact

USSR-controlled before Pact

German-occupied after Pact

Soviet-occupied after Pact

—— Molotov–Ribbentrop line

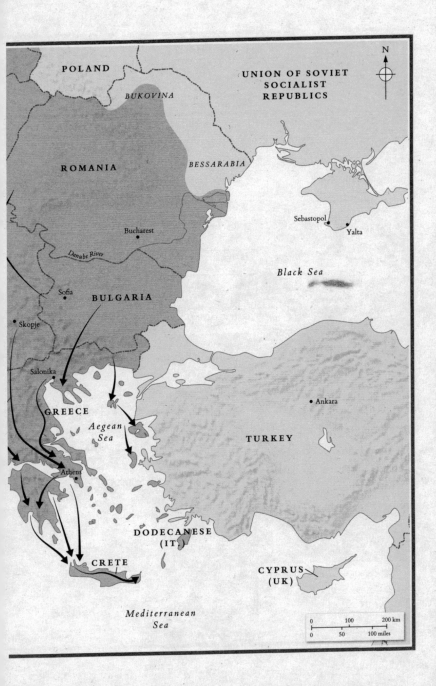

The Eastern Front, 22 June–9 July 1941

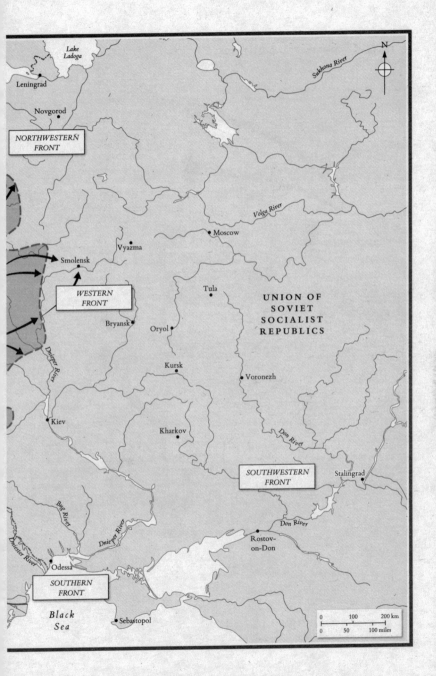

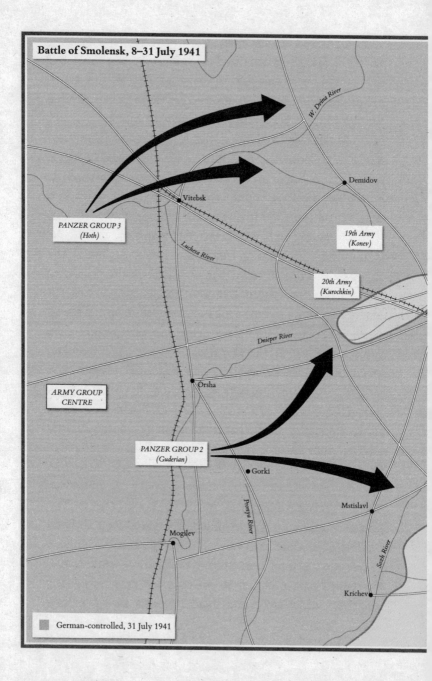

Battle of Smolensk, 8–31 July 1941

W. Dvina River

Demidov

PANZER GROUP 3
(Hoth)

Vitebsk

Luchesa River

19th Army
(Konev)

20th Army
(Kurochkin)

Dnieper River

ARMY GROUP
CENTRE

Orsha

PANZER GROUP 2
(Guderian)

Gorki

Pronya River

Mstislavl

Sozh River

Mogilev

Krichev

German-controlled, 31 July 1941

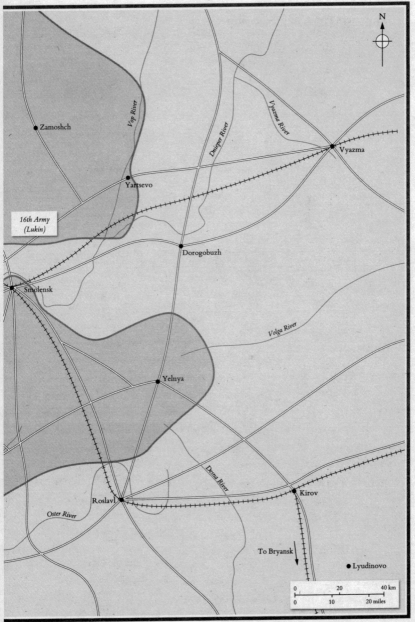

The Eastern Front, July–September 1941

Helsinki

SWEDEN

Stockholm

ESTONIA

Tallinn

LATVIA

Riga

Dvina River

LITHUANIA

Kaunas

Vilnius

Minsk

EAST PRUSSIA

Danzig

Niemen River

Białystok

Berlin

Vistula River

Bug River

Warsaw

Brest-Litovsk

Pripet Marshes

GERMANY

Oder River

POLAND

Dubno

Prague

CZECHOSLOVAKIA

Lvov

Bratislava

Vienna

AUSTRIA

Budapest

HUNGARY

ROMANIA

Belgrade

Bucharest

YUGOSLAVIA

To 9 July
To 1 September
To 9 September

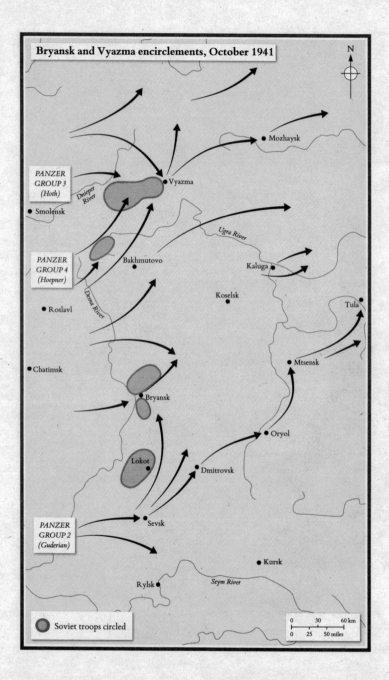

Bryansk and Vyazma encirclements, October 1941

N

PANZER
GROUP 3
(Hoth)

Dnieper
River

Smolensk

PANZER
GROUP 4
(Hoepner)

Desna River

Roslavl

Chatimsk

Bakhmutovo

Vyazma

Mozhaysk

Ugra River

Kaluga

Koselsk

Tula

Bryansk

Lokot

Mtsensk

Dmitrovsk

Oryol

PANZER
GROUP 2
(Guderian)

Sevsk

Kursk

Rylsk

Seym River

Soviet troops circled

0   30   60 km
0   25   50 miles

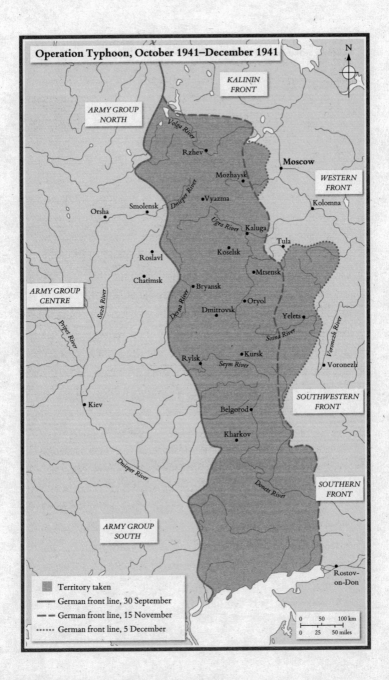

Operation Typhoon, October 1941–December 1941

N

KALININ FRONT

ARMY GROUP NORTH

Volga River

Rzhev

Moscow

Mozhaysk

Dnieper River

Vyazma

WESTERN FRONT

Orsha

Smolensk

Kolomna

Ugra River

Kaluga

Koselsk

Tula

Roslavl

Mtsensk

Chatimsk

ARMY GROUP CENTRE

Bryansk

Oryol

Desna River

Dmitrovsk

Yelets

Sosna River

Pripet River

Sozh River

Voronezh River

Rylsk

Kursk

Seym River

Voronezh

Kiev

SOUTHWESTERN FRONT

Belgorod

Kharkov

Dnieper River

SOUTHERN FRONT

ARMY GROUP SOUTH

Donets River

Rostov-on-Don

Territory taken

German front line, 30 September

German front line, 15 November

German front line, 5 December

| 0 | 50 | 100 km |
| 0 | 25 | 50 miles |

German advance on Moscow, June–December 1941

SWEDEN

Stockholm

Helsinki

Tallinn

ESTONIA

Riga

LATVIA

Dvina River

LITHUANIA

Kaunas

Vilnius

Minsk

EAST
PRUSSIA

Danzig

Niemen River

Białystok

Berlin

Vistula River

Bug River

Warsaw

Brest-Litovsk

*Pripet
Marshes*

GERMANY

Oder River

POLAND

Dubno

Prague

CZECHOSLOVAKIA

Lvov

Bratislava

Vienna

AUSTRIA

Budapest

HUNGARY

ROMANIA

Belgrade

Bucharest

YUGOSLAVIA

German-occupied, 9 July
German-occupied, 9 September
German-occupied, 5 December

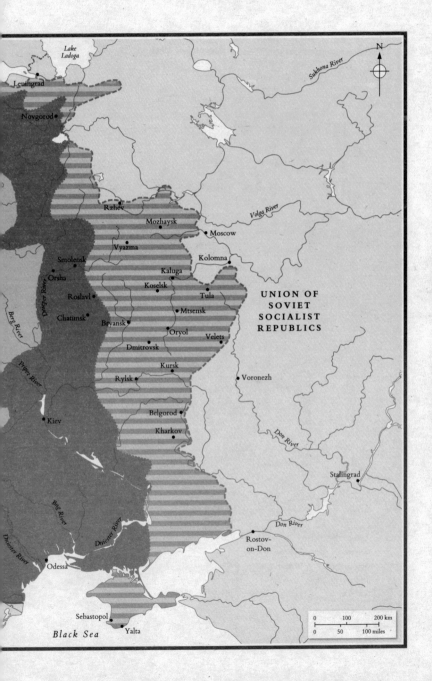

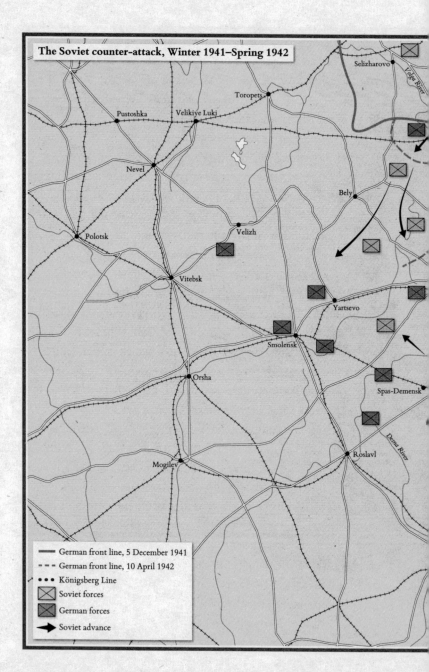

The Soviet counter-attack, Winter 1941–Spring 1942

Selizharovo
Toropets
Pustoshka
Velikiye Luki
Nevel
Bely
Polotsk
Velizh
Vitebsk
Yartsevo
Smolensk
Orsha
Spas-Demensk
Mogilev
Roslavl
Volga River
Desna River

- ———— German front line, 5 December 1941
- – – – German front line, 10 April 1942
- • • • Königsberg Line
- ⊠ Soviet forces
- ⊠ German forces
- → Soviet advance

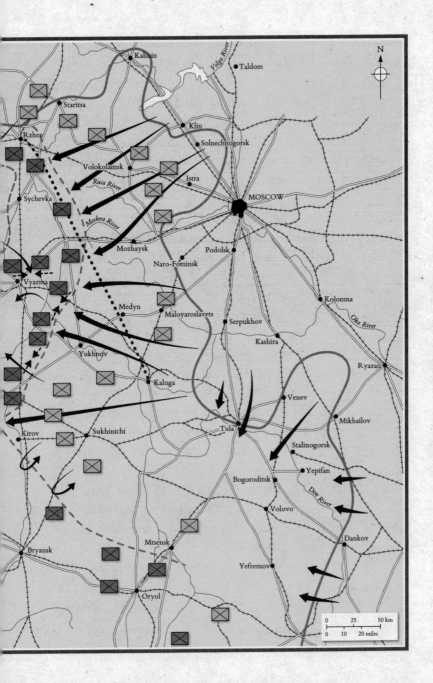

The Soviet counter-attack, Winter 1941–Spring 1942

SWEDEN

Stockholm

Lake
Ladoga

Leningrad

Tallinn

ESTONIA

Novgorod

ARMY GROUP NORTH
(Leeb)

Riga

LATVIA

Dvina River

LITHUANIA

Kaunas

ARMY GROUP CENTRE
(Bock)

Smolensk

Vilnius

Danzig

EAST
PRUSSIA

Niemen River

Minsk

Dnieper River

Białystok

Bug River

Vistula River

Warsaw

Brest-Litovsk

Pripet River

Pripet
Marshes

Oder River

POLAND

Bug River

Dubno

Kiev

CZECHOSLOVAKIA

Lvov

ARMY GROUP SOUTH
(Bock)

Bratislava

Budapest

Dniester River

Bug River

HUNGARY

Odessa

--- Spring 1942
.... Winter 1941
——— 22 June 1941
▨ Soviet gains Winter 1941–Spring 1942

ROMANIA

Black
Sea

Bucharest

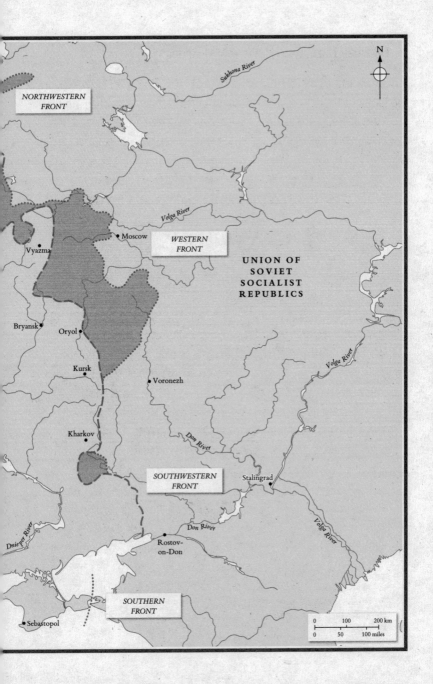

Operation Torch, 1942

FRANCE

Atlantic Ocean

PORTUGAL

SPAIN

Madrid

Lisbon

EASTERN TASK FORCE (Allied forces) Nov 1942

CENTRAL TASK FORCE (US forces) Nov 1942

WESTERN TASK FORCE (US forces) Nov 1942

Gibraltar

Algiers

Oran

MOROCCO (SP.)

Rabat

Fez

Casablanca

Safi

MOROCCO (FR.)

ALGERIA (FR.)

→ Allied advance
⇢ German advance
✳ Allied victory
✷ German victory

Massacres and death camps, 1941–2

North Sea

NORWAY
Oslo

SWEDEN
Stockholm

DENMARK
Copenhagen

NETHERLANDS
Amsterdam

Danzig

Berlin

GERMANY

Warsaw

Chełmno

POLAND

Auschwitz-Birkenau

Brussels

BELGIUM

LUXEMBOURG

Prague

CZECHOSLOVAKIA

FRANCE

Bern

SWITZERLAND

Vienna

Bratislava

AUSTRIA

Budapest

HUNGARY

ITALY

YUGOSLAVIA

Belgrade

Sarajevo

○ Einsatzgruppen massacres
□ Death camps

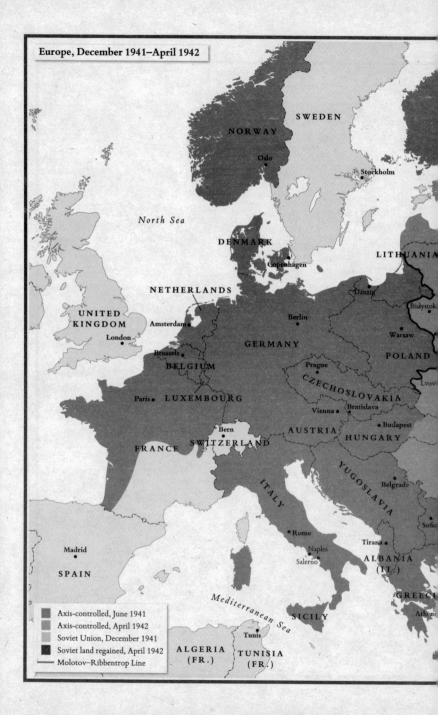

Europe, December 1941–April 1942

SWEDEN
NORWAY
Oslo
Stockholm

North Sea

DENMARK
Copenhagen

LITHUANIA

NETHERLANDS
Danzig
Białystok

UNITED
KINGDOM
Amsterdam
Berlin
Warsaw

London
Brussels
GERMANY
POLAND

BELGIUM
Prague
Lvov

CZECHOSLOVAKIA

Paris
LUXEMBOURG
Vienna
Bratislava

Bern
AUSTRIA
Budapest

FRANCE
SWITZERLAND
HUNGARY

ITALY
YUGOSLAVIA
Belgrade

Madrid
Rome
Sofia
Tirana

Naples
ALBANIA
Salerno
(IT.)

SPAIN
GREECE

Mediterranean Sea
SICILY
Athens

Tunis

ALGERIA
TUNISIA
(FR.)
(FR.)

Axis-controlled, June 1941
Axis-controlled, April 1942
Soviet Union, December 1941
Soviet land regained, April 1942
Molotov–Ribbentrop Line

N

FINLAND

Helsinki
Tallinn
ESTONIA
Riga
LATVIA
Vilnius
Kaunas
Minsk
Brest-
Litovsk
Dubno
Kiev

Leningrad

UNION OF
SOVIET
SOCIALIST
REPUBLICS

Rzhev
Mozhaysk
Moscow
Vyazma
Kolomna
Orsha
Kaluga
Smolensk
Roslavl
Koselsk
Tula
Chatimsk
Mtsensk
Bryansk
Oryol
Velets
Dmitrovsk
Rylsk
Kursk
Voronezh
Belgorod
Kharkov
Stalingrad

Rostov-
on-Don
Odessa
ROMANIA
Sebastopol
Bucharest
BULGARIA

Black Sea

Caspian Sea

Ankara
TURKEY

DODECANESE
(IT.)
CYPRUS
(UK)
SYRIA
IRAQ

0   100   200 km
0   50   100 miles

Preface

Hitler's invasion of the Soviet Union on 22 June 1941 was the biggest, bloodiest and most barbarous military enterprise in the history of warfare. The specific purpose of Operation Barbarossa, as the Führer codenamed this cataclysmic venture, was also the most decisive campaign of the Second World War. Had Hitler achieved its objective – the annihilation of the Soviet Union – he would have been the master of Europe's destiny. As it was, by the time his armies had reached the gates of Moscow less than six months later, any prospect he might once have had of realizing his delusional vision of a Thousand Year Reich had already vanished.

The Wehrmacht – the collective name for the German army, navy and air force – would, of course, go on to launch further major offensives and secure many dramatic victories as the war progressed. But these were ephemeral triumphs. By the end of 1941 at the very latest, the Nazis had already lost any realistic chance of winning the war. For three and a half more years the soil of Eastern Europe would be saturated in the blood of tens of millions of people, victims of a hideous endgame the outcome of which had already been ordained. Disconcerting though it may be for those who, for understandable reasons, assert that the valiant Allied troops who landed on the Normandy beaches in June 1944 became the principal agents of victory over Hitler, the evidence is otherwise.

It was the 'Great Patriotic War', as Stalin called the struggle on Germany's Eastern Front, not D-Day that settled Hitler's fate. This is not remotely to suggest that those who offered their lives in that latter endeavour did so in vain. On the contrary: it is to them above all that countless millions of their fellow citizens in western Europe owe the freedom and democracy that the Soviet dictator was to deny to their neighbours who were later to fall under the Kremlin's 'sphere of influence'. That Stalin was able to bend so much of post-war Europe to his will sprang from the fact that it was his soldiers, not his Western allies, who broke the Third Reich on the battlefield. Although the timing and the manner of the final destruction of the Nazis was determined in concert by the United States, Britain and the Soviet Union, the failure of Operation Barbarossa was the most important terminus of the war in Europe, the point at which – after less than six months of intense struggle – Nazism's demise became inevitable.

It is also not to diminish the scale of suffering endured during the First World War (when the Battle of the Somme alone claimed more than a million casualties in a little under five months), or in other struggles during the Second World War (when the Battle of Stalingrad claimed a similar number of casualties in the same period), to note that the long history of military conflict cannot yield a scale of carnage to compare with that of Operation Barbarossa when, within a comparable time-span, around six times that number of young men were listed as killed, wounded, or missing in action.

The Nazi invasion of the Soviet Union took Stalin by surprise and sent shock waves around the world. It was almost universally assumed that the Red Army would crumble within weeks. But the German triumphalism proved premature. This book charts the progress of Operation Barbarossa from its inception until Hitler's armies reached the capital at the end of the year. It does not attempt to explore every one of the scores of battles fought on three fronts in a vast military theatre; in this respect, its focus is on Army Group Centre, the force that spearheaded the invasion and which was to lead the assault on Moscow. In charting the progress of this army group, I draw extensively on the reports, diaries, letters and memoirs of its leading protagonists, including its commander, General Fedor von Bock, his field commanders (who included the Third Reich's most celebrated panzer general, Heinz Guderian) and the officers and men serving under them. Many of these men wrote to their loved ones with guileless candour: about the fear and elation of battle, the killing, the camaraderie, their longing for home, their endless marches across an arid terrain in searing summer heat, the cloying mud of autumn that brought vehicles to a standstill and trapped foot soldiers and the horses that were used to pull artillery carriages in its glutinous embrace, and the arctic winter, when temperatures fell to −35°C and tens of thousands lost limbs to frostbite.

Far from proving to be a recipe for certain victory, Operation Barbarossa became a cauldron of bitter disputation between the generals at the front and Army High Command at the rear. As this schism deepened, the army chief of staff, Franz Halder, sought in vain to mediate between them and the Wehrmacht's mercurial commander-in-chief, Hitler, a nightmare task about which he wrote openly in his daily war diary. Like those battles fought by army groups North and South, Army Group Centre's campaign against the Soviet armies – led, for the most part, by Stalin's greatest commander, General Georgy Zhukov – was relentless, arduous and ferocious, but it was not a conventional conflict either in scale or in character.

The Eastern Front was a battlefield on which courage was conspicuous and duty was sacrosanct but where neither side paid more than scant regard to the niceties of common humanity. In place of chivalry there was hatred, a reductive atavism that was inflamed by the peremptory and implacable directives that poured forth from Hitler and Stalin. These not only sought to direct the course of the military struggle but also insisted that no quarter should be given and no mercy shown. The rules of warfare as defined in the prevailing Geneva Conventions were ignored in this titanic struggle between the continent's two tyrannical behemoths.

The invading armies had been repeatedly instructed that their enemy belonged to an inferior species of humanity and their troops reacted accordingly. On and off the battlefield, Soviet soldiers and civilians alike were routinely subjected to acts of horrific brutality. Torture and murder by the troops under their command were routinely overlooked by the Wehrmacht's senior officers, who on frequent occasions presided over what was effectively the summary execution of those found to be political commissars, spies or partisans. Such murderous excesses by the Ostheer (Army of the East) were reciprocated in full measure by Soviet troops, who had no qualms about treating Germans as violent criminals against whom no punitive measures were too extreme to merit sanction. On both sides, a lethal combination of loathing and fear gave licence to rare savagery. The descriptions of such incidents proffered by those who participated in them or who watched on without demur were notably self-serving, often defiant and only occasionally laced with shame or disgust. No account of Operation Barbarossa can afford to sidestep this overwhelming evidence of a terrible truth.

Most of those serving in the Red Army fought either from patriotism or to recover their homelands, others from ideological conviction, but all in the knowledge that Stalin's regime ruled as much by terror as by consent. The Soviet dictator's paranoid conviction that he was surrounded by ideological saboteurs was allied to a pitiless indifference to the life of others. In war, as in peace, he was swift to exact mortal retribution on those who displeased him. Generals were subjected to summary execution or arbitrary imprisonment. Those who fled the battlefield or surrendered – even in the face of insuperable odds – faced the death penalty, their families punished not only by that disgrace but also by losing livelihoods and pension rights. At Stalin's behest, the Stavka (the Soviet military high command) established 'blocking units' that were deployed behind the front to shoot down those men who withdrew en masse rather than be mown down by the advancing enemy.

Yet the Soviet leader managed to secure the allegiance of the overwhelming majority of the population as they rallied to the cause. As their letters and memoirs (some of which have only recently been recovered from the secret depths of the Soviet archives) reveal, soldiers and civilians endured with the stoic resolve of men and women who were united against the invaders. Many of Moscow's major landmarks were shrouded by camouflage and the city was placed under curfew. Under constant aerial bombardment, workers managed to dismantle thousands of strategically vital industrial plants, transporting them to safety in the Urals, where they were soon back in full production and at a rapidly accelerating rate of output. In the autumn of 1941, as the Germans threatened the outer ring of Moscow's inadequate defences, the capital was placed under a state of siege; miscreants or those who breached the curfew were shot on sight. Under Zhukov's overall direction, tens of thousands of ill-equipped volunteers – men and women, young and old – worked with dogged resolve to shore up the city's inner barricades, digging trenches and tank traps in the deep mud or frozen ground of a harsh Russian winter. A regime that ruled by terror alone would never have been able to command the allegiance of a people without whose commitment defeat would have been certain.

The crimes against humanity committed on the battlefield by both sides were dwarfed in scale by the atrocities committed by the Nazis behind the lines. Soviet troops who survived to become prisoners of war were force-marched into captivity. Abused, beaten and whipped along the way, they were also denied medicines, food and water. Tens of thousands died before reaching the makeshift prison camps into which they were herded like animals to huddle behind barbed wire and where they lacked shelter or sanitation or any other of the most basic means of survival. Denied nourishment, some prisoners resorted to cannibalism, but the great majority starved to death. This book chronicles a pitiless brutality that formed an integral part of Operation Barbarossa. By May 1945, some 3 million Soviet soldiers had died in captivity. Two-thirds of these men died from starvation or at the barrel of a gun before the end of 1941.

And there was even worse. In the eastern territories that the Wehrmacht brought under Nazi control in 1941, four Einsatzgruppen (task forces or 'action squads'), led by senior commanders, roamed from city to city and town to town authorized to commit mass murder. The establishment of the Einsatzgruppen was approved by Hitler and organized by Heinrich Himmler and Reinhard Heydrich, who, as head of the SS and chief of the Reich Main Security Office respectively, were the principal architects of the Holocaust. Initially under orders to execute 'Jews in Party and state positions', the death squads were soon encouraged to kill any Jews – men, women and children – with indiscriminate fervour. The commanders of the Einsatzgruppen were competitive zealots, striving to outdo one another with higher and higher rates of execution. At their instruction, the victims were rounded up, robbed of their belongings, killed by firing squads and buried in mass graves. These killers did not operate alone. The most senior generals in the Wehrmacht – despite their vehement post-war protestations to the contrary – were not only aware of the Einsatzgruppen's role but also, in many cases, complicit in facilitating it. In every one of the countries invaded by Hitler during Operation Barbarossa, regular soldiers, indigenous police forces and local militia combined to assist the killers in their task. There is copious evidence of this from official orders and accounts as well as reports from the perpetrators themselves and statements from eyewitnesses and those few victims who survived. These testimonies are as incontrovertible as they are dreadful. No adequate description of Operation Barbarossa should exclude them.

In the early weeks of the invasion, this commitment to murder was not matched by efficiency. Gradually, though, the killers streamlined their operations until they perfected a systematic means of shooting large numbers of men, women and children at speed – macabre achievements which they reported to their superiors in cold statistical detail.

Within six months of the Nazi invasion, and after a series of gruesome experiments with various kinds of poison gas, the first death camps, among them Auschwitz-Birkenau, came into operation; the industrial-ization of mass murder had begun. By Christmas 1941 the first million victims of Hitler's 'final solution' had been exterminated, either with guns or in gas chambers. It is a grotesque irony that the most unspeak-able crime of the twentieth century was the sole element in the Führer's apocalyptic vision for the Third Reich that, until the closing months of the war, was not unduly impeded by defeat on the battlefield. To bypass this aspect of Operation Barbarossa would be to avoid identifying one of its most direct and immediate outcomes.

A full account of Hitler's invasion of the Soviet Union requires con-sideration of its cause as well as its effect. Operation Barbarossa did not take place in a historical vacuum but was the direct outcome of a high-wire political drama that began following the First World War and the unresolved miseries that engulfed Europe in its aftermath. For that reason – perhaps to the surprise of some readers – Part One of this book opens in the spring of 1922, when the Soviet Union and Germany, so recently at each other's throats on the First World War battlefields and treated thereafter as pariah states by the rest of Europe, signed a treaty of reconciliation. The European democracies were aghast. The treaty was a diplomatic coup de main that left the British prime minister, Lloyd George, floundering; his painstaking efforts to build a continent-wide consensus in favour of sustainable economic development, and thereby peace and security, was in tatters.

To disentangle the interwoven strands of the political drama that was played out subsequently on the European stage – it is hard to make any sense of Operation Barbarossa otherwise – is to lay bare the arrogance and fear that led the disunited democracies of western Europe to regard the Soviet Union with an aversion that not only precluded a meaningful dialogue with the Kremlin but also led most of them to regard Ger-many's unhinged Führer as the lesser of two evils. From the ruins of Versailles to the rise of Hitler in Germany and Stalin's murderous con-solidation of power in the Soviet Union, all the way to the shock of the Molotov–Ribbentrop Pact in August 1939, the official papers, letters, diaries and memoirs of the chief protagonists illuminate only too starkly the irreconcilable or unobtainable objectives that left Europe's leaders at a loss while the continent drifted ineluctably towards a second conflagration that no one wanted – except Hitler and possibly Stalin (whose main objective was to avoid direct involvement) – but which none of them could stop.

Within a year of starting the Second World War, not only had the German panzers subjugated most of western Europe but Hitler had also decided to postpone the invasion of Britain in favour of destroying the Soviet Union first. There were multiple reasons for this fateful decision, but the trigger for launching Operation Barbarossa lay in the Balkans. This book therefore highlights the bitter contest between Moscow and Berlin to control that combustible and strategically vital region of Europe. When the direct negotiations between the Soviet foreign minister, Vyacheslav Molotov, and Hitler reached a testy impasse at the end of November 1940, the Führer ordered his generals to make detailed plans for the invasion of the Soviet Union for the following spring. In June 1941, by which time he had occupied Yugoslavia and driven the British out of Greece, he found himself at war on two fronts at once.

Operation Barbarossa was thus not quarantined from what was rapidly becoming a global conflict, which is the crucial context within which I have framed the invasion. Within hours of the news that the Wehrmacht was on the warpath within the Soviet Union, Churchill, followed in less grandiloquent terms by Roosevelt a few days later, declared his unequivocal support for the Soviet cause. Before long, both Washington and London found themselves in an unlikely alliance with the world's only communist state, the three leaders soon becoming known as the 'Big Three'. This was a seismic rapprochement that not only had a direct impact on the war on the Eastern Front but on the post-war history of Europe. For that reason, my account of Operation Barbarossa also focuses on the intense human and political drama of this turbulent, often acrimonious but critically important three-way partnership as diplomatic emissaries from Washington and London traipsed into the Kremlin to parley with the mercurial Soviet dictator.

Hitler's invasion of the Soviet Union changed the course of history. As its subtitle suggests, this book was conceived in the belief that the last six months of 1941 were of greater moment than any other period in the twentieth century. Operation Barbarossa was not only a fatal gamble but it was also how Hitler lost the war.

PART ONE

The Slide to War

1. Paving the Way

Over the Easter weekend of 1922, the elegant resort of Rapallo, on the Italian Riviera, was thronged with affluent Italians who favoured the balmy climate along this part of the Mediterranean coast. The town's quietude and lack of vulgarity had long appealed to foreigners as well, and especially to those with cultural sensibilities. It was in the lanes around Rapallo that the philosopher Friedrich Nietzsche first incubated the ideas that were later to form the basis for his magnum opus, the novel *Thus Spoke Zarathustra*, which was widely regarded as impenetrable. Among others to have enjoyed the town's reticent streets and discreet cafes were Guy de Maupassant and Lord Byron. Its contemporary habitués included Ezra Pound and the English essayist Max Beerbohm, who was renowned for his dandified caricatures of the English upper classes.

Rapallo was graced by a ruined monastery, an ancient basilica with a leaning bell tower, numerous medieval churches and the remains of two castles, one of which was on a rocky promontory at the edge of the harbour, where it had once stood sentinel against marauding pirates. For the louche, there was also a sprinkling of discreet casinos and an occasional night club. The most imposing building of all was the neo-Palladian Excelsior Palace hotel, which boasted more than 140 rooms and a 'bathing establishment' overlooking the sea. The hotel was greatly preferred by the reticent rich and international diplomats in search of privacy and discretion.

It was here on that Easter weekend that the German foreign minister, Walther Rathenau, and the Soviet Union's Commissar for Foreign Affairs, Georgy Chicherin, sat down together with their delegations to put the final touches to an agreement between their two governments that had been in secret negotiation for several weeks. As they would certainly have been aware, the Rapallo treaty, as it was called, was a diplomatic time bomb which was primed to detonate on Easter Monday just under forty kilometres along the coast in the city of Genoa. Its effect was to be devastating, the collateral damage irreparable.

As he strode through the jostling mass of cameras and newsmen into the great conference chamber in the thirteenth-century Palazzo San Giorgio in Genoa on the afternoon of Monday, 10 April 1922, the British prime minister, Lloyd George, was quite unaware of what was being hatched in Rapallo. He exuded confidence and resolve. After a sustained bout of shuttle diplomacy he had managed to cajole thirty-four fractious European nations into attending a great conference at which he hoped their deep animosities would be reconciled by an international treaty that – under his presiding genius – would finally restore order and prosperity to a fractured continent.

The scale of Lloyd George's ambition was boundless. In the House of Commons before his departure for Italy he declared that Europe was 'broken into fragments by the devastating agency of war', and that his purpose at Genoa was nothing less than the 'reconstruction' of the entire continent.[1] In that spirit, he had timed his entrance into the palazzo for maximum impact, confident that the assembled delegates would rise to reward his endeavours with a prolonged ovation – as they did.

The British prime minister was not only a flamboyant politician who shone in the limelight but also a man of genuine strategic vision and imagination. As one of the leaders of the four Allied Powers – Britain, France, Italy and the United States – who had wrangled their way towards the Treaty of Versailles three years earlier, he had been among the first to realize that the Paris Peace Conference had done nothing to heal the gaping wounds of the Great War and very little to prevent them festering with potentially cataclysmic consequences.

At best, the Versailles treaty had wrapped a bandage around a suppurating lesion. It had imprinted new boundaries on the map of Europe, carving out a myriad independent states from diverse regions that, for the last half century or more, had suppressed their internal ethnic and cultural animosity under the tutelage of four competing imperial autocracies. The European 'balance of power' – a concept forged by the Austrian chancellor, Prince Klemens von Metternich, and his Holy Alliance in the early nineteenth century and elaborated by the German Empire's 'Iron Chancellor', Otto von Bismarck, with his proclamation of the Second Reich in 1871 – was already crumbling well before 1914. By the end of the Great War it had collapsed entirely.

At Versailles, the Austro-Hungarian Empire that had once held chaotic sway over a swathe of central and southern Europe was dismembered; only its fairy-tale capitals, Vienna and Budapest, served as reminders of the lost imperial splendour of the Habsburgs. Similarly, the Ottoman Empire – 'the sick man of Europe' – which had been fraying at the edges well before the outbreak of war saw its Balkan possessions confiscated by the victors and redistributed among its quarrelsome constituent parts. The turbulent despotism of the Russian Empire had succumbed to a Bolshevik revolution; Czar Nicholas II, the last of the Romanovs, had been assassinated and the largest nation on the continent was now consumed by civil war. No less spectacularly, the German colossus that, under the last of the Kaisers, Wilhelm II, had bestrode Europe for a generation, was broken and humiliated.

The peoples of Europe who had previously endured the certainty of imperial edicts were adrift amidst the swirling detritus of a war in which there had been more than 40 million casualties, including some 10 million soldiers killed on the battlefield and more than 6 million civilians behind the front lines. A further 10 million people had been internally displaced or were criss-crossing the new borders – hastily established at Versailles – as refugees in search of safety, shelter and food. Though some countries enjoyed a post-war boom that engendered a cautious optimism, much of Europe's economy lay in ruins. With unemployment rampant and destitution commonplace, grief and misery prevailed. It gradually became clear that Versailles, foundering on the rocks of high-minded self-delusion, had failed to achieve its brave purpose: the creation of a bedrock for the resolution of this existential crisis.

The most ambitious vision to be mooted at the Paris Peace Conference had been the creation of an international forum for global security based on the assumption that all states might be persuaded to replace their instinct for self-preservation with the disinterested quest for international harmony. In deference to President Woodrow Wilson's romantic notion that thereby the world could finally be made 'safe for democracy', this morally impeccable vision was embodied at Versailles by the formation of the League of Nations. This was a grandiose scheme but far too fragile to withstand the violent aftershocks of the 1914–18 earthquake.

Its fragility had become cruelly apparent soon after President Wilson returned from Versailles to Washington boasting to the Senate that 'at last the world knows America as the saviour of the world'.[2] This hubris may have flattered some American egos – relieved to be advised that their sons had not died on the European battlefield in vain – but the great majority of US senators were underwhelmed. More than that, they chose to adopt the guiding precept of their most revered founding father, George Washington, that the United States should in future avoid 'entangling alliances' with any other nation. Congress therefore refused either to endorse Wilson's commitment to the League of Nations (which, in consequence, was terminally enfeebled) or to ratify the Treaty of Versailles wherein it had been begotten.

For almost two decades thereafter, the United States all but withdrew from the front line of European diplomacy in favour of a policy of detached neutrality, intervening only spasmodically – and self-interestedly – in the affairs of what for many Americans had become a faraway continent about which they knew little and cared rather less. It would not be until the outbreak of the Second World War in 1939 that President Roosevelt felt strong enough politically to inform a reluctant Congress that 'entangling alliances' had once again become unavoidable.* In the meantime, the Europeans would have to find their own salvation.

Far from making Europe 'safe for democracy', the Versailles treaty served only to aggravate the tensions that, for numerous reasons, were very soon to envelop Europe. After many weeks of anguished and often angry wrangling, the victors finally confirmed the tribute to be exacted from the vanquished German leviathan. In the hope of eliminating for ever the threat of German revanchism, the newly constituted Reich – whose leaders had been excluded from the negotiations that sealed their fate – was to be stripped of all its conquests, hobbled militarily, weakened economically and punished financially.

When the elected leaders of the Weimar Republic were summoned to hear the sentence imposed on them their worst premonitions were confirmed. Their nascent democracy was required to surrender a great swathe of territory that either had formed part of Germany's nineteenth-century empire or had been conquered during the war: Alsace and Lorraine were to be returned to France, the Rhineland was to be occupied by the Allies, the Saarland was to be placed under French administration for fifteen

---

* However, it took a further two years before the US legislators formally agreed that America should join the anti-Axis alliance.

years and further territories were to be surrendered to Belgium, Czechoslovakia, Poland and Lithuania. It took five years before all the complex
cessions of territory devised at Versailles were finally put in place. Though
Versailles left the Reich still in possession of the largest landmass in Europe to the west of the Soviet Union, the Germans felt as though their
great nation had been dismembered – an indignity compounded by the
decision of the Allied Powers to confiscate their African colonies as well.
The Reichswehr (the German Defence Force) was to be so pinioned as to
turn an imperial war-making machine into a military police force,
equipped with no more than 100,000 men and forbidden to manufacture
or maintain armoured cars, tanks or warplanes. Even more controver-
sially, the so-called 'War Guilt' clause imposed a punitive scale of financial
reparations to compensate for the destruction that the Kaiser's belliger-
ence had provoked.

In the relevant section of the Versailles treaty, the opening paragraph –
Article 231 – stated: 'The Allied and Associated Governments affirm
and Germany accepts the responsibility of Germany and her allies for
causing all the loss and damage to which the Allied and Associated Governments and their nationals have been subjected as a consequence of the
war imposed upon them by the aggression of Germany and her allies.'
The hapless leaders of the Weimar Republic faced a simple choice: either
to accept these surrender terms or face invasion and occupation by the
Allied Powers. They duly signed along the dotted line. Although this
retribution was less extortionate than the victims would claim – Germany
was not left quite as 'prostrate and helpless'[3] as was widely presumed – it
was enough to incubate a deep bitterness in the national psyche at what
was generally regarded as a cruel and vindictive punishment for crimes
for which they believed they had not been responsible.

For different but no less divisive reasons, Russia had also been excluded
from the Paris Peace Conference. Like President Wilson, Lloyd George
was prone to sympathize with the uprising of the Russian proletariat
against the tyranny of the Czars, which, he believed, sprang from a legitimate demand for a radical change from centuries of oppression. 'To say
that we ourselves should pick the representatives of a great people was
contrary to every principle for which we had fought,'[4] he advised the
French prime minister, Georges Clemenceau. In so saying, he reflected a
widespread popular attitude across Europe as well as in Britain. However,

Clemenceau, who had been unyielding in his insistence that Germany deserved the punitive measures imposed at Versailles, insisted that any diplomatic dalliance with the Bolsheviks would feed a nascent appetite for revolution among Europe's impoverished and alienated working classes.

The French leader's disdain was echoed with great force by the British Secretary of State for War, Winston Churchill, who did not shrink from giving public expression to his animosity in the most colourful terms. 'Civilization', Churchill boomed into a crowd at an election rally in November 1918, 'is being completely extinguished over gigantic areas, while Bolsheviks hop and caper like troops of ferocious baboons amid the ruins of cities and the corpses of their victims.'[5] Unlike Lloyd George, Churchill believed that, far from being biddable, the new regime in Moscow was hell-bent on revolutionary conquest. 'Of all the tyrannies in history, the Bolshevik tyranny is the worst, the most destructive, the most degrading,' he instructed an audience in London, an outburst that prompted Lloyd George to reflect drily, 'His ducal blood revolted against the wholesale elimination of Grand Dukes in Russia.'[6] Ducal blood or not, in due course the future prime minister would be forced by events to adopt a very different tone towards the regime in Moscow.

The European consensus in favour of excluding the Russians as well as Germany from Versailles had been too strong for Lloyd George to resist. Even as the Paris delegates dotted the i's and crossed the t's of the treaty, 180,000 Allied troops drawn from Western armies were still meddling in the Russian Civil War, which had erupted following the 1917 revolution. The Allied support for the White Russians against the Bolsheviks did not lack purpose but was without a coherent strategy. In the course of twelve months the troops had managed to advance in a crab-like fashion towards an obscure objective, only to be withdrawn soon after Versailles for no discernible reason except to demonstrate their lack of resolve. Thereby they not only failed to divert the leaders of the fledgling communist state from their revolutionary path but also confirmed Moscow's deepening sense that the West was united in seeking to frustrate and, if possible, undermine the revolution by any means that might from time to time come to hand. In the years ahead, Stalin's paranoia served merely to aggravate this well-grounded suspicion.

*

By the time of the Genoa Conference it was clearer than ever to Lloyd George that the two largest states on the continent could no longer be treated as outcasts. They were too big, too populous and too explosively unstable to ignore. Both pariah states would have to be brought in from the cold. Without their presence at the negotiating table, he believed it would be impossible to reconnoitre a way out of the worsening European crisis or to construct a sustainable framework for stability across the continent. Conversely – with a foresight evidently denied his fellow leaders – he feared that perpetual isolation would drive Germany and the Soviet Union to put aside their ideological differences in favour of forming a close economic and strategic partnership, which – were it to prosper – would destroy Europe's fragile equilibrium. In the months leading up to Genoa he had therefore expended a great deal of political capital in arm-twisting the French into accepting Germany's presence at the conference table while simultaneously overriding the repugnance of several other participants – not least Conservative members of his own rickety coalition – at the very thought of sitting alongside Bolshevik revolutionaries.

Although Moscow and Berlin were not strong enough to boycott Genoa, neither was gratified by the invitation to attend Lloyd George's conference. They arrived in Italy with little expectation of being released from the handcuffs the Allied Powers had placed on them at Versailles. A few days earlier the prime minister had informed Chicherin that the Soviet Union would receive economic assistance only if the Kremlin agreed to repay the huge debts and loans to the West accumulated by the Czarist regime before the revolution.[7] Chicherin was a cultivated intellectual who had inherited great wealth. He had travelled widely and spoke every major European language. He had written a book about Mozart and he admired Nietzsche (though whether he was aware that Rapallo was one of the philosopher's favourite watering holes was not known). He had also been one of Lenin's closest confidants and a dedicated Bolshevik. He was evidently thin skinned as well and quick to sense a slight. Inadvertently, the Italians gave him an opportunity to take offence by billeting his party – along with the Germans – well away from the main conference centre in Genoa. Before his arrival, the *Manchester Guardian*'s well-connected Moscow correspondent, Arthur Ransome (soon to become famous as the author of the Swallows and Amazons series of children's books), wrote that Chicherin had formally protested that 'the only communication with Genoa is a long road especially convenient for assassination . . . it may be impossible for us to go to Genoa if we have to run a daily gauntlet'.[8] His protest was ignored. If he needed proof, this was yet one more example of the West's disdain for the Soviet Union.

Chicherin's German counterpart, Rathenau, who had only been appointed to the post in January, was a prominent Jewish industrialist. A liberal intellectual, he was renowned for his tolerance and integrity. He was also insistent that Germany should honour the terms of the Versailles treaty, disagreeable as these were. For this, as well as for advocating dialogue with the Soviet Union, he was regarded politically as being on the extreme left. He had every bit as much justification to fear assassination as Chicherin: in the run-up to the Genoa Conference he had even written of his premonition that he might be murdered by one or another group of fanatics. Though he abhorred Bolshevism – which he mocked for seeking to impose 'compulsory happiness' on the Russian people – he believed that economic and political co-operation with the Soviet Union would prevent German ultra-nationalists from seizing the political agenda to demand the creation of a 'Greater Germany'.

From the Reich's perspective, a deal with the Kremlin also made practical sense. France had not relented in the three years following Versailles. The Quai d'Orsay, as the French foreign ministry was universally known, continued to insist that the Reich would have to pay the reparations bill in full – an intransigence which had severely constrained Lloyd George's room for diplomatic manoeuvre. Although the British prime minister had been much influenced by the eminent economist John Maynard Keynes, who had resigned from the Treasury in protest at the 'abhorrent and detestable' punishment inflicted on the Reich at Versailles, he had little choice but to tell the German government that – whatever else he might conjure out of the ether – it would not be possible to negotiate any reduction in what he regarded as a crippling drain on the Reich's exhausted Treasury.

Despite their differences, Moscow and Berlin thus had more than enough common ground to negotiate an agreement that might allow them jointly to circumvent the humiliations of Versailles and to liberate themselves from the perpetual impoverishment of isolation and debt imposed on them by the victors of the Great War. Their search for reconciliation required only that the continent's two behemoths reopen ancient links and adapt them to fit these different times.

Before the First World War, when Austro-Hungary, the Ottomans, Russia and Germany – the Central Powers that still held sway across the continent – circled one another, making and unmaking alliances to balance their overlapping but competitive interests, the relationship between Russia and Germany had been artfully calibrated to avoid conflict. Thanks to Bismarck's ingenuity, they had even signed a secret treaty in 1887, aptly named the Reinsurance Treaty, under which they agreed to maintain a relationship of benevolent neutrality and, under certain circumstances, to offer each other military support. Though the treaty itself collapsed with the Iron Chancellor's dismissal three years later, cordial diplomatic relations – underpinned by family bonds and mutually advantageous economic ties – persisted until the eve of the First World War.

The 1922 Rapallo treaty was thus a revival of a Bismarckian realpolitik that required Moscow and Berlin to see beyond the bitter legacy of the First World War. Only four years earlier, in February 1918, German troops had crossed the Russian border, threatening to occupy a great swathe of a country already crippled by civil war. With this sword of Damocles hanging over him, Lenin had been forced by Berlin to sign the Treaty of Brest-Litovsk on 3 March 1918, the terms of which were every bit as harsh as those that, soon afterwards, Germany was required to accept at the Paris Peace Conference.* Yet almost as soon as the Versailles treaty had been agreed neither the Reich nor the Soviet Union – in true nineteenth-century style – had qualms about opening secret talks to re-establish the pre-war economic ties that had been so valuable to both states before 1914.

Bizarrely, these negotiations were initially masterminded from a Berlin prison. In December 1918 Karl Radek, a Marxist revolutionary, had been sent to Germany at Lenin's behest to assist the nascent Communist Party led by Rosa Luxemburg in fomenting revolutionary change in a nation seething with discontent. Radek was not discreet. Soon after his arrival the tension between the dominant socialist party and the communists erupted into open warfare on the streets. The Spartacist uprising

---

* The treaty was annulled at the Armistice in November 1918, following the Kaiser's formal surrender to the Allied Powers.

in January 1919 led to the deaths of at least 160 insurgents and civilians as well as more than thirty casualties among the paramilitaries sent in by the government to crush the rebellion. Luxemburg was captured and summarily executed. Radek was more fortunate: he was arrested and incarcerated in a Berlin jail.

Despite the punitive terms of the Brest-Litovsk treaty (which had been nullified by Germany's defeat in the war), Berlin's attitude towards Moscow was guided by a new realpolitik. Since both Germany and the Soviet Union saw themselves as victims of Versailles, a mutually beneficial relationship began to seem highly desirable. To mark this shift, the German authorities moved Radek to distinctly superior surroundings in another part of the Moabit prison, where he was treated like a senior diplomat rather than a dangerous criminal. He was allowed to establish what he described as a 'political salon',[9] where leading German industrialists and government officials came to confer with him, including the foreign minister, Rathenau. By the time of his release from prison and his return to Moscow in 1920, his diplomacy had started to bear fruit.* A succession of trade delegations – which notably included Europe's largest company, the arms manufacturer Friedrich Krupp AG – were soon hustling back and forth between the two countries to restore their lucrative pre-war operations.

In the post-Versailles period, numerous reports of these burgeoning commercial ties surfaced in the European and American press. In the months before Genoa, a flurry of rumours and press reports had started to circulate in Berlin to the effect that a formal agreement between the Soviet Union and Germany was in the offing. Despite this, the idle and incompetent British ambassador in the German capital, Lord D'Abernon, either failed to read the runes or was remarkably insouciant about their import. Either way, he neglected to alert London. As a result, the prime minister

---

* Radek's reward was to become secretary of the Comintern – the Communist International. However, he made the dangerous mistake in the 1920s of criticizing Lenin's successor, Stalin. Though later rehabilitated – he helped draft the 1936 Soviet Constitution – he was one of the most prominent victims of Stalin's paranoia. At the notorious 'Trial of the Seventeen' he confessed to treason and was sentenced to ten years' penal labour. He was prevented from serving his full term by an NKVD agent who murdered him on the orders of its boss, Lavrenty Beria. Radek was exonerated of any offence in 1988.

was in blissful ignorance of the Soviet–German negotiations until he was told about the Rapallo treaty on that fateful Easter Monday. His dismay at the news was matched by his fury. As a 'pioneer of personal diplomacy',[10] he had staked his credibility as an international statesman on a successful outcome to the Genoa Conference. Nor was it ever far from his mind that a new pan-European treaty would do much to restore his own reputation at home, giving much-needed new life to the tarnished glitter of his prime ministerial career. The 'Welsh wizard', who was widely held to have 'won the war', had every intention of being crowned as the man who also won the peace. As soon as he heard of the Moscow–Berlin deal that had been sealed behind his back in Rapallo, he knew that these hopes were in ruins. He was not yet aware of the terms of the treaty. Nor did he need to be: it was enough that it had been signed.

He was outraged, but he should not have been surprised. Three years earlier, in the days before the leaders of the United States, Britain, Italy and France put their signatures to the Versailles treaty, he had sent a private note to Georges Clemenceau, warning him that the harsh punishment France wished to inflict on the defeated aggressor would drive Germany to 'throw in her lot with Bolshevism and place her resources, her brains, her vast organizing power at the disposal of the revolutionary fanatics whose dream it is to conquer the world for Bolshevism by force of arms'.[11] On Easter Monday 1922, it looked very much as if something of that kind had just been agreed.

Lloyd George's chagrin was intense. At a formal dinner for the delegates, he berated the leaders of the German delegation and publicly accused Rathenau of 'duplicity'.[12] The prime minister's wrath was laced with despair. All that he had worked to achieve in ten fraught weeks of international diplomacy lay in tatters. When he heard what had happened, even the notoriously two-faced Foreign Secretary, Lord Curzon – who loathed Lloyd George – was moved to note disgustedly 'we seem to be relapsing . . . into the deepest slime of pre-war treachery and intrigue'.[13]

Characteristically Lloyd George soon recovered his poise, contriving to paste over the truth with a glossy varnish of Welsh oratory that deceived no one. After a further three days of rambling debate, the *New York Times* reported that 'the conference has seemed to feel itself in the shadow of failure, and the various delegations have been casting about to decide upon whom to fix the responsibility. It is like a party broken up by a mischievous boy, and the question is, Who must be pronounced the guilty one?'[14] By the time the diplomats filed out of the Palazzo San Giorgio for the last time on 19 May, it was plain to all that nothing of note had been achieved.* Not only had Genoa been an irredeemable flop, doomed to be the last conference of its type for a generation, but Lloyd George returned to London without that 'peace for our time' message he required to convince colleagues in his already disintegrating coalition that he had any future as prime minister. He was duly ousted in October 1922, never again to return to the front line of British politics. The man he had castigated for 'duplicity' also paid dearly for putting his name to the Rapallo treaty, but his was the ultimate price. On 24 June 1922, as Walther Rathenau was being driven to work, a large Mercedes drew up alongside his car. One of its occupants opened fire with a sub-machine gun, killing the foreign minister instantly. He was not the first honourable politician in Germany to lose his life in this way, nor would he be the last. It was becoming the 'new normal' in a country still traumatized by both war and peace.

At both Versailles and Genoa, the governments of Europe had demonstrated that, although they had the will to heal the wounds of the Great War, they were riven by too many competing visions and conflicting agendas to realize that purpose. In the absence of the Western world's most powerful state, they proved incapable of devising a coherent blueprint for recovery, without which, as Lloyd George had forewarned, further convulsions were all but inevitable. The shock of Rapallo was a portent, serving notice on their adversaries that the two largest nations on the continent would not allow themselves to be chained by the will of others; that, by one means or another, the two former foes, whose soldiers had so recently been slaughtering one another on the battlefield, were quite ready to collaborate in constructing a way out of the predicament imposed upon them. Rapallo did not cause Europe's downward spiral but – with the benefit of hindsight – serves to illuminate the harsh truth that the 'war to end wars' had achieved nothing of the kind.

Although the formal wording of the Rapallo treaty was confined to

---

* The delegates did agree to a partial return to the gold standard. This applied only to the banks, not to Europe's citizens.

promises of diplomatic and economic co-operation – the normalization of relations, the mutual renunciation of all territorial claims and an agreement to stimulate trade and investment – the understandings between the two sides went much further and were of far greater import. In defiance of Versailles, the deal provided diplomatic cover for secret military talks between Germany and the Soviet Union designed to circumvent the restrictions imposed at Versailles, which were intended to make it impossible for the Reich's armed forces to take offensive action.

Britain was unable to establish firm evidence of this menacing prospect but the Foreign Office was suspicious. In a note to Curzon, ten days after the news of the Rapallo treaty burst on the world, an astute Whitehall official warned, 'I am convinced that . . . there is a perfect understanding between the two parties that the Germans will help to build the Russian army and especially the Russian navy: such a co-operation revolutionizes the outlook in Europe.'[15] His warning was not quite on the mark. Although the Soviets gained important military insights, the main effect of the treaty was to provide the Germans with the opportunity to evade the terms of the Versailles treaty by rebuilding their armed forces far away from the prying eyes of western Europe.

Within weeks of Rapallo, Moscow agreed that the Reichswehr could establish a flying school at Lipetsk (460 kilometres to the south of the capital) and a chemical weapons plant at Volsk (300 kilometres to the south of Samara). Under the guise of building 'tractors', weapons manufacturers such as Krupp and Junkers set up factories near Moscow and Rostov-on-Don to build tanks. At a training ground near Kazan, German commanders tested battlefield manoeuvres that would be adapted by panzer commanders to slice through the French defensive lines in 1940 and – in the grimmest of ironies – to devastate the Soviet forces that would be ranged against them in the early summer of the following year. Heinz Guderian, who would become famed as one of Hitler's most brilliant panzer commanders on both fronts, later paid oblique tribute to this most cynical of compacts, writing, 'Since 1926, a testing station had been in existence abroad where new German tanks could be tried out . . .'[16] In return for Moscow's largesse, an exchange programme allowed Soviet officers to be trained at German military academies, where both sides learned a great deal about the other's organization and methods.

This military entente was underpinned by a trading agreement between the two nations. In return for extensive loans, the Bolshevik government exported huge quantities of grain to the Reich. In 1923 alone – in the immediate aftermath of a famine in which 5 million Soviet citizens in western Russia died from starvation and related diseases – this amounted to more than 3 million tons. In return, Moscow used the credits extended by the German banks to buy industrial machinery and supplies to reconstruct its own 'military-industrial' complex, which had been ravaged by war and revolution.

Disconcerted by the rapport between the two continental giants, the British watched from the sidelines, baffled and anxious. 'We cannot afford . . . to have Germany or an eventual Russo-German combination supreme on the continent,'[17] Austen Chamberlain, the British Foreign Secretary, noted as his officials sought to shape a countervailing policy that was framed by a deep aversion to communism. A widespread prejudice in the Foreign Office against the 'incessant, though shapeless menace'[18] of the Soviet Union led London to conclude that Moscow posed a greater threat to European security than Berlin. Notwithstanding Versailles, Britain set about prising the Weimar leaders away from the Russian Bear. Supported by France, Belgium and Italy, London devised a series of interlocking agreements to reassure the Germans that the Reich was no longer regarded by the other European democracies as an outcast.

The 1925 Treaty of Locarno was the fruit of this diplomatic offensive. Under the terms of the treaty, the Germans and the French agreed their common border and renounced the use of force against one another; the French, together with Belgium, withdrew from Germany's industrial heartlands in the Ruhr (which they had occupied in 1923 following the Reich's failure to pay its annual reparations bill); the demilitarization of the Rhineland imposed at Versailles was confirmed; and Germany was formally accepted back into the family of western Europe with an invitation to join the League of Nations. Locarno was hailed for delivering that 'peace for our time' which had proved so elusive at Genoa three years earlier, but it was a fragile chalice within which to contain the grudges and fears that Europe still incubated.

The Russians, who had put intense pressure on Berlin to reject the Locarno terms, were aggrieved by the Reich's decision to succumb to London's blandishments. Anxious to reassure a paranoid Moscow that they had no intention of joining an anti-Soviet cabal, the Germans moved swiftly to reaffirm the economic and military ties established by the Rapallo treaty. In April 1926, four months after the Locarno treaty came into force, the Soviet foreign minister, Chicherin, arrived in the German capital, where the two sides pledged themselves, in the form of the Berlin treaty, to renew their neutrality pact for a further five years. As Austen Chamberlain complained, the Germans had opted 'to run with the hare and hunt with the hounds'.[19]

Though frustrated by the Weimar leadership, British ministers were far more acerbic about the Bolshevik regime in Moscow, which they abhorred and feared, seeing in the Kremlin leadership the personification of the urge to subvert freedom and democracy in the West and to replace capitalism with communism and its accompanying 'dictatorship of the proletariat'. This was a justifiable attitude but it was also blinkered. In the febrile years following the rise of Hitler, it had a profoundly adverse effect on diplomatic relations between London and Moscow, which ill-served British interests. Contemptuous of the Kremlin's pretensions to 'great power' status, Austen Chamberlain not only rebuffed Soviet efforts to secure Western loans, but, adopting the patronizing tone prevalent in Whitehall, noted 'they really are suffering from swollen heads. They are of less consequence to us than they suppose and they grossly flatter themselves when they suppose that British policy is dictated by thought of them.'[20]

Like their European counterparts, British ministers were irked by Moscow's determined if clumsy efforts to undermine Western democratic institutions while demanding equality of status with their ideological adversaries. In Britain's case this was exemplified by Moscow's symbolic support for the 1926 General Strike by means of a modest donation to the Trades Union Congress. Citing this breach of diplomatic propriety by Soviet diplomats based in London, Lloyd George's successor as prime minister, Stanley Baldwin, severed diplomatic relations with Moscow.* Following Locarno – where, according to the Foreign Secretary, the government had been 'battling with Soviet Russia for the soul

---

* On 12 May 1927, British police raided the offices of the Soviet trade delegation (ARCOS), searching for government documents that were alleged to have been stolen from the War Office. The Russians claimed – with justice, but to no avail – that the police action constituted a breach of diplomatic immunity.

of Germany' – Britain's overriding objective was unambiguous: in Austen Chamberlain's words, it was 'to attach Germany solidly to the Western powers' and to prevent the Reich 'succumbing to the temptation' to slip back into the Soviet embrace.[21]

Though formal relations with the Soviet Union were restored by Ramsay MacDonald's incoming Labour government in 1929, the icy stand-off between London and Moscow aggravated Stalin's conviction that Britain was intent on mobilizing the European democracies to destroy Bolshevism. Mutual distrust and incomprehension so disfigured Anglo-Soviet relations as to make a constructive dialogue between London and Moscow all but impossible for the next decade.

A more immediate – and far more dangerous – challenge to Europe's fragile stability came not from Bolshevism but in the form of the Wall Street Crash in 1929. For the previous five years, following a series of complex negotiations, the US banks had been keeping the German Reichsbank afloat with massive loans that had helped offset the cost of reparations imposed on the Weimar Republic at Versailles. As a result, the faltering German economy had started to recover and the great manufacturing industries to thrive once more. The financial firestorm of hyperinflation that ruined lives and livelihoods in the mid-1920s had been doused. German citizens began to enjoy relative prosperity and stability. But with the sudden meltdown of the global financial system, those US loans were withdrawn, the life-support system taken away. The German economy went into free fall, industrial output collapsed and, within three years, 6 million or more Germans – both white-collar workers and those who laboured on the factory floor – were out of work. Stricken by the Great Depression, families lost their savings and went hungry, malnutrition was rife and children were ravaged by disease. Feeding on this human misery and resentment, a foetid virus – one that had been incubating in the post-war turbulence of a defeated nation and for which there was no apparent antidote – rampaged across the entire nation, rapidly infecting a huge proportion of the population.

An obscure fringe political movement, founded on 5 January 1919 with a membership of twenty-four and calling itself the German Workers' Party, had in little over a decade become the largest party in the Reichstag. Known by then formally as the National Socialist German Workers'

Party – the NSDAP or Nazi Party – its ideology was anti-Semitic and racist and its methods were violent. Its adherents were led by an unemployed Austrian veteran of the First World War who had won an Iron Cross (1st and 2nd Class) for gallantry but then failed in his attempt to earn a living as an artist. Mesmerized by Adolf Hitler's pseudo-Darwinist theory that the Germans were a racially pure people who would in due course master Europe by subjugating or extirpating any of the non-Aryan races that stood in the path of this apocalyptic vision, his followers were as fanatical as he in their devotion to his cause. Before long, seduced by Hitler's gift for messianic oratory, huge crowds attended Nazi Party rallies, listening to him in rapt attention before raising their outstretched right arms in tribute as they chanted '*Sieg Heil!*' while he incited them towards a perdition far more terrible than anything imposed on them by the victors at Versailles.

No one who had waded through the leaden repetitions of *Mein Kampf* would have been surprised by their leader's boundless hatred of 'the Jew', whom he described repeatedly as, inter alia, 'a parasite', 'a pernicious bacillus' and a 'mortal enemy' that had to be expunged.[22] In a grotesque perversion of history, Hitler asserted that it was this 'subhuman' species that had snatched victory from Germany in 1918 and handed it to the Allies. Subsequently, their 'corrupt and degenerate' collusion with their Marxist colleagues in the Weimar government had produced the Versailles treaty, which was an 'instrument of boundless extortion and abject humiliation'.[23] Hitler's abomination of 'international Jewry' was entwined with a loathing of Bolshevism and a limitless appetite for Lebensraum – living-space – without which the German 'master race' would be unable to re-establish its proper destiny.

In *Mein Kampf* these themes formed a common though inchoate thread. It was an all-or-nothing imperative:

> The right to possess soil can become a duty if without extension of its soil a great nation seems doomed to destruction . . . Germany will either be a world power or there will be no Germany . . . If we speak of soil in Europe today, we can have in mind only Russia and her vassal border states. Here Fate itself seems desirous of giving us a sign. By handing Russia to Bolshevism, it robbed the Russian nation of that intelligentsia which previously brought about and guaranteed its existence as a state . . . [That]

was not the result of the political abilities of the Slavs in Russia but only a wonderful example of the state-forming efficacy of the German element in an inferior race . . . For centuries Russia drew nourishment from this German nucleus . . . Today it can be regarded as almost totally exterminated and extinguished. It has been replaced by the Jew . . . The giant empire in the east is ripe for collapse. And the end of Jewish rule in Russia will also be the end of Russia as a state . . .[24]

Hitler had an unrivalled gift for exploiting the festering grievances and prejudices of a defeated people and to offer them salvation with a messianic vision of the nation rising from the ashes to become a great world power once again. His vast audiences were roused to a pitch of almost orgasmic hysteria. After little more than a decade of street thuggery and political manipulation, the National Socialists had commandeered the nation, through first the soap box and then the ballot box.

Initially, however, the Nazis appeared to have no chance of becoming a mass movement. On 8 November 1923 they made their first move by initiating a violent coup d'état attempt against the local state commissioner, who was speaking at a Munich bierkeller. On the following day, in the hope of inciting the local garrison of the Reichswehr to join them in toppling the Weimar government, they staged a march in the city aimed at seizing key state installations. In the ensuing mayhem, the Bavarian police shot and killed fifteen marchers as well as an innocent bystander. Along with Rudolf Hess, one of his co-conspirators responsible for orchestrating the shambolic so-called 'Beer Hall Putsch', Hitler was arrested, charged and found guilty of treason. But instead of imposing a long incarceration in a common jail, the judge – who was a Nazi sympathizer – sentenced him to just five years of *Festungshaft* (house arrest) in a fortress, where he lived in relative comfort until he was released nine months later. As he was not required to exert himself in physical labour, he had plenty of time in which to complete the turgid but terrifying manuscript that was published as *Mein Kampf*.

In the December 1924 election the Nazis could garner only 3 per cent of the vote, which gave them a mere thirty-two seats in the 472-seat Reichstag. But within six years, as the Great Depression began to ravage the country, they achieved a six-fold increase in their share of the vote, securing 18 per cent in the 1930 elections. They were now a force to reckon with. Tensions were high. Running battles in the streets between the Nazi Party's Storm Troopers (the SA, or Brownshirts, as they were known), and their social-democratic SPD and Communist Party rivals gave a dangerous edge to the worsening political crisis. In July 1932, the Nazis won 37 per cent of the vote, which made them the largest party in the Reichstag with 230 seats. The SPD (the former governing party) and the Communist Party trailed far behind with, respectively, a 21 per cent and a 14 per cent share. The Nazis had attracted more votes – 13,745,680 – than the other two parties put together. However, as no other party was willing to work with them, they were as yet unable to form a governing majority. The result was political gridlock.

Four months later, in November, in an attempt to break out of this impasse, President Paul von Hindenburg – who had been in office since 1925 – decided to dissolve the Reichstag and call another election. On this occasion, popular support for the Nazis fell by 4 per cent but they once again emerged as the largest party with the highest share of the popular vote. As the smaller parties were still unwilling to form a bloc large enough to keep Hitler out of power, the Reichstag was once again paralysed. Hindenburg, who was revered as the wartime commander-in-chief of the Kaiser's army and who had been, since the autumn of 1916, the de facto head of government, was at a loss. Although he had become a father figure to the nation, he was tired and enfeebled by age, and certainly no match for Hitler. On 30 January, seeing no other way to break the political deadlock, Hindenburg summoned the Nazi leader to confer on him the title Chancellor of Germany. Hitler was sworn in on 30 January 1933.

It had been a remarkable coup de théâtre. With a rare gift for populist rhetoric, Hitler told his listeners what they wanted to hear: that the most powerful state in Europe had been robbed of its rightful place in the firmament, expelled from its own lands, denied the right to bear arms and humiliated by financial reparations, which – though they had ceased in 1932 – he blamed for their impoverishment.

When he added into that toxic mix that the principal agency of their current misery was a conspiracy of Jewish plutocrats, a great many other-wise rational citizens did not pause to question the proposition, let alone to ask whether the 'plutocrats' were really to blame and, if so, what was the difference between a Jewish and a gentile plutocrat. Nor did they choose to recall that, while some Jews were indeed bankers, most were shopkeepers, traders and artisans earning modest incomes in what would today be called 'the service sector'. In a Europe which had long been disfigured by anti-Semitism, Hitler merely confirmed their prejudices and gave them focus. In the ferment of that time, little by little, distortion by distortion, lie by lie, he acquired for himself a high enough share of the popular vote to give him the authority to incinerate the very democratic institutions that had brought him to the highest office in the land.

Aside from his ideological rantings that made their pulses race so violently, the voters had little idea of what their Führer would do with the power they had bequeathed him. His first formal address to the nation, on 1 February 1933, left them little the wiser. Highlighting the 'most profound distress' of millions of German men and women, which, if it continued, would lead to 'a catastrophe of unfathomable dimensions', he declared that his 'first and foremost duty' was 'to re-establish the unity of spirit and will of our Volk'. To this end, he promised to wage a 'merciless war against spiritual, political and cultural nihilism'. There was, though, no mention either of the Jewish 'bacillus' or of Lebensraum.

Had the voters been present at a secret meeting of military leaders two days later, they would have been privy to a much clearer and uglier vision. Opposition to the Nazis, he advised the assembled generals, had to be 'crushed', while 'extermination' was the only means of containing Marxism. Democracy was a 'cancer' that had to be extirpated. The need for Lebensraum would probably require military conquest and Germanization, for which purpose the rapid build-up of Germany's armed forces was an essential precondition. Some of his listeners enthused, others were nonplussed. None uttered a word of dissent. As Hitler's eminent biographer Ian Kershaw has written, 'However disdainful they were of the vulgar and loud-mouthed social upstart, the prospect he held out of restoring the power of the army as the basis for expansionism and German dominance' accorded with the long-held objectives of Germany's military elite.[25]

Hitler turned next to the nation's leading industrialists, inviting – instructing – them to join him on 20 February in a villa belonging to Hermann Goering, an ace fighter pilot in the First World War and the Führer's most trusted accomplice. Goering had joined the Nazi Party in 1922 after hearing one of Hitler's rants. Wounded when marching alongside the other leaders of the Beer Hall Putsch, he had been smuggled out of Munich to the Austrian city of Innsbruck. Treated with morphine to relieve the pain, he became addicted to the drug and, for a while, was confined to an asylum. On his return to Germany, he was elected to the Reichstag in the 1928 elections. By virtue of becoming the majority party in the July 1932 elections, the Nazis had the constitutional right to appoint the Reichstag's president. Hitler chose Goering. When the Nazi leader became Chancellor, he appointed Goering as Prussia's interior minister, which gave him control of the largest police force in Germany. By dint of amalgamating a plethora of units, he had soon established a new secret police organization, the Gestapo (control of which he would later pass on to Heinrich Himmler).

The industrialists were well aware that Goering, like Hitler, was not a man to be ignored with impunity. Once Hitler had finished telling them that the days of parliamentary democracy were numbered and the revolutionary left would be crushed by force if necessary, he left Goering's villa and his number two picked up the theme. Demanding their financial support, he urged them to help fill the party's severely depleted coffers in order to secure victory in the forthcoming election scheduled for 5 March 1933. This election, Goering advised them, 'will surely be the last one for ten years, probably even for the next hundred years'.[26]

For some of those present this was an irresistible incentive, notwithstanding the fact that it would involve collaborating with the forces of darkness. For those with an internationalist outlook, the prospect was far from enticing, but virtually impossible to evade. Seventeen leading companies duly contributed to an election fund of 3 million Reichsmarks, a huge boost to the Nazi Party's campaign in the days leading up to the vote.

At the end of the month Hitler took one further step towards consolidating his power. On the pretext of suppressing a mythical communist insurrection, the non-existent authors of which he blamed for the fire that had gutted the Reichstag on 27 February, he had no difficulty in persuading Hindenburg – a deeply conservative figure – that civil liberties should be suspended forthwith.* In an atmosphere polluted by

---

* Four men were arrested and charged with causing the Reichstag Fire. One of them, a twenty-four-year-old Dutch communist named Marinus van de Lubbe, confessed to the crime and was sentenced to death. The other three were acquitted. There was

intimidation and violence by Nazi vigilantes, more than 17 million voters cast their ballots for the National Socialists in the 5 March election – during which opposition parties were banned from campaigning. This gave Hitler a 43.9 per cent share of the popular vote. Armed with this rigged mandate, he went even further. Barring Communist Party deputies from attending the parliamentary session of 23 March (which was held in the Kroll Opera House following the Reichstag Fire), he steamrollered the appropriately named 'Enabling Act' onto the statute book. He thereby acquired the power to rule by decree and to use force as he saw fit to maintain public order. There would be no more elections in Germany until the end of the Second World War.

On 2 August the following year, Hindenburg died from lung cancer at the age of eighty-seven. There was an outpouring of national grief. At his state funeral, Hitler was careful to play a prominent role. By that time, however, he had already destroyed any remnants of German democracy. Following a shoo-in plebiscite, he abolished the role of president and, by assuming its powers, acquired direct control over every institution of the state, including the armed forces. The Führer and the Nazi zealots who clustered around him were now free to impose their fanatical will on a population of 67 million. And they knew what they wanted to do: establish Germany as the dominant power in Europe, regain the territories 'stolen' from them at Versailles, destroy communism, eliminate the Jewish 'bacillus' and create Lebensraum for the superior Aryan race in lands currently inhabited by an inferior Slavic people in eastern Europe and beyond. To achieve these goals, the German economy would have to be put on a war footing, and any treaties or undertakings that inhibited this would have to ignored or abrogated. The ways and the means, no less than the timetable by which all these objectives were to be realized, were as yet unclear, but that they were deeply embedded in the Nazi psyche was not in doubt. Few Germans resisted. To differing degrees the great majority from all sections of society were to be complicit, compliant or cowed into submission. The Third Reich had come of age.

---

speculation that the fire was started by the Nazis, but the consensus among historians is that the Dutchman was guilty and that he probably acted alone.

2. Dictators and Democrats

On 25 March 1933, two days after Hitler's Enabling Act was approved by the Reichstag, an unattributed article appeared in the *Manchester Guardian*. It was a dispatch from the Soviet Union from a British journalist, Malcolm Muggeridge, who had been posted to Moscow the previous year. He had arrived with his wife, Kitty, 'resolved' he wrote later 'to go where I thought a new age was coming to pass' and with the intention of surrendering his British passport for a Soviet one. His starry-eyed vision was far from unique. Among many left-wing British intellectuals to share his view were Kitty Muggeridge's aunt, Beatrice Webb, who, with her husband, Sidney, was co-founder of the London School of Economics, the *New Statesman* and the Fabian Society, and that society's most luminous supporter, the playwright George Bernard Shaw.

As a fervent admirer of the Soviet Union, Shaw had been invited to Moscow two years earlier for a nine-day 'fact-finding' mission. Lionized by the regime, he was driven around the capital in an open-topped limousine with his fellow travelling companions, Lord and Lady Astor. The family owned the vast Cliveden estate on the banks of the Thames. Nancy Astor was a renowned socialite who, in 1919, became the first woman to be elected as a Westminster MP. The aristocratic couple and the socialist playwright were bedazzled by what they were allowed to see of Moscow. Feted by revolutionary writers and artists, they were invited to meet Joseph Stalin at the Kremlin. Shaw was quite overcome. Flattered to be treated as though he were an old friend, he emerged from his three-hour encounter with the Soviet leader to declare on his departure for London, 'Tomorrow I leave this land of hope and return to our Western countries – the countries of despair.'[1]

As one of the Western world's most prominent public intellectuals, his approbation mattered to the Kremlin and, on his return to London, the great man did not disappoint. Asked about reports of food shortages and famine in parts of Russia at a press conference, he declared that he had not seen 'a single undernourished person in Russia, young or old', and then added sardonically, 'Were they padded? Were their hollow cheeks distended by pieces of rubber inside?'[2]

Such aperçus from so eminent a figure played no small part in tempting liberal opinion in the West to join communism's fellow-travellers in vilifying critics of the Soviet Union as reactionary capitalists or diehard members of a ruling class that was fearful lest the virus of communism should infect those millions of hungry men and women who had lost their jobs in the Great Depression. In the absence of contrary evidence, it was tempting to believe that the Soviet Union offered the rest of the world an earthly Nirvana.

Malcolm Muggeridge was not so credulous. Already disillusioned by six months in Stalinist Russia, he decided to find out for himself if there was any substance to the rumours of a mass famine. Early in 1933 he travelled into the North Caucasus and Ukraine, where he was soon confronted by a horrifying reality. In one small market town, he reported, 'the civilian population was obviously starving . . . ; not undernourished as, for instance, most Oriental peasants are undernourished and some unemployed workers in Europe, but having had for weeks next to nothing to eat'. One of these wretched individuals, looking round anxiously to ensure that he could not be overheard told him, 'We have nothing, absolutely nothing. They have taken everything away.' Muggeridge passed mile after mile of empty fields. The land was untilled and the livestock had died. The granaries were empty and there was no seed to plant for the next harvest. Everywhere he went he found only 'despair and bewilderment'.[3] It did not take long for him to realize that he was witness to a humanitarian crisis caused by the regime's determination to secure, in the implacable language of the revolution, the 'liquidation of the kulaks as a class' and to establish collective farms on their expropriated lands. The kulaks – small landowners often owning upwards of five acres (and therefore large enough to employ labourers) – were presumed by the Bolsheviks, often correctly, to be viscerally hostile to the revolution as well as being unwilling to surrender their homesteads and their livelihoods to the state.

This 'liquidation' – which was an essential component of Stalin's first Five Year Plan – required party officials to seize all the kulaks' assets and to expel them from homes that had often been in their ownership for generations. The operation was not confined to the Caucasus and Ukraine. In January 1933 party officials across the fertile grain lands of central Russia came under intense pressure to accelerate the programme of requisition and expulsion. As enthusiastically obedient as his counterparts elsewhere to meet the targets set by the Kremlin, the First Secretary of the Central Black Earth Regional Party, Commissar Juozas Vareikis, instructed his comrades that they were to 'dekulakize' between 90,000 and 105,000 households, and that between 12,000 and 13,000 kulak families were to be exiled and their 'counter-revolutionary' ringleaders jailed or executed.[4]

Within weeks, the chaos caused by this official form of ethnic cleansing meant that bread supplies in this richly fertile region began to run out. Six months later, the director of the regional branch of OGPU (the national secret police agency) was forced to cable Vareikis to report that the spring sowing had not been harvested and the crop was 'rotting and going to seed'. In May 1933 OGPU's director reported: 'In just the village of Borisovska more than a thousand have died of starvation . . . In whole numbers of villages the corpses of those who have died are not being collected for long periods . . . The collective farm workers are abandoning the villages and heading for the towns.'

So far from being distressed by such reports, which flowed into the Kremlin in an unending stream, the regime demanded even tougher action. Vyacheslav Molotov was Stalin's chosen instrument for this task. As chairman of the Council of People's Commissars and Stalin's closest confidant, he was directly responsible for overseeing the 'liquidation' and 'collectivization' programme. The Black Earth region was critical to the success of the programme. Covering around 350,000 square kilometres of high-yielding soils some 700 kilometres south-west of Moscow, it was one of the capital's primary grain baskets. In his icily indifferent fashion, Molotov ignored the starving peasantry but insisted that the expropriations in the Black Earth region should be neither suspended nor modified. In a personal message to Vareikis he instructed the troubled commissar that 'no diversions from the plan . . . can be contemplated, [and there are] no mitigating circumstances'.[5] Those peasants who threatened to resist were to be sent into exile elsewhere in the Soviet Union or, if they resisted, executed on the spot.

For ardent communists like Lev Kopelev,* who, like many thousands of other young party functionaries, was dispatched to the countryside to dekulakize the land, this was a price worth paying:

> In the terrible spring of 1933 I saw people dying from hunger. I saw women and children with distended bellies, turning blue, still breathing, but with vacant, lifeless eyes. And corpses, corpses in ragged sheepskin coats and cheap felt boots . . . I saw all this and did not go out of my mind or commit suicide . . . Nor did I lose my faith. I believed because I wanted to believe.[6]

Many years later, he was to recant but, at the time, the young intellectual believed that

> world revolution was absolutely necessary so that justice would triumph . . . [there would be] no borders, no capitalists and no fascists at all . . . Moscow, Kharkov and Kiev would become just as enormous, just as well-built, as Berlin, Hamburg and New York . . . We would have skyscrapers, streets full of automobiles and bicycles . . . All the workers and peasants would go walking in fine clothes, wearing hats and watches.[7]

This vision, as he would acknowledge, so clouded his judgement that he found himself 'hating' the kulaks, seeing himself and his comrades as 'warriors on an invisible front, fighting against kulak sabotage . . . and for the souls of these peasants who were mired in unconsciousness . . . who did not understand the great truths of communism'.[8]

The great majority of the famine victims lived in Ukraine and it was here that kulak resistance to the collectivization of their lands was most stubborn. Knowing that their produce was to be confiscated from them by local officials – in line with the arbitrary and unachievable quotas drawn up by Molotov to ensure a surplus for the cities – many peasants

---

* Lev Kopelev went on to serve as an intelligence and propaganda officer in the Second World War. A scholar and writer, he remained loyal to the Soviet system even after he was sentenced to ten years' hard labour in the Gulag in 1945 for complaining about atrocities committed against German civilians. It was there that he met Alexander Solzhenitsyn (becoming the model for Rubin in *The First Circle*). Released in 1954, it was not until 1968 that he finally broke with communism. He was fired from his academic post and expelled from the Writers' Union for supporting prominent dissidents. In 1980, while he was out of the country, his Soviet citizenship was revoked. This was restored to him by President Mikhail Gorbachev in 1990. Kopelev died in 1997.

downed tools and refused to till their fields. Those kulaks with the courage and cunning to conceal their harvest faced 'liquidation' in its most gruesome sense. A Politburo decree authorized personally by Stalin in 1932 had made it a capital offence for the farmers to 'steal' grain. A peasant had but to hoard a single sack to face the firing squad.

Hundreds of thousands of those peasants who were spared immediate execution perished from hunger, thirst and disease on the long, life-sapping journey from their villages to internal exile in the faraway interior. When the trains carrying these victims came to a halt, their corpses were laid out beside the tracks for instant burial. Untold numbers in unmarked graves. Those who survived the journey – 'administrative' exiles, as they were officially designated – had to scavenge for food in alien and inhospitable lands.

The suffering of the exiles was acute. In May 1933 an unnamed state official, evidently appalled by what he witnessed, reported seeing men and women

> haunting the villages like shadows in search of a piece of bread or refuse. They eat carrion, slaughter dogs and cats. The villagers keep their houses locked. Those who chance to enter a house drop on their knees in front of the owner and, with tears, beg for a piece of bread. I witnessed several deaths on the roads between villages, in the bathhouses, and in the barns. I myself saw hungry, agonized people crawling on the sidewalk. They were picked up by the police and died several hours later.[9]

Despite the clinical diligence with which party functionaries compiled the raw statistics, it never became possible to establish the precise number of those who perished in the Great Famine of 1932–33. Stalin may not have intended to liquidate the peasantry in the same manner as he did the kulaks, but starvation was the direct result of the policies he devised and unleashed on them. It is probable that at least 10 million Soviet citizens died as a result of either execution, starvation, disease or deportation into internal exile.*

---

* These estimates are based on figures that have been exhaustively analysed since the fall of the Soviet Union, when access to the relevant files became possible for the first time. For authoritative, detailed, and haunting accounts, see Timothy Snyder, *Bloodlands: Europe Between Hitler and Stalin* (Vintage, 2011), pp. 21–58 passim, and Anne Applebaum, *Red Famine: Stalin's War on Ukraine* (Penguin, 2018).

That so few people in the West appreciated the scale of this catastrophe owed much to a highly tuned Soviet propaganda network at home and abroad that feted, favoured and sometimes financed the biddable and the gullible. Thus, at the peak of the genocide, Bernard Shaw, along with twenty other well-known names, was inspired to pen an angry letter to the *Manchester Guardian*, protesting that on their respective visits to the Soviet Union none of them had seen evidence of

> economic slavery, privation, unemployment and cynical despair of betterment . . . Everywhere we saw a hopeful and enthusiastic working-class . . . [which was] free up to the limits imposed on them by nature and a terrible inheritance from [the] tyranny and incompetence of their former rulers . . . We would regard it as a calamity if the present lie campaign were to be allowed to make headway . . .[10]

Shaw was not alone. Other international luminaries were no less ideologically fixated – among them the novelists H. G. Wells and André Gide. Although he would not acknowledge it for many years, Arthur Koestler, who was living in Moscow at the time, witnessed starving children for himself. He described them as 'horrible infants with enormous wobbling heads, stick-like limbs, swollen, pointed bellies'[11] and the famine victims as 'enemies of the people who preferred begging to work'.[12]

The most influential of these fellow-travellers was a Liverpool-born journalist, Walter Duranty, who was the Moscow correspondent of the *New York Times*. An unashamed apologist for the Soviet Union, Duranty was motivated less by ideological conviction than by an appetite for the good life in Moscow, for which he depended on the Kremlin's indulgence. To preserve his privileged status he went out of his way to vilify anyone who challenged his own Panglossian coverage of Soviet affairs for America's most prestigious newspaper. When his reportage was challenged – even indirectly – he was merciless.

In the spring of 1933, a young reporter for the *New York Evening Post*, Gareth Jones, defying the ban on travel to Ukraine, walked for ten days through village after village, where he saw distraught peasants 'eating cattle fodder'. Jones had managed to acquire a visa to enter the Soviet Union courtesy of the Soviet ambassador Ivan Maisky, who wished to ingratiate himself with the former prime minister David Lloyd George, for whom Jones was working as a foreign affairs advisor. This had not impaired Jones's integrity. When the peasants told him 'There is no bread. We are dying,' he did not fail to describe their pitiful state. In other circumstances his harrowing report, which was printed in a number of newspapers, both in the United States and in Britain, might well have made a significant impact.[13] However, Duranty – who a few months earlier had been awarded a Pulitzer Prize for his coverage of Soviet affairs – was swift to pounce, using his pre-eminent status to censure the tyro journalist for writing 'a big scare story'.[14] In a craven determination to protect their own access to the Soviet leadership, most of Duranty's colleagues in the Western press corps based in the Russian capital scurried to take his part.* Though he was grudgingly to admit for the first time that Russia was facing 'a food shortage' which, he conceded, had indeed caused widespread malnutrition, Duranty reassured the readers of the *New York Times* that 'any report of a famine in Russia' was 'an exaggeration or malignant propaganda'.[15] While the Pulitzer Prizewinner's stock in America rose higher than ever, Jones was completely (and in the end, it appears, literally) outgunned by his opponents.†

In Britain, Muggeridge was similarly eclipsed. After witnessing a column of hungry peasants being marched out of their village by a squad of militiamen, he wrote, 'The worst of the class war is that it never stops. First individual kulaks shot and exiled; then groups of peasants; then whole villages.'[16] And he had asked, 'How is it that so many obvious and fundamental facts about Russia are not noticed even by serious and intelligent visitors?'[17] In so far as his challenge was even acknowledged, it was met with incredulity rather than shock. Beatrice Webb, who had herself returned from an eight-week trip to Moscow some months earlier, was perplexed by what she described as 'Malcolm's curiously hysterical denunciation of the Soviet Union . . . drawing a vivid and arrogantly expressed picture of the starvation and oppression of the peasants of the North Caucasus and Ukraine'.[18] Webb's eagerness to swallow the Kremlin's propaganda was widely shared not only by the liberal intelligentsia but also – more tellingly – in the chancelleries of Europe. Western

* For an illuminating account of this episode, see Anne Applebaum, 'How Stalin Hid Ukraine's Famine from the World', *The Atlantic*, 13 October 2017.

† Gareth Jones was murdered by 'bandits' on 12 August 1935 while on a reporting assignment in Mongolia. It was suspected by some that he was targeted by the secret police, anxious to get rid of so turbulent a reporter.

governments had access to enough independent evidence to conclude that Muggeridge and Jones were not exaggerating. But, for the most part, diplomacy dictated that they should be ignored.

In line with the British government's policy of balancing its aversion to the Soviet Union with its apprehension about the rise of Hitler, a senior Foreign Office diplomat, Laurence Collier, was brazenly insouciant. In response to a British MP's anxious query, he wrote, 'The truth of the matter is, of course, that we have a certain amount of information about famine conditions . . . We do not want to make it public, however, because the Soviet government would resent it and our relations with them would be prejudiced.'[19] Thus, as in the Caucasus and other parts of Russia itself, the murderous famine in Ukraine – which was held by many Ukrainians to be a deliberate act of genocide to wipe out their nation – was all but ignored by the outside world.

It would be several decades before Muggeridge's indictment of the Great Famine as 'one of the most monstrous crimes in history, so terrible that people in the future will scarcely be able to believe that it happened'[20] was finally accepted as the truth.* For the most part, those who evinced any curiosity at all were disposed to share Duranty's breezy assertion that (in the phrase variously attributed to Robespierre and Napoleon) 'you can't make an omelette without breaking eggs'.[21] In preparing this dish, Stalin had been responsible for breaking 10 million eggs. He would soon break many more.

In the United States, the newly elected president, Franklin D. Roosevelt, had assumed office in March 1933 with one overriding objective: to bring an end to the Great Depression. Europe was in turmoil, Hitler was supreme in Germany and the Soviet Union was subjecting the Russian people to merciless persecution. Unlike his immediate predecessor, Herbert Hoover, Roosevelt was an internationalist, but he inherited an isolationist Congress and a nation stricken by poverty and hardship. Seeking to inspire hope in the midst of an economic calamity, he began his Inaugural Address with one of his most famous aphorisms. 'Let me assert

---

* The Soviet Union was never to acknowledge the existence of the famine. Even after the fall of communism the Russian authorities continued to downplay its significance.

my firm belief that the only thing we have to fear is . . . fear itself,' he declared, making clear that his priority was to 'conquer' what he described as the 'emergency at home'.[22] With social dislocation, unemployment, hunger and, in some areas, near-starvation threatening to tear apart the social fabric of the nation, foreign relations were bound to come a distant second to the vital need to reboot America's broken capitalist system.

The New Deal was Roosevelt's chosen solution and in the early months of his presidency, it consumed his attention. Europe's post-war predicament did not entirely pass him by, however. Nor was he content merely to watch the evolving crisis from the sidelines. After the failure of their earlier efforts at Versailles and Genoa, and the limited achievement at Locarno, the European chancelleries were once more making tentative efforts to reconcile their competing interests in the hope, yet again, of constructing a framework for economic stability and strategic security. Determined to protect US interests in a global economy, Roosevelt dispatched emissaries to two ambitious international conferences that were running in parallel but with different agendas, one in London and the other in Geneva.

At the World Economic Conference in London, which opened in June, it soon became clear that the US negotiators, at the president's behest, were no more willing to forgo protectionism as the principal means of combating the Great Depression than their European counterparts. As a result, on 27 July 1933 the conference was torpedoed by its most important participant. In Geneva, an ambitiously entitled 'World Disarmament Conference' had opened in February 1932. It was soon deadlocked after France insisted that security should precede disarmament while the Germans argued, conversely, that they should be released from the shackles of Versailles in order to rearm for their own security. After a six-month break, the delegates reconvened in February 1933, under the ominous shadow of the newly established Nazi government in Germany. This stiffened Roosevelt's determination to make 'a very, very definite' success of Geneva.

As evidence of his good faith, he ordered that the size of the US Army be cut from its already modest complement of 140,000 men (only 40,000 more than the level imposed on Germany at Versailles), a gesture that was fiercely resisted by the US War Department. In an angry confrontation at the White House, the army chief of staff, General Douglas MacArthur, was reputed to have told his president that, when the

United States lost the next war, he hoped that as 'an American boy, lying in the mud with an enemy bayonet through his belly and an enemy foot on his dying throat spat out his last curse' the name of Roosevelt, not MacArthur, would be the words he would utter.[23] Roosevelt was enraged by this flagrant defiance and MacArthur backed down. But the general was not appeased. Many years later, he recalled, 'I just vomited on the steps of the White House.'[24]

The president's initiative had no impact. Despite his message to all fifty-four participants urging them to seek 'the complete elimination of all offensive weapons', the diplomats in Geneva demonstrated the same diligent commitment to military protectionism as their counterparts in London had displayed in the name of economic protectionism. The logjam could not be broken. The final blow came in October 1933, when, at Hitler's behest, the German delegation – which was led by Joseph Goebbels, the recently appointed Minister of Public Enlightenment and Propaganda – walked out of the negotiations. For good measure, the Germans simultaneously quit the League of Nations (to which the Weimar government had been admitted in 1926), blaming the refusal of the other powers to grant the Third Reich military parity with them. Chastened by his failures in both London and Geneva, Roosevelt decided to detach the United States – at least temporarily – from the political cauldron on the other side of the Atlantic, noting languidly, 'We shall go through a period of non-co-operation in everything . . . for the next year or two.'[25]

There was one major exception to this retreat: the Soviet Union. In October 1933 the president summoned two of his most trusted aides, Henry Morgenthau, head of the Farm Credit Association and very soon to be appointed Treasury Secretary, and William Bullitt, an experienced diplomat who had been sent to Moscow in 1919 in an attempt to broker a peace deal to end the Civil War (he secured a draft agreement for Wilson but Congress refused to endorse it). In the absence of harmony elsewhere in Europe, Roosevelt instructed them to approach Moscow with a view to improving relations between the White House and the Kremlin, or, as he put it at a press conference to explain this unexpected overture, between 'two great nations, two great peoples'.[26] Gifted with more strategic imagination than his isolationist adversaries in Congress, he judged that rapprochement with Moscow would send a clear warning to the militaristic regime in Tokyo that any further aggression in a region where Soviet and US interests overlapped would not be tolerated. In 1931 the Japanese had occupied Manchuria, reigniting a longstanding border dispute with the Soviet Union and – in the name of 'Asia for the Asians' – seemed set on yet more territorial expansion that threatened to bring them into direct conflict with the United States in the Pacific.

Moscow did not hesitate. After sixteen years of diplomatic isolation (following the US decision to sever relations after the Bolsheviks took power in 1917), the lure of restoring formal links with the world's most powerful state – and the last major nation still to withhold formal recognition – was irresistible. Within days, the Soviet Commissar for Foreign Affairs, Maxim Litvinov – a sinuous negotiator of whom it was said 'he could come dry out of the water', was on a plane to Washington, where he arrived on 8 November. Litvinov was an ideal choice for the task. As a revolutionary émigré, he had lived a chequered life, criss-crossing Europe and secretly buying weapons to smuggle into Russia for the Bolshevik faction of the banned Social Democratic Labour Party (SDLP). He had lived in London, where, in 1903, he had a meeting with Lenin in the London Library, shared a house with Stalin during the SDLP's 5th Congress in 1907 and took an English wife.★ At the age of fifty-seven, he was now an urbane and cultivated Bolshevik diplomat, well acquainted with the ways of the world and unusually well equipped to form easy relations with his Western peers. He was accompanied by the ubiquitous Walter Duranty, whose effusive articles about Stalin's dicta-torship in the *New York Times* had earned him not only the lasting gratitude of the Kremlin but also the US State Department's admiration.

At first, the omens were not encouraging. The talks at official level faltered almost as soon as the pleasantries were over, and within two days reached deadlock. This prompted Roosevelt to intervene personally by inviting Litvinov to a presidential tête-à-tête at the White House. The two men swiftly established a rapport, each charming the other so effect-ively that by the end of that evening they had sketched out a draft for a 'gentlemen's agreement' between the two governments.

★ The couple's grandchildren became distinguished Soviet dissidents. According to the historian and former British ambassador to the Soviet Union Rodric Braithwaite, one of these settled in Devon, in the south-west of England.

Litvinov happily conceded two key demands. The first required him to confirm that his government would refrain from interfering in the internal affairs of the United States, through either propaganda or subversion – a concession that was unlikely to be worth the paper it was written on except as a gesture of goodwill. The second demand – that the religious rights of American citizens living in the Soviet Union would be respected – was more significant. The issue of religious freedom was of great importance to the Catholic Church and therefore mattered greatly in Washington, politically as well as morally.

During the Great Depression several thousand US citizens had been lured away from the vanishing promises of the American Dream to the seductive image of the workers' paradise fed to them by the likes of Duranty. Among other rosy portraits of life in the Soviet Union, he reassured his readers that each of the Gulag's concentration camps 'forms a sort of "commune" where everyone lives comparatively free, not imprisoned but compelled to work for the good of the community . . . They are certainly not convicts in the American sense of the word'.[27]

And there was work. In 1931 Henry Ford had signed a $40 million deal to build a plant at Nizhny Novgorod (some 320 kilometres from Moscow) in which to assemble 75,000 outdated Model A saloon cars. More than 100,000 Americans applied to work there; 10,000 were hired. By 1931, there were enough Americans living in Moscow to sustain an English-language newspaper, the *Moscow News*. English language schools were opened in four Russian cities – Moscow, Leningrad and Kharkov (the site of a tractor factory), as well as Nizhny Novgorod.[28]

Though many of these adventurers were soon disillusioned with life under Bolshevism, it was not their unhappy experiences that shaped the American attitudes towards the Soviet Union. More importantly, there were plenty of legislators as well as churchmen whose aversion to communism and atheism would ensure that any apparent agreement with Moscow would be under persistent and sceptical scrutiny.

To appease the doubters in Congress, Litvinov readily agreed to repay up to $150 million of debt owing since the end of the First World War, which was somewhat less than the $600 million the State Department believed was due. It was enough, though, for a deal to be done. In the early hours of 17 November 1933, Litvinov and Roosevelt signed their concordat, thereby formally establishing diplomatic relations between their two governments for the first time since the Bolshevik revolution. Duranty's persuasive falsehoods in the *New York Times* did not determine Washington's attitude towards the Kremlin but they assuredly cleared away some notable obstacles that would otherwise have stood in its way. Had American public opinion been roused by the truth about Stalin's 'liquidation' of the kulaks and the mass starvation of the Soviet peasantry it entailed, Roosevelt – ever sensitive to the national mood – would have been obliged to use a far longer spoon to sup with the Soviet foreign minister.

As it was, any fears that Roosevelt might have harboured about the public reaction to his announcement that America was about to embrace the world's first communist state were swiftly dispelled. The agreement was widely welcomed by business leaders and, save for a few sceptics, by Congress as well. No less pertinently, the major churches, reassured that their own communicants – if not the Russian faithful – would be spared persecution by the Bolshevik regime, did not protest. Roosevelt's acute political antennae had served him well.

The president's first official envoy to the Soviet Union arrived in Moscow committed to forging a new era of harmony between the two ideological adversaries. William Bullitt, whose first visit to the Soviet Union in 1919 had not been forgotten, was greeted like an old friend by the Kremlin. With a bonhomie and extravagance rare even by the standards of those days, the new ambassador opened the doors of the US Embassy to anyone who mattered in Moscow. His parties became the talk of the town. On at least one occasion he treated some 500 guests to a culinary orgy of spectacular delights that were said to rival the most lavish pre-revolutionary banquet.[29]* But the more Bullitt learned about the regime, the less enthusiastic he became. The pervasive secrecy, suspicion, surveillance and repression that hung like a fetid pall over the life of the city came to disgust him. He returned to Washington three years later to re-emerge as an ardent and outspoken anti-communist.

Roosevelt did not allow Bullitt's volte-face to deter him. Neither the Kremlin's reluctance to honour its outstanding debts, nor the continued activities of Soviet intelligence agents in America, let alone the failure of

---

* Bullitt's famous banquet is said to have inspired a climactic episode in Mikhail Bulgakov's wonderful novel *The Master and Margarita*.

Moscow's trade czars to facilitate lucrative deals with US exporters or the growing evidence that Stalin was a murderous tyrant – caused him to revise his view that a strategic relationship with the Soviet Union was critically important to US interests and should be preserved, even at high cost.

It was not by accident, therefore, that he chose Joseph Davies to succeed Bullitt. A skilful lawyer, an experienced diplomat and a personal friend of long standing, Davies shared Roosevelt's outlook but with a loyalty that evidently shrivelled his critical faculties. Determined to strengthen Washington's ties with the Kremlin, he blindfolded himself to the evidence of Stalin's brutality with legalisms that shredded the ethical values he might have been supposed to represent. Whether or not this nonchalance pleased the White House, his reports were never subjected to serious challenge – an oversight that protected the president from any searching scrutiny of his strategic imperative: the maintenance of a cordial transatlantic relationship with that 'great nation'.

During the Great Famine Stalin had discovered how easy it was to suborn international opinion with a confection of repeated denials and a carefully crafted infusion of half-truths with which to dupe the credulous. This did not mean that he believed his tenure to be secure.

The Soviet dictator was born in 1878 in the Georgian town of Gori. The son of an impoverished wife-beating shoemaker, Joseph was a diminutive child who was clever enough to win a scholarship to the spiritual seminary in the town of Tiflis. He was a chorister who wrote poetry of sufficient quality to be included in various Georgian anthologies. But at the age of twenty, by which time he had read Karl Marx's recently published *Das Kapital* and steeped himself in radical thought, he walked out of the seminary as a committed atheist and nascent revolutionary. He was soon at the centre of a web of ideologues, committed to overthrowing the repressive czarist regime of Nicholas II. Working underground to foment unrest, he was arrested and imprisoned on more than one occasion.

Following the notorious St Petersburg Massacre in 1905, he formed armed squads that raided government arsenals, extorted funds from local businesses and launched guerrilla attacks on government forces. Later that year, as a delegate to a Bolshevik conference in St Petersburg, he met Lenin and soon became one of his prominent comrades. By 1912 he was not only a member of the Central Committee but also the editor of the then underground party newspaper, *Pravda*. Throughout his rise to power, he was frequently either in jail or forced into internal exile. By the time of the 1917 revolution, with Lenin and Trotsky he was a member of the triumvirate who shaped the course of Soviet history.

During the Civil War he demonstrated an unmatched readiness to use the violence of the state to terrorize any suspected counter-revolutionary into submission. Often falling out with colleagues, mortally so in the case of Leon Trotsky, he was as profoundly insecure as he was ruthless and ambitious. Lenin, who did not care for Stalin's boorish nature and disapproved of his offensive and cavalier manner, nonetheless trusted him sufficiently to appoint him as the party's general secretary. Following Lenin's stroke later that year and his death in 1924, Stalin's rise to absolute power was gradual but inexorable. During his ascent he had made many enemies and he feared those about him might either seek to subvert his authority or – as he had done to others on so many occasions already – find ways of terminating his life.

Thus, using the pretext provided by the assassination of Sergei Kirov, a leading member of the Soviet Politburo (in circumstances so murky as to implicate Stalin himself), the Soviet leader unleashed what became known officially as the Great Purge. Within two months of Kirov's murder on 1 December 1934, almost 200 senior communists had been shot. No Soviet voice could be heard in protest, while once again the regime's apologists abroad found reason to justify these atrocities. As Bernard Shaw breezily explained, 'The top of the ladder is a very trying place for old revolutionists who have had no administrative experience, who have had no financial experience, who have been trained as penniless hunted fugitives with Karl Marx on the brain and not as statesmen. They often have to be pushed off the ladder with a rope around their necks.'[30]

In operational terms, the Great Purge was a simple project. Stalin already had the means readily to hand: a well-established police state bequeathed to him by Lenin, who had established the Cheka to oversee and execute the Red Terror campaign in the early days of the revolution, when between 150,000 and 250,000 'counter-revolutionaries' were executed.* Lenin had also established scores of labour camps to incarcerate

---

* The Cheka: 'The Extraordinary Commission for Combating Counter-Revolution and Sabotage'.

political dissidents alongside 'common' criminals, where they endured conditions of extreme hardship and brutality. Those who survived were treated to a punishment regime by prison officers licensed to go far beyond the bounds of common humanity into the realms of unconstrained sadism.

Stalin expanded this network of surveillance, arrest, detention, torture, summary execution and penal servitude (notably creating the state-wide Gulag) when he inherited Lenin's crown in 1922. The names changed (in 1922, the Cheka was transmogrified into OGPU, which was in turn subsumed into the NKVD in 1934*) but the vengeful purpose did not. By the mid-1930s the Stalinists in the Politburo had total control of the levers of state power. Aside from a handful of deviationists from left and right, who muttered in protest but had almost no influence, all significant opposition had been crushed. Though formally he was no more than primus inter pares, Stalin was virtually unassailable. His paranoia told him otherwise, however: he would need to liquidate many more subversives in the vain hope of exorcizing the psychotic demons that assailed him. Thoughts were as dangerous to him as any other threat. When they were wrapped in the ironies of a poem, they posed a viral menace. When the great Soviet poet Osip Mandelstam wrote, 'Only in Russia is poetry respected. It gets people killed. Where else is poetry so common a motive for murder?' he was charged with 'counter-revolutionary activities'. In 1938 he was sentenced to five years' hard labour, though he died from cold and hunger in a Siberian transit camp before he could reach his final destination. Among many of Mandelstam's fatal crimes was to circulate a poem, which became known as 'The Stalin Epigram', in which he directly attacked the dictator as a gleeful killer who 'rolls the executions on his tongue like berries. / He wishes he could hug them like big friends from home.'[31]

Though the entire Politburo was complicit in the terror that Stalin now unleashed upon the Soviet Union, he was its presiding genius. It was he who instigated the purge of lowly members of the Communist Party, he who authorized the routine use of torture to extract 'confessions' from alleged 'enemies of the people' and to incriminate colleagues

---

* OGPU: 'The Joint State Political Directorate'; NKVD: 'The People's Commissariat for Internal Affairs. In 1946 it was replaced by the KGB: 'The Committee for State Security'.

of crimes they had not committed, and he who conceived the show trials at which, after a travesty of due process, the Supreme Court – proceedings that he occasionally observed from a gallery overlooking the courtroom – delivered verdict and sentence in a pantomime of public justice.

At the first of these show trials, it took the Supreme Court no more than six days to find sixteen defendants guilty of conspiring to overthrow the government; each one, as had been preordained, was then executed in the cellars of the NKVD headquarters in central Moscow, the Lubyanka, where innocents were routinely tortured to extract false confessions.* At the second show trial, in January 1937, the court similarly took six days before ordering that thirteen of the seventeen defendants should be forthwith executed by firing squad; the other four were sentenced to many years of hard labour.

The US ambassador took it upon himself to attend the entire trial and to take detailed notes of the proceedings. On the basis of these, Davies sent a lengthy missive to the US Secretary of State, Cordell Hull, who had been appointed in 1933 (and would remain in that post until his retirement in 1945). In this report he described how, in their 'despair', the defendants sat 'holding their heads in their hands or burying their heads upon the rail' as they listened to the state prosecutor reading out their already-signed confessions to the military triumvirate who stood in judgement over them.[32] His sensibilities were clearly offended.

Nonetheless the ambassador informed Hull that he had 'arrived at the reluctant conclusion that the state had established its case, at least as to the existence of a widespread conspiracy and plot among the political leaders against the Soviet government', adding that 'to have assumed that this proceeding was inevitable and staged as a project of dramatic political fiction would be to presuppose the creative genius of Shakespeare'.[33] Shakespeare had his Fools; in Davies, Stalin had his Useful Idiot.

One of the three defendants to avoid the death penalty was Karl Radek, who received a sentence of ten years' penal servitude in return for implicating some of the most senior figures in the Soviet hierarchy in acts of alleged treason. Among these thus identified were the leading

---

* It retained that reputation after the NKVD became the KGB. Today the building is the headquarters of the Russian Federation's FSB security service.

Marxist theoretician Nikolai Bukharin and Marshal Mikhail Tukh-achevsky, one of the Red Army's most formidable generals.

As a twenty-seven-year-old commander during the 1920 Russian–Polish War, Tukhachevsky had proved himself to be a brilliant tactician and his stock rose rapidly. By the late 1920s he had emerged as a pioneering military theorist and a radical reformist. Unhappily for him, he once had cause to reprimand Stalin, who was then the political commander of the Southwestern Front, for interfering in what were purely military matters. Stalin did not forget that clash. By the time he had been formally anointed as party leader in 1929, the charismatic military commander had risen to become army chief of staff. Seeing him as a potential threat to his own authority, the dictator at once set about undermining Tukhachevsky's totemic status.

In 1930 spurious allegations that he was planning a coup led to an investigation, which, despite the assiduous efforts of OGPU, failed to find a scintilla of evidence against him. Stalin's moment did not arrive, therefore, until the January 1937 show trial where Radek chose to save his own skin by accusing Tukhachevsky of treason. The marshal's fate was sealed. Under interrogation and torture he signed a confession (stained with his own blood) in which he admitted to the preposterous charge that he was a German agent who was collaborating with Bukharin to overthrow the Soviet government.* His conviction was a foregone conclusion. On 11 June 1937, at a specially convened military tribunal, which no defence attorneys were permitted to attend and to whose verdict no appeal was allowed, he was sentenced to death along with eight Red Army generals.

Later that evening, after Stalin had approved the death sentence, Tukhachevsky was taken from his cell in the Lubyanka and shot once in the back of his head by the NKVD's chief executioner, Major General Vasily Blokhin, who had had been appointed to this coveted role by Stalin in 1928. He led a company of official killers which, at the NKVD's behest, carried out numerous mass executions, for which Blokhin was garlanded with honours including the Order of Lenin.

---

* For a full account of this episode, see Simon Sebag Montefiore, *Stalin: The Court of the Red Tsar* (Weidenfeld and Nicolson, 2003), pp. 196–201. Sebag Montefiore's revelations, the product of an assiduous examination of the Soviet archives, throw a memorable and merciless light on the Soviet dictator.

After Tukhachevsky's execution, the general's wife, Nina, and his two brothers, who were military instructors, were also shot. Three of his sisters were dispatched to the Gulag and his young daughter was similarly expelled once she had come of age (remaining in exile until after Stalin's death in 1953). Long before that, in a gruesomely accidental form of retributive justice, five of the eight judges who condemned Tukhachevsky to death had themselves been executed.

Stalin's paranoia was buttressed by a no less obsessive belief in the higher echelons of the party that the Soviet Union had been in a virtual state of siege ever since the revolution, threatened from without and from within. By the mid-1930s, as the international war clouds gathered across Europe, this dread had become contagious. In the absence of any evidence, the source of the virus was pinpointed to the Soviet High Command – some of whose most senior commanders had indeed served in the Czar's Imperial Army during the Great War or with the White Russians during the Civil War – which stood accused of incubating an 'enemy within' that was conspiring to subvert Bolshevism by collaborating with the agents of foreign powers like Britain, Poland, Japan or Germany.

A swathe of marshals, generals, corps commanders and divisional commanders along with a senior admiral were accordingly purged. Within a month of Tukhachevsky's execution more than 1,000 senior officers had been 'exposed' as conspirators in a 'military-fascist' plot against the Soviet State. Some were executed, some were imprisoned, and others expelled from the party. By the late autumn of 1938, 10,000 army leaders had been arrested and a further 35,000 had been discharged (although 11,000 of these were later reinstated).[34] The culture of terror reached into every rank. Junior officers avoided suggesting initiatives or showing leadership, preferring instead to behave like zombies, automata merely carrying out instructions and avoiding the limelight. The decapitation of the Red Army not only removed or crippled many of the brightest and best but caused a seismic disruption that had a corrosive effect on the overall morale of officers and men alike. More broadly, though its intended purpose may not have been '*pour encourager les autres*', the purges had precisely that effect on every Soviet citizen, suppressing any prospect of challenge or defiance.

By now the agents of the Great Purge were on the rampage across the Soviet Union to eliminate all 'anti-Soviet elements' wherever they could be found. After the 'exposure' of Tukhachevsky's plot, scores of thousands were swept up by NKVD agents working with frantic energy to meet the arbitrary quota of arrests set by the Politburo. Under the overall supervision of the head of the NKVD, a dwarfish sadist called Nikolai Yezhov, confessions were routinely extracted from the accused using torture. Beatings were so harsh that the eyes of the victims 'literally popped out of their heads'.[35] Three-man tribunals – troikas – dispensed summary justice with the stroke of a pen. To run the NKVD was to wield immense power. It was also an extremely dangerous post to occupy. Yezhov had succeeded Genrikh Yagoda (who had overseen the mass executions of the kulaks) in 1936. The following year Yagoda was found guilty of treason and executed. The year after that Yezhov was removed in favour of Lavrenty Beria, who immediately found cause to have him shot as an 'enemy of the people'. Beria was to last much longer – it would not be until 1953, following the death of Stalin, that he was to meet a similar fate – and was responsible for many more targeted killings than any of his predecessors.

Stalin was as brazenly resolute in the commission of mass murder as Adolf Hitler would later show himself to be. Along with Molotov and other senior members of the Politburo, the Soviet leader personally authorized the execution of tens of thousands of those who had been rounded up by the NKVD merely by writing the word 'Approved' against their names on the death lists routinely submitted to the Kremlin. On one day alone in late 1938, he sat with Molotov as together they dispatched 3,167 people to their deaths by this means.[36] As his loyal henchman was airily to concede, 'Haste ruled the day . . . Innocent people were sometimes caught.'[37] By the end of the year, when Stalin suspended the Great Purge, at least 750,000 victims had thus been 'liquidated', not because they had committed any identifiable crime but to ensure that they could not do so in the future. Defining 'enemies of the people' as those who dared to question 'the rightness of the Party line' not only in words but also 'in their thoughts, yes even in their thoughts',[38] Stalin presided over the destiny of 160 million people in the name of a socialist revolution with the authority of a despot. Such was the state of the Soviet Union as Europe slipped at an accelerating rate towards the abyss of the century's second great military conflagration.

3.   Shuttle Diplomacy

In London, the government's policy of appeasement had by this time seized the political agenda. Strategically, the bloodletting in Russia was a sideshow which merely confirmed the Cabinet's view that the Soviet Union was in thrall to a tyranny exercised by revolutionary barbarians. Since his arrival in London in 1932 Ivan Maisky, the urbane and club-bable Soviet ambassador, had gone out of his way to cultivate some of the most influential figures in London's political establishment. While he was careful to demonstrate that he was a loyal servant of his masters in Moscow, his personal diaries reveal him to have been an astute and acerbic observer. '[Neville] Chamberlain', he noted on 8 March 1938, 'is a consummate reactionary with a sharply defined anti-Soviet position . . . who feels with his every fibre that the USSR is the principal enemy and its communism is the main danger to the capitalist system that is so dear to his heart . . . Such is the prime minister we have to deal with now in England.'[1] Maisky might have been even less enamoured of the British leader had he known that, following their first meeting in 1932 (at which time Chamberlain was Chancellor of the Exchequer) – the 'consummate reactionary' had casually described the new Soviet ambassador as a 'revolt-ing but clever little Jew'.[2]

Chamberlain's view that Moscow was both ideologically beyond the pale and strategically irrelevant had come to prevail in both Whitehall and Westminster. Ministers and civil servants shared the view that the only way to prevent Britain being sucked into another ruinous war in Europe was to appease rather than provoke the German Führer. The thought that the Soviet Union might play a constructive role in con-taining Nazism – thereby stabilizing Europe – barely registered in the Cabinet's collective mind.

Only a tiny proportion of Conservative MPs failed to succumb to this governmental groupthink. Among this minority, only Churchill – now in his 'wilderness years' – and, to a lesser degree, Anthony Eden (who had resigned as Foreign Secretary in February 1938 in protest at

Chamberlain's stance) – were able to strike any chord with the public beyond Westminster. Hitler's rise to supreme authority in Germany had tempered Churchill's loathing of Bolshevism. Four years earlier, in July 1934, in a speech endorsing the Soviet Union's successful application to join the League of Nations, Churchill had argued for reconciliation with Moscow to counter what he regarded as the far graver threat posed to the British Empire by the Nazis. His was not an ideological volte-face but a strategic assessment of the teetering balance of power in Europe. In the same month, he had commanded the attention of the House of Commons as he urged his colleagues to understand that Russia was 'most deeply desirous of maintaining peace' and could become 'a stabilizing force in Europe'. Conversely, he warned that the militaristic regime in Germany not only was bent on rearmament but also 'might easily plunge into a foreign adventure of the most dangerous and catastrophic character to the whole world'.[3]

Britain's future prime minister had judged Nazi Germany only too well. As anyone who had paid attention to the relevant passages in *Mein Kampf* would have known, Hitler's imperial vision was in no doubt. The Führer's demotic genius had been to find a language that would chime with the 'stab in the back theory' popular among Germans – that the Versailles treaty had been an 'instrument of unlimited blackmail and shameful humiliation' which had fallen like a 'whip-lash on the people'[4] – and with his obsessive appetite for territorial expansion. As he had indicated at the secret meeting with his generals as soon as he became Führer, Germany's only way to acquire Lebensraum was by invasion and conquest. Soon afterwards, in a speech to a gathering of rural policy makers,* one of his most zealous adherents, his agriculture minister, Richard Darré† – a high-ranking member of the SS – described the proposed geographical contours that would shape the Nazi Empire:

> The natural area for settlement by the German people is the territory to
> the east of the Reich's boundaries up to the Urals, bordered in the south

* The Reichsnährstand – RSNT – the German Reich's rural and agricultural policy body, established in 1933 and abolished at the end of the war.
† Darré was arrested in 1945 and sentenced to seven years' imprisonment at the Nuremberg 'Ministries Trial' (1947–49). He was released in 1950 and died from liver cancer three years later.

by the Caucasus, Caspian Sea, Black Sea and the watershed which divides the Mediterranean basin from the Baltic and the North Sea. We will settle this space, according to the law that a superior people always has the right to conquer and to own the land of an inferior people.[5]

There would be arguments about the Reich's military priorities, options and timing, but no backsliding was permitted by those required to establish this new European order. In August 1934, on the death of Hindenburg, all members of the armed forces had been required to swear an oath of allegiance to 'Mein Führer'. Seven months later, Hitler renounced the military prohibitions imposed on Germany at Versailles. A year after that, in March 1936, after formally abrogating the Locarno treaty, German troops reoccupied the Rhineland. With the exception of the Soviet Union, Europe (like the United States) chose to avert its troubled gaze from these persistent violations.

In London there was no appetite for a military response. The absence of any significant protest or demonstration reinforced the judgement of the Secretary of State for War, Duff Cooper, that the public did not care 'two hoots' about the remilitarization of the Rhineland.[6] Similarly, most British MPs, according to one of their number, the diarist Harold Nicolson, were 'terribly pro-German, which means afraid of war',[7] while Chamberlain's predecessor as prime minister, Stanley Baldwin, observed bleakly that Britain did not in any case have the military forces needed to enforce its treaty obligations.[8] At a private meeting with senior Conservative parliamentarians in July 1936, Baldwin was complacency personified. When a deputation from both the Lords and the Commons arrived, he airily dismissed Churchill's warnings about Hitler, opining that

> none of us knows what goes on in that strange man's mind . . . We all know [his] desire, and he has come out with it in his book, to move east, and if he should move east it should not break my heart . . . If there is any fighting in Europe to be done, I should like to see the Bolshies and the Nazis doing it.[9]

In his clumsy way, the prime minister had articulated an attitude that was becoming commonplace in Whitehall and which – as Moscow had long suspected – would shape Britain's negotiating stance towards the Bolshevik regime in the next few years.

That November in the House of Commons, Churchill, insistent that Britain should rearm against the Nazi threat, had been at his most withering about Baldwin's vacillating leadership:

> Everything, he assured us, is entirely fluid. I am sure that is true. Anyone can see what the position is. The government simply cannot make up their mind, or they cannot get the Prime Minister to make up his mind. So they go on in strange paradox, decided only to be undecided, resolved to be irresolute, adamant for drift, solid for fluidity, all powerful to be impotent.[10]

Two years later, on 12 March 1938, by which time Hitler had appointed himself Commander-in-Chief of the Wehrmacht, the German 8th Army marched triumphantly into Austria. To great rejoicing in Vienna, Hitler proclaimed his delight in his acquisition of 'the newest bastion of the German Reich'. But there was much further to go. Within days of the Anschluss, Hitler set about finalizing plans for his next conquest, telling his generals on 28 May, 'I'm utterly determined that Czechoslovakia should disappear from the map.'[11] The Czech president, Edvard Beneš, was informed that, unless he ceded the Sudetenland (where the majority of the population was German), he would face the military consequences of his defiance.

This prompted the other major European powers, led by Britain, to begin a bout of frenzied but despairing international diplomacy to avert that prospect. Willing to make almost any accommodation with Hitler to avoid another struggle on the European battlefield, Neville Chamberlain even boarded an aeroplane for the first time in sixteen years to begin his own form of shuttle diplomacy, until – less a peer than a supplicant – he arrived in Munich in the last week of September to confirm that neither Britain nor France would offer any significant resistance to Hitler's demands. There were 3.5 million disaffected ethnic Germans living in the Sudetenland, most of whom relished the thought of being 'liberated' by the Nazis. Their relative economic deprivation had been exploited by their own leaders to produce a groundswell of nationalism and demands for autonomy. In an attempt to broker a compromise with the Czech government, Chamberlain had dispatched a mission to Prague in August 1938, led by the National Liberal peer Lord Runciman.

Unbeknown to the British, the German Sudeten leaders were under orders from Berlin to avoid making any such deal. Runciman failed but, on his return to London, reported that the Sudeten minority's urge to turn to 'their kinsmen' in Germany for help was a 'natural development under the circumstances'.

More significantly, no Western government – least of all Britain's – was willing to sacrifice its own armed forces in a military venture that was fraught with uncertainty; the prevailing view in London and Paris was that nothing could be done by arms to save Czechoslovakia from the panzers. Yet, despite the fact that the Nazis had increased military expenditure to the point where, by 1938, armaments consumed by far the greater part of the Reich's GDP, the Wehrmacht was not nearly so potent as the anti-appeasers believed. Ironically, Churchill's exaggerated claims about the Third Reich's military strength had the opposite effect to what he intended: they increased the support for appeasement. Thus, in his crassly worded BBC broadcast on 27 September, Chamberlain spoke for many who feared bombardment by the Luftwaffe when he said, 'How horrible, fantastic, incredible it is, that we should be digging trenches and trying on gas masks here because of a quarrel in a faraway land between people of whom we know nothing.' And there was very little dissent when he added, 'However much we may sympathize with a small nation confronted by a big and powerful neighbour, we cannot in all circumstances undertake to involve the whole British Empire in war simply on her account. If we have to fight on, it must be on larger issues than that.'

Beneš was both humiliated and devastated. Excluded altogether from the Munich negotiations, he had no choice but to acquiesce in the deal agreed over his head the following day by the British prime minister, joined by the leaders of France and Italy, as they signed away the Sudetenland to the Nazis.

Within Germany itself, the Nazis had been working simultaneously to realize Hitler's vision for the Third Reich on the home front. From the moment he came to power, those who dared to oppose Nazism were persecuted by the state police for violating new treason laws and incarcerated in their thousands. Not content with this, Goering, Himmler (who had now been given command of the SS) and Heydrich (whom Himmler had chosen as his successor to run the Gestapo) drew up a hit

list of those Nazis they regarded as threats to Hitler's supreme authority. During the Night of the Long Knives at the end of June 1934, the
SS and the Gestapo, supported by members of Goering's personal battalion, killed eighty-five Stormtroopers – members of the Nazi
paramilitary organization led by Ernst Röhm, whom Hitler feared as a
rival. Röhm himself was arrested, imprisoned and shot dead at point
blank range. Hitler justified this purge on the grounds of Röhm's
'treason'.

These killings coincided with a wave of repressive measures taken
against those who failed to meet the Aryan ideal. Among those to be
rounded up and incarcerated in prison camps were vagrants, drug addicts
and homosexuals (Himmler had toughened the pre-existing law crimin-
alizing homosexuality). This persecution and purification of Germany
bore a similarity to the methods adopted by the NKVD in the Soviet
Union. Although the numbers thus imprisoned were far smaller than
those who filled the Soviet Gulag, the underlying principle was chill-
ingly similar.

Likewise, with terrifying intensity, Hitler's determination to liquidate the Jewish 'bacillus' had acquired accelerating momentum. By 1938,
only 9,000 of the 50,000 Jewish companies that had been in operation
when Hitler came to power still survived. The rest – large and small –
had been forced to sell up or close down (greatly to the advantage of
firms such as Mannesmann, Krupp and IG Farben, who bought these
assets at rock-bottom prices). In the same year a host of other restrictions
was imposed. Jewish doctors and lawyers were forbidden to practise, and
in August a decree was issued instructing all Jews to add either the word
'Israel' or 'Sara' to their official papers. From October of that year, the
single letter 'J' was stamped in all Jewish passports.

The assassination in Paris on 7 November 1938 of Ernst vom Rath, a
Nazi diplomat, by the seventeen-year-old Herschel Grynszpan, a
German-born Polish Jew, became the trigger and excuse for an anti-
Semitic pogrom forty-eight hours later. Kristallnacht – the Night of
Broken Glass – was an orchestrated eruption of popular hatred. As the
authorities watched on approvingly, many hundreds of Jewish homes,
schools and hospitals in cities across Germany and Austria (following
the Anschluss earlier in the year) were vandalized; more than 1,000 synagogues and 7,000 Jewish businesses were destroyed or ransacked. At

least a hundred Jews were killed in a murderous spree led by the SA, (now headed by Röhm's chief of staff, Victor Lutze), much diminished in influence following the Night of the Long Knives, but no less useful as an instrument of state brutality. Many more Jewish families were subjected to physical abuse and random beatings. More than 1,300 individuals are estimated to have died either from their wounds or by their own hand, so terrified were they by the pogrom.

Following that atrocity, 30,000 Jewish men were rounded up and arbitrarily detained in concentration camps at Dachau, Sachsenhausen (both established in 1933) and the recently opened Buchenwald. Here they endured abuse and other cruelties designed to 'persuade' them that their only prospect of salvation was to flee Germany. To tighten the screw still further, the government issued a raft of decrees under which Jews were forbidden to own cars, enter public libraries, theatres, cinemas, concert halls, lecture theatres or swimming pools, have a telephone or even own a pet.

In the ensuing panic, long queues formed outside foreign embassies and consulates as tens of thousands of Jews scrambled to find a way of escape. Victor Klemperer was the son of a rabbi, a cousin of the conductor Otto Klemperer and a notable scholar who had been dismissed from his post as a professor of Romance languages following a ban on Jewish academics. On 6 December 1938, fearing that it would take years for him and his disabled wife to acquire the necessary visas or to buy emigration papers, he wrote in his diary that, under the accumulating pressure, 'our nerves have gone to the dogs'. He had heard alarming whispers about the concentration camps, one of which came from his friend Alfred Aron, who had just been released from one of them. 'Frightful hints and fragmentary stories from Buchenwald', he noted that evening, '. . . no one comes back from there a second time, between ten and twenty people die every day anyway.'[12]

Kristallnacht and its aftermath were widely reported abroad, shocking civilized opinion in the rest of the world. The persecution of German Jewry could no longer be dismissed as a perverse ideological aspiration: it was, unambiguously and overtly, a flagrant crime against humanity. Klemperer, who was one of only a handful of Jews to survive the war without leaving Germany, was dismayed by those of his peers who were ready to collaborate with the Nazi authorities in the hope of finding an escape route through the establishment of a Jewish state in some remote corner of the world. 'The solution to the Jewish question', he wrote 'can only be found in the deliverance from those who invented it. And the world – because this really does concern the world – will be forced to act accordingly.'[13] His optimism was premature. In the 1930s 'the world' – at least in the form of its European governments – had no more intention of confronting Hitler over the persecution of the Jews than it had had of confronting Stalin over the persecution of the kulaks. When human rights were weighed in the balance against national self-interest, they were inevitably found wanting.

By the autumn of 1938, Nazi triumphalism was rampant. A short while before putting his name to the Munich Agreement, Hitler addressed 15,000 members of the Nazi Party in the Berlin Sportpalast. In the words of the US correspondent William Shirer, who had been in Germany since 1933, he was 'shouting and shrieking in the worst state of excitement I've ever seen him in. Full of more venom than even he has ever shown . . . For the first time in all the years I've observed him he seemed tonight to have completely lost control of himself.' As the Führer sat down, 'Goebbels leapt up to shout "one thing is sure: 1918 will never be repeated!"' At this, according to Shirer, 'Hitler looked up to him, a wild eager expression in his eyes, as if those were the words which he had been searching for all evening and hadn't quite found. He leapt to his feet and with a fanatical fire in his eyes that I shall never forget brought his right hand, after a grand sweep, pounding down on the table and yelled with all the power in his mighty lungs: "Ja!" Then he slumped into his chair exhausted.'[14]

4. Self-Delusion and Bad Faith

Chamberlain appeared genuinely to think that he had secured 'peace for our time' at Munich. As he wrote soon afterwards to the Archbishop of Canterbury, 'I sincerely believe that we have at last opened the way to that general appeasement which alone can save the world from chaos.'[1] Judging by the euphoria that greeted his return, most British people were initially only too eager to share his delusion. More than 20,000 laudatory letters poured into 10 Downing Street along with an astonishing array of gifts, which ranged from fishing rods and umbrellas to a grand piano and a pair of Dutch clogs. King George VI and many of his family wrote to congratulate the prime minister. In Parliament there was similar adulation. In this feverish atmosphere the minority of anti-appeasers, in and out of the chamber, were rounded on for allegedly betraying their country. Duff Cooper (who resigned from the Cabinet the day after Munich in protest) was among those to be denounced as a 'traitor'. When Churchill was similarly traduced, he gave as good as he got, apparently berating one fellow Tory 'like a Billingsgate fishwife'. Beyond the Westminster hot-house, the public mood was no less intemperate. The novelist Barbara Cartland observed that people who were 'ordinarily calm and unpolitically minded lost their tempers, were furious with those who disagreed with them, rude and offensive at the slightest provocation'.[2]

The mood was short lived. As though the nation had imbibed excessively from a heady cocktail, the jubilation was followed by a hangover. As the doubts began to surface, the thin-skinned prime minister became peevish, turning on his critics in the Commons who had the temerity to insist that the Nazis should no longer be indulged and that Britain should rearm to confront the aggressor. In one of several similar letters to his sister Ida, to whom he frequently confided his innermost thoughts, Chamberlain betrayed the petulance that so often marred his judgement, complaining that Churchill and his followers were 'carrying on a regular conspiracy against me'.[3]

Chamberlain's gall was breathtaking. In a clear breach of the very values he accused Churchill of violating, he was himself about to initiate a conspiratorial venture of his own. Though he shared the widespread disgust at the anti-Semitic rampage on Kristallnacht, he refused to allow the outrage it provoked in Britain to divert him from his resolve to keep the embers of appeasement glowing. Given the febrile atmosphere, though, he had to move by stealth. Without informing his Foreign Secretary, Lord Halifax – who had started to have second thoughts about appeasement – he sanctioned the opening of secret channels to Berlin through which a succession of amateur emissaries sought, on his behalf, to encourage the Führer to abandon his territorial ambitions and instead work with Chamberlain to consolidate the peace that the prime minister still thought he might construct on the rickety foundations of Munich. On one occasion (29 November 1938) after the Foreign Office – via MI5 – found out about a particularly egregious example of this prime ministerial subterfuge, Halifax confronted Chamberlain with the evidence but without revealing his source. The prime minister affected to have no knowledge of any such contact, claiming that the Foreign Secretary's revelation left him 'aghast'. Halifax chose to believe him.[4]*

By now Hitler did not bother to conceal his demented world view. Addressing a gathering of 3,600 young officers in the grand Mosaic Hall of Albert Speer's new Reich Chancellery on 18 January 1939, he demanded their 'unconditional belief' that 'our Reich will one day be the dominant power in Europe', declaring his 'unshakeable will that the German Wehrmacht should become the strongest armed force of the entire world'.[5] Twelve days later, on 30 January 1939, addressing a fervently enthusiastic Reichstag, he went further, explicitly linking his vision for Lebensraum with his readiness to 'annihilate' the Jews.† If the warmongering 'Jewish media' and its political allies in the United States and Britain sought to thwart German aspirations, the Third Reich was

---

* For a carefully researched and illuminating account of the years leading up to Munich, see Tim Bouverie, *Appeasing Hitler: Chamberlain, Churchill and the Road to War* (Bodley Head, 2019).

† As Ian Kershaw has pointed out, the German word for annihilation – *Vernichtung* – is 'a conveniently ambiguous term' that can denote physical extermination or extirpation by either expulsion or genocide. See Ian Kershaw, *Hitler, 1936–1945: Nemesis* (Penguin, 2001), pp. 152–3.

ready to resist: 'If international-finance Jewry inside and outside Europe should succeed in plunging the nations once more into a world war', he warned, 'the result will not be the Bolshevization of the earth and thereby the victory of Jewry, but the annihilation of the Jewish race in Europe.'[6] And on 10 February 1939 he told a gathering of senior commanders that Germany's future was contingent on the acquisition of more Lebensraum – the thought of which, he promised, 'will dominate my entire being . . . I will . . . never draw back from the most extreme measures.'[7]

A month later, as though he had never signed the Munich agreement, Hitler summoned the elderly president of the Czech state, Dr Emil Hácha, to Berlin. Barely pausing for the diplomatic niceties, Hitler told him brusquely that German troops were about to march on the Czech capital. According to his interpreter, Paul Schmidt, he went on, 'The entry of German troops cannot be stopped. If you want to avoid bloodshed you had better telephone to Prague at once and tell your Minister for War to order Czech forces to offer no resistance.'[8] With that, the Führer terminated the interview. Having no choice but to comply, the ailing Hácha signed a joint communiqué (which had been drafted by Hitler before the meeting) that incorporated Czechoslovakia into the 'Greater German Reich'.

Hitler's elation at this bloodless triumph was unbounded. Such was his hubris that he evidently required his two female secretaries to plant a kiss on either cheek as he said, 'This is the happiest day of my life . . . I will go down as the greatest German in history.'[9]

As British officials were well aware, the Führer's appetite was far from sated. A Whitehall memorandum from Gladwyn Jebb, whose task was to collate the intelligence from a range of European sources for the Foreign Office, was as prescient as it was unequivocal:

> Germany is controlled by one man, Herr Hitler, whose will is supreme, and who is a blend of fanatic, madman and clear-visioned realist . . . he regards Germany's supremacy in Europe as a step to world supremacy . . . At present he is devoting special attention to the eastward drive, to securing control of the exploitable riches of the south, and possibly more, of Russia . . . But Herr Hitler is *incalculable*, even to his intimates.[10]

Hitler's next target was Poland. In 1934, at Berlin's invitation, the Poles had signed a ten-year non-aggression pact with Germany that was designed to deter the Soviet Union. They had co-operated in the dismemberment of Czechoslovakia by annexing parts of Moravia and Silesia. But they reckoned without Hitler's vulpine treachery. When Warsaw refused to surrender Danzig in April 1939, Hitler decided that Poland should be obliterated by force. On this occasion, though, his thuggery did not go unchallenged. Belatedly appearing to acknowledge that to appease Hitler was to feed an insatiable appetite, Chamberlain had stood in the House of Commons on 31 March 1939 to give the Poles a formal undertaking that if they came under attack and sought assistance, it would be provided. At last, the prime minister had laid down a red line: were Hitler to march on Warsaw, he would face a military confrontation with both Britain and France as well as Poland. Chamberlain's warning drove Hitler into paroxysms of fury. But he was not to be thwarted. On the contrary: it stimulated him to ramp up an alternative means to the same end.

Hitler had been careful not to sever relations with the Soviet Union when he came to power. Although he had repeatedly used the most bellicose language in different places at different times to express his loathing for the 'Bolshevik wire-pullers' who had their 'international Jewish headquarters in Moscow',[11] his anti-communist tirades were directed principally at his domestic opponents rather than the Kremlin. While warning that rapid rearmament was necessary to avoid 'a victory of Bolshevism over Germany [that] would lead not to a Versailles treaty but to the final destruction, indeed to the annihilation, of the German people',[12] he was well aware that the Reich's industrial output was still heavily dependent on Soviet raw materials. Similarly, although the Kremlin routinely used *Pravda* as its mouthpiece to ridicule the German chancellor as variously an 'idiot' or a madman who was 'possessed by a demon',[13] Stalin was careful to ensure that this war of words should not be misconstrued as evidence of belligerent intent. Like Hitler, he was shadow boxing, not fighting but sparring.

Faced with Chamberlain's ultimatum, a truce in the war of words with the Kremlin appeared to offer Hitler a possible solution to his immediate frustrations. Poland – which had re-emerged as a nation state in 1918 but since 1926 had been under military dictatorship – formed a buffer between the two European behemoths. If he could secure a compact with Moscow, the threat of a Soviet military response to a German invasion of Poland would be greatly reduced. Despite their ideological animosities, the framework for such a deal was already in place. The Third Reich merely had to rekindle the still-glowing embers of an old fire. From 1922, when the Weimar leaders signed the Treaty of Rapallo, until Hitler became Führer in 1933, Germany's special relationship with the Soviet Union had flourished to the benefit of both. Very soon after his accession – despite persecuting communists within Germany and repeatedly advising his Cabinet that the primary goal of his foreign policy was the eradication of an international 'Jewish-Bolshevist plague'[14] – Hitler had renewed the 1926 Berlin treaty, which itself reaffirmed the neutrality pledges embodied in the Rapallo treaty signed by Chicherin and Rathenau in 1922. Under the terms of their trading relationship, Germany was still able to import precious raw materials (including manganese, chrome, oil and iron ore) from the Soviet Union's vast store of mineral wealth in return for the provision of sorely needed industrial machinery. Hitler was not so lacking in reason as to overlook the fact that, without a secure supply of such imports, it would be impossible for Germany to create a war machine capable of any offensive action, let alone powerful enough to establish hegemony over the entire continent. Even with these resources and a massive rearmament programme, he was aware of the statistics, which revealed that in an arms race with the Western democracies – even if the United States were to remain on the sidelines – Germany would very soon become the loser. In these circumstances, the attractions of renewing an economic and strategic partnership even with the devil incarnate were irresistible. Realpolitik still prevailed.

Hitler did not rush to embrace Stalin, but his tone began to soften markedly. During a two-hour harangue at the Reichstag on 28 April 1939, he denounced Britain and mocked Roosevelt but refrained from delivering his usual diatribe against the Soviet Union. Four weeks later, on 23 May, at a private meeting with his most senior generals, he re-asserted his determination to carry out the destruction of Poland, which, as they already knew, was timetabled for the late summer. At some point after that, he advised them, he would turn on Britain: 'Britain is our enemy and the showdown with England is a matter of life and death,'[15] he told his pliant listeners. Once again, though, he refrained from delivering one of his familiar anti-Soviet tirades. Instead, he suggested – albeit obliquely – that a political and economic understanding with Moscow might be in the offing.

Hitler's timing was fortuitously exquisite. By May, Stalin had come to the view that to open a dialogue with his ideological nemesis in Berlin might be judicious. Faced with the threat of an expansionist Germany, he had to make a choice between seeking an Anglo-French alliance or forming a compact with Hitler. This was not the first time that he had nurtured such a thought. As early as 1934 he had spoken admiringly of Hitler's methods, which so nearly mirrored his own. At a meeting of the Politburo, a few days after the Night of the Long Knives, he said, 'Have you heard the news from Germany? About what happened, how he got rid of Röhm? Good chap that Hitler! He showed how to deal with political opponents!' And in January 1937, he had authorized his chief negotiator in Berlin, David Kandelaki, to sound out the prospects for Soviet–German political agreement as an alternative to confrontation. At that point, however, Hitler had been unresponsive.[16]

Stalin did not take Berlin's 'nein' to be Hitler's final word but – in the spirit of realpolitik – he decided to try another means to avoid the Soviet Union being dragged into a European conflagration. Despite his abiding suspicion of Britain's political establishment – he had not forgotten that only twenty years earlier Britain had been fighting against him and his fellow revolutionaries on the Civil War battlefield, or that London had treated the Soviet Union as a potential adversary ever since – he opted to recalibrate Moscow's relationship with the British government. He had just the man for the task in his foreign minister, Maxim Litvinov (who had successfully negotiated the reopening of diplomatic relations with the United States in 1934). It had been Litvinov's guiding hand that had steered the Comintern away from its subversive role as an agent of global revolution to become an instrument to promote 'popular fronts' against fascism, and it was his polished diplomacy that, in the name of 'collective security', had secured the Soviet Union a place in the European sun as a member of the League of Nations in 1934. Despite the show trials and the purges – the Great Terror, as this period became known – he had skilfully managed to avoid committing the Kremlin to any foreign policy initiatives that might further have fuelled Britain's animosity.

Litvinov had taken the diplomatic initiative a few days after the Anschluss, by using a press conference in Moscow on 17 March 1938 to float the proposal for an anti-Nazi alliance that might deter Germany from any further actions of that kind. Chamberlain's response was bleak and hostile. In a rambling speech in the House of Commons, the prime minister brusquely dismissed the Soviet proposal as an attempt to nego-tiate a 'mutual undertaking in advance to resist aggression . . . [which] His Majesty's government for their part are unwilling to accept'.[17] When the Soviet ambassador, Maisky, noted that the prime minister 'feels with his every fibre that the USSR is the principal enemy',[18] he was close to the mark. In a private letter to his sister Ida, written a few days before that Commons performance, Chamberlain wrote of his belief that the Russians were 'stealthily and cunningly pulling all the strings behind the scenes to get us involved in war with Germany'.[19]

Litvinov did not give up. A year later, in April 1939, as Europe slid closer to the cataclysm of a war over Poland, he tried once again. On this occasion he proposed the formation of an Anglo-French-Soviet pact to deter Hitler from further aggression by providing 'mutual sup-port and guarantees' to the nation states of central and eastern Europe. According to Halifax's permanent secretary, Alexander Cadogan, the Foreign Secretary was 'almost unrecognizable from the H. of a year ago' and evidently ready to 'warm up' relations with Russia and, in due course, to dispatch a minister to Moscow.[20] Nonetheless, Britain's initial response to the Soviet overture – which took three weeks to deliver – was glacial. Disdain and mistrust still prevailed. With a mandarin's dry detachment, Cadogan summed up the Foreign Office view, noting, 'The Russian proposal is extremely inconvenient. We have to balance the advantage of a paper commitment by Russia to join a war on one side, against the disadvantage of associating ourselves openly with Russia.'[21] According to one senior official in the department, Laurence Collier, the Cabinet's attitude was even more brutally cynical. In a note to his colleague William Strang, he wrote that Chamberlain's policy was being driven by 'the desire to secure Russian help and at the same time to leave our hands free to enable Germany to expand eastward at Russian expense'.[22]

The prime minister, who had yet to lose his appetite for appeasement, remained adamantly opposed to closer ties with the Soviet Union. Maisky's sour observation that 'for psychological reasons, the prime minister is still unable to swallow such a pact, since it would throw him into the anti-German camp once and for all, thus putting an end to all projects aimed at reviving "appeasement"' was nonetheless acute.[23]

Stalin was a victim of paranoia, but in the case of the British prime minister his suspicions were not without foundation. By the spring of 1939, despite Britain's guarantee to Poland, it was not at all fanciful for him to imagine Hitler and Chamberlain trying once more to settle their differences around the conference table at the expense of the Soviet Union. Such brooding fuelled his obsessive fear that London would be content to stand aside while the Nazis launched a blitzkrieg against the East that would inevitably suck the Soviet Union into a military conflict for which the Soviet Union was ill-prepared. Frustrated by Britain's reluctance to engage in more than a diplomatic skirmish, the Kremlin – as Britain's intelligence services were by now aware – had already decided to respond positively to Berlin's cautious overtures.

Driven by the compelling need to avoid being drawn into war, Moscow thus initiated a twin-track strategy that led in opposite directions, one to London, the other to Berlin. Early in May, to further the Berlin option, Stalin sent a very clear message to the Nazi leadership by publicly and brutally sacking Litvinov, the long-serving advocate and architect of collective security whose Jewish heritage had long been the butt of anti-Semitic sneers in Germany, where he was mockingly referred to as Finkelstein-Litvinov. With his usual callousness, Stalin fabricated treasonable charges against his foreign minister which were so far-fetched that even his kangaroo court was unable to sustain them. Possibly as a result of this, or, more probably, because he had nurtured valuable contacts in the West, Litvinov's life was spared. Instead he became a 'non-person' until two years later he was rehabilitated as the Soviet ambassador to the United States.

Litvinov's replacement as the People's Commissar for Foreign Affairs was the chairman of the Council of Ministers, Vyacheslav Molotov, who had distinguished himself earlier in the decade as one of Stalin's most tyrannical acolytes. 'Stone Arse'– allegedly so named because Stalin kicked his posterior so often and because he could outsit any interlocutor – was an immensely powerful figure in the Politburo. Cold, cynical and uncompromising, his style and outlook were in sharp contrast to those of his predecessor. Where Litvinov was emollient, Molotov was abrasive; where the former disdained dialogue with Nazis, the latter had no such aversion; where the outgoing minister believed that 'collective security' – in the form of a partnership with Britain and France – offered the most promising way of avoiding war, his replacement was scornful of his predecessor's floundering attempts to join hands with London and Paris.

The sacking of Litvinov and the advent of Molotov set the dovecotes fluttering in Westminster. So much so that Churchill found himself supported by a swelling lobby when, on 19 May 1939 in the House of Commons, he argued powerfully in favour of a British alliance with the Soviet Union to counter the dangerous promise of Berlin–Moscow co-operation. 'The [prospective] alliance is solely for the purpose of resisting further acts of aggression and of protecting the victims of aggression,' he insisted, before in mocking tones asking rhetorically, 'What is wrong with this simple proposal? It is said "Can you trust the Russian Soviet Government?" I suppose in Moscow they say "Can we trust Chamberlain?" I hope that we may say that the answer to both questions is in the affirmative. I earnestly hope so.'[24] The chiefs of staff – who had hitherto been vehemently averse to any talk of an alliance with the Soviet Union (though simultaneously fearing a rapprochement between Moscow and Berlin) – had also, in Cadogan's words, come round to a 'whole hog' alliance with the Soviet Union. Even the Foreign Office, where anti-Bolshevik sentiment was still intense, was reluctantly drawn to the same conclusion. As much of the Cabinet felt the same way, the prime minister found himself under growing pressure to change tack.[25]

But Chamberlain was obdurate. On 20 May Cadogan came away from a meeting with him to note, 'In his present mood PM says he'll resign rather than sign alliance with Soviet[s].'[26] Mirroring Stalin's suspicion that Britain would collude with the Nazis to overthrow the Soviet Union, Chamberlain wrote, 'I cannot rid myself of the suspicion that they [the Soviets] are chiefly concerned to see the "capitalist" powers tear each other to pieces while they stay out themselves.'[27] Yet even he could not ignore the groundswell of public and parliamentary opinion, or the shift in his Cabinet's attitude. A few days after Churchill's acerbic onslaught in the Commons, he reluctantly authorized a formal attempt to secure a tripartite alliance between Britain, France and the Soviet Union. Moscow clearly believed that in the face of this putative coalition Hitler would back off. Similarly, Halifax recorded the prime minister's opinion that 'Herr Hitler was not a fool and would never enter a war which he was bound to lose. The only thing he understood was force.'[28] Halifax was minded to agree.

Maisky urged the Foreign Secretary to lead the British negotiating team himself. Halifax was tempted but, under pressure from Chamberlain, he refused to go to Moscow in person lest it suggest that the British were overly eager to secure a deal. In his stead he elected to send a middle-ranking Foreign Office official, William Strang. A tall, donnish, bespectacled figure, Strang was an accomplished diplomat who had already served in Moscow and was most unlikely to be intimidated by an 'ignorant and suspicious peasant', as Molotov was deemed to be by the ever-waspish Cadogan.[29] However, Churchill's scathing comment that Strang was 'without any standing outside the Foreign Office'[30] echoed Moscow's sense that the Soviet Union was being fobbed off with a negotiating nobody.

The mutual distrust between London and Moscow (and to a lesser extent between Paris and Moscow) was exemplified by the icy welcome given to the Anglo-French negotiating team by the new Soviet foreign minister when the talks opened on 15 June. What started badly was destined to get worse. To his great frustration, Strang was straitjacketed by Chamberlain's refusal to allow him to discuss a comprehensive treaty that would entail the provision of mutual support in the face of 'indirect' as well as 'direct' aggression. For Moscow this was a sine qua non for any meaningful co-operation. While the British feared that the Comintern was still a dangerously subversive force that would foment communism in the region, the Russians feared a Nazi-inspired uprising in one or other of Latvia, Lithuania or Estonia – the three Baltic States that bordered the Soviet Union. An impasse became inevitable. Molotov's diplomatic style was disconcerting. By turns thuggish and unyielding, he was only too ready to slice through the diplomatic veneer with a crudity that might have dumbfounded a less resilient interlocutor. As Strang would recall, Molotov interrupted one of their exchanges with the words 'If Her Majesty's government and the French government [whose emissaries in Moscow played a secondary role] treat the Soviet government as nitwits and nincompoops, then I myself can afford to smile. But I cannot guarantee that everyone will take so calm a view.'[31] Whether or not this was intended as a threat, it hardly contributed to progress. There was no meeting of minds. Each demanded compromises that the other was unwilling to make, rather as though they were haggling over the price of a carpet in an oriental bazaar rather than seeking to settle the fate of nations.

In London, Cadogan gave vent to his personal antipathy towards Moscow: 'The Russians are intolerable. We give them all they want, with both hands, and they merely slap them.'[32] Conversely, as the talks blundered into the quicksands, Molotov, infuriated by London's obstinate determination to limit any agreement to a political declaration of mutual support likened the British to 'crooks and cheats'.[33] From the Soviet perspective, a political entente without a military commitment was barely worth the paper it was written on. Strang, who was frustrated by Molotov's insistence on 'stubbornly and woodenly' repeating his arguments, nonetheless had some sympathy with the Russian position. On 20 July, exercising admirable restraint, he advised the Foreign Office that the British negotiating stance by which he was straitjacketed had 'created an impression that we may not be seriously seeking an agreement . . . We should perhaps have been wiser to pay the Soviet price for this agreement at an earlier stage.'[34] As Strang well knew, he had been sent on something of a fool's errand as bagman for a British strategy that possessed neither candour nor good faith.

The looming collapse of the Moscow talks did not in any way appear to disconcert Chamberlain or Halifax (who had evidently shifted his ground). On the very day that Strang reproached his Whitehall counterparts for the unhelpful procrastinations imposed on him by London, the Foreign Secretary coolly informed his Cabinet colleagues that the prospect of a breakdown in negotiations did not cause him 'very great anxiety, since whatever formal agreement is signed, the Soviet government will probably take what action best suits them if war breaks out'.[35] Chamberlain, who was still intent on reopening a productive dialogue with Hitler that might lead the German dictator to abort his plans to invade Poland was even less concerned by the impasse in Moscow.

On 19 July Sir Horace Wilson – the head of the Home Civil Service, Chamberlain's trusted confidant and an indefatigable appeaser – held the first of two secret meetings with Dr Helmuth Wohlthat, a senior German trade official sent to London by Goering, who had been appointed the Third Reich's economic supremo three years earlier. Wilson's apparent objective – which he subsequently denied – was to bribe Hitler with a huge loan to opt for peace instead of war. Immediately after their second meeting the following day, Wohlthat was invited to a private meeting with Robert Hudson, Britain's Minister for Overseas Trade. Hudson evidently proposed a number of ways by which Hitler might be induced to choose peace rather than war. Unhappily, the minister was notoriously indiscreet and could not refrain from boasting about this initiative to two prominent journalists. The following day the *Daily Telegraph* and the *News Chronicle* blazoned their front pages with reports that, along with other economic stimuli, Britain would indeed provide the Third Reich with a huge loan in return for German disarmament under international supervision. The impact was immediate and predictable: pandemonium in the press, questions in the Commons, dismay on the Quai d'Orsay and, according to Britain's ambassador to Italy Sir Percy Loraine, ridicule at Britain's 'shark-like mania of [sic] buying the world'.[36] The reports could hardly have come at a worse moment. Halifax's private secretary, Oliver Harvey, who was both fiercely opposed to appeasement and a gifted diarist, noted bleakly that these reports were 'calculated to do infinite harm to Soviet negotiations . . . Whether the story is true or not . . . it is a very silly proposal.'[37]

The prime minister similarly regarded Hudson's indiscretions as 'disastrous' but for very different reasons. His focus was not on the Soviet reaction but the reaction from Berlin. Not for the first time, he complained, the trade minister had taken ideas 'on which other people had been working for years and put them forward as his own'. It was particularly galling on this occasion as Hudson had evidently filched his proposal for 'an economic arrangement' with Germany from 10 Downing Street. It was also infuriating to have his scheme for renewing a secret dialogue with Hitler so rudely pre-empted by the 'semi-official air' which Hudson's incontinence had bestowed on his own nascent ideas for avoiding war.[38]

Despite the scorn that was now heaped on his government, Chamberlain was not willing to alter course. In a letter to his sister Hilda, he spoke of opening

> discreeter channels by which contact can be maintained for it is import-
> ant that those in Germany who would like to see us come to an
> understanding should not be discouraged . . . My critics of course think
> it would be a frightful thing to come to any agreement with Germany
> without first having given her a thorough thrashing . . . But I don't
> share that view.[39]

His obstinate resolve was fortified by a firm conviction that an alliance between Hitler and Stalin was inconceivable. He could hardly have been more wrong.

With the invasion of Poland still scheduled for late August, Hitler was in a hurry. Rather than seeking a peace dividend with Britain, his overriding objective now was a pact with the Soviet Union that would – in effect – license the Polish offensive. By weaning the Russians away from any diplomatic or military entanglement with the British, he hoped to avoid an unpalatable choice: either to postpone Operation White (as the invasion of Poland was codenamed) or risk prosecuting a war on two fronts, the prospect of which was anathema to the German High Command. At the Führer's behest, his foreign minister went on the dip-lomatic warpath. In a strongly contested field, Joachim von Ribbentrop was as repellent as any of Hitler's many odious acolytes. As the German ambassador to Britain between 1934 and 1938, he had managed to alien-ate almost everyone except the sillier members of the pro-German lobby. Widely derided as coarse and ridiculous, he was aptly described by his personal secretary, Reinhard Spitzy, as 'pompous, conceited and not too intelligent'.[40] Nonetheless, he was slithery enough to ingratiate himself with the Führer and thus to acquire growing influence in those critical months of 1939. Bitterly Anglophobic, he was only too anxious to broker a deal between Berlin and Moscow.

In early June Berlin had initiated a discreet and cautious flirtation with Moscow. At first the Russians responded coolly, but it did not take long before they started to show an interest. By the middle of the follow-ing month Ribbentrop felt confident enough to press matters further. On 21 July he dispatched a senior member of his staff, Karl Schnurre, to meet the Soviet chargé d'affaires in Berlin, Georgi Astakhov. While

Chamberlain fantasized about a peace deal with Hitler and the Anglo-Soviet talks headed towards the buffers, Schnurre sketched out the contours of a far-reaching proposal: the re-establishment of economic ties, the normalization of relations and a political treaty that would be buttressed by their shared antipathy towards the capitalist democracies. The Kremlin was tempted. The flirtation became a proposition.

In the Soviet capital the British negotiators had no inkling of Ribbentrop's dramatic overture, but Strang had long foreseen that – in his overriding urge to avoid war – Stalin would have few scruples about seeking solace in an alternative embrace with Nazi Germany in the absence of an agreement with Britain. Accordingly, he cabled Cadogan to warn that 'if we want an agreement with them [the Soviets] we shall have to pay their price or something very near it'.[41] That price was Molotov's insistence that Britain open military talks alongside the political negotiations forthwith. Echoing Strang, the British ambassador, Sir William Seeds, pressed the point, insisting, 'the arrival in Moscow of a British military mission is the only proof of our sincerity which the Soviet government is likely to accept . . . every member of the Politburo consider [sic] the present British government is imbued with a spirit of "capitulation" if possible to [the] Axis powers.'[42]

To preserve an illusion of purpose and progress Chamberlain reluctantly agreed that a joint Anglo-French military mission be dispatched to the Soviet capital, ostensibly to discuss ways in which their forces could collaborate to deter Hitler from further military adventures. The mission was to be led by Admiral the Hon. Sir Reginald Aylmer Drax, who had enjoyed 'a good war' but had no significant experience as a negotiator at a senior level – let alone on behalf of his government in the heat of a diplomatic stand-off. He was astute enough both to be aware of his limitations and to suspect that he was being sent on a mission impossible. On the eve of his departure, he sought guidance from Halifax. What should he do, he asked, if the negotiations in Moscow began to falter? The Foreign Secretary paused before telling him that, in such circumstances, he should 'draw out the negotiations as long as possible'.[43] The urge to keep the Russians dangling on the diplomatic hook while Chamberlain – as the Politburo had suspected – persisted in his attempts to appease Hitler was not merely a clumsy manoeuvre but spectacularly ill judged.

The House of Commons was about to rise for the summer recess. Halifax himself prepared to spend the 'Glorious Twelfth' of August, which marked the start of the grouse-shooting season, at his Yorkshire estate. Chamberlain looked forward to a spell of fishing in Scotland. On 2 August, their holiday plans were momentarily called into question when Churchill, reflecting a widespread sentiment, used the Adjournment Debate to join Labour in demanding that the House should curtail its summer recess (which was due to last until 3 October). Warning his colleagues that there would soon be 'a supreme trial of willpower, if not indeed a supreme trial of arms', the rebellious backbencher castigated Chamberlain, declaring 'it would be disastrous, it would be pathetic, it would be shameful for the House of Commons to write itself off as an effective and potent factor in the situation'. At his acerbic best, he added that he hoped the government would not say to the House, 'Begone! Run off and play. Take your gas masks with you. Do not worry about public affairs.'[44]

Churchill's sarcastic rebuke was to no avail. Guns, fishing rods, buckets and spades disappeared with their owners to various country retreats while, on 5 August, Drax and his delegation – accompanied by a French negotiating team – set off for the Soviet Union. As though to demonstrate his intent, Halifax instructed the admiral that they should travel at a leisurely pace in a cargo vessel (capable of thirteen knots) rather than a British or French cruiser (capable of thirty knots) or even an aircraft.* As a result the delegation did not reach Moscow until 11 August.

The Russians were already aggrieved by what they regarded as persistent and deliberate distortions of their foreign policy by Chamberlain's apologists in the House of Commons. A few days before his empty-handed return to London, Strang was summoned to the Kremlin by Molotov to be reprimanded in the chilliest manner: 'You appear to be deliberately misunderstanding us. Do you not trust the Soviet Union?

---

* Later Drax justified this decision on the grounds that the government was unwilling to divert a warship or bomber from their vital military tasks.

Do you think we are not interested in security too? It is a grave mistake. In time, you will realize how great a mistake it is to distrust the government of the USSR.'[45] As soon became clear, the Soviets had no more intention of negotiating in good faith than the British. Nonetheless, such ominous language did little to suggest that Drax – whose lowly diplomatic status was, like that of Strang, interpreted by a prickly Molotov as a gesture of British disdain – would lift the darkening mood in the Soviet capital.

For the British 'political' team, it was a momentary relief to discover that the military negotiating baton was to be passed from the Commissar for Foreign Affairs to Marshal Kliment Voroshilov, the imposing but ostensibly genial Commissar for Defence. The relief was short lived. The cordial reception Voroshilov gave the Anglo-French negotiators rapidly gave way to irritation when he discovered that his interlocutors had no negotiating mandate, let alone the authority to sign a military accord. Nothing could have been better calculated to confirm Moscow's growing conviction that the British (and their junior partners the French) were merely toying with the Soviet Union while – in Britain's case at least – seeking to repair the fraying ties with Hitler. Earlier in the year Stalin had used a speech to claim that the capitalist democracies wished to foster a war between Germany and Russia in the course of which the combatants would so 'weaken and exhaust one another' as to force them, as 'enfeebled belligerents', to accept a peace imposed on them by their Western adversaries.[46] The sentiment was crudely expressed but the Soviet leader's words contained more than a kernel of truth: from London's perspective it was indeed better, if there were to be war and blood spilled – as Baldwin had said – it should be that of 'the Bolshies and the Nazis' rather than the British.

It rapidly emerged that any residual hope Moscow may still have nurtured for a triple alliance with the British and French was doomed. A 'killer' question from Voroshilov settled the matter. If Hitler were to invade Poland, he wanted to know, would the government in Warsaw permit the Red Army to cross Polish territory – in co-ordination with the two Western democracies – to confront the Wehrmacht? Unable to give a clear answer, the embarrassed leaders of the Anglo-French delegation sought advice from respectively London and Paris. The response from the Quai d'Orsay was swift: the French delegation should sign a draft agreement forthwith. In Whitehall, the deputy chiefs of staff met on 16 August to urge their political masters that 'the strongest pressure' should be put on Warsaw to permit the Russians to fight the Germans on Polish soil. In so advising, they demonstrated a woeful ignorance of the toxic history of Polish–Russian relations. They may have been right to argue that this was 'the best way of preventing a war' and avoiding the profoundly undesirable alternative of 'a possible Soviet–German rapprochement',[47] but they ignored the fact that there were no circumstances in which Warsaw would permit Soviet troops to enter Poland's sovereign territory. As it happened, their advice was ignored in any case.

The prime minister was still fly fishing in Scotland, where the salmon were evidently in plentiful supply – enough, at any rate, for him to send one back to London to a gratified Cadogan, who had so far refused to burden his political master with affairs of state. The permanent secretary was adamant about this. When Sir Robert Vansittart – the government's 'chief diplomatic advisor' – rang him on 18 August, in what he described acidly as 'a high state of excitement', to pass on a warning from a source in Berlin that Hitler was about to invade Poland, Cadogan was unmoved. After consulting Halifax, he decided that Chamberlain should not be disturbed over what he dismissed as a 'war of nerves'.[48] Cadogan's insouciance was pervasive. In Moscow, the British ambassador, William Seeds, waited in vain for a reply to his urgent request for an answer to Voroshilov's question.* After nine days of fruitless discussion, the defence commissar brought the talks to a shuddering halt by declaring bluntly that 'further talks can lead merely to a lot of chatter'.[49] As a leading historian of this period has put it, 'the Western policy of procrastination had run out of tomorrows'.[50]

---

* The telegram from Seeds was eventually discovered in the relevant Foreign Office archive by Anthony Read and David Fisher while researching *The Deadly Embrace*. A caustic note had been scribbled in the margin: 'It was not possible to send an answer to this telegram as no decision was taken.' It was in the handwriting of William Strang, who had by then returned to London. See Anthony Read and David Fisher, *The Deadly Embrace: Hitler, Stalin and the Nazi-Soviet Pact, 1939–1941* (W. W. Norton, 1988), p. 234.

If the British had been perfidious, so too had the Russians. Stalin was not only cynical but adept at pursuing two competing options at once. While Voroshilov was still ostensibly seeking to negotiate a military pact with the British and French, German and Russian officials were simultaneously putting the finishing touches to an economic treaty between the Third Reich and the Soviet Union worth in the order of 200 million Reichsmarks a year ($7.5 billion in 2019 dollars) for a decade – one of a series of economic accords that had followed the 1922 Rapallo treaty and its renewal in Berlin four years later. Seen in purely economic terms, it was a commonplace 'win–win' commercial transaction: Germany urgently needed raw materials for the Third Reich's rapidly expanding armoury and Stalin was hungry for the modern technology required to meet the Soviet Union's ambitious third economic Five Year Plan. But, in the summer crisis of 1939, the very fact that such a deal was done was a harbinger of a far more significant and more ominous relationship.

After a fortnight of intense negotiations the German ambassador, Friedrich-Werner Graf von der Schulenburg, told Molotov that Berlin was in a position to draft a formal pact with Moscow. In response, the Soviet foreign minister handed his German counterpart an aide-memoire suggesting that the two governments reaffirm in writing the non-aggression treaty initially agreed at Rapallo in 1922. For those with a sense of the continent's recent past, the ghost of Rapallo (along with its secret military codicils) must have sent shivers through the chancelleries of Europe when the news broke that the continent's two behemoths – bitter ideological adversaries that had not spared one another the lacerating language of mutually hostile tyrannies – were once again finding common cause.

Stalin's unwavering priority was still to keep the Soviet Union out of any European war for as long as possible. Torn between the option of an anti-Nazi alliance with Britain and France and a military pact with his German nemesis, he now opted to clasp the 'bird in the hand' offered by Berlin. If the result were to be a war between the two 'capitalist' states it would, he argued, at least serve to strengthen communism at no cost to the Soviet Union. Unmindful or forgetful of the ominous warnings in *Mein Kampf*, the Soviet leader allowed himself to dream that such a deal would lead to the righting of historic wrongs which, deep in the Russian psyche, were held to have been imposed on them as far back as the nineteenth century and, more recently, at Versailles. Collaboration between the Soviet Union and the Third Reich, he hoped, might satisfy their competing aspirations and thereby, with luck, remove the cause of significant tension between them. In any case, in his urge to postpone war with Germany for as long as possible, inevitable as it might one day become, he had very little alternative: Hitler's version of 'peace for our time' seemed irresistible. Though each viscerally abhorred the ideology of the other, they were kindred spirits: not only ruthless and unprincipled but consummate opportunists, at one in their readiness to use any available means to secure their immediate ends. For both, a deal that Hitler would liken a few days later to 'a pact with Satan' had become compelling.[51] For the time being at least, a shotgun marriage made in hell was more desirable by far than a premature *Götterdämmerung*.

On the day their economic treaty was signed, Hitler sent a flattering note to Stalin asking if he would be willing to receive Ribbentrop in Moscow with a view to endorsing a major strategic pact between their two countries. Stalin could not know that, ten days earlier, he had confided to a trusted German diplomat, 'Everything I do is directed against the Russians. If the West is too stupid and blind to grasp this, then I shall be compelled to come to an agreement with the Russians, beat the West and then after their defeat turn against the Soviet Union with all my forces.'[52] Now he waited impatiently for Stalin's response. When this was handed to him, the Führer was at supper in the Berghof, his residence in the Bavarian Alps where he spent much of the war. According to one of his guests, Albert Speer, he 'stared into space for a moment, flushed deeply, then banged the table so hard that the glasses rattled, and exclaimed in a voice breaking with excitement, "I have them! I have them!"'[53]

The prospective meeting of unholy minds was announced on 21 August, when the official Soviet News Agency TASS reported blandly that Germany's foreign minister, Ribbentrop, would depart imminently for Moscow as 'the exchange of views between the two governments has made apparent the desire of both parties to bring about the lessening of tension between them, to remove the threat of war and to conclude a non-aggression pact'. The implications were at once apparent. With the stroke of a pen, Hitler was about to be released from any lingering fear that the 'annihilation' of Poland by the Nazis would unleash a war on two fronts. As soon as Seeds saw the TASS report, he requested a meeting with Molotov. It became an angry confrontation when the British ambassador accused the Soviet minister of acting in bad faith by negotiating a pact with Germany behind Britain's back. Molotov was coldly aggressive, countering that 'the height of insincerity had been reached when military missions arrived in Moscow empty-handed'.[54] Relations between London and Moscow had reached a low ebb. They would soon sink lower.

A great burden of responsibility for what followed lay with Chamberlain. An Anglo-French military alliance with the Soviet Union would by no means have guaranteed peace in Europe. However, with such a formidable array of firepower and manpower ranged against him, it is possible that Hitler might have been deterred from an all-out attempt to eliminate the Polish state. His High Command, with grimly vivid memories of the First World War, would assuredly have argued strenuously against such a hazardous and premature undertaking that might have led to a dreaded war on two fronts. Even if a confrontation between the Western Allies and the Nazis on the battlefield was almost inevitable, an alliance with the Soviet Union in the east would have put Britain and France in a far stronger position to prevail in the west. Chamberlain's vindictive attitude towards his domestic critics at Westminster and his thin-skinned refusal to heed alternative advice even from his supporters betrayed the short-sighted and narrow-minded obstinacy of mediocrity. At no point did he give serious consideration to a strategic partnership with a Bolshevik regime that he loathed and which – with some justification – he regarded as a rogue state. This, combined with his overweening arrogance, duped him into the conviction that he could single-handedly deliver 'peace for our time' by appeasing Hitler while cold-shouldering Stalin. His motives may have been honourable but, in guaranteeing precisely the opposite outcome from that for which he had so assiduously and demeaningly striven, his judgement was fatally flawed.

5. A Pact with Satan

When Ribbentrop strode self-importantly down the steps of Hitler's personal aircraft onto the tarmac in Moscow at 1 p.m. on 23 August 1939 he and his entourage were treated as though they were Heroes of the Soviet Union. To the German foreign minister's evident satisfaction, the airport terminal was bedecked with the swastika flying alongside the hammer and sickle while a military band struck up 'Deutschland über alles'. The formalities over, the Nazi delegation was whisked into the city, where that afternoon in the Kremlin Stalin accorded Ribbentrop the rare honour of greeting him in person alongside Molotov.

Even by the prevailing standards of diplomacy, the cynicism with which the two men sat down together with a map to carve up the nations of eastern Europe between them was breathtaking. The draft pact committed each party not to wage war against the other or to ally itself to an enemy of the other. Far more significantly, it also contained a secret protocol, the existence of which would not be revealed publicly until the Nuremberg trials in 1945. In addition to clauses which ceded Latvia, Estonia and (later) most of Lithuania along with Finland and Bessarabia (which formed part of Romania) to the Soviet Union's 'sphere of influence', the protocol licensed the partition of Poland into two neat halves, the western slice falling to the Germans, the eastern slice to the Soviets.

This diplomatic surgery did not take long to accomplish. After returning to the German Embassy to cable the Berghof for Hitler's approval for his handiwork, Ribbentrop was back in the Kremlin by 10 p.m. that evening to inform Stalin that he was empowered to sign the formal agreement. Stalin responded by proposing a toast to Hitler, observing 'I know how much the German nation loves its Führer . . . I'd like to drink his health.' At 2 a.m. on 24 August, watched benignly by the Soviet leader, the two foreign ministers put their name to what would become known as the Molotov–Ribbentrop Pact. Cameras clicked and toasts were drunk before Stalin bade goodnight to his guests, reassuring

Ribbentrop, 'I can guarantee on my word of honour that the Soviet Union will not betray its partner.'

Stalin was jubilant that his 'sphere of influence' restored to the Soviet Union so much of the territory of the nineteenth-century Russian Empire that had been lost in the First World War. He was also as spectacularly steeped in bad faith about the deal itself as Hitler. That night, as he celebrated with Molotov and other senior members of the Politburo at his dacha in the forest near Kuntsevo, he was heard to say, 'Of course it's all a game to see who can fool whom. I know what Hitler's up to. He thinks he's outsmarted me but actually it's I who's tricked him.' War, he opined, 'would pass us by a little longer'.[1]

The initial reaction of the Russian people to the news of the pact ranged from astonishment to incredulity. 'It left us all bewildered and groggy with disbelief,' one Soviet official, Victor Kravchenko, was to write. 'The villainy of Hitler had become in our land almost as sacred an article of faith as the virtue of Stalin . . . The swastika and the hammer-and-sickle fluttering side by side in Moscow! And soon afterwards Molotov explaining to us that Fascism was, after all, "a matter of taste".'[2] Very soon however, shock yielded to relief that Stalin had indeed appeared to save them from the horror of war.

The German public was similarly bewildered, and in some cases alarmed, by the news. It was 'an incredible turnabout, confusion . . . Incalculable danger for all Jews', Victor Klemperer noted. 'Everyone guesses, waits, the tension is too great . . .'[3] Even a number of the Führer's most devoted acolytes were dismayed that their ideological enemy was suddenly to be treated as an ally. So powerful was this aversion that Hitler felt obliged to reassure his own military leadership. At a meeting with his senior generals in Berlin on 28 August, looking 'worn, haggard' and 'preocupied', his voice 'croaking' with exhaustion, he explained – somewhat opaquely – that his deal with Stalin was 'a pact with Satan to cast out the devil'.[4] Seeking to boost their faith in his judgement, he insisted that ruthless military action against Poland had become an urgent political and economic imperative. 'Essentially, all depends on me, on my existence . . . no one will ever again have the confidence of the whole German people as I have,' he boasted. 'We have nothing to lose, we have everything to win . . . our economic situation is such that we can only hold out for a few more years . . . We have no other choice.' All that now mattered was victory: 'Close your heart to pity . . . Act brutally . . . The stronger man is right.'[5]

According to Churchill, the 'sinister news' of the Molotov–Ribbentrop Pact 'broke upon the world like an explosion'.[6] This was true enough of a bewildered Western public, but it should not have come as a surprise to the British or French governments, which had been repeatedly warned not to dismiss the very real danger that the Bolsheviks and the Nazis would find common cause. Finally, though, even Chamberlain had to face the reality that a deal with Hitler was no longer an option. On 25 August, Halifax and his Polish counterpart, Edward Raczyński, signed an Agreement of Mutual Assistance in which both governments promised to give military support to the other in the event of an attack on either by another European country.

The unlikely speed of Britain's unequivocal stand clearly startled Hitler. His immediate response was to postpone the invasion of Poland by six days from the original target date of 26 August. But, a little before dawn on 1 September, the Wehrmacht launched the long-planned Operation White. Supported by the Kriegsmarine and the Luftwaffe, some 1.5 million well-armed German soldiers crossed the border in a three-pronged assault, the focal point of which was Warsaw. Spearheaded by six panzer divisions with a total of some 2,400 tanks between them, the German invasion force had overwhelming firepower against which the Polish army could not possibly prevail. The liquidation of the state of Poland was only a matter of time.

Two days later, on 3 September, Chamberlain broadcast solemnly to the British people and to the world. With a sorrowfully self-regarding reference to 'the bitter blow' it had been to him personally that his 'long struggle to preserve peace' had failed, he announced that Britain was now at war with Germany. That same evening, a British passenger ship, the *Athenia*, en route to the United States, with refugees from Nazi Germany, was torpedoed by a German U-boat off the coast of the Irish Republic with the loss of 117 lives. 'The Battle of the Atlantic', as Churchill was to call it, had begun. On land, it was different. For the next six months, the French and British armies faced the German forces across the Maginot Line★ in what became known as the 'phony war', watching on from the Western sidelines as the Nazis and the Soviets carved up eastern Europe between them.

As the Germans consolidated their conquest in the west, the Russians invaded the broken remains of Poland from the east. A little over two weeks after the Wehrmacht's aggression, more than 800,000 Red Army troops swept into 'their half' of Poland on 17 September. By 6 October they had crushed the last vestiges of Polish resistance. The two armies made initial contact in the city of Brest, nearly 800 kilometres from Berlin and a little over 1,000 kilometres from Moscow. The Polish forces had battled against the Wehrmacht for six days before surrendering the city's ancient fortress to the invaders. When the Russians arrived, the Germans were required to retreat from the forward positions they had established on the eastern side of the demarcation line agreed in the secret protocol of the Molotov–Ribbentrop Pact, including the fortress at Brest, which commanded a strategically important position overlooking the River Bug. For the commander of 19th Army Corps, General Heinz Guderian, whose panzers had been the first to enter Brest, this was irksome in the extreme. The Polish campaign, he wrote later, had been 'a baptism of fire for my armoured formations' and the capture of the fortress 'had cost us much blood'; moreover, the speed at which they were expected to withdraw meant 'we could not even move all our wounded or recover damaged tanks'. Despite this, the two armoured groups managed to put on a show of mutual amity, clambering on each other's tanks and using sign language to communicate that they were on a shared mission.[7]

In Warsaw, where the homeless and terrified refugees huddled in the ruins of their former homes in streets strewn with masonry, broken glass, and human body parts, the respective heads of the German–Soviet 'Border Commission' were in jocular mood as they celebrated their conquest. Sharing a post-prandial cigarette with his Soviet counterpart, Alexander Alexandrov, Hans Frank, who would soon emerge as one of the Holocaust's most committed engineers, joked, 'You and I are smoking Polish cigarettes to symbolize the fact that we have thrown Poland

---

★ The line of concrete fortifications and gun emplacements installed by France in the 1930s to deter a German invasion.

to the wind'.[8] The crimes and cruelties that were now unleashed upon that benighted nation by both tyrannies were unconstrained by the international rules of warfare as defined by the Geneva Conventions at that time.

The atrocities on the German side of the Molotov–Ribbentrop Line began within days of the invasion. The explicit Nazi policy was to establish Lebensraum in Poland by 'ethnically cleansing' the territory of its Slavic population. According to two of Hitler's most senior military commanders – Field Marshal Wilhelm Keitel, the craven Commander-in-Chief of the Wehrmacht, and Franz Halder, the somewhat less subservient army chief of staff – the Führer's explicit intention, in the words of the latter, was to 'annihilate and exterminate' the Polish people.[9]

From the beginning, the Wehrmacht played a much fuller part in this enterprise than its apologists would later claim. In the city of Bydgoszcz on 3–4 September, German troops participated in a pogrom, allegedly in retaliation for the harsh treatment meted out to some of their comrades who had been taken as prisoners of war along with pro-Nazi saboteurs to be summarily executed or lynched by angry Polish mobs. The Wehrmacht, accompanied by a force of SS troops, responded to these crimes in kind, but on a far more vindictive scale – executing between 600 and 800 Polish hostages and later massacring more than 1,000 civilians.

Hitler's troops also went on the rampage in the city of Częstochowa, which fell without a struggle at the same time: 3 September 1939. Over the course of the next three days, the soldiers torched shops and houses, looting and pillaging without restraint. In one such operation, the troops rounded up some 10,000 citizens, forcing them to lie face down in the main square in front of the cathedral before separating the men from the women. Any male found in possession of a firearm, or even a razor or pocket knife, was shot on the spot. The rest were lined up as though to be driven into the cathedral. Instead, the troops opened fire on them with machine guns, killing or wounding several hundred in what was officially described by the Wehrmacht as an 'anti-partisan' operation.

Nor were these isolated incidents. By the end of September more than 500 towns and villages had been incinerated with flame throwers and their inhabitants terrorized. Initially, these violations of military discipline were treated as serious offences by Wehrmacht commanders.

When the perpetrators could be identified they were brought before military tribunals and sentenced to severe punishment. They might as well have been released without charge: within weeks, Hitler had nullified the authority of these courts by granting amnesties to the guilty men on the grounds that the suffering they had endured at the hands of the Poles during the invasion was punishment enough.

If some Wehrmacht commanders sought to restrain the men under their command, the SS leadership in Poland encouraged such excesses. Hitler had made it clear that 'only a nation whose upper levels have been destroyed can be pushed into the ranks of slavery' – the role he had allotted to the Polish people within the newly extended Third Reich.[10] In the months leading up to the invasion, two of Hitler's most trusted and depraved lieutenants took up the challenge of executing the Führer's will. Unprepossessingly dumpy in appearance, with a receding chin, sagging jawline and rimless spectacles, combined with a receding hairline and a wispy imitation of a 'Hitler' moustache, Himmler would have fitted ideally the role of anti-hero in a film about a failed bank clerk. However, he wielded immense power. As Reichsführer-SS he had overall command of the Third Reich's entire police, security and intelligence apparatus. Under Himmler's leadership, Reinhard Heydrich ran the Reich Main Security Office, which gave him operational control over the Gestapo, the Kriminalpolizei, or Kripo (criminal police), the SS and the SD (the Nazi Party's intelligence organization). Physically, he offered a faintly absurd contrast to Himmler. Tall, lean and upright, with a long, aquiline nose, his face narrow and stern, Heydrich conveyed that sense of menace which Himmler's appearance belied. Together, though they were never close personally, they formed a formidable double act. As the leading architects of the Holocaust, no killers in all history would rival their intensely focused and diligent commitment to mass murder.

Poland was to provide the testing ground. With meticulous attention to detail, they drew up a list of 61,000 members of the Polish cultural and social elite: academics, judges, teachers, social workers, priests, former military officers, civil servants and any other individuals who could plausibly be regarded as belonging to the Polish intelligentsia. The SS was enjoined to hunt down and execute every one of them. Under Heydrich's direct oversight, this task was allotted to seven paramilitary murder squads, totalling 4,500 men. Heydrich's Einsatzgruppen (task forces), as they were euphemistically christened, relished the chance to demonstrate their commitment. For the most part, these killers were not ignorant thugs. Their leaders belonged to the German elite, often as graduates of universities armed with doctorates. Such education had the signal advantage of equipping them with the intellectual clarity to identify their targets with precision. They did not operate in isolation: in addition to the units of the German army, the SS and the SD, they were supported by the Volksdeutscher Selbstschutz, a home-grown 'self-protection' force of ethnic Germans that had operated covertly as a pro-Nazi fifth column before the war. The SS had no difficulty in persuading them that Hitler's purpose was also theirs: 'You are now the master race here. Nothing was yet built through softness and weakness . . . Don't be soft – be merciless and clear out everything that is not German,'[11] Ludolf von Alvensleben, one of Himmler's SS-troopers, instructed them. They needed no further encouragement.*

Illustrating the scale of the operational challenge, even the combined efforts of the Einsatzgruppen, the Selbstschutz and army regulars were unable to execute their Polish victims at the rate required to meet the schedule set by Heydrich. By the end of October they had managed to find and execute only 20,000 individuals. Yet, either because they became more proficient or less selective, their rate soon accelerated. By the end of the year, they had killed even more than the quota of 61,000 allotted to them by Heydrich.

One group among the 35 million population of Poland was singled out for special treatment. Jewish communities had been established in the country for a thousand years and, despite periodic waves of anti-Semitism which swept through their ghettoes, had established deep roots there. By September 1939 the Polish diaspora of some 3.4 million souls had grown to become one of the largest in the world. Following the Nazi–Soviet partition, more than two-thirds of these found themselves under German occupation. But their very existence in what was intended to become an Aryan Nirvana was regarded with particular odium by the Nazis. Whereas any Slav could expect to become a slave

---

* So extreme was the behaviour of the Volksdeutscher Selbstschutz that, in due course, even their Nazi overseers were embarrassed. In consequence, with much of their task accomplished, the squads were disbanded early in 1940.

labourer, the Jews had a different destiny. Although they too might be similarly exploited and some had artisanal roles as well, these were temporary reprieves. Regarded as vermin by the Nazis, their survival was contingent. Their eventual fate, if they did not die of hunger or exhaustion beforehand, was to be eliminated, either by expulsion or by extinction.

Poland's Jews were not hard to identify. For the most part they congregated in their own communities, clustering around their places of worship and nurturing their own traditions. By burning down their synagogues, humiliating their women with intimate body searches and killing some 7,000 of their men, the Einsatzgruppen and their partners managed to terrorize a few hundred thousand families into fleeing their homes for the uncertain haven of the Soviet zone of occupation. This exodus, however, barely grazed the surface of the problem confronting the invaders. More than 1.5 million of the remaining Jews in Nazi-occupied Poland lived in the central zone of occupation known as the General government. This region, which incorporated the cities of Warsaw, Lwów (Lviv) and Kraków, had been earmarked for colonization by German settlers and was therefore to be cleansed of Jews.*

Hitler had made it clear that Poland should be purged not only of Jews but also of all Poles except those required as serfs. It was essential, he ordered, for the Nazi authorities 'to seal off these alien racial elements so that the blood of its people will not be corrupted again . . . it must without further ado remove them and hand over the vacated territory to its own national comrades'.[12] This was more easily said than done. The 9 million Poles living in the regions annexed by the Nazis greatly outnumbered the ethnic Germans already living there. Mass movements of population, mass incarcerations and mass killings of these 'stateless persons', as they had been designated, would be required to make good on Hitler's edict.

The murderous campaign in Poland did not go entirely unchallenged. In November 1939 a small number of Wehrmacht commanders in the field belatedly but courageously alerted the army's commander-in-chief, Walther von Brauchitsch, to what was being perpetrated in the name of

---

* For a meticulously researched and chilling account of this period, see Timothy Snyder's *Bloodlands*, pp. 131–2.

the Third Reich. The military governor of the German occupying forces, Colonel General Johannes Blaskowitz, reported that 'criminal atrocities' were being committed by men with 'animal and pathological instincts' whose 'blood lust' was becoming an 'epidemic'. This, he insisted, could be arrested only by 'bringing the guilty and their followers at the greatest speed under military command and jurisdiction'.[13]

Brauchitsch's reaction was instructive. Apart from a mealy-mouthed reference to the 'regrettable mistakes' made by the SS and its acolytes, he failed to demand any further restraint. His feebleness was cowardly but not inexplicable. Hitler had already cut the ground from the Wehrmacht. Ridiculing the 'childish attitude' of his generals, and their 'Salvation Army methods' in Poland, he not only removed the SS and the police forces from the jurisdiction of the military occupation forces but further weakened the Wehrmacht by transferring its administrative authority to a civilian body in which Nazi zealots held all the key posts.[14] This shift of responsibility was of ominous import. Not only was the fading status of the military High Command terminally undermined but, as his biographer has noted, Hitler's decision 'pointed the way to the accommodation between army and SS about the genocidal actions to be taken in the Soviet Union in 1941'.[15]

In that half of Poland annexed by the Soviet Union, the authorities were no less zealous than their Nazi counterparts and, although their purposes and means differed, they were only marginally less murderous. In Stalin's case, a determination to eliminate the Polish hierarchy was not animated by racial hatred or the search for Lebensraum (of which the Soviet Union had more than enough), but by a paranoid desire to stamp out any vestiges of opposition to his communist state. In the course of imposing its military stranglehold on their swathe of the country, the Soviets took 100,000 prisoners of war. Weeding out the rank and file, who were soon released, they held some 15,000 officers in captivity before deporting them to the Soviet Union. That total included military reservists, among them the civil servants, doctors, lawyers, scientists and teachers who formed Poland's educated and administrative elite. These officers were held in three camps, all within the Soviet Union.

By the spring of 1940 Lavrenty Beria, who had proved so effective as Stalin's executioner-in-chief during the Great Terror, had turned his attention to these prisoners of war and others held elsewhere. Arguing that they would join the Polish resistance if they were allowed to return to their homes, he proposed in early March that they should be executed instead. Stalin, with the endorsement of Molotov and others in the Politburo, concurred. Using the methods of summary justice that had proved so successful before, Beria created a new set of troikas – three-man committees – who duly condemned to death some 14,700 Polish military and police officers, government officials, prosecutors, judges, intellectuals, landowners, as well as a further 1,000 'spies and saboteurs'.

The killings took place in various locations. In April 1940, 4,500 officers were taken to the outskirts of Russia's Katyn Forest, some twenty kilometres west of Smolensk. There they were lined up, shot neatly in the back of the head, stacked in piles and buried in mass graves concealed among the trees. Over the following weeks, in a variety of secret locations nearby, a further 17,500 individuals who were regarded by Stalin as potential threats to the Soviet Union's tyrannical occupation, were slaughtered. Altogether these killings, known collectively as the Katyn massacre, accounted for 22,000 individuals. At one of these sites, an NKVD prison near the town of Kalinin, 180 kilometres north-west of Moscow, more than 7,000 were executed. It was a meticulous operation. One by one the victims were marched into a specially constructed soundproof cell, where they were pinioned by two agents while a third shot them in the back of the head. It was an arduous process that could not be hurried. It took some twenty-eight days to kill them all at an average of only 250 every twenty-four hours. To ensure that his men did not falter, Major General Vasily Blokhin, the psychopathic commander of the NKVD's Lubyanka prison in Moscow, travelled from the capital to participate in the operation. Wearing his trademark butcher's apron to avoid his clothes being spattered with the blood of his victims, he set about his task with tireless resolve.[16]

In a separate move, reminiscent of what happened during the pogrom against the kulaks less than a decade earlier, the Soviet occupiers encouraged the Polish peasantry to rise up against their landlords. Not all heeded the summons but others went on the rampage, wielding axes to hack their former masters to death; in at least one documented case a landowner was tied to a stake and flayed alive, after which he was forced to witness the execution of his family.[17] To eliminate any vestige of resistance, the NKVD rounded up thousands of families who were judged to pose a potential threat to the Soviet occupation. In March 1940, in a single operation, 139,794 men and women, old and young, were taken from their homes at night and loaded into freight trains at gunpoint. In wagons normally used to transport cattle, they huddled together for the long slow journey into the Soviet Union, where they were destined for the Gulag. In temperatures that fell well below freezing, and sometimes as low as −40°C, they trundled across the steppe, half-starved of food and water. Some 5,000 of them froze to death before they reached their various destinations deep in Siberia or Kazakhstan. At various halts along the way the dead were thrown out of the trucks to be buried beside the track in shallow mass graves. Within six months of trying to eke out an existence as labourers in an alien land, a further 11,000 Polish deportees would die from hunger and disease.[18]

Between September 1939 and June 1941, the Bolsheviks deported 315,000 Polish citizens and arrested a further 110,000. Of these, at least 30,000 were executed, while a further 25,000 died in custody.[19] Albeit for different reasons, these victims were treated by the Soviet leadership as though they were every bit as subhuman as the Slavs and Jews were held to be by the Nazis.

With Poland subjugated, the Soviet Union – exercising its 'rights' under the Molotov–Ribbentrop Pact – moved to secure its northern frontiers by commandeering the Baltic buffer states of Latvia, Lithuania and Estonia. Taking a step-by-step approach, Moscow began by bullying them into concluding 'mutual assistance pacts' before exercising a clause in those agreements to establish Red Army bases in all three states. Any further moves to impose its hegemony over the Baltic had to be suspended in November 1939, when Finland proved less amenable to similarly thuggish inducements.

For more than a year the Soviet Union had sought to persuade Helsinki to cede territory on the seaward approaches to Leningrad (which was a mere thirty-two kilometres from the Finnish border), allegedly to counter the risk of an attack on the Soviet Union by the Nazis. But Helsinki had refused to oblige. Moscow lost patience. On 30 November, upwards of half a million Red Army troops, supported by some 6,000 tanks and almost 4,000 aircraft, advanced to the border, the Mannerheim Line, so-called because its defensive fortifications had been constructed at the orders of Field Marshal Baron Carl Gustav Emil Mannerheim, the Commander-in-Chief of the Finnish Army. The Soviet High Command assumed that the Finns – who had a little over 300,000 soldiers but no more than thirty tanks and sixty aircraft – would collapse within a fortnight. Instead they fought with great skill and tenacity. Facing highly motivated and well-trained troops, appropriately equipped for a sustained guerrilla campaign in deep snow and freezing conditions (on one day the temperature fell to –43°C), the Soviet armies suffered a succession of humiliating reverses. Poorly led by generals who lacked strategic vision or operational coherence, the Soviet troops were inadequately trained, badly supplied and easily demoralized.

The Finns sought help from the British but Chamberlain dithered, veering indecisively between confronting the Soviet Union militarily or using diplomatic means to demonstrate his disapproval. In December 1939 Cadogan advised the Foreign Secretary that, 'if we who talk so much about resisting aggression, do nothing about Russia, we shall be displaying considerable inconsistency, to put it at its lowest'. However, he offered no advice about what should be done except to suggest that Britain might have to afford 'such assistance to Finland as we can',[20] without identifying what that might entail.

In response to an urgent request from Helsinki, the British contemplated the dispatch of a task force – 50,000 British soldiers with supporting ships and aircraft – to confront the Soviet Union on the Finnish battlefield. There were those in Whitehall and Westminster, notably including appeasers, who found it far more gratifying to contemplate war against the Bolsheviks than against the Nazis. Their voices, inside and outside government, were loud enough to oblige the War Cabinet to give serious consideration to that option. The Foreign Office supported such a move, advising that 'the complete downfall of Russian military power' would be to Britain's advantage as 'the collapse of Russia was likely to contribute materially to the early defeat of Germany' – though quite how Whitehall's bureaucrats were drawn to this bizarre conclusion is unclear.

The government's military advisors were less fanciful, arguing that any such operation would be an act of military folly, almost impossible to mount or sustain, and that, on balance – contra the Foreign Office – it would 'make it more difficult to achieve our primary object in this war, the defeat of Germany'.[21]

Plans were eventually laid for the dispatch of a modest military contingent by sea but – to the relief of Cadogan, who judged these to be 'amateurish and half-hatched by a half-baked staff'[22] – Chamberlain delayed until it was too late. As with the Nazi invasion of Poland, the British once more ingloriously watched from the sidelines as, by sheer force of numbers, the Red Army began to grind the Finns into submission. Moscow did not entirely escape retribution, however: the Western Allies were able to agree that by way of punishment the Soviet Union should be expelled from the League of Nations – a move whose impact was somewhat blunted by the fact that the League was a moribund body that had long ceased to have any diplomatic or strategic relevance.

It took three months, one week and six days from the day of the invasion before the Soviet armies were finally able to declare victory in what became known as the Winter War and, in March 1940, to force Helsinki into signing the Moscow Peace Treaty. The Finns had suffered 66,000 casualties, including 22,700 killed or missing in action, but these numbers were less than a fifth of the losses endured by the invaders, who suffered 380,000 casualties, including 125,000 men killed or listed as missing in action.[23] It was a heavy price to pay for the small girdle of security that Moscow thus acquired in the approaches to Leningrad. Militarily, it had been an expensive fiasco. Politically, it was a humiliation that confirmed the impression in every Western capital – crucially, in Berlin – that the Red Army was incompetently led, poorly structured and badly trained: a military machine that was ill suited to modern warfare and liable to fall apart under sustained pressure.

Stalin reacted to his pyrrhic victory over the Finns with characteristic venom. After one particularly inglorious failure early in the campaign, he had dispatched his Red Army's political commissar, Lev Mekhlis (who had previously served as a quasi-grand inquisitor during the earlier military purges), to the front line, where the shambolic 44th Division had lost 1,000 men, 1,170 horses and 43 tanks. The commissar knew what was required of him. Eschewing the niceties of a formal court martial, he ordered the execution of the division's most senior commanders, a sentence carried out publicly in front of their demoralized men, who had been summoned, for their presumed benefit, to witness the shootings.[24]

In the debriefing that followed the end of hostilities, Stalin invited his defence commissar, Kliment Voroshilov, to his Kuntsevo dacha. According to Nikita Khrushchev, who was one of those present, the Soviet leader lost his temper with Voroshilov, charging him with personal responsibility for the multiple disasters of the Finnish campaign. Voroshilov's oversight of the fiasco had indeed been lamentable but – as a notoriously brutal satrap whom Stalin had once endorsed as 'the legendary Red Marshal'[25] – he dared on this occasion to defy the dictator. Apparently forgetting that he had himself advocated and overseen the decimation of the Red Army during the Great Purge, while personally signing at least 180 execution warrants, he yelled back at Stalin, 'You have yourself to blame for all this. You're the one who annihilated the old guard of the army; you had our best generals killed.' The row soon escalated to the point where Voroshilov evidently 'picked up a platter with a roast suckling pig on it and smashed it on the table'.[26]* To confront Stalin so openly was to risk mortal censure but Voroshilov was spared. Though sacked as Commissar for Defence (to be replaced by Marshal Semyon Timoshenko), he was allowed later to return to front-line duties, where his mediocrity would be on full display once again.

Relations between London and Moscow, which had deteriorated sharply following the Molotov–Ribbentrop Pact seven months earlier, were now in free fall. The Cabinet debated whether the subjugation of Finland prefigured further aggression that might force Britain into a military conflict with the Soviet Union. The Foreign Office – anxious perhaps to demonstrate that appeasement was not its default option – was hawkish. Endorsing the British ambassador's opinion that the Soviets had 'settled down into an undeclared war' against Britain and should be placed alongside the Nazis as 'partners in crime',[27] the diplomats went so far as to suggest that it had become politically desirable 'to bring about the complete downfall of the Russian military power',[28] though without specifying how this might be achieved. With the French pressing London to sever diplomatic relations with Moscow, a gesture was judged to be important. Cadogan proposed that the government 'pick a quarrel' with the

---

* It should be noted that Khrushchev's self-serving memoirs are not always reliable. Perhaps in this case the 'suckling pig' should be taken with a metaphorical pinch of salt.

Russians by dispatching the RAF on a bombing raid against the Baku oil wells – even though he suspected that this would only serve to provoke Moscow to elevate the non-aggression pact into a formal alliance with the Third Reich.[29]

With the House of Commons rousing itself to a frenzy of impotent anti-Soviet rhetoric – 'vivid, seething, overflowing fury', as the Soviet ambassador described the debate[30] – very few voices were raised in opposition to the advocates of a belligerent stance towards the Soviet Union. But these were not without influence. Once again, Churchill – who had returned to government as First Lord of the Admiralty a few months earlier – used his place in the War Cabinet to argue against the demonization of the Soviet Union. Nor was he alone in his readiness to overlook the Red Army's occupation of Finland in Britain's wider strategic interests. More surprisingly, a junior Foreign Office minister, Rab Butler, an erstwhile appeaser, broke ranks with his officials. Displaying a subtlety that had evidently been denied his more excitable colleagues in the Commons, he commented drily that although a 'certain noble purity' attached to a policy 'which tends to add one enemy after another to those opposed to us', it would be wiser to establish a dialogue with Moscow to prevent Berlin presuming that the Soviet Union was 'a completely subservient ally'.[31]

That strategic debate was brought rudely to a halt in April 1940, when the Germans launched their drive to occupy Denmark (which succumbed in a single day) and to invade Norway. This not only consumed the attention of the War Cabinet but served as a brutal reminder that the Nazis posed a direct threat to Britain far graver and more immediate than any action that might conceivably be taken by the Soviet Union: the 'phony war' was over. In its place Britain faced an existential challenge for which it was as yet ill prepared. The rapid occupation of the two Scandinavian countries was swiftly followed by a panzer blitzkrieg that overran the Low Countries before circumventing the Maginot Line to advance deep into France. Paris was occupied on 14 June. By that time, the British Expeditionary Force, which had stood alongside the French on the border with Belgium for the last nine months, had been driven into a helter-skelter retreat to Dunkirk, and had scrambled back across the Channel to the relative safety of Britain: it was a heroic but humiliating evacuation from the European mainland that left more than 40,000 troops on the beaches of northern France to be swiftly incarcerated as prisoners of war. It would be four years before a British army (under the overall command of the United States) was prepared to set off in the opposite direction to play its part in the final destruction of the Third Reich. For now, Hitler was master of Europe.

If there was any cause for Western optimism it was that Chamberlain had been replaced as prime minister by Churchill. Ironically, Chamberlain's resignation was triggered by a disastrous naval campaign to retake Norway which had been masterminded by Churchill in his role as First Lord of the Admiralty. Chamberlain self-destructed in the House of Commons with an aggressively defensive account of the debacle. His days were already numbered, but his failure to master the House at a critical moment – the German panzers were simultaneously rolling into Belgium – was the final humiliation. After delivering a withering critique of the prime minister, the Conservative MP Leo Amery administered the coup de grâce by quoting Oliver Cromwell's words to the Long Parliament, 'Depart, I say, and let us have done with you. In the name of God, go.'

On 10 May Chamberlain tendered his resignation. Churchill was the only credible candidate to succeed him. Three days later, in his first speech in the Commons as prime minister, the new leader declared, 'I have nothing to offer but blood, toil, tears and sweat.'[32] Mercifully, from Britain's perspective, he in fact had a great deal more to offer. At this point, though, he barely had time to give the Soviet Union a moment's thought, let alone to formulate a coherent strategy that might wean Moscow away from Berlin's embrace and turn it towards Britain instead. That task was left to the Foreign Office, where it was presumed that any such effort was pointless. Fortuitously – but, as it would prove, greatly to Britain's advantage – the Molotov–Ribbentrop Pact was already starting to unravel.

6. Thieves Fall Out

A little after 11 a.m. on 12 November 1940, Stalin's foreign minister arrived in Berlin for a meeting with Hitler. For his first venture beyond his country's borders in fifty years, Molotov travelled by train, accompanied by a retinue of more than sixty staff. At the behest of the Führer's propaganda minister, Joseph Goebbels, a sinister master of manipulation, he was given a muted welcome, in notable contrast to the warmth with which Ribbentrop had been received in Moscow fifteen months earlier. 'I ensure that there is no SA guard of honour. That would be going too far. Also no deployment of the general public . . . Moscow places great importance on this visit. We shall know how to exploit it . . . Cool reception,' Goebbels noted in his diary.[1] The Anhalter station was bedecked with flowers and swastikas, which all but concealed the hammer and sickle of the Soviet flag that fluttered in the background. Molotov was greeted by Ribbentrop, the Wehrmacht's commander-in-chief, Keitel, and SS leader Heinrich Himmler. In the square outside, a military band played the 'Internationale', but at double speed, lest any closet communist who might stray onto the set should be tempted to join in.[2]

His delegation – all wearing 'identical dark blue suits, grey ties, and cheap felt hats', which some wore 'like berets, some on the back of their heads like cowboys and some low over the eyes like Mafiosi'[3] – was put up in the splendour of the newly renovated Schloss Bellevue, a neo-classical imperial palace used to accommodate high-profile guests in some luxury. This may have compensated for the cool welcome and the absence of cheering crowds in the streets, though Molotov later claimed to have no recollection of his arrival in the German capital.

Ostensibly, the Molotov–Ribbentrop Pact was still intact. On the face of it, it had been reinforced by a further trade deal signed the previous February which committed the Soviet Union to provide raw materials worth 650 million Reichsmarks in return for a huge cache of military hardware to a similar value – including the *Lützow*, one of the

Kriegsmarine's small fleet of heavy cruisers. Although the negotiations had been hampered by ill humour, sharp practice and bad faith, they offered the illusion that all was well between these unlikely bedfellows. It was not. Far from burying the two sides' deep-seated and longstanding antipathies, the Molotov–Ribbentrop Pact had merely suppressed them. As one astute British official noted, 'neither dictator dare turn away lest the other stab him in the back'.[4] Their bad-faith concordat was about to spawn a poisonous set of intractable disputes.

The ostensible purpose of Molotov's visit to Berlin was to discuss what his German counterpart, Ribbentrop, had described in a letter to Stalin as a new 'delineation of mutual spheres of influence'[5] designed both to refresh and to revise the Molotov–Ribbentrop Pact. This was disingenuous. Berlin's real purpose was to distract Moscow from Hitler's European game plan, in which the Soviet Union was to be not a partner but a victim.

Following his conquests in northern and western Europe, Hitler was deflected from the invasion of the Soviet Union by the need to shore up his southern flank, which, following Italian failures in the Balkans, he feared would be threatened by a British invasion that might choke off one of the Reich's vital arteries. It was not enough for him to conquer new lands in the east and colonize their peoples. Lebensraum would depend upon the economic as well as the human exploitation of these territories and a means of importing and exporting goods of all kinds from them. To this end, mastery over the Danube – the major navigable artery that fed into the Black Sea and thence via the Dardanelles and the Aegean into the Mediterranean – was crucial.

This fact put Nazi Germany on a collision course with the Soviet Union. There were other issues – notably the formation in August 1940 of an informal military agreement between Berlin and Helsinki that permitted the Wehrmacht to station troops in Finland close to the border with the territories occupied by the Soviet Union after the Winter War – but by the autumn of 1940 it was not the Baltic States but the Balkans that had become by far the most combustible source of conflict between the two 'non-aggressors'. Since the time of Peter the Great, free access to the Danube and control of the 'warm water' Black Sea ports had been regarded by the Russians as essential to national prosperity and security. Any threat to this strategic 'right' had long been regarded by Moscow as an assault on the very fabric of the Russian state and a justifiable casus belli.

Churchill understood this. In a remarkably prescient but often over-looked passage of his famous broadcast depiction of Russia as 'a riddle, wrapped in a mystery, inside an enigma',[6] only a month after the outbreak of Britain's war with Germany, he added, 'perhaps there is a key. That key is Russian national interest.' He went on to declare, 'It cannot be in accordance with the interest of the safety of Russia that Germany should plant herself upon the shores of the Black Sea, or that she should overrun the Balkan states and subjugate the Slavonic peoples of south-eastern Europe. That would be contrary to the historic life-interests of Russia.' In June 1940, Molotov confirmed that Churchill's judgement was spot on. In a meeting with the Italian ambassador, the Soviet for-eign minister explained that the Soviet Union had 'the legitimate right to full control of the Black Sea, which must be exclusively Russian'.[7] Romania, which bordered the estuary of the Danube and the Black Sea – an important junction at the crossroads of central, eastern and south-eastern Europe – was a case in point. Under the terms of the secret protocols of the Molotov–Ribbentrop pact, the historical region of Bessarabia – cur-rently occupied by Romania – fell into the Soviet 'sphere of influence'. As evidence of Moscow's determination to reinforce its presence in the region, Stalin had recently strongarmed Bucharest into relinquishing the neighbouring provinces of Bukovina and Bessarabia, which straddled the border between Romania and Ukraine.

Hitler did not formally protest at Stalin's pre-emptive strike, but with a guile that wrong-footed the Soviet leader he acted indirectly but decisively. In August 1940 he unilaterally announced the abolition of the International Commission, which for more than eighty years had been responsible for the administration of the lower reaches of the Dan-ube.* In effect, this amounted to a declaration that henceforth the Danube was to be a German river, a Nazi waterway giving Berlin control over all access to and from the Black Sea. When the Soviet Union (which had not been a member of the International Commission) protested

---

* The members of the commission were the two riparian states of Romania and Bulgaria plus Britain, France and Italy as well as Germany.

vigorously at this coup de main, Berlin affected to be perturbed by Moscow's reaction and suggested that the two sides work together to find a resolution to avert a damaging confrontation. Not surprisingly, given their incompatible objectives, the Danube talks soon became grounded in the diplomatic mud.

The implications of this impasse were in little doubt. A report produced by the Soviet Union's foreign military intelligence agency, the GRU, quoting the Soviet ambassador in Belgrade, was blunt and to the point: 'For Germany the Balkans are the most significant asset and ought to be included in the new order of Europe; but since the USSR would never agree to that, a war with her is inevitable.'[8]

The diplomatic tension was ratcheted up further when, within days of surrendering Bukovina and Bessarabia to the Soviet Union, King Carol II of Romania was overthrown in a military coup. Its leader, General Ion Antonescu, was a fascist who at once assumed dictatorial powers by appointing himself as prime minister and planting Carol's inept teenage son, Michael, on the throne as the titular head of state. His first move was to forge an alliance with Nazi Germany. Hitler was more than happy to co-operate. On 12 October, at Antonescu's invitation, German troops established a garrison in Romania, thereby nullifying the impact of Stalin's twin annexations (which for the time being remained in Soviet hands). Just over two weeks earlier, Germany, Italy and Japan had concluded the Tripartite Pact.* Antonescu, who was soon to prove himself as murderous as any of Hitler's henchmen, was eager to demonstrate his credentials. His application to join the pact was accepted on 23 November, ten days after Molotov's arrival in Berlin.

Stalin's troubles deepened following the ill-judged decision by the Italian dictator, Benito Mussolini, to invade Greece on 28 October. This led King Boris III, who ruled the quasi-fascist kingdom of Bulgaria (which sat on the opposite bank of the Danube from Romania and was also nominally neutral) to judge it politic to tilt towards Berlin. Eager to signal his support, the king invited a contingent of German troops to

---

* The Tripartite Pact, signed on 27 September 1940, committed the signatories to provide political, economic and military support to any one member that came under attack from any other power not currently engaged in the European or Sino-Japanese War. It was aimed principally at the United States. It had more symbolic purpose than practical utility.

establish a base in the country. A few months later, in March 1941, he joined Antonescu in the Tripartite Pact's warm embrace. Stalin had been comprehensively outmanoeuvred.

Reports from the Soviet Embassy in Berlin on the eve of Molotov's visit raised the stakes further with a dispatch advising that the Nazi leadership now regarded the Balkans as 'a new bridgehead for a military engagement against the Soviet Union'.[9] The head of the GRU, the Soviet foreign intelligence service, General Filipp Golikov, who had recently returned from a fact-finding mission to the German capital, simultaneously warned that Germany was 'continuing to transfer its troops to the Balkans'[10] – albeit, he advised (correctly as it would transpire), in readiness for a possible attack on Greece rather than directly against the Soviet Union.

With his antennae on full alert, Stalin's instructions to his foreign minister reflected his acute concern about the way events were unfolding. Molotov was left in no doubt about his prime objective in Berlin. As a prosaic and dogged diplomat, 'Stone Arse' was exceptionally unlikely to be sideswiped by any vision of the sunlit uplands that Hitler might invite him to contemplate. His overriding task was to make it clear that Stalin would never relinquish Russia's imperial right to control the Black Sea. But he was also mindful of the fact that, following the debacle in Finland a year earlier, the Red Army was in no state to conduct a war against the all-conquering Wehrmacht with any hope of success. An escalation of the Balkan crisis was therefore to be avoided.

Hitler was no less keen than Stalin to avoid a premature confrontation that might inadvertently flare into an untoward military conflict. The planning for the invasion of the Soviet Union was at a preliminary stage, the 'war-games' needed to test those plans had not been scheduled, and the logistical challenge of redeploying scores of divisions that were currently occupying much of western Europe had yet to be examined in any detail. Moreover, the success of the invasion would depend upon surprise: an attack launched at a moment of Hitler's choosing and certainly not to be dictated or potentially scuppered by events that had slipped out of his control. It was essential, therefore, that his meeting with the Soviet foreign minister should appear to be conciliatory.

Before his appointment with Hitler, Molotov met his German counterpart in his suite of offices in the former presidential palace, which, according to Hitler's interpreter Paul Schmidt (who attended this meeting as an observer), had been decorated by Ribbentrop in an excessively vulgar fashion.[11] In sharp contrast to the Soviet foreign minister, Ribbentrop was invariably reluctant to use one word where ten would do. So it was on this occasion. In the course of a portentous monologue that lasted over an hour, Ribbentrop laid out a vision of the future in which the Soviet Union might join the Tripartite Pact and share in the spoils that would accrue from the inevitable defeat of Britain and the dismemberment of its global empire. For most of this meandering soliloquy Molotov listened impassively, intervening on only three occasions when, in sharp contrast to his host's ingratiating grandiloquence, he spoke with 'a certain mathematic precision and unerring logic . . . and, as though he were taking a class, gently rebuking the sweeping, vague generalities of Ribbentrop'.[12] It was clear that Molotov was keeping his powder dry for the encounter with Hitler that afternoon.

Along with his negotiating team and his interpreter, Valentin Berezhkov,* the Soviet foreign minister was escorted through a maze of marbled halls before reaching Hitler's office. It was a moment of pure fascist theatre: 'Two tall blond SS men in black, tightly belted uniforms with skulls on the caps clicked their heels and threw open the tall, almost ceiling-high doors with a single well-practised gesture. Then, with their backs to the door jambs and their right arms raised, they formed a kind of arch, through which we had to pass to enter Hitler's office, a vast room which was more like a banqueting hall than an office.'[13]

Being well acquainted with the Kremlin palaces, Molotov was undaunted by this display of Nazi magnificence. Hitler was seated at his desk but rose to greet Stalin's emissary with an elaborate show of courtesy. The talks began conventionally, with both men expressing their commitment to the importance of Soviet–German collaboration, before Molotov seized the initiative, calmly but persistently seeking clear answers to a set of detailed questions about the precise character of the future relationship that Hitler was proposing. In particular he asked, 'How do matters stand with regard to the safeguarding of Russian interests in the Balkans and the Black Sea . . . And how does the Tripartite Pact stand with regard to it?' Paul Schmidt was taken aback: 'No foreign visitor had ever spoken to him [Hitler] in this way in my presence.' The

* Berezhkov was Stalin's interpreter, loaned to Molotov for the occasion.

interpreter half-expected the Führer to leap up and bring the meeting abruptly to a close, as he had seen him do in past encounters which had become disagreeable. Instead, Hitler responded almost apologetically, 'The Tripartite Pact will regulate conditions in Europe according to the natural interests of the European countries themselves and that is why Germany now approaches the Soviet Union, so that she can express her views on the territories that are of interest to her.'[14] Since this rejoinder was as vague as his opening remarks, Molotov pressed for more detail. At one point he said bluntly that the Soviet Union would not consider joining the Tripartite Pact unless 'we are to be treated as equal partners and not mere dummies'.[15] Hitler was not accustomed to such a robust interrogation and was evidently unable to endure it for long. After a while, advising somewhat lamely that a British air raid might be in the offing, he suggested that they suspend their dialogue for the evening. Their meeting had achieved precisely nothing – and, of course, there was no air raid.

Later that evening, Ribbentrop hosted a dinner for Molotov, who sparred and joshed with the Führer's deputy, Rudolf Hess, and Hermann Goering, now elevated to Reichsmarschall. He might have displayed rather less camaraderie had he known that, a few hours earlier, Hitler had issued Directive No. 18, which – somewhat buried in an updated blueprint for the Nazification of Europe – contained the following instruction:

RUSSIA: Political discussions for the purpose of clarifying Russia's attitude in the immediate future have already begun. Regardless of the outcome of these conversations, all preparations for the East for which verbal orders have already been given will be continued. Further directives will follow on this subject as soon as the basic operational plan of the Army has been submitted to me and approved.[16]

Only a very small number of Hitler's most senior generals were aware of this injunction. It was a well-kept secret. As a result, none of Moscow's agents in Berlin had been able to alert the Kremlin. Stalin was completely unaware of what was afoot. Had Molotov known about Directive No. 18, he would certainly have been better prepared for the serial obfuscations with which Hitler was to disguise his real purposes at their next meeting on the following day. As it was, in a late-night exchange of telegrams, he reassured Stalin he would find a way to 'press [Hitler] on the Black Sea, the Straits and Bulgaria', but would avoid

saying anything that might undermine the pact he had crafted with Ribbentrop fifteen months earlier.[17] This attempt to square the circle would
rapidly prove fruitless.

The second meeting opened in a chilly fashion, with both men alleg-
ing that the other side had violated the pact – the Germans by stationing
troops in Finland and the Russians by acting similarly in Bukovina.
When Molotov claimed that the Soviet presence in Bukovina was 'irrelevant' to their wider relationship, Hitler did not respond directly. Instead
he said – as though seeking sympathy – that 'the Soviet Government
would have to understand that Germany was engaged in a life and death
struggle' but that, so long as they did not fall out, 'there was no power on
earth which could oppose the two countries'.[18] When Molotov changed
tack to chide Hitler for stationing troops in Finland, pointing out that
under the Pact, the Baltic States fell into the Soviet 'sphere of influence',
the Führer was again evasive. But he was clearly nettled, warning that
any conflict between them over the Baltic would impose 'a strain on
German-Russian relations with unforeseeable consequences'.[19] Molotov
was not deterred but repeated that the German presence in Finland constituted a violation of the Pact.

Hitler reacted to this impasse by changing the subject to dilate upon
a more congenial topic. Britain, he declared, would very soon be defeated
and the British Empire – a 'bankrupt estate' – would then be ripe for
them to plunder. 'Let's divide the whole world,' he suggested.[20] The
Soviet diplomat was not known as 'Stone Arse' for nothing. In his precise and obdurate way, he brought the discussion back to Europe and
the intractable issue of the Balkan states and the Black Sea. 'I persisted.
I wore him down,' Molotov recalled with satisfaction.[21]

The two men sparred testily until Molotov asked how Germany would
respond if the Soviet Union gave a military guarantee to Bulgaria on
similar terms to that given by Germany to Romania. Hitler was yet
again evasive, saying only that he would need to discuss the issue with
Mussolini. Molotov persisted: the Soviet Union needed protection from
any attack 'on the Black Sea through the Dardanelles', as Russia had
faced in the Crimean War and more recently in the Civil War. Hitler
could stand no more. Once again praying in aid the RAF, he advised
that there might very well soon be an air raid on the capital. The meeting ended without agreement. It would be their last.

On this occasion the RAF was happy to oblige. That evening, Molotov's guests were feasting on the world's best caviar and consuming liberal quantities of vodka at the 'return' banquet for his German hosts when the sirens started to wail. As the Soviet Embassy lacked an air-raid shelter, Goering, Hess and others hurried to their limousines in search of a place of safety. Ribbentrop escorted Molotov to his bunker in the Foreign Ministry, where – against the distant chatter of anti-aircraft guns, the thump of exploding bombs and the ceaseless lament of the sirens – they reopened their fruitless dialogue about their rivalrous aspirations for the division of the spoils once Britain had been forced to surrender.★

The next morning Molotov left Berlin for Moscow with even less ceremony than when he'd arrived. There had been no meeting of minds. Nothing had been achieved. Although the Molotov–Ribbentrop Pact was not yet in tatters, it was frayed beyond repair. Hitler had been seeking to play a twentieth-century version of the nineteenth-century 'Great Game' by luring Moscow into compliance with his vision for world domination until he was fully prepared to turn the entire might of the Wehrmacht against the Soviet Union. In the weeks following his abortive meeting with Molotov, he appeared still to hope that he could maintain the charade for a while yet. It soon became clear, though, that Moscow was no longer willing to play: Hitler's unyielding policy was not merely to confine the Soviet Union to the margins of Europe but to seize control of the entire Balkan region. There were no circumstances – except for defeat on the battlefield – under which the Kremlin would tolerate this takeover. The gulf between Moscow and Berlin was unbridgeable.

Hitler very soon lost patience. On 5 December, he summoned the army commander-in-chief, Brauchitsch, and Halder, his powerful chief of staff, to a meeting at which – with unbounded confidence – he sketched out his vision for the year ahead. Although he had abandoned plans for a cross-Channel invasion of Britain, he boasted that very soon

★ Churchill claimed later that the air raid had been timed deliberately. 'We had heard of the conference beforehand,' he quipped, 'and though not invited to join in the discussion did not wish to be entirely left out of the proceedings.' According to Stalin (as reported by the prime minister following their first meeting in August 1942), when Ribbentrop vouchsafed that 'England is finished', Molotov retorted, 'If that is so, why are we in this shelter, and whose are these bombs which fall?' Winston S. Churchill, *The Second World War*, vol. II: *Their Finest Hour* (Cassell, 1949), pp. 516–17.

'every inch' of Gibraltar would be 'pulverized', the Mediterranean would be under Axis control and the threat of a British attack on the Reich from the south via the Balkans would be eliminated – if necessary by dispatching the Wehrmacht to overrun Yugoslavia and occupy Greece. The way would thereby be cleared for a full-scale invasion of the Soviet Union in the spring of 1941. A year earlier, well before his triumphs in the west, both Brauchitsch and Halder had been so appalled by Hitler's military adventurism that they had contemplated his overthrow; now, both men – like the overwhelming majority of their fellow generals – found themselves in awe of the Führer's apparent invincibility. Similarly, the Wehrmacht's most senior commanders shared not only his political and military aspirations for eastern Europe but also what the German historian Gerhard Hirschfeld has described as 'his fanatical disdain for Judeo-Bolshevism'.[22] Thus, though they may have had reservations about the dangers of conducting a war on two fronts, the army's two most senior generals listened dutifully on 5 December as their Führer instructed them to plan in detail for a military operation on such a scale and fraught with such hazard as to be more reckless by far than any enterprise that he had yet undertaken.

Hitler's decision to move so swiftly against the Soviet Union – even though it would entail fighting a war on two fronts – was motivated by his apprehension that the British, the Americans and the Russians might form a military alliance with enough combined power to crush his European imperium. Following the fall of France nine months earlier, the mood had shifted in the United States. Roosevelt's landslide re-election victory in November 1940 had put him in a much stronger position to see off the isolationists and to persuade Congress to authorize the greatest surge in military expenditure in the history of the United States. He was also far better placed to support Britain – and any other of Hitler's adversaries – with more than warm words and tough trade deals.★

For Hitler the destruction of the Soviet Union was no longer a theoretical vision but a pressing necessity. Had he been given advance sight

★ In September 1940 Churchill and Roosevelt had concluded the 'Destroyers for Bases' deal. In exchange for fifty redundant US destroyers (which had been in mothballs) that were urgently needed to protect the British coastal waters, Britain was obliged to grant ninety-nine-year leases to the US for bases on seven UK possessions in the Caribbean. It was not an equal exchange.

of Roosevelt's 29 December 'Fireside Chat' with the American people before his meeting earlier that month with Brauchitsch and Halder, he would have been yet more convinced that he was right to press ahead. The president used his broadcast to promote a vision of the United States as 'the great Arsenal of Democracy'. Mocking America's 'appeasers', he warned that Hitler sought to 'enslave the whole of Europe', to 'dominate the rest of the world'; if Britain were defeated, the American continent would be at the mercy of the Axis powers, 'living at the point of a gun – a gun loaded with explosive bullets, economic as well as military'. To avoid that fate, he told the American people, the United States had no choice but to support its allies with as much weaponry as their great democratic arsenal could produce.[23]

Hitler had convinced himself that if the Soviet Union could be eliminated from the war before 1942 – by which time he judged that the United States would be ready to intervene against him militarily – Britain would be deprived of her 'continental sword' (in the form of an alliance with the Soviet Union) and, in consequence, the United States would think twice before waging war in Europe while simultaneously facing the Japanese. If these factors helped determine the timing of Barbarossa, his overriding objectives were unchanged: the establishment of Lebensraum for the Aryan peoples of the Third Reich and the annihilation of 'Judeo-Bolshevism'. The strategic priorities were at the service of, and dovetailed with, his deranged ideological obsessions.

It would be a straightforward victory, he told his generals:

> The Russian is inferior. The army lacks leadership . . . We will have in the spring a perceptibly better position in leadership, material, troops while the Russians will be at an unmistakable low point. When the Russian army is battered once, the final disaster is unavoidable . . . We must use attack methods which cut up the Russian army and allow its destruction in pockets . . . The anticipated time for execution is the end of May.[24]

On 18 December he confirmed his decision formally with the issue of Directive No. 21:

> The German Armed Forces must be prepared, even before the conclusion of the war against England [sic], to crush the Soviet Union in a

rapid campaign . . . In certain circumstances I shall issue orders for the deployment against Soviet Russia eight weeks before the operation is timed to begin. Preparations which require more time than this will be put in hand now, in so far as this has not already been done, and will be concluded by 15th May, 1941. It is of decisive importance that our intention to attack should not be known.

The directive was named after the twelfth-century Holy Roman Emperor Frederick I, a German-born warrior king also known as Barbarossa. Cast in the heroic mould, Frederick I Barbarossa was renowned for his wisdom as well as courage on the battlefield. His overriding goal during a long reign was to restore the empire to the status it had last enjoyed under Charlemagne, if necessary by force of arms.*

To conceal the preparations for Operation Barbarossa (for which both Finland and Romania were identified as 'probable allies'), the Führer instructed his commanders-in-chief to involve only the smallest number of staff officers possible. As a further effort to guarantee secrecy, all their instructions were to be phrased as though they were 'precautionary measures undertaken in case Russia should alter its present attitude towards us'.[25]

Rumours of the impending invasion had already been swirling around the capital for several days. On 5 December – the day of Hitler's meeting with Halder and Brauchitsch – the Soviet ambassador in Berlin, Vladimir Dekanozov, received from an undisclosed source a warning which he took seriously enough to forward to Moscow: 'To comrades Stalin and Molotov – very urgent. Russia, please be alert, as Hitler is soon going to attack you. It will soon be too late.'[26]

A little over three weeks later, after the issue of Directive No. 21, the head of the GRU, Golikov, was alerted to a report from Berlin that Hitler was actively preparing to invade Russia. The source was a German diplomat, Rudolf von Scheliha (who had been recruited by the NKVD while serving in Warsaw, where he was given the code name

---

* Along with Richard I of England and Philip II of France, Frederick I led the Third Crusade in 1189 in a bid to retake Jerusalem from Saladin's infidels. He died en route when crossing a river in southern Anatolia. See Kennedy Hickman, 'Biography of Frederick I Barbarossa', ThoughtCo, 26 August 2020; www.thoughtco.com/crusades -frederick-i-barbarossa-2360678.

Ariets). According to Ariets, who had since been transferred to the Information Department of the Ministry of Foreign Affairs in Berlin, 'highly placed sources' had told him that 'War will be declared in March 1941'.[27] Pressed for more details by Golikov (who was terrified of rousing Stalin's ire by proffering evidence that might force the Soviet Union onto a premature war footing), Ariets replied five days later to confirm that his source was 'a friend in the military' and that the warning 'was based not on rumours but on a special order of Hitler that was especially secret and known only to a few people' – very probably a reference to the slightly garbled version of Directive No. 21, which had presumably been leaked to him by his 'friend'.

At the end of February, Ariets added further details, reporting – with uncanny accuracy – that the invasion would be mounted by three army groups led respectively by three field marshals: Fedor von Bock, Gerd von Rundstedt and Wilhelm Ritter von Leeb. The date, he had advised, was 'provisionally set for May 20'. And he added, 'Preparatory measures have resulted in the assignment of Russian-speaking officers and non-commissioned officers to various headquarters. In addition armoured trains are being constructed with wide gauges as in Russia.'[28]

Ariets was one of scores of spies around the world to provide such early – and increasingly detailed and accurate – warnings of Hitler's plans. Like many spies on all sides of the conflict, Rudolf Scheliha's – motives were complex and mercenary. He was known to enjoy a lifestyle that his salary could not sustain. He was thought to have a gambling addiction and to maintain a number of mistresses. But whatever the financial motive for his 'treachery' may have been, his abhorrence of Nazism was not in doubt.* Moscow was dismayed by the growing evidence of Hitler's intentions, but far from galvanizing the Kremlin into an immediate reaction, they induced a form of collective catatonia in which the relevant officials dutifully recorded the plethora of reports from capitals all over Nazified Europe but failed to give them the credence they deserved. The raw data was usually passed upwards. Much of it reached Stalin's desk, but it was rarely sifted to assess its credibility or

---

* On 29 October 1942, Ariets was arrested and interrogated by the Gestapo. Charged with being a member of an anti-Nazi conspiracy, he was found guilty and executed two weeks later. In 2000, he was honoured as a resistance fighter at a formal ceremony in the German Foreign Office. There is a street named after him in the city of Hamburg.

value, although reports were routinely bowdlerized to align them with what it was presumed Stalin wanted to hear or to exclude conclusions that he might find unpalatable. The GRU's desk officers knew only too well that bearers of bad tidings were unwelcome, and how easily the dictator could be provoked to fury by any suggestion that the Molotov–Ribbentrop Pact might be imperilled by countervailing intelligence evidence. Living as they did in terror of his censure, it proved wiser to soothe the anxious brow of the mercurial dictator with half-truths than to draw attention to unassailable facts. With his customary precision, Molotov described Stalin's attitude thus:

> I think that one can never trust the intelligence. One has to listen to them but then check on them. The intelligence people can lead to dangerous situations that it is impossible to get out of . . . one cannot count on the intelligence without a thorough and constant checking and double checking. People are so naïve and gullible indulging themselves and quoting memoirs.[29]

Stalin's disdain was underpinned by the conviction that the Soviet Union was too important to the German economy for Hitler to risk a formal breach. The Soviet Union currently supplied 74 per cent of the Reich's phosphate, 67 per cent of its asbestos, 65 per cent of its chrome ore, 55 per cent of its manganese, 40 per cent of its nickel imports and 34 per cent of its imported oil. Far from diminishing, the inflow of vital raw materials from the country since the 1940 trade agreement had grown to the point where Germany had become dependent on the Soviet Union for some 70 per cent of all its imports. In January 1941, following an acrimonious but eventually successful round of negotiations, Berlin and Moscow signed a new commercial agreement worth a further 650 million Reichsmarks. Under this deal, Germany became even more dependent on Russia – not only for oil but also for grain, copper, nickel, platinum, chrome and manganese, all of which were crucial to the Reich's wartime economy. Although he was aware that these exports enabled Germany to circumvent an otherwise effective British naval blockade, Stalin was unable to accommodate the thought that Hitler might be preparing other means of securing these supplies than by a trade agreement. As a result, he continued to delude himself that he had far greater leverage over German policy than a careful scrutiny of the intelligence should have allowed.

Paradoxically, Stalin's dismissive attitude towards these warnings was also infused by a gnawing fear that they might be accurate. It was less distressing to presume the spies had based their reports on rumour and gossip, or even deliberate falsehoods designed to provoke war between Germany and the Soviet Union, for which the Red Army was entirely unprepared. Despite starting preparations for a potential conflict in the late autumn of 1940, the Soviet High Command had yet to receive any coherent instructions for the defence of the nation. In December the defence commissar, Marshal Timoshenko, became so alarmed by the lack of direction from the top that he complained to the Central Committee of the Communist Party. The Chief of the General Staff, General Kirill Meretskov, was evidently unaware of mounting evidence from Ukraine and Belorussia that the Germans were establishing command posts, transferring troops towards the Soviet border, turning civilian buildings into army barracks and installing anti-aircraft defences close to the frontier. A report warning of the 'dismal state' of the Red Army troops on the front line had been produced but no remedial action had yet been taken. Eventually Stalin summoned his generals to a conference at which, in addition to discussing a wholesale reorganization of the armed forces, he charged them to devise 'new war ideologies' without indicating what their purpose might be. By the end of 1940, the atmosphere in the military was laden with gloom, uncertainty and confusion.[30]

In January 1941, these glaring inadequacies were harshly exposed when the Red Army conducted two 'war games', one simulating a German invasion from the north and the other from the south. In both paper exercises the Russians were defeated. This shook the confidence of the High Command and drove Stalin to a paroxysm of anguished frustration. Summoning the participants to appear before the full Politburo, he demanded an explanation. Meretskov stumbled through a semi-coherent account before Stalin brutally interrupted him. 'The trouble is we do not have a proper chief of staff,' he said, dismissing the dumfounded Meretskov on the spot. As if that were not enough punishment, the sacked general went to the Bolshoi Theatre a few nights later only to be confronted once more by Stalin, who humiliated him yet again in front of Molotov, Timoshenko and others, saying, 'You are courageous, capable, but without principle, spineless.'[31]

By that time General Zhukov, one of the few commanders to have emerged from the war games with any credit, had been summoned to the Kremlin and on 1 February was told he was to replace Meretskov as chief of staff. His brief was to place the Soviet armed forces on a sound defensive footing. Zhukov was a formidable figure. He had displayed his qualities of generalship in 1939 during the undeclared war against the Japanese on the Mongolian border in the Soviet Far East; during the abortive war games in January he had secured a reputation for strategic clarity, tactical audacity and ruthlessness.

His challenge in the spring of 1941 was immense: to devise a military strategy and establish an operational plan to arrest and reverse any German onslaught that might be launched on almost any section of the 2,900-kilometre front line between the Baltic and the Black Sea. On paper the resources available to him – 171 divisions at the front with 57 more as a second echelon in reserve – constituted a formidable if not an invincible military force. He had weaponry in abundance. By the spring of 1941, the Red Army had some 20,000 tanks of various types and sizes – notably more than the Germans. However, fewer than half of these were stationed on the front line and most were obsolete, in need of repair or unsuited to the terrain. Although their replacements (especially the KV-1 and T-34) would prove to be far more effective than their German counterparts, these were not yet available in sufficient numbers to make a significant impact. Their crews were ill trained and their drivers very often had no more than two hours' experience at the wheel before heading to the front. The mechanized corps, with some 1,000 tanks each, were scattered widely in unwieldy formations. They were far from combat-ready.

The Soviet air force had almost four times as many fighters and bombers as the Luftwaffe, but these too were unreliable and in poor repair. Lacking radio transmitters, their navigators were – for the most part – without the means to maintain contact with ground control. The pilots were inexperienced and this, combined with the delivery of new aircraft that had not been adequately flight tested, led to a great many fatal accidents – at the rate of several a day.

The situation was so serious that in April Timoshenko and Zhukov complained to Stalin, demanding that senior heads should roll. A few weeks later, on 10 April, the commander of the Soviet air forces, Pavel Rychagov, was summoned to the Kremlin to explain these failures to a star chamber court of senior military figures and Politburo members. Angered by the criticism, and his tongue evidently loosened by alcohol, he made the fatal error of answering back, bursting out in exasperation, 'The accident rate will go on being high as long as you make us fly in coffins.' The former fighter pilot had gone too far. Stalin, who had been pacing up and down sucking on his pipe, stopped, turned, went up to Rychagov and said ominously, 'You shouldn't have said that.'[32] Stalin, who was unforgivingly punitive, meant what he said.*

Zhukov's greatest task was to oversee the training, equipping and deployment of a conscript army of often raw recruits, led by officers among whom experience, motivation and commitment were in short supply. His problems were exacerbated by the baleful presence of Communist Party apparatchiks at every level. Despite modest reforms in the late 1930s, the political commissars still retained an iron grip on the military, authorized by the Central Committee to second-guess front-line officers. Although they were well drilled in techniques of indoctrination, they knew precious little about warfare. Their diktats were not only ill-informed but also carping, demoralizing and intimidating. Bitter memories had not faded; between 1937 and 1940 almost 50,000 Red Army officers had been purged and, though many of them were subsequently reinstated, 90 per cent of the district commanders had been replaced by their subordinate officers. Instead of relishing the prospect of leadership, young officers shied away from taking initiatives; instead of shouldering responsibility, they frequently chose to be invisible, beneath the radar.

An alarming number became clinically depressed by the tension between obeying the doctrinaire whims of the commissars and exercising the initiative, flair and flexibility that the realities of life and death on the battlefield required. The official suicide statistics revealed that a

* Rychagov was arrested on 24 June, two days after the start of Operation Barbarossa. Held responsible for the catastrophic failure of the air force to mount any resistance to the Luftwaffe's devastating onslaught, he was held in custody, tortured and, on 28 October, executed along with his wife and twenty brother officers. He was pardoned posthumously in 1954.

tragically large number were driven to take their own lives. In one particularly poignant case, a loyal young communist who, according to the official archives, had been 'living in an earth dugout for months', wrote a final message:

> I am not able to go on living this hard life . . . I love my country and I would never have betrayed it. I believe in an even better future, when a bright sun will shine on the whole world. But here there are enemies who sit and threaten every step an honest commander tries to take. I decided to take my own life, even though I am but 21 years old.[33]

There could have been little doubt that the enemies to which he referred were the omnipresent commissars.

For those who chose to soldier on but who lacked adequate training or experience, life was made even harder. As Catherine Merridale has noted in her vivid and scholarly *Ivan's War*, 'Men in the ranks were quick to spot incompetence. While the culture of purging and denunciation did a lot to damage officers' prestige, their own ineptitude was fatal.'[34] Insubordination, born of contempt, was commonplace, an attitude the fiasco of the Winter War against Finland had served only to exacerbate.

All these factors made it hard to find high-quality recruits to fill the empty spaces in an army which had been purged but was seeking rapidly to expand. By the late spring of 1941, the shortfall was 36,000 and rising. Despite Zhukov's tireless and ruthless efforts, the Red Army was an arthritic leviathan which was still far from being 'fit for purpose'.

This fact permeated Stalin's thinking to the point where the more warnings he received about Hitler's aggressive purpose, the more reluctant he became to accept them. In relation to Hitler, his paranoid instincts appeared to desert him. Noting the irony of this, Alexander Solzhenitsyn was to write that Stalin did not trust his own mother, God, fellow party members, peasants, workers, intellectuals, soldiers, relatives, wives, mistresses, or even his own children: 'In all his long suspicion-ridden life he had only trusted one man . . . This man whom Stalin trusted was Adolf Hitler.'[35] This double-edged indictment was potent, but did not allow for the fact that the Soviet dictator nurtured the self-deluding hope that by placating his Nazi nemesis he might postpone an invasion he now regarded as inevitable, at least until the Red Army was in a better state of readiness.

★

In Berlin, the German High Command was rather less sanguine about Operation Barbarossa than the Führer, who repeatedly instructed them that victory was certain. In one such meeting he declared, 'I am convinced that our attack will sweep over them like a hailstorm';[36] at another, 'The Russians will crumple under the massive impact of our tanks and planes'.[37] Nor could his generals have been in any doubt about the means required to deliver the Führer's ends. As he never tired of telling them, the invasion had a far greater purpose than military victory alone: it would be a 'war of extermination' in which the traditional rules of engagement would have no meaning. He used the term 'exterminate' so wantonly and with such relish as to eliminate all doubt in their minds that, for him, the 'annihilation' (another favoured term) of Judaeo-Bolshevism was every bit as important as the acquisition of raw materials or the establishment of Lebensraum for the peoples of the Third Reich.

He spelled out the gruesome implications of these objectives in the Reich Chancellery on 30 March, where he addressed more than 200 senior officers, including the commanders-in-chief of all three services. In the words of one of the most senior officers present, General Walter Warlimont,* deputy chief of OKW (Wehrmacht High Command) Operations, he made it clear that 'the German soldier need not be bound by the letter of the laws of war or of disciplinary instructions but that, on the contrary, "any type of attack by the inhabitants against the Wehrmacht" should be dealt with with the utmost severity, including summary execution without court martial procedure'.[38] Queasiness about the treatment of the enemy would not be an option: 'Commanders must make the sacrifice of overcoming their personal scruples.'[39]

Whatever qualms they may have had, the generals did not dare even to question the Führer, let alone express any dissent. General Warlimont's defence of this supine reaction – that some of them knew that 'opposition generally did more harm than good' while others 'had not followed

---

* As deputy chief of OKW, Warlimont was privy to, and immersed in, the development of the military plans for Barbarossa. For his part in drafting the Commissar Order of 6 June and the Barbarossa Order (which codified the 30 March directives from Hitler) he was convicted of war crimes at Nuremberg in 1948 and sentenced to life imprisonment. Three years later the sentence was commuted to eighteen years. Released in 1954, he subsequently wrote a self-exculpatory – but illuminating – biography which was published ten years later.

Hitler's long diatribe in detail' and thus 'had not grasped the full meaning of his proposals' – was so feeble as to beggar belief.[40] But feebleness was collusion's handmaiden. On 6 May 1940 the army's commander-in-chief, General Brauchitsch, published a draft set of formal instructions designed to give quasi-legal authority to Hitler's requirements. At its core was an order that all political 'offenders' captured by the Wehrmacht should be 'liquidated if possible at prisoners-of-war collecting points or at the latest on passage through the transit camps'.[41] The official 'Guidelines for the Behaviour of the Fighting Forces in Russia' (19 May) that were to be issued to all ranks on the eve of Barbarossa demanded 'ruthless and vigorous action against Bolshevik agitators, guerrillas, saboteurs, Jews and the complete elimination of all active and passive resistance'.[42] There was to be no part of Hitler's 'war of annihilation' from which his generals would be permitted to exclude themselves, an obligation which they accepted without demur and in some cases with enthusiasm.

Though planning for the invasion was accelerating sharply following Directive No. 21, the generals had qualms about the scale and speed with which they were required to accomplish their Führer's objectives. At the end of January, following a meeting with Brauchitsch, Halder had noted, 'Barbarossa: purpose is not clear. We do not hit the British . . . Risk in the West must not be underestimated.'[43] Their anxiety about fighting a war on two fronts was sharpened by an avalanche of analyses detailing the enormous strategic and tactical challenges that would face their commanders on the battlefield. Reams of documents laid bare the logistical, organizational and operational complexities of structuring, mobilizing, training, equipping, deploying and sustaining an army of more than 3 million men on alien terrain far from the heart of the Fatherland. It was, at best, a daunting enterprise. At worst, they feared, it would be a disaster.

Their assessment of the Soviet Union's military potential was also sobering. The more thoroughly they examined the evidence about the Soviet Union's material and human resources, the more obvious it became that their enemy had the potential to offer formidable resistance. For all its evident shortcomings and failures, they judged the Red Army to be a 'gigantic war-machine' whose structural and organizational weaknesses were offset by its size, the quality of its weaponry and, they were advised by their own observers on the spot, by 'the frugality, toughness and bravery of its individual soldiers'. Internal documents based on close observation of the Red Army warned against the temptation to be misled by its woeful performance against the Finns. In contrast to Hitler's instinctive disdain for the 'inferior' quality of the Russian soldier, these reports argued that he 'would fight to the death' to protect his Motherland and that, in defence, 'he is tough and gallant, and usually allows himself to be killed at the spot where his leader has placed him'.[44]

Yet, if the German High Command feared that Hitler's reach so far exceeded his grasp as to render Barbarossa a perilous or foolhardy venture, they refrained from saying so. As Commander-in-Chief of the Wehrmacht, the Führer was constitutionally omnipotent; as the conqueror of the West, and someone who had overridden his cautious military advisors, he was also politically unassailable. He had made it abundantly plain that he would brook no dissent and that he had no intention of leaving Operation Barbarossa in the hands of his generals: it was his war, he was its mastermind, and he was resolved to control its direction as unequivocally as he had defined its purpose in terms they could not possibly misunderstand.

For Hitler, the security of the Third Reich's southern front was an essential precondition for the launch of Barbarossa. Any risk of internal upheaval, or that any Balkan state might reach out to either the Russians or the British had to be eliminated first. In late February, with this risk yet to be averted, he was confronted by a rapidly accelerating regional crisis that promised to derail his timetable for the invasion of Russia. Although Bulgaria was about to follow Romania by joining the Tripartite Pact,* Yugoslavia had yet to succumb to Berlin's heavy-handed enticement. Even worse, a significant part faced imminent defeat at the hands of the Greeks. Rather than marching in triumph on Athens to claim his slice of the Balkan cake as Mussolini had imagined when he launched his hubristic invasion four months earlier, his troops had started to flee across the mountains into Albania. Hitler feared that this blundering retreat would reinforce the Anglo-Greek alliance and thereby threaten his southern flank: the British would acquire a foothold in the Balkans from which to launch a major assault on the Reich

---

* Bulgaria joined on 1 March 1941.

or to bomb the Romanian oilfields that were crucial to the Reich's ability to sustain a war economy.

On 24 February, as though to confirm Hitler's apprehension, the British prime minister ordered General Archibald Wavell, the Middle East commander-in-chief, to transfer four divisions from the Desert Campaign to Greece. The impact of this decision on the campaign in North Africa was immediate. The 'Army of the Nile', as Churchill liked to call the 8th Army, was at that moment poised to destroy the Italian 10th Army in the Libyan Desert and to seize Tripoli. To the fury and dismay of the British commanders in the field, the redeployment of four divisions meant this mission had to be aborted. Churchill's decision – which an initially reluctant Wavell had finally endorsed – coincided to the day with the arrival of General Erwin Rommel in the Libyan capital at the head of two panzer divisions in a bid to prevent Hitler's Axis partner from facing humiliation in North Africa as well as in Greece.[45]

However, Churchill was driven by what he regarded as a far more important strategic objective: to secure an alliance with Greece and Yugoslavia that – with the tacit and, he hoped, the active support of Turkey – would safeguard Britain's imperial interests in the Middle East and Africa from a Wehrmacht offensive. As yet, this was no more than a gleam in Hitler's eye but, urged on by the Commander-in-Chief of the Kriegsmarine, Admiral Erich Raeder, he was already toying with the thought of 'a detour through the Mediterranean and Africa on the way to world empire'.[46]

The explosion of violence that was about to erupt in the Balkans owed much to their strategic location as a stronghold for whichever power could master their convulsive rivalries and enmities. At this pivotal moment in the Second World War, it owed no less to the fateful irony that the British and the Germans both feared that each intended to use the region as a launch pad from which to open a second front against the other. As it happened, neither – at that point – intended to adopt any such offensive strategy. But by now it was no longer possible to avert a military confrontation with the Wehrmacht that the prime minister's most senior advisors knew was bound to end disastrously.

'The Germans could overrun Greece with the utmost ease if they wanted to,' the director of military operations, Major General John Kennedy, had warned, noting tartly, 'we stood to gain more by winning the African coast for ourselves than by denying Greece to the Germans'.[47] Similarly, the Chief of the Imperial General Staff, Sir John Dill, advised that, if the troops were sent in, 'they would be certain to be annihilated or driven out again'.[48] However, he had been persuaded during a visit to Athens with Anthony Eden that diplomacy should prevail over narrow military logic. Churchill conceded that there was no more than 'a good fighting chance', but he was determined to show the world, and especially President Roosevelt, that Britain would honour its commitments, and thereby, he hoped, stiffen his allies' resolve to join Britain against the Nazis.* For that reason, the prime minister judged it was better to try and fail rather than not to try at all.

On 2 March 1941 the first contingents of a British Expeditionary Force landed at the port of Piraeus. Within two days, more than 60,000 troops were on their way north to join the Greeks in resisting the threatened German blitzkrieg. Churchill had hoped that the presence of British troops on Greek soil would encourage neighbouring Yugoslavia to resist the growing threats from Berlin. But on 25 March Belgrade buckled. As acting head of state, Prince Paul joined Romania and Bulgaria to become a fellow signatory to the Tripartite Pact. Events now moved rapidly towards a conflagration as the Yugoslav army, in close co-operation with the British, staged a military coup. Paul was forced to cede the throne to his teenage cousin, King Peter II, for whom he had been acting as regent. Serb nationalists took to the streets to dance in celebration and to wave British flags in fraternal triumph. The cry went up, 'Rather war than the Pact: rather death than slavery.' Churchill was almost as elated as the crowds, reflecting, 'A people paralysed in action, hitherto ill-governed and ill-led, long haunted by the sense of being ensnared, flung their reckless, heroic defiance at the tyrant and conqueror in the moment of his greatest power.'[49] The rejoicing did not last long.

Yugoslavia's impertinent defiance enraged Hitler. His blandishments and threats had come to naught. Barbarossa could no longer proceed as planned. His southern flank was suddenly and unexpectedly exposed in the most alarming fashion. He sent a telegram to Mussolini: 'I do not consider this situation as being catastrophic, but nevertheless it is a

---

* In a 1939 treaty with Greece, the British government had pledged British support in the event of an attack on Greek territory.

difficult one . . .'[50] To launch a blitzkrieg against the Soviet Union with both Greece and Yugoslavia ranged against him alongside the British would be too foolhardy for even Hitler to contemplate. His only alternative was to crush both countries at once or to postpone Barbarossa sine die. On the very day of the military coup, he issued Directive No. 25, which stated bluntly: Yugoslavia 'must be regarded as an enemy and beaten down as quickly as possible'. It was not good enough merely to defeat the Yugoslavs on the battlefield but – as punishment for their insolence – their capital city was to be 'destroyed from the air by continual day and night attack'. In the same directive, he coupled this with the order 'simultaneously' to begin operations against Greece.[51]

On 6 April some 350,000 German troops, supported by 700 aircraft, marched on Belgrade from their staging posts in Romania. In a single day of low-level bombing 17,000 Yugoslavs were killed (almost as many as died in Dresden during the entire month of February 1945).[52] After eleven days and 100,000 casualties the capital was in ruins. Yugoslavia surrendered. The brutality of Hitler's resolve had been demonstrated with pitiless clarity.

On the same day, 680,000 German troops, supported by 1,000 tanks and 700 aircraft, blitzed their way into northern Greece. Exhausted and demoralized by the onslaught, the Greeks fell back in disorder. To avoid its own annihilation, the British Expeditionary Force had to beat a more or less orderly retreat to the coast. Since the port at Piraeus had been virtually obliterated by the Luftwaffe, the troops made for the beaches, where a hastily assembled fleet of British warships, flying boats and fishing smacks waited to rescue them. In an operation reminiscent of Dunkirk, they destroyed what was left of their artillery, tanks, trucks and even pack animals before trying to make their escape under fire from the German bombers. Some 43,000 men made it to the boats but 15,000 – a quarter of those who had landed at Piraeus six weeks earlier – were killed, wounded or captured. On 23 April, as the British survivors extricated themselves from this debacle, the Greek army laid down its guns. Four days later, the swastika was flying over the Acropolis.*

* The British survivors were given sanctuary in the British garrison on Crete. Their respite was short lived. On 20 May, 22,000 German parachutists, backed up by ground troops, landed on Crete in an airborne invasion supported by more than 500 warplanes. The islanders joined the British and Commonwealth troops to mount a valiant

Hitler had made himself the undisputed master of the Balkans. Strategically, however, it was to prove a pyrrhic victory, secured at exorbitant cost. Though it was true that, with his southern flank secured, Hitler could now proceed with the invasion of the Soviet Union, the target date of late May for the launch of Barbarossa could no longer be met. The destruction of Yugoslavia and the occupation of Greece had required the mass redeployment of men and weaponry – infantry and armoured divisions – from Poland, where they had been mustering for Barbarossa. The invasion could not start before they had returned to their positions close to the Polish front line. This was a daunting logistical task that would take four precious weeks.

Though he did not know it at the time, Churchill's decision to come to the aid of Greece thus had a significant if fortuitous impact on the Barbarossa campaign. Although the British effort to resist the Nazi takeover of the Balkans had ended in humiliating failure, it had not been entirely in vain. The perceived threat to Berlin's Balkan hegemony led Hitler to postpone the launch of Barbarossa. As a result, the number of optimal war-fighting weeks on the Eastern Front before the onset of the Russian winter was sharply and alarmingly curtailed.

---

resistance. It was to no avail. Crete fell one week later. Though the Germans paid a heavy price for their victory, the British suffered a humiliating defeat at the cost of some 23,000 casualties. Those who survived were evacuated by the Royal Navy's Mediterranean fleet, but not before nineteen vessels had been sunk and a further twenty-two damaged by the Luftwaffe's bombers. It was a very high price to pay for an honourable enterprise.

7. Stalin Ignores the Warnings

The Molotov–Ribbentrop Pact had so aggravated relations between London and Moscow that negotiations between the two governments had stalled. The animosity and distrust provoked by the breakdown of talks in August 1939 continued to fester. The British government was so preoccupied with the struggle against Germany that the conduct of Soviet policy was largely delegated to the career civil servants who ran the Foreign Office, where both leadership and clarity of purpose were noticeable by their absence. In this vacuum, the British ambassador in Moscow, Sir Stafford Cripps, was trapped between the mandarins in Whitehall and the hard men in the Kremlin. Cripps had been in this pivotal post since May 1941, despite the fact that he and the prime minister – who likened him disparagingly to 'a cage in which two squirrels [were] at war, his conscience and his career' – had very little in common except an instinctive mutual aversion.[1]

Sir Stafford Cripps was not a conventional diplomat. His otherwise admiring aunt, Beatrice Webb, thought he was 'oddly immature in intellect and unbalanced in judgement'.[2] Elegant in style but not emollient by nature, he was clever, arrogant, ascetic, rich and ambitious. A left-wing MP who had briefly been expelled by Labour, he had flirted with the British Communist Party and had been forgiving of Stalin's purges. While Churchill was an unapologetic imperialist, Cripps believed fervently that the war's overriding triumph would be the creation of a new world order in which socialism would be the victor. On one issue, however, they were at one: in 1940, with Britain fighting alone against Nazism, it would be the height of folly to cold-shoulder the Soviet Union any longer.

The Foreign Office bureaucrats did not agree. Their collective view, stiffened by the Soviet invasion of Finland, was that the Russians had 'settled down definitely into an undeclared war' against Britain, and were Hitler's 'partners in crime'.[3] Cadogan, who wielded great influence, regarded the Soviet Union as beyond redemption. Under Chamberlain the Cabinet did not dissent. Once Churchill had installed himself in

Number 10, however, the Cabinet's attitude changed abruptly. With France almost certain to crumble and the debacle of Dunkirk already in prospect, the atmosphere in the early summer of 1940 was grim with foreboding, even despair. The restoration of relations with the Soviet Union to counter Hitler's growing stranglehold on Europe came rapidly into focus.

Cripps had virtually appointed himself to Moscow. After sounding out Maisky, he seized the moment to let it be known that he would like to go to the Soviet capital as a 'special envoy' to fill the diplomatic void which had opened up between the two governments. He certainly seemed to have the right credentials. Four months earlier, he had travelled to Russia on a 'fact-finding' mission, when he had detected that the bond between Moscow and Berlin was more fragile than the propaganda from both capitals suggested. He had met Molotov, who left him with the impression that, if 'the British government would adopt a friendly attitude towards Russia', Moscow was ready to restore cordial relations with London.[4]

Three months on, in the crisis of May, Halifax – a most unlikely advocate of friendship with the Soviet Union – was persuaded that the Cripps mission might serve a useful purpose. Overriding his officials, he put the idea to the prime minister. With little time to deal with anything other than the imminent Nazi invasion of France, Churchill waved through the appointment, persuaded – erroneously as it transpired – that Cripps's reputation as a radical socialist might help him to penetrate Stalin's carapace of suspicion and hostility towards Britain.

Foreign Office officials, fearful that, with Cripps as 'our man' in Moscow, their influence would wane, grumbled about the appointment of such a wayward ideologue who was so clearly 'not one of us'. The tone was set by Cadogan, who noted disdainfully that Cripps was 'an excellent lawyer and a very nimble debater' but had 'not yet won his spurs in diplomacy'.[5] With very few exceptions, he and his colleagues not only deplored Cripps's ideological convictions but also were tempted to regard him as a 'willing tool' of the Bolsheviks.[6] This put them at odds with the junior Foreign Office minister Rab Butler, the former arch-appeaser who was one of the few with enough influence to press the case for Cripps. Butler's private secretary, Sir Henry 'Chips' Channon, who shared his minister's outlook, noted that the Foreign Office 'have learnt nothing and forgotten nothing: in fact they are still asleep, dreaming in a pre-Hitler, pre-dictator world, foolish, carping, finicky, inefficient and futile'.[7] An exaggeration but a telling one: the mandarins were out of step with their ministerial masters.

By the end of May 1940, even before his accreditation had been approved, Cripps was in the air bound for Moscow. The Kremlin, fearful that Hitler might suspect that a diplomatic shift towards London was in the offing, insisted that Britain's emissary should not be granted the status of 'some astral special envoy' but merely that of a routinely appointed ambassador.[8] His journey was anything but routine. Required to fly via Athens to avoid the Luftwaffe fighters that now patrolled the direct route between London and Moscow from their newly acquired bases in Norway, he almost failed to make it when his plane flew into a storm, was hit by lightning and overturned in mid-air. It was not a good augury.

He arrived in Moscow on 12 June without fanfare or official welcome, to be met at the airport by the embassy staff and his official Rolls-Royce. The embassy itself stood grandly on the edge of the River Moskva, looking across towards the ornate towers and spires of Red Square and the Kremlin. Built on a scale that did not appeal to Cripps's aesthetic sensibilities, his new home was drearily decorated and stuffed with ugly and uncomfortable furniture. He was disheartened at the thought that much remedial work would be required to make it congenially habitable. And then there was the food. As the teetotal vegetarian noted dejectedly, 'It looks like being very expensive and difficult living for me here as vegetables are unattainable almost and fruit is worse.'[9] It was but the start of what would prove a dispiriting venture. Though his culinary needs were soon met easily enough, he discovered that his ambassadorial ambitions would be far harder to achieve.

To stress the importance of Cripps's mission, Churchill wrote his first letter to the Soviet leader. Addressing him as 'Monsieur Stalin', he urged that, 'when the face of Europe is changing hourly', the deep political divisions between Britain and the Soviet Union should 'not prevent the relations between our two countries in the international sphere from being harmonious and mutually beneficial', so that they could face together the threat of Germany's 'hegemony' in Europe.[10] He received no reply. It was an eloquent response. For the time being, Stalin had nailed his diplomatic colours to the Nazi mast and had no intention of pulling them down.

A few days later, after a brief and formal meeting with Molotov, the new ambassador presented Churchill's letter to Stalin at the Kremlin. It was a frosty encounter that lasted almost three hours. In the course of a 'severely frank discussion', Stalin insisted that the Soviet Union did not feel threatened by Germany and that he could not agree 'to restore the old equilibrium' with Britain.[11] The two men would not meet again for another year. Cripps's subsequent requests for high-level meetings with members of the Politburo were similarly rebuffed.

The closest he got to the Kremlin's corridors of power was when, three months after his arrival, he was granted an audience with Molotov's deputy, Andrei Vyshinsky, who, despite presiding over the murderous show trials in the 1930s, was no longer influential. 'Yesterday's great thrill(!!)', Cripps noted drily, 'was a very long talk that I had with Vyshinsky last evening.' As lawyers by profession, the two men swiftly found enough common ground on which to build a congenial relationship, but their meetings were to accomplish nothing of note.* To his intense frustration, Cripps's days were marked only by the conventions of diplomacy: a cycle of cocktail parties, dinners, and 'one-to-ones' with fellow ambassadors to pick over the entrails of the rumours, gossip and titbits of intelligence that came their way.

Cripps had long believed that war between Germany and the Soviet Union was inevitable and he had said so frequently. He also advised the Foreign Office that mere words would not be enough to restore Anglo-Soviet relations. But he was resolutely stonewalled. In private correspondence he railed against what he detected as 'the distrust and hatred of the Russian government' in Whitehall.[12] In more measured terms he advised Halifax that 'the history of the last twenty years' had taught the Russians to regard the present British Cabinet 'as fundamentally hostile to the Soviet Union' and that they distrusted Britain's desire to 'divorce them from the Axis'. Explaining that a 'great and ever-present fear of Germany' dictated Soviet foreign policy, he insisted that a demonstrable change in approach was required to acknowledge Soviet interests and to find a way of accommodating them.[13]

His advice was ignored, his proposals rejected. Cadogan set much

---

* As Gabriel Gorodetsky, editor of his diaries, has noted, Cripps was evidently unaware of Vyshinsky's role as chief prosecutor during the purges.

greater store by securing the support of the United States, where anti-Bolshevism was still rampant, than on constructing any form of partnership with the Soviet Union that might provoke Washington's irritation. Halifax had initially endorsed Cripps's appointment, but with a mind that, in Butler's waspish phrase, was 'always open to the last comer'* – readily succumbed to his permanent secretary's insistent opinion and told the Cabinet that the support of the United States mattered far more than the 'somewhat illusory benefits of the goodwill of the USSR'.[14] Cripps was told that he was to take no initiatives of his own but should 'sit tight'. Cadogan, whose loathing for the 'cynical, blood-stained murderers'[15] in Moscow was unabated, evidently relished delivering these snubs: after an earlier meeting with the ever-biddable Halifax, he had sneered that Cripps 'argues that we must give everything . . . and trust to the Russians loving us. This is simply silly . . . Extraordinary how we go on kidding ourselves.'[16]

Cripps was thus left on the sidelines, an impotent observer of a rapidly unfolding drama. His counterpart in London, Maisky, did not fail to notice his isolation. 'It looks as though Cripps is turning into our enemy due to his political failures, failures resulting from the British Government's reluctance to move towards rapprochement with us,' he noted in March 1941, adding that an ambassador 'is akin to a travelling salesman. When he sells good commodities, he will be successful even if his personal qualities are quite ordinary. When he sells bad commodities, he is doomed to fail even if his personal qualities are excellent. Cripps has basically had nothing to sell for these past ten months.'[17]

Britain's apparent indifference to the fate of the Soviet Union confirmed Stalin's brooding but well-founded belief that Britain's strategic objective was to draw Moscow into war with Germany. As a result, any communication from London that could be interpreted as evidence of this duplicity carried no weight with the Kremlin. In significant part this explains the Soviet leader's response to what Churchill described as the 'cryptic' message he sent to Stalin on 3 April alerting him to Hitler's

---

* 'Edward Halifax's mind was always open to the last comer; but after hearing new ideas, he would commune with himself, with his Maker, and with Alec [Cadogan],' Rab Butler, *The Art of the Possible: The Memoirs of Lord Butler* (Penguin, 1973), p. 77.

intentions. It was the prime minister's first direct communication with Stalin since the telegram he had sent introducing the Cripps's mission the previous summer.

In the absence of any firm evidence, Churchill's uncanny intuition had led him many months earlier to believe that Germany might in due course invade the Soviet Union. In June 1940, soon after Dunkirk but before Hitler had abandoned his plans for the invasion of Britain, he wrote, 'If Hitler fails to beat us here he will probably recoil eastwards. Indeed, he may do this without trying invasion, to find employment for his Army [which had just crushed most of western Europe into submission].'[18] In October of that year, in the course of briefing his senior commanders, he said that Germany would inevitably turn on Russia during 1941 'for the sake of her oil'.[19] Apart from Cripps, he was virtually alone among his colleagues in showing such foresight. By the spring of 1941 – notwithstanding the prevailing view in the intelligence community and the Foreign Office – he became convinced that such an invasion was imminent.

The prime minister was an assiduous student of military intelligence, especially of the spasmodic data from Enigma signals decrypted by the code breakers at Bletchley Park. These revealed that as soon as the Yugoslav government had joined the Tripartite Pact, trainloads of troops (including three panzer divisions) had been ordered to redeploy from the Balkans to southern Poland, but that, following the anti-Nazi coup in Belgrade, they were turned back before they had even crossed the Polish border. This was enough for Churchill. 'Your Excellency will readily appreciate the significance of these facts,' he advised Stalin in his 3 April message.[20] The prime minister had presumed – correctly as it turned out – that the to-and-fro of the German troop movements was evidence that Hitler intended to launch an attack on the Soviet Union, but that he would do so only after Yugoslavia had been crushed. Unhappily, though, he refrained from elaborating this interpretation for Stalin's benefit, apparently believing both that his insight was of unique significance and that the arresting brevity of his message was bound to alert Stalin to a very real danger. In truth, it was so wrapped in ambiguity and contained so little fresh information as to be of very little intrinsic value. Nonetheless, and not surprisingly, Churchill was infuriated to be told that Cripps had failed to deliver the message on the grounds that the Kremlin had already been

inundated with similar reports and that he had himself just alerted Vyshinsky to the danger at greater length and more emphatically. For this reason,
as Cripps told Eden (who had returned to the Foreign Office in place of
Halifax three months earlier), it would be both 'ineffectual' and 'a serious
tactical mistake' to deliver the prime minister's message.[21]

Eden was easily persuaded. He had already cautioned Churchill
against saying anything to Stalin that might 'imply that we ourselves
required any assistance from the Soviet Government or that they would
be acting in any interests but their own'.[22] Now, he advised the prime
minister, 'I think there may be some force in Stafford Cripps's arguments
against the delivery of your message.'[23] Churchill was not mollified.
Cripps's refusal to pass on 'this extremely pregnant piece of information'[24] was unpardonable. In the event, the message eventually reached
the Kremlin almost three weeks after its dispatch, though there is no
evidence that Stalin bothered to read it; had he done so, it would assuredly
have served only to confirm his belief that the perfidious British hoped
to provoke the Soviet Union into war against Germany.

In the meantime, on 9 April, Churchill made a speech in Parliament
which had precisely that effect. In one of his familiar tours d'horizon,
he reported on the severe British setbacks in North Africa (where Rommel had launched a lightning counter-attack against the British 7th
Armoured Division and laid siege to Tobruk), the disasters in Greece
and Crete and the grave threat to the Atlantic lifeline posed by German
U-boats. It was what he went on to say, however, that had MPs on the
edge of their green benches:

> It is, of course, very hazardous, to try to forecast in what direction or
> directions Hitler will employ his military machine in the present year.
> He may at any time attempt the invasion of this island. This is an ordeal
> from which we shall not shrink ... But there are many signs which
> point to a Nazi attempt to secure the granary of the Ukraine and the
> oilfields of the Caucasus as a German means of gaining resources where-
> with to wear down the English-speaking world.[25]

This startling assertion − when in the secret circles of the British
intelligence community it was still firmly believed that the Moscow–
Berlin Axis was indissoluble − garnered widespread coverage in the
press. The impact on the Russians was predictable. As Maisky put it, the

Kremlin concluded that the British were seeking 'to frighten us with Germany [but] the prime minister's remarks . . . produce an effect in Moscow quite opposed to the one he intends'.[26] Discovering that Churchill's warning was little more than surmise merely reinforced his view that 'the campaign of the British Government and the English Press was unsubstantiated . . . and evidence that "*Der Wunsch ist der Vater des Gedankens*" – the wish is father to the thought'.[27]

At this point, Cripps's intense frustration led him greatly to compound the damage. Anguished by the fact, as he later put it, that 'not only Stalin but even Molotov' avoided him 'like grim death', and that Stalin 'did not *want* to have anything to do with Churchill, so alarmed was he that the Germans [might] find out', he made the impetuous and arrogant decision to break the conventional rules of diplomatic engagement.[28] In a long and well-argued message to Molotov (which he sent via Vyshinsky) he warned that a German invasion was now inevitable. In this case, he added, Britain would assuredly wish to collaborate with the Soviet Union against the Nazis. He followed up with a number of proposals for Anglo-Soviet co-operation (which he had failed to clear with London), which were so vague as to be without useful content. Even worse, he went on to imply that, in the absence of an agreement with the Soviet Union, Britain might in due course feel bound to make peace with Germany. It was, he wrote, 'not outside the bounds of possibility if the war were protracted for a long period that there might be a temptation for Great Britain (and especially for certain circles in Great Britain) to come to some arrangement to end the war'.[29] As a servant of the Crown this was an egregious diplomatic offence. It was also counterproductive: nothing could have been better calculated to deepen the Kremlin's paranoia about Britain's real intentions. Golikov, who was at the centre of the GRU web in Moscow collating such evidence and who knew that his career, if not his life, depended on telling Stalin what he wanted to hear, was adept at nurturing his leader's belief that Britain's principal objective was to provoke a war between Germany and the Soviet Union. As he put it in one of his regular briefings to the Kremlin, any report emanating from British sources was 'undoubtedly' intended 'to seek the worsening of relations between the USSR and Germany'.[30]

Stalin was by now more determined than ever to regard the Molotov–Ribbentrop Pact as inviolable and even more likely to repudiate any intelligence from any source – like those that had started to reach him over three months earlier from the likes of Ariets in Berlin – which suggested that he might be deluding himself. Churchill's 'cryptic' warning about Barbarossa was as nothing compared with far less ambiguous evidence from the growing cascade of intelligence now pouring into the Kremlin, all warning of an imminent Nazi invasion. These came from agents in Berlin, from Hitler's satellite capitals in eastern Europe and occupied western Europe as well as Soviet agents in Britain. But Stalin had so inured himself against the very thought that Hitler might use force to bend Moscow to his will as to dismiss all evidence to the contrary.

By April these communications were being supplemented by even more persuasive reports from both within and without the borders of the Soviet Union. On 10 April the NKGB – the military intelligence arm of the Soviet secret service – reported on a build-up of German forces on the Soviet border: 'Information from agent sources and statements by border crossers have established that the concentration of units of the German army on the border of the Soviet Union is continuing. At the same time there is accelerated construction of defensive positions, airfields, strategic branch lines, highways and dirt roads'.[31] A detailed report, using even stronger terms, arrived from Ukraine, where the First Secretary of the Communist Party, Nikita Khrushchev, was warned by the regional head of the NKGB, 'Agent reporting and debriefing of border crossers establishes that the Germans are intensively preparing for war with the USSR, for which purposes they are concentrating troops on our borders, building roads and fortifications, and bringing munitions.'[32]

Stalin chose to look in the opposite direction, comforting himself with the fact that on 13 April (the same day that Belgrade fell to the Nazis) he had just signed a non-aggression pact with the regime in Tokyo. He was so elated by the thought that, despite Japan's membership of the Tripartite Pact, he would not now have to contemplate a war on two fronts that he went in person to say farewell to the Japanese foreign minister, Yōsuke Matsuoka, who had come to Moscow to sign the agreement on Tokyo's behalf. Bystanders at Moscow's railway station were astonished to see the two men whose countries had so recently been at war walking arm-in-arm down the platform, deep in conversation. Embracing Matsuoka, Stalin was overheard to say 'we are Asiatics, too, and we've got to stick together'. So carried away was he by the moment that he strode about with great bonhomie, shaking hands with railway workers, government officials and a gaggle of invited diplomats. Noticing Colonel Krebs, the German military attaché, he walked over and threw his arms round him, saying, 'We are going to remain friends, won't we?'[33]

This did not mean that the Soviet leader had opted in favour of pacifism. On 4 May the Politburo approved a resolution naming Stalin as chairman of the Council of People's Commissars to ensure that local officials should have 'every conceivable reinforcement in order to support their task of defending the country'. The next day, with his supreme authority thus confirmed, he addressed the annual graduation ceremony for military cadets at the Kremlin. In a closed session, he spoke for some forty minutes without a script. Accounts of what he said differ, but that it was of significant moment was not in doubt. He spoke of a Red Army that was far better trained, armed and equipped, more mobile and more powerful than it had been three years earlier and more than able to defend itself against attack. As the young officers would soon discover, his bullish review bore little relation to reality. Whether his purpose was simply to inspire the graduates or give Hitler pause for thought, his message had little impact on either the Commissar for Defence, Timoshenko, or the Head of the General Staff, Zhukov, both of whom were well aware that the Red Army was still ill prepared to face a full-scale German onslaught.

On the same day, Richard Sorge, a Soviet spy based in Tokyo (where his cover was as a correspondent for the German newspaper *Frankfurter Zeitung*), sent a microfilm transcript of a phone call between Ribbentrop and the German ambassador to Japan. In the course of their conversation the German foreign minister was recorded as saying 'Germany will begin a war against the USSR in the middle of June 1941.' Ten days later, on 15 May, Sorge was more precise, reporting that the date had been fixed for 20–22 June. Stalin's ostrich-like response was to denounce Sorge – who had, it was true, acquired a reputation for avarice and debauchery – as 'a little shit who's set up factories and brothels in Japan'.[34] Once again, he chose to look the other way. Knowing that he was risking Stalin's wrath, Beria decided to forward an alarming intelligence report that had been compiled for the Central Committee, the Council of People's Commissars and the Defence Commissariat. This document detailed a massive build-up – three motorized divisions, six infantry divisions, nine or ten artillery regiments and seven tank battalions – close to the Soviet Union's northern frontier in East Prussia. Stalin ignored it.

By now the Politburo was aware that the NKGB believed that no fewer than 130 German divisions were massing along the long front from the Baltic to the Balkans. With almost daily reports of the German build-up both from the border itself and from within Nazi-occupied Poland, Hungary, Romania and Bulgaria, Timoshenko and Zhukov made a concerted attempt to persuade Stalin that more units should be sent to the front. Still obsessed by the fear that such a response would provide Hitler with a casus belli, Stalin turned them down. Instead, he chose to interpret the German military build-up as sabre-rattling designed to intimidate him into granting further economic and political concessions than those agreed the previous January.

The Soviet leader's refusal to face reality was hardened by his paranoid misinterpretation of one of the most bizarre incidents of the Second World War. On 10 May Hitler's deputy, Rudolf Hess, piloted himself to Scotland and parachuted to the ground on a crazed mission to broker a peace deal with Britain. Far from being Hitler's envoy, he was acting in defiance of his Führer, who was aghast at his mission. 'The Führer is absolutely shattered,' Goebbels noted. 'He is very bitter. He never expected anything like this. One can be prepared for anything except the aberrations of a lunatic.'[35] London was bewildered and responded at once by imposing a news black-out on the media. Churchill was at Ditchley Park in Oxfordshire, when he was told about Hess's arrival.* His first instinct was to announce (in the words of his draft text) that Hess had flown to Britain 'in the name of humanity', but Cadogan and Eden protested that this would make it 'look like a peace offer' from Hitler. They argued, conversely, that 'we may want to run the line that he had quarrelled with Hitler'.[36]

According to Cadogan, this suggestion provoked Churchill to fly into 'a raging temper' from which he did not recover until the next morning, when he conceded that they were probably right after all.[37] However, it was only after the rest of the War Cabinet made it clear they too opposed what the ever-scathing Cadogan called Churchill's

---

* Ditchley Park was deemed to be safer from the Luftwaffe than Chequers, which was set on high ground in Buckinghamshire, but where he nonetheless spent far more time during the war, or than his own home at Chartwell in Kent.

'stupid [draft] statement' that, four days later, he finally agreed to drop it.[38] Instead, as Cadogan had advised, the government gave informal briefings to the effect that Hess had indeed fallen out with Hitler over the Soviet Union. Any hope that London might have had that this would soften Stalin's attitude towards Britain was doomed. Nothing would persuade him that the Hess mission was anything less than incontrovertible evidence that Berlin and London were hatching an anti-Russian plot to destroy Soviet communism.*

Stalin's belief that Hitler's objective was to blackmail rather than bludgeon the Russians into compliance was not confined to his inner circle in the Kremlin. In London, the Joint Intelligence Committee (JIC) – overriding Enigma evidence to the contrary – persistently dismissed rumours of an imminent Nazi assault on the Soviet Union. Instead, the security chiefs stressed the 'overwhelming' advantages to Germany 'of concluding an agreement with the USSR' while judging that the Kremlin would 'endeavour by every means in her power to avoid a clash by yielding to German demands'.[39] Still convinced that Operation Sealion – the invasion of Britain – remained Hitler's prime objective, and that he would not contemplate launching a war on two fronts, the JIC found a ready audience in the Foreign Office. Sharing the widespread assumption – for which there was no evidence – that Berlin and Moscow were engaged in intensive political and economic negotiations, Whitehall managed to convince itself that a German invasion of the Soviet Union was virtually inconceivable.

In a reference to these phantom negotiations, Cadogan noted on 9 May, 'I believe that Russia will give way and sign on the dotted line,' adding, 'I wish she wouldn't, as I should love to see Germany expending her strength there. But they are not such fools . . .'[40] In the absence of unequivocal evidence to the contrary, the prevailing view both at the Foreign Office and the War Office continued to be driven by the phantasmagorical belief that the build-up of German forces along the Soviet border was designed to intimidate Moscow into making concessions that, as it happened – following their stand-off over the Balkans – Berlin had not in fact demanded.

* That suspicion remains to the present. Although there has been no evidence of any collaboration between the British intelligence services and Berlin, some of the relevant British documents are still withheld and are not due to be released – under the hundred-year rule – until 2041.

It was not until the middle of June, only days before the date set for the launch of Operation Barbarossa, that the JIC finally accepted that an invasion was imminent. Blindsided by a 'well-nigh complete' absence of information about the Soviet Union,[41] but well served by Enigma code breakers at Bletchley Park, the entire Whitehall machine leapt to another conclusion. As the official historian of British Intelligence during the Second World War, Professor F. H. Hinsley (who had himself been at the apex of the Ultra operation at Bletchley Park), has magisterially observed, 'doubt about Russia's readiness to withstand German pressure was replaced by certainty that she could not long survive a German attack'.[42] The Cabinet was therefore formally advised by every relevant arm of the Civil Service that it would take the Germans between three and eight weeks to reach Moscow. Only the prime minister declined to share the almost universal pessimism that now prevailed in London.

On 14 June, in an increasingly desperate effort to persuade himself as well as the rest of the world that all was well between Moscow and Berlin, Stalin ordered TASS to issue a communiqué rebutting 'false and provocative' rumours which were being 'widely circulated in the English press as well as in the foreign press in general' to the effect that 'Germany has begun to concentrate its troops on the borders of the Soviet Union with the objective of an attack on her' and that 'the Soviet Union in its turn has begun to prepare intensively for war with Germany and is concentrating troops on the latter's frontier'. It was, the communiqué stressed, 'ridiculous' to present the Red Army's forthcoming manoeuvres (Stalin had just authorized a cautious redeployment of reservists to positions nearer the western border) as being 'hostile to Germany'. Both Germany and the Soviet Union were 'unswervingly observing the provisions of the Soviet–German non-aggression pact'.[43]

In Berlin, the Nazi leadership greeted the release of the TASS communiqué with delight. 'A torrent of rumours is pouring out of London to the world. All to do with Russia. And, in fact, fairly accurate. But on the whole, the world continues to believe in bluff or blackmail. We do not react at all . . . In any event, Moscow seems to be doing nothing to counter any aggression. Marvellous!' Goebbels noted.[44] It was clear from the TASS communiqué that the Kremlin had chosen to swallow Berlin's explanation for the build-up of troops in Poland as forming part of the Wehrmacht's preparation for Operation Sealion, which – like the British – the Russians presumed to be Hitler's primary military objective: they had no inkling that the plans for the invasion of Britain had been discarded nine months earlier or that the Soviet Union had been in Hitler's sights for almost as long.

On the same day, 14 June, the Führer summoned his senior commanders to the Chancellery. In the course of an hour-long address, he told them, 'we will have the worst of the fighting behind us after about six weeks', and he reiterated that 'every soldier must know what it is we are fighting for. It is not the territory we want, but rather that Bolshevism is destroyed.'[45] It was a familiar refrain: the troops were engaged in a 'war of extermination' in which the traditional rules of engagement would have no meaning. As he said to Goebbels later that day, 'Bolshevism will collapse like a house of cards. We face victories unequalled in human history . . . Right or wrong, we must win. It is the only way. And victory is right, moral and necessary. And once we have won, who is going to question our methods?'[46] In the meantime Goebbels' task was 'to continue to invent rumours: peace with Moscow, Stalin coming to Berlin, an invasion of England is imminent, so as to conceal the real situation. I hope we can keep it up for a while yet.'[47]

That Berlin was able to maintain one or other of these fictions with less than a week to go before the start of the invasion was a triumph of propaganda and planning. But it would not have been successful without Stalin's purblind refusal, even at this late stage, to accept the truth. He had invested every ounce of his diplomatic and political energy into averting or at least postponing a conflict with Germany until the Red Army was in a much stronger position to drive the invaders from Soviet territory: until the borders were adequately fortified with carefully positioned and well-concealed artillery units; until heavy concrete tank traps had been embedded across the likeliest lines of attack as well as wide and deep ditches from which no panzer could escape; until minefields had been laid; until the armour had been overhauled and repaired; until the troops had been adequately trained and armed; and until their commanders had agreed upon not only the most likely invasion routes but also how best to deploy their divisions accordingly. But as Stalin had also forbidden his generals to take any steps that might be interpreted as provocative, the Soviet Union's defences were in disrepair, and its armies were almost totally unready for what was about to happen. Like Chamberlain before him, Stalin opted to appease the Nazi monster; unlike Chamberlain, however, he could not bear to contemplate the thought that his strategy had disintegrated. Under a burden of stress that even his thuggishly resilient character could barely sustain, he chose instead to close his mind to reason and to retreat into foul-mouthed tirades against those who persecuted him with the facts.

On 13 June Richard Sorge – who had hitherto proved uncannily reliable – warned from Tokyo (possibly in response to Golikov at the GRU), 'I repeat: nine armies with a strength of 150 divisions will begin an offensive at dawn on 22 June 1941.'[48] Stalin yet again dismissed the warning, as he had done a month earlier when the same 'little shit' had sounded an identical alarm. Three days later, on 16 June, a source in the German Air Ministry, Starshina ('Sergeant Major' in Russian), aka Major Harro Schulze-Boysen, who had been recruited by the NKVD in 1940, confirmed Sorge's warning from another perspective. Starshina frequently provided accurate information about Luftwaffe reconnaissance flights along the border. Now, only six days before the planned invasion, he reported, 'all preparations by Germany for an armed attack on the Soviet Union have been completed, and the blow can be expected at any time'.[49] When this message landed on Stalin's desk, he scrawled a furious note on it: 'Tell the source in the staff of the German Air Force to fuck his mother! This is no source but a disinformer.'[50]

The Red Army's two most senior commanders, Timoshenko and Zhukov, were close to despair. Though not privy to the bulk of the foreign intelligence, they already had more than enough evidence from their own sources to confirm Starshina's warning. On 13 June, not for the first time, they had tried without success to alert Stalin to the German manoeuvres on the other side of the border. The next day, though, he peremptorily dismissed their request to mobilize their forces. 'That means war. Do you understand that or not?' he barked at them. When they tried to reason with him by explaining that the Germans were clearly on a war footing, he accused them of being duped by the intelligence, adding dismissively, 'You can't believe everything in intelligence circles.'[51] A couple of days later, he again refused their request to move troops to stronger defensive positions, saying, 'We have a non-aggression pact with Germany. Germany is up to her ears with the war in the west and I am certain that Hitler will not risk creating a second front by attacking the Soviet Union. Hitler is not such an idiot and understands that the Soviet Union is not Poland, not France, and not even England.'[52]

There was nearly a showdown at a meeting with the Politburo on 18 June. Timoshenko and Zhukov arrived in the Kremlin laden with detailed maps of the military dispositions on the front line as they sought to make the case for putting the army on full alert. The more compellingly they made the case, the more obdurate and intemperate Stalin became. Accusing them of warmongering, he eventually lost patience altogether, rose to his feet, walked over to where Zhukov was standing among the assembled satraps and started to abuse him: 'Have you come here to scare us with war, or do you want a war because you're not sufficiently decorated or your rank isn't high enough?' he sneered. The chief of staff abruptly resumed his seat.

Timoshenko persisted, insisting that there would be chaos at the front if the Wehrmacht were to attack. His temerity roused Stalin to a paroxysm of malevolence. Gesturing towards the defence commissar, he railed, 'It's all Timoshenko's work . . . He ought to have been shot, but I've known him as a good soldier since the Civil War.' When Timoshenko persisted, pointing out that Stalin had himself referred to the possibility of war with Germany at the military graduation ceremony on 5 May, Stalin looked around the room and, according to the commander-in-chief's own account, said, 'Timoshenko's a fine man but apparently a small brain,' adding, as he raised his thumb to illustrate this, that he had spoken in those terms on that occasion only to 'raise their alertness, while you have to realize that Germany will never fight Russia on her own'. At this he evidently stalked out of the chamber. A moment later, he reappeared, putting his head round the door, shouting, 'If you're going to provoke the Germans on the frontier by moving troops there without our permission, then heads will roll, mark my words.'[53] He then slammed the door, leaving his audience flummoxed and intimidated. As all of them knew, a threat from Stalin was rarely a casual aside.

Zhukov later defended his failure to defy the dictator by issuing the order 'deploy'. While admitting that he had been frightened to do so in case Stalin had handed him over to Beria for punishment, he also insisted that it was not fear alone that held him back: 'I didn't regard myself as cleverer or more far-sighted than Stalin . . . I sensed the danger of a

German attack, the feeling was gnawing at my vitals. But my faith in Stalin, and my belief that in the end everything would come out in the way he suggested, was stronger.'[54] It was a fatal error of judgement.

On 21 June, a Russian spy, Leopold Trepper, codenamed Otto, who had infiltrated the German command system in Nazi-occupied Paris, reported, 'Wehrmacht command has completed the transfer of its troops to the Soviet frontier and tomorrow, 22 June, will suddenly attack the Soviet Union.' When he read this, Stalin wrote in the margin, 'This is an English provocation. Find out who the author of this provocation is and punish him.'[55]

A few hours later, the first shots were fired in what was to become the most devastating conflict in recorded history.

PART TWO

Invasion

8.   The Blitzkrieg

On the midsummer evening of 21 June 1941, the Belorussian city of Brest-Litovsk appeared to be at ease with itself. All military exercises had been cancelled for the weekend. Off-duty soldiers strolled with girlfriends and mingled with families enjoying the late-evening warmth. Bands played in the well-tended parks, crowded with young people who laughed and danced until darkness fell. 'It was lovely and pleasant,' one of these revellers, Georgy Karbuk, noted, although he had also detected 'a certain tension within the town'. As he and his friends left the park, his sense of foreboding was heightened when the electric lights suddenly went out. 'This had never happened before. We continued on further to Pushkin Street, about half a kilometre, and the lights went out there too.'[1] Karbuk went home to bed, little knowing that the phone lines had also been cut: the work of German saboteurs preparing the ground for the cataclysm that was about to befall the city.

From his forward observation post on the other side of the River Bug, General Heinz Guderian, the leader of Panzer Group 2, as the 19th Army Corps had been renamed, could see that the city's defenders who were still on duty had no idea of the gathering storm. 'We had observation of the courtyard of Brest-Litovsk citadel and we could see them drilling by platoons to the music of military bands. The strong points along their bank of the Bug were unoccupied.'[2] The peace was disturbed only by a German goods train which rattled across the bridge, steaming away from the Russian side on its way to Warsaw and the Third Reich. Even the pre-battle religious service for the men of the 45th Infantry Division waiting at the river's edge for the order to cross into the Soviet Union was conducted so quietly as barely to ruffle the twilight calm.

Brest-Litovsk lay on the Northern Bug, which flows through the country in a north-westerly direction. Less than 100 kilometres from the Polish border with Belorussia and Ukraine, it was not only a major river crossing point but also an important strategic stronghold. It was for this reason that Guderian had been so aggrieved when forced to hand over the fortress to the Russians after Panzer Group 2 had seized it from the Poles two years earlier. Now, as the panzers prepared to remedy that frustration, a war correspondent, Gerd Habedanck, embedded with the 45th Infantry Division as they edged their way to the river bank, noted, 'Silently, absolutely silently we crept up to the edge of the Bug. Sand had been strewn across the roads so that our hobnailed boots made no sound.'[3]

In Berlin, the German propaganda minister, Joseph Goebbels, could barely contain his elation as the clock ran down to zero hour. Rumours of the invasion were still just that: the Red Army was not yet on a war footing. He could congratulate himself that in large measure it was due to his brilliance as a custodian of half-truths and lies that the German people and foreign states might speculate but none of them could be certain. Surprise had been guaranteed. 'The business of Russia is becoming more dramatic by the hour,' he noted; 'our enemies are falling apart . . . The operation is being ushered in with magnificent skill. We shall have a good start.'[4] When he went to see Hitler later that evening, he was pleased to discover that the Führer was keen to listen to a selection of 'fanfares' that he had chosen for him. After sifting through them all, Hitler chose a version of the 'Horst Wessel Song', the Nazi Party's triumphalist anthem. As his theme for Barbarossa he chose a passage from Franz Liszt's *Les Préludes*.

On the face of it, Hitler had just cause for optimism. Under his orders the Wehrmacht had mobilized the greatest invasion force in history. By the early hours of Sunday, 22 June 1941, some 3.3 million soldiers equipped with 3,350 tanks, 7,184 pieces of artillery, 600,000 trucks and 600,000 horses, all supported by 2,500 warplanes, were lined up along a 1,800-kilometre front that stretched from the Baltic to the Balkans. No fewer than 148 troop divisions marshalled into three army groups: North, Centre and South, commanded respectively by Field Marshals von Leeb, von Bock and von Rundstedt, just as the Soviet agent Ariets had predicted four months earlier. All three commanders were in their sixties, scions of military families reared in the Prussian tradition, graduates of leading military academies, veterans of the First World War, where they served with distinction, senior generals for the invasion of Czechoslovakia and Poland in 1939 and the Low Countries and France in 1940. Whatever their initial qualms may have been, they were at one in their readiness to put themselves fully at the service of Hitler's vision, strategy and ideological convictions.

Under their leadership, a battle-hardened phalanx of field commanders led troops that were well drilled and highly motivated. They too had proved themselves in occupied Europe; their armoury – panzer tanks, artillery and aircraft – were battle-tested; they were poised for action; they had the overwhelming advantage of surprise; and they believed themselves to be invincible. They had also been indoctrinated by Nazi propaganda. With few exceptions they revered their Führer. His prejudices had become their own. Hitler's struggle for 'the liquidation of Jewish Bolshevism' was not only endorsed by the SS, the SD and the Wehrmacht High Command but force-fed to the troops who, on the eve of Barbarossa, were issued with the Wehrmacht's 14 May guidelines reminding them that Bolshevism was 'the mortal enemy of the National Socialist German people' and specifying the 'ruthless' measures that they would have to take to assure its destruction.

In the days leading up to the invasion, the crudity of this propaganda intensified: 'Anyone who has ever looked into the face of a Red commissar knows what Bolsheviks are,' one Wehrmacht publication advised. 'There is no need here for theoretical reflections. It would be an insult to animals if one were to call the features of these, largely Jewish, tormentors of people, bestial . . . In the shape of these commissars we witness the revolt of the subhuman against noble blood.'[5]

In the lead-up to Operation Barbarossa, as their units were moved piece by piece towards the Soviet border, very few soldiers paused to contemplate the full import of their Führer's search for Lebensraum or the 'annihilation of Judaeo-Bolshevism'. Nor did many of them know where they were heading or the immensity of the undertaking before them.

Wilhelm Prüller, who had been conscripted in Austria to serve as a dispatch rider in a tank battalion, discovered that his unit was on the move from its base in central Poland only on the day he returned from leave. 'I'm not yet sure what's happening,' he wrote in his diary, 'but we are to go to the East and quite certainly Russia later on. But as what? I cannot believe that the Führer would sign a non-aggression pact, only to break it two years later.' Assuming that their advance was therefore bound to be a defensive move against a Soviet incursion, he wondered if Stalin might have 'made a deal with England', in which case, 'of course it's clear that we've got to crack down'.[6]

Karl Fuchs, a tank sergeant in Army Group Centre's Panzer Group 3, was similarly in the dark. Fuchs was an aspiring teacher who was given to writing in semi-mystical terms. In a letter home to his pregnant wife as his division began its move to the border, he wrote:

> My dearest sweetheart . . . Important, beautiful and holy things don't simply happen, you have to fight for them, fight for them with all your might . . . the struggle for existence, whether we are talking about a man or a woman, creates proud, free, honest and upright people. All others will remain repulsive creeps, inferior individuals.[7]

Fuchs's love for his wife was matched by his devotion to his Führer. He wrote in another letter,

> My dearest darling . . . I can understand your pain and sorrow because you have to be so alone now. Yet, I can't provide any comfort or any consolation; indeed, I must ask you to be strong and firm. Look, my dear, your husband stands in the midst of a proud and difficult time. He is a soldier – not a civilian – as a soldier he has duties to his Fatherland. These duties are important and sacred . . . we are engaged in a struggle that will assure us the well-being of our growing children and our nation.[8]

Late on the evening of the 21st, Hitler composed a long and rambling letter to Mussolini, which the Italian dictator received the following morning. Until that moment, the Führer's Axis partner had been given no inkling of what was afoot. Perhaps because he was aware that Mussolini's principal aim was to secure a large slice of Britain's African empire once London had been forced to sue for peace, Hitler refrained from referring to his deepest motives for Barbarossa. He did not mention his craving for the Soviet Union's bountiful supply of raw materials and its huge supplies of oil in the Caucasus; his hunger for the rich food-producing soils of western Russia and Ukraine; and, overarching all those territorial ambitions, his compulsive urge to create an Aryan empire for the Third Reich, cleansed of all Bolsheviks, in which the Slavs would either perish or become a servant class and from which the Jewish 'bacillus' would be eliminated by whatever means might be required.

Instead, he elaborated a military strategy designed to secure his fellow dictator's endorsement. Although Mussolini had joined the Axis in 1937, it was not until 22 May 1940 that he signed the 'Pact of Steel' (the military alliance with Germany). By this time, with France about to fall, he was confident that Britain would soon follow suit, and he hoped to share in the carve-up of the world's largest empire that would assuredly follow. His opportunism was overt: 'I only need a few thousand dead so that I can sit at the peace conference as a man who has fought,' he confided to his chief of staff, General Pietro Badoglio.[9] Hitler's rationale for invading the Soviet Union rather than Britain was a fragile structure of convoluted and contradictory suppositions, yet it provided his clearest exposition of the strategic case for a monumentally risky venture.

'England [sic] has lost this war,' Hitler wrote, but added that he could defeat Britain only by eliminating the Soviet Union. The danger, he explained, was that London might forge an alliance with Moscow. Both adversaries would then be reinforced by abundant supplies of materiel from the United States. In these circumstances, Britain might well survive. It followed that since he had 'no chance of eliminating America', he had to 'exclude Russia . . . [which] . . . does lie in our power'. With Russia out of the equation, he explained, Britain would soon be finished: 'we can, with our rear secured, apply ourselves with increased strength to the dispatching of our enemy [Britain]'.[10]

At least on paper, Hitler's armies faced a formidable foe on the other side of the line: more than 4 million men – 170 Red Army divisions – deployed in three overlapping layers to a depth of 400 kilometres from the border. But Stalin's fear of causing a 'provocation' on the border and the resulting General Staff Directive of 15–18 June 'forbidding any concentration of troops in the frontier areas'[11] meant that only fifty-six of these divisions were stationed along the front line. And, although the Russians had a numerical superiority in tank numbers of 7:1 and of planes up to 5:1,[12] these statistics meant little when measured against the war-fighting potential of the two sides on the eve of battle.

Although the Soviet leadership did not yet know for sure that Hitler was at the point of unleashing Barbarossa, the mood at the Red Army Headquarters was far from sanguine. Reports from the front line were pregnant with alarm: the Germans were removing wire entanglements from their side of the border; German reconnaissance aircraft were openly violating Soviet airspace; German tanks could be distinctly heard rumbling along the front.

When this was transmitted to the Kremlin, Stalin was nonplussed, irresolutely veering from the insistence at one moment that war could still be avoided to the recognition that it was all but inevitable at the next. Thus, even as he demanded that the Paris-based spy Otto be punished for reporting that the invasion was imminent, he simultaneously contacted the commander of the Moscow Military District, General Ivan Tyulenev, to ask, 'How do things stand with the anti-aircraft defence measures?' When Tyulenev told him that they were not yet ready for action, he ordered, 'You should bring the troops of Moscow's anti-aircraft defence to 75 per cent of combat readiness.'[13] Similarly he instructed the Moscow party leaders to order all party secretaries to stay at their posts, advising cryptically, 'The Germans might attack.' Once again, though, when he was told soon afterwards that a German NCO had crossed the border in the Kiev Special Military District to warn that the Germans would invade in the early hours of the following morning, he dismissed the deserter as an agent provocateur.

That evening, Stalin summoned a meeting of the Politburo to discuss the crisis. Both the defence commissar, Timoshenko, and the chief of staff, Zhukov, were in attendance. After some desultory debate, Stalin repeated his wishful thought that the deserter who had come across the line at Kiev was trying to provoke a conflict. For once, his commanders contradicted him openly, saying they thought he was telling the truth. Stalin asked what could be done. There was silence until Timoshenko spoke up, urging that the armed forces on the front line should be put on full alert. Stalin objected, insisting that it was too soon for such a provocative order.

On this occasion, Zhukov was not to be fobbed off. He had brought with him a draft order which advised that a surprise attack by the Germans was 'possible' and instructed that the border forces be put on full alert. Again Stalin hesitated. This time, though, he gave his reluctant approval to a watered-down directive ordering that all units be brought to a state of combat readiness and that all aircraft should be dispersed and camouflaged. But, 'in order to avoid complications', the directive added that in no circumstances should Red Army soldiers 'be incited by any provocation'.[14]

There were other intimations of the approaching conflagration. Staff at the German Embassy along with their wives and children were reported to have packed their bags to leave the city. This intelligence prompted Molotov to summon the German ambassador, Friedrich-Werner Graf von der Schulenburg, to his office to demand an explanation. Schulenburg stonewalled, reminding the foreign minister that both he and his wife were still in the capital. Molotov did not press the point further.

At the Army Club in Minsk, the Belorussian capital, some 770 kilometres south-west of Moscow and 340 kilometres from Brest-Litovsk, the Commander-in-Chief of the Soviet Western Front, Colonel General Dmitry Pavlov, was enjoying a relaxed evening with his staff. They had gathered to watch a popular comedy by the famous Soviet playwright Oleksandr Korniychuk. In the middle of the performance they were rudely interrupted by the head of the intelligence department for the Western Military District, Vasily Blokhin, who entered their box and whispered in Pavlov's ear. He had just been informed that Red Army reconnaissance had reported seeing German troops readying for action and that they had even 'shelled some of our positions'. 'It can't be true,' Pavlov muttered before turning to his deputy, General Ivan Boldin, to pass on the message, adding, 'Seems nonsense to me' – at which he tapped his number two on the hand as though to indicate that they should continue to watch the play.[15]

Before the curtain came down, another German soldier, Alfred Liskow, swam across the Bug to the Soviet lines to warn his captors that an artillery barrage was to open up within a few hours, and that at first light, 'rafts, boats, and pontoons' would be thrown across the river as a bridge for the invading troops to cross over into Soviet-occupied Poland.[16] After a lengthy interrogation by a Russian border patrol, it emerged that the deserter was a Bavarian factory worker who had braved the crossing to alert 'his proletarian brothers' to the danger.[17] This counted for nothing. His warning was reported to the Kremlin, allegedly prompting Stalin to order that the hapless informant be shot for 'disinformation'.* By that time, however, Guderian's assault troops had advanced to the very edge of the Bug and were waiting for the final order to cross.[18]

The Politburo meeting finally broke up as Timoshenko and Zhukov headed back to the Defence Commissariat to oversee the transmission

---

* Stalin was so promiscuous with such orders that it is not clear whether he had thus targeted Liskow or another 'provocateur'. As it happened, events now unfolded at such a speed that it was impossible to carry out the order before Liskow's veracity was proved beyond doubt. He was put in prison and survived at least for some months. His eventual fate is unknown.

to all military districts of the directive they had cobbled together on Stalin's behalf and which stressed that 'the task of our forces is to refrain from any kind of provocative action'.[19] The directive was not ready for dispatch until after midnight. Most military headquarters never received the warning and, for those that did, it was far too late to be of any value.

At 11 p.m. Stalin and his confidants repaired to the Soviet leader's dining room, where, according to one of them, Anastas Mikoyan, he tried to convince the gathering that Germany did not intend to start a war: 'I think Hitler's trying to provoke us. He surely hasn't decided to make war?'[20] None of the gathering dared challenge this self-delusion. Instead, just after midnight, they clambered into their armoured Zil limousines and left in a motorcade for Stalin's dacha at Kuntsevo. Once there – according to a competing range of reports from the participants – they either watched a film or merely sat drinking and dining until, in the early hours of the next morning, 22 June, they went home or back to their desks. Stalin went to bed.

In Minsk, when the play came to an end, Pavlov returned to his office to be briefed on the situation at the front. He was unable to sleep. At around one o'clock in the morning he received a call from Moscow. It was Timoshenko, asking for an update. Pavlov passed on what he had been told, which was very little: a build-up of German motorcycle units and special forces had been seen on the German side of the river but there was no more than that to report. Pavlov must have sounded anxious because the defence commissar sought to reassure him: 'Just try to worry less and don't panic.' It cannot have given Pavlov much comfort, however, to hear him add, 'Get the staff together anyway this morning, because something unpleasant may happen, perhaps, but don't rise to any provocation. If there is a specific provocation, ring me.'[21]

With the invasion now only hours away, the Red Army commanders in the military districts nearest the border were not only unaware of what was about to happen but also in no condition to respond effectively when it did. They had yet to mobilize their troops. Some were on weekend leave, others were participating in exercises away from the front. Those who were in place lacked supplies and were often hamstrung by the absence of transport or, if they had the vehicles, an acute shortage of fuel. Tank crews were disabled by inadequate training and qualification; infantrymen, for the most part, had their rifles but had yet to be issued with ammunition. The defences from which these troops were supposed to arrest an invading army had still not been completed. A scatter of pill boxes and gun emplacements, some of them still unmanned, was all that stood between them and the blitzkrieg that was about to engulf them.

A little before 2 a.m. on 22 June, yet another German deserter crossed the line. He reported that the invasion would begin within two hours. The news never reached Moscow. German sappers had already cut the telephone wires. Combined with an acute shortage of radio equipment and trained operators, this led to a mass breakdown of communications. Front-line officers lost contact with their men and their headquarters at the very moment that the invading armies were forming up in their starting positions to attack. As they waited for the order, the three German army commands transmitted their unique call signs to signal their 'full and final readiness' for action.[22]

It was not until 3 a.m., following an exceptionally imprecise instruction from Timoshenko, that Pavlov sent out the code word 'GROZA' – storm – authorizing front-line commanders to assume 'full combat readiness'. He little knew that he had issued this order too late for it to reach enough formations in time to have much effect.[23] He did, though, make contact with Brest-Litovsk to be told that saboteurs had cut the phone lines and severed the water and electricity supply to the 9,000 men stationed inside the citadel. Half an hour later, Pavlov was on the line to Brest-Litovsk again to inform the garrison that 'a provocative raid by Fascist bands onto Soviet territory' might soon occur. Yet again, though, he instructed his commanders not to respond to the 'provocation' and that their men should not cross the border in hot pursuit.[24] A similar combination of caution and chaos prevailed along the entire front.

Operation Barbarossa began with an artillery barrage that shattered the silence of the dawn sky in a blaze of exploding shells. As the first wave of the 3.3 million-strong invasion force began to swarm in highly organized and tightly disciplined units across the border, a mighty aerial armada screamed down out of the clouds to rain high explosives on key targets, demolishing the border defences and destroying bridges, railheads, command posts and power stations. In the days leading up to the invasion, Luftwaffe spotter planes had not only mapped every square kilometre of the terrain along the 3,000-kilometre border – the tracks, the roads, the bridges – but had pinpointed the location of every airfield. With meticulous care, they had identified the locations of the Soviet Union's warplanes, stacked in neat rows out in the open and easily visible from the air, as though offered up for target practice for the Stuka dive-bombers. As the Luftwaffe struck, bemused Red Army commanders were left muttering to one another, *Eto nachalo* – 'this is the beginning'.[25]

In Berlin, Goebbels was awake. 'Now the guns will be thundering. May God bless our weapons. Outside on the Wilhelmplatz, it is quiet and deserted. Berlin and the entire Reich are asleep . . . I pace up and down in my room. One can hear the breath of history. A glorious and wonderful hour has struck, when a new empire is born.'[26] Thus inspired, he went into the Propaganda Ministry studio, where he was to read out a proclamation to the German people in Hitler's name, which the Führer had drafted a few hours earlier. In the pseudo-spiritual terms favoured by the Nazis, he was to declare that 'the reawakening of our people from despair, misery and an abusive disregard is the sign of a pure inner rebirth'.[27]

For the benefit of a nation which might otherwise have been shocked at waking to such news, Hitler's explanation was as convoluted as it was meretricious: he had been obliged to jettison the 1939 pact with the Soviet Union in response to British attempts to strangle the Third Reich through encirclement and to counter the threat now posed by the Soviet divisions massing along the German frontier. The moment had arrived 'to counter this conspiracy of the Jewish-Anglo-Saxon warmongers and the equally Jewish rulers of the Bolshevik headquarters in Moscow'.[28]

About half an hour earlier, the Soviet ambassador to the Reich, Vladimir Dekanozov – who had been trying with increasing urgency to see Ribbentrop, only for his office to be told repeatedly that he was unavailable – was woken by his staff. An unnamed official had rung saying, 'Herr Reichsminister von Ribbentrop wishes to see representatives of the Soviet government at the Foreign Office.' When told that the ambassador was asleep and it would take time to arrange a car, the official said, 'The Reichsminister's motor car is already waiting outside your embassy. The Minister wishes to see Soviet representatives immediately.'[29]

Dekanozov – a dwarfish figure, beak-nosed, and bald save for a few strands of oily black hair plastered across his shiny pate – was unprepossessing at the best of times. Nonetheless he was a senior NKVD official and justly feared as one of Beria's most vicious interrogators. In defiance of diplomatic protocol, he had installed a secret chamber in the Soviet Embassy where members of the Soviet community in Berlin suspected of disloyalty could be tested, tortured and, if found wanting, executed. He was as unswervingly obdurate as Stalin in his belief that Hitler would not breach his commitment to the Molotov–Ribbentrop Pact. Even when he was shown the proofs of a Russian phrase book for the troops (delivered secretly to the Soviet consulate by a German communist) that contained the Russian words for 'Surrender!', 'Hands Up!', and 'I'll shoot!' he had failed to pass on the warning to Moscow.[30] Now, in the early hours of 22 June, Ribbentrop was about to shatter Dekanozov's faith by informing him that the agreement between the Soviet Union and Nazi Germany, which he had himself so proudly and carefully crafted, was unilaterally to be abrogated.

The German foreign minister was ill at ease. According to the First Secretary, Valentin Berezhkov, who accompanied Dekanozov, 'His face was scarlet and bloated, his eyes were glassy and inflamed', as though he had been drinking.[31] When the two men sat down, Ribbentrop interrupted the ambassador's opening words to say, 'The Soviet Government's hostile attitude to Germany and the serious threat represented by Soviet troop concentrations on Germany's eastern frontier have compelled the Reich to take military countermeasures.'[32] It was clear to Dekanozov that, under the guise of taking 'defensive measures', the invasion was already underway. Ribbentrop rose to leave. Dekanozov was speechless, but finally he too stood. Looking up at the vast bulk of the foreign minister, he found the torturer's presence of mind to retort, 'You'll regret this insulting, provocative and thoroughly predatory attack on the Soviet Union. You'll pay dearly for it.'[33] He did not offer to shake hands but made to return to the embassy just as Ribbentrop, recovering his notoriously oleaginous poise, hurried up to him to say, 'Tell Moscow I was against the attack.'[34]

A crescendo of reports now cascaded into the Russian capital from across the front line that even the Kremlin could not ignore. The Soviet Union was under all-out attack, from the Baltic to the Balkans. At the Defence Commissariat there was alarm and pandemonium. The news could hardly have been worse. Field Marshal Leeb's Army Group North – battle-hardened veterans of the Wehrmacht's victories in western Europe – was scything a path towards Leningrad, which Hitler had vowed to raze to the

ground. At the other end of the front, Field Marshal Rundstedt's Army
Group South was launching a two-pronged attack from Poland and
Romania deep into Ukraine towards Kiev; and Field Marshal Bock's
Army Group Centre was locked in a ferocious battle at Brest-Litovsk en
route for Moscow.

As Timoshenko tried to digest the enormity of what he was hearing,
he took a phone call from Boldin, who only a few hours earlier had
been relaxing beside Pavlov at the theatre in Minsk. Boldin informed
him that reports reaching Western Front Headquarters indicated that at
least eight cities (up to a depth of eighty kilometres from the border)
were being attacked by Luftwaffe bombers, that fighters were strafing
both troops and civilians and that German units had crossed the frontier
in many sectors. He urged an immediate military response. Timoshenko
would still not hear of such a move, insisting 'no actions are to be started
against the Germans without our consent'. Goaded beyond endurance,
Boldin shouted down the line, 'But our troops are retreating, towns are
in flames, people are dying.' When Timoshenko still failed to react,
Boldin insisted, 'Comrade Marshal, we must act. Every moment is precious. This is no provocation. The Germans have started a war.'[35] The
defence commissar merely repeated his previous instruction.

But such reports could not be ignored for much longer. With great
reluctance Timoshenko decided that Stalin, who was still asleep at
Kuntsevo, had to be woken to hear the news. Reluctant to make the call
himself, he instructed his deputy, Marshal Semyon Budyonny, to ring
Stalin's dacha on his behalf and – as though to cover himself – told Zhukov to do likewise. The chief of staff got through first but the duty
officer at Kuntsevo didn't want to disturb Stalin's sleep. 'Wake him,
immediately. The Germans are bombing our cities,' Zhukov ordered.
Three minutes later Stalin was on the phone. He listened to the chief of
staff but said nothing. After a long pause, Zhukov asked, 'Did you
understand what I said?'[36] There was another silence. Then, by now
clearly fully awake, Stalin gave instructions that the Politburo should
gather in the Kremlin immediately.

Stalin hurried back to Moscow. Soon after 4 a.m., looking haggard
and bewildered, he was joined in his office by, among others, Molotov,
Beria, Timoshenko, Lev Mekhlis (Stalin's 'military enforcer' as head of
the army's Political Department), and Zhukov.[37] Still unwilling to face

the facts, he once again tried to persuade himself that the attack was not Hitler's doing. 'Could this be a provocation by the German generals?' he asked, prompting a sardonic Zhukov to recall, 'Relying on his own wisdom, he had outwitted himself.'[38]

Soon after 5 a.m. the German ambassador, Schulenburg, who had been so coy with Molotov a few hours earlier, rushed to the Kremlin seeking an urgent meeting with the Soviet foreign minister. He was hurried into Molotov's office, where he read out virtually the same message that Ribbentrop had handed to Dekanozov. Molotov could scarcely believe what he had heard. He was silent for a moment and then stammered, 'Is this supposed to be a declaration of war?' Schulenburg did not speak but shrugged his shoulders as if to say that it was not his doing and that he deplored Hitler's act of aggression – which was true.* Molotov suddenly found his voice and shouted angrily, 'The message I have just been given couldn't mean anything but a declaration of war . . . [It is] a breach of confidence unprecedented in history . . . Surely we haven't deserved that.'[39] At that, Schulenburg shook hands and left the Kremlin for the last time to join the exodus of German citizens from what was now an enemy capital.

It was not until 7.15 a.m. on 22 June that Stalin finally permitted Zhukov to issue Directive No. 2, which stated:

1. Our troops are to attack the enemy forces with all the strength and means at their disposal, and to annihilate them wherever they have violated the Soviet border.
2. Our reconnaissance and combat aircraft shall ascertain where enemy aircraft and land-forces are concentrated. By striking mighty blows our aircraft are to smash the main enemy troop concentrations and their aircraft on its airfields . . .[40]

Stalin had at last acknowledged the facts, but in the process had demonstrated the gulf of ignorance that separated the Soviet High Command from the disaster that was already unfolding on the battlefield.

---

* In 1944 Schulenburg was executed for his role in the July 1944 plot to assassinate Hitler.

9.   Hatreds and Horrors

At 3.15 a.m. on 22 June 1941, the Soviet border guards protecting one of the bridges spanning the Bug fifteen kilometres south of Brest-Litovsk, were startled by shouts from their German counterparts on the other side of the river, asking them to come out to discuss 'important business'. As soon as the Russians came into view, they were gunned down. The bridge was secured without delay and Guderian's panzers were soon across it, facing almost no resistance as they scorched deep into Soviet territory. At Brest-Litovsk itself, German sappers had crept up under cover of darkness to remove the primitive explosives attached to the railway bridge by the Soviets. Wave upon wave of infantrymen crossed over to lay siege to the fortress, where thousands of soldiers were soon cowering under an unremitting barrage of artillery fire. 'This all-embracing barrage literally shook the earth. Great fountains of thick black smoke sprang up like mushrooms from the ground . . . we thought that everything in the citadel must already have been razed to the ground,' the 45th Infantry Division's chaplain, Rudolf Gschöpf, recalled.[1]

A number of servicemen had their wives and children living with them in the fortress, which was equipped with schools, shops and hospitals. The wife of one Russian officer recalled:

> Early in the morning I was woken up with my children by a terrible noise. Bombs and shells were exploding. I ran barefoot into the street with my children . . . what a dreadful scene outside. The sky above the fortress was full of aircraft dropping bombs on us. Totally distracted women and children were rushing about looking for a place to hide from the fire. Before me lay the wife of a lieutenant with her young son; both had been killed.[2]

Although most of the troops stationed at the fortress had taken advantage of the licence given them to leave for a midsummer weekend break, 3,500 of their comrades remained behind on duty. Now besieged by the enemy, they and their families were effectively incarcerated. They began to run out of food and water. German sappers had cut off their electricity and severed the telephone lines to Minsk. The German High Command might have expected them to surrender. However, they resisted with a ferocity and enterprise that took their attackers by surprise – an early harbinger of how resilient the Russian soldiers would prove in defence of the Motherland.

The wider city was engulfed by flames. Dead and wounded lay on the streets. Buildings were on fire. The main hospital's operating theatre was incinerated. The sky was red with flames that roared menacingly above the debris. The noise, the smoke and the dust provided a lurid backdrop for Guderian's infantry, who advanced like 'a great avalanche with no start or finish . . . their sleeves rolled up, hand-grenades stuck in belts and machine pistols hanging from their necks or rifles at the ready'.[3]

Fifty kilometres to the east, in Kobrin, Colonel I. T. Starinov, a mining specialist, was on his way to Brest from Pavlov's headquarters at Minsk. He was awoken by a loudspeaker which blared, 'Everyone is to leave the building immediately!' Pausing only to put on their uniforms and boots, the men rushed into the street just in time to see a bomber squadron diving towards them. Starinov flung himself into a ditch. Amidst an eardrum-shattering cacophony, bombs started to land around them. When the columns of smoke cleared, Starinov saw that part of a building close by was in smithereens. In the silence, he heard a sound: 'a high-pitched, hysterical female voice was crying out a desperate, inconsolable "aaaaaa"'.

He and a fellow officer decided to press on for Brest. Hitching a lift in a staff car, they passed a long line of women fleeing the epicentre of the bombardment, 'carrying hastily dressed, sleeping children, bundles and baskets'. In Kobrin's main square another loudspeaker imperiously boomed out the early morning news from Moscow. Everyone paused expectantly, wondering what the radio announcer would say. The bulletin informed them of many things, notably that the Soviet harvest was ripening well and that a factory had fulfilled its production quota ahead of schedule. Starinov listened intently, expecting a special announcement, but, to his astonishment and dismay, there was no mention of any invasion or any bombing raid. Instead, the weather forecast that concluded the bulletin was followed by a chirpy fitness instructor with his daily calisthenics lesson. To the cheery accompaniment of 'Stretch your arms out, bend! Livelier! Up, down, up, down,' Starinov watched as several trucks, laden with 'weeping women and children', rumbled through the square heading to what might or might not prove a place of safety.[4] The colonel and his colleague decided to return to Minsk for further instructions.

On the way they passed a military airfield near the town of Pinsk. It had been severely damaged. 'It was painful to see the smashed and burning planes . . . Yet still we stubbornly believed that it was only here that the enemy had caught our troops unawares and that elsewhere Soviet aeroplanes were bombing the enemy.'[5] In fact, not only around Brest but along the entire front the Luftwaffe had the freedom of the skies from which to inflict torment with impunity. Scores of Soviet airfields were littered with the smouldering metal carcases of warplanes, which, far from confronting the enemy as instructed by Stalin, had been wrecked in the early hours of 22 June before their pilots had even got out of bed. By midday, with more than a thousand aircraft put out of action, the Soviet air force had effectively been eliminated as a serious fighting arm. By nightfall a total of 1,800 aircraft had been lost. Those Soviet pilots who did manage to scramble into the air were generally outflown, outsmarted and outgunned. They proved incapable of striking any significant blow against the invaders, let alone the 'mighty blows' demanded by Moscow that morning.

The Luftwaffe pilots could scarcely hide their delight at this bonanza. Hans-Ulrich Rudel, a Stuka pilot who was to become a war hero for his derring-do exploits,* described the ease with which the dive-bombers picked off their targets, whether they were 'tanks, motor vehicles, bridges, fieldworks and AA sites . . . the enemy's railway communications or armoured trains'.[6] A fighter pilot, Pilot Officer Heinz Knoke,

---

* Credited with destroying more than 500 tanks, 2,000 ground targets as well as a battleship, two cruisers and a destroyer, Rudel – an ardent Nazi – flew more than 2,500 missions and survived countless near-death experiences. He was decorated by Hitler with the Third Reich's highest military honours. After the war he lived in various parts of South America, where he remained an active neo-Nazi until his death in 1982. (I am reliably informed that Rudel's memoirs are not always reliable!)

rejoiced at the scene below: 'Vehicles have been stripped of their camouflage and overturned by the blast. The Ivans at last come to life. The scene below is like an overturned ant-heap, as they scurry about in confusion. Stepsons of Stalin in their underwear flee for cover in the woods.' After returning to his base to refuel, Knoke was soon on the offensive again, relishing the impact of strafing a fleeing enemy: 'Thousands of Ivans are in full retreat, which becomes an utter rout when we open up on them, stumbling and bleeding as they flee from the highway in an attempt to take cover in the nearby woods.'[7]

If it was exhilarating, it was also dangerous. The pilots took risks that even the most foolhardy of their number would not have attempted if there had been Soviet warplanes to confront them. On one occasion Rudel thought to rescue the crew of a plane forced down after being hit by Soviet anti-aircraft fire as it strafed a column of Russian troops. Accordingly, he lowered his flaps and went in to land:

> Whang! A burst of M.G. [machine gun] fire hits my engine! There seems no sense in landing with a crippled aircraft; if I do we shall not be able to take off again. My comrades are done for. Their waving hands are the last I see of them. The engine conks like mad, but picks up and is running just sufficiently to allow me to pull out on the other side of the copse. The oil has plastered the window of my cockpit and I expect a piston seizure at any moment. If that happens my engine will stop for good.[8]

The plane and Rudel survived to return to base.

The German pilots were highly trained and motivated. Flying eighteen hours at a stretch, they paused only for the twenty minutes it took to land, refuel and take off again. Rudel noted, 'Every spare minute we stretch out underneath an aeroplane and instantly fall asleep. Then if a call comes from anywhere we hop to it without even knowing where it is from. We move as though in our dreams.'[9] Like many of their fellow pilots – most of whom were in their early twenties – Rudel and Knoke had been infected by Nazism. Knoke did not attempt to conceal his loathing for the enemy: 'We have dreamed for a long time of doing something like this on the Bolshevists. Our feeling is not one of hatred, so much as utter contempt. It is a genuine satisfaction for us to be able to trample the Bolshevists in the mud where they belong.'[10]

*

The citizens of Moscow, the Wehrmacht's ultimate destination, had as little inkling of what was about to befall the Motherland as their counterparts in Brest-Litovsk, 1,000 kilometres to the west. After several days of rain, the weekend weather was fine, the temperature balmy. Those who had not left the city for their dachas relaxed after the shortest night of the year. Some tended their allotments or fished for their suppers on the banks of the Moskva. Others strolled in Gorky Park, relishing the start of a summer break. Potential delights abounded. In one of the capital's many theatres, Chekhov's *The Three Sisters* was playing to full houses. Opera lovers could choose between two Verdi tragedies: *Rigoletto* and *La Traviata*.[11] Those who preferred the cinema could see, among other offerings, the popular *If War Should Come Tomorrow*, which reassured them that, if the Germans were to attack, 'the Red Army would carry the fighting into the aggressor's homeland within days, the German workers would rise to greet them, and victory would come with a minimum expenditure of blood'.[12]

On the morning of 22 June, Muscovites were instructed by a state radio announcement to interrupt their weekend at midday for an important broadcast. Such alerts were not uncommon, but generally not to be missed. At the appointed time, small crowds duly huddled around the loudspeakers that with disconcerting authority bedecked every public place. If they had expected to hear the voice of their leader, they were disappointed. Instead it was Molotov's monotone that echoed across the expectant city as he informed them tremulously that Germany had launched an invasion against the Soviet Union. 'This unheard-of attack on our country is an unparalleled act of perfidy,' he intoned querulously, 'made despite the fact there was a non-aggression pact between the Soviet Union and Germany.' Concealing the enormity of the disaster and minimizing the loss of Soviet lives (allowing only that 'more than two hundred' soldiers had died), he sought to rouse the nation: they were about to embark on a 'Patriotic War for our beloved country, for honour, for liberty . . . The government calls on you, men and women citizens of the Soviet Union, to rally even more closely around the glorious Bolshevik Party.' He concluded with a passage that was apparently crafted by Stalin: 'Our cause is just. The enemy will be beaten. Victory will be ours.'[13] Quite why Stalin had eschewed the chance to address the nation himself was unclear, though it is possible that he was using his foreign minister – who had signed the pact with Germany – as a shield to protect himself from any opprobrium that he might otherwise have incurred. Although he was clearly grateful to Molotov, telling him that the 'speech went well', he could not resist jibing, 'You sounded a bit flustered . . .'[14]

The news stunned the Soviet Union. People were in tears, speechless, confused, incredulous, angry and fearful. Reflecting the insecurity of a totalitarian state, the NKVD was on full alert, monitoring the mood closely through its unrivalled network of informers, to find answers to critical questions: would the nation fall in line and fulfil its patriotic duties or would dissidents, subversives, saboteurs and foreign agents sow seeds of disquiet and resentment against the Kremlin for its failure to predict the invasion or to protect the borders of the Soviet Union? Would fascist propaganda seep through the carapace of newspeak with which the state bombarded its citizens? The secret state went into overdrive, tapping phones, eavesdropping on gossip and intercepting personal correspondence.

Some of the findings were disconcerting, but, as the regime needed the truth, the NKVD did not dissemble. Its reports revealed widespread criticism and even contempt for the government that 'was often expressed with surprising – and surprisingly – incautious freedom, force and perspicacity'.[15] In his lacklustre attempt to rally the public to the Soviet cause, Molotov had inadvertently exposed a raw nerve. A doctor noted bleakly that 'the prisons were full, the peasants were ill-disposed and half the population was opposed to the government'; one woman was relieved that the war had started because 'life in the USSR had become unbearable – everyone was sick of famine and forced labour – the sooner it was over the better'; an employee of Intourist (the State travel agency) who had once believed that the Civil War was a struggle for freedom now thought that 'there was nothing for them to die for'; a government official, named Danilov, supposing that the Germans were already in control of Kiev and other cities, expressed his delight at the prospect of a Nazi victory: 'Now at last we can breathe freely. Hitler will be in Moscow in three days and the Intelligentsia will be able to live properly.'[16] And there was much more in a similar vein.

The regime was swift to crush any threat of open dissent. More than a thousand people who had been fingered under the categories of 'terrorism, sabotage, wrecking, German, Italian, and Japanese espionage, other forms of espionage, bacteriological sabotage, Trotskyism, former members of anti-Soviet political parties, sectarians and conscientious objectors, various anti-Soviet elements' were rounded up and imprisoned.[17] They were not the first and they would not be the last.

Mercifully for the Kremlin, such 'enemies of the state' were not in the ascendant. As the news began to sink in, a combination of genuine patriotism and government propaganda created a surge of anger at the perfidy of the Nazis. Volunteers from across the Soviet Union came forward to offer themselves to the cause. 'We will put up with any hardships to help our Red Army ensure that the Soviet people utterly destroys the fascists,' one promised. Another, expressing himself in the leaden terms of a party apparatchik, nonetheless clearly spoke from the heart when he said, 'Hitler has violated the sacred borders of the first socialist country in the world . . . We will win because there is no power in the world that can vanquish a people who have risen up in patriotic War.'[18]

Somewhat more ambivalently, Victor Kravchenko, listening to Molotov's broadcast with colleagues at the Commissariat for Foreign Trade, mused subversively that, under the terms of the trade deal between Moscow and Berlin, he and his colleagues had been responsible for overseeing the dispatch of 'sorely needed food, metals, oil and munitions' to facilitate Hitler's invasion. The thought was unpalatable. When they twiddled the knobs on the office radio for other news, they heard a voice booming out of the ether in flawless Russian:

> Citizens of Russia! Russian people! Listen! Listen! This is the headquarters of the German Army . . . For 24 years you have been living in hunger and fear. You were promised life and got slavery. You were promised bread and got famine. You are slaves without any human rights. Thousands of you die every day in concentration camps and in the frozen wastes of Siberia . . . Death to the parasites of the Russian people! Overthrow your tyrants![19]

They switched off the radio in disgust. Next day, lest a more gullible public be contaminated, the authorities ordered all private radios to be handed over to the police.

Despite their misgivings, the great majority of Russian citizens rallied to the flag. While Molotov's broadcast was still echoing across the Soviet Union, Nikolai Amosov, a military surgeon based in the city of

Cherepovets, was ordered to join a team of doctors at a local school (School No. 2). Their task was to assess the fitness of prospective recruits and reservists who had already responded to the call-up. Those judged too weak or too old to bear arms were swiftly dismissed. The rest were subjected to a cursory medical examination. The commander of the local 'call-up' commission told them, 'Please judge responsibly and strictly. You don't need, as is your normal custom, to send them for consultations or investigations. There is no time for that. We have two days to mobilize our contingents.' Amosov inspected the young men as they stood awaiting examination and he was touched by their appearance:

Here they are in front of me, defenders of the Motherland, aged between 20 and 35. They are collective farmers from nearby villages, workers from our industries – saw mill, the port, timber farm, employees from offices, shoemakers and tailors . . . They are not at all well-dressed but they take care of their appearance and their shirts are clean. Most of them are thin . . . They don't talk much . . . They undressed by the entrance of the classroom . . . They cover up their private parts when approaching the doctor. A naked person is defenceless.

As the evening wore on, the throng of recruits waiting in the corridor outside the classroom became boisterous. The cause was apparent. Before long, a good many of the men were so drunk on vodka that they had to be sent to another room to sleep off the effects. Those who passed inspection were formed into platoons and lined up in the courtyard outside, where wives, sweethearts and children, ignoring the shouts of a corporal trying to impose order, pushed and shoved their way into the ranks to embrace their departing loved ones. As the new recruits marched away from the school towards the railway station or a local barracks, Amosov noted, 'Men are holding the hands of children, women hang onto their shoulders . . . There is noise, exclamations and sobbing . . . Later the women will come back home, alone, lost.'[20]

In Minsk, Colonel General Pavlov was psychologically paralysed by the scale of the emergency. Reports from the front suggested that his Western Front was under assault from thirty infantry divisions, five tank divisions and two motorized divisions, supported by forty artillery and five aviation regiments. For weeks, at the Kremlin's behest, he had refused to contemplate any measures to increase the readiness of the combat troops under his command. Now he was at a loss. His troops were scattering before the onslaught and almost everywhere on the retreat. His deputy, Boldin – a far more decisive and clear-minded figure – pressed for permission to fly to the city of Białystok, 120 kilometres north of Brest-Litovsk, to find out what was happening for himself. Somewhat reluctantly Pavlov and Timoshenko approved his request.

Accompanied by his ADC, Boldin left Minsk at around 3 p.m. As they flew closer to the epicentre of the battle, he looked down to see fires raging at a railway station, trains burning and warehouses on fire. Ahead, the horizon was ablaze:

> Enemy bombers were continuously streaking through the sky . . . Our pilot . . . flew the plane at the lowest possible altitude. Skirting the populated areas, we neared Belostok [Białystok]. The further we went, the worse it became. There were more and more enemy planes in the air. It was impossible to continue the flight. Up ahead there was a small airfield with planes burning beside a metal hangar.

Boldin ordered the pilot to land there. As they began their descent, a Messerschmitt fighter plane detected them. Roaring up from behind, it unleashed several machine-gun rounds but was forced to bear away before it scored a hit.

Within minutes of landing they heard the roar and shriek of nine aircraft (almost certainly Junkers Ju 87s – the Stukas) as they dived towards them. They just made it to cover before the earth shook with the impact of the bombardment. When they looked out from their shelter they saw that several aircraft on the ground – including Boldin's – had been engulfed in flames. They were thirty-five kilometres from Białystok. Boldin commandeered an army truck, picked up a stray group of soldiers who were slogging their way towards the front and headed on. He came upon a gaggle of workers standing disconsolately by the roadside. 'Who are you?' he asked. An elderly man replied, 'We had been working on fortifications. But the place where we worked is now a sea of flames.' They had no idea what to do or where to go. A little further on, Boldin halted a column of cars heading towards them. An aspidistra was protruding from the window of one of the vehicles, a luxury Zil 101, to which only senior officials could aspire. Inside there were two women and two children. Boldin reproached them: 'Surely at a time like this you might have more important things to transport than your aspidistra. You might have taken some old people or children.' The women and their driver looked away in embarrassment. As they spoke, a German fighter swooped overhead, strafing this sitting target. Three volleys hit Boldin's truck, killing the driver and everyone in it apart from Boldin himself, his ADC and a dispatch rider who had leapt out just in time. Nearby stood the remains of the Zil. 'Everyone inside was dead,' noted Boldin. 'Only the evergreen leaves of the aspidistra were still sticking out of the window.'[21]

As they entered Białystok, they found a city in chaos. Fuel depots and grain warehouses were ablaze; a railway station had been bombed, killing many women and children waiting there to escape the city; fleeing civilians streamed down the road towards them. Navigating their way through this anarchic muddle of humanity, they reached the 10th Army's regional headquarters. It was deserted. They were directed to a field command post, which they found at the edge of a small wood twelve kilometres south-west of the city. It was minimally appointed: two tents, each with a wooden table, some stools and one telephone. A truck with radio equipment was parked nearby. It had broken down. Dusk was starting to fall.

Boldin was met by Major General K. D. Golubev and a group of staff officers who confirmed his forebodings: heavy losses of men and equipment, tanks wrecked or inoperable, aircraft and artillery destroyed, ammunition and fuel almost exhausted. Golubev bent over a map and sighed, 'We have remarkable people – strong-willed, dedicated and with great fortitude . . . the situation is grave, very grave.'[22]

This distressing sitrep was interrupted by the general's communications officer. The link to Minsk had been re-established. Pavlov was on the line. The commander-in-chief listened to Boldin's report before giving him what were clearly preordained and detailed instructions that took no account of what he had just been told. Boldin was to reorganize the front forthwith and, with what was left of two mechanized corps and one cavalry corps, to mount a major counter-offensive. He was to drive the invaders back and to prevent any further attempt by any enemy unit to break through the line. Pavlov continued, 'This is your immediate assignment, and you are personally responsible for carrying it out.' The operation was to begin that night. It was a preposterous order.

Boldin tried to explain that, in the present 'grave' circumstances, it would be quite impossible to carry out Pavlov's instructions. His commander-in-chief paused before saying with an air of finality, 'That's all I have to say. Get started on the assignment.' Pavlov had begun to inhabit a fantasy world, where fear of Stalin and wishful thinking had replaced all military logic in favour of a stream of absurd commands. But, to avoid facing a court martial and the firing squad, Boldin had no option but to comply. It was the start of a nightmarish forty-five days from which, against all odds, he emerged to become a national hero. Pavlov was to fare less well.

At 9.15 that night Timoshenko issued Stalin's Directive No. 3, which was as ludicrous as that which had just been issued to Boldin but on a far greater scale. The Red Army was to launch a simultaneous counter-offensive across the entire 1,800-kilometre front against all three German army groups. The apparent objective was to hurl the invader back in one great counter-blow – much as a world champion wrestler might throw off a novice fighter who had temporarily pinned him to the ground. The recipients of Directive No. 3 were well aware that, with their forces in disarray, on the retreat or facing encirclement, this feat was beyond them. But Red Army commanders – like Boldin – had little choice but to obey Stalin's orders unquestioningly.

At 10 o'clock that night, as though to proclaim that it had lost touch with reality, the Soviet General Staff released its first operational summary of the campaign:

> Regular troops of the German Army during the course of 22 June conducted operations against frontier defence units of the USSR, attaining insignificant success in a number of sectors. During the second half of the day, with the arrival of forward elements of the field forces of the Red Army, the attacks of the German troops along most of the length of our frontiers were beaten off and losses inflicted on the enemy.[23]

Even by Soviet standards, this was a breathtaking catalogue of delusionary falsehoods that concealed the catastrophe that was already engulfing Stalin's armies.

*

The young men who had volunteered for the front did not yet realize quite how severely their patriotism would be put to the test. Their papers told them they had just joined the Red Army. They might have expected a welcome. Instead, they found confusion. In the absence of barracks or transport or unit commanders, they found themselves tramping the streets or dossing in classrooms. In Moscow some slept on station platforms, waiting for trains that might in due course take them to the front. They mingled there with reservists who knew the realities of military service and advised them accordingly. It was a sobering experience. These old hands were unmoved by radio propaganda or exhortations from party commissars. Some of their comrades had been unable to face the prospect of a return to the battlefield; police reports spoke of self-mutilation and even suicide among their number. However, most were doggedly fatalistic. Like the raw recruits they had started to educate, they lingered obediently, an army-in-waiting without direction, support, or inspiration. In this military limbo-land, the streets of the capital were 'thronged with groups of men, several hundred at a time, just sitting, waiting, talking, drinking, and reflecting on their fate'.[24] Any illusions these young men may still have harboured were soon to be dispelled, violently and terrifyingly.

Churchill was asleep at Chequers when the news of the German invasion reached Britain in the early hours of 22 June 1941. The prime
minister had endured a particularly gruelling few weeks of military setbacks, during which even his extraordinary resilience had been put
severely to the test. Following the debacle in Greece and the loss of
Crete, he had sought to restore British fortunes in the Middle East,
where Rommel had seized the initiative in the desert war. Overriding
an unusually assertive Chief of the Imperial General Staff, General Dill,
he instructed Wavell to launch a counter-attack to drive the Desert Fox
back from the Egyptian border, insisting that he should persist 'until
you have beaten the life out of General Rommel's Army'.[1] Churchill's
impetuosity was Wavell's undoing. Much against his will, the Middle
East commander-in-chief launched Operation Battleaxe on 15 June. His
objective was to lift the siege of Tobruk and once again to drive the Axis
forces back across the desert to Tripoli. The operation was a dismal failure. The British suffered severe losses on the first day. By the second day
the 'Army of the Nile' was under intense pressure; on the third day, it
crumbled. Rommel was stronger than ever.

Churchill had set such store by Battleaxe that he retreated to Chartwell, his country home in Kent, as he wished to wait alone to hear
the first report of its outcome. Yet another British defeat in a battle in
which he had invested so much authority was, he wrote, 'a most bitter
blow . . . I wandered about the valley disconsolately for some hours.'[2]
Had he been aware of Hitler's Draft Order No. 32, written a week earlier, which called for the destruction of the British position in the Middle
East and the Gulf 'by converging attacks from Libya through Egypt,
from Bulgaria through Turkey, and possibly from Transcaucasia through
Iran'[3] – which would have confirmed the CIGS's worst fears about Hitler's objectives – he might have been even more disconsolate. As it was,
he returned to London and peremptorily sacked Wavell (with whom he

had frequently been at odds), reflecting harshly that 'we had ridden the willing horse to a standstill'.[4]

With Wavell removed, the PM swiftly bounced back. His guests at Chequers on the following weekend included Eden, Cripps and the US ambassador, John G. Winant. During dinner on the evening of Saturday, 21 June, the prime minister – as usual – held court. With characteristic self-assurance, he not only declared that the Germans would inevitably attack Russia but, equally inevitably, that the Russians would be defeated. In so saying, he did no more than reflect what was now the collective view of the government's most senior advisors, among whom General Dill said dismissively that 'the Germans would go through them like a hot knife through butter'.[5] Even Cripps, who had flown back from Moscow to brief the government a few days earlier, did not dissent, advising the War Cabinet that the Red Army would not 'hold out for more than three or four weeks'.[6] Calculating that the Nazis would probably reach Moscow within six weeks, the Joint Intelligence Committee advised that, very soon after that, Hitler would be ready to launch an invasion of Britain.[7] Eden went to bed that night reflecting that even if such fears were realized, the Russians would at least inflict enough damage on the Wehrmacht to 'ease some of the strain upon us'.[8]

Before heading to bed, the prime minister took his customary nocturnal stroll around the garden. His private secretary, John ('Jock') Colville, accompanied him. As they mused on the prospect of a German invasion, Colville suggested that for an 'arch anti-Communist' like Churchill to support the Soviet Union against the Nazis would be tantamount to 'bowing down to the House of Rimmon [by surrendering his principles on the grounds of expediency]'. Churchill replied that he had 'only one purpose – the destruction of Hitler. If Hitler invaded Hell he would at least make a favourable reference to the Devil.'[9]

In the early hours of 22 June, Colville was woken by a phone call with the news that Germany had indeed just launched an attack on Russia. He padded around to wake Churchill, who greeted the information with 'a smile of satisfaction'; it was the first good news for a long time. Soon afterwards Eden was woken by the prime minister's valet bearing a silver salver with a large cigar and a message: 'The prime minister's compliments and the German armies have invaded Russia.' The Foreign

Secretary put on his dressing gown and (sans cigar) joined the prime minister in his bedroom to discuss their next move. Churchill said he would address the nation later that day and would tell the people that the Russians were now 'partners in the struggle against Hitler'.[10]

Before Churchill's broadcast, Moscow still harboured the suspicion that Britain, even at this late date, might side with Germany. According to the former foreign minister, Litvinov (who, despite still being a 'non-person', remained remarkably well informed), this suspicion ran so deep that, when certain that the German invasion was in earnest, the Kremlin leapt to the conclusion that 'the British fleet was steaming up the North Sea for [a] joint attack with Hitler on Leningrad and Kronstadt'.[11] In London, an anxious Maisky contacted the Foreign Secretary for reassurance that 'our war effort would not slacken', comfort that Eden was happy to provide.[12] Nonetheless it was with 'bated breath' that the Soviet ambassador tuned in for the broadcast that evening.

Churchill laboured at his address for most of the day, completing the final draft only twenty minutes before it was due for live transmission by the BBC at 9 p.m. To avoid any attempt by either Eden or Cadogan to tone down his words, he refrained from showing it to either of them. The result was vintage Churchill. It was orotund in language, potent in imagery and – delivered in his inimitable cadences – calculated to uplift and inspire the listener with the breadth of his prime ministerial vision:

> No one has been a more consistent opponent of communism than I have for the last twenty-five years. I will unsay no word that I have spoken about that. But all this fades away before the spectacle which is now unfolding. The past, with its crimes, its follies, and its tragedies, flashes away. I see the Russian soldiers standing on the threshold of their native land, guarding the fields which their fathers have tilled from time immemorial . . . I see the ten thousand villages of Russia where the means of existence is wrung so hardly from the soil, but where there are still primordial human joys, where maidens laugh and children play. I see advancing upon all this in hideous onslaught the Nazi war machine, with its clanking, heel-clicking, dandified Prussian officers . . . I see also the dull, drilled, docile, brutish masses of the Hun soldiery plodding on like a swarm of crawling locusts . . .
>
> We have but one aim and one single, irrevocable purpose. We are resolved to destroy Hitler and every vestige of the Nazi regime. From

this nothing will turn us – nothing. We will never parlay, we will never negotiate with Hitler or any of his gang. We shall fight him by sea, we shall fight him in the air, until, with God's help, we have rid the earth of his shadow and liberated its people from his yoke . . . That is our policy and that is our declaration. It follows therefore that we shall give whatever help we can to Russia and the Russian people.[13]

His choice of language had been carefully calibrated to give heart to the Soviet leadership but not to make any precise commitment. And it worked. When Churchill proclaimed that he would never 'parlay' with Hitler, Maisky's elation was unbounded. 'A forceful speech! A fine performance!' he chortled. 'Bellicose and resolute: no compromises or agreements.'[14] In his relief he failed to note that the prime minister had carefully refrained from referring to the Russians as 'allies', or to the form or scale of the 'help' Britain intended to provide.

The sincerity of Churchill's blistering attacks on Hitler in his BBC broadcast – which prompted a patronizing Cadogan to note that 'he was overdoing the mudslinging'[15] – was not matched by a similar resolve to save Russia. He was still preoccupied with the struggle in the Western Desert. He could not know what was in the Führer's mind but his fear – shared by the chiefs of staff – that the Middle East was almost certainly in his sights was not without reason. So confident was Hitler of a swift victory over the Red Army that the Deputy Chief of the General Staff, Friedrich Paulus, who had played a large part in planning Barbarossa, was already putting the final touches to a strategic operation that would see three panzer divisions spearhead an invasion of Syria and Palestine (via Turkey). The army would reach the Suez Canal in November 1941, from where they would open a land route to India via Persia. Far-fetched as this project might seem, Hitler not only endorsed it but proposed to facilitate it by imposing a stranglehold on the Mediterranean, which in turn would mean seizing Malta and Gibraltar.*

The prime minister dreaded what he feared to be Hitler's imperial ambitions. His anxiety was reinforced by the Joint Intelligence Committee, which predicted an invasion along very similar lines to that

---

* In 1943 Paulus commanded the 6th Army, which surrendered at Stalingrad. He was captured, survived imprisonment, and after the war lived in Dresden until his death in 1957.

simultaneously being planned by Paulus.[16] Churchill – who was to declare 'I have not become the King's First Minister in order to preside over the liquidation of the British Empire'[17] – had no intention of squandering precious military hardware in a losing struggle for the Soviet Union if there was any risk that the price would be the loss of the Middle East. The imminent arrival of General Claude Auchinleck to replace Wavell as that front's commander-in-chief was not expected to turn the tide against Rommel for some months.* For these reasons, Churchill was willing only to provide Stalin with enough support to convince him that Britain shared his pain. A gesture was required.

This took the form of a delaying tactic in the guise of a military mission, which was dispatched to Moscow on 24 June. It had no clear remit or mandate, and it lacked any sense of urgency. Eden confessed he had no idea what its role might be while Dill, the CIGS, openly expressed his abhorrence at the thought of collaboration with the Bolsheviks. The attitude of the War Office was illuminated by one of its junior ministers, Edward Grigg, who told his friend Harold Nicolson over lunch that '80 per cent of the War Office experts think that Russia will be knocked out in ten days', and that this 'would give great triumphs to Hitler and leave him free to fling his whole force against us'.[18] Reflecting on this, Nicolson noted, 'I cannot but feel that the W.O. view is coloured by political prejudice and by the fact that Stalin murdered most of his senior officers.'[19] From the British perspective, the only useful role of the Red Army before its imminent defeat was to slow the German advance, deplete its forces and wear down its men, thereby providing Britain with the crucial breathing space necessary to rebuild its depleted defences on the home front and strengthen the frontiers of the Empire in the Middle East – against either or both of which a Nazi onslaught was expected within weeks.

The military mission's inglorious purpose was conveyed succinctly by Sir John Kennedy, the Director of Military Operations, to its reluctant leader, General Noel Mason-MacFarlane, who had a well-earned

---

* Auchinleck, who had hitherto spent most of his professional career in India, had been Commander-in-Chief of the Indian Army. A little before his arrival in Cairo, Wavell left to become Commander-in-Chief, India. Both men were at least as able as any of their peers, some of whom, like Montgomery, sought and achieved a much higher public profile.

reputation for being tough, clever and courageous. 'We don't think this is anything more than an off-chance,' Kennedy told him. 'But we can't afford to miss even a poor chance like this . . . Your job will be to keep the Russian war going, and so exhaust the Boche.'[20] Under no circumstances, Mason-MacFarlane was told, should he make any 'political commitment'[21] or agree to any form of military or other support. His primary role would be to assess the performance of the Red Army and the state of morale among its senior leadership.

Had Stalin been aware of these prevailing sentiments, his abiding suspicion that London was only too happy to see Russians die on the battlefield to secure a British victory over Nazism would have been abundantly confirmed. And had the political and military elites in London been less contemptuous of the Soviet Union, they might have noted that their cavalier prediction that the Red Army would be a pushover was, at the very least, premature.

The first evidence for this was at the fortress in Brest-Litovsk, where it took three days for Guderian's panzer group to gain the upper hand. The fighting was bitter and brutal, an early foretaste of the future. Instead of raising their hands in surrender, the defenders took desperate measures. They concealed themselves behind walls and rubbish tips, in cellars and sheds, from where they emerged suddenly to fire bursts of machine-gun fire into German soldiers as they forced their way into the citadel. Snipers occupied the upper floors, waiting to pick off individual targets. By this means, Lance Corporal Hans Teuschler was hit in the chest from 300 metres away and knocked unconscious. When he came round, with his shirt and tunic 'soaked with blood', he saw another member of his unit lying beside his machine gun. His eyes had glazed over and he was clearly close to death. Teuschler struggled across to offer the dying man a canteen of water. To his right, another gunner 'sat bolt upright, unmoving'; he was already dead. A 'sad concert of cries from the helpless wounded could be heard from all sides. "Medic, medic, God in Heaven, help me!"' he recalled. The commander of the 45th Infantry Division reported that it was 'impossible to advance . . . because the highly organized rifle and machine-gun fire from the deep gun emplacements and horse-shoe-shaped yard cut down anyone who approached'. Within twenty-four hours, he was to report, his division had lost 21 officers and 290 NCOs, who had been 'picked off by snipers and machine guns wielded with great accuracy by the defenders'.[22]

Providing 'a ghastly but epic illustration of how Russian infantrymen could fight traditionally in ferocious style',[23] the defenders yielded only after a murderous hand-to-hand struggle that left only a few hundred of them alive once the battle was over. According to a Russian nursing sister from the local hospital, who witnessed what happened when the German troops overran the compound, the invaders were not merciful:

> They took all the wounded, children, women, soldiers, and shot them all before our eyes. We sisters, wearing our distinctive white hats and smocks marked with red crosses, tried to intervene, thinking they might take notice. But the fascists shot 28 wounded in my ward alone, and when they didn't immediately die, they tossed in hand-grenades among them.[24]

This was not the kind of resistance Guderian had expected. 'The important citadel of Brest-Litovsk held out with remarkable stubbornness for several days, thus depriving us of the use of the road and rail communications across the Bug,'[25] he noted in frustration. Reviewing progress across the entire front on the first day of Barbarossa from his headquarters at OKH (Army High Command), the army's chief of staff, Halder, was already sounding cautious: 'After the first shock, the enemy has turned to fight. There have been instances of tactical withdrawals and no doubt also of disorderly retreats, but there are no indications of an attempted operational disengagement. Such a possibility moreover can be discounted.'[26]

Nonetheless the panzers were soon advancing at blitzkrieg speed. Although both Army Group Centre's panzer groups, under Generals Guderian and Hermann Hoth, met more resistance than they had expected, it was not enough to arrest their progress. A German pilot, flying in a Stuka at 800 metres, witnessed the Soviet retreat from Brest on the road towards Minsk:

> Bulky tanks of all sizes, motorized columns, carts pulled by horses, and artillery in between – all frantically making their way east . . . The squadron dove down and we spattered the road with machine-gun fire . . . Our bombs fell by the side of the tanks, guns, between vehicles and panic stricken Russians running in all directions. It was total panic down there – nobody could even think of firing back. In order to leave the road intact

for our own advance, we dropped the bombs only at the side of the road. The effect of the incendiary and splinter bombs was awesome. With a target like this there are no mistakes. Tanks were turned over or stood in flames, guns with their towing vehicles blocked the road, while between them horses, thrashing around, multiplied the panic.[27]

The almost total absence of Russian warplanes and the leaden-footed reactions of the Soviet commanders, still paralysed by the shock of what was happening, gave the Luftwaffe pilots free rein to slaughter. However, the advance was not without cost, sometimes of the most ghastly kind. As the Russians retreated from Białystok towards Smolensk, 600 kilometres to the east, the ease with which the panzers cut through the faltering resistance of Pavlov's forces seduced some junior officers into taking devil-may-care risks. One young lieutenant, ignoring wiser counsel, raced his panzers forward before the infantry had time to clear the trees on either side of the main road ahead of them. After the tanks had disappeared from view, there was a silence. Then the air was rent by piercing screams and excited voices shouting in Russian. An infantry platoon, led by Lance Corporal Gottlieb Becker, was sent to investigate. They found that the entire unit had been massacred. 'Here and there a body jerked convulsively or danced around in its own blood,' Becker recalled. 'The majority of the German soldiers had their eyes gouged out, others their throats cut. Some had their bayonets stuck in their chests. Two soldiers had their uniform jackets and shirts ripped apart and their naked stomachs slit open; glistening entrails hung out of the bloodied mass. Two more had their genitals cut off and laid on their chest.'[28] When evidence of such incidents was sent back to Berlin, the facts were exaggerated and recycled for public consumption in dramatic and lurid newsreels and documentaries that portrayed the Russians as having more in common with beasts than human beings.

In the months ahead, such butchery would become so prevalent as to seem humdrum. Further along the front to the south, a 180-man infantry battalion was trapped by an unexpected Russian counter-attack. The prisoners were led off in groups and taken into a field beside the road, where they were ordered to strip. As they did so, their captors began to beat them around the head with their rifles and to pierce their exposed flesh with bayonets. Some had their hands tied behind their backs and were ordered to lie down. One infantryman, Hermann Heiss, described what happened to him: 'A Russian soldier stabbed me in the chest with his bayonet, at which point I turned over. I was then stabbed seven times in the back. I did not move any more. The Russians evidently assumed I was dead . . . I heard my comrades cry out in pain and then I passed out.'[29] The following morning, after the Russian counter-attack had been repelled, Heiss was discovered. He was still alive, lying in the midst of 153 half-naked corpses, twelve of which had been genitally mutilated. Heiss was one of only fourteen survivors.[30]

Some Soviet commanders ignored such acts of depravity, regarding them as the inevitable price of close combat. Others were less sanguine. Major General Mikhail Potapov, commanding the 5th Army, reported in dismay, 'It has frequently occurred that Red Army soldiers and commanders embittered by the cruelties of the Fascist thieves . . . do not take any German soldiers and officers prisoner but shoot them on the spot.'[31] He was not so bothered by the inhumanity of such reprisals as by their counterproductive consequences: 'I categorically forbid shootings on individual initiative . . . [it is] – detrimental to our interests.' To murder prisoners of war was not only to destroy a possible source of intelligence but would assuredly deter enemy troops from deserting.[32]

News of the horrors began to spread like a virus through the ranks on either side. Atrocity was piled upon atrocity. Retaliation begat retaliation until the field of battle was contaminated by so much fear and hatred as to obliterate any vestige of common humanity. Robert Rupp, an NCO serving in a motorized infantry unit, kept a diary in which he described a typical attack on a village that had been overrun by the panzers but which was still infested with Russian troops.

With a tank unit strategically placed to cut off any escape, a small contingent of infantrymen fanned out into the village to hunt down any Russians who might have concealed themselves in the tumbledown cottages and outbuildings which surrounded them. With two homes already ablaze, the terrified peasants scurried to rescue their meagre possessions and to drive their animals as far from danger as possible. It took a while but, by the time they had completed their search, the German soldiers had rounded up fifty men. A number of these were wounded: 'One of them had his cheek torn open by a hand-grenade,' Rupp noted. 'He asked me for water and greedily slurped down some tea.' Others had to sit in the street 'for a long time' before they received any treatment.

Later, two of the prisoners were shot, one because he had allegedly used dumdum bullets [which were deemed illegal by the Hague Conventions of 1899, a ruling that was routinely ignored] and because he had apparently fired his weapon after initially raising his hands in surrender.⋆ Their bodies were thrown into a grave dug for them by their comrades. 'One of them was still alive,' Rupp noted. 'He continued to wheeze even beneath a thick layer of earth, which rose up as an arm worked itself up into the air.'[33] Later, four Russians were instructed to dig another grave. A prisoner was marched forward and made to lie in it, whereupon he was shot by a fellow NCO. The victim was the same man to whom Rupp had earlier given some tea. His misfortune was to be identified as a commissar, and thus subject to Hitler's Commissar Order's ruling that such individuals were to be executed on the spot.

Though killings of this sort, often on a far larger scale, were commonplace, they did occasionally cause the invaders a frisson of disquiet. When a motorcycle battalion 'shot the entire inhabitants of a village, women and children too, and cast them into graves they were made to dig themselves', allegedly because 'the whole village had been involved in an ambush that had cost the motorcyclists dearly', Rupp reported that this retaliation had provoked 'differences of opinion'.[34] One of the few (unnamed) German soldiers to be aghast at such crimes against humanity wrote, 'Here war is pursued in its "pure form" . . . The scenes which one observes border on insane hallucinations and nightmares.'[35]

In the absence of any recognized rules of warfare, there were no boundaries to restrain even the worst excesses. For German soldiers, who had been indoctrinated to believe that Slavs lacked those traits which made them worthy of treatment as human beings, murder was not only a means of assuaging the red rage of battle against a hated enemy but also a simple way to dispose of unwanted detritus.

Hitler's diatribes had anaesthetized the sensibilities of both rank and file soldiers and their leaders alike. Even the commander of 43rd Army Corps, General Gotthard Heinrici – an otherwise sophisticated and thoughtful officer – was culpable. When he led his troops into Poland – 'such an awful country' – he became obsessed by the filth, which he attributed to the

---

⋆ Dumdum bullets are designed to expand on impact, mushrooming rather than passing through the body and thereby causing a much larger wound.

character of the Slavs as much as to their poverty. Describing the General Government – where some 12 million Poles, including more than a million Jews had been corralled and redefined as 'stateless people' – as the 'scrapheap of Europe', he was revolted by the serf-like living conditions they were forced to endure. Holding these victims of Nazi racism responsible for the miseries the Nazis had imposed on them, he looked with horror at their half-ruined homes. They were 'dirty, with shreds of curtains at the windows, filthy . . . It feels as if we attract lice and fleas merely by walking through the streets. In the Jewish quarters it stinks so much that we have to blow our noses and spit out in order to get rid of the inhaled dirt.'[36]

Once on the Russian battlefield, this generalized revulsion merged toxically with an awed outrage at the obduracy of the enemy soldiers, which he described variously and repeatedly as 'cunning', 'devious' and 'deceitful'. Heinrici was incensed by the fact that instead of surrendering to superior might, they hid behind trees and in foxholes, from where 'they shoot every German from behind'. In punishment for this egregious tactic, he noted coolly, 'our men have cleaned up among them on various occasions, without mercy'; and since 'the Russian was like a beast towards our injured soldiers', he was content to observe that 'our men shot and beat to death everything in brown uniforms . . . with the result that hecatombs of people lose [sic] their lives'.[37] His dispassionate account of such atrocities – in marked contrast to the paternal concern he showed towards his own men – was a measure of how swiftly and how far Barbarossa had descended into barbarism.

While other commanders similarly either averted their gaze or acquiesced in these outrages, a few – at least in the early days – sought to stop them. General Joachim Lemelsen, serving under Guderian as the commander of 42nd Panzer Corps, was appalled by the brutality of his own men. On 25 June he issued them with a formal rebuke: 'I have observed that senseless shootings of both POWs and civilians have taken place. A Russian soldier who has been taken prisoner while wearing uniform and after he put up a brave fight, has the right to decent treatment.'[38] When this made little impact, he tried again: 'in spite of my instructions . . . still more shootings of POWs and deserters have been observed, conducted in an irresponsible, senseless and criminal manner. This is murder! The German Wehrmacht is waging this war against Bolshevism, not against the Russian people.' He had been not only dismayed by the barbarism but also alarmed by its consequences, noting that 'scenes of countless bodies of soldiers lying on the roads, clearly killed by a shot through the head at point-blank range, without their weapons and with their hands raised, will quickly spread in the enemy's Army'.[39]

But Lemelsen's authority – like that of his peers who held a similar view – had been fatally undermined by OKW's own collusion in the murderous means by which the Nazis had elected to conduct their 'war of extermination' against Bolshevism, which Hitler had outlined in a meeting with his generals on 30 March. After several iterations these had been enshrined in the Führer's notorious Commissar Order of 6 June, which stated:

> In the struggle against Bolshevism, we must not assume that the enemy's conduct will be based on principles of humanity or of international law. In particular, hate-inspired, cruel, and inhumane treatment of prisoners can be expected on the part of *all grades of political commissars*, who are the real leaders of resistance . . . To show consideration to these elements during the struggle, or to act in accordance with international rules of law, is wrong and endangers both our own security and the rapid pacification of conquered territories . . . Political commissars have initiated barbaric, Asiatic methods of warfare. Consequently, they will be dealt with *immediately* and with maximum severity. As a matter of principle, they will be shot at once, whether captured *during operations or otherwise showing resistance*.[40]

These 'guidelines' had been an injunction, not a suggestion. Along with the Barbarossa Decree (issued by the Wehrmacht High Command three weeks earlier), which specified the jurisdiction of martial law and 'special measures' to be taken by the troops, the Commissar Order authorized murder as a weapon of war. Only a handful of senior generals found the courage to express their disquiet at such measures. Among these was the commander of Army Group Centre, Field Marshal Bock. 'It is so worded,' he noted in relation to the Barbarossa Order, 'that it virtually gives every soldier the right to shoot at – from in front or behind – any Russian he takes to be – or claims that he takes to be – a guerrilla. The order rules out any constraint towards punishment of any offences in this regard.'[41] He raised his concern with the army's commander-in-chief, Brauchitsch, who – true to his pusillanimous character – reassured him that such orders were not incompatible with the prevailing regulations under which a soldier was answerable to a military court for his actions on and off the battlefield. Instead of pressing his point, Bock seized on this comforting interpretation with alacrity. Withdrawing his objections, he thereby joined his fellow generals by giving his tacit consent to what Ian Kershaw has aptly described as the 'premeditated barbarism'[42] that was unleashed on the peoples of the Soviet Union.

Heinz Guderian was to claim subsequently that Hitler's Commissar Order was never sent to him by Bock. For this reason, he asserted, it was 'never carried out by my troops'.[43] As Lemelsen could have testified, this was untrue. Yet, notwithstanding his dismay at the excesses of his men, even Lemelsen felt obliged to qualify his rebuke to them with the reminder that 'The Führer's instruction calls for ruthless action against Bolshevism and any kind of partisans! People who have been clearly identified as such should be taken aside and shot only by an order of an officer.'[44] In attempting to conceal these extrajudicial killings beneath a veneer of military discipline, commanders like Lemelsen − reluctantly or not − were, as the historian Omer Bartov has noted, 'simultaneously engaged in furnishing them with arguments lifted directly from Hitler's ideological arsenal as a means to motivate them in battle and make them believe that the murders they were ordered to carry out were an unavoidable existential and moral necessity'.[45] Pumped up with battlefield adrenalin, Hitler's brutalized soldiers were, in any case, unlikely to be deterred from dispensing their own summary 'justice', especially when they knew that they were unlikely to be detected or punished.

On a significantly smaller but equally barbarous scale, extrajudicial killings by the Germans were reciprocated by the Red Army. Wounded men were frequently executed to save the trouble of treating them; likewise those who refused to co-operate under interrogation. These casual murders, along with revenge killings, became so commonplace as barely to merit comment in official Soviet reports. In a mirror image of the prevailing attitude among Wehrmacht commanders, General Mikhail Potapov, the Commander-in-Chief of the Soviet 5th Army, serving in Ukraine, casually signed off a report dated 30 June which stated, 'It has frequently occurred that Red Army soldiers and commanders embittered by the cruelties of the Fascist thieves . . . do not take any German soldiers and officers prisoner but shoot them on the spot.'[46]

11. Stalin's Rallying Cry

As his panzer divisions sped eastwards, Guderian hastened from one to another of them, chivvying them on to ever greater efforts. Deliberately taking risks that few of his peers (with the exception of Rommel in North Africa) would contemplate, he frequently put his life in danger. On 24 June, as he was driven to the town of Slonim to meet up with the 17th Panzer Division, Guderian stumbled on a firefight between a Russian infantry unit and one of the 17th's artillery batteries. 'I joined in this action and by firing the machine-gun in my armoured command vehicle succeeded in dislodging the enemy from his position. I was then able to drive on,' he wrote with the self-regarding bravado that this buccaneering commander could not resist.[1]

When he arrived at the 17th Panzer Division's headquarters, Guderian joined its commander, General Hans-Jürgen von Arnim, Lemelsen, the Corps Commander, and a group of their subordinates.

> While we were discussing the situation there was a sudden outburst of lively rifle and machine-gun fire in our rear; our view of the road from Białystok was blocked by a burning lorry, so we were in ignorance of what was going on until two Russian tanks appeared out of the smoke. They were attempting to force their way into Slonim, with cannons and machine-guns blazing, and were pursued by German Panzer IVs which were also firing heavily.[2]

Catching sight of this gathering, both Soviet tanks opened fire: 'We were immediately subjected to a rain of shells, which, fired at such extremely close range, both deafened and blinded us for a few moments.' They threw themselves to the ground but a commanding officer was killed and another wounded. Guderian was unscathed. The Russian tanks drove on into the town, where they were destroyed.

Later that afternoon, after issuing instructions to maintain the forward momentum, Guderian left Slonim to return to his headquarters. Almost at once he ran into a Russian infantry unit on the edge of the city: 'I ordered my driver, who was next to me, to go full-speed ahead and we drove straight through the Russians; they were so surprised by this unexpected encounter that they did not even have time to fire their guns.' Guderian was flattered to discover that he must have been recognized as he noted with satisfaction that 'the Russian press later announced my death; I felt bound to inform them of their mistake by means of the German wireless'. Guderian's self-regard was boundless as was his ability persuasively to exaggerate his own role as a pioneer in the development of modern tank warfare. However, his aggressive attitude and personal courage on the battlefield gave him a degree of operational independence, influence and authority that, to their chagrin, was denied his peers.

The Soviet forces were in disarray but pockets of resistance abounded. Two days after the first panzers crossed the border, the army's chief of staff, Franz Halder, was driven to note, 'The enemy is making a stand almost everywhere in the border area. Our troops do not fully grasp this because resistance was disorganized . . . there are still substantial enemy forces broken up in smaller groups . . . There are no signs of an operational withdrawal by the enemy.'[3]

The relentless German bombardment nonetheless took a severe toll, pushing the Soviet troops up to and sometimes beyond the limits of human endurance. On 25 June the chief of staff of the 4th Army, Colonel Leonid Sandalov, reported that several of his divisions had been so battered by Guderian's tanks that they 'no longer had combat capability'. When his front-line commanders strove to persuade their men, who were 'demoralized and not showing stubbornness in defence',[4] to hold their collective nerve they were frequently ignored. Some panicked.

The poet Konstantin Simonov, serving as a war correspondent, watched as a terrified soldier fled down the Minsk highway, shrieking 'Run! The Germans have surrounded us. We're finished.' An officer shouted, 'Shoot him, shoot that panic-monger!' When a volley of shots failed to arrest the would-be deserter, a captain 'jumped out in his path, and trying to hold him, grasped his rifle. It went off, and, frightened still more by this shot, the fugitive, like a hunted animal, turned round and with his bayonet rushed the captain. The latter took out his pistol and shot him. Three or four men silently dragged the body off the road.'[5]

The Wehrmacht had a carefully planned and well-rehearsed battlefield tactic for breaking the Red Army's resistance. Advancing at speed, Panzer Groups 2 and 3, supported by infantry and artillery, were to break through the Soviet defences with flanking attacks designed to trap the Soviet divisions inside an ever-tightening noose until they were militarily asphyxiated and forced to surrender. This operation depended on close co-operation and co-ordination between the various attacking forces. However, the speed with which the panzers advanced became a source of growing friction between OKH in Berlin and the commanders on the ground. Both Guderian's Panzer Group 2 and Hoth's Panzer Group 3 advanced so rapidly that the supporting infantry divisions – travelling by truck, on foot and with horses – soon fell far behind.

Bock faced a dilemma. His instinct was to allow the panzers to press forward as fast as possible but, as he noted on 25 June, the 'Führer is debating whether . . . the encircled area will be so large that our forces will be insufficient to destroy the trapped Russians or force them to surrender'. Later that day he was instructed by Halder to reduce the area of the encirclement from that which they had previously agreed. This was bound to slow the panzers' advance and, in Bock's judgement, would give the enemy precious time to regroup. 'I am furious,' he noted; 'the order significantly narrowed the army's area of attack'. He was still seething the following morning when Brauchitsch arrived from Berlin: 'I was still so annoyed by the order to close the pocket prematurely, that when he congratulated me I replied gruffly, "I doubt there's anything left inside now!" '[6]

Bock's anger highlighted a persistent tension in the Army High Command's approach: there was the urge, on the one hand, to press on towards Moscow as fast as possible but, on the other, to capture or kill as many Soviet troops as could be netted by encirclement. The theory of kettling the enemy in pockets was clear enough. As the historian Robert Kershaw has noted, 'the centres of resistance were bypassed, overtaken and ringed by panzers and motorized infantry until the pocket "killers", the marching infantry divisions, came up with heavy artillery to reduce them.'[7] Impatience and a lack of co-ordination between different branches of the Ostheer (the Army of the East) meant that, in practice, these operational principles were often stress-tested to the point of destruction. Nonetheless, when they worked, they were devastating.

As it happened, both Halder and Brauchitsch sympathized with Army

Group Centre's frustration. As they still had the authority to bypass what Halder described disparagingly as the Führer's 'old refrain . . . [that] we are operating too far in depth', the chief of staff instructed Bock to close an 'inner ring' around Białystok but allowed him to press on eastwards to establish a far larger 'outer ring' of encirclement around Minsk, 240 kilometres further towards Moscow. In this way, they hoped to meet Hitler's strictures without squandering the advantages to be secured by the speed of the panzer onslaught.

As the smaller noose tightened around Białystok, General Boldin did his best to mount the counter-offensive ordered by Pavlov. As he had warned, it proved to be an impossible task. The remnants of the 10th Army had been sliced up by the panzers and had all but run out of ammunition; the troops, subjected to a ceaseless bombardment by the Luftwaffe, were drained of energy. The last operational tank corps – under the command of General Mikhail Hatskilevich – was effectively immobilized. An agitated Hatskilevich arrived at Boldin's field headquarters with a bleak message: 'We are firing our last shells. Once we've done that, we shall have to destroy the tanks.' Boldin replied, 'Yes. I do not see what else we can do.'[8]

With virtually every corps and division under his command now surrounded, Boldin's only hope of survival was to break out of the 'inner ring' in which they were trapped. The commander seized the initiative. Ordering his generals, officers and men to split into small groups, he instructed them to find their own means of escape from the tightening noose. Boldin managed to steer his own unit into the no-man's land beyond the Białystok encirclement but well shy of the panzers' forward units. As they skirted the German lines, they were joined by other units that had also found a way of escape into the vastness of the Belorussian forest. Like a military pied piper, Boldin gradually accumulated a bedraggled following of 1,600 exhausted men, whose morale sank even lower when they picked up Nazi propaganda leaflets which read, 'Moscow has surrendered. Any further resistance is useless. Surrender to victorious Germany.' Boldin had rare qualities of leadership – formidable self-confidence, personal courage, a clear mind and a resolute will to succeed. Against all the odds, he somehow managed to galvanize his followers to join him in an epic attempt to reach the city of Smolensk.[9]

By 28 June, Guderian's panzers had advanced from Brest-Litovsk to seize Minsk, the Western Front's former headquarters. Pavlov had already fled the city, withdrawing 180 kilometres east to set up a new operations base in the forest outside the city of Mogilev. In a state of near panic, he had contacted Moscow to report that 'up to 1,000 tanks are enveloping Minsk from the north-west; there is no way to oppose them'.[10] With his entire front in disarray, he now instructed every division under his command to withdraw. In the absence of telephones and radios, Pavlov attempted to deliver this instruction to his front-line commanders by means of an elderly biplane (which was swiftly shot down), and then by a succession of armoured cars (all of which were also destroyed). Eventually, two intrepid liaison officers managed to parachute into what remained of the 10th Army's command centre, where they were at once arrested under suspicion of spying for the Germans. Unhappily, the 10th Army's cipher clerks were unable to read the orders the two officers had brought from Pavlov as the codes had just been changed and had yet to reach this benighted outpost. The two officers were shot on the spot.[11]

Exasperated and demoralized, Pavlov decided he should head closer to the front to find out for himself what was happening. It was a desultory effort that yielded nothing of note. He returned to Mogilev in time to welcome a delegation from Moscow headed by General Andrei Yeremenko, who had been summoned from his Siberian command for the purpose. Yeremenko arrived on 29 June while Pavlov was eating breakfast. Looking anxiously at his guest, Pavlov asked, 'What fate brings you here? Are you staying long?' In reply, Yeremenko said nothing but handed him a piece of paper. This informed him he had been removed from his command forthwith and that Yeremenko was there to replace him. Looking bewildered, Pavlov asked, 'And just where am I going?' Yeremenko replied, 'The People's Commissar [for Defence, Timoshenko] has ordered you to Moscow.'

Pavlov became voluble in his own defence, complaining with some justification that the collapse of his front-line forces had been caused in large part by 'the tardy receipt of the order to put the troops on combat alert'. However, he conceded that 'the stupefying strikes of the enemy caught our troops unawares. We were not prepared for battle. We were living peacefully, training in camps and on ranges. Therefore, we sustained heavy losses.'[12] Such unpalatable facts would carry no weight in

Moscow, where on the same day Stalin was railing against 'the monstrous crime' committed by Pavlov's armies in failing to withstand the German onslaught, adding ominously that 'those responsible must lose their heads'.[13]

That afternoon, flanked by four of his most powerful henchmen in the Politburo – Molotov, Georgy Malenkov, Beria and Mikoyan – Stalin strode into the defence commissar's office to confront Timoshenko and Zhukov. Neither general was able to give a coherent account of the unfolding catastrophe. Incensed, Stalin turned on Zhukov and spat, 'What kind of chief of staff panics as soon as the fighting starts, loses contact with his forces and represents nothing and commands nobody?' Even Zhukov was crushed by the savagery of Stalin's onslaught. It was enough to cause the chief of staff to break down in tears and leave the room. A little later he was persuaded to return for a rather more sober assessment of a crisis that none of those present knew how to contain. On his way out of the building, Stalin turned to Mikoyan and the others and, according to all of them, said one or another version of 'Lenin founded our state, and we've fucked it up!'[14]

Stalin was evidently close to despair. He retreated to Kuntsevo to be alone. Exhausted and humiliated by a failure of judgement for which even his most loyal acolytes could hardly avoid holding him responsible, he isolated himself at the dacha, holding no meetings and answering no phone calls for a full twenty-four hours. Whether he feared that the Politburo would remove him from office or, more cunningly, had decided that this was the best way to test their loyalty, was never to be clear. Either way, reassurance soon arrived in the form of a deputation from the Politburo. 'Why have you come?' he asked them anxiously, as though they were about to take him into custody. Molotov answered for his comrades, saying, 'I tell you here and now that if some idiot tried to turn me against you, I'd see him damned. We're asking you to come back to work.' Stalin apparently responded by saying, 'Yes, but think about it. Can I live up to people's hopes any more? Can I lead the country to final victory? There may be more deserving candidates.'

This unlikely display of humility was an effective ploy which at once elicited the response he must have craved. As the others nodded in a display of fervent agreement, Voroshilov said, 'I believe I shall be voicing the unanimous opinion. There's none more worthy.' Molotov then said that his comrades had discussed the creation of a new State Defence Committee, the GKO.* At this, Beria, one of its architects, stepped forward to confirm that they wanted the new body – which was to have supreme authority for the conduct of the war – to be led by Stalin.[15] This confirmation of his undisputed leadership made the dictator more powerful than ever. With only Molotov, Voroshilov, Malenkov and Beria as its other members, the decisions of this inner cabinet were not open to challenge. Its terms of reference were explicit: 'All citizens and all Party, Soviet, Komsomol† and military bodies [are to] carry out the decisions and provisions of the State Committee for Defence without question.'[16] The 'dictatorship of the proletariat' was now formally vested in one man and, with his status thus reaffirmed, he was more than ready to obey the summons.

On 3 July Stalin finally addressed the Soviet people, who crowded around loudspeakers in offices, factories and civic squares across the Soviet Union to listen, many of whom were evidently 'nervous, and often frightened and bewildered'.[17] Hitherto, the instigator of the Great Purge and the Great Terror had inspired a distant awe and admiration among the masses, who were largely unaware of the true horror for which he had been responsible. Now, though, he adopted a tone they had never heard before. They were astonished when, forswearing wooden communist clichés, he addressed them less as a domineering Bolshevik than a brotherly patriot. 'Comrades, citizens, brothers and sister, fighters of our Army and Navy! I am speaking to you, my friends,' he began in a speech that was devoid of ideological platitudes but, in words that carried an echo of Churchill's masterly 'We shall fight on the beaches' speech following the calamity of Dunkirk, did not shrink from acknowledging that they faced 'a life-and-death struggle' against a 'wicked and perfidious enemy'. To defeat these 'cruel and merciless' invaders, the entire Soviet population would need 'to fight for every inch of Soviet soil, fight to the last drop of blood, for our towns and villages'.[18] In comfortingly calm tones, he concluded by reassuring his listeners that they were not alone; that theirs was not merely a defensive struggle but a war of liberation

---

* In full, Gosudarstvenny Komitet Oborony, established jointly by the Praesidium of the Supreme Council, the Council of the People's Commissars and the Communist Party's Central Committee on 30 June 1941.
† The All-Union Leninist Young Communist League.

for all Europe in which (somewhat prematurely) he claimed that Britain and the United States would stand shoulder to shoulder with the Soviet people: 'Our arrogant foe will soon discover that our forces are beyond number . . . Forward – to Victory.'[19]

By almost every contemporary account from every standpoint, the effect of Stalin's words was transformative. Like other leaders facing similar crises, he inevitably glossed over the true scale of the military disaster but he had spoken with the clarity and conviction of a leader in whom the nation could place its trust. Only the most jaundiced or defeatist citizen could doubt their leader's belief that eventual victory was not just possible but inevitable. Konstantin Simonov, by no means a communist sycophant, wrote:

> I felt that was a speech hiding nothing, concealing nothing, relating the truth to the end, and telling it the only way it could be told in such circumstances. That made me glad. It seemed to me that to tell such bitter truth in such circumstances meant to bear witness to one's strength . . . It pleased me and touched my heart to hear the address 'My friends!' This had not been heard in our speeches for a long time.[20]

Wandering the streets of the capital, the British journalist Alexander Werth detected 'a confident, determined look on all faces' as they pored over the text of the speech, which had been reprinted in *Pravda* and widely distributed to be read out in the workplace or stuck on walls and windows. Posters sprang up across the city. They were not subtle but effective: one portrayed a Russian tank 'crushing a giant crab with a Hitler moustache'; another, 'a Red Soldier ramming his bayonet down the throat of a giant Hitler-faced rat'.[21]

Stalin's broadcast had burnished his image as a patriot, but behind the comradely carapace the dictator was as ruthless as ever. His anger at the collapse of the Western Front had already hardened into an unforgiving urge to find scapegoats for his own fatal errors of judgement. Pavlov, by now a broken man, was first in line. On 4 July he was arrested and, along with eight of his senior commanders, charged with forming an 'anti-military conspiracy' which had 'betrayed the interests of the Motherland'. The military tribunal did not allow itself to be sidetracked by legal niceties but, after a summary trial, found the officers guilty of 'lack of resolve, panic mongering, disgraceful cowardice . . . and fleeing in terror in the face of an impudent enemy'.[22] The 'conspirators' were duly sentenced to death and executed. In a characteristically vindictive act that ensured that his family could not escape his disgrace or inherit his pension, Pavlov was also stripped of his military rank. For good measure his property was confiscated as well. It was his unfortunate distinction to be the first but very far from the last commander to pay the ultimate penalty for failing to conjure victory out of defeat on the Barbarossa front line.

Such punitive measures could do nothing of course to halt the German advance. Within days of Stalin's broadcast, Bock's two panzer groups – Hoth attacking from the north and Guderian from the south – had not only advanced more than 350 kilometres from their starting positions but had trapped the bulk of the Red Army's 3rd, 4th, 10th and 13th armies inside an oval pocket that covered thousands of hectares between Białystok and Minsk. So rapid was the speed of their advance that – as Hitler had warned – the German infantry fell a long way behind the panzers. As a result, Bock lacked the numbers required to seal the pocket hermetically. Although several thousand men escaped, most elected to stand and fight. Instead of raising their arms in surrender, the Soviet gun crews remained obstinately in their bunkers, firing at the encircling troops until they ran out of ammunition. Bock was taken aback by their fortitude. 'In spite of the heaviest fire and the employment of every means the crews refuse to give up,' he noted, adding grimly, 'Each fellow has to be killed one at a time.' As for the thousands whom he presumed to be hiding in the forests 'far behind our front', he comforted himself with the thought that they had only postponed the inevitable as they would be forced to emerge 'when they get hungry'.[23]

By 8 July the battles in and around the Białystok–Minsk pocket were all but over. Twenty of the Western Front's forty-four Soviet divisions had been annihilated while the remaining twenty-four were so depleted – with up to 30 per cent of their original complement destroyed – as to be incapable of offensive action. Of the 671,000 men who had faced the initial German thrust, some 420,000 had been killed or wounded or were missing in action. The survivors – hungry, bedraggled and exhausted – were rounded up to be force-marched into captivity, where they awaited new horrors as prisoners of war in a conflict that Hitler had decreed should not be constrained by any of the prevailing international rules of engagement.

The panzers did not pause but pressed on towards Smolensk. For the infantry, it was a wearisome advance. Their starting positions were already 600 kilometres behind them but Moscow was still the same distance away. The long daily marches interspersed with bitter fighting were starting to exact a heavy toll. A German war correspondent, Arthur Grimm, who was attached to one of Bock's infantry divisions, described a landscape that 'stretches flat ahead with wavelike undulations. There are few trees and little woodland. Trees are covered in dust, leaves a dull colour in the brilliant sunshine. The countryside is a brown grey green with occasional yellow expanses of corn. Over everything hangs a brown-grey pall of smoke, rising from knocked-out tanks and burning villages.'[24]

Weighed down by heavy backpacks under a relentless sun, the soldiers plodded across the bleak Russian steppe, sweat pouring from their brows, muscles aching, feet blistering. To march from dawn to dusk for up to fifty kilometres a day was gruelling for the infantry and for the supply columns – laden with medical supplies, spare parts, fuel, oats and hay for the horses – that followed behind them. It was a logistical enterprise of great complexity that depended on open roads and an efficient train service. The advance would have been greatly hampered if the troops had been forced to rely exclusively on food supplies from the rear rather than the vast quantities of meat and grain that – in defiance of the rules of warfare – they stole from the farms of peasants through whose lands they passed.

The more deeply Hitler's armies penetrated into Russia, the longer and more vulnerable to adverse weather and sabotage these routes would become. Under the clear skies and in the baking heat of the Russian summer, though, that was not yet apparent. The men just kept on marching. 'Our feet sank into the sand and dirt, puffing up into the air so that it rose and clung to us. The horses coughing in the dust produced a pungent odour. The loose sand was nearly as tiring for the horses as deep mud would have been. The men marched in silence, coated with dust, with dry throats and lips,' noted Siegfried Knappe, an artillery officer riding alongside the horse-drawn gun carriages that carried the heavy guns.[25] The monotony was unrelenting: 'As we marched, low hills would emerge from the horizon ahead of us and then slowly sink back into the horizon behind us. It almost seemed that the same hill kept appearing in front of us. Kilometre after kilometre. Everything seemed to blur into uniform grey because of the vastness and sameness of everything.'[26] The men trudged three abreast, heads down, looking to neither left nor right, not talking or singing, but seeming to retreat into their own private worlds within which they might insulate themselves from an alien and hostile land.

As an officer, Knappe was privileged to ride on horseback and, from this vantage point, he was not entirely unappreciative of the vastness of the country that he presumed would soon belong to the Reich. As a student of the natural world, he noted that

> in some forested places, the earth was squeaky and springy beneath our boots. The leaves on the surface were little and brittle, but underneath lay leaves that had withered many years before and created a brown spongy mass in which many tiny insects scurried . . . The living trees usually smelled fresh and damp, and the odour of the dead trees was dry and rich.

Out in the open, he watched yellow butterflies and blue-back beetles while grass snakes 'rustled through the grass, practically invisible . . . Grasshoppers were plentiful and could not seem to tell a moving soldier from a stationary tree, often hitching free rides. Swarms of gnats plagued us, and darting flies were everywhere.'[27]

At midday, the men would halt for a meal, usually of stewed vegetables and whatever meat the catering corps had been able to pillage along the way, all cooked in a horse-drawn canteen. When they had eaten, they were allowed to lie down and rest. Most fell instantly asleep: a jumble of bodies spread-eagled on the bare earth beside the road. According to Heinrich Haape, a surgeon serving in the 18th Infantry Regiment, this brief respite was of little value: 'The hour and a half's sleep had done more harm than good. It had not been easy to wake the dog-tired men. Our bones were cold, muscles stiff and painful and our feet were swollen. We pulled on our field boots only with great difficulty.'[28]

One evening, Knappe was summoned to have dinner with his divisional commanding officer, Major General Helfrid von Studnitz, whom he held in high regard as an administrator and intellectual. After asking after the morale of Knappe's men and the condition of the horses under his command, Studnitz said, 'How do you think the campaign has gone?' Knappe replied, 'Great.' Studnitz paused before saying, 'I was in Russia during the last war. I have experienced the Russian winter. It is savage, like nothing we have ever experienced. It will come, and it will come soon. We are just in this little part of Russia. We have a vast country ahead of us, and if we do not take Moscow before the weather turns bitter cold, I worry about what will happen.'[29]

While Guderian's panzers accelerated towards Smolensk, Army Group North, under the command of General Leeb, made similar progress. Within three weeks of the invasion his panzer divisions had advanced 450 kilometres, overrunning Lithuania, Latvia and Estonia before reaching the Leningrad *oblast* (province) on the southern outskirts of the city. Overwhelmed by the ferocity of this blitzkrieg, General Kuznetsov's Northwestern Front collapsed. His three armies retreated in chaos, losing 90,000 men and more than 1,000 tanks and 1,000 aircraft in the process. As a result, the armies under General Popov on the Northern Front came under intense pressure.[30] Within six weeks, the totemic city, founded by Peter the Great in 1703, would be under siege.

The progress made by Rundstedt's Army Group South was less dramatic but no less threatening. It was an arduous campaign which led through difficult terrain to the south of the Pripet Marshes, a 270,000-square-kilometre area of rivers, wetlands and forests covering most of southern Belorussia and north-western Ukraine. Extending 230 kilometres from north to south, the marshes were virtually impenetrable except on foot. Army Group South was confronted by much stiffer resistance from General Mikhail Kirponos's Southwestern Front than Leeb had to face in the Baltic. The Stavka – the Soviet High Command – had presumed that any attack against Russia would be launched on this front. Not only did Kirponos have the four strongest and best equipped armies in the Red Army but he was also far abler – bolder, more imaginative and more flexible – than either Popov or Kuznetsov. Despite making a number of tactical errors, he succeeded in launching a powerful counter-attack around the city of Dubno, 430 kilometres west of Kiev. In what was to prove the largest such battle of the Second World War, some 3,000 Soviet and more than 700 German tanks pounded one another in a confused swirl along a seventy-kilometre front for seven days before Rundstedt's panzers eventually broke through Russian lines. It was a devastating setback: Kirponos had lost more than 241,000 men, 172,000 of whom were killed, captured or missing in action, as well as 800 tanks, 6,000 guns and mortars, and more than 1,200 aircraft. The way was now open for Army Group South to accelerate towards the Ukrainian capital, Kiev – and beyond that, to the Caucasus and Stalingrad.[31]

By 3 July Halder was so elated by the progress of all three army groups that he felt able to note – on the same day that Stalin broadcast his rallying cry to the Soviet people – that it was 'probably no overstatement to say that the Russian campaign has been won in the space of two weeks'.[32] The speed with which the invaders had advanced and the scale of destruction they had inflicted on the Soviet forces appeared to justify his hubris. Although (according to his calculations) the Ostheer had lost more than 54,000 men, including 11,822 killed, 38,809 wounded, and 3,961 missing, the Red Army had fared far worse: 750,000 losses, of whom 590,000 were dead, wounded, or missing, as well as 10,000 tanks and almost 4,000 aircraft.[33] In a little over a fortnight, the Soviet Union had suffered a devastating series of defeats. It was an epic humiliation but, though it might have seemed so, *Götterdämmerung* it was not.

12. A Shaky Alliance

The leader of the military mission in Moscow, General Mason-MacFarlane, and the British ambassador who accompanied him, Stafford Cripps, were given an unusually warm welcome when their Catalina flying boat docked in the Russian port of Archangel on 26 June 1941 at the end of a seventeen-hour journey from the Shetland Isles. After a fine dinner and a comfortable night aboard a waiting yacht, they were flown to Moscow in the defence commissar's personal aircraft. This was a signal honour which did not escape Cripps's notice. He was even more gratified when Molotov – who had cold-shouldered him for almost a year – asked to see him twice within a day of his arrival in the capital. 'The atmosphere is so different here that it is difficult to realize it is the same place politically,' he noted happily.[1]

Nonetheless it soon became clear that Moscow sought what neither Mason-MacFarlane nor Cripps was authorized to deliver: a sustained supply of military hardware and, no less importantly, a joint commitment by both governments to refrain from making a separate peace agreement with Germany – the thought of which, despite Churchill's broadcast less than a week earlier, still troubled a suspicious Kremlin. The underlying tensions that had bedevilled Anglo-Soviet relations since the revolution still hovered only a little below the surface of the fragile bonhomie of their new relationship.

On 29 June Zhukov laid his military cards on the table. His detailed shopping list included '3,000 fully equipped fighters, a similar number of bombers, 20,000 anti-aircraft guns and technical information on numerous secret devices'.[2] Mason-MacFarlane – who, like Cripps, felt instinctively that the Red Army was likely to perform far better than the gloom-mongers were still predicting – forwarded Zhukov's demands to London. Judging by the response of the chiefs of staff, he might have sent them a bowl of cold porridge. He was told that the only item on Zhukov's agenda that could be spared for the time being was one – only one – night fighter. Meanwhile, he was to keep the talks going but to make no commitments.

On 8 July Cripps was granted an hour with Stalin. It was only their second meeting and, on this occasion, the ambassador found him 'much more friendly and frank' than the last time. 'It is a relief', he noted, 'to be able to talk to someone who can say what he thinks and whose word you know is the last word.'[3] Cripps's ostensible purpose was to hand over a copy of a letter from Churchill in which the prime minister reiterated, 'We shall do everything to help you that time, geography and our growing resources allow.'[4] Beyond that there was no tangible commitment but rather a reminder that Bomber Command was at full stretch in Britain's efforts to obliterate major targets in Germany. As Stalin was far too shrewd not to have noticed, the prime minister might just as well have written 'We can do very little to help you. We are under severe threat ourselves but we hope you realize that by bombing Germany – which we have to do for our own sakes – we will also help your cause. I hope you fight with all your might. Your efforts on the battlefield are of inestimable value to us.'

Stalin concealed his disappointment, merely telling Cripps that the Russians 'were under extremely heavy strain' and that he needed a very public agreement with Britain to ensure that there could be no separate Anglo-German peace settlement. Cripps had already pressed Churchill directly

> to demonstrate our desire to help even at some risk to ourselves if necessary ... They realize what their fighting means to us and not unnaturally they look to us to do something practical to reciprocate the help they are giving ... We are in danger of encouraging the collapse if we do not fully and frankly give the Russians everything possible to help and strengthen their resistance.[5]

Now, he transmitted Stalin's desire for a joint declaration to London. Whitehall was profoundly sceptical but Churchill overrode the naysayers to jump at Stalin's proposal. Since the Soviet leader sought little more than a broad commitment to a common purpose, it was in effect a cost-free means of encouraging the Russians to fight Britain's war. Telegramming his agreement to Stalin, Churchill summoned a special meeting of the War Cabinet, which duly endorsed his decision. On 12 July, after a further flurry of messages, Molotov and Cripps signed what became the first major agreement between London and Moscow since the formal establishment of the Soviet Union in 1921.* It was a turning point. Cripps was so elated that when Molotov offered him a celebratory drink, he accepted at once: 'I definitely and ostentatiously broke my teetotalism for the occasion. So champagne was brought in and I took one large gulp of it as a toast to Down with Hitler.'[6]

Three days later Churchill announced the Anglo-Soviet 'Agreement for Joint Action' in the House of Commons. It was, he declared,

> a solemn agreement . . . to undertake the war against Hitlerite Germany to the utmost of our strength, to help each other as much as possible in every way and not to make peace separately . . . The Agreement . . . cannot fail to exercise a highly beneficial and potent influence on the future of the war. It is of course an Alliance, and the Russian people are our allies.[7]

It was somewhat stretching the terms of their 'Agreement' to describe it as an 'Alliance', since it entailed no military commitment by Britain to the Soviet Union. Nonetheless it served its purpose both by humouring Stalin and by appeasing British public opinion, which strongly favoured such an initiative.

To demonstrate Britain's newfound solidarity, Churchill knew that a gesture was needed. In a note to the First Lord of the Admiralty and the First Sea Lord, he proposed that the Royal Navy conduct a joint exercise with the Soviet navy. To win their support, he once again underlined the benefits that would accrue to Britain from such a boost to Soviet self-esteem. 'The advantage we should reap if the Russians could keep in the field and go on with the war, at any rate until the winter closes in, is measureless,' he wrote, adding, 'These people have shown themselves worth backing, and we must make sacrifices and take risks . . . to maintain their morale.'[8]

As he surveyed the collapse of his armies before the Nazi blitzkrieg, Stalin could also take comfort from the United States, where the White House was in no doubt about the need to keep the Russians 'in the field'. Roosevelt's carefully constructed rapprochement with the Soviet Union had come to an abrupt end with the Molotov–Ribbentrop Pact. Even so,

---

* Britain had signed a trade agreement with the Bolshevik state in 1921, the first of its kind between the Soviet Union and any Western state.

though mindful of the electorate's ideological and moral aversion to Bol-shevism, he had been careful not to isolate Moscow entirely. Though he had described the Soviet invasion of Finland as a 'dreadful rape' he had resisted the pressure to cut off either diplomatic or commercial ties in the fear that it would drive Moscow even further into Berlin's embrace. How-ever, even after the Nazi invasion, he was still constrained to move cautiously towards a détente with Stalin. Whereas it cost Churchill little to promise 'whatever help we can' to the Soviet Union, Roosevelt felt obliged to hedge, saying nothing in public about the invasion until two days after-wards, when he felt confident enough to make a similar commitment, albeit in answer to a correspondent's question at a press conference rather than in a direct address to the nation. And when pressed by a reporter as to whether the defence of the Soviet Union was essential to the security of the United States, he sidestepped, replying opaquely, 'Oh, ask me a different type of question – such as "How old is Anna?"' (his eldest daughter).[9]

The president's caution sprang in part from his reluctance to alienate the voters, who as yet showed no enthusiasm for offering support to a com-munist dictatorship, and in part from the fact that the military establishment in Washington shared Whitehall's consensus that the Red Army would rapidly collapse under the German onslaught. However, this did not mean that he was content to sit on the sidelines. He not only believed strongly that to support Britain effectively entailed supporting the Soviet Union but, more pertinently, he was convinced that America's own security was entwined with the Soviet Union's ability to defeat the Nazis. Roosevelt's assessment was undoubtedly influenced by his former ambassador to the Soviet Union, Joseph E. Davies, who still carried weight in Washington. Davies had already made it clear that, in his judgement, the Red Army 'would amaze and surprise the world'.[10] Moreover – as Roosevelt made clear on 26 June in a letter to his close friend, Admiral William Leahy* – he was rather more optimistic about what he called 'this Russian diversion' than his advisors. 'If it is more than just that,' he wrote, 'it will mean the liberation of Europe from Nazi domination – and at the same time I do not think we will need to worry about any possibility of Russian domination.'[11]

* At that time, Leahy was serving as ambassador to Vichy France. The following year Roosevelt recalled him to Washington, where he served as his personal chief of staff and as head of the Joint Chiefs of Staff.

On 24 June, as a first step towards improving relations with Moscow, Roosevelt authorized the release of $39 million of frozen Soviet assets. The following day he declared that the Neutrality Act would no longer apply to US ships transporting supplies to Soviet ports, any more than it did to any other allied state. On 10 July, for the first time since the start of the Second World War, he summoned the Soviet ambassador, Konstantin Umansky, to inform him that $1.8 billion in supplies that had been formally requested would be delivered as soon as possible, and that the first tranche was expected to reach the Soviet Union by the end of September. In making these commitments he was more forthcoming but just as hard-headed as Churchill. 'If the Russians could hold the Germans until 1 October', he explained, 'it would be of great value in defeating Hitler since after that date no effective military operations with Russia could be carried on and the consequent tying of a number of German troops and machines for that period of time would be of great practical value in assuring the ultimate defeat of Hitler.'[12] In the event it would prove much harder to deliver the promised supplies by the end of September than the president hoped, but his public commitment to the Soviet cause mattered every bit as much to Stalin as the military hardware itself.

The Soviet leader's relationship with Churchill was pricklier by far, and for good reason. Although the prime minister had been eloquent in support of the Russian people, he was ambivalent about the means with which to demonstrate this. He was frustrated by Stalin's failure to appreciate that Britain's bombing campaign against German cities and the battles against the Axis forces in the Middle East were in themselves a means of siphoning off German resources from Barbarossa. He was also easily bruised by what he regarded as Stalin's grudging expressions of gratitude and, on occasion, his open displays of ingratitude. For his part, Stalin made little attempt to dispel the abiding belief in London that he was a brutal dictator who for more than a decade had been stimulating Bolshevik revolution in Europe until he cynically sided with the Nazis against Britain in her time of greatest peril. Stalin's cynicism irked the prime minister. As Churchill put it:

> They had given important economic aid to Nazi Germany . . . Now, having been deceived and taken by surprise, they were themselves under the flaming German sword. Their first impulse and lasting policy was to

demand all possible succour from Great Britain and her Empire, the possible partition of which between Stalin and Hitler had for the last eight months beguiled Soviet minds from the progress of German concentration in the East.[13]

Churchill's underlying resentment found a petty outlet in his refusal to allow the BBC to broadcast the 'Internationale', not least because it was not only the Soviet state anthem but also the 'marching song' of the British Communist Party. The prime ministerial edict was imposed in defiance of the fact that the anthems of every other British ally were broadcast routinely on Sunday evenings immediately before the nine o'clock news. That Britain had formed what he called an 'alliance' with the Soviet Union made no difference.

The omission of the 'Internationale' from this musical pageant was widely noticed. It bemused Maisky. Affecting to regard the decision as a 'tragicomic controversy', he noted drily that 'the hair of thousands of British Blimps stands on end when they hear it'. But when his wife rushed out of the room one evening in tears of fury when the BBC broadcast in its place a little-known Russian song, he changed his own tune to complain that Churchill's decision was an act of 'cowardice and foolishness'.[14] According to Maisky, the Minister of Information, Duff Cooper, explained that Churchill had growled, 'I am ready to do anything for Russia, but I will not allow the communists to make political capital from the "Internationale".'*

The prime minister was easily offended by Stalin. When the Soviet leader did not deign to respond either to his 22 June broadcast or to his two personal messages (in all of which he promised every support to the Russian people) for almost a month, he was mightily put out. He was further aggrieved that the reply, when it did arrive, contained an expression of gratitude that was brusque to the point of churlishness. Even more gallingly, the Soviet leader would insist on writing to demand that Britain open a second front against Germany, either in northern France or in the Arctic. At this stage in the war, with Britain still 'standing alone', neither option was even a remote possibility. On 18 July, the Soviet leader had the temerity to tell him that a second front in France 'would be popular with

---

* After he was mocked in the press and elsewhere, Churchill relented. The ban was lifted in January 1942.

the British Army, as well as with the whole population of Southern England'.[15] Churchill was outraged: Stalin was not only wrong but his interference in British affairs was unforgivable.

Offended by the presumptuous tone of Stalin's missive, Churchill was goaded into a blunt response: 'The Chiefs of Staff do not see any way of doing anything on a scale likely to be of the slightest use to you,' he wrote. Nor could he resist adding pointedly, 'You must remember that we have been fighting alone for more than a year . . . we are at the utmost strain.' However, he leavened his rebuke by advising that the British were planning a naval operation against the Germans around Russia's 'Arctic flank' and would soon be sending supplies to Archangel, which was, he wrote, 'the most we can do at the moment'.[16]

Later he reflected ruefully and bitterly on the long series of telegrams between the two leaders that now ensued:

> I received many rebuffs and only rarely a kind word . . . The Soviet Government had the impression that they were conferring a great favour on us by fighting in their own country for their own lives. The more they fought the heavier our debt became. This was not a balanced view. Two or three times in this long correspondence I had to protest in blunt language.[17]

It was, however, quite true – as Churchill was initially reluctant to acknowledge – that the more the Russians fought, the 'heavier our debt' did indeed become. He was among the many who, despite their vivid memories of the First World War, found it hard to grasp quite how bloody and barbarous the struggle for the soul of the Soviet Union had already become.

As the German panzers cut a swathe through the Soviet defences, Nikolai Moskvin, a young political commissar and a fierce patriot, had the task of sustaining the wavering morale of his beleaguered regiment, which had come under heavy fire on the Belorussian front. He hurried into the firing line to join his men. Just before his departure, he wrote in his diary on 22 June, 'I love my motherland, I will defend it to the last ounce of my strength, and I will not begrudge my life for my people.'[18] It was a widely shared sentiment that, after three weeks of death and destruction, came under severe strain. On 15 July Moskvin made plans to summon his unit to hear him read out Stalin's rallying cry to the nation (made in his radio broadcast ten days earlier), but so heavy was the German bombardment that the meeting had to be aborted. That evening, he noted gloomily, 'It is possible that we are not completely defeated yet, but the situation is extremely difficult . . . The enemy's aviation is destroying absolutely everything. The roads are littered with the bodies of our soldiers and the civilian population. Towns and villages are burning. The Germans are everywhere – in front, behind, and on our flank.'[19]

A little over a week later, by which time his regiment had been kettled inside Bock's encircling noose, he made a further attempt to stiffen morale. He was not optimistic. 'What am I to say to the boys?' he wondered, before gathering them together that evening. Whatever advice he gave himself, it was evidently inadequate. The following morning, he asked himself despairingly, 'How can I get their approval? How? Am I to say that Comrade Stalin is with us . . . ?' His chagrin was not hard to explain: soon after hearing his homily, thirteen of his men had stolen away into the surrounding forest.[20]

The retreat was chaotic across the entire front. In many instances, discipline broke down. Thousands panicked and fled. Not infrequently, young men who had been rushed to the front with little training and worn-out weapons and who were witnessing the brutality of war for the first time – maimed bodies and bloated corpses – opted in favour of a bullet in the back for desertion over the continuing agony of battle. Their commanders were unprepared for the scale or savagery of the German onslaught but had no time to draw up plans for an orderly withdrawal. Lines of communication collapsed. Spasmodic and often contradictory orders arrived from army command posts either too late or not at all. With phone lines down and without radios, neighbouring units had no means of making contact with one another. They were easy prey for a mobile, flexible and fleet-footed adversary that could surround isolated groups and pick them off at leisure. Their predicament was aggravated by an acute shortage of trucks to transport ammunition or fuel for the tanks and an absence of repair facilities for vehicles that were damaged in battle or broke down from normal wear and tear. The Luftwaffe strafed and bombed the Soviet retreating columns with impunity, their victims the more easily identifiable because – to avoid the risk of causing provocation before the invasion – commanding officers had resolutely failed to provide them with adequate camouflage.

The shambles was observed with dismay by General Ivan Fedyuninsky, commander of the 15th Rifle Corps serving on the Southwestern Front, who might have been describing any part of any front. 'Sometimes on narrow roads, bottlenecks were formed by troops, artillery, motor vehicles and field kitchens, and then Nazi planes had the time of their life . . . Often our troops could not dig in, simply because they did not even have the simplest implements . . . trenches had to be dug with helmets, since there were no spades.'[21] Although Fedyuninsky had detected 'the enormous enthusiasm and patriotic uplift' that Stalin's broadcast had aroused – lauding the way in which his message to the troops had been reinforced by the Red Army's political commissars, who explained that 'the whole Soviet people were rising like one man to fight the holy Fatherland War'[22] – the evidence was markedly less reassuring.

For the most part, it was true that the Soviet infantry – whether driven by Moskvinesque patriotism or fear of the firing squad – fought with astonishing valour, careless of their own lives. Brandishing antiquated rifles with fixed bayonets, they charged directly into the implacable precision of the German artillery, steeling themselves with mass cries of fury, as though that terrifying sound alone would silence the guns. Instead, though some German units were indeed intimidated by such ferocity and the sight of so many bayonets, they were felled by the thousand. Those who survived very often ran out of ammunition. Many units ran out of rifles. With breathtaking effrontery, Anastas Mikoyan, the Politburo member responsible for military supplies, blithely conceded later, 'We surely thought we had enough for the whole army . . .' but, thanks to his quartermasterly oversight, 'reservists going to the front ended up with no rifles at all.'[23] This oversight made no difference to his upwardly mobile status.*

---

* Anastas Mikoyan, who was deeply implicated in Stalin's rule of terror, later became foreign trade minister in the post-war Soviet regime. After Stalin's death in 1953, he became a Khrushchev loyalist, serving as first deputy premier, helping to draft the 'Secret Speech' to the 20th Party Congress in which Khrushchev denounced Stalin, and playing a prominent 'soft-power' role on the international stage. Following the Politburo coup which forced Khrushchev to step down in 1964 (and which he opposed), he re-emerged during Brezhnev's reign to become chairman of the Praesidium of the Supreme Soviet. He was forced to retire in 1965 and died thirteen years later in October 1978 at the age of eighty-two.

1. The craven and irresolute Commander-in-Chief of the Wehrmacht, Field Marshal Wilhelm Keitel, never dared to challenge Hitler openly. He survived in his post throughout the war.

2. Field Marshal Fedor von Bock, Commander-in-Chief of Army Group Centre, charged with the assault on Moscow. Within a fortnight of the invasion, he noted: 'If the Russians don't soon collapse somewhere, the objective of defeating them so badly that they are eliminated will be difficult to achieve before winter.'

3. Field Marshal Wilhelm Ritter von Leeb, Commander-in-Chief of Army Group North, led the assault on Leningrad. The siege began on 8 September and lasted for 900 days. In December, during the Wehrmacht's retreat, he defied Hitler's order to 'stand fast' and was sacked.

4. An ardent Nazi, Field Marshal Gerd von Rundstedt, Commander-in-Chief of Army Group South. His objective: the capital of the Ukraine, Kiev. In November 1941 he insisted his troops were too exhausted to press on to the Caucasus. Hitler sacked him.

5. Commander-in-Chief of the German Army, the pusillanimous Field Marshal Walther von Brauchitsch (*right*), was held in contempt by Hitler, who regarded him as a 'cowardly wretch'. The Army High Command's Chief of Staff, Franz Halder (*left*), the go-between for Hitler and the front line commanders wrote: 'Führer's interference unendurable'. But he endured it.

6. In October, General Gotthard Heinrici, commander of the 43rd Army Corps, wrote to his wife promising 'Christmas presents from Moscow', but in December he noted: 'We are going to our doom.'

7. Heinz Guderian was the Third Reich's most celebrated panzer general. Headstrong, fearless, rebellious and ambitious, he acquired mythic status. Stalin was alarmed by the exploits of a man to whom he referred as 'that villain'.

8. On the day Hitler launched Barbarossa, Joseph Goebbels, Minister of Propaganda and a fanatical Nazi, wrote: 'One can hear the breath of history. A glorious and wonderful hour has struck, when a new Empire is born.'

9. Himmler, the commander of the SS (here inspecting Soviet prisoners of war) was a principal architect of the Holocaust. He established the Einsatzgruppen (killer squads) that – in collaboration with the Wehrmacht – executed more than a million civilians during Operation Barbarossa.

10. Hans-Ulrich Rudel, a Stuka pilot, was a Nazi war hero, credited with destroying 500 tanks and 2,000 ground targets. Like so many young men in the Wehrmacht he was besotted with Hitler.

11. Defence Commissar Marshal Semyon Timoshenko (*left*) posing with General Georgy Zhukov (*right*), the Soviet Union's greatest military commander. On the eve of Operation Barbarossa, they pressed Stalin to put the Red Army on a war footing. The Soviet dictator reacted in fury: 'Do you want a war because you're not sufficiently decorated or your rank isn't high enough?'

12. Lieutenant General Konstantin Rokossovsky (*second left*), 16th Army Commander, was widely revered. With Moscow under assault, he withdrew his forces from an untenable position. Zhukov threatened to have him shot for defying orders. Rokossovsky appealed to Stalin, who reassured him of his personal support.

13. Commander-in-Chief of the Western Front, Colonel Dmitry Pavlov, was at the theatre when he was told that the German invasion had started. Paralysed by the scale of the emergency, he issued preposterous orders that exacerbated the crisis. In July, along with others, he was found guilty of 'disgraceful cowardice' and executed.

14. Marshal Kliment Voroshilov, dubbed 'the legendary Red Marshal' by Stalin, was a courageous but incompetent commander. Sacked for his inadequate defence of Leningrad, he was reprieved but held only titular authority thereafter. He drank heavily. At a Kremlin banquet in honour of the British Foreign Secretary, Anthony Eden, he slumped into Stalin's lap and had to be carried from the hall.

15. Deputy Commander of the Western Front, General Ivan Boldin was incisive and fearless. As the Germans launched Barbarossa, he phoned Timoshenko to demand an immediate military reaction. When the Defence Commissar demurred, he shouted: 'But our troops are retreating, towns are in flames, people are dying . . . Comrade Marshal, we must act'.

16. General Boris Shaposhnikov became Chief of Staff when Zhukov was sent to shore up the crumbling frontline. In November 1941, he ordered Boldin to head south from Moscow to confront Guderian, whose 'vandals' had allegedly 'dared to defile the people's holies of holies – the grave of Leo Tolstoy' at Yasnaya Polyana.

17. Foreign Affairs Commissar Maxim Litvinov, surrounded by reporters in New York in November 1933. After a genial tête-à-tête in the White House with President Roosevelt, the two men signed a concordat formally establishing diplomatic relations between their respective governments for the first time since the Bolshevik revolution.

18. Roosevelt's personal envoy to Stalin, Harry Hopkins (*left*), with the British ambassador, Sir Stafford Cripps, in Moscow, August 1941. The two men established a strong rapport. Churchill regarded Cripps, with whom he had an abrasive relationship, as an apologist for the Soviet Union.

19. Churchill with the urbane and astute Soviet ambassador Ivan Maisky, who charmed London's political and social elite. Maisky was feted by those crusading for a Second Front. One of his key tasks was to temper the animosity between Churchill and Stalin. He sometimes succeeded.

Despite the best efforts of commissars and commanding officers, morale plummeted in many units. By July, untold numbers of officers as well as men were on the run, despite the risk of being caught behind the lines by the NKVD and put before a firing squad. Nor was it only the infantry. Tank crews deserted as well. The Soviet engineers had already developed what would prove to be some of the most formidable armoured vehicles of the Second World War (including the heavy and virtually indestructible KV-1 and the lighter and faster medium T-34) but the great majority of the 15,000 tanks with which the Red Army started the war on the Soviet Union's Western Front were both outmoded (like the T-26 and the T-28) and in need of renewal or repair. Poorly maintained by ill-trained mechanics and operated by inexperienced crews, they may have looked impressive in a military parade but were arthritic in battle. Constrained by an outmoded military doctrine, the armoured brigades were arranged in fragmented units behind the ground troops – not concentrated in formations like the panzers – supposedly to provide the infantry with heavy covering fire while the foot soldiers fought the German advance to a standstill. In the event, transfixed by the relentless speed of the advancing panzer squadrons, they were stunned into vulnerable immobility: sitting targets for the German guns. Rather than waiting to be incinerated, many tank crews opted to leap out and flee for the uncertain safety of the forest.

Gabriel Temkin, a raw recruit making his way to a training camp just behind the front line, bore witness to this rout. Travelling partly by train but more often on foot from his home in Gomel to the town of Oryol more than 300 kilometres away, he saw railway stations in ruins, roads blown up and Stuka bombers, their terrorizing sirens screaming, descending on defenceless columns: 'I saw people killed, some of the bodies twisted together. The wounded, especially the lightly wounded, were crying for help, which was rarely available.'[24] He noticed in awe the speed with which the contents of entire factories were loaded onto transporters that trundled past him, taking them to be reassembled on safer sites far behind the lines. Interspersed with these great trucks but heading in the same direction was a stream of civilians under near-constant bombardment by the Luftwaffe: 'the planes, having dropped their bombs, were flying low, shooting their machine guns indiscriminately . . . many houses were bombed and turned into rubble, or, being wooden, were burned out so that only chimneystacks and piles of ashes remained of them.'

The bombers also made a point of targeting the woods on either side of the roads with incendiary bombs, rightly presuming that men and horses would shelter under the trees at night. In one such bombardment Temkin noticed that 'the burning greyish-white trees were turning reddish, as if blushing and ashamed of what was going on. It was in that beautiful birch forest that for the first time I smelled burned flesh. I could not distinguish between the smell of burning horse-flesh from that of human.' As he passed the sorry columns of troops similarly retreating from the front, he noticed 'their outdated rifles hanging loosely over their shoulders. Their uniforms were worn out, covered with dust, not a smile on their mostly despondent, emaciated faces with sunken cheeks.'

Temkin resisted any inclination to join them. When he arrived at the base on the outskirts of Oryol, he joined a large number of other conscripts who had made similar journeys. They were given new uniforms but soon discovered that they would be unable to learn how to fire a rifle as there were none; instead the young conscripts were required to march up and down on a parade ground shouldering wooden imitations. He had been earmarked for training as a wireless operator, but before he had a chance to discover whether the camp possessed a radio he was summoned to appear before his superiors. They told him that his military training was at an end. He was to be transferred to a labour battalion. As an immigrant from Nazi-occupied Poland, he was deemed too untrustworthy to carry a weapon on the battlefield. Like many others – and for similar reasons – he was ordered to hand back his uniform, which was replaced by a hand-me-down set of quasi-military clothes and a pair of well-worn shoes. With bemused resignation, he reflected later that the 'greenish half-padded coat' he was also given was to serve him well for the next year – 'not only as a coat but also as a blanket, and even – its sleeves – as a pillow'.

In Moscow, the newly formed State Defence Committee, with Stalin indisputably at its head, decided that urgent steps were needed to shore up the capital's defences. On 4 July Stalin authorized the formation of twenty-five volunteer divisions – a total of 270,000 men aged between seventeen and fifty-five – that were to be sent to the front once they had been taught the basics of warfare. The men – many of whom were at the older end of that spectrum – were enlisted within days. The speed with which they were enrolled was impressive but the process was shambolic. Medical students were enlisted as infantrymen when there was a dire shortage of doctors and nurses at the front. In some cases, Komsomol leaders, ever anxious to fulfil their quotas, managed to enlist as volunteers individuals who were already subject to the draft. Thus redesignated, these unfortunates were later to be registered as deserters, despite the fact that they were serving as volunteers and in some cases were already dead or missing in action. It was widely rumoured, though not confirmed, that other young men were press-ganged into becoming volunteers by the simple expedient of rounding them up on the streets.[25]

The training given to the volunteers was rudimentary, their 'uniforms' were the clothes in which they stood and their weapons – if any were available – were antiquated rifles or pistols that often predated the First World War. A notable example of this awesomely disorganized response to the invasion was a militia unit – the 8th People's Volunteer Division – which was blessed with a disproportionate number of writers, artists, actors and musicians. Among these cultural luminaries was the novelist Alexander Bek (who was to write a vivid chronicle of the Battle of Moscow later in the year). Bek had earned a reputation as a prankster who dressed with an eccentric disregard for convention. 'He wore great big boots, puttees which kept unwinding and trailing on the ground, a grey-coloured uniform, and most absurd of all, a forage cap which sat on top of his head like a bonnet,' one of his colleagues noted.[26] Among the 250 musicians from the Moscow conservatoire who joined the division were the pianist Emil Gilels and the violinist David Oistrakh, who played for the troops and survived to be feted as twentieth-century maestros. The conservatoire's rector, Abram Diakov, who was also renowned as a pianist, was less fortunate. His fate was never discovered, but as one of the 7,500 men serving with the 18th, when it was shredded at the Battle of Vyazma-Bryansk in October, he was either killed in action or, more probably, died in captivity as a prisoner of war, very possibly shot because he was a Jew. His only legacy, poignantly enough, were the few recordings of his public performances which survived the war.[27]

Realizing that Moscow itself might be in danger, the authorities also mobilized hundreds of thousands of its citizens into civil defence programmes within and around the city as well as much further from the capital. Their task was to construct defensive barriers to protect the capital's outer perimeter. Initially a task force of some 50,000 students – both male and female – were sent to construct trenches, tank traps, pill boxes and gun emplacements at strategic locations along a hundred-kilometre arc from Roslavl, almost 400 kilometres south-west of Moscow, northwards to Smolensk, a similar distance away. The mobilization itself was straightforward. The party had a long-established system, which had been tried and tested during the Great Famine, for forcing people unquestioningly to leave their homes for unknown destinations at short notice and without explanation. The students dutifully and in most cases with unswerving loyalty left their homes and their studies to obey the summons.

First by train and then on foot, one group of students found itself in a large village about forty kilometres from Roslavl. After a few days without any instructions, and at first without implements either, the students were ordered to dig a large ditch alongside the banks of the river near to where they had been billeted. They set to work in a frenzy of energy, fortified by a plentiful supply of eggs and meat offered to them by peasants who were retreating in long columns from the distant sound of gunfire, herding their animals before them. Listening to this and watching enemy reconnaissance planes circling overhead, the students approached their leader, Mikhail Gefter, a history student and one of the few Komsomol officials to eschew an excuse to be anywhere but at the front. Anatoly Chernyaev, a fellow historian, asked Gefter on their behalf if they could be given rifles to defend themselves. He was told that this was not permitted but that, as it happened, there were no weapons to spare anyway.

After completing their trench, the students were forced to withdraw some ten kilometres to the rear, where they started to dig once more. It was the first of many such retreats which would eventually end with their arrival back at the Kiev station in Moscow from which they had departed less than two months earlier. Chernyaev was furious at so much wasted effort. He was also fortunate. As the German panzers overran or circumvented their fragile barricades, he was one of the second-, third- and fourth-year students to be pulled back before their positions were overrun.*

---

* Chernyaev survived to become a distinguished academic, first as an historian and later, from 1986 to 1991, as President Gorbachev's senior foreign policy advisor. An

The first and fifth years – for unexplained reasons – were left to continue their fruitless task. Most of these were soon to be trapped in one or another of the pockets formed as the German panzers either bulldozed through or bypassed the Red Army's crumbling front. When the German infantry, which followed the panzers, began to tighten the noose around these trapped Soviet armies, the Moscow students were among those hundreds of thousands of young men who either died in last-ditch hand-to-hand struggles or were force-marched into captivity, where they were to perish from hunger and disease.★

Those who belonged to the older generation of volunteers fared no better. In the middle of July, Konstantin Simonov looked pityingly at a forlorn group of middle-aged militiamen heading for the front:

> I found it hard to bear. I thought: do we really have no other reserves besides these volunteers, dressed anyhow and barely armed? One rifle for two men, and one machine gun . . . They marched without supply wagons, without the normal regimental and divisional support – naked men, to all intents and purposes, on naked ground. Their uniforms were second- or third-hand tunics: some had once been dyed blue. Their commanders were not young either, reservists who had not served for many years. They all still needed to be trained, formed, made to look like soldiers.[28]

early advocate of a post-Soviet world in which the Cold War would yield to an era of harmony between East and West, he drafted and co-wrote many of Gorbachev's most visionary speeches. He died in 2017 at the age of ninety-five with that vision far from realization.

★ For a full account of this and other similar episodes, see Rodric Braithwaite's superb *Moscow 1941: A City and Its People at War* (Profile, 2007), pp. 126–9.

13. Hideous Realities

The temptation to believe that Soviet soldiers were automata, blindly obeying orders, was widespread and penetrated deep into the psyche of the invading armies. Men whose minds were already poisoned by Nazi propaganda found it only too easy to accept that the people they were fighting belonged to a subhuman species that resembled the Aryan races only in bodily form and thus were akin to vermin, as cunning as they were vicious. The guileless diary written by Wilhelm Prüller, the dispatch rider, reveals him to be a tender husband, a vivid observer, a brave soldier and an ardent Nazi who was simultaneously horrified and exhilarated by the intimacy of death.

They were always on the move. On 7 July he wrote:

Everyone's in a fever of excitement, the way we always are before an attack. Our cheeks glowing, our eyes sparkling, our hearts beating faster, and our thoughts concentrated on one thing: to get them, to destroy them! By chance I remember that Lorli's [Lore, his daughter] birthday is today. But I haven't time to think about it long. Orders are given, the attack begins, the fight sweeps me into its course. On the dot of 5.15 the steel giants move off: 140 of them! The Russians will soon be ready to shit.

At one point, he watched as a solitary Russian tank appeared over the horizon and careered towards his unit with its turret open. Its commander stood upright. Ten Russian soldiers – 'including women' – sat on its outer shell. It was soon incinerated:

Some of the women, completely nude and roasted, were lying on and beside the tank. Awful. All along the whole road you see Russians who have been mashed up by our lorries or tanks. If you look at them, you can't believe that it was ever a human being. An arm there, a head there, half a foot somewhere else, squashed brains, mashed ribs. Horrible.[1]

In Prüller, as in so many of his companions, relish and disgust were shockingly entwined.

A few days later, his battalion was following a panzer unit as it rolled eastwards through ripening cornfields. He kept his eye on the tanks until they disappeared over a hill in front of them. It was only then that he realized that the hillside was infested with Russian soldiers who had hidden themselves in well-camouflaged foxholes. 'The Russians don't dare stick their heads out of the holes,' Prüller noted. 'They simply stick their carbines out and press the trigger, or throw their grenades out without looking where to aim them.' After a while a number of tanks returned. They followed what became a familiar routine, driving back and forth over the enemy foxholes:

> Mash up and back a few times over them, so you'd think the people in the holes had turned into soup; but no. They're still there all over the place . . . We have to creep up to each hole, hurl a grenade inside and then finish them off with pistols or rifles. No calls of surrender: the Russians prefer to be flattened out in their holes. Here and there a steel helmet with two raised dirty hands appears. But we don't recognize any pardon.

In retaliation for a young German trooper, apparently shot dead by a Russian soldier even as his wound was being dressed, Prüller's unit did not pause but acted. 'It isn't a fight any more that we're conducting now, it's a massacre. It takes a long time for us to mop up, hole after hole, till there are no more shots.'[2] By the time they paused for breath, they had killed 135 Soviet soldiers at a cost of eleven of their own men. It was a satisfying tally for a young Nazi who had been taught to regard the Russian people as 'disgusting creatures' and 'dirty beasts'.

The young artillery officer Siegfried Knappe, similarly following the panzers on another part of the same front, was likewise complicit in extrajudicial killings that would have been regarded as war crimes had the Wehrmacht, under Hitler's orders, not disavowed the prevailing Geneva Conventions. In this Kafkaesque nightmare, Knappe sought to justify such atrocities by condemning the enemy's failure to abide by rules of engagement that his own commander-in-chief had explicitly repudiated. But he had greater sensitivity to the consequences than the dispatch rider.

On one occasion, as his regiment advanced along the road from Minsk to Smolensk, his platoon was ordered to fan out to clear a way through a heavily wooded area where the Russian defenders had concealed themselves, hiding in trenches covered with twigs, branches and leaves. Knappe expected them to 'stand and raise their hands in surrender'. On this occasion, though, they remained hidden until his unit had passed over their positions, at which point they rose up suddenly to fire at his patrol from behind. While acknowledging that these Russians were 'desperate' men, Knappe was outraged that, in shooting his men in the back, the Russians had 'broken a code of honour'.

Unlike Prüller, however, he was dismayed by the overreaction of his soldiers, and even more by his own failure to deter them:

> In a combat situation, the soldier is under inhuman stress to begin with and when he sees a friend he has been sharing his life with suddenly drop because he was shot in the back, it is too much . . . It is not just friendship, and it is stronger than flag and country . . . Our soldiers went berserk, and from that point on during the attack they took no prisoners and left no one alive in a trench or foxhole. I did not try to stop them, nor did any other officer, because they would have killed us too if we had. They were out of their minds with fury . . . they were all killed, without mercy or remorse.[3]

In the calm of that evening, his men sat around the field kitchen, eating their rations or smoking and drinking coffee that bubbled on top of a log fire. Some mended their boots or wrote letters home. Knappe wondered what they might tell their loved ones after 'the horror and exhaustion' of that day, noting resignedly, 'They had clearly adapted to this new type of warfare better than I had.' Knappe was troubled enough to demand an audience with his immediate superior, Major Walter Krüger. The major was in his command tent inspecting a map in preparation for the Soviet counter-attack expected the following day. Knappe must have betrayed his unease as Krüger, looking up from the map, paused before saying, 'You did not like what you saw today.' Knappe replied, 'No, but I understood it.' Krüger paused again before saying, 'Good. That is important. There is nothing that you or I can do about an incident like that. The Russians took control of the situation out of our hands.'[4] Across the length of the front, similar 'incidents' were sanctioned by a collective shrug of the shoulders.

Barbarity begat barbarity in a downward spiral that led otherwise civilized men to forsake humanity in a daily orgy of savagery. But there was a significant distinction between the attitudes on either side. From the perspective of the Russian soldier, the Nazi invaders were bent on destroying their Motherland, their homes and their families. This engendered a hatred so intense as to justify in their minds any means of stopping the advance, however bestial. In the case of a great many German soldiers, the red rage of battle was not the sole explanation for the atrocities they inflicted on their hated enemy. Such men viewed Slavs as an inferior life form that had no right to be treated as human. For their commanders, many of whom shared that opinion, the murderous rampages in which their men indulged also provided a swift and simple way of releasing them from the burden of force-marching their victims to prisoner-of-war camps hundreds of kilometres behind the ever advancing front lines. It was easy to turn a blind eye to any excess – especially as their commander-in-chief, the Führer, had no qualms about such atrocities.

Even so, by mid-July, hundreds of thousands of Soviet soldiers had been taken prisoner. Across the entire front, roads became clogged by ragged columns of exhausted and broken men shuffling towards the perdition that awaited them. On their way, they passed regiment upon regiment of German troops marching in the opposite direction. Among these was a young rifleman, Benno Zieser. Soon after advancing through Poland into Ukraine – a stop-start journey on foot and by train that had taken a fortnight – Zieser's company was resting at a railhead well inside the Soviet Union. He had already witnessed enough to temper his youthful exuberance at the prospect of the victorious battle ahead. He had seen a hospital train filled with wounded comrades 'with missing limbs, blood-streaked uniforms, blood-soaked bandages on legs, arms, heads and chests'; a ruined town, with chimneys sticking grotesquely from the rubble and iron girders 'snapped like matches'; burned-out tanks, decapitated tanks, overturned tanks and tanks inextricably bogged in marshland.

Now, as he and his comrades (most of whom, like him, were still teenagers) wandered idly about the marshalling yard, their attention was arrested by the sight of

a broad earth-brown crocodile slowly shuffling down the road towards us. From it came a subdued hum, like that from a bee-hive. Prisoners of War. Russians, six deep. We couldn't see the end of the column. As they drew near the terrible stench which met us made us quite sick; it was like the biting stench of the lion house and the filthy odour of the monkey house at the same time.

They went to move away from 'the foul cloud which surrounded them', but found themselves transfixed by the spectacle: 'Were these really human beings, these grey-brown figures, these shadows lurching towards us, stumbling and staggering, moving shapes at their last gasp, creatures which only some last flicker of the will to live enabled them to obey the order to march?' Zieser saw a prisoner stumble and fall out of line. A guard drove him back into the column with a rifle butt. Another, with an open head wound, ran out to beg a scrap of bread from a local bystander until a guard 'yanked him back into line' using 'a leather whip lashed around his shoulders'.[5]

Not yet hardened by conflict, these teenagers watched uneasily as the prisoners were goaded with rifle butts and leather thongs into the open wagons of a nearby freight train. One had so little strength that he was unable to climb aboard and 'just fell back on the track'. There was a sudden pistol crack and 'as if struck by lightning, the Russkie cramped all up in a heap and was still, blood from his half-opened lips oozing down in his left ear'. One young recruit yelled out in spontaneous protest. He was silenced by the guard who had fired the fatal round: 'Pull yourself together, man. Can't you control yourself? Fresh out, I suppose, aren't you? But you'll soon get that baby-talk knocked out of you.'[6] Such incidents were not rare. Very often, the last moment of life for any prisoner who was sick or wounded or merely exhausted was to watch helplessly as a guard pulled a pistol from his holster, took aim at his forehead and pulled the trigger.

Many prisoners had untreated wounds of the most ghastly variety. At one holding camp, Edwin Erich Dwinger – a nationalist writer by profession but now writing as a war correspondent for the benefit of SS-Reichsführer Heinrich Himmler – had enough sensitivity to be horrified by the sight of a group of prisoners sitting on the ground awaiting transport into captivity. One, the right side of whose jaw had been blown away by a bullet, had tried to wrap some rags around his neck: 'Through the rags his windpipe, laid bare, was visible and the effort it made as his breath snorted through it.' Another's arm was 'a ragged mass of flesh. He had no bandages and blood oozed from his wounds as if from a row of tubes'. Many had been so badly burned by flame-throwers that 'their faces had no longer any recognizable human features but were simply swollen lumps of meat'.[7] They sat in silence, not even a moan or whimper between them.

For Dwinger there was a sight yet more tragic. Some of his fellow soldiers took pity on the victims and began to distribute bread and margarine:

> They began their distribution more than thirty metres distant from the place where the most badly wounded were lying and these rose up, yes, even the dying rose up quickly and in an inexpressible stream of suffering hurried towards the distribution point. The man with a jaw swayed as he stood up; the man with the five bullet wounds raised himself by his good arm . . . and those with burned faces ran . . . but this was not all; half a dozen men who had been lying on the ground also went forward pressing back into their bodies with their left hands the intestines which had burst through gaping wounds in their stomach wall. Their right hands were extended in gestures of supplication . . . as they moved down each man left a smear of blood upon the grass . . . and not one of them cried . . . none of them moaned . . . they are all dumb, as dumb as the poorest of God's creatures.[8]

Within the first two months of the war, at least 150,000 and perhaps 200,000 prisoners of war died before they reached the dumping grounds that served as prison camps. They were beaten or starved to death, either on forced marches or on the transport trains, which would stop from time to time to throw piles of corpses out. Few German soldiers – even those who were not directly implicated – showed sympathy for their victims. In one of his letters home, the tank gunner Karl Fuchs expressed a common sentiment:

> Hardly ever do you see the face of a person who seems rational and intelligent. They all look emaciated and the wild, half-crazy look in their eyes makes them appear like imbeciles. And these scoundrels, led by Jews and criminals, wanted to imprint their stamp on Europe, indeed on the world. Thank God that our Führer, Adolf Hitler, is preventing this from happening.[9]

★

On the assumption that Operation Barbarossa would be swiftly accomplished, Hitler had moved into new headquarters deep in the forests of East Prussia on 24 June. Wolfsschanze (Wolf's Lair) was a sprawl of wooden huts and bomb-proof concrete bunkers, some eight kilometres east of the town of Rastenburg. The complex was divided into three security zones, the innermost of which, heavily guarded and ringed by a fence of steel, surrounded Hitler's personal compound. His bunker adjoined others for his most trusted acolytes: his vainglorious deputy, Hermann Goering; OKW's sycophantic commander-in-chief, Field Marshal Wilhelm Keitel; its no less deferential chief of operations, General Alfred Jodl; and the sinisterly manipulative Martin Bormann, whose role as Hess's successor had been dignified by the title of Deputy Führer of the Nazi Party Chancellery. So far from enduring the rigours of a normal 'field' headquarters, these senior members of the entourage lived in some comfort. According to one of their number, the concrete walls of the bunkers were lined with brightly painted wooden panels and their spacious bedrooms enjoyed the luxury of 'built-in cupboards, glazed basins and baths with water laid on, central heating and every type of electrical gadget'.[10]

In addition to staff quarters, meeting rooms and an operations centre from where Hitler could follow Barbarossa's progress, the complex contained a large dining hall. There, in a series of rambling monologues over dinner, 'the coarsest, cruellest, least magnanimous conqueror the world has ever known' as he was described by the historian Hugh Trevor-Roper, expounded his ideological and political theories to his fawning entourage. His aperçus were dutifully recorded by the obsequious Bormann, who acted as his official Boswell. Much of what he said – at inordinate length – would have been familiar to students of *Mein Kampf*, where he had written, as Trevor-Roper was to summarize, that 'the struggle between Germany and Russia was to be the decisive battle of the world . . . a war of life and death, empire or annihilation, deciding the fate of centuries; a war not *against* the past – that was already dead – but between two Titans disputing its inheritance'.[11]

In early July 1941, fifteen years after the publication of *Mein Kampf*, when victory seemed imminent, such sentiments must have had peculiar force. 'Bolshevism must be exterminated . . . Moscow, as the centre of the doctrine, must disappear from the earth's surface as soon as its riches have been brought to shelter,' the Führer avowed at dinner on 5 July.[12] 'After a meeting with Hitler, two days later, Halder noted, 'It is the Führer's firm decision to level Moscow and Leningrad and make them uninhabitable.' In addition to depriving 'not only Bolshevism but also Muscovite nationalism of their centres', he told Halder that both cities were to be 'razed by the air force', which would 'relieve us of the necessity of having to feed the populations through the winter'.[13] The reason for that was well understood: those among the 7 million citizens who survived the aerial bombardment would either starve to death or flee eastwards towards Siberia, where their chances of scavenging a living were as remote as the wastelands they would inherit.

The insouciance with which Hitler's High Command accepted the fate their leader had allotted to the civilian population of the Soviet Union is horrific, but not inexplicable. Even those generals who did not entirely share Hitler's maniacal precepts were aware of the immense challenge posed by the need to provision an invading army of nearly 3 million men. In the weeks leading up to Barbarossa the planners had come up with a solution. Unlike the variety of nascent ideas then being proposed for the extermination of European Jewry, the Hunger Plan, as it was known, was not shrouded in secrecy but was overt and explicit. It had much in common with principles applied during Stalin's Great Famine, which had been visited on the same benighted region less than a decade earlier. It entailed the mass starvation of millions of people.

Concocted by senior officials who were, for the most part, ardent Nazis, the prospect of a subhuman species dying in large numbers raised few qualms. The fundamental challenge for them was to feed the invading troops without rationing the supply of basic foodstuffs to the Reich's civilian population. Germany, like much of Europe, had not been self-sufficient even in peacetime, and the war had exacerbated this deficit. Though the Nazis were plundering the territories they had occupied in western Europe for a wide range of raw materials and industrial goods, they were unable to requisition a significant quantity of surplus food for the very good reason that there was none. Agricultural output had slumped across the continent. The blitzkrieg across the Low Countries and through France had not only caused hideous human dislocation but also disrupted the production and distribution of foodstuffs. Already aggravated by Britain's naval blockade, Germany's food shortages looked

certain to be further exacerbated by Operation Barbarossa unless an alternative solution could be found. Grim memories of the First World War
and its aftermath – when millions went short of food and many were
brought to the verge of starvation – were still fresh in the German mind.

In popular European mythology, Ukraine's bountiful soil held the
elixir of life. The region was held to be a 'bread basket', overflowing
with enough grain to feed all Europe. The Third Reich's Ministry of
Agriculture knew better. Not only did Ukraine produce a modest
annual surplus but, since collectivization, this had been requisitioned by
Bolshevik bureaucrats (sometimes at the point of a gun) to feed the
workers in the Soviet Union's industrial heartlands. Appreciating this,
the ministry's overlord, Herbert Backe, who was a zealous Nazi, came
up with a swift and simple fix. In the spring of 1941 he proposed that the
food chain between Ukraine and the cities of central and northern Russia be severed and grain redistributed among the invading armies.

Backe found a ready ally in OKW's economic guru, General Georg
Thomas, who was far less committed to Nazism but, as a soulless administrator, merely saw the Hunger Plan as a solution to a looming logistics
problem.* If the soldiers were allowed to plunder Ukraine's granaries,
tens of thousands of trucks would be liberated for the crucial task of
maintaining a steady flow of men, weapons, ammunition and fuel to
the front. On 2 May 1941 the heads of the Reich's key ministries were
summoned to a meeting at OKW, where the Hunger Plan was duly
endorsed. An official minute of the meeting confirmed that its implications were well understood: 'If we take what we need out of the country
[Ukraine], there can be no doubt that many millions of people will die
of starvation.'[14] Backe was more precise. By his estimate, the 'surplus
population' of Soviet citizens who would perish as a result of the Hunger Plan was likely to be in the order of 20–30 million. The German
High Command did not shrink from this prospect; in fact it was fully
complicit in it. A little before the invasion OKW's guidelines for the
implementation of the Hunger Plan were published in a 'Green Book'.
The forecast was unequivocal:

---

* Thomas was later to be implicated in planning a coup against Hitler in 1939 that
fizzled out. When this plot was revealed following the failed attempt on the Führer's
life in July 1944, he was imprisoned in Dachau. He was released by the US 5th Army
in May 1945.

Many tens of millions of people in this territory will die or must emigrate to Siberia. Attempts to rescue the population from death by starvation by drawing on the surplus from the Black Earth regions can only be at the expense of the food supply to Europe. They diminish the staying power of Germany in the war and the resistance of Germany and Europe to the blockade. There must be absolute clarity about this.[15]

Mass starvation was not an accidental by-product of the invasion but an essential component of it.

Nor was that all. From Hitler's perspective the Hunger Plan had a further benefit. It would not only resolve an economic and operational quandary but also play a critical role in delivering Lebensraum. As well as shelling Moscow into oblivion to destroy Bolshevism, Hitler intended to bring every part of the Soviet Union west of the Urals under permanent Nazi suzerainty. At dinner on 27 July he dilated specifically on the future of Ukraine, whose indigenous inhabitants were destined for the role of rural helots. 'Nothing would be a worse mistake on our part than to seek to educate the masses there,' he explained. 'It is to our interest that the people should know just enough to recognize the signs on the road,' though he conceded that to ensure they would be able to perform their allotted purpose, 'they must be allowed to live decently'. In the southern part of Ukraine, he proposed to go further. This particularly verdant and fertile region would be designated as 'exclusively a German colony'. Explaining that 'there'll be no harm in pushing out the population that's there now', Hitler expounded his vision for the Aryan region: in place of the subhuman Slavs, the Reich would allocate the land to tens of thousands of German 'soldier-peasants' who would till the soil, marry fecund countrywomen – it would be forbidden to marry a townswoman – and produce large numbers of children, whose own offspring would steadily repopulate the region. As guardians of the Reich, the 'soldier-peasants' would bear arms 'so that at the slightest danger, they can be at their posts when we summon them'. For all Germans, 'the beauties of Crimea' would become 'our Riviera' and in Croatia they would be able to relax in an exclusively German 'tourist's paradise'. Given the chance, Hitler's favourite film-maker, Leni Riefenstahl, would doubtless have provided the images required to promote this Aryan vision of bucolic perfection. If any of the toadies at his dinner table were moved to ponder that their Führer had become totally insane, they refrained from expressing even the mildest degree of scepticism.[16]

Hitler's notion of Lebensraum had seeped into the collective psyche of the German nation. When the family-loving Wilhelm Prüller wrote home he was sometimes engulfed by a wave of homesickness, contrasting his native Austria with the homesteads they passed on their way east – 'Peasant houses with straw roofs which look more like dog huts; a ragged dirty, animal-like people.'[17] Yet, he also looked beyond the immediate squalor to the future that Barbarossa would deliver to him and his family: 'You simply cannot imagine what a happy feeling it is to see such a country, Henny! As far as the eye can see: fields, corn, wheat, field after field. This great country we are capturing for our children. This earth! This wreath! This wealth! It's simply wonderful'[18]

Whether or not Prüller might have become one of his Führer's 'soldier-peasants', Hitler's freedom to fantasize was unbounded by any external pressure to contemplate reality. Issued from his cocoon-like inner sanctum at Wolfsschanze, Hitler's diktats – however aberrant they might have seemed to front-line commanders – went unchallenged by his immediate entourage. This thraldom served to exacerbate the Führer's urge to interfere from a position of ignorance in the detailed decisions that in a more conventional conflict would have been left to the generals. OKW's deputy chief of operations, Walter Warlimont, who was not exempt from blame, attributed Hitler's obsessive need to make every significant decision himself to his 'limitless suspicion and overriding determination to exercise his authority, the glaring inadequacies of his self-taught generalship and his incapacity to subordinate to well-tried military principles his own wishful thinking, based on politics, economics, and prestige *desiderata*.'[19]*

In the months leading up to the invasion Hitler failed to resolve what he already knew to be the potential tension between two distinct military objectives: the seizure of the Ukrainian heartlands (for their abundant industrial, mineral and agricultural resources) and the eradication of the roots of Bolshevism by way of annihilating the Soviet capital. This

* Before the war, Warlimont had played a crucial part in devising the structure of OKW, which rubber-stamped Hitler's unassailable military authority. Though Warlimont was at Wolfsschanze with constant access to Jodl, there is no evidence that he expressed any such reservations at the time, let alone such a scathing indictment.

apprehension had been camouflaged by the Wehrmacht's confidence that the Red Army would be crushed so rapidly that both objectives could be secured simultaneously. By the middle of July, a cursory look at the campaign cartography might have seemed to confirm their judgement.

Taken in isolation and at a glance, these maps offered a snapshot of an overwhelming military triumph that appeared to foreshadow the realization of Hitler's maniacal dreams. All three army groups were well on the way to their allotted targets: Army Group South was advancing steadily on Kiev, Army Group North was closing on Leningrad, and Army Group Centre was scything its way towards Moscow. Such snapshots, though, concealed some disconcerting facts: that the advance had slowed, that in some areas it had stalled altogether, and that it had been made at an unexpectedly heavy price in men and materiel. On all three fronts the fighting had become fiercer and the enemy's counter-attacks more frequent. By contrast with the invasions of the Balkans and western Europe, when troops who had been surrounded opted to surrender rather than face certain death, Soviet soldiers facing a similar predicament usually chose to die rather than surrender. Already, to the Ostheer's most discerning commanders, victory no longer promised to be as swift or certain as the High Command had predicted.

The spectacular progress of Bock's Army Group Centre had come at a particularly high price. As the general commanding 43rd Army Corps, Gotthard Heinrici was under pressure to close the gap between his infantry and Guderian's panzers, which had advanced so rapidly eastwards from Minsk that they were already encircling the retreating Soviet armies in another huge pocket around Smolensk. Despite marching up to fifty kilometres a day, however, his men were lagging some 200 kilometres behind the leading tanks. The strain on his men was intense. On 11 July, in one of his many letters to his wife, he wrote that they were 'utterly exhausted', and two days later that 'the heat and the dust are killing us. It gets hotter and more humid each day. We do not feel like eating, just drinking. We try to march only during the afternoon and at night. It is simply not bearable during the day. Today the heat is so bad that I can hardly write a letter.'[20]

At OKH headquarters Halder noted on 15 July that 'the enemy . . . is doing all he can to avoid being pushed back any further to the east. The Russian troops now . . . are fighting with savage determination.'[21] This, combined with the fact that large numbers of the enemy had managed to escape the Smolensk pocket, began to alarm Brauchitsch. In turn this prompted Halder to note that OKH's commander-in-chief had been plunged into a 'severe depression' by the unexpected strength of the Soviet resistance.[22]

The first signs of the rift that was about to open up between the generals at the front and their superiors at OKH came when a rumour reached Bock on 13 July of a proposal to divert some of his panzer divisions to reinforce Army Group North and Army Group South. This alarmed Bock, who believed with great passion that the overriding priority was 'to completely smash' the Russian forces around Smolensk and then for his entire armoured strength 'to drive quickly to the east until I can report that the enemy is offering no more resistance in front of Moscow!'[23] Bock was not to know that on the same day Hitler had decided that 'the dash toward Moscow' should be put on hold and had already made it clear to a disgruntled Halder that 'a quick advance to the east is less important than smashing the enemy's military strength.'[24]

The army chief of staff's frustration was matched by his impotence: the Führer's 'perpetual interference in matters the circumstances of which he does not understand is becoming a scourge which will eventually become intolerable', he noted.[25] By confiding such criticism exclusively to the pages of his diary, Halder, of course, ensured that Hitler's arbitrary diktats would rarely be challenged. Two days later, Brauchitsch, who was little more than the Führer's mouthpiece, delivered unpalatable news to Bock: 'a further advance to the east by the panzers after the capture of the area around Smolensk is out of the question'.[26] Once again, the generals failed to challenge Hitler's mercurial strategic whims.

On 19 July, as Supreme Commander of the Armed Forces, Hitler issued Directive No. 33, instructing that Army Group Centre's advance towards Moscow should be 'with infantry formations' only. Three days later, on 23 July, to put the matter beyond doubt, he issued a more detailed 'supplement to Directive No. 33', ordering that this advance should not begin until Bock had completed 'mopping-up operations around Smolensk and further south'. Meanwhile, Army Group South was to extend its operations beyond Kiev to the Caucasus and into the Crimea, while Army Group North, which he judged would very soon take Leningrad, was to make preparations to send 'considerable forces' back to Germany – presumably for rest and recreation before relieving and reinforcing the Reich's Western Front, perhaps before a renewed attempt to invade Britain.[27] In what one of his senior acolytes at OKW described as a 'flight of fancy', the Führer also ordered the Luftwaffe to launch air attacks on Moscow, not yet to raze the Soviet capital but as a reprisal for Russian bombing raids on Helsinki and Bucharest.[28]

On 24 July Brauchitsch advised Bock that Guderian's Panzer Group 2 and Hoth's Panzer Group 3 were to be temporarily removed from his command, respectively to reinforce Rundstedt's Army Group South and Leeb's Army Group North. Bock was furious at this sudden shift in strategic focus. In a sharply worded reaction, he retorted that if the High Command persisted with this plan it might as well abolish his command altogether. 'Perhaps they will correctly construe from this suggestion that I am "piqued",' he wrote angrily in his diary, 'but if the army group is to be carved up into three parts there will be no need for the headquarters.'[29]

Bock was not alone. The generals under his command shared his contempt for the craven way in which Keitel and Jodl were content to be Hitler's errand boys, rubber-stamping rather than questioning his judgement. As Commander-in-Chief of Luftflotte 2, General Albert Kesselring had acquired a reputation for strong leadership and sound strategic judgement during the 'pre-invasion' bombing campaign against Britain in 1940–41. Now in command of the Luftwaffe's operations on the Eastern Front, he was similarly offended – and for a very simple reason that Hitler had clearly overlooked in his enthusiasm to punish Moscow. Commiserating with Bock, Kesselring complained that it would be quite impossible for him to mount an effective aerial attack on the capital until the Luftwaffe had established bases much closer to the city. Both men agreed that this would be possible only once the two panzer groups that were about to be removed from Bock's command had between them broken up the Red Army's reserve formations that were beginning to regroup between Smolensk and Moscow.

From their perspective the core purpose – the liquidation of Bolshevism via the destruction of the Soviet capital – was being jeopardized by the Führer's caprice. At the end of a long meeting with Hitler, which left him bitterly critical of the Führer's 'long-winded' and 'unjustly critical' comments about the Ostheer's front-line commanders, Halder commented that the Führer's fiat would allow 'the enemy to dictate our policy' and would 'mark the beginning of the end of the decline of our initial strategy of imaginative operations'. He had tried to make the case for pressing ahead with the advance on Moscow rather than pausing to round up the enemy 'in small encircling actions of a purely tactical character', as the Führer now ordained. It was to no effect. 'My representations stressing the importance of Moscow are brushed aside without any valid counterevidence,' he noted glumly.[30] This time, though, it was not the end of the matter.

The battles around Smolensk – the springboard for the final attack on Moscow – had started to exact a heavy toll on the German infantry. Again and again front-line officers reported 'the absolute exhaustion' of their troops. When Heinrici's four divisions finally caught up with Guderian's panzers, they were at once embroiled in a ferocious Soviet counter-attack south-west of Smolensk. On 22 July the general wrote despairingly of finding '[artillery] carriage drivers sleeping like the dead in front of their horses' and of 'the huge mental stress' endured by men who had to face challenges 'that have never been experienced before in any other campaign'. In a telling note that foreshadowed worse to come, he wrote, 'no one knows how long this battle will last. There is no sign of an end at the moment, despite all the victories we have won . . . it does not seem as if the Russians' will to resist is already broken or that the people want to be rid of their Bolshevik leaders.'[31]

The fatigue was eating away at morale. On 27 July – the day that Hitler was dazzling his dinner guests at Wolfsschanze with his crazed vision of how Germany's 'peasant-soldiers' would transform Ukraine into a land fit for Aryan heroes – a surgeon serving in the 18th Panzer Division's motorcycle battalion wrote that the men in his unit had to endure a

> far too great mental and nervous strain . . . under a powerful barrage of heavy artillery . . . The enemy charged them . . . penetrated their positions and was repulsed in hand-to-hand fighting . . . The men could not shut their eyes day and night. Food could be supplied only during the few hours of darkness. A large number of men, still serving with the troops at present, were buried alive by artillery fire . . . the men were promised a few days of rest . . . But instead found themselves in an even worse situation . . . The men are indifferent and apathetic, are partly suffering

from crying fits, and are not to be cheered up by this or that phrase. Food is being taken only in disproportionately small quantities.[32]

Over the course of three weeks, the 18th Panzer Division would lose 150 of its original complement of 200 tanks – an unsustainable rate of attrition. Bock was baffled by the strength of the Red Army's resistance:

Astonishing for an opponent who is so beaten; they must have unbelievable masses of materiel, for even now the field units still complain about the powerful effect of the enemy artillery. The Russians are also becoming more aggressive in the air, which is not surprising, for we can't yet get at their air bases near Moscow.[33]

A few days later, he noted, 'I have almost no reserves left to meet the enemy massing of forces and the constant counter-attacks.'[34]

From his front-line headquarters, General Heinrici was even more disconcerted. 'My corps has got to get out of this messy situation. The endless fights in the forests will be the end of the troops . . . even the best troops cannot fend off an attack in the forests and the swamps,' he wrote on 30 July.[35] With 43rd Army Corps bogged down to the south-west of Smolensk, he noted bitterly:

We are still left with this thankless task . . . with all these obstacles – the atrocious forests and swamps, the dreadful state of the roads – so many things are not happening which would be a matter of course under normal circumstances. We have all underestimated the Russian. It was always said that his leaders are pathetic. Well, they have proved their leadership skills with the result that our operations have come to a halt . . . There is no doubt it would be a blessing for the whole world if Bolshevism, its methods and repercussions would vanish from the face of the earth. It is awful. It is a disgusting beast, but it is furiously defending itself.[36]

At this point, the realization that the 'disgusting beast' was far from the point of collapse, forced Hitler to reverse the major operational decision he had made only one week earlier. In Directive No. 34, released on 30 July 1941, he cancelled Directive No. 33, and ordained that Army Group Centre's panzers would not after all be diverted to the northern and southern fronts. Explaining this astonishing volte-face, he cited 'the appearance of stronger enemy forces on the front and to the flanks of Army Group

Centre, the supply situation and the need to give 2nd and 3rd Armoured Groups about ten days to rehabilitate their units [which] make it necessary to postpone for the moment further tasks and objectives'. This was not only an unexpected reverse but also a startling acknowledgement that Operation Barbarossa, which by now was supposed to be at the point of annihilating the Red Army, had been put 'on hold'. Hitler's self-congratulatory boast on 4 July (which echoed Halder's of the day before) that 'to all intents and purposes the Russians have lost the war' had proved to be recklessly premature.[37] Within six weeks of launching Barbarossa, his clarity of vision had succumbed to doubt and indecision.

The Smolensk crisis was the first significant setback for Hitler's armies since the invasion of Poland and it began to have a baleful effect. The semblance of harmony, easy to preserve when their armies seemed to be invincible, gradually gave way to discord, confusion and recrimination – all of which was exacerbated by the flow of conflicting orders that now started to emanate from the Wolfsschanze.

On 28 July Hitler confided to his army adjutant, Major Gerhard Engel, that

> he was not sleeping at night since he was uncertain about many things. Within his breast two souls wrestled: the political-strategic and the economic. Politically he would say that two suppurating boils had to be got rid of: Leningrad and Moscow. That would be the heaviest blow for the Russian people and the Communist Party . . . Economically speaking there were quite different objectives . . . the south was more important, where oil, wheat, more or less everything was located necessary to keep the country going. A land where milk and honey flowed. One thing at least was absolutely required, and that was a proper concentration of forces.[38]

Hitler had identified this potential dilemma before Barbarossa but had suppressed it in the conviction, shared by the Wehrmacht High Command, that both objectives could be secured simultaneously and within weeks. With his options narrowing, he now leapt to the conclusion that he had a binary choice: it was one or the other. His vacillation between the two options opened up a strategic vacuum which the generals belatedly found the courage to fill. The stage was set for a fundamental, fateful and bitterly contested reappraisal of the entire campaign.

At 6.30 p.m. on 30 July 1941, a gaunt and sickly American was driven through the gates of the Kremlin and ushered into Stalin's office. Harry Hopkins was the personal envoy of Roosevelt and, in addition to the bag of medicines that accompanied him wherever he went, he was armed with a letter from the president. It asked the Russian leader 'to treat Mr Hopkins with the identical confidence you would feel if you were talking directly to me'.[1] The meetings between the president's envoy and the Soviet leader over the next two days were to prove of lasting moment.

Hopkins was Roosevelt's closest confidant. His wartime home was at the White House, where the president had given him his own private quarters. As a principal architect of Roosevelt's New Deal and its associated relief and works programmes, he had earned a reputation as a clear-minded and decisive administrator. For a while his success in these roles had tempted him to consider running for the presidency, but any such hopes were abandoned when he was diagnosed with stomach cancer in 1937. He had been dogged by ill health throughout his life (he was forty-nine at the time of the diagnosis) and it was widely presumed that the disease would soon carry him away; in 1939, he was so ill that Roosevelt wrote to a friend, 'The doctors have given up Harry for dead.'[2] After treatment at the already famous Mayo Clinic, he survived on a diet consisting largely of pills and intravenous injections from his ever-present supply, a combination that accounted for his cadaverous appearance. As a younger man he had managed to acquire a reputation as a playboy, but, with the outbreak of war, he surrendered the high life to serve Roosevelt as his most intimate and influential friend. Though his detractors regarded him as 'a sinister figure, a backstairs intriguer, and an Iowan combination of Machiavelli, Svengali and Rasputin', the president's faith in him was absolute.[3]

The arrival of Hopkins in Moscow was as unexpected as it was sudden. He had been in London for two weeks, leading an intensive and testing round of talks between the two governments. He had first met Churchill earlier in the year, when, at Roosevelt's behest, he flew to London on a fact-finding mission, not least to discover more about the prime minister.* On that occasion, he had travelled widely, witnessing the 'courage' of the British people at war. He also forged a strong personal bond with Churchill, who, he reported back to the president, was 'the government in every sense of the word . . . and . . . I cannot emphasize too strongly that he is the one person over here with whom you need to have a full meeting of minds'.[4] No one else really mattered.

In July 1941, that 'meeting of minds' had yet to be established. The US chiefs of staff were disdainful of what they regarded as Churchill's anachronistic obsession with sustaining the British Empire; in particular, they resented having to dispatch scores of US vessels laden with military hardware to the Middle East to bolster what they regarded as Britain's *folie de grandeur*. A few weeks earlier Roosevelt had intimated that he shared their view, advising the prime minister in May that the loss of Egypt and the Middle East would not be an unmitigated disaster to the Allied cause. When Churchill reacted badly, the president hastened to mollify him, but insisted that,

> should the Mediterranean prove in the last analysis to be an impossible battleground . . . I do not feel that such a fact alone would mean the defeat of our mutual interests. I say this because I believe the outcome of this struggle is going to be decided in the Atlantic and unless Hitler can win there he cannot win anywhere in the world in the end.[5]

As Hopkins swiftly appreciated, this underlying Anglo-US tension was bound to be aggravated by Barbarossa. The dynamics of a 'special relationship' – which for twenty years had been marked as much by doubt and suspicion as by mutual regard – were bound to be affected.

In London, the president's emissary exuded charm, but he was tough. Flanked by three senior US commanders, he told Churchill and the British chiefs of staff at 10 Downing Street that the American Joint Chiefs of Staff thought that 'the British Empire is making too many sacrifices in trying to maintain an indefensible position in the Middle

---

* Although Churchill and Roosevelt had met one another casually almost two decades earlier, Roosevelt – though not Churchill – had forgotten the occasion.

East', and that it was essential for 'the people in authority in Washington' to be given a good reason why they 'must get supplies to the Middle East'.[6] With the Russians fighting for their very survival, both Western leaders had pledged (in Churchill's words) to provide the Soviet Union with 'whatever help we can'. Since both Washington and London believed at the time that the Red Army would collapse within weeks, this expression of support cost little. By late July, though, with the Soviet armies by no means yet broken, the sincerity of London's and Washington's commitment could no longer be taken for granted.

The defence chiefs in both capitals were exceedingly reluctant to dispatch precious supplies from their own arsenals to shore up the Soviet Union. Roosevelt's 'Arsenal of Democracy' – which was not yet overflowing with weaponry – was coveted by the Joint Chiefs for the defence of the United States and the protection of US interests in the Pacific. It was difficult enough for Roosevelt to justify the diversion of military hardware for Britain's 'imperial' campaign in the Middle East. To divert further resources to the Soviet Union was certain to meet resistance from the Department of War but, more especially, in Congress, where isolationists and anti-communists found common cause in their aversion to the Bolsheviks in Moscow. And there was a further problem for the president: the inevitable competition between Britain and the Soviet Union for whatever largesse the White House might bestow on America's two unlikely allies.

Roosevelt's own instinct was to provide the Soviet Union with generous quantities of material as well as political support. In the back of his mind was the thought that the Russians were likely to play a greater part in the defeat of Nazism than the British. This led to a further calculation: the British were heavily dependent on America's generosity and had nowhere else to turn. Nor was Churchill's commitment to the defeat of Hitler in doubt. The same could not be said for Stalin. It was widely believed in both Western capitals that a rapprochement between Moscow and Berlin could not be ruled out. While Roosevelt's emissary in London knew little of the Soviet leader, Assistant Secretary of State Adolf Berle, an outspoken and influential advocate of that view, warned him that Moscow was unpredictable: 'there might be a military coup in Germany with a general emerging as dictator and an immediate Russo-German alliance. Judging by their propaganda, the Russians are apparently playing for something like this now . . . So for God's sake warn the sentimentalists to watch themselves.'[7]

Roosevelt was not a sentimentalist, but he was inclined to the somewhat romantic view that an undertaking by the United States to provide sustained political and military support was likely to cause Moscow to pause before pursuing such an alarming option. And there was another thing: he nurtured the pragmatist's hope that American largesse might in due course steer the Soviets away from their ideological cul-de-sac towards the primrose path of social democracy and thereby, following the defeat of Nazism, establish a sound basis for a post-war global settlement.

In London, Hopkins and Churchill discussed the final preparations for the first summit between the two Western leaders, which it had been agreed, should be held aboard a warship in Canadian waters early in the following month. The main purpose of the Atlantic Conference, as it was to be known, would be to draw up a charter embodying a set of guiding principles for a new world order that would secure broad, if not universal, approval. As Hopkins was well aware, though, the summit would take place in something of a vacuum without a clearer appreciation of the Soviet Union's ability to prevail against Germany.

It was arranged, therefore, for Hopkins to meet Ivan Maisky, the Soviet ambassador to Britain, at the US Embassy in London. They had a desultory conversation in which each sparred genially with the other until, apparently out of the blue, Hopkins asked 'what could be done to bring Roosevelt and Stalin closer'. Maisky was nonplussed. Hopkins explained that, for Roosevelt, the Soviet leader was 'little more than a name . . . There is nothing concrete, material or personal in Roosevelt's perception of Stalin.'[8] It was at this point that Hopkins evidently conceived a bold diplomatic initiative. Mindful that the Anglo-US summit was imminent, he asked the prime minister if it was possible to get to Moscow and back within a week. Churchill affirmed that it was, but only via the long and hazardous flight (on the route taken by Mason-MacFarlane's military mission in a Catalina flying boat a month earlier) that, he intimated, was too arduous for someone as frail as Hopkins to contemplate.

Hopkins was not deterred. With the assistance of John Winant, the US ambassador in London, he drafted a telegram to Roosevelt asking for permission to make the journey:

I have a feeling that everything should be done to make certain the Russians maintain a permanent front even though they may be defeated in the immediate battle. If Stalin could in any way be influenced at a critical time I think it would be worth doing by a personal envoy. I think the stakes are so great that it should be done. Stalin would then know in an unmistakable way that we mean business on a long-term supply job.[9]

Roosevelt gave his assent at once. Two days later Hopkins was on his way. Among those to wave him off was Averell Harriman,* the newly appointed presidential envoy to the United Kingdom. Later Harriman wrote that 'his flight seemed as much of an adventure as a trip to the moon today'.[10]

The flight was every bit as arduous as Churchill had warned. The conditions in the Sunderland flying boat were spartan and the journey took even longer than expected. Hopkins spent twenty-four hours either sitting on the machine gunner's stool at the rear of the plane or trying to sleep in one of the canvas stretchers slung along the fuselage for the crew. It was extremely uncomfortable, and when they entered the Arctic Circle also exceptionally cold. Owing to a navigational error they failed to make the expected landfall on the Russian coast. For a while they were lost, and without charts of one of the remotest regions on the planet. Only a faint radio signal from the White Sea port of Archangel, their intended destination, put them back on track. Roosevelt's envoy was evidently unperturbed. After a brief stopover, he flew on to Moscow in a lavishly appointed Douglas airliner owned by the government.

At the US Embassy, he was briefed by the ambassador, Laurence Steinhardt. The ambassador's pessimistic dispatches to Washington reflected the views of the US defence attaché, Major Ivan Yeaton, who had convinced himself that the Red Army was doomed to imminent defeat. Hopkins was sceptical about this. Before his arrival, he had read a long and well-argued memorandum from the former US ambassador, Joseph Davies (whose sanitized version of Stalin's rule of terror had done much to sustain US–Soviet relations in the mid-1930s). Davies not only

* Harriman had just been appointed by Roosevelt as a special envoy to Britain with particular responsibility for overseeing the Lend Lease programme. He had just returned from a visit to the Middle East that had convinced him, contra the Joint Chiefs, that the US should continue to supply the means to prosecute that campaign.

claimed that the Russians were far more resilient than was widely supposed but warned that it was essential to convince Stalin that the United States was not 'a capitalist enemy'; otherwise there remained a risk that he might yet make peace with Hitler 'as the lesser of two evils'.[11]*

More significantly, Hopkins also had a long conversation with the British ambassador, who was at the airport with his US counterpart to greet him. Roosevelt's envoy was due to have his first meeting with Stalin that evening and Cripps was anxious to engineer a private conversation with him beforehand, 'without mortally offending' Steinhardt, whom he held in low esteem.[12] Hopkins was evidently no less anxious to meet Cripps. When the two Americans visited the British Embassy later that morning, the envoy contrived to get rid of Steinhardt 'on the plea that he [Cripps] had to tell me a lot of things from the PM'. Cripps wasted no time before letting his guest know exactly what he thought of both Steinhardt and Yeaton. This prompted Hopkins to say – on the basis of his earlier briefing – that he agreed that both men 'entirely failed to take any broad view of the situation'. Cripps was much relieved to discover that he and the president's envoy 'saw very much eye to eye' on every important issue and he was delighted when Hopkins told him that 'Roosevelt was all out to help all he could even if the Army and Navy authorities in America didn't like it'. It was, noted Cripps, 'a great joy to have the opportunity of talking to him'.[13]

Before his meeting with Stalin, Steinhardt took Hopkins on a sightseeing tour of Moscow. He could hardly have missed the way in which the city had been elaborately camouflaged against aerial attack. Iconic buildings had been given a variety of disguises: the Bolshoi Theatre was draped in canvas which was decorated by false doors; Lenin's mausoleum in Red Square was covered with sandbags and dressed up as a two-storey cottage; the bright red stars that illuminated the spires of the Kremlin churches were hidden under grey cloth; and a graffiti specialist had done his best to turn the walls of the Kremlin itself into a row of apartment buildings. The effort was impressively strenuous but of limited value, as it was impossible to conceal the route of the River

---

* Although it was written on his departure from Moscow in 1938, Davies, whose views still commanded respect in Washington, regarded the memorandum as remaining highly pertinent.

Moskva, which snaked through the heart of the city. By the time of Hopkins's arrival the capital had been under bombardment by the Luftwaffe for just over a week. Hopkins (who had once worked for the American Red Cross as a Director of Civil Relief) was impressed by the measures taken by the city's authorities to protect its inhabitants.[14]

The first bombs had fallen on the night of 21 July. Around 200 aircraft, in wave after wave, took part in the raid. The British journalist Alexander Werth was in his apartment when the attack started just after 10 p.m. He was mesmerized by the dazzling array of searchlights arcing across the sky, air-raid sirens, the roar of approaching aircraft and then the violent crunch of bombs landing followed by the rat-tat-tat of anti-aircraft guns. As what he described as 'the real fun' started, he looked out of his kitchen window to see 'a fantastic piece of fireworks – tracer bullets, and flares, and flaming onions, and all sorts of rockets, white green and red; and the din was terrific; never saw anything like it in London [which he had witnessed first-hand during the Battle of Britain]'.[15]

Werth's colleague, the Associated Press correspondent Henry Cassidy, was in his room on the top floor of a five-storey wood-and-plaster apartment block. The building started to shake and shudder as bombs began to fall. The cascade of incendiaries that rained down in bundles sent him rushing to the 'house committee room' on the ground floor, where he found an air of remarkable order and calm. A woman was on the phone calling neighbouring house committees to ask if they needed help. A group of teenagers had been deputed to climb up to the roof in relays to act as fire-watchers. At midnight, a second wave of bombers arrived directly overhead, 'scattering incendiaries up and down the streets, like postmen delivering mail'. One landed on the roof of the building. 'Soaking wet with sweat, his red shirt open at the throat, rubbing his elbow-length asbestos gloves', one of the boys told the assembled women how he had tossed a bomb into the yard below. He was at once a hero. 'The women brought him a stool, made him sit down, despite his own objections, and petted him like a world heavy-weight championship winner in his corner.' Cassidy ventured up to the roof to find that the bomb had fallen immediately above his bedroom.[16]

Nor did the British Embassy escape. Cripps was preparing for bed when four incendiaries landed on the embassy roof. The staff managed to extinguish three of them but the fourth had landed in an inaccessible corner and set the building alight. Fire hoses were rushed in and very soon a cascade of water was pouring down the main stairs. The worst of the blaze was above Cripps's bedroom and its ceiling was soon dripping water. He was not greatly put out: 'I was able to sleep there to the accompaniment of water dripping into two buckets and the firemen hammering away in the roof as well as the fighters flying over and a few final bombers coming. No real damage was done to anything that matters.'[17]

Despite the cacophony and the casualties on that first night, Werth saw 'no signs of any devastation' as he wandered through the city the following morning. He noted that the tramcars 'were clattering along merrily' and that 'everyone looked quite cheerful – perhaps rather startled at the results of the blitz'.[18]

Not everyone was so fortunate. Ambulances raced back and forth across the city ferrying to hospital those who had been caught in the open or trapped beneath falling masonry. Altogether upwards of 370 Muscovites were either killed or severely wounded on that night, some of the latter being brave but foolhardy young men who tried to remove the bombs by picking them up with their bare hands.[19]

More than a thousand buildings had been hit in that bombardment but the impact was muted by the efficiency of the firefighters and the speed with which well-drilled teams of civil defence volunteers and others dragooned forcibly by the NKVD and other city authorities cleared the damage: craters were filled in, tram lines repaired, glass windows replaced, and streets swept of debris. These volunteers were doubtless encouraged in their task by the knowledge that three of their comrades – fighters found guilty of neglect for allowing a warehouse to burn down – were summarily executed.[20]

Compared with the ravages inflicted on London, the damage wrought by the Luftwaffe was modest in scale. However, many of the capital's most prominent landmarks were to be destroyed or badly damaged in the following weeks, despite the camouflage. They included Moscow University, the Pushkin Art Gallery, the Bolshoi Theatre, Tolstoy's house and the offices of *Pravda* and *Izvestia*. Only the metro stations were truly safe during a raid. As in London, these became bomb shelters at night. Muscovites, mostly women and children, queued patiently as they waited to file down on to the platforms. As one local doctor observed, order prevailed:

They lie in careful order. Each family has its area. They spread out news-papers, then blankets and pillows. Children sleep, adults amuse themselves in various ways. They drink tea, even with jam. They visit each other. They talk quietly. They play dominoes. There are several pairs of chess players, surrounded by 'fans'. Many read books, knit, darn stockings, repair linens – in a word, they were set up well and for a long time. Places are permanent, 'subscribed'. Along both sides of the tunnel stand trains, where on the seats small children sleep.[21]

N. Erastova (her full name remains unknown) was among the thousands of young women who had 'signed on' to join the Red Army as a volunteer in the hope of being sent to the front as medical orderlies and nurses. Instead she was sent to a metro station to administer first aid to the sick and wounded. During a rudimentary training programme, she had almost fainted at her first sight of blood. In the crowded gloom of the underground she was relieved that she did not have to assist at one of the many premature births that the crisis appeared to induce. But she was busy throughout the night: 'With our medical bags and Red Crosses on our sleeves we were in constant demand. The most common request was for some sedative.' So great was the need that the nurses took to mixing the sedative – valerian – with water.* It appeared to be just as effective. 'There was so much gratitude – "thank you, dear nurse, I feel better now" – it was pure psychotherapy.' Before long, Erastova's wish to be at the front would be granted. She would join the 6th People's Militia Division, where – as she put it – 'I saw so much blood that I became quite used to it.'[22]

During the early days, the stations were crammed with up to 750,000 sleeping bodies, but as the bombing became a routine event, the fear began to evaporate. Many citizens elected to emulate the British ambassador and sleep in their own beds, evidently judging their lives to be at little greater risk in their lath-and-plaster apartments than underground. They were not, of course: figures produced by the Soviet authorities put the total death toll for the first nine months of the Luftwaffe's bombing campaign at upwards of 2,000, with almost three times as many wounded. The number would have been far higher without the

---

* Valerian is a herbal remedy for pain, tension and insomnia manufactured from the root of the plant *Valeriana officinalis*.

heavy guns that girdled the city and the scores of Soviet fighters that patrolled the skies overhead, between them downing an estimated 10 per cent of the attacking aircraft.★

Roosevelt once said of his envoy, 'Harry is the perfect ambassador for my purposes. He doesn't even know the meaning of the word "protocol". When he sees a piece of red tape he just pulls out those old garden shears and snips it. And when he's talking to some foreign dignitary he knows how to slump back in his chair and put his feet up on the conference table and say "Oh, yeah?"'[23] Hopkins adopted that approach – if not that posture – when he was ushered into the presence of Stalin for the first time. He was neither overawed nor intimidated but he was immediately impressed. 'He welcomed me with a few, swift Russian words. He shook my hand briefly, firmly, courteously. He smiled warmly. There was no waste of word, gesture, nor mannerism.'[24]

After the preliminaries, during which Stalin spoke of the interests shared by their two nations, Hopkins cut to the chase. This meeting, he said, was about aid to the Soviet Union – both the immediate supplies required by the Red Army and those that would be needed if the war were to last a long time. Stalin did not hesitate before rattling off a detailed shopping list in both categories. His urgent need was for 20,000 pieces of anti-aircraft artillery (both large and small), machine guns for the defence of his cities and more than a million rifles. In the case of a long war he would need aviation fuel and aluminium. 'Give us the anti-aircraft guns and the aluminium and we can fight for three or four years,' he declared as their first meeting came to an end.[25] The two men arranged to meet again the following evening.

On the next day, 31 July, Cripps and Hopkins again had lunch together unaccompanied. It was a crucial occasion at which Hopkins listened closely as the British ambassador outlined his strong personal view – which was by no means yet endorsed by London – that the future of Europe depended on the establishment of an Anglo-US-Soviet alliance, and that this could be achieved only 'by immediate military co-operation sustained by long-term political agreements'. Knowing that endorsement

---

★ These figures were dwarfed by those for the London Blitz, in which nearly 30,000 people were killed and a further 50,000 injured.

by Hopkins would be crucial, Cripps advocated a tripartite conference between Britain, the United States and the Soviet Union. Hopkins agreed.

At his second meeting with Stalin, the Soviet leader once again demonstrated his mastery of detail and his clarity of strategic purpose. In an office lined with elaborate maps of the battlefront, he listed at much greater length the weaponry required to withstand the German onslaught. It was, noted the US ambassador afterwards, the first time that the paranoid and secretive Soviet leader had opened up with 'such unparalleled frankness' to any foreign official.[26] Thus encouraged, Hopkins responded by elaborating the proposal floated by Cripps over lunch. He suggested that the tripartite conference should be held in Moscow to allow the three great powers 'fully and jointly [to explore] the relative interests of each front as well as the interests of our several countries'.[27] Stalin responded enthusiastically, asking Hopkins to convey a personal message to Roosevelt:

> The might of Germany was so great that, even though Russia might defend herself, it would be very difficult for Britain and Russia combined to crush the German military machine . . . the one thing that could defeat Hitler, and perhaps even without firing a shot, would be the announcement that the United States is going to join in the war with Germany.

Hopkins was careful to remain non-committal about that, but he was heartened by Stalin's tone, and especially by his flattering assertion that the president and the United States 'had more influence with the common people of the world today than any other force'.[28]

Roosevelt's envoy was too steely to be seduced by the Soviet leader's blandishments, but he was not unmoved by his force of personality and commanding presence. In as vivid a portrait as any other, he wrote subsequently:

> No man could forget the picture of the dictator of Russia as he stood watching me leave – an austere, rugged, determined figure in boots that shone like mirrors, stout baggy trousers, and snug-fitting blouse. He wore no ornament, military or civilian . . . His hands are huge, as hard as his mind. His voice is harsh but ever under control. What he says is all the accent and inflection his words need . . . He curries no favour with

you. He seems to have no doubts. He assures you that Russia will stand firm against the onslaughts of the German Army. He takes it for granted that you will have no doubts, either.[29]

After breakfast on the day of his departure, 1 August, Hopkins made time for a further meeting with Cripps. The British ambassador had not been idle. Encouraged by Hopkins's account of his meeting with Stalin, Cripps handed him the draft of a joint message that he had crafted the previous evening for Churchill and Roosevelt to send to Stalin. It contained a formal proposal for representatives of the American and British governments to meet Stalin in the Soviet capital. To press his case further, Cripps sent a memorandum, via Hopkins, for the two Western leaders to discuss at their forthcoming summit, which was due to start within a few days. Advising that the Russians should be given 'all the supplies that we can raise because that is at the moment the weakest point of the enemy and therefore our best chance of success',[30] he added that it would be an act of 'supreme folly' to deprive the Soviets of materiel, the absence of which might turn their retreat into a 'rout'.[31] Cannily enclosing with his memorandum a tin of Russian caviar and two bottles of vodka for the president, he also added a note in which he expressed his hope that the two Western leaders would 'implement the suggestion that I know he [Hopkins] is going to put forward'.[32]

Cripps's plea on Stalin's behalf could hardly have been interpreted as other than an ill-concealed dig at his own prime minister's curmudgeonly exchanges with the Soviet leader. By contrast, the American president was – as he knew from Hopkins – very likely to be sympathetic. On the very day that Cripps was colluding with the American envoy to push their joint initiative, Roosevelt was goading his officials to accelerate the delivery of aid to the Soviet Union. Berating the Secretary of War, Henry L. Stimson, at a Cabinet meeting for failing to dispatch the 200 aircraft and other 'token' shipments which had already been promised to Moscow, he evidently said that he was 'sick and tired of hearing that they [the Russians] are going to get this and they are going to get that . . . he wanted to hear what was on the water'.[33] In Hopkins's absence he summoned another senior administrator, Wayne Coy, and instructed him to free the logjam: 'Please . . . with my full authority, use a heavy hand – act as a burr under the saddle and get things moving.' And, on the eve of his own departure for his summit with Churchill, he told Coy that if the German invasion could be held for the next two months, 'Russia is safe until the spring. Step on it.'[34]

Hopkins flew back to London elated by his triumphant visit to Moscow but forgetting the bag of medicines on which his very life depended. Buffeted by strong headwinds, the flying boat took twenty-four hours to reach Scapa Flow in Orkney. By the time the pilot touched down in a rough seaway close to the shore, Hopkins was not merely exhausted but so ill that, according to his biographer, there were renewed fears for his life. Doctors were summoned and he was sent to bed with enough drugs to ensure he had a long sleep.[35] When he awoke, it was time to join the prime minister aboard HMS *Prince of Wales* for the voyage across the Atlantic for the first summit between the two Western leaders.

Churchill noted solicitously that his friend was 'much exhausted',[36] though he soon recovered enough to fill the spare hours on the five-day crossing playing backgammon with the prime minister, despite seas so rough that the destroyers escorting the battleship were forced to turn back, leaving the *Prince of Wales* to steam alone to the rendezvous in Placentia Bay – at a speed no marauding U-boat could possibly match.★

The Anglo-American summit took place aboard the cruiser USS *Augusta*. The two leaders had been in correspondence but it was their first meeting as the heads of their respective governments. Each regarded the other with wary respect. According to Churchill's aide-de-camp, Sir Ian Jacob, their initial conversation 'had something of the nature of the first meeting between two stags; the two great men wanted to have a good look at each other'.[37] They were both aware that – aside from a shared abhorrence of Nazism – their priorities did not yet align. Moreover, the balance of power between them was not as even as the cavalcade of military chiefs and government officials accompanying them might have suggested: Churchill's private secretary, John Colville, noted sniffily that his boss had brought with him 'a retinue which Cardinal Wolsey might have envied'.[38] When Hopkins told friends, 'You'd have thought Winston was being brought up to the heavens to meet God,' he was merely

---

★ On 10 December, three days after the attack on Pearl Harbor, the *Prince of Wales* was sunk by Japanese aircraft in the Pacific.

giving expression to the fact that the British prime minister arrived aboard *Augusta* as more supplicant than peer.[39]

Among the papers Hopkins had carried with him from Washington on his trip to London and Moscow was a one-line aide-memoire, which he had jotted down following his pre-departure meeting with Roosevelt. It was blunt and unambiguous: 'No talk about war.' At Number 10, Hopkins had made this very clear to the prime minister: he was not to raise the issue during the summit. The subject was taboo. Churchill was disinclined to heed this injunction. On his very first evening aboard the US vessel in Placentia Bay, he seized the moment with characteristic chutzpah. At an informal 'getting-to-know-you' session with the Americans, who barely knew their British counterparts, he held forth without restraint. Even Roosevelt's Anglophobic son, Elliott, was captivated by the prime minister's artistry: 'Churchill reared back in his chair . . . slewed his cigar from cheek to cheek . . . his hands slashed the air expressively, his eyes flashed. He held the floor that evening and he talked. Nor were the rest of us silent because we were bored. He held us enthralled.'[40] The president listened intently without once interrupting his guest. Churchill's tour d'horizon was clearly also a tour de force conveying the clear if unstated message that it would be in the interests of the United States, no less than those of the United Kingdom, to take up the cudgels against Nazi Germany. A short while later, during a conversation with Roosevelt's most senior advisors, he made the point unambiguously, telling them, 'I would rather have an American declaration of war now and no supplies for six months than double the supplies and no declaration.'[41]

Churchill's hyperbole reflected the intensity of the sentiment. He knew that without America's direct participation, the challenge of securing Britain's global needs against the threats posed by both the Japanese in the Pacific and the Nazis in Europe was likely to prove insuperable. His purpose at Placentia was therefore to seduce the president into making public commitments that would inevitably draw America openly into war. Roosevelt was sympathetic, but far too wily to succumb. Although he foresaw that, in due course, the United States was bound to take up arms against the enemies of freedom and democracy, he was also a cunning politician who recognized that ambiguity and duplicity had crucial roles to play in steering the American voters towards that

inevitability. His political antennae were acutely sensitive to the isolationist sentiment that still held sway across the nation and in Congress.
According to Churchill, the president explained that he was 'skating on
pretty thin ice in his relations with Congress' and any request for a declaration of war would only produce a long-drawn-out and inconclusive
debate.[42] From Roosevelt's standpoint, therefore, the purpose of the
Atlantic Conference was merely to alert American opinion to the threat
to their own values and interests posed by the Nazis. It was not, as
Churchill had hoped it might become, an undertaking to mobilize the
United States for war.

Both sides had agreed that their summit needed to conclude with an
Anglo-American declaration of intent that might form the constitutional basis for the establishment of future global peace and security.
Officials on both sides spent three days wrangling over the wording of
every line of what was to be called the Atlantic Charter. They drafted
and redrafted until, on 12 August, they produced a document to which
the two leaders were able to give their approval. The 'Joint Declaration'
was something of a damp squib. The principles it enshrined (which
would later form the blueprint for the 1948 Universal Declaration of
Human Rights) were couched in such innocuous terms as virtually to
guarantee universal consent; only the most purblind dictators would
fail to see the cost-free advantages of putting their names to a grandiose
statement of intent that could be ignored with impunity.

To Churchill's disappointment, Roosevelt refused to commit himself
to the establishment of an international organization to police the post-
war order which the Joint Declaration envisaged. However, he managed
to draw some comfort from the 'astonishing' fact that the leader of an
ostensibly neutral power (the US) had joined with a belligerent state
(the UK) to endorse a charter that included a reference to the 'final
destruction of the Nazi tyranny'.[43] In truth, these were thin pickings
and he knew it. Though he and Roosevelt did their best to promote the
global significance of their eight-point charter with their respective
electorates, it made little impact. As Eden's private secretary, Oliver
Harvey, noted, it was a 'terribly woolly document full of all the old
clichés of the League of Nations'.[44] A few days later the well-connected
diarist Harold Nicolson observed that the 'eight points have fallen very
flat'.[45] The American voter was similarly unmoved. Moreover, the

polls – which came as no surprise to Roosevelt – showed that 70 per cent of the public remained stubbornly resistant to the idea that 'our boys' should be sent into battle against the Germans.

On his return to London, Churchill tried to rally the nation in a broadcast to the British people. He was at his most mellifluous and grandiloquent, claiming to have returned 'across the waves, uplifted in spirit, fortified in resolve' as a result of his meeting with 'our great friend the president of the United States'.[46] He also allowed himself to indulge in an unwarranted degree of wishful thinking by interpreting the Atlantic Charter's reference to 'the final destruction of the Nazi tyranny' as a presidential pledge 'which must be made good'. He was therefore cast into gloom when he heard Roosevelt insist firmly and publicly that the United States was not on the brink of declaring war on Germany. If his broadcast was designed to bounce the president into war, it failed lamentably.

In a bleak note to Hopkins a few days later, Churchill wrote, 'The president's many declarations with regard to the United States being no closer to war and having made no commitments have been the cause of concern here in London and in the Cabinet . . . I don't know what will happen if England [sic] is fighting alone when 1942 comes.'[47] Neither Hopkins nor Roosevelt was sympathetic, though the former did appreciate that the president's often opaque interventions could easily be misinterpreted by a wishful thinker as conveying more than was intended. He was also worried enough by Churchill's gloom to warn Roosevelt that if the British came to believe that the United States had no intention ever of becoming a belligerent 'it would be a very critical moment in the war and the British appeasers might have more influence on Churchill'.[48]

As it was, the prime minister's disappointment should have been tempered by knowing that Roosevelt had every intention of steering the United States towards belligerency at his own pace and in his own way. At a meeting of the War Cabinet on his return to London, Churchill reported the president as telling him that 'he would wage war, but not declare it, and that he would become more and more provocative'.[49] This was precisely Roosevelt's strategy: to advance crabwise towards a confrontation with Germany rather than to make public declarations of belligerency.

Nor was the Soviet Union excluded. On the contrary. Nearly every significant decision made at Placentia Bay was made behind closed port-holes and without any attendant publicity. And almost every one of these decisions related either directly or indirectly to the Soviet Union. Roosevelt's impatience with his officials for the tardy implementation of his commitment to provide the Soviets with aid sprang from a grow-ing sense of urgency. Convinced that Germany's eventual defeat hinged as much – if not more – on the outcome of Operation Barbarossa as on Britain's indomitability, he was determined to ensure the delivery of US aid to both allies as swiftly and safely as possible. The principal threat to the provision of this support came from the U-boats prowling the Atlantic in search of merchant convoys to sink. Nothing was now more important to him than combating this menace. If, in the process, he were to engineer a confrontation with the U-boats in the Atlantic for which the blame could be pinned on German aggression, he was confi-dent he could secure the approval of Congress to accelerate the preparations for war without laying himself open to the charge of warmongering.

Even before Hitler's invasion of the Soviet Union, Roosevelt had unilaterally – in April 1941 – extended the geographical boundaries of the US Security Zone in the Atlantic well beyond the western hemi-sphere as far out as longitude 26°W, a north–south line on the chart between Greenland and the Azores and some 2,600 miles from the American coastline. Within that vast expanse, US air and maritime patrols were charged to monitor the movement of hostile vessels and alert the Royal Navy to any perceived threat to the Allied convoys. At the Atlantic Conference, he went much further.

In a private meeting aboard *Augusta*, he told his military and naval advisors that, as from 1 September, US warships would be required to escort any merchant convoys through the hazardous seas between the Atlantic seaboard and Iceland, which was the stop-off on the main sea route from the United States to Britain and the Soviet Union. This was tantamount to warning Berlin that an attempt to sink any vessel in such a convoy between the United States and Iceland would be treated as an act of aggression against the United States. All he needed was a pretext to provoke such an act. He soon found it.

On 4 September, a German U-boat – under strict orders from Hitler to avoid attacking any US vessel – was goaded into attacking the USS

Greer. The US warship escaped unscathed but the president seized on the incident to deliver a Fireside Chat in which he ridiculed 'the tender whisperings of appeasers that Hitler is not interested in the Western Hemisphere' and insisted that this skirmish in the Atlantic represented 'one determined step towards creating a permanent world system based on force, on terror, and on murder'. As righteous as it was disingenuous, his performance was vintage Roosevelt. While insisting that the United States did not seek 'a shooting war with Hitler', he advised his listeners that, henceforth, 'if any German or Italian vessels of war enter the waters, the protection of which is necessary for American defence, they do so at their own peril'.[50] This 'shoot on sight' policy, as it became known, was the logical escalation of the plan he had hatched with his officials during the Atlantic Conference. His Fireside Chat was an unofficial – not de jure but de facto – declaration of a not-so-phony war. It could only hearten both London and Moscow.

Stalin had even greater cause to be gratified by another decision reached in the seclusion of Placentia Bay. Although neither Churchill nor Roosevelt made any public reference to the memorandum drafted by Cripps and endorsed by Hopkins at their meeting in Moscow, it had landed in the president's in-tray at an opportune moment. Unlike Churchill, who had no choice but to endorse what he described begrudgingly as the 'arrival of Russia as a welcome guest at [a] hungry table',[51] Roosevelt was genuinely committed to providing the Soviet Union with as much materiel as his 'Arsenal of Democracy' could provide. Churchill had to conceal his pique at the thought that every piece of weaponry dispatched to the Soviet Union was one less for Britain.

On 14 August, using Cripps's draft almost verbatim, the two Western leaders sent their first joint message to Stalin. Describing 'the long and hard path to be traversed before there can be that complete victory without which our efforts and sacrifices would be in vain', and warning that 'our resources, though immense, are limited and it must become a question of where and when those can best be used to further to the greatest extent our common effort', they proposed 'a meeting which should be held in Moscow, to which we would send high representatives who could discuss these matters directly with you'.[52]

Stalin was elated and gave his ready consent to the suggestion. He would have been even happier if he had been privy to the private letter that the president sent to his Secretary of State for War, Stimson, at the end of August. 'I deem it to be of paramount importance for the safety and security of America', he wrote, 'that all reasonable munitions help be provided for Russia, not only immediately but as long as she continues to fight the Axis powers effectively. I am convinced that substantial and comprehensive commitments must be made.'[53]

It was a transformative moment in the relationship between the Western Allies and the Soviet Union from which can be traced a series of events that would shape the course of the Second World War and the fate of the Third Reich.

15. Disarray on the Soviet Front

In his meeting with Hopkins, Stalin may have spoken with 'unparalleled frankness', but he had been decidedly economical with the truth. His measured and cautiously optimistic account of the Red Army's prowess on the battlefield was belied by the facts and by his own agitated response to a growing crisis at the front. More especially, but not surprisingly, he made no mention of his stormy encounter with his chief of staff on the very day of the American envoy's arrival in Moscow.

Summoned to the Kremlin on 30 July, Zhukov laid out his maps before Stalin and the ever-attentive and always sinister political commissar, Lev Mekhlis. His appreciation of the Red Army's predicament was candid. He did not disguise the scale of Soviet losses or the weakness of the reserve forces at his command. He was in the midst of predicting where the next German thrust might threaten when he was interrupted by Mekhlis, who, in his silkily subversive fashion, asked on what basis he had derived his assessment. Not unreasonably, the chief of staff replied that he was unaware of the enemy's plans but his conclusions were drawn from a considered analysis of the enemy's current deployments. Stalin prompted him to continue.

Zhukov did not hold back. The Soviet armies were under severe pressure at 'the most dangerous and weakest sector of our line . . . the Central Front'. 'What do you suggest?' Stalin demanded. Again, unlike most of his peers, Zhukov did not hesitate to speak his mind. Three armies – two from the southern front and another from the headquarters reserve protecting the approaches to Moscow – should be redeployed to plug the gap. Pressed brusquely by Stalin, he explained that this would not weaken the capital's defences as at least eight divisions could be summoned from the Far East as replacements. Stalin interjected roughly: 'And hand over the Far East to the Japanese?' Zhukov was not to be deflected but insisted that forces on the Southwestern Front protecting Kiev should be withdrawn from their positions east of the River

Dnieper and that five divisions be moved from there to support the southern edges of the Central Front. Stalin became belligerent: 'And what about Kiev, in that case?' The chief of staff retorted that the appropriate tactical move would be to allow the city to fall. Stalin erupted, 'You are talking rubbish.'

At this, Zhukov became incensed. If Stalin really believed that was so, he shot back angrily, then he should be relieved of his post and sent to fight at the front. Stalin did not back off. Telling him to calm down, he sneered, 'Since you mention it, we will get by without you.' After further heated argument, Zhukov gathered up his maps and stalked out. Forty minutes later Stalin summoned him back, but only to tell him formally that he was indeed to be released from his post. He would take command of the Reserve Front armies, where, Stalin told him mockingly, he was to plan a counter-attack on the salient at Yelnya, fifty kilometres south-east of Smolensk, which the chief of staff had identified as a likely launch pad for the next stage of the German assault on the capital. As Stalin would soon discover, far from speaking rubbish, Zhukov had been spot on.[1]

The Red Army's predicament was acute. With Army Group North approaching Leningrad's outer defences from the south, and seven Finnish infantry divisions advancing towards the city's northern suburbs, the Northern Front's four Soviet armies under General Popov were in mounting disarray. Leningrad was clearly going to be besieged and might even be encircled. At the other end of the 1,000-kilometre front, Army Group South's armies had advanced relentlessly through eastern Ukraine and, despite suicidally brave counter-attacks by the Soviet infantry, were poised to cross the Dnieper; like Leningrad, Kiev too was threatened by encirclement. It was no better on the Central Front. As both Zhukov and Timoshenko were aware, Bock's armies, though themselves wearied by the stubborn resistance of the Soviet troops, were exacting a fearful toll in lives and military hardware.

At the outbreak of war, Vasily Grossman, already renowned as writer and novelist, was seconded to the Red Army newspaper, *Krasnaya Zvezda* (Red Star) to serve as a special correspondent. He was disappointed to have been turned down for active duty, although, as he was both short-sighted and distinctly overweight, his rejection was perhaps not surprising. Since this forcibly liberated him to become the finest chronicler of the Nazi–Soviet campaign, however, it was to prove an invaluable reprieve.

Grossman was not only intrepid but also astonishingly careless of his own safety. His determination to play a full part in the Great Patriotic War was assuredly influenced by his intense anxiety and guilt about his mother, who had been trapped in the Ukrainian city of Berdychiv by the invading German troops.* On 5 August, after repeatedly pressuring his editor, he was finally allowed to head for the town of Gomel, 560 kilometres south-west of Moscow, where Pavlov's replacement, Yeremenko, had set up his Western Front headquarters after his forced withdrawal from Minsk. Grossman, who was thirty-five, was accompanied by two younger war-hardened colleagues who had been deputed by his editor to look after the eminent writer.

Grossman was a humane and gifted observer who rarely missed a telling detail. At Bryansk, where they had to change trains, Grossman noted that 'every corner' of the railway station was 'filled with Red Army soldiers. Many of them are badly dressed in rags. They have already been "there". Abkhazians [from the North Caucasus] look the worst. Many of them are barefoot.'[2] On the next stage of their journey, the three men had a disconcerting encounter with a female nurse, who used her boots and her fists to try to force them off the steps of a train steaming at full speed, shouting, 'Jump off this second! It is forbidden to travel on hospital trains.'[3] She did not succeed. In Gomel, they were welcomed by an air-raid siren. Once the bombs had fallen and the planes had left, Grossman went for a stroll. 'What sadness there is in this quiet green town, in these sweet public gardens, in its old people sitting on the benches, its sweet girls walking along the streets. Children are playing in the piles of sand brought here to extinguish incendiary bombs . . . The Germans are less than fifty kilometres away,' he noted.[4]

At Yeremenko's headquarters, he was told by the chief of the front's political department, Brigade Commissar Kozlov, that 'the Military

---

* According to Grossman's daughter, Katya, he had wanted to bring his mother, Yekaterina Savelievna, to Moscow when the war began, and he had had the opportunity to rescue her before the Germans reached the city. However, his second wife, Olga Mikhailovna, evidently objected and he did not press the issue. Along with 12,000 other Jews, his mother was murdered by a squad of SS killers on 15 September 1941. Grossman never forgave himself.

Council was very alarmed by the news' that had just reached them: Roslavl, only 150 kilometres to the north-west, had just fallen to Guderian's panzers. Already the mere mention of that name sent a frisson of fear throughout the Soviet High Command. His pre-war book, *Achtung! Achtung!* – in which he had assiduously promoted and exaggerated his own contribution to revolutionary ideas about modern tank warfare – had been widely read by military strategists across Europe. Their successful application of the blitzkrieg through the Low Countries and France, as well as on Soviet soil during the previous six weeks, had given Guderian near-mythical status. The capture of Roslavl appeared to be one more milestone on his way to Moscow. Grossman's gloom and disillusion were not dispelled by picking up a copy of the brigade newspaper to read its leading article: 'The much-battered enemy continued on his cowardly advance.'[5]

Accompanied by one of his colleagues, Oleg Knorring, Grossman was driven to a military airfield outside Gomel, where the 103rd Red Army Aviation Fighter Division was based. On the way, they passed wagons, carts and peasants retreating from the German bombardment. He arrived in one village that seemed to be 'full of peace – nice, calm, village life – with children playing, and old people and women sitting on benches', until suddenly three German bombers appeared overhead. 'Bombs exploded. Screams. Red flames with white smoke.' Grossman himself came under fire and hurried to hide on the edge of a cemetery. Some nearby soldiers, digging a grave for a fallen colleague, rushed to hide in a ditch. This displeased the officer in charge. 'The lieutenant shouts: "Carry on digging, otherwise we won't finish until evening . . ." They ignore him. Everyone runs in different directions. Only the dead signaller is lying full length. And machine guns are chattering above him.'[6]

At the airbase, where many buildings had been destroyed, he was impressed by the bravado of a young pilot. 'I've shot down a Junkers 88 for the Motherland,'[*] the pilot told Grossman, adding, 'There's no anxiety [but] anger, fury. And when you see he's on fire, light comes into your soul . . . Who's going to turn away? Him or me? I am not going to. I have become a single whole with the plane and don't feel anything any longer.'[7]

---

[*] The Junkers Ju 88 was a versatile twin-engine medium-range bomber, highly effective in a variety of roles; 15,000 were produced between 1939 and 1945.

Bravado went hand-in-hand with self-delusion. The regiment's commander, Nikolai Nemtsevich, wanted Grossman to believe that no German aircraft had appeared over his airbase for ten days. His explanation for this was categorical: 'The Germans have no fuel, the Germans have no aircraft, they have all been shot down.' Grossman was drily impressed: 'I've never heard such a speech – what optimism! This trait of character is both good and harmful at the same time, but at any rate he'll never make a strategist.'[8]

That night he was put up in a large, empty multi-storey building at the airbase. 'It was deserted, dark, frightening and sad. Hundreds of women and children were living here a short time ago, families of pilots.' He did not sleep easy. At one point he was woken by 'a frightening low humming' and went outside: 'Squadrons of German bombers were flying eastwards over our heads, evidently those very ones Nemtsevich spoke about during the day, the ones he said had no fuel and were destroyed.'[9]

The Soviet pilots raced to their aircraft. Grossman described 'the roar of engines starting up, dust, and wind . . . Aircraft went up into the sky one after another, circled and flew away. And immediately the airfield became empty and silent, like a classroom where the pupils have skipped away.' Later, they returned:

> The lead aircraft had human flesh stuck in the radiator. That's because the supporting aircraft had hit a truck with ammunition that blew up at the moment the leader was flying over it. Poppe, the leader, is picking the meat out with a file. They summon a doctor who examines the bloody mass attentively and pronounced [it] 'Aryan meat!' Everyone laughs. Yes, a pitiless time – a time of iron – has come![10]

The laughter did not last long. A few days later, Grossman was forced to join the flight from Gomel, which fell soon after to Guderian's panzers.

A little further to the north, Nikolai Amosov, the army surgeon, was setting up his field hospital in the village of Zhuzdry, a mere eight kilometres from Roslavl. The staff of Field Hospital 226 had travelled 180 kilometres over six days with twenty-two horse-drawn carts carrying their equipment as well as those nurses who were unable to walk because their blisters were too severe or because they had not been provided with boots. The medical team was stoical. 'We only drive on small dirt roads as we want to avoid bombings and vehicles . . . We don't even know the news as we have no radio . . . We sleep on the ground, we fall asleep in the evening but the cold wakes us at night, the nights are so terribly cold,' Amosov noted.[11] They only realized how close they were to the front when they began to see Red Army soldiers, artillery and ammunition trucks. At one point, Amosov went forward to find out what was happening. He found confusion and contradiction: 'There is fighting in Roslavl'; 'our men are defending the line ten kilometres west of Roslavl'; 'the Germans have broken through and are pushing forward, it is scary!'; and 'Don't you see? Roslavl is on fire.'

As dusk fell, Amosov and his team reached the main highway. They saw soldiers setting up their artillery and firing in the direction of the smoke. Obeying his original orders – which had dispatched them to a front that, though they did not yet know it, had already fallen – Amosov continued along the highway towards Roslavl. The road was crowded with vehicles. An officer in a command truck stopped them: 'Show me your map and the order,' he demanded. He read it briefly and then instructed, 'Turn around and go back as fast as you can.' In his confusion, Amosov stood in silence. 'Come on, I give the orders! I am responsible. I am Colonel Tikhonov . . . Is that clear?'

Field Hospital 226 duly turned to retreat eastward until they reached the village of Sukhinichi, twenty kilometres down the road. There they pitched camp and set up a dressing station. As they were doing so, bombs started to fall nearby. A nurse rushed in. 'The wounded are here!' she shouted. Three trucks packed with injured soldiers drove into the compound. 'Here they are,' Amosov noted. 'Sunken cheeks, dirty, most of them in their tunics, no greatcoats. Slit sleeves or trouser legs. Most of them have fresh bandages, many of them are falling asleep while leaning against the wall, or on the floor . . . we take them to the bathhouse.' The hot water evidently raised their spirits. 'There are smiles and even jokes. "Comrade Military Doctor, thanks for the banya! I've not washed since I was in the reserve regiment." '[12]

On another part of the same front, the young political commissar Nikolai Moskvin was in a very different state of mind. Three weeks earlier he had shot his first deserter. Maddened by the accumulating terror of shelling, lack of sleep and long retreating marches, the soldier suddenly took it upon himself to urge his comrades to lay down their arms. He came up to Moskvin. 'He made a salute to, I suppose, Hitler, shouldered his rifle and walked off towards the scrub . . . Red Army private Shulyak brought him down with a bullet in the back.' The man fell to the ground. 'They'll kill the lot of you,' the soldier swore, before looking up at Moskvin to spit out, 'And you, you blood-stained commissar, they'll hang you first.' Trained to be ruthless, the commissar took out his revolver and fired into the writhing body. 'The boys understood. A dog's death for a dog.'[13] It was a duty, not a pleasure.

Stalin's reaction to reports that large numbers of troops were either deserting the front or surrendering prompted him to a characteristic response. On 16 August he issued Order No. 270. In leaden and repetitive language, he began by commending those commanders who had behaved 'courageously – and sometimes heroically' in leading their men out of one or another of the encirclements. Among others, he singled out the deputy commander of the Western Front, General Boldin, who had led more than 1,000 men not only out of the encirclement at Białystok but also eastwards behind enemy lines until they managed to rejoin the main force forty-five days later near Smolensk.★ In the course of this epic venture, Stalin noted they 'destroyed the headquarters of two German regiments, twenty-six tanks, 1,049 passenger vehicles, transport vehicles and staff cars, 147 motorcycles, five batteries of artillery, four mortars, fifteen machine guns, one aeroplane at the airport and a bomb arsenal'. Even if the figures Stalin gave were suspiciously precise, there was no doubt that it had been an heroic achievement.

But there had also been 'shameful acts of surrender', and 'certain generals' had been 'a bad example to our troops'. Among these, he cited the commander of the 28th Army, Lieutenant General Vladimir Kachalov, whose troops were encircled at Smolensk. According to Stalin, Kachalov had 'showed cowardice and surrendered to the German fascists . . . [choosing thereby] to defect to the enemy'. Although this accusation was entirely false – Kachalov had in fact been killed in action – he was, in absentia, posthumously sentenced to death.

Stalin also singled out Major General Pavel Ponedelin, the commander of the 12th Army during the defence of Kiev. Along with the 6th Army,

★ See Chapter 11.

Ponedelin's troops had been trapped on open ground to the west of the Dnieper at Uman by the overwhelming firepower of Rundstedt's Army Group South. On 1 August, after repeated attempts by both Soviet armies to break out, Ponedelin sent a message to the Southern Front Command which was copied to Stalin: 'The situation has become critical. The encirclement of the 6th and 12th armies is completed . . . There are no reserves. There is no ammunition, the fuel is running out.'[14] By 6 August, Rundstedt's troops had closed the noose so tightly that both armies were under artillery fire on all sides from a distance of no more than ten kilometres. Rather than being mown down where they stood, 100,000 Soviet troops surrendered. Instead of falling on his sword, Pone-delin allowed himself to be taken prisoner when his tank was hit by enemy fire. By 'deserting to the enemy' he had, in Stalin's book, commit-ted 'the crime against the country of breaking a military oath'.*

Order No. 270 continued, 'Can we put up with the Red Army cow-ards, deserters who surrender themselves to the enemy as prisoners, or their craven superiors, who at the first hitch at the front tear off their insignia and desert to the rear? No, we cannot.' There followed a list of punishments for such criminals. In future they would be considered as 'malicious deserters' who should be shot on the spot while their families would be arrested for this 'betrayal of their homeland'. All 'encircled units and formations' were 'to selflessly fight to the last'. Any unit that 'prefers to become a prisoner' would be 'destroyed by all means possible on land and air, and their families deprived of public benefits and assistance'.

The practice of punishing a soldier's family by withholding his pen-sion and other entitlements was not new but, as Catherine Merridale has pointed out, the prospect of imprisonment in a system 'where, even a child's schooling depended on a family's collective honour in official eyes' was peculiarly harsh. One of the cruellest side-effects of these vin-dictive measures was the Kafkaesque ruling that those who were 'missing in action' – whether they had been 'shot down over rivers and marshes, blown to pieces or gnawed away by rats' – were, like those who surren-dered, to be treated as 'malicious deserters' with similar consequences

---

* Ponedelin was held by the Germans until the end of the war. In 1950, Stalin ordered his execution by firing squad. He was 'rehabilitated' in 1956 after Stalin's death.

for their families.[15] So that no one could be in doubt about its meaning, Stalin instructed that Order No. 270 be read out in full to 'all companies, squadrons, batteries, teams and staffs'.[16] The promulgation of these regulations was a mark not only of Stalin's merciless nature but also of his deepening fear that the Soviet Union was in extreme peril. If the nation's soldiers were not inspired by patriotism to choose a suicidal death on the battlefield then they would be terrorized into doing their duty for the Motherland.

There was another means of instilling terror into any soldier contemplating surrender. It was just as potent and entirely beyond Stalin's ability to control. It was the growing awareness of what would happen to you if you fell into enemy hands. Commissar Moskvin found this out, by chance, soon after he had dutifully executed a deserter – 'a dog's death for a dog' – when his unit came under fierce attack once again. This time, virtually the entire regiment was annihilated. Moskvin and two comrades found themselves alone in the forest. Moskvin was seriously wounded, and despairing. Unable to sleep and fearful of gangrene, he nonetheless found the strength to make a note in his diary: 'I am on the verge of a complete moral collapse . . . I feel guilty because I am helpless and because I know I should pull myself together.'[17] In the event the men were found by a group of peasants who evidently thought that, once they had recuperated, they could be put to work in their fields.

It was then that Moskvin met the first of several Soviet soldiers he would encounter who had escaped the Nazi prison camps. He was horrified by what he was told: 'They say there's no shelter, no water, that people are dying from hunger and disease, that many are without proper clothes or shoes. They are treated like slaves, shot for the slightest misdemeanour, or just from mischief, for a kind of fun.'[18] This was not an exaggeration. The word soon spread. As thousands of their comrades had already discovered, to be taken prisoner, herded onto a train or frogmarched into captivity, was to suffer a fate equally bad as, if not worse than, being killed on the battlefield.

On paper the prisoner-of-war camps were coated with a veneer of traditional military propriety. They were given official designations: the Dulag (transit camp), the Stalag (for enlisted men and non-commissioned officers) and the Oflag (for officers).[19] In reality these distinctions were meaningless. Had the German High Command chosen to treat their prisoners according to the minimal standards required by the prevailing 1929 Geneva Conventions, they would have been obliged to provide housing conditions 'similar to those used by the belligerent's own soldiers in base camps' along with food 'of a similar quality to that of the belligerent's own soldiers', 'adequate clothing', 'medical facilities'. If they died, they were to be 'honourably buried' in clearly marked graves. None of these rights was either available or even considered by the Nazis, who chose to argue that, since Moscow had failed to sign up to the Geneva Conventions, its standards did not apply to Soviet prisoners of war.

The three grades of prison camp were thus as indistinguishable from each other as they were from the surrounding terrain. Facilities were rudimentary or non-existent. There were few medical supplies or health clinics. Latrines, if they existed, were holes dug on open ground. There was little or no shelter. Prisoners very often had to sleep in the ragged remains of their uniforms in temperatures that could fall well below freezing at night. Most cruelly of all, there was very little food. The provision of starvation rations dovetailed neatly with the Hunger Plan, which foresaw the deaths of millions of 'subhuman' Slavs but in the case of the prisoner of war camps only fortuitously so. It was not so much by design as from indifference that the German High Command presided over the deaths of millions of Soviet soldiers held in captivity.

The daily calorie intake mandated by the OKH was well below the levels required for survival. In one characteristic camp, each prisoner was allocated a daily ration of two bowls of watery cabbage soup and one pound of bread. Hot water, not tea, was available at breakfast. These rations were provided only to those with the strength to work as slave labour. Their death from starvation was thus postponed for a little longer than for their weaker peers.

In August 1941, following the encirclement at Uman, between 15,000 and 20,000 wounded Soviet soldiers lay in the open at one camp. Benno Zieser was among the guards set over them. He noted, 'Nearly every day we had men die of exhaustion. The others would take their dead back to camp to bury them. They would take turns carrying corpses. The camp graveyard was very large; the number of men under the ground must have been greater than that of those still among the living.'[20]

At another 'collection point' nearby, 8,000 prisoners were herded into a compound designed to hold between 500 and 800 men. The heat was extreme and so was their hunger. One day, a group of prisoners decided to make a run for the perimeter fence in the forlorn hope of escaping this torment. Soon afterwards, one of the guards, Leo Mellart, heard the sound of heavy-calibre gunfire, followed by shouts and cries of terror. The shooting was directed at a grain silo in which a number of prisoners had been locked up following the thwarted attempt to escape. When the guns stopped firing, he recalled, the body count was between 1,000 and 1,500 men, killed or severely wounded.[21]

Sometimes, starving men were driven to extreme measures to survive. One week in August Hans Becker, a young NCO, was instructed to go to the prisoner-of-war camp in the town of Dubno, the scene of a major tank battle during the first week of the invasion. Becker had believed himself to be fighting against 'a uniformly brutish and impoverished people, nearer to beasts than men [who] fought like a pack of hungry wolves'. It was his first visit to the camp where he was under instructions to find twenty men who were strong enough to join a working party. The prisoners were housed in what had previously been a school.

'The first room I entered was large and bare: the prisoners in it were Mongols. The atmosphere, lacking light, was murky and sinister and what air there was had become indescribably offensive. I gulped and was nearly sick. It was a pigsty, except that all the pigs I had ever seen had been far cleaner than these men.'

Becker knew that people would find it hard to believe what he witnessed in that room, but later – by which time his disgust for the enemy had turned to remorse and horror at the brutalities inflicted on Barbarossa's victims – he wrote, 'If truth sits on the lips of dying men, as we are told, it sits on mine.' As he peered into the gloom he heard 'a savage scream'. He watched as a 'whirling mass of bodies staggered through the gloom, grunting, biting and tearing at each other. A figure was hurled onto a plank bed, and I realized that they were all attacking one man. They were gouging his eyes out, twisting his arms right off and tearing the flesh from his bones with their nails. He was knocked down and literally torn apart.' Becker tried to intervene, but to no effect. As the famished men began to tear at their victim's flesh, he called for a guard but no one came. He rushed out to find the camp's commanding officer, who simply shrugged, saying, 'Tell us something new. This happens every day. We stopped worrying about it a long time ago.'

For Becker's benefit, a Russian prisoner, who spoke a little German, explained that the 'Mongols' had a code word which was used as a command. 'When this was spoken,' Becker wrote, 'they all pounced on the one who had previously been selected to provide the day's meat ration: he would be murdered so that the rest of them could stave off for another day the hunger which their scanty camp food could not satisfy.'[22]

By the end of August, some 800,000 Soviet soldiers had been taken prisoner. Within a few months their number would swell to more than 3 million. Of these only a million survived. Of the rest, some 600,000 died from exposure, starvation and disease. The remainder would be executed.

16. Hitler's Hiatus

The disarray in the Soviet High Command was more than matched by the confusion, doubt and disillusion that, at all levels, had started to permeate the German front line. Wilhelm Prüller, who only three weeks earlier had written lyrically of 'the great country we are capturing for our children', noted on 4 August that it had been 'a terrible day'. His battalion had come under 'murderous fire' from a Soviet unit that was so 'well dug into the corn and sunflower fields [that] you could barely show yourself without a bullet whistling over your head'. Even the combination of light artillery and heavy machine guns was unable to dislodge the enemy. It was only when the tanks, which had gone on ahead, were withdrawn to add their firepower that the Russians finally surrendered the salient his unit was trying to capture. Even then it was not over. Before his unit reached its destination – across yet one more hill – three of Prüller's friends had fallen, two from rifle fire and one, Schöber, after a splinter from a grenade pierced his cheek just below the eye and penetrated his skull.

It was late evening before the battalion finally forced its way into the town of Ternovka. Late that night a 'dog tired' Prüller lay down on a bed of straw, reflecting on the accident of fate that was allowing him to survive while a growing number of his friends perished.[1] Although his battalion had taken 3,000 prisoners on that day, fifteen of his comrades (including one officer) had been killed, fifty (including three officers) were wounded and two more were missing. Altogether, since the start of Operation Barbarossa the battalion had suffered 350 losses, a severe haemorrhage of increasingly scarce manpower.[2] Losses on this scale affected morale. Prüller did not doubt that victory was inevitable, but he now asked himself, 'How long will it last?' He was weary and homesick. 'How wonderful it would be to be at home again! To be in peace and quiet again. No thoughts about the war, or death and destruction, or the advance, the attack, the enemy artillery and rifle fire, or dead and wounded. No! To have none of that, just quiet.'[3]

The growing realization that the moment of victory was receding into an uncertain future was summed up by an infantryman serving in Army Group Centre, who wrote, 'Our losses are immense . . . One day we have the road, then the Russians, and so it goes on, day after day.'[4] Another, serving in the 35th Infantry Division, wrote home to report wearily, 'At the moment we are part of the Army reserve – and high time – we have already lost fifty in the company. It shouldn't be allowed to continue much longer otherwise the burden will be really heavy. We normally have four men on the [anti-tank] gun, but for two days at a particularly dangerous point, we had only two.'[5] Some began to contemplate what had so recently been inconceivable: that the war might last for many months. 'If we ended up here in the winter, something the Russians would dearly have us do, it would not do us a lot of good,' a lance corporal in a transport battalion noted gloomily.[6]

The mood of the men at the front found an echo among their commanding officers. General Heinrici, who was well aware that his men were close to exhaustion, could scarcely believe the stubborn defiance of the Soviet infantry. In a letter to his wife, he wrote:

> We are amazed about how tough the Russian fights. His units are half-destroyed, but he stuffs in new men on the attack again. I have not the slightest idea how the Russians do it. The prisoners insist that it is the pressure of the commissars who shoot everyone who does not comply. But this cannot go on forever to keep the troops in line. Our swift advances turned into a slow stumble. It is unforeseeable how far into Russia we get this way, as long as resistance is as fierce as it has been so far. Maybe it will collapse one day. At the moment it is all in limbo.[7]

Even Heinrici's commanding officer, Guderian, normally so audacious and swashbuckling, was affected. Constantly on the move, hurrying from unit to unit, urging on his commanders to even greater efforts, he had acquired a reputation for inexhaustible energy and fearlessness. In correspondence with his wife, though, he allowed the strain to show. On 1 August he wrote, 'how long heart and nerves can stand this I do not know'; and a few days later:

> Have I not become old? These few weeks have imprinted their marks. The physical exertions and battles of the will make themselves felt.

Occasionally I have a tremendous yearning for sleep which I can seldom satisfy . . . by and large, I am feeling very fit when something is going on – also quick and able. But as soon as the tension is relaxed comes the relapse.[8]

He concealed this well. According to the 4th Army's chief of staff, General Günther Blumentritt, he was regarded by the 300,000 men under his command as the 'Rommel of the Armoured Command'.[9] His Luftwaffe adjutant, Oberleutnant Karl-Henning von Barsewisch, was clearly besotted. Guderian, he recalled, was 'a superman, a ball of energy and brainy too . . . When his eyes flash Wotan seems to hurl lightning or Thor swings the hammer.'[10] Like Rommel in the North African desert, he seemed to lead an enchanted life. Again and again, he came close to death, invariably emerging both unscathed and insouciant. On 5 August, as a large body of Soviet troops attempted to escape the encirclement at Roslavl, Barsewisch watched as he 'rushed immediately to the point . . . full of rage, and closed the gap with a battery which he led personally into battle. There was this fantastic man, standing by a machine-gun in action against the Russians, drinking mineral water from a cup and saying, "Anger gives you thirst." '[11]

If he was fearless, he was also ruthless. As the casualty list grew longer so did the reluctance of some soldiers to face another day of battle. Guderian's commanders became ever more mindful of his stern ruling on the eve of Barbarossa that breaches of discipline should be punished severely and that 'deserters should be shot on the spot'.[12] Lieutenant General Walther Nehring, leading the 18th Panzer Division under the overall command of Lemelsen, instructed his officers to remind their troops that 'cowardice is not only the most disgraceful, but also one of the most dangerous crimes a soldier can commit, for it not only undermines discipline, but weakens the striking capacity of the troops. This danger will be dealt with in every instance with the heaviest punishment – the death penalty.'[13]

In a mirror image of the way in which the Russian commanders treated their miscreants, those who deserted from Nehring's command or who deliberately inflicted wounds on themselves were automatically guilty of a treasonable offence. His troops were told that three of their comrades who had been captured by the Russians had committed a capital offence by allegedly telling their captors 'that they had been forced to fight'.[14]

The mood at OKW echoed that in the ranks of the Ostheer. With Barbarossa on hold while Hitler wrestled with the 'two souls' in his breast,* front-line commanders chafed at the absence of clear-cut orders and their inability to plan the next stage of Barbarossa. As victory receded towards the middle distance, Halder had to confront a host of growing pressures. High among these was 'a clamour' of demands for men to replace those who had fallen. He totted up the casualty figures: so far the three army groups had lost 179,000 men between them; they had received only 47,000 replacements. Army Group Centre – which had suffered the highest number of casualties – was demanding 10,000 replacements 'within eight–ten days'. Even if this demand were met, Bock would still be short of 54,000 men.

And then there was the weather. For the time being, the sun still shone and the roads were dry. Even that, though, had become a problem. Many of those tanks and other armoured vehicles not destroyed in battle were often irreparably damaged by the invasive clouds of dust stirred up by their advance along unpaved roads. This combination had crippled the 18th Panzer Division, which had lost almost a third of its original complement of motorized armour. Even more worryingly, OKH had to face the prospect of doing battle during the onset of the Russian winter – now less than two months away – when roads would be churned into unpassable quagmires or frozen into impenetrable barriers of ice and snow. Nothing could be done about the climate but, on 2 August, Halder felt bound to draw up a list of clothing that each man would require to survive sub-zero temperatures: 'two woollen vests, toques [warm close-fitting hats], earmuffs, gloves, scarves, chest warmers'.[15]

Even to contemplate fighting in these conditions sent a shiver through the ranks of the German High Command, which had originally presumed to be in Moscow well before the winter. In the hope of averting this worst case, the Ostheer's generals supported by OKH belatedly began to acquire the collective backbone to challenge Hitler openly. Rather than grousing divisively behind his back, they contrived to form

* See p. 214.

a united front with the intention of seizing the high ground from their wavering supreme commander. Their hope was to persuade him that the only way to resolve his strategic dilemma was to authorize the resumption of the offensive on Moscow even at the expense of Ukraine. It was to prove an excessively frustrating task for such a fragile coalition of the willing.

In the closing days of July Hitler had fallen ill. He did not turn up for meals or attend the daily situation conferences. According to his adjutant Nicolaus von Below, 'it was quite obvious from his appearance how miserable he was'. His personal physician, Dr Theodor Morell, reported that the Führer's 'heart and circulation were not in a good order' and that he might have suffered internal bleeding or 'apoplexy', as Morell described it as he applied his patent remedies.[16] Although this treatment did not help his patient resolve the strategic dilemmas he had brought upon himself, he was soon well enough to begin a round of visits to all three army groups to hear the views of their commanders.

He started with Army Group Centre. On 4 August, accompanied by Brauchitsch and Halder, he met Bock at his headquarters. It was an inconclusive encounter from which Army Group Centre's C-in-C emerged to note that, although Hitler raised the idea of focusing on Moscow, 'it appears that he is not yet clear on how the operations should now proceed'.[17] Hitler also spoke separately to the two panzer group commanders, Guderian and Hoth, who, like Bock, both stressed the case for Moscow. Had Hitler hoped to divide and rule by seeing them individually, he clearly failed. The only difference between Hoth and Guderian was that the former believed he would be ready to launch the attack on the capital on 15 August while the latter favoured delaying the advance until the 20th.

Later that day, Hitler added to the uncertainty by telling Halder – who had thought that he was veering in favour of Moscow – that Leningrad and the south (including Crimea) were more important. The confusions and contradictions in the Führer's mind greatly irked the OKH's chief of staff, who found himself trapped between the Führer's vacillations and the frustration of the generals. Without 'a clear idea of what the political command regards as the prime objectives in the campaign', he noted, it was impossible to provide the front-line commanders with either operational orders or the appropriate resources to fulfil them.[18]

On 5 August, however, Halder was momentarily cheered when Brauchitsch returned from a meeting with Hitler at Wolfsschanze to report that the commander-in-chief had been 'deftly steered' towards the army's view, though he noted acidly that 'a radical improvement in the future is not to be hoped for unless operations become so fluid that his [Hitler's] tactical thinking cannot keep step with developments'.[19] The next day, though, these hopes were dashed when he heard that, at a meeting with Army Group South's commander-in-chief, Gerd von Rundstedt – who had been briefed by Halder to emphasize the import-ance of Moscow – Hitler once again veered back to his old theme that victory in the north and the south were the most important objectives, and therefore 'Moscow comes last'.[20]

Halder was not deterred. On 7 August he had a rare meeting with Jodl, from which he came away 'convinced' that he had persuaded the Wehrmacht's head of operations that OKH's ideas were sound and that 'he will pull with us in the same direction'. Yet, in his ambiguous fash-ion, Jodl failed to sign up unequivocally to Halder's insistence that Bock should 'drive with all his forces on Moscow'. As ever, Jodl, who lived in terror of Hitler's disapprobation, was hedging his bets.[21] The Führer's front-line tour had done nothing to help him make up his mind. 'One sees clearly how indecisive F. [the Führer] is regarding the continuation of the war. Ideas and objectives keep on changing. One emerges from the situation conferences as nonplussed as one went in,' his adjutant noted wearily on 8 August.[22]

In the absence of direction, Army Group Centre's 147 divisions, which had been expected to spearhead the assault on Moscow, were still advan-cing but slowly and irresolutely, scattered across a 700-kilometre front. Bock was increasingly troubled by the resistance they were meeting: 'In spite of his terrific losses in men and materiel the enemy attacks at several places daily, so that any regrouping . . . has so far been impossible. If the Russians don't soon collapse somewhere, the objective of defeating them so badly that they are eliminated will be difficult to achieve before the winter.'[23] Hitler's strategic vacillations and tactical meddlings had ex-acerbated a worsening predicament.

Halder grew ever more exasperated. As army chief of staff, he was on the receiving end of a succession of disturbing reports about the condi-tion of all three army groups. The 'plain truth', he noted, was that on many parts of the front, the troops, forced to fight pitched battles day after day and suffering 'heavy losses', were 'exhausted'.[24] The essential reason for this was not hard to discern: the Wehrmacht could no longer field enough men to counter the growing strength of the Red Army. 'The whole situation makes it increasingly plain that we have underestimated the Russian colossus, who consistently prepared for war with the utterly ruthless determination so characteristic of totalitarian states,' Halder noted. 'At the outset of the war, we reckoned with about 200 enemy divisions. Now we have already counted 360 . . . if we smash a dozen of them, the Russians simply put up another dozen. The time factor favours them, as they are near their own resources, while we are moving farther and farther away from ours.'[25]

Halder was clear: the only way to break out of this paralysing prospect was to subordinate all other objectives to the immediate task of taking Moscow. At his prodding, Jodl was finally persuaded to present this case to Hitler. Armed with a sheaf of maps and statistics showing that the Soviet forces were at their strongest on the Central Front, he advised Hitler that 'the most important objective was the annihilation of this enemy grouping, followed by the capture of Moscow [which] would begin at the end of August'.[26] On this occasion – with all his senior commanders for once in unison – Hitler did not demur. On 12 August, he issued a 'Supplement to Directive No. 34', which gave conditional approval to the advance on the capital. The directive went on to state specifically that 'the object must then be to deprive the enemy before the coming of winter, of his governmental, armament, and traffic centre around Moscow, and thus prevent the rebuilding of his defeated forces and the orderly working of governmental control'.[27]

OKH's relief was short lived. A powerful Soviet counter-attack against Leeb's Army Group North was threatening his advance on Leningrad. On Hitler's orders, Bock was instructed to dispatch a panzer division and two motorized divisions to help arrest a Soviet breakthrough on that front. Already irked by a succession of confusing and contradictory decisions made over his head, which, he complained, had rendered 'rational command . . . impossible',[28] Bock was aghast at this new instruction. Complaining that his tanks were either undergoing repair and maintenance in preparation for the advance on Moscow or were required for the protection of the group's infantry divisions in the centre, he protested vehemently against yet another 'impossible demand'. The Führer's order, he told Halder, would jeopardize any future offensive by Army Group Centre.[29]

Halder sympathized with his 'furious' field marshal but was at a loss, replying, 'I don't know myself what I should do. I am utterly desperate.'[30] Bock, he noted in his diary, 'had been playing an all-out gamble with the numerically superior [Soviet] army, but that calculated risk was justified in that it permitted him to pass to the offensive at any moment. Now army group is compelled to pass to the defensive, and all it accomplished to date is wasted.'[31] Brauchitsch, whose absence of a backbone was well attested, did his best to talk Bock round but, so far from backing down, Bock replied stiffly that he was 'quite aware that sacrifices had to be made [but] the potential consequences were so serious that it was my duty to state my opinion'.[32]

From Halder's perspective, the worst possible option was for Army Group Centre to abandon the attack on Moscow in favour of digging in behind fortified barricades and fighting small battles or, as he put it, reverting to 'position warfare'. Bock explained to both Brauchitsch and Halder that 'going over to the defensive was no simple matter, considering the large frontages held by my weak divisions'.[33] Reluctant as ever to provoke Hitler's wrath, Brauchitsch was non-committal, but Halder had no doubt that 'changing to the defensive position is quite impossible . . . The front of Army Group [Centre] . . . is exceedingly overextended, and a changeover to determined defence entails far-reaching planning, to which no prior thought has been given.'[34]

Guderian was even more frustrated. Soon after his victory at Roslavl on 8 August, he wrote, 'I would not wish to be in this area in the autumn . . . waiting always brings the dangers of immobility and static warfare: that would be terrible.'[35] He had already prepared detailed plans for the next phase of his advance on Moscow only now to find himself thwarted by the hiatus at the highest levels of the Wehrmacht. The panzer commander was always ready to ignore or sidestep unpalatable instructions, but on this occasion even he could not disobey an order that he must have realized emanated directly from Hitler's capricious bunker at Wolfsschanze. He paid a disconsolate visit to his men, who had been poised to advance along the main highway east of Roslavl towards their objective. 'It was with a heavy heart' that he noticed 'my soldiers, confident that they would soon be advancing straight towards the Russian capital, had put up many signposts marked TO MOS-COW'.[36] His indignation spilled over in a letter to his wife on 18 August: 'This indecision has had a bad effect upon the troops, for everyone is aware of the absence of harmony. This is the product of unclear orders and counterorders, absence of instructions sometimes for weeks . . . we are missing so many opportunities.'[37]

As a result of Hitler's dithering, Moscow was in danger of becoming a lost cause. If Halder's despairing comment that 'everything that has so far been achieved is for nothing' was to be confounded, something had to give.[38] And it did. After almost a month of turbulent irresolution, the simmering tension between Hitler and his generals finally came to a head when the high commands of both the Wehrmacht and the army presented Hitler with the case for an immediate advance on Moscow. But if they hoped that their démarche, blandly entitled 'The Further Operations of Army Group Centre', would sway the Führer, they reckoned without his troubled assessment of the complex challenges that now faced the Third Reich.

Hitler's global vision – which entailed the destruction of Bolshevism, the annihilation of international Jewry and the establishment of Lebensraum – was unhinged, but his strategic anxieties were not. On 14 August he 'flew into a passion of rage' when he read a copy of the Atlantic Charter, which Churchill and Roosevelt had just negotiated in Placentia Bay.[39] His ire was particularly aroused by Point 6, which promised 'the final destruction of the Nazi tyranny'. Combined with the US occupation of Iceland – the transit point for the transatlantic convoys – and Roosevelt's provocative naval strategy in the Atlantic, he interpreted the charter as evidence that Germany now faced the prospect of an extended war on two fronts.* His earlier delusion that the United States would watch on as Churchill was forced into capitulation was no longer tenable: the Western democracies were clearly resolved to fight to the finish. On the Eastern Front it was equally clear that the Jewish/Bolshevik conspirators were proving

---

* On account of its strategic position, Iceland was occupied militarily by Britain in May 1940, despite Reykjavík's voluble protests. A year later, the garrison was transferred to the United States.

alarmingly resilient: not only had the Red Army survived the initial blitzkrieg, it was also quite obviously capable of conducting a far longer campaign than he had ever imagined.

These twin challenges affected his physical as well as his mental well-being. On the same day that the generals made their pitch for Moscow, he was visited by Goebbels at Wolfsschanze. The Führer had been ill again, this time suffering from a severe bout of dysentery that had left him looking 'somewhat assailed and sickly'.[40] He was also downcast. Goebbels was taken aback when Hitler talked dispiritedly about the progress of Barbarossa, and even indicated that he thought it might in due course be possible to negotiate a peace deal with Stalin. This startling admission was explicable only as tacit acknowledgement of his huge strategic error in leading the Third Reich into a simultaneous confrontation with two powerful antagonists each resolved to destroy Nazism and with the combined potential to overwhelm the Wehrmacht. He had trapped himself in a grave predicament for which he alone was responsible.

And there was more: to sustain a war on two fronts the Wehrmacht would have to secure both the grain and raw materials of Ukraine and outright control of the Baltic, without which – as Adam Tooze has pointed out – 'Germany could not guarantee its delivery of iron ore production from Scandinavia'.[41] In the absence of a swift victory on the battlefield, the essential needs of Germany's wartime economy would have to take precedence over the purely political or military objectives on which his generals had set their sights. It was a worsening dilemma from which he still found it almost impossible to escape.

There was a further psychological factor looming in the back of his megalomaniacal mind, to which he referred during this stand-off with his generals: Napoleon's march on Moscow almost 130 years earlier.[42] Like Hitler, the French emperor had also launched his invasion in June (two days after the date chosen by Hitler for Barbarossa). His Grande Armée was similarly the largest military force that had ever been assembled. He had also won a major battle at Smolensk, from where he went on to prevail upon the blood-soaked field of Borodino, a mere 110 kilometres from Moscow. But when his victorious troops marched into the city, they found it abandoned and on fire. By the end of the year, six months after launching his campaign, what was left of his half-starved and frost-bitten forces was driven out of Russia never to return. It was a humiliation from which Napoleon's reputation never recovered, while France's hegemonic sway over Europe began to crumble: a salutary warning that was rarely far from Hitler's mind.

Such nebulous parallels from the distant past weighed as little with his generals as Hitler's economic case for abandoning the attack on the Soviet capital. They argued that a decisive breakthrough to Moscow could still be achieved before the onset of the Russian winter, and thereby the decapitation of Judaeo-Bolshevism and the collapse of the Soviet Union. To divert forces from Army Group Centre to support the flanking operations of Army Group South and Army Group North, they insisted, would not only sabotage that objective but would entail a long and inconclusive struggle on adverse terrain and in worsening weather, with supply lines that would become dangerously over-extended. Victory would be postponed indefinitely.

But Hitler's 'two souls' had at last – though temporarily – ceased to wrestle with one another. He had made up his mind. On 21 August he barked out his decision in the form of another directive: 'The proposals of OKH for the continuance of the operation in the East, dated 18 August, do not conform to my intentions.' In the five brutally succinct paragraphs that followed, he reverted to his earlier insistence that Moscow was of secondary importance:

> The principal object that must be achieved yet before the onset of winter is not the capture of Moscow, but rather in the south, the occupation of the Crimea and the industrial and coal region of the Donets,* together with the isolation of the Russian oil regions in the Caucasus and, in the North, the encirclement of Leningrad and junction with the Finns.[43]

Army Group Centre was to remain on the defensive and postpone any thought of taking Moscow. OKW's irresolute commander-in-chief, Keitel, and his pliable head of operations, Jodl – both of whom were besotted by the Führer's 'genius' – reacted by retreating into their customary roles as supine and subservient acolytes. But it was not quite the end of the matter.

Halder was devastated. He was also furious. Hitler's orders constituted a crushing rejection of the strategy he had crafted, which had so

---

* More generally known as the Donbass region.

recently been agreed by both OKH and OKW. Equally galling was the Führer's decision to rub salt into the wound the next day by sending Brauchitsch a searing critique of his judgement and leadership, a personal attack that his chief of staff viewed as 'absolutely outrageous'.

'I regard the situation created by the Führer's interference unendurable for OKH,' Halder confided to his diary. 'No other than the Führer himself is to blame for the zigzag course caused by his successive orders, nor can OKH, which is now in its fourth victorious campaign, tarnish its good name with these latest orders.'[44] He was in mutinous mood. At a meeting with Brauchitsch later in the day, he tried to persuade the army's commander-in-chief that they should both resign in protest. To Halder's regret, Brauchitsch – ever the temporizer – refused on the enfeebled grounds that 'the resignations would not be accepted'.[45] In effect, like Keitel and Jodl, he buckled before the prospective wrath of the Führer.

Bock, who was at the point of issuing orders for the renewed advance towards Moscow, was as appalled as Halder. 'I want to smash the enemy army and the bulk of this army is opposite my front!' he noted. 'Turning south is the secondary operation – even if it is just as big – which will jeopardize the execution of the main operation, namely the destruction of the Russian armed forces before winter.'[46] When he made this point to Brauchitsch, he was firmly rebuffed, despite warning that, were he to follow Hitler's latest directive, he would be unable to hold the centre line for more than a maximum of ten days, and that, he warned, would itself be 'an emergency solution'.[47] He could have saved his breath. That evening – 22 August – he received the formal order to divert a significant proportion of his armour and infantry to the south. He consulted Guderian to determine which of the Panzer Group 2 units should be thus redirected. Guderian rebelled and, according to Bock, 'flatly rejected the operation' on the grounds that he was unwilling to 'dissipate his forces for a secondary operation'.[48]

In the face of this defiance, Halder convened a meeting the next day, 23 August, with Bock, who invited Guderian to join them. Halder was clearly still beside himself with rage at the Führer's attack on Brauchitsch (in which he must have felt himself traduced by association). Although the three of them did not discuss Hitler's order in any detail, they were in no doubt that it would entail at best a long drawn-out conflict, that the Ostheer would be left floundering in the depths of a Russian winter and that none of the Führer's objectives would be secured. Immediately afterwards, Bock took it upon himself to call Hitler's adjutant, Rudolf Schmundt, to ask if the Führer would at least 'listen to Guderian' before making a final decision.*

Guderian and Halder arrived at Wolfsschanze that evening. What transpired next was to be the cause of bitter dispute. For reasons that neither elected to explain, both Brauchitsch and Halder chose to exclude themselves from the meeting with Hitler. In the former's case this was probably because, like Keitel and Jodl, he did not dare openly to challenge the Führer. In Halder's case, it may have been because he thought that, as the most lauded commander in the German army and much touted by Goebbels, the panzer leader would make a greater impact on his own. As it was, Guderian was left without flanking support, a fact he greatly resented.

Before he was ushered into Hitler's presence, Guderian was confronted by Brauchitsch, who had already crumbled to the point where he allegedly told him, 'I forbid you to mention the question of Moscow to the Führer. The operation to the south has been ordered. The problem now is simply how it is to be carried out. Discussion is pointless.'[49] At those words, Guderian flared up, demanding to be flown back to his panzer group as it was now obvious that the proposed meeting would be 'a waste of time'. Brauchitsch refused but, once again, told him not to mention Moscow.

Before leaving for Wolfsschanze, the panzer leader had displayed an iron resolve to make the case for Moscow as the only viable alternative. On his departure, as if to confirm his reputation for fearless straight talking, he was overheard to say that Hitler would abandon the Moscow option only 'over my dead body'.[50] By his own assuredly self-serving account, he was true to his word. Once in the room with the Führer, who was flanked by Keitel and Jodl, he immediately went on the offensive, outlining the wearied and depleted state of his panzer group. When

* Schmundt was to suffer an untimely end. He was at Hitler's side when the bomb planted by Colonel Claus von Stauffenberg on 20 July 1944 exploded. The assassination attempt failed to kill its intended victim but Schmundt was mortally wounded and died two months later. At Hitler's instructions, he was buried in the Invalidendom – the 'heroes' cemetery' – in Berlin.

he had finished, Hitler asked, 'In view of their past performance, do you consider that your troops are capable of making another great effort?' Guderian seized the moment: 'If the troops are given a major objective, the importance of which is apparent to every soldier, yes.' Hitler knew exactly what that meant and responded, 'You mean, of course, Moscow?' Later Guderian would report what he claimed to have told Hitler:

> Moscow was the great Russian road, rail and communications centre: it was the political solar plexus; it was an important industrial area; and its capture would not only have an enormous psychological effect on the Russian people but on the whole of the rest of the world as well . . . The troops of Army Group Centre were now poised for an advance on Moscow; that before they could start on the alternative operation towards Kiev a great deal of time would be wasted in moving to the south-west; that such a move was towards Germany, i.e. in the wrong direction . . . Finally I touched upon the enormous difficulties which must arise if the proposed operation [to the south] were not terminated as fast as now planned and were to be protracted into the period of bad weather. It would then be too late to strike the blow for Moscow this year.[51]

Mindful perhaps of Guderian's iconic status, Hitler heard him out in silence before replying at similar length to reiterate his oft-repeated arguments in favour of going south. In the course of his disquisition, the Führer went out of his way to disparage his most senior commanders, saying, 'My generals knew nothing about the economic aspects of war.'[52] Guderian watched contemptuously as those self-same generals nodded solemnly 'in agreement with every sentence that Hitler uttered'. In the face of this united front, Guderian would claim to have judged that the better part of valour would be discretion. 'I did not think it would then be right to make an angry scene with the head of the German State when he was surrounded by his advisors,' he reflected. It was the end of the discussion.[53]

It is possible that there was a further factor in his decision to back down. Guderian was ambitious as well as headstrong. He was almost certainly aware that he was under consideration as a replacement for Brauchitsch. To earn the displeasure of an unforgiving Führer was hardly calculated to enhance his prospects.

Whatever the reason for Guderian's retreat, Halder was scathing when the panzer leader told him what had transpired. 'My reply to him is that I had [sic] no sympathy for such a 100% change of mind,' he noted that evening.[54] As Guderian recalled their exchange, Halder's reaction was very different. Rather than remonstrating with him, the chief of staff suffered 'a complete nervous collapse'.[55] Neither man would ever forgive the other.

The die had been cast. For the moment, the muddle, confusion and indecision of the past month was over. Hitler's authority as Supreme Commander of the Armed Forces was once again undisputed and the abiding myth of his genius was once again not to be questioned. This did nothing to restore the fortunes of the armies with which he had launched Barbarossa barely two months earlier. The combat strength of the infantry divisions along the entire Eastern Front had been reduced by 40 per cent and the panzer divisions by 50 per cent. In Army Group Centre, where only 34 per cent of the panzers were ready for action, the armoured forces as a whole, according to its War Diary for 22 August, were 'so battle-weary and worn-out that there can be no question of a mass operative mission until they have been replenished and repaired'.[56]

No such reality checks were allowed to frustrate the Führer's maniacal vision, which – to a degree that defied military reason – was still widely shared by his senior generals. Bearing in mind that, by the end of August 1941, the Red Army was growing rapidly in both manpower and weaponry, forethought might well have reasoned that Operation Barbarossa already looked as though it was destined to fail, that the Soviet Union would not be annihilated and, therefore, that Hitler's vision of establishing a 'Reich for a Thousand Years' was similarly doomed. But forethought and reason were in short supply, and there was no turning back.

PART THREE

Counterstrike

17. Between the Lines

The August hiatus had no effect on the Third Reich's official murder squads, which were working assiduously behind the lines to complete their allotted task. On the contrary, they were making the most of the pause to fulfil their duties in the territories that had been 'liberated' in the first six weeks of the invasion. No hamlet, no village, no town and no city was safe.

By the middle of the month, the four Einsatzgruppen that had already demonstrated their prowess in that part of Poland occupied by the Reich in 1939 had been reinforced by 5,500 members of the so-called Ordnungs-polizei (Order Police) as well as an additional two SS brigades, each of 5,000 men, supplied by Himmler.[1] Spearheaded by the Einsatzgruppen, some 20,000 killers now roamed behind the lines in well-organized units. Heydrich had drawn up a list of those they were to target: 'Comintern functionaries (and Communist professional politicians generally); higher, middle and lower functionaries of party central, regional, and local committees; People's Commissars; Jews in party and state positions; other radical elements (saboteurs, propagandists, snipers, attempted political murderers, agitators, et cetera.)'[2] The 'et cetera' was telling. Heydrich's apparently precise order was in effect an invitation for the killers to rampage wantonly against the population whose lands had been occupied by the Nazi invaders.

Hitler had made his own attitude clear enough on 16 July 1941, when, in a reference to the 'Garden of Eden' that would be created in the regions designated to provide Lebensraum, he said, 'the vast area must be pacified as quickly as possible; this will happen best by shooting anyone who even looks sideways at us'.[3] As so many individuals – men, women and children – were judged to be 'looking sideways', the task of 'shooting' them not only acquired the attributes of mass murder but rapidly turned into the first stage of the Final Solution.

As chief interpreter and enforcer of Hitler's will, Himmler left no doubt in the minds of his subordinates that every Jew was to be exterminated. The instructions were unequivocal: 'Explicit order by the RF-SS [Himmler]: all Jews must be shot,' the 3,500 men serving in the SS Cavalry Brigade – which operated under Himmler's personal supervision – were told on 1 August 1941. That afternoon, for the avoidance of any doubt, Gustav Lombard, one of the SS Cavalry Brigade's unit commanders, confirmed, 'Not one male Jew is to remain alive, not one family in the villages.' Soon afterwards Lombard was able to report that several Jewish communities had been cleansed by these means.[4]

A further order from Himmler that all female Jews should be drowned in the Pripet Marshes proved harder to fulfil. As another unit commander, Franz Magill, explained, 'Driving women and children into the swamps did not have the success it is supposed to have [sic] as the swamps were not deep enough for sinking under to occur. After a depth of one metre a person for the most part hit firm ground so that sinking is not possible.'[5] Despite these setbacks, Himmler's personal death squad reported on 13 August that they had killed 13,788 'plunderers', most of whom were Jews. There had been some resistance: two members of the SS Cavalry Brigade had been killed when they drove over a mine.[6]

In the territories conquered by Army Group Centre, Einsatzgruppe B was led by SS-Gruppenführer Arthur Nebe. As the former head of the Kriminalpolizei, Nebe was particularly loyal to Heydrich, who had direct authority over all four Einsatzgruppen. Assiduous in pursuit of the murderous objectives of both Himmler and Heydrich, Nebe was assisted by a notably zealous battalion of the Order Police. Following the encirclement at Białystok, Battalion 309 herded the city's Jews into the central marketplace and the main synagogue. From the former, they were taken to a local park, where they were put up against a wall and shot. The 700 individuals in the synagogue were incinerated when the police poured petrol on the entrance doors and then tossed a grenade inside. Those who tried to escape were shot down. In this tightly packed part of the city, the fire spread rapidly to neighbouring houses in which a number of Jews had taken refuge; they too were burned to death. It required thirty trucks to transport the corpses of between 2,000 and 2,200 Jews for burial in a mass grave just outside the city.[7]

A few days later, a further 3,000 Jews were rounded up and taken to the city's sports stadium, where they sweltered in the fierce summer heat without food or water while they were divested of their valuables.

Later they were shuttled in trucks to some conveniently located anti-tank ditches in a wood outside the city. It took many hours but eventually, the firing squads drawn from Battalions 316 and 322 shot and buried at least 3,000 Jews to add to the 2,000 that their comrades in Battalion 309 had already murdered.[8]

Within the next few days, as Battalion 322 advanced from Białystok towards Minsk (which it reached a little before the end of the month), the 3rd Company distinguished itself on several occasions, notably in the village of Narevka-Mala, where, along with one Polish citizen who was found guilty of 'plundering', 232 Jews were dispatched 'smoothly and without incident'.[9] The clinical satisfaction with which such atrocities were logged was in line with police regulations: precise, measured and detailed.

Battalion 322's polished performance may have been influenced by Himmler, who had visited the unit a few weeks earlier during a whistle-stop tour of the conquered territories. Following the SS leader's visit, Lieutenant Colonel Max Montua (one of the Reichsführer's senior commanders) issued a 'Confidential' order:

(1) All male Jews between the ages of seventeen and forty-five convicted as plunderers are to be shot according to martial law. The shootings are to take place away from cities, villages and thoroughfares. The graves are to be levelled in such a way that no pilgrimage site can arise. I forbid photographing and the permitting of spectators at the executions. Executions and grave sites are not to be made known.

(2) The battalion and company commanders are especially to provide for the spiritual care of the men who participate in this action. The impressions of this day are to be blotted out through the holding of social events in the evening. Furthermore the men are to be instructed continuously about the political necessity of the measures.[10]

Later in August, Battalion 322 arrived in Minsk to participate in an extensive operation to round up 700 people, including seventy-four women from the city's Jewish ghetto. All of them were shot. The explanation given for this execution was that they 'had been encountered without the Jewish Star during the roundup . . . in Minsk it has been discovered that especially Jewesses removed the markings from their clothing'.[11] As the momentum of killing increased, the death squads no longer discriminated by gender or age. Nor was any attempt made any longer to offer justification for their actions. For men who 'saw themselves as legitimized by the authority of their Führer', it was enough that the victims were Jewish.[12]

In every region of the Soviet Union occupied during the first weeks of Barbarossa – from the Baltic to the Balkans – the killing squads operated with similar conviction. In many erstwhile independent states, they were ably assisted by the 'self-cleansing' enthusiasm of local inhabitants, either forming themselves into vigilante groups or merely operating as ad hoc lynch mobs who were eager to join in the orgy of Nazi killing. Their hatred for the Jews in their midst appeared to spring from an ugly combination of nationalism and xenophobia. A bigoted loathing for the alien customs of a different culture made them particularly susceptible to those Nazi propagandists who told them that the Jewish intelligentsia had been the principal agents of the worst excesses inflicted on them by the Stalinist occupation.

Thus, soon after the invasion, a detachment from Einsatzgruppe A collaborated with a mob of enthusiastic 'nationalists' who had rounded up a large group of Jews and had started to massacre them on the forecourt of a garage in the Lithuanian town of Kaunas (Kovno). By chance, the operation was witnessed by a much-decorated and hardened regular officer, Lieutenant Colonel Lothar von Bischoffshausen:

> On the concrete forecourt of the petrol station a blond man of medium height, aged about twenty-five, stood leaning on a wooden club, resting. The club was as thick as his arm and came up to his chest. At his feet lay about fifteen to twenty dead or dying people. Water flowed continuously from a hose washing blood away into the drainage gully. Just a few steps behind this man some twenty men, guarded by armed civilians, stood waiting for their cruel execution in silent submission. In response to a cursory wave the next man stepped forward silently and was beaten to death with the wooden club in the most bestial manner, each blow accompanied by enthusiastic shouts from the audience.[13]

Onlookers at the scene told Bischoffshausen that the killer was known locally as 'the death dealer of Kovno'. His self-appointed task was to ensure that all 'traitors and collaborators [with the Soviets]' would receive a punishment that fitted that crime. Bischoffshausen was appalled not only by the slaughter but also by the ghoulish density of the crowd, among which some parents were lifting their little children onto their shoulders to afford them a better view of the action. However, not all Lithuanians were so pitiless. A young factory worker, Laimonas Noreika, later described how he watched in horror as 'a group of well-dressed, spruce, intelligent-looking people held iron bars which they used to viciously beat another group of similarly well-dressed, spruce, intelligent people . . . They kept hitting them until they finally lay inert.' By the end of that afternoon, between forty and sixty Jews had been beaten to a pulp. According to a German photographer who took pictures of the scene, soldiers in the unit to which he was attached watched on as 'the Death Dealer fetched an accordion, climbed to the top of the pile of the corpses, and played the Lithuanian national anthem'. The crowd joined in by singing and clapping.[14]

In one of more than twenty such incidents witnessed in just one area to the south of Białystok, an anti-Semitic vigilante group in the Polish town of Jedwabne rounded up local Jews and – under the supervision of the SS – corralled them in the main square. According to several overlapping testimonies, the victims were instructed to wrap themselves in talliths (prayer shawls) and to jump up and down or dance while they were beaten with cudgels and rubber whips. The local rabbi was then forced to lead a procession of some forty men into a hay barn, where they were killed by rifle fire. They were followed by a further 250 to 300 victims – women and children as well as their menfolk – who were driven into the same barn. As both SS and regular soldiers watched on, the vigilantes poured kerosene on the building and set it ablaze. The bodies of those who were burned to death were buried in two mass graves close by.[15]

No people in Europe suffered more than the Poles at the hands of the Nazis following the launch of Barbarossa. However, this predominantly Catholic country was not immune to anti-Semitism. The country's turbulent past, and its struggle to establish a distinct identity after the First World War, provided fertile soil for a form of xenophobia in which the Jews (who had formed a third of Warsaw's pre-war population) were seen as an existential threat to that identity. Moreover, many Poles had come to believe that Jews had collaborated with, or were beneficiaries of, the Soviet occupation from 1939 to 1941. Some of their pogroms may therefore be attributed to what historian Roger Moorhouse has described as 'a spontaneous spasm of revenge'.[16] There was more to it, however. Although in Poland more Christians risked their own lives to protect their Jewish neighbours than in any other country in Nazi-occupied Europe, a great many of their fellow countrymen supported – actively as well as passively – the persecution and the extermination of the Jews.

The most visible expression of Polish collaboration with the Nazis in this period was the 20,000-strong auxiliary militia officially known as the Granatowa Policja (Blue Police). Co-opted into the service of the Reich by Hans Frank's General Government, they operated under the supervision of the SS. Not all of them shared the anti-Semitic attitudes of their commanders. Some used their unique access to the Nazis to pass on intelligence to the Polish underground and – like those individual Poles who did their best to protect their Jewish neighbours – paid with their lives when their 'treachery' was exposed. However, most members of the Blue Police not only collaborated in the persecution of Poland's Jews but willingly enforced the humiliating and punitive restrictions imposed on them by the Nazi authorities.

Further south, in Ukraine, anti-Semitism was rife and deep seated. Many Ukrainians, with bitter memories of Stalin's Great Famine a decade earlier, regarded the Nazi invasion as a liberation. Here too, local activists were only too willing to work alongside the Einsatzgruppen as fellow executioners. Another of Himmler's creations, the Ukrainische Hilfs-polizei (Ukrainian Auxiliary Police), played a particularly prominent role in a succession of massacres throughout the region which began at the end of July. Earlier that month a Hungarian army unit travelling through the town of Kamianets-Podilskyi reported seeing long columns of Jews who had been force-marched out of Hungary after the pro-Nazi regime had classified them as 'stateless'. They had only been allowed to take with them their personal possessions, three days' supply of food and a meagre amount of cash. Many had 'collapsed from exhaustion and hunger' along the way and were seen to be crawling along the roads leading into the town; others had bandaged their feet with rags torn from their clothes. Tens of thousands crammed into the already overcrowded Jewish quarter, where they lived in 'unspeakable and indescribable dirt . . . the streets stink, unburied bodies are lying in some of the houses'.[17]

On 27 August, under the orders of its commander, Otto Basch, who answered to Heydrich, Einsatzgruppe C, supported by the Order Police, marched a long column of Jews from the town into the nearby forest. What happened there was witnessed by the drivers of a Hungarian military convoy. They were transfixed by horror. Gabor Mermall was one of them:

> We saw hundreds of people undressing there . . . we were passing a row of maple trees – practically over the mess of naked corpses . . . suddenly we glanced at a square-shaped ditch, at all four sides of which people were standing. Hundreds of innocent people were gunned down. I'll never forget what I saw and felt: the scared faces, the men, women and children marching to their own graves without resistance.

A German officer sought to restore discipline. 'Don't worry,' he reportedly reassured the drivers, 'there are enough Jews left in the world.'[18] The guns did not fall silent for three days. By that time, according to the official report filed by Friedrich Jeckeln, the higher SS and police leader for the southern region, an estimated 23,600 Jews had been murdered in those Ukrainian woods.

By this time, few citizens of the Reich would have been unaware that Jews were being targeted on the Eastern Front. The Gestapo was greatly encouraged to see that the German public was gratified by newsreels that showed Jews being arrested and taken into custody. According to the Gestapo's Berlin Office, people reacted to 'images of the arrest of the Jews' with 'enthusiastic approval'.[19] Even if they were not familiar with all the metaphors deployed by Hitler to characterize a Jew – 'a maggot in a rotting corpse', 'a pestilence far worse than the black death', 'a germ-carrier of the foulest kind', 'mankind's internal bacteria', 'a parasite in the body', 'the eternal bloodsucker' and more[20] – it was virtually impossible for them to have been unaware of the fact that Jews were in the Third Reich's firing line. There was, though, a distinction to be made between endorsing the humiliation of the Jews and sanctioning acts of genocide against them. As in other parts of western Europe, latent and often overt feelings of anti-Semitism were widespread in Germany but these did not mean that most Germans gave their 'enthusiastic approval' to the mass murders perpetrated in their name. More insidious was a notable absence of curiosity or concern about the fate of the Jews – a 'national conspiracy of silence'.[21] As Ian Kershaw has put it so memorably, 'the road to Auschwitz was built by hatred but paved with indifference'.[22]

The Wehrmacht had no excuse. From the most senior general to the lowest foot soldier, no member of the Ostheer had been left in any doubt about Nazism's mission to eradicate the Jewish presence in Europe. Not only had they been systematically indoctrinated with Hitler's hatred for the Jews, but also very many of them clearly shared his sentiments. Lest they had any doubt about the opinions they were expected to hold, they had the Wehrmacht's official publication – the *Mitteilungen für die Truppe* (Troop Announcements) – to guide them. Distributed to every military unit, one of its editions stated, 'Anyone who has ever looked in the face of a Red commissar knows what the Bolsheviks are like. Here is no need for theoretical expressions. We would insult the animals if we describe these mostly Jewish men as beasts. They are the embodiment of the satanic and insane hatred against the whole of noble humanity.'[23]

Moreover, the formal distinction between the roles of the SS and the Wehrmacht was sharply eroded by the readiness of the latter to over-look, endorse or frequently to participate in the crimes of the former. Despite the initial qualms of some officers who sought vainly to impose the military discipline of the pre-Nazi era on their men, the generals played a critical role in facilitating the Holocaust on the Eastern Front. Some, like the commander of the 6th Army, General Walther von Rich-enau, shared Hitler's vision. When he went out of his way to order 'harsh but just atonement of Jewish subhumanity',[24] he earned the gratitude of the Führer, who had this order distributed to all combat formations on the Eastern Front.[25] Others – like the commander of Army Group Cen-tre, Bock – chose rather to avert their gaze from the disagreeable excesses of the SS and its agencies. In his 600-page war diaries, which cover the entire Second World War, Bock made not a single mention of the Ein-satzgruppen. His only reference to their activities was in one oblique entry on 4 August 1941, when he noted:

> On the basis of rumours, *which later turned out to be exaggerated* [my italics] I had Police General Nebel [Nebe], who was responsible for my rear area but who was not under my command, issue instructions that within the limited bounds of my headquarters executions were only to be carried out if they involved armed bandits or criminals.

That was all. It was apparently enough for Bock that the commander of Einsatzgruppe B 'had promised to do so'.[26]

18.   The Carnage of Kiev

The opening days of September offered the Red Army a flicker of hope. On the 9th, a trainee nurse in Moscow, Irina Krauze, who was not an optimist by nature, was momentarily elated. 'The bulletin is very good today: the Germans have been knocked out of Yelnya and are being chased even further.'[1] For the first time since the start of Operation Barbarossa, the Germans had been forced to retreat. This was essentially attributable to Zhukov.

Dismissed as chief of staff by Stalin for daring to insist that Kiev should be abandoned, the mercurial Soviet leader had almost immediately given him command of the newly expanded Reserve Army – another opportunity to show that his strategic judgement was indispensable. For much of August, under Zhukov's overall guidance, Timoshenko's armies had been mounting a series of fierce assaults against German strongholds along the Central Front. So great was the pressure on his forces that by the end of that month Bock was driven to conclude that 'the centre of my army group is so dispersed and so weakened by the tough defensive fighting that it is no longer capable of attacking on its own'.[2]

The Yelnya bridgehead, eighty kilometres to the south-east of Smolensk, had been seized by Guderian's 2nd Panzer Group in July as a launch pad for the next stage of Army Group Centre's now postponed advance on Moscow. With orders to hold this position at all costs, the Germans who had dug themselves in on either flank of the salient found themselves under a sustained artillery bombardment that had pulverized the sixty-kilometre front into a hideous moonscape. And their situation was steadily deteriorating. Halder was soon well aware of this. After a tour of the front he noted starkly, 'Troops very strained. Enemy artillery activity very unpleasant. Our munition use is limited. Mines and wire absent.'[3] Even during a lull towards the end of August, Bock was losing an average of 200 men a day at Yelnya, a rate of attrition which meant that every unit was badly under strength; in what Halder described as a 'highly excited' state, he called up the chief of staff to say,

'Defences near breaking point. Army Group cannot hold its eastern front if the Russians continue attacking.'[4]

The lull was no more than that. Zhukov had prepared a four-pronged counter-attack with the full might of his Reserve Army with Yelnya as his prime objective. On the last day of August, two tank divisions, eight rifle divisions and one motorized infantry division with the support of 800 guns, mortars and multiple rocket launchers were unleashed against the salient. Their objective was encirclement.[5] Within a day, the Russians had penetrated ten kilometres into Bock's southern flank. With his divisions 'being bled white' and facing the very real threat of encirclement, he made the decision on 2 September to abandon Yelnya.[6] The bridgehead was retaken by the Red Army four days later.

It was just possible for OKH to present this defeat as a tactical withdrawal. In fact, it was anything but. The loss of 23,000 men in the space of a month to secure a stronghold that for some weeks the commanders in the field had judged to be of little strategic value did not impress the rank and file, who were the victims of the High Command's incompetence. Many were bitter. Officially it was called a 'planned withdrawal', Franz Frisch wrote later:

> But to me it was so much bullshit. The next day, we heard on the radio, in the 'news from the front' [the *Wehrmachtbericht*] about the 'successful front correction' in our Yelnya defensive lines and the enormous losses we inflicted on the enemy. But no single word was heard about a retreat, about the hopelessness of the situation, about the mental and emotional numbness of the German soldiers. In short, it was again a 'victory'. But we on the front line were running back and forth like rabbits in front of the fox. This metamorphosis of the truth from 'all shit' to 'it was a victory' baffled me, and those of my comrades who dared to think.[7]

The Russians were as anxious to exaggerate the scale of their achievement as the Germans were to minimize it. The victory, such as it was, served greatly to raise morale on the home front, where the Russian people had become jaundiced by the bowdlerized versions of a dire reality pumped out by the state-run media. For once they could be told the truth, albeit in a distinctly optimistic form. As the Moscow-based British journalist Alexander Werth was to observe, 'Here was not only, as it were, the first victory of the Red Army over the Germans; here was also

20 and 21. Walther Rathenau (*above*), the German foreign minister, at the Genoa Conference of thirty-four European Nations in April 1922. He had just detonated a diplomatic time bomb by signing the Rapallo treaty with his Soviet counterpart, Georgy Chicherin, the Commissar for Foreign Affairs (*below, third from left*).

22. The Genoa Conference was the brainchild of the British prime minister, David Lloyd George. With his vision in tatters, he was enraged. At a formal dinner, he publicly berated Rathenau for 'duplicity' in negotiating with the Soviet Union behind his back. Politically the 'Welsh Wizard' never recovered.

23. The German Führer, Adolf Hitler, and the British prime minister, Neville Chamberlain, at Munich in September 1938, affecting to inspect a map of Czechoslovakia, which – with British and French acquiescence – was about to be dismembered by the Nazis. Chamberlain was feted when he returned to London promising 'peace for our time'.

24. In the early hours of 24 August 1939, a benign Stalin presided when the German foreign minister, Joachim von Ribbentrop (*left*) – as repellent as any of Hitler's odious acolytes – signed the Non-Aggression Pact with the Soviet Foreign Affairs Commissar, Vyacheslav Molotov (*right*), known as 'Old Stone Arse'. The Soviet dictator celebrated by toasting Hitler.

25. Following the Molotov–Ribbentrop Pact, Eastern Europe was carved up between the Soviet Union and Nazi Germany. At Brest-Litovsk, troops from both sides fraternized on the demarcation line between the two occupied zones in a cynical display of mutual amity.

26. On 22 June 1941, Wehrmacht troops stormed across the River Bug near Brest-Litovsk, taking the Soviet defenders totally by surprise.

27. The German invasion was spearheaded by the panzer divisions that blitzed eastwards along a 3,000-kilometre front so rapidly that London and Washington concluded that the Soviet Union would collapse within weeks.

28. In trepidation and near-disbelief, Muscovites gathered around street radios to hear Molotov's monotone voice announce that in 'an unparalleled act of perfidy' the Germans had launched an invasion against the Motherland.

29. Soviet soldiers could expect little mercy from German troops, who had been indoctrinated to believe that they were an inferior species of humanity. In a conflict marked by an unprecedented scale of barbarism and depravity, the invading troops frequently executed their captives on the spot.

30. Huge numbers of Soviet prisoners of war were marched into captivity. Scores of thousands died en route from hunger, disease, beatings and shootings. More than three million soldiers died in Nazi prison camps during the war. Two thirds of these were taken prisoner before the end of 1941.

31. Roosevelt and Churchill on board USS *Augusta* in Placentia Bay, August 1941. They signed the Atlantic Charter (the blueprint for the 1948 Universal Declaration of Human Rights) but Churchill returned to Britain disappointed by the president's refusal to commit the United States to war.

the first piece of territory – perhaps only 100 or 150 square miles – in the whole of Europe reconquered from Hitler's Wehrmacht.'[8] It was a good story, and one the regime was anxious to share with the world. So great was the propaganda value that, for the first time, a group of foreign correspondents was allowed to leave the comfortable incarceration of Moscow to see the front for themselves.

Werth was among eight journalists from the United States and Britain selected for this privilege. Chaperoned by an escort of minders from the Ministry of Foreign Affairs, they left Moscow in a convoy of cars heading for Yelnya. On the way they passed a semblance of normal life: peasants with cart-loads of vegetables heading for the capital; old ladies sitting by the roadside selling mushrooms; crows and starlings wheeling in the skies above. Only the convoys of military vehicles and the rumble of heavy tanks suggested that all was not well in the empty vastness of rural Russia. After six hours, the correspondents reached the town of Vyazma, which had come under sporadic attack from German bombers. 'Why bomb it?' Werth asked himself:

> It seemed such a harmless little town . . . a mass of quiet little provincial streets, with wooden houses and little gardens in front of them, and rows of rough wooden fences. And in the gardens grew large sunflowers and dahlias; and old women, with scarves around their heads. The place cannot have changed much since the days of Gogol.[9]

One old woman, 'yellow and haggard' and wearing a black knitted shawl around her head, wept as she talked to him, a reminder that the war was psychologically, if not yet physically, close at hand. 'Oh! this war, this war, these cursed Germans: I could scratch every German's eyes out . . . 300 people killed in the last raid on Vyazma. Oh God, oh God!' This expletive provoked another matron to retort, 'Oh stop it! And where is your God anyway?' 'Up there. He is looking down on us.' A teenage boy joined in. 'Up there is a long way. And anyway it isn't true that there were 300 . . . There were fifty-two, all buried in the common grave.'[10] As though that were not tragedy enough.

That evening the correspondents were accorded the honour of a meeting with Timoshenko's chief of staff, General Vasily Sokolovsky. He was handsome, charming and upbeat. 'The German blitzkrieg has become a blitzkrieg for the destruction of German men and equipment,' he told them; the 'grinding down' of the German war machine 'was in full swing'. He was confident that the Germans would suffer severely in the coming winter: 'All our troops have their *polushubki* (thick, sheepskin coats) and other adequate clothes, and they can stand even 50 degrees of frost; the Germans will not stand up to it.' He expected the Germans to renew the offensive but, he said, it would be 'a last desperate gamble . . . I don't think they will ever get to Moscow.'[11]

They reached the new front line by passing through a wide wooden gate decorated with portraits of Stalin and Timoshenko and posters exhorting the troops to 'do their duty to the last', promising that 'Victory will be ours' and instructing them that 'the Fascist Reptile must be crushed'.[12] The road was thick with young soldiers. On either side, tank traps sprouted from the ground. Artillery batteries were hidden in the trees. And yet, though they could hear guns blazing close by, Werth noticed cows grazing quietly and a girl who was hanging out washing and two small boys who waved at their convoy.

They were driven to a large clearing in the trees, where they were welcomed by a regimental colonel and his fellow officers. As they ate their way through a great spread of Russian hors d'oeuvres washed down with so much vodka that one of his colleagues half-disappeared under the table, Werth was reminded how greatly these young *voyaki* (fighters) resembled 'the simple, brave, unassuming men whom Tolstoy drew so well in *War and Peace*'. After the obligatory toasts to Stalin, the Red Army, Great Britain and the United States, this incongruous luncheon was brought to an abrupt end by a bout of heavy shelling so uncomfortably close to their tent that they were ordered to hurry to an underground bunker.

Over the next few days, the correspondents had a foretaste of a phenomenon that would soon come to play an important part in the campaign. As soon as they left the main road, their small four-wheel-drive vehicles became bogged down in cloying mud a foot deep. They repeatedly had to pull and push them free of the glutinous sludge. Werth noticed however that, although large trucks also became stuck and could be extricated only with great difficulty, heavy tanks managed to slither through without problem and were able to maintain normal speed over even the roughest surfaces.

One evening they visited a field hospital less than ten kilometres behind the front, where they witnessed 'some of the horrors of war': 'a young fellow, scarcely conscious, with both his legs amputated; another who had lost both eyes, and whose head, a mass of bandages, was like the head of an eyeless snowman. He lay completely silent, uttering only faint groans from time to time.'[13] The staff of seven surgeons, six doctors and forty-eight nurses was handling 300 cases a day. Werth was impressed that a well-equipped operating theatre had been constructed in a dugout alongside an X-ray machine and a number of blood-transfusion units. As frequently happens, Werth, being a foreign correspondent, was almost certainly taken to a 'showcase' field hospital. X-ray machines were not to be found in the peasant houses that generally served as field hospitals and where operations were performed on kitchen tables.

Later, Werth and his fellow journalists met Captain Lebedev, a university graduate who had been a teacher but was now serving in the army. The captain was unusually ready to speak his mind. He had little sympathy with the self-delusions fed to the Russian public by the Soviet state media:

> The flag-waving – the Hurrah-patriotism – of our press is all very well for propaganda purposes, to keep up morale; but it can be overdone . . . we just don't know how much farther the Germans are going to push . . . If you people have got any influence with the British government, for God's sake don't say all is splendid . . . we shall need help from abroad . . . before we are finished.[14]

Had a commissar overheard such a downbeat assessment, Lebedev might well have been charged with a treasonable offence. As it was, he went on to describe the

> hatred the Germans have stirred up among our people. We are easy-going, good-natured people, you know; but I assure you in the Red Army now, men [are] thirsting for revenge. We officers sometimes have a job in keeping our soldiers from killing German prisoners . . . those arrogant, fanatical Nazi swine. I have never known such hatred before.[15]

They eventually reached Yelnya after many detours through villages and towns that had been obliterated in the fighting. In one of these, Werth noted, 'There wasn't a house standing; not a fragment of a house, not a single plank . . . An old tin samovar, lying on the ground, was the only remnant of the actual village.'[16] There were mass graves for the several hundreds of Russian soldiers who had been killed there; the Germans were buried in shell holes. Yelnya was also utterly destroyed. Before retreating, the Germans had rounded up most of the able-bodied men and women and carted them back into their own rear to serve the Third Reich as slave labourers. The old and the children were locked up in the church while the invaders set fire to every single house in the town until all that was left was 'rubble and ashes'.[17] By the time Werth and his companions were back in Moscow, the 'story' of the war was elsewhere. Kiev had fallen.

With Bock's front at Yelnya collapsing, the internecine warfare that erupted between the generals following Hitler's decision that Army Group Centre should go over to the defensive intensified. The smouldering animosity between Halder and Guderian in the wake of the panzer leader's failure to stand his ground against Hitler at Wolfsschanze soon spread to ignite a bitter conflict between Guderian and Bock as well. With great reluctance the headstrong panzer commander had obeyed Bock's order that his Panzer Group 2 should be diverted to link up with the left flank of Rundstedt's Army Group South to complete the encirclement of the Soviet armies protecting Kiev. However, Guderian resolved to do it in his own way.

To the barely concealed fury of both Halder and Bock, he entirely ignored them when they sought to steer the direction and temper the speed of his blitzkrieg. At the end of August his panzers came under severe pressure from enemy flanking attacks. To counter these, Guderian peremptorily demanded reinforcements that Bock could ill spare. Halder – who was still smarting from Hitler's rejection of the 'Moscow option' – also wanted to hold these panzer units in the centre for the final thrust for Moscow, which he still regarded as the overriding priority. As though writing an unruly pupil's school report, he complained, 'G[uderian] will not tolerate any army commander and demands [that] everybody up to the highest position should bow to the ideas he produces from a restricted position.'[18]

It was with a certain relish that, on 31 August, he noted:

This morning is dominated by a decidedly uncomfortable development in Guderian's group. Carrying out his drive as a flank movement along the full length of the enemy front, he squarely invited heavy attacks on his eastern flank; then his advance, striking far to the east and leading him away from the Second Army [which was too distant to offer covering fire] produced a gap which was exploited by the enemy for attacks also from the west. These two developments have reduced his power to strike south to a point where his movements are paralysed. Now he is blaming everyone in sight for his predicament and hurls accusations and recriminations in all directions.[19]

On the same day, Bock referred to an 'unpleasantly worded' radio message from Guderian in which he both reiterated and expanded his demand for more reinforcements. When Bock hedged, the panzer commander insisted 'that the Führer decide'. This breach of military protocol – in effect a threat to leap the chain of command – further outraged Halder, who described it as 'unparalleled cheek', adding after a later conversation with the Army Group Centre commander, 'Guderian is striking a tone which Bock cannot tolerate on any account.'[20] When the Panzer leader complained yet again that 'too few forces had been given to him, and these too late', Bock finally lost patience. He contacted Brauchitsch and asked the commander-in-chief to relieve the 'headstrong' panzer leader of his command. 'Brauchitsch asked me to think things over again,' he noted in frustration.[21] By the following day Bock had simmered down. Conceding that Guderian was an 'outstanding and brave commander', he told Brauchitsch, 'I was agreeable to his settling the affair by talking to him.'[22]

Guderian emerged victorious from this stand-off. Though his relations with both Halder and Bock were now irreparably damaged, he was given most of the reinforcements he had demanded. Despite a succession of mini-crises provoked by unexpected if minor Soviet lunges, he was thus able to maintain his chosen route to the south. Soon, though, driving rain turned the roads into mud baths. In contrast to the relative mobility of the Soviet armour, his vehicles – accustomed to proceeding in orderly columns – slithered into gluey bogs. Before long Guderian's divisions were strung out for many miles as men and machines struggled to extricate themselves from the mire. Motorcyclists could no longer ride their machines. Guderian's four-wheel-drive staff car was brought to a halt and had to be recovered by a towing vehicle borrowed from the artillery. On some days average speed fell to less than ten kilometres an hour; fifteen was the best they could achieve. He recalled:

> Only a man who has personally experienced what life on these canals of mud we called roads was like can form any picture of what the troops and their equipment had to put up with and can truly judge the situation at the front and the consequent effect on our operations. The fact that our military leaders made no attempt to see these conditions for themselves and, initially at least, refused to believe the reports of those that did, was to lead to bitter results, unspeakable suffering and many avoidable misfortunes.[23]

In Moscow, the triumph at Yelnya was soon forgotten, a mere blip on a receding strategic horizon. A mood of gloom and anger once more pervaded the Kremlin, where the imminent collapse of Kiev was all-consuming. Stalin was as frustrated by Guderian as Bock and Halder were, but for entirely different reasons. Guderian's contemptuous waywardness which so aggrieved his senior officers was for Stalin a disconcerting unpredictability that confused and wrong-footed his own generals. The Soviet leader, who could not resist interfering in the operational detail in a spasmodic and arbitrary fashion, was so bemused by the panzer leader's speed and dexterity that he was reduced to referring to Guderian simply as 'that villain' as he goaded Andrei Yeremenko, for failing to arrest the panzer leader's advance towards Kiev. The fact that General Yeremenko lacked the manpower and firepower to do this – a deficiency that was aggravated by muddled and contradictory orders emanating from Zhukov's successor as chief of staff, General Boris Shaposhnikov – did not weigh with the Soviet leader. On 2 September, as Guderian once again sidestepped the blundering attempts by Yeremenko's depleted forces to stand in his way, he let fire at the commander of the Bryansk front line: 'The Stavka is much displeased with your work . . . you are just nibbling at the enemy, but you can't shift him. Guderian and the whole of his group must be smashed to smithereens. Until this happens, all your statements about success are worthless.'[24]

Two days later, recognizing the grave danger now facing Kiev, the commander-in-chief of both the Southern and Southwestern fronts,

Marshal Semyon Budyonny, asked Stalin for immediate reinforcements and the authority to rearrange the disposition of his forces the better to avoid encirclement. He got nowhere. On 7 September, with the front threatening to cave in, he asked for permission to withdraw the 5th Army, which was in imminent danger of collapse. By the time the authorization came through, it was too late: the 5th Army was trapped.

By 11 September it was clear to Budyonny that he had little hope of stopping Panzer Group 2 from joining forces with Panzer Group 1 to spearhead a pincer movement that threatened to encircle five Soviet armies. His only option was to withdraw. Rebuffed by Shaposhnikov, who was too frightened to tell Stalin the truth, he decided to signal the Soviet leader directly with his unpalatable assessment: 'Delay with the withdrawal will lead to losses in men and a huge quantity of equipment.'[25]

Stalin reacted in character. Summarily dismissing Budyonny, he ordered General Timoshenko, who was commanding on the Western Front, to head south to take his place. He then phoned General Kirponos, commanding on the Southwestern Front, forbidding him to withdraw any of his troops from their front-line positions. In a final attempt to change Stalin's mind, Budyonny tried to enlist his successor to join him in a last-minute effort to explain the facts to Stalin. As a cavalry officer who became a hero of the Civil War (and after whom a popular military march had been named), the famously moustachioed Marshal of the Soviet Union, who had long been one of Stalin's most trusted allies, was evidently confident enough to know that he would be spared the ultimate penalty for such defiance.* Timoshenko was less sanguine, reportedly responding, 'I don't want to put my head in a noose.'[26]

On 14 September – by which time Guderian was at the point of linking up with Panzer Group 1 – the Southwestern Front's chief of staff, General V. I. Tupikov, radioed Shaposhnikov in one more attempt to change Stalin's mind. He did not fudge the issue: 'The catastrophe which is clear to you will occur in a matter of several days.'[27] Stalin's response was to dismiss Tupikov as 'a panic-monger'[28] and to instruct Shaposhnikov to 'instil the entire front with the necessity to fight on stubbornly,

---

* Budyonny's 'punishment' was not severe: he was given command of the Reserve Front.

and, without looking back, to fulfil the orders given to you by Stalin [sic] on 11 September'.[29]

The Russian armies who fought to save Kiev did so with a fanatical disregard for their own lives. In one sector, the crew of a T-34 tank that had been disabled by a German artillery battery managed to scramble out through the turret. Instead of raising their arms in surrender, however, the men drew their pistols to fire in vain at their tormenter. In another sector, a German infantry regiment was astonished by 'a lunatic and reckless cavalry attack which rode through our machine-gun fire' and then 'galloped through German outposts with drawn sabres, slashing down with such force that troops caught in the open had their helmets cleaved to the skull.' Just as disconcertingly, the Cossacks were followed by 'mass human-wave attacks, which we had not experienced until now'.[30]

In their hopeless attempt to arrest the inevitable, these counter-attacks were as fearless as they were suicidal. Yelling their rage and hatred, some ran at speed towards the German lines with bayonets at the ready. Others careered forward in trucks. Once they were within range, they came under blistering fire from artillery, anti-tank weapons and machine-guns. Soon the dead were lying in heaps, the wounded writhing among them. According to a report by the German 45th Infantry Division, 'The dead covered the length of the embankment in countless masses.'[31]

The invaders did not entirely escape the carnage. Max Kuhnert, who served in a cavalry reconnaissance unit, was for ever haunted by one image:

> I could not avoid seeing the truckful of young corpses. It was just ghastly . . . Blood was literally running down the side from the floorboards of the trucks, and the driver was, despite the heat, white as a sheet. Shells were still flying about . . . We marched on . . . We saw so many corpses lying there by the roadside. And pieces of bodies, some of them scorched or charred from the heat of guns or exploding shells . . . The dream of glory diminished.[32]

In the middle of September, as Budyonny had foreseen, Panzer Group 1 and Panzer Group 2 joined forces a hundred and fifty kilometres to the east of Kiev at Lokhvytsia to close their pincers around four Soviet armies (the 5th, 21st, 26th and 37th). By 18 September, the Ukrainian capital was in German hands. As the Russian troops tried to escape, they were either mown down in their scores of thousands or taken prisoner in their hundreds of thousands. The encirclement at Kiev was larger than that at Smolensk, and arguably the largest in the history of warfare. Four armies containing forty-three divisions had been virtually obliterated. In a little over three weeks, the Southwestern Front had suffered at least 700,000 and perhaps more than a million casualties, including 616,000 killed, wounded, or taken prisoner* during the Battle of Kiev itself; only 15,000 men broke out of the encirclement to make it back to their own lines. In addition to these fearful losses, the Germans seized more than 2,600 guns and mortars along with sixty-four tanks. In effect, at a cost of a (relatively) modest 128,000 casualties, they had destroyed the Southwestern Front.

In the mayhem, Kirponos, who was renowned for his steadfastness and audacity, was wounded when his retreating command column was caught in an ambush on 20 September. Later that day he was hit in the head by the splinters from an exploding mine. He died within two minutes. Budyonny and Timoshenko were more fortunate. They escaped with their lives, but only to survey an unprecedented but avoidable catastrophe. As a result of Stalin's obstinate blundering, Rundstedt's Army Group South was now well positioned to launch a two-pronged attack towards Stalingrad and the Crimea while Guderian was already hastening north again to prepare for the belated attack on Moscow which Hitler was now ready to authorize.

Once Kiev had been secured, Einsatzgruppe C was free to move into the city to execute Heydrich's orders. On 27 and 28 September posters were pasted up across the city:

> All Jews in the city of Kiev and its surroundings will present themselves on Monday, September 29, at 8am on the corner of Melnik and Dokterivshaya Streets (beside the [Jewish] cemetery). Documents, money, and valuables as well as warm clothing, underwear, and so on are to be brought. Any Jew not carrying out this order and found elsewhere will be shot.[33]

Thanks to 'our very special talent of organization' – as the local Einsatzkommando chief, Paul Blobel, boasted – some 30,000 Jews duly

---

* German and Soviet figures differ. According to the Germans, 665,000 prisoners alone were taken, including militiamen and labour battalions.

showed up at the collection point believing that they were destined for 'resettlement'.[34] Carrying their belongings in sacks, suitcases and boxes, which were sometimes loaded on handcarts, they were marched into the forest, urged on by Ukrainian policemen who 'formed a corridor and drove the panic-stricken people towards the huge glade' that edged a large ravine or yar, known as Babi Yar.[35] Threatened by curses and urged with sticks and snarling dogs, they were forced to undress until they were naked. Instructed to place each item of clothing on one pile and their valuables on another,[36] they were ordered to proceed to the mouth of the ravine. What happened next was witnessed by, among others, a Ukrainian watchman:

> they found themselves on the narrow ground above the precipice, twenty to twenty-five metres in height, and on the opposite side there were the Germans' machine guns . . . the killed, wounded and half-alive people fell down and were smashed there. Then the next hundred were brought, and everything repeated again. The policemen took the children by the legs and threw them alive down into the Yar.[37]

Another witness reported seeing members of the Schutzpolizei (a branch of the Order Police) descending into the pit, forcing those whom the machine guns had failed to kill to lie down on top of those who had already been shot:

> The corpses were literally in layers. A police marksman came along and shot each Jew in the neck with a sub-machine gun . . . I saw these marksmen stand on layers of corpses and shoot one after the other . . . The marksman would walk across the bodies of the executed Jews to the next Jew, who had meanwhile lain down, and shoot him.[38]

Even then, the number of victims was so great that the killers were not entirely successful. That evening, according to the watchman's testimony, 'the Germans undermined the walls of the ravine and buried the people under thick layers of earth. But the earth was moving long after, because wounded and still alive Jews were still moving. One girl was crying: "Mammy, why do they pour sand in my eyes?"'[39]

Astonishingly, there were survivors. Yelena Yefimovna Borodyansky-Knysh was among that handful. It was midnight when she and her four-year-old daughter were ordered to line up on the edge of the ravine.

She did not wait to hear the next command but threw her child onto the heap of bodies and then fell on top of her.

> A second later bodies started falling on me. Then everything fell silent. There were more shots, and again bloody, dying and dead people began falling into the pit.
>
> I sensed my daughter wasn't moving . . . To keep her from suffocating, I made fists out of my hands and put them under her chin. She stirred. I tried to raise my body to keep from crushing her . . . there was blood all over the place. We were sandwiched between bodies.
>
> I felt someone walk across the bodies and swear in German. A German soldier was checking with a bayonet to make sure no one was still alive. By chance he was standing on me, so the bayonet blow passed me.

When he departed, Yelena walked and crawled out of the ravine carrying the little girl, who was unconscious. She found her way to the yard of a brick factory, where they hid for four days with no food or clothing until, with the help of a kindly Ukrainian woman who took pity on them, they managed to escape.[40]

Another survivor, Dina Pronicheva, also chose to jump into the pit before being shot. She lay there pretending to be dead. All around and beneath her she could hear 'strange submerged sounds, groaning, choking and sobbing . . . The whole mass of bodies kept moving slightly as they settled down and were pressed tighter by the movements of the ones who were still living.'

When the German soldiers descended into the pit and began to shoot anyone who still showed signs of life, Dina drew on her skills as an actress in the Kiev Puppet Theatre. She recognized one of the killers as the man who had examined her papers and taken her bag in the clearing by the ravine. To test whether she was alive or dead, he picked her up and struck her with his fist. She hung limply in his arms as though dead. He dropped her, kicked her in the breast and trod on her foot until the bones cracked but still she did not move. He left. Soon afterwards she heard the sound of shovelling and of sand falling ever closer to where she lay. She was soon half smothered and started to choke. She panicked and began to struggle. Mercifully the killers chose that moment to down tools and leave. Dina managed to pull herself out of the pit by clinging onto a small bush.

At the top she was startled by a child's voice. A small boy had also managed to climb out of the unholy sepulchre. He was trembling and shivering. She told him to follow her and they both crawled away. As they were leaving the area the boy, who was some way ahead, suddenly shouted a warning that Germans were there. The Nazis who had caught him could not understand what he had said, so simply killed him and went on their way. Dina survived to record her testimony for posterity.[41]

In the course of two long days, the men of Sonderkommando 4a of Einsatzgruppe C, the 3rd Company of the 'Special Duties' Waffen-SS supported by the [Ukrainian] Police Battalion Number 9, had worked with a commitment, efficiency and speed calculated to earn the approval of their superiors. A few days afterwards, they were able to report, 'In retaliation for the arson in Kiev, all Jews were arrested and on 29 and 30 September, a total of 33,771 were executed.'[42] As the overall commander of this operation, SS-Obergruppenführer Friedrich Jeckeln, fresh from his triumph at Kamianets-Podilskyi, now had further cause to celebrate. His upwardly mobile career was to lead him subsequently to preside over the murder of perhaps 100,000 Jews, for which achievement he was to be garlanded with medals and in due course promoted to the rank of general.★

The Babi Yar massacre was better documented than most, but similar atrocities occurred throughout the summer and autumn of 1941. By the end of September more than 100,000 Jews had been exterminated by such means. The Holocaust had begun in earnest.

★ In January 1942 he was awarded the War Merit Cross with Swords for killing 25,000 Jews at Rumbula in Latvia. He was appointed to the rank of general in the Waffen-SS. In April 1945 he was taken prisoner by Soviet troops. He was sentenced to death and hanged in Riga on 3 February 1946.

19. Leningrad

Here and there are men lying in the field, all around the field. At first it looks as if everyone is immobile, dead. But then I look closer and see that some are turning, lifting their heads. They saw our vehicle and there is more movement, they rise, they get up. How many people are here? 100, 200? How many are alive? What can we do, we are just a handful of medics?

It was late September. Nikolai Amosov (who had set up a field hospital just outside the village of Sukhinichi six weeks earlier) looked around incredulously. He was momentarily at a loss. 'We should give them water but there is no water . . . I say to the driver: "Go back to the hospital, bring flasks of water, bring nurses, stretchers, bandages, materials."' The surgeon and the rest of his team pressed on into the village, following the trail of bodies until they reached the local railway station.

German bombers were still circling above them. After a lull earlier in the month, the Ju 88s (so-called 'fast bombers') had just returned to attack the railhead, which had become a staging post close to the main Kiev–Moscow railway line some 270 kilometres south-west of the capital. The bombers had scored a direct hit. Five carriages were burning, others had been derailed. There were hundreds of casualties. 'As you come close the sight is terrifying,' Amosov noted. 'People are trapped in the distorted smouldering carriages. No, these are no longer people, these are corpses . . . Mutilated bodies, blood that has gone black from the fire, remains of bandages and metal frames. Stench of burnt flesh and paint.'

It was his first such experience and he strove to control his revulsion and sense of hopelessness. Then he forced himself to recall the war surgeon's maxim: 'One should not do long and complex operations if the wounded are many. Only help when your help will be effective . . . It is tough but it's the only way.' Most of the wounds were so grave as to be untreatable except by specialists. For those victims death was the only possible outcome.

In the early hours of the following morning, while he was still at work in his makeshift operating theatre, Amosov was interrupted by his commanding officer ordering him to stop operating on the wounded. Those who could be moved were to be evacuated on foot or in farm carts to a major railhead at Kozelsk, forty kilometres nearer to Moscow. Amosov watched them leave: 600 young men, bowed over sticks or hobbling on crutches, bandages on their arms and heads, and, in the case of those unable to get their boots on, cloth wrappings to protect their feet: 'It was painful to look at them . . . how are they going to make it if they are so weak? How many will get there?'

Later that morning, Amosov sat under an apple tree with the commander. The leaves were falling. 'You should get some sleep,' the commander said. 'I am not sleepy . . . My head feels very empty. As if something has ended my life,' Amosov replied. A moment later a lone Soviet fighter flew overhead, just as they saw eight German bombers approaching from the west. They stood up to warn the pilot, gesticulating and shouting as though he could hear them: 'Just go away. What can you do on your own!' The Russian continued flying towards the enemy aircraft. They watched the battle. It did not last long. 'He catches fire, there is black smoke and the plane falls behind the hills. The parachute did not emerge. We are standing there feeling lost, shaken, tears in our eyes. They [the Germans] fly past us in regular formation. Damn them!'[1]

The Luftwaffe was once more on the offensive, softening up the Red Army's defences along the route from Kiev towards Moscow. Following the fall of the Ukrainian capital, Panzer Group 2 was heading north again, advancing at speed towards Oryol and Bryansk, which were still in Soviet hands. Vasily Grossman was not far in front of them as he too headed in the same direction, passing through a landscape devastated by human misery. He was greatly affected by the plight of the peasants: 'They begin to cry as soon as they begin to speak, and one feels an involuntary desire to cry too . . . There's so much grief.' Many of the peasants were on the move. Dust was everywhere: 'White, yellow, red dust. It is stirred up by the feet of sheep, pigs, horses, cows, and by the carts of refugees . . . Dust is hanging, swirling, whirling over Ukraine.' At night the Luftwaffe flew overhead, Heinkels and Junkers: 'They spread among the stars like lice. The blackness of the air is filled with their humming. Bombs are crashing down. Villages are burning all round.'[2]

Grossman only paused in Oryol for a day before his editor, David Ortenberg, dispatched him to Bryansk, where – after failing to arrest Guderian's drive on Kiev – Yeremenko's forces were now trying to hold the line against the 17th Panzer Division. On a visit to one unit, Grossman witnessed a commonplace incident which was nonetheless chilling for that: the interrogation of a 'traitor' who had been caught by his own comrades as he tried to smuggle himself back into his own lines. His disguise did not deceive them. 'He has an overgrown beard and is wearing a torn brown russet coat, a big peasant hat. His feet are dirty and bare, his legs naked to the calf.' The Germans had 'bought' him for one hundred marks. 'He thinks the modesty of this sum might make them more forgiving.' It didn't. He knew then what his fate would be:

> He isn't a human being any more, all his movements, his grin, his glances, his noisy, greedy breathing – all that belongs to a creature that senses a close and imminent death . . . When he looks at the soldiers and their rifles there's an animal fear in his eyes.
>
> The colonel slaps his face, shouting and crying at the same time: 'Do you realize what you've done?' The guard, a Red Army soldier, then shouts at him, too: 'You've disgraced your son! He won't be able to live with this shame.' The harangue over, the unfortunate wretch was shot where he stood.[3]

Grossman also met the commander of the 50th Army, Major General Mikhail Petrov. The general had escaped from the Smolensk encirclement in full dress uniform, refusing to conceal himself as a civilian. Petrov had earned a reputation for cruelty as well as courage. He took Grossman to the front at a point where one of his regiments had just failed to seize a German-held salient. Petrov was not happy. Amidst the blazing guns and the whistling bullets, he reprimanded the regimental commander:

> 'If you fail to capture this village within an hour, you will have to give up your regiment and take part in the attack as a private.' The regimental commander answers: 'Yes, Comrade Army Commander.' His hands are shaking. There isn't a single man walking upright. Men are running, stooping low or crawling on all fours from one hole to another. They are afraid of bullets and there aren't any bullets [at that moment]. They

are all covered in mud and wet. [Nikolai] Shlyapin [Petrov's regimental commissar] is walking around as if on a country stroll and shouts to the soldiers: 'Bend lower, cowards, bend lower!'[4]

That evening, a military prosecutor arrived from Petrov's rear headquarters. Grossman and Petrov were drinking tea sweetened with raspberry jam as he gave the general a list of names – individuals charged with a range of capital offences, including cowardice, desertion and, in the case of a number of local peasants, circulating enemy propaganda. Grossman watched closely. 'The general did not hesitate. Petrov pushes his glass aside. In the corner of the document, he approves the death sentence in red capitals written in a small childish hand.' He spared only one of the offenders, an 'old maid' as the prosecutor put it, whose crime had been to encourage her friends to offer the Germans bread and salt. Her sentence was cut to ten years in jail. Grossman was not impressed by 'the short and large-nosed' general who was dispensing justice so nonchalantly.[5] Even in recording this episode Grossman was taking a grave risk. As the editors of *A Writer at War*, Antony Beevor and Lyuba Vinogradova, have pointed out, if the NKVD had read his notebooks, 'he would have disappeared into the Gulag'.[6]

Nothing would have caused him more trouble than to report – as he noted – that many Ukrainian peasants appeared to regard the German invaders as liberators. But Stalin's Great Famine, the expropriation of their lands, and the 'dekulakization' of their communities only a decade earlier were still fresh torments. He met a group of women who had only sackcloths to protect them from the bitingly cold wind that blew from the east. Nor was their persecution over. To clear the forward areas for the Red Army better to face the Nazi 'hordes', the regional commissars planned to evacuate these peasants to the far side of the Volga, a journey of more than a thousand kilometres from their homes. The Volga German Autonomous Republic, as it was known until its abolition in August 1941, was then inhabited by 400,000 'Volga' Germans. Perhaps to make way for the new arrivals, but certainly because their loyalties were suspect, these unfortunates were deported to Kazakhstan and Siberia, where they were dumped in a wasteland without means of subsistence. According to some estimates, a little under 40 per cent of the deportees were to perish – yet another testament to Stalin's propensity to commit genocide in the name of an allegedly higher cause. The Ukrainians did not want to inherit the lands the Volga Germans were to leave. Grossman noted:

> They are rebelling . . . They raise their sickles. The sickles shine dully in the grey autumn light. Their eyes are crying. The next moment the women laugh and swear, but then the anger and grief return . . . 'We won't leave, we'd rather die here. If any lousy snake comes to force us out of our homes, we'll meet him with sickles.'[7]

There were frequent reminders that the war was ominously close. In one village he took note of a grotesque incident: 'The head of the driver of a heavy tank had been blown off by a shell, and the tank came back driving itself because the dead driver was pushing the accelerator. The tank drove through the forest, breaking the trees, and reached our village. The headless driver was still sitting in it.'[8]

A few days after that incident, Grossman woke up suddenly in the middle of the night, got dressed and walked out into the yard of the compound where he was staying. All was silent. But the Germans were only fifteen kilometres away. At daylight, he and his companions about-turned from Bryansk and headed back to Oryol, unaware that units of Panzer Group 2 were heading for the same destination – and at a speed which, yet again, would take the Soviet commanders by surprise.

These were dark days for Stalin. He not only presided over the collapse of the Southern Front but an emergency on the Northern Front as well. As Kirponos fought in vain to prevent the fall of Kiev, the Germans virtually sealed Leningrad from the outside world. By the end of the first week in September the last road and rail links to the city had been severed.

A Soviet volunteer, Daniel Granin, was in one of the few remaining battalions defending the Dudergof Heights, ten kilometres to the south-east of the city, when the bombers dived at them:

> [W]e came under air attack which caused heavy casualties. The rest of the soldiers in my unit scattered and I was left alone – without an army. So I boarded a tramcar and drove back home, with my machine gun and hand-grenades. As far as I was concerned the German army was going to be in Leningrad in a few hours.[9]

The attackers were inclined to the same opinion. After clearing the heights of what remained of the Soviet artillery, the 18th Army's infantrymen advanced into the city's suburbs. An artillery observer, Hans Mauermann, was with them: 'Our company had in fact stopped a tramcar that had driven out of Leningrad, and ordered them to get out. We considered whether or not to hang on to the driver, so they could drive into Leningrad the following day.'[10]

Fearing – wrongly, as it turned out – that Leningrad was about to crumble, Stalin's immediate reaction was to find a scapegoat. It did not take him long. The commander of the Leningrad defences, Kliment Voroshilov, had great personal courage – leading one counter-attack on the front line at Ivanovskoye brandishing a pistol – but he displayed little tactical or organizational acumen. Stalin railed at him (and the powerful Second Secretary of the Soviet Communist Party, Andrei Zhdanov, who was with him): 'We're so indignant about your conduct. You tell us only of losses . . . What'll be the end of our losses? Have you decided to surrender Leningrad?'[11] His fury was followed by a familiar denouement. Voroshilov had already been sacked once by Stalin following the Finnish debacle; now the legendary 'Red Marshal' was to suffer the same fate for the second time. Stalin summoned Zhukov from the Central Front on 8 September and ordered him to make haste for Leningrad.

Zhukov arrived on 13 September. He did not waste time with the niceties but, without saying a word, handed Voroshilov a note from the Soviet leader. It was to the point: 'Hand over command to Zhukov and fly to Moscow immediately.' The Red Marshal, who retained the dignity of an earlier generation, summoned his staff. 'Goodbye, comrades . . .' he said. 'That's what an old man like me deserves. This isn't the Civil War. Now we have to fight differently . . . But don't doubt for a minute that we'll smash the Fascist scum!'[12]

It did not take long for Zhukov to grasp the scale of the crisis. He reacted with speed, tactical brilliance and ruthlessness. Bullying those around him and threatening them with the firing squad if they didn't deliver Leningrad from the perdition of a German breakthrough, he concentrated on reinforcing and extending the existing barricades until they formed an impenetrable shield against any German onslaught: the city was to be held at any cost. The penalty for failure was harsh. On 17 September he signed Order No. 0064, which decreed that 'all commanders, political officers, and rank and file who leave the line of defence without prior written instruction of the Front or Military Council are to be shot on sight'.[13]

Before his arrival, Peter the Great's fantastical masterpiece had already been transformed into a people's citadel. Almost every apartment block, every house and every shop was boarded up or sandbagged. Buses and trams were commandeered to block roadways. No interchange was without a barricade. Machine-gun posts protected every avenue. A 36,000-strong workers' army was drilled in the use of a rifle and stood ready for hand-to-hand combat.

Zhukov went further. The city would be defended in depth to the maximum extent possible. Every route into the city was to be mined. Anti-aircraft guns were to be installed in the suburbs for use against panzers rather than the Luftwaffe's bombers. High explosives were to be stockpiled to demolish factories and bridges. In line with Order No. 0064, those who failed to act as though their lives depended on it – looters, slackers, deserters – were to face summary execution by the NKVD. It all happened and at great speed. The city was on alert twenty-four hours a day. Under Zhukov's iron fist, there was no evidence of panic. Leningrad was marked by a rare stoicism and resilience. Even Zhukov, not known for any excess of emotion even on reflection, was to recall that the 'courage, endurance and tenacity' of its citizens 'impregnated itself in my memory for life'.[14]

It so happened that, before the new defences were fully in place, Hitler had abandoned his plan to raze Peter the Great's masterpiece. The commander of Army Group North, Leeb, was ordered to call off the attack and to divert most of his Panzer Group 4 to Army Group Centre (where it was destined to play a leading role in the final assault on Moscow). Those of his soldiers who could see the city shimmering in the distance were baffled. Walter Broschei, whose company was poised for the final onslaught from a chain of hills to the south-west of Leningrad, noted, 'In the distance the city pulsed with life. It was bewildering – trains ran, chimneys smoked and a busy maritime traffic ran on the Neva river.' But as he reflected on the decision to call off the attack, he concluded that Leeb lacked the numbers required to assure success: 'We had twenty-eight soldiers left from 120 normally in the company and had now been gathered into so-called "combat battalions" – unsuitable to attack Leningrad.'[15]

Hans Mauermann was relieved when the order came: 'Every day it had been attack, with all its uncertainties and not knowing what might happen. From the perspective of even further hardship this was very much welcome. The emotion swung between shame we had not pulled it off to "thank God" we did not have to go in there.'[16]

By late September Zhukov could claim that the German advance had been arrested. But Leningrad was now almost totally encircled. The only route in and out of the city was via a narrow belt of land on the edge of Lake Ladoga that became famous around the world as the city's 'Road of Life'. Unhappily it was only a road of life for some. Although more than 450,000 citizens had already been evacuated, 2.2 million were still trapped inside the city. The stranglehold was devastating. As food supplies ran out they began to starve. At first in their tens, then in their hundreds, then in their thousands and then in their tens of thousands. Corpses – sometimes mutilated for human consumption – piled up in the streets. By the winter of 1941–42, when the temperature dropped well below freezing, the death rate reached 100,000 a month. In the course of what became an 872-day siege, many more died. The total number of victims was never precisely established but, by the end of January 1944, when the siege was finally lifted, Hitler could claim to have presided over the deaths of perhaps a million civilians in Leningrad alone.

As one disaster followed on the heels of another, brutality continued to provide one avenue for the release of Stalin's frustrations. On 11 September General Vasily Goncharov, the artillery commander of the 34th Army, was accused of cowardice for allowing a number of units to be encircled. In line with Stalin's Directive No. 270 against 'deserters, cowards and panic-mongers', he was sentenced to death. The order was pronounced jointly by Mekhlis and General Kirill Meretskov, who had himself been arrested with Pavlov in July. Unlike General Pavlov, the erstwhile Commander-in-Chief of the Western Front, Meretskov had been spared the firing squad but – as one of his interrogators later confessed – only after 'continuous torture was applied . . . he was beaten with rubber rods'. Thus chastised, he not only confessed to crimes that he had not committed but denounced Pavlov as a 'traitor' for good measure.[17] Now rehabilitated by Stalin, he became an enthusiastic advocate of the ultimate penalty for 'cowardice'.

The elderly major instructed to shoot Goncharov was more squeamish.

Ordered to stand in a row of staff officers alongside the general, he watched as Mekhlis – in his role as army commissar – walked along the line until he stopped in front of the doomed man. After a brief exchange, he read out the dread words, 'In accordance with Order No. 270 of the People's Commissar for Defence . . .' When he finished he turned to the major and ordered him to execute his own commanding officer. The major was overwhelmed with horror at the thought. As a brother officer recalled, he was unable to overcome his emotion, and with great daring refused. 'A firing squad had to be summoned instead.'[18]

None of this was enough to deter a growing number of soldiers – either individually or en masse – from choosing to face a firing squad rather than the meat-grinding impact of the German guns. In the absence of more effective ways of securing the loyalty of their troops, their commanders were reduced to repeating Stalinist slogans like 'Stand to the death' or 'Not a step back'. Something more was required. Stalin was only too ready to come to their aid.

On 12 September he and Shaposhnikov signed a joint order instructing every division in the Red Army to establish 'blocking detachments'* of battalion strength and to be fully armed and equipped with transport and tanks.[19] Shorn of its legalistic niceties, these units were tasked to mow down any soldiers who were judged to be inciting panic or trying to flee the field of battle. Twelve days later, on 24 September, the tactic was put to the test at Chernevo, a village near the city of Glukhov, where the Russians were under severe pressure from units of Guderian's Panzer Group 2, closing in on Bryansk and Oryol. In the face of what he judged to be intolerable losses, Major Hamazasp Babadzhanian, commanding the 395th Rifle Regiment, sought permission from his divisional commander, Colonel A. Z. Akimenko, to withdraw from the west bank of the River Kleven to the east. Akimenko refused, using the words, 'Not a step back. Stand to the death.'[20] Babadzhanian obeyed.

Soon afterwards, between seventy and eighty tanks burst through the line being held by the 395th and two other regiments. At that point, according to Akimenko,

---

* 'Blocking detachments' had existed from the beginning of the Great Patriotic War. This order greatly expanded their role; instead of being formed by small NKVD units, they were to be established in every infantry division as part of the regular army.

an extraordinary incident occurred . . . about 900 men committed treachery to the interests of our homeland. As if by command, this group rose up, threw away their rifles and, with raised hands, they proceeded to the side of the enemy tanks. The enemy tanks quickly edged up to the traitors and, under cover of other tanks, began to take the traitors away.

Unable to 'take control of the traitors for future punishment' himself, Akimenko opted to obey Stalin's newest edict: 'I gave an order for two artillery battalions to open fire on the traitors and the enemy tanks. As a result a considerable number of traitors were killed.'[21]

In the course of that battle (according to the contemporary records kept by Akimenko's division), Babadzhanian lost 605 men killed, wounded, or missing in action; a further 850 were described as having 'surrendered as prisoners of war'. There was no mention of the 'considerable number' who had been executed by their own artillery.

Babadzhanian's courage in the face of this disaster so impressed Grossman (who had been forced to leave the area while the battle was still underway) that he lionized him as the hero of his best-selling novel *The People Immortal*, published a few months later, in which he was killed, fighting to his last drop of blood. Soon afterwards, the author found himself at dinner with a brigade commander on the Ukrainian front. They reminisced about dates and names until it dawned on Grossman that he was talking to the character in his novel. 'Yes, I was there,' Babadzhanian confirmed, 'but you killed me.' Grossmann, rarely at a loss for words, replied, 'I killed you but I can resurrect you, too.'[22]★

★ In 1944 Babadzhanian was made a Hero of the Soviet Union for his role in helping to drive the Germans out of Ukraine. After the end of the war he was promoted to the rank of major general. In 1956 he played a leading part in crushing the Hungarian uprising. Later he became Chief Marshal of the Soviet Tank and Armoured Troops. He died in 1977 and was buried in Moscow with full military honours.

20.   Wars of Words

On 28 September, ominous snow clouds piled up over Moscow. The British ambassador and his American counterpart were wrapped against the cold as they waited on the tarmac to greet the arrival of a joint Anglo-American delegation. There was a Soviet guard of honour (500 soldiers, apparently rushed from the front). The Stars and Stripes, the Union Jack and the Hammer and Sickle were clustered together to wave in unison as Lord Beaverbrook (representing Churchill) and Averell Harriman (representing Roosevelt) descended from their aircraft to the formal welcome of their respective national anthems.

Aside from the fact that they were both millionaires, the two emissaries had little in common. Harriman, the son of an industrial magnate, had inherited a fortune, graduated from Yale University, gone into banking, and, as a friend of the Roosevelt family, gravitated into public service, where he helped deliver the president's New Deal. He was elegant, debonair and charming. His credentials as an international diplomat were impeccable.

By contrast, Beaverbrook was diminutive, rotund and graceless. More significantly, he was a self-made bruiser, a bundle of ferocious ambition and energy. Born William Maxwell Aitken in Canada in 1879, he was one of ten children of a Scottish-born Presbyterian minister. Brought up in poverty, he left school with no formal qualifications and worked variously as a local reporter, a life-assurance salesman and a debt collector. His passion was for newspapers, and he had the guile and chutzpah to make enough money to buy several of them. In 1910 he moved to England, where he was befriended by Bonar Law, a fellow Canadian and a junior Conservative minister. Beaverbrook, ever alert to an opportunity for personal advancement, exploited the future prime minister's contacts to win a seat in the Westminster Parliament that same year and, six years later, a controlling stake in an ailing British newspaper, the *Daily Express*, which he turned into the largest selling newspaper in the world. As a media baron, he was soon feted by the rich, the fashionable and the talented, whether or not they shared his reactionary political views.

In May 1940, by now Lord Beaverbrook, he was appointed by Churchill as Minister for Aircraft Production. His readiness to shoulder his way through apparently insuperable bureaucratic and industrial obstacles earned him promotion to Minister of Supply by a clearly besotted prime minister. Those of his peers who sensed that dishonesty came to him as second nature were less enthusiastic. Churchill's wife, Clementine, who was a rather better judge of character than her husband, could not abide the 'little imp', as she called him.

'Try ridding yourself of this microbe which some people fear is in your blood,' she was later to advise him after a particularly egregious example of Beaverbrook's duplicity.[1] In September 1941 he enjoyed the full confidence of the prime minister, who wrote to Stalin on the eve of the Anglo-American delegation's departure for Moscow, describing him as 'one of my oldest and most intimate friends'.[2]

If they were not natural cronies, Beaverbrook and Harriman had a common purpose: to persuade Stalin that the two Western allies were united in their resolve to extract the Soviet Union from what was still widely regarded in their respective capitals as the jaws of defeat. Their mission had originated with the joint letter Churchill and Roosevelt had sent the Soviet leader during the Atlantic Conference a little over six weeks earlier, in which they had suggested such a meeting in Moscow.

In the intervening period, the Red Army's predicament had worsened sharply. On 30 August, in a highly unusual move, Stalin sent a personal telegram to Ivan Maisky in London. The Soviet leader had just read his ambassador's report of a meeting with Eden a few days earlier in which he urged the British Foreign Secretary to open a second front (which Stalin had demanded a month earlier) as well as pressing for the early delivery of an increased volume of military hardware. Stalin had clearly been impressed by his ambassador's stance. 'The Hitlerites want to beat their opponents one by one – Russians today, English tomorrow. English passivity helps the Hitlerites,' Stalin wrote. 'The fact that England applauds us and curses the Germans does not change anything. Do the English understand that? I think they do. So what do they want? I think they want us to weaken.'[3]

Emboldened by his leader's readiness thus to confide in him, Maisky responded with his own personal message the following day. Notwithstanding Stalin's paranoid tendencies, he knew that his suspicion of Britain was not entirely without foundation and, in his wily fashion, he sought to unravel the 'complicated knot of motives' by which British policy towards the Soviet Union was ensnared. Among these conflicting impulses he detected both a 'desire to weaken us' and an 'unshakeable belief in German invincibility on land'. These factors, combined with their awareness that 'the Russians fight well' had led the British Cabinet to conclude that, for a year or two, it could avoid sending ground troops into Europe to open a second front. The most effective way to combat this 'complacency', Maisky urged, was plain-speaking: 'Churchill and others must understand at long last that if the USSR leaves the stage, the British Empire is finished.'[4]

Stalin needed little encouragement. On 3 September he wrote to Churchill in the bluntest terms to warn that the Soviet Union faced a 'mortal menace' that could be averted only if the Allies opened 'a Second Front somewhere in the Balkans or France' with forces 'capable of drawing away from the Eastern Front 30 to 40 [German] divisions'.[5] The very thought of a second front – which was starting to attract widespread public support in Britain and notably from Beaverbrook's *Daily Express* – was anathema to Churchill.* The prime minister not only loathed any thought of diverting scarce resources from Britain's own hard-pressed armed forces but also had grim memories of earlier attempts to mount a major seaborne invasion of the European continent. In July, he had told Eden, 'Remember that on my breast are the medals of the Dardanelles, Antwerp, Dakar, and Greece', four disasters for which he had direct responsibility – and to which, as Andrew Roberts has pointed out, he might have added Norway and Crete.[6]

In the same letter, Stalin also demanded '30,000 tons of aluminium by the beginning of October next and a minimum monthly delivery of aid amounting to 400 aircraft and 500 tanks (of small or medium size).' He went on to warn that in the absence of such support 'the Soviet Union will either suffer defeat or be weakened to such an extent that it will lose

---

* So great was Churchill's regard for the 'little imp' that he tended to overlook the rampant disloyalty of his capable minister.

for a long period any capacity to render assistance to its Allies by its actual operations on the fronts of the struggle against Hitlerism'.[7]

On 4 September Churchill replied in equally blunt terms:

> Although we should shrink from no exertion, there is in fact no possibility of any British action in the West, except air action, which would draw the German forces from the East before the winter sets in. There is no chance whatever of a second front being formed in the Balkans . . . Action, however well meant, leading to costly fiascos would be of no help to anyone but Hitler.[8]

Stalin's letter had been delivered personally to the prime minister by Maisky at 10 Downing Street. In the course of their conversation Maisky, who had himself been shaken by the contents of Stalin's letter, warned that without the aid demanded by Stalin, 'the USSR will face the risk of defeat with all the ensuing consequences'.[9] This lightly veiled threat hit a raw nerve in Churchill, who, until the Molotov–Ribbentrop Pact, had argued strenuously for an alliance with Moscow against the Nazis. Angered by what he sensed to be 'an underlying air of menace' in the Soviet ambassador's tone, he retorted, 'Remember that only four months ago we in this Island did not know whether you were not coming in against us on the German side. Indeed, we thought it quite likely that you would . . . Whatever happens, and whatever you do, you of all people have no right to make reproaches to us.'[10]

Nonetheless, he was troubled enough by Maisky's words to send an urgent message to Roosevelt advising that he and Eden (who was also present) had been driven to conclude that they 'could not exclude the impression that they [the Russians] might be thinking of separate terms'.[11] The fear that Moscow could yet be driven to sue for peace with Berlin in the hope of securing a modified version of the Molotov–Ribbentrop Pact was never far from the minds of strategists in London and Washington. The implications for Britain's efforts to break Hitler's stranglehold on Europe – let alone to protect the Empire – were almost too ghastly to contemplate but, as Churchill's message to Roosevelt made clear, they could not be ignored.

In Moscow, Stafford Cripps had also been handed a copy of Stalin's letter by the junior foreign minister Andrei Vyshinsky. Cripps was as devastated by its import as Maisky and took it upon himself to send a 'MOST IMMEDIATE' message to the Foreign Office in London:

> [The letter] shows that unless we can now at the last moment make a super-human effort we shall lose the whole value of the Russian front, at any rate for a long period, and possibly for good . . . I fear it is now almost too late unless we are prepared to throw everything in, in an effort to save the front.[12]

Churchill, already smarting from the tone of Stalin's missive, was incensed by his ambassador's endorsement of it. Determined to quash any prospect of a second front, he replied personally to Cripps in terms calculated to cause maximum offence: 'When you speak of "a superhuman effort", you mean, I presume, an effort rising superior to space, time, and geography. Unfortunately these attributes are denied us.'[13] It was the beginning of a long and acrimonious correspondence between two competitive egos who held markedly different views about the best means of securing the defeat of Nazism – a mutual antagonism aggravated by Churchill's blunt denial of Cripps's request to brief the government in person on his appreciation of the Soviet Union's predicament.

Ten days later, on 14 September, Harriman arrived in London for a series of meetings with Beaverbrook to discuss their agenda for the Moscow Conference. Within two hours of the plane landing, Beaverbrook – who was accustomed to getting his own way – summoned the US delegation to a meeting in the War Cabinet rooms. In his crudely direct fashion, he tried to seize the initiative, demanding to know what quantities of munitions and raw material the United States was willing to supply to the Russians. The urbane Harriman would have none of it and refused politely but firmly to tell him. Beaverbrook persisted, asserting that there was no time to be lost. According to Harriman, Beaverbrook – who was under stern instructions from Churchill 'to make sure we are not bled white'[14] – appeared to think that, if he could extract a specific US commitment before they departed for Moscow, he would be able to postpone making any British commitment until the negotiations with the Russians were underway. Harriman was far too canny to fall into Beaverbrook's trap. Once again he demurred, retorting drily that for him to make such a commitment at this stage 'would relieve the

Americans of the necessity of going to Moscow'. At this, Beaverbrook backed off in alarm. 'Oh, no, no, no,' he replied. 'We must go together.'[15] It was not a good beginning.

When Churchill heard a rather exaggerated account of the stand-off between the two would-be envoys, he moved swiftly to invite Harriman to dinner. 'I know how difficult he [Beaverbrook] can be. But it's a vital matter. I depend on you,' he said soothingly.[16] Harriman confirmed that he would, of course, still go to Moscow, adding firmly that 'it was just as well that the equal standing of the British and American delegations had been settled before they left London'.

Beaverbrook was too thick-skinned to feel deflated, but at least for the next six days he conducted himself with somewhat greater decorum as the two teams discussed what might reasonably be available for the Russians. Nonetheless the relationship between the two men remained strained. After dinner one evening, Harriman's wife wrote a letter to her sister: 'Dinner tonight [with Beaverbrook] was in rather sharp contrast to last night – with the P.M. One's a gentleman and the other is a ruffian. Ave[rell], luckily can talk both languages.'[17]

At Beaverbrook's insistence the two emissaries travelled to Moscow by sea via the Soviet port of Archangel. The voyage, in the cruiser HMS *London* through waters that were dangerously exposed to German air and sea attack, was uneventful but not particularly congenial. Harriman noted that, although Beaverbrook had given up 'bullying' him, he turned on his own team – which included General 'Pug' Ismay, Churchill's personal representative on the Chiefs of Staff Committee, and Sir Charles Wilson, Churchill's personal physician – telling them 'that they were coming along for the ride; he and Harriman would handle all the important negotiations with Stalin'.[18]

As soon as the diplomatic courtesies at the airport had been observed, Molotov presented the two envoys with an invitation to meet Stalin at the Kremlin later that evening. A little after 9 p.m., they were ushered into the Soviet leader's expansive office. Stalin greeted them courteously but without effusion. Harriman was struck by the fact that he rarely looked them in the eyes, preferring to address his remarks to Maxim Litvinov (sacked as Commissar for Foreign Affairs in the spring of 1939 during the purge of diplomats but resuscitated for this meeting as Stalin's interpreter). Molotov, who was also present, remained silent throughout the meeting.

According to the American envoy, Stalin was remarkably forthcoming, even to the point of volunteering that if Hitler had concentrated his assault on the capital rather than on three fronts simultaneously, 'the city would certainly have fallen'. As it was, were Moscow to fall, 'he was prepared to go on fighting a defensive war from behind the Ural Mountains'. However, he warned, the loss of 'the nerve centre of all Soviet operations would gravely handicap any offensive action in the future'.[19] Thus unburdened, Stalin produced a very long shopping list, at the top of which was a demand for the delivery of more than 1,000 new tanks a month, though, as Harriman observed drily, he was willing to reduce this to 500 to avoid being charged with 'asking for astronomical quantities'.[20] Although they made no progress during the five-hour meeting, both Harriman and Beaverbrook nonetheless left the Kremlin 'more than pleased' to have been given such a genial reception.[21]

For quite different reasons, both envoys had agreed to exclude their respective ambassadors from the negotiations with Stalin. Harriman had been alerted by Harry Hopkins to the fact that Steinhardt was deeply pessimistic about the Red Army's prospects. He had also been told that the Soviet leader could not abide the ambassador – a report that was confirmed when Stalin denounced him in a casual aside as 'a defeatist, a rumour-monger, and a man chiefly interested in his own safety'.[22] The American envoy had also taken against the British ambassador because Cripps, somewhat prissily, had objected to the inclusion in the delegation of a prominent American journalist, Quentin Reynolds, whom Harriman had himself chosen to be its spokesman. Beaverbrook – whose 'second front' sympathies led him to identify more closely with Cripps than with Churchill over the urge to make 'superhuman' efforts to help the Soviet Union – was nonetheless delighted to exclude Cripps from the talks. He had every intention of delivering his own personal report to the War Cabinet without any risk that the forceful and opinionated British ambassador might steal some of his thunder. He was also disagreeably inclined towards Cripps's asceticism, telling Harriman that he was 'always ill at ease with teetotallers . . . particularly socialist teetotallers who were candidates for sainthood'.[23]

His exclusion from the negotiations greatly irked Cripps, who was still smarting not only from Churchill's slights but also from the fact that he had been systematically cut out of the diplomatic loop between

London and Moscow at such a critical period. But he did pick up one or two important tit-bits. In his indiscreet fashion, Beaverbrook let slip that he had been significantly hobbled by the War Cabinet, an admission which led Cripps to a gloomily acerbic prognosis:

> He [Beaverbrook] is certainly out to do everything possible to give immediate help and he would have liked to have given full information about our production etc., but the Cabinet refused to allow it. The result is that the whole thing comes down to a sort of Father Christmas party with America and England [sic] declaring what they are prepared to do to help poor Russia, which is the wrong atmosphere altogether.[24]

The next day, at the second Kremlin meeting, Cripps's foreboding proved frustratingly accurate. Stalin was in a very different mood. He was truculent, disdainful and aggressive. It was, noted Harriman, 'very rough going' as the Soviet leader castigated the two men for the dearth of assistance they appeared to be offering. According to the American envoy, he virtually accused the two Western allies of bad faith; at one point in what had become 'a deeply discouraging talk' he made the point explicitly, charging that 'the paucity of your offers clearly shows that you want to see the Soviet Union defeated'.[25] When Beaverbrook handed him a letter from Churchill, he made a show of indifference, barely glancing at it before dropping it on the table beside him. When Molotov murmured that he had not read it, he merely picked it up and handed it to a clerk, still unread. It was a discourtesy designed to be noticed. The meeting ended as badly as it began. It was scant consolation that, instead of aborting the conference at that point, Stalin sullenly agreed that they should meet again.

Beaverbrook, who had returned from their first meeting to send a triumphalist telegram to Churchill, was chastened. According to Harriman, 'Max was rattled' – though less by the impasse itself than by the damage it might do him at home. 'Beaverbrook', he wrote, 'was constantly thinking of his own reputation with his colleagues in the British government.'[26]

For the third meeting, on 30 September, Beaverbrook – who had taken the lead in the first two – allowed Harriman to present the Allied case. Technical teams from both sides had combed every detail of Stalin's original shopping list, so the American cut to the chase. The conference needed to come to a rapid conclusion, he told Stalin, who concurred at once, observing that Berlin radio was already claiming that the talks had ended in failure and acrimony. Point by point, they went through a list of seventy items as Harriman explained what the Allies were able and willing to provide. It was a significant package, worth, in total, $1 billion ($18 billion in 2020 dollars). As they ticked off item after item, the atmosphere became harmonious. So much so that, when everything had been agreed, Beaverbrook could not resist asking Stalin if he was pleased by the offer they had made. Stalin smiled and nodded. At this, the former Foreign Affairs Commissar, Litvinov – forgetting for this occasion he had merely been summoned from obscurity to act as interpreter – leapt up to declare 'Now we shall win the war!'[27]*

There was one further hurdle to be cleared. Stalin insisted that the two sides sign an official protocol confirming their agreement. Unfortunately, neither Harriman nor Beaverbrook had been authorized to put their names to any such document. When Harriman parried that written agreements were unnecessary, they agreed to a meeting with Molotov the next day to resolve the issue. However 'Old Stone Arse' proved to be unbending: a protocol was required. Beaverbrook countered that a protocol was no more than a 'glorified memorandum'. Eventually, they concocted a face-saving form of words which found expression in a formal communiqué as sonorous as it was vapid. Complete with references to 'fascist aggression' and the atmosphere of 'understanding, confidence, and goodwill' that had prevailed throughout, it declared the 'conference of the three great powers had successfully accomplished its work, passed important resolutions in conformity with the aims set for it, and manifested the perfect unanimity and close co-operation of the three great powers in their common efforts to gain the victory over the mortal enemy of all freedom-loving nations'.[28]

Beaverbrook was so elated by the outcome that he raced to the conclusion that Stalin was 'a kindly man' who 'practically never shows any impatience at all'. This flight of fancy carried over into an impromptu press conference to which he summoned the five Western correspondents

---

* A month later, Litvinov was rehabilitated to become the Soviet Union's ambassador to the United States. This followed a private conversation with Stalin at which Harriman was sharply critical of the current ambassador, Konstantin Umansky, who had become deeply unpopular in Washington on account of his arrogant and intemperate demands for American aid.

based in Moscow. Elaborating on a communiqué that he had issued jointly with Harriman, he implied that Stalin was as delighted by the success of the conference as he was. Alexander Werth caught his mood, noting wryly that Beaverbrook was 'bursting with exuberance. Slapping his knees he was saying that the Russians were pleased with Beaverbrook, and the Americans were pleased with Beaverbrook – "Now aren't they, Harriman?" to which Harriman replied, "Sure you bet." '[29]

In a self-serving cable to Churchill, Beaverbrook reported that the conference had led to 'an immense strengthening of the morale of Moscow'. Though the prime minister sent 'heartiest congratulations . . . No one could have done it but you,'[30] his own reflections later were distinctly jaundiced. The reception given to the mission in Moscow 'was bleak and discussions not at all friendly. It might almost have been thought that the plight in which the Soviets now found themselves was our fault . . . It might almost have been we who had come to ask for favours.'[31]

The Gala Banquet at the Kremlin, which followed the formal end of the conference on 1 October, was held in the old Imperial Palace. Harriman was impressed by the grandeur of his surroundings and the lavish quantities of food and alcohol with which their table was laden. He wondered at 'the endless hors d'oeuvres beginning with caviar and various forms of fish, cold suckling pig, then the dinner of hot soup, chicken and a game bird, with ice cream and cakes for dessert . . . In front of each man there were a number of bottles containing pepper vodka, red and white wine, a Russian brandy – and champagne.' As there were so many guests – 120 or so in all – a great many reciprocal toasts were drunk during the two-hour feast. From time to time, Stalin, who had Harriman and Beaverbrook on either side of him, would rise from his place to clink glasses with those further down the table.

Harriman was struck by the contrast between the Kremlin and 10 Downing Street, where, he claimed – not entirely accurately – Churchill was 'always careful to conform to British rations'. Later, he declared that he had been 'disgusted' watching Soviet officials eat like gluttons when the Russian people went hungry.[32] As protocol demanded, Cripps – who was still smarting at his exclusion from the conference and was as yet unaware of what it had (or had not) achieved – had a place near the head of the table. Despite himself, he enjoyed the occasion: 'It was an extremely good show . . . in a lovely suite of rooms . . . the food was excellent and too much of it.' If he was momentarily tempted to overindulge, asceticism restrained him: 'I was grateful for my vegetarianism and my teetotalism!' he noted.[33]

The following day the British ambassador – who by this time had been finally briefed on the contents of the agreement – was coldly realistic. The Allied communiqué, he judged,

> was quite false in saying that we had satisfied the wishes of the Russians. It is true that eventual lists were agreed but this does not mean that we have promised anything like all they wanted . . . I am afraid that after the spectacular success of the conference, the time of disappointment will come when the things do not arrive. In fact I do not think that there is any chance of our delivering more than a fraction of what we have actually promised, unless some very drastic steps are taken to spare them shipping. This will be the great struggle now for those who want to help Russia.[34]

His forecast was to prove only too accurate. Beaverbrook and Harriman had been careful to distinguish between an undertaking to 'make available' the supplies and a commitment to ensure their safe delivery. There were good reasons for this: the fierce competition within the Allied camp for what was available; an acute shortage of merchant shipping; the threat posed by the U-boats and the Luftwaffe in the war-torn seas between the United States, Britain and the Soviet Union; and the natural hazards of winter storms, heavy fog and drifting icebergs. It would have been impossible to guarantee the promised deliveries even with the best will in the world and, as Cripps had hinted, the British at least were decidedly lukewarm benefactors. In the months ahead, these promised deliveries – or their absence – were to become the source of much misunderstanding not only with Moscow but also between London and Washington.

As the conference came to an end, Cripps's protégé, Geoffrey Wilson, who was back in London at the Foreign Office following a stint in the Moscow embassy, wrote a letter to his friend John Cripps, Stafford's son. In a downbeat assessment of Anglo-Soviet relations, he peered into the future with rare prescience:

> One of my nightmares is that if the Russian armies are eventually successful, as I think they may well be, they will end this war by marching

to Berlin and occupying all points of Europe east. And then how are we going to get them out? . . . It seems to me that the influence that we shall have on them depends very much on the way in which we treat them now, and it is for that reason that I think it is so desperately important to 'get alongside of them' somehow, quite apart from any question of military or economic supplies . . . unless there is a change, there is going to be a most unholy row between us when this thing is over, and the final atmosphere of suspicion and mistrust will be far worse at the end than it was two or three years ago.[35]

The words could well have been written by Cripps himself.★

Such thoughtfulness did not form part of Beaverbrook's intellectual repertoire. He was a doer, not a thinker. He was also incontinently offensive to those around him. He preened himself with great bonhomie in off-the-record briefings with Moscow's corps of foreign correspondents, but he did not conceal his disdain for embassy officials. Even Cripps was treated as though he were a lackey rather than a senior colleague. Although Beaverbrook slept and entertained in a lavish suite in the National Hotel (which overlooked Red Square), he decided to commandeer Cripps's office at the embassy during the day. When the ambassador's presence was required, he evidently 'opened the door and bellowed "Cripps!"'[36] More galling, though, than Beaverbrook's boorish behaviour was his refusal to share any information with the British ambassador. 'I have held myself at B[eaverbrook]'s disposal every day and all day but he has not vouchsafed anything to me at all,'[37] Cripps lamented at the end of the conference.

Harriman was more forthcoming. 'The very small amount of information that I have as to the happenings of the last week are entirely from him,' Cripps noted after a productive two-hour meeting from which each emerged with a high opinion of the other.[38] During their tête-à-tête, the two men agreed that the three great powers should explore the prospects for a 'tripartite arrangement' within which to establish a framework for peace and stability in the post-war world.[39] Though

★ Sir Geoffrey Wilson rose to become permanent secretary at the Ministry of Overseas Development and then, successively, vice-president of the World Bank, chairman of the Race Relations Board and chairman of Oxfam. He died in 2004 at the age of ninety-four.

Cripps sensed that Roosevelt's envoy set greater store than he did by the Atlantic Charter, it was clear to him that they had at least identified a beginning, a point of departure.

The issue had been raised head-on by Stalin at the end of the third session of the Kremlin talks. Once the war was over, he argued, the United States, Britain and the Soviet Union should turn their military partnership into a formal peacetime alliance. This was treacherous territory that neither envoy was authorized to explore. Beaverbrook responded by saying simply that 'it would be enough to win the war' and Harriman observed that the Atlantic Charter 'constituted a programme for peace to which the United States and Britain had already subscribed'.[40]

The little-noticed final paragraph of the conference communiqué was carefully worded to avoid entering this diplomatic minefield while acknowledging that it could not be sidestepped indefinitely: 'In concluding its session, the conference adheres to the resolution of the three governments that, after the final annihilation of the Nazi tyranny, a peace will be established which will enable the world to live in security in its own territory in conditions free from fear and need.'[41]

Within days, such diplomatic forethought began to look wilfully hypothetical, if not wildly premature. Moscow was soon to be threatened by an all-out military assault designed to throttle the Soviet capital.

21. Operation Typhoon

On 3 October Hitler went to the Sportpalast in Berlin to open Kriegswinterhilfswerk, the annual winter campaign by the Nazi Party's 'charitable arm', which raised funds to provide essentials for the poor, operating under the heart-warming banner 'None Shall Starve or Freeze'. The masses had gathered, arms raised to salute him. The Führer looked jaded but, wrapped in the devotion of his disciples, soon became jubilant. He had just arrived back from Wolfsschanze after launching a new offensive, telling the troops at the front that this would be 'the last decisive battle of this year'; that their enemy 'did not consist of soldiers but a majority of beasts'; and that their names 'will be associated for all time with the most tremendous victories in history'.[1] In front of a rapturous audience in Berlin, he went further. At the end of a long rambling speech, punctuated by frequent applause, he roused them to a frenzy of delight – tinged perhaps by relief – by declaring that the Soviet Union was 'already broken and will never rise again'.[2]

For the most part, his senior generals did not dissent. Barbarossa had been hard fought, with 185,000 of the Ostheer's soldiers killed in a little over three months, but they had penetrated more than 800 kilometres into the heart of the Soviet Union along a front over 1,600 kilometres in length. They had taken Kiev, put Leningrad under siege and, following their victories at Minsk and Smolensk, were now poised to strike at the capital, a mere 300 kilometres away.

However, despite his public assurance that the Soviet Union was 'broken', Hitler was exceptionally anxious to destroy the Red Army as a significant threat before the onset of the vicious Russian winter. There was little time and he was in a hurry. The plan – codenamed Operation Typhoon – was simple enough: to force a massive breach through Stalin's armies that were drawn up as a defensive shield in front of Moscow, to advance at blitzkrieg pace to the outskirts of the capital and then rapidly to strangle the nerve centre of Judaeo-Bolshevism. The Soviet Union would not have been physically destroyed but, Hitler hoped, the Leviathan would indeed 'never' rise again.

To this end the Ostheer had been fundamentally restructured to focus 'the highest concentration of panzer, motorized, and infantry divisions ever assembled by Nazi Germany'.[3] With units transferred from Army Group North and Army Group South, the final drive on Moscow was to be spearheaded by a greatly strengthened Army Group Centre. With seventy-five infantry divisions at his disposal and three of the Ostheer's four panzer groups (2, 3 and 4), including more than 1,000 tanks, 14,000 pieces of artillery, all supported by 1,390 combat aircraft, Bock had command of what appeared to be a formidable, if not invincible, fighting force.[4]

Operation Typhoon began with a sudden and immense artillery bombardment at 5.30 a.m. on 2 October. Thirty minutes later Helmut Pabst, a signals NCO attached to an artillery unit in Panzer Group 3, leapt onto the top of a dugout: 'There are tanks! Giants rolling slowly towards the enemy. And the planes. One squadron after the other, unloading their bombs across the way.' Ten minutes later, he was transfixed by a barrage of mortar fire: 'Dammit, it's really something worth seeing; the rockets leave a black trail, a dirty cloud which slowly drifts away. The second salvo goes off! Red and black fire, then the projectile emerges from the cone of smoke . . . the things fly straight as arrows through the morning air.' At a little after 8 a.m. he counted hundreds of tanks as they rolled past his position followed by line upon line of assault guns and motorized infantry. 'It looks like chaos but it works to the minute, like clockwork . . . tomorrow it'll be Moscow,' he chortled. Soon after midday, his unit reached the shattered remains of the Red Army's forward defences. It was deserted apart from the corpses of those who had fallen: 'A system of trenches, a stretch of scarred earth, one crater after another. The dead look horribly mangled . . . Above the troops on the march fly the formations of bombers; then the fighters, swift and silver – Eastward, ho!'[5]

It had started to look as though Hitler's blitzkrieg would live up to the billing he had given it in the Sportpalast. That evening, Guderian (whose Panzer Group 2 had started its attack two days before the main body of Army Group Centre, and had already advanced eighty-five kilometres) advised that 'he was sure he had broken clean through the enemy line'. Halder was elated. 'Typhoon has started with smashing force,'[6] he noted. An equally exultant Bock wrote, 'The Army Group went to the attack according to plan. We advanced so easily that doubts arose as to whether the enemy had not in fact decamped.'[7]

The mood was much the same among the rank and file. Hitler's Sportpalast speech was relayed to the troops at the front. Wilhelm Prüller was among those listening intently. He was entranced. 'No one knows what this beloved voice means to us,' he noted that evening, 'how our cheeks glow, our eyes sparkle . . . What a lift his words give us, as we crowd round the wireless set, not wanting to miss a single word! Is there a finer reward after a day of battle than to hear the Führer? Never, we thank him!'[8] Some were rather less besotted. Hans-Jürgen Hartmann was not alone in wondering whether it was 'only "talk" that our enemy is broken and will never rise again. I cannot help myself – I am totally bewildered. Will the whole war still be over before winter?'[9]

It was a question that perpetually agitated Hitler. His conviction, which he shared with Goebbels on the day of his Sportpalast speech, that 'the Soviet army will be essentially smashed within fourteen days' contained a meteorological caveat. Victory would be assured, he confided, 'if the weather stays moderately favourable'.[10] It was an uncharacteristic note of caution. For the moment, such concerns could be put aside; the weather was still fine and the skies were clear. There was an autumn chill in the air but no rain or snow to prevent the panzers and the infantry divisions from advancing at speed towards Moscow.

There was just one problem: although the Soviet forces had already endured 2 million battlefield casualties, the Stavka was still able to muster fifteen armies along the crucial 350-kilometre front: 1,250,000 men – 40 per cent of the Red Army's total strength – deployed in three separate fronts that, between them, were equipped with 1,000 tanks, 7,600 guns and mortars and 667 combat aircraft. The heaviest concentration was clustered along a 140-kilometre north–south axis between two crucial salients at Vyazma and Bryansk (respectively 240 and 350 kilometres from the capital). To reach Moscow, Bock's armies would have to break through at both those points. Despite the formidable array of firepower at his disposal, Bock faced a daunting challenge. Operation Typhoon was a massive and fateful gamble.

At first glance, the odds appeared to be in Hitler's favour: not only was the Red Army ill-prepared for a major campaign but also, the armies at Stalin's disposal in the Central Front had yet to complete the large-scale redeployments and reorganizations required to reinforce Moscow's outer defensive ring, which was still highly vulnerable. This task was complicated by the wholesale changes that Stalin had instigated at the top of the command structure. Colonel General Ivan Konev had only just taken command of the Western Front (replacing Timoshenko, who had been rushed south in the vain bid to save Kiev). Similarly, Budyonny – scapegoated by Stalin for his failure to hold the Kiev line – was newly in command of the Reserve Front (replacing Zhukov, after he was sent north to save Leningrad). Only Yeremenko's Bryansk Front, defending the area most immediately exposed to Guderian's breakneck advance, had been under the command of the same general for more than a month. Stalin's game of military musical chairs, which smacked less of strong leadership than suppressed panic, could hardly have been played at a more inopportune moment.

The herculean task that faced the three Soviet commanders was aggravated by the dire state of their forward defences and the debilitated condition of their men and machines. Despite the back-breaking efforts of civilian engineers and raw recruits, the fortifications on the approaches to Moscow were only partly finished and in many places too fragile to arrest a determined panzer onslaught. Many of the front-line units were close to exhaustion after a series of sustained and frenzied counter-attacks in September. The recruits summoned from the rear to replace those who had been killed or captured were either raw conscripts or volunteers who in either case were ill trained and badly equipped. Their morale was equally poor. At the Bryansk Front Major Ivan Shabalin, commanding the political section in the 50th Army, found it hard to galvanize his men. 'At night time,' he noted, 'when the Germans conduct their reconnaissance, the men in our forward positions simply sleep. We fail to take any active measures . . . this is a travesty of how war should be conducted – I despair! Someone needs to take hold of this situation urgently.'[11]

The ravages of Barbarossa had left every Red Army division in the Western Front grievously short of its full complement of men and machines. Most rifle divisions were at no more than half strength. The armoured divisions should have presented an awesome prospect, but many of their tanks were in disrepair. Only a handful, notably the T-34s – which were truly capable of striking dread into the attackers – remained operational.

To make matters worse, the patchy and unreliable radio communications network linking front-line commanders with both each other and their headquarters made 'command and control' – exceptionally challenging in any rapidly developing campaign – virtually impossible on a fluid battlefield along such a long front. On top of that, the initial intelligence about the German preparations for Typhoon had been sketchy and vague. The Stavka was not only unprepared for the forthcoming onslaught but also unaware of the direction from which the German thrust might come – though Stalin was convinced, in the absence of evidence one way or the other, that it would come from Army Group South rather than Army Group Centre. In this cloud of unknowing, confusions and contradictions abounded.

It had been clear since mid-September that a full-scale German offensive was imminent. For this reason, with his forces engaged in a series of counter-offensives, Konev had been ordered to 'go over to the defensive' and to 'dig in'. Simultaneously though, his Western Front commanders were somewhat vaguely instructed to prepare for an offensive 'in the future'.[12] On 27 September Konev was told that 'the course of combat with the enemy has made it apparent that our forces are still not prepared [to face] a serious offensive operation',[13] and that he was to redouble his efforts to establish a strong defensive line. On the following day, with Operation Typhoon's artillery already in place, Stalin ordered Shaposhnikov to instruct the Red Army about the need to plan, organize and prepare to conduct offensive operations.[14] The spray of competing commands from Moscow was at best perplexing.

Vasily Grossman, who had hurried away from Bryansk to return to Oryol a few days earlier, reached the city in the last week of September, unaware that Guderian's panzers were close at hand. German warplanes were circling above. A frightened colleague who had just arrived told him that the Germans were 'rushing straight towards Oryol. There are hundreds of tanks.' Word soon got round and the citizens started to collect their belongings and flee. 'The city is rumbling all night long. Vehicles and carts move without stopping,' Grossman wrote. 'In the morning the city is gripped by horror and agony, almost like typhus. There's weeping and commotion in our hotel . . . People with sacks and suitcases are running past in the street, some carrying children.' He and his colleagues did not join the rush but, displaying admirable sangfroid, took themselves to a local *banya* to relax in a steam bath. Only after that refreshment did they leave Oryol, heading back along the Bryansk road once more, unaware that they were heading for even more trouble.[15]

Panzer Group 2 had advanced so rapidly that later the same day Guderian was able to inform Bock that his tanks had reached Oryol, the hub of a major rail and road link to Moscow.[16] 'Our seizure of the town', he wrote, 'took the enemy so completely by surprise that the electric trams were still running as our tanks drove in. The evacuation of industrial installations, carefully prepared by the Russians, could not be carried out. Along the streets leading from the factories to the station lay dismantled machines and crates filled with tools and raw materials.'[17] In fact there were not 'hundreds of tanks', as Grossman's panicked colleague had announced but four. They drove unopposed into a main square that was bereft of defenders. The commander of the tank squadron, Arthur Wollschlaeger, recalled, 'When the citizens of Oryol saw us, they fled into the streets and side streets, white as ghosts.'[18] The four tanks held the city, unchallenged, for three hours before reinforcements arrived.

As he surveyed the speed with which the Soviet defences were crumbling along the whole front, Halder was uncharacteristically smug. Army Group Centre's progress 'continues its classic course', he noted.[19] To the German High Command, Moscow seemed tantalizingly close: one last thrust and the Soviet capital would be in Nazi hands. Hitler's quartermaster general, Eduard Wagner, reflecting the exuberance which had started to consume his fellow staff officers, wrote:

> we have the impression that the last great collapse is imminent . . .
> Operational aims are set that would once have made one's hair stand on
> end . . . Over and over again, I'm amazed at the Führer's military judgement. He is intervening this time, one could say decisively, in the course
> of operations, and up to now he has always been right.[20]

From Oryol, Grossman and his colleagues hurried along the highway towards Bryansk, following the route taken by the retreating Soviet forces a few hours earlier. It was an eerie experience to travel through the deserted no-man's land that separated the Soviet and German lines. They found shelter at the headquarters of the 50th Army in the Bryansk forest ten kilometres or so south of the city. No one there was yet aware that they were about to be encircled by a pincer movement conceived by Army Group Centre and executed by Guderian's Panzer Group 2, which was advancing on Bryansk from the rear (cutting off Oryol) and from the west.

As the disaster unfolded, Major Ivan Shabalin (the NKVD head of the 50th Army's political section) watched on in dismay. 'The situation is chaotic,' he noted on 3 October. '[O]ur signal corps works badly, our command structure likewise. The generals in our neighbouring armies [13th and 15th] keep to the rear, already making plans for their own escape. We hear that Oryol has been evacuated, and that town is 150 kilometres behind our own position – such hopeless disorder.'[21] The following day he and Petrov met to discuss ways in which they might arrest the offensive. They found a divisional commander who claimed he had received no orders and had therefore taken no action. Soon afterwards they met his commissar, who claimed to be on his way to the front but was heading in the opposite direction. As they drove on they met groups of soldiers who had clearly left their posts without permission. They ordered them to return.

A little later, however, they saw why the troops had voted with their feet. Their defence positions had been laid waste by a combination of Kesselring's bombers and Guderian's artillery. Machine-gun emplacements and trenches were in smithereens. Without air support, they had been unable to mount any kind of counter-attack. As Shabalin wrote:

> The division I am with is smashed. We have lost contact with the regiment on our right flank, and have no idea whether anyone remains alive. The regiment on our left is down to twenty men, and the division as a whole can scarcely muster 300. The Germans are making fresh probing attacks and our forces are in total disorder.[22]

That evening Petrov, who was renowned for fortitude in the face of enemy fire as well as cruelty, asked Shabalin a rhetorical question to which he in any case supplied his own answer: 'Are we really supposed to go on shooting people for retreating without permission in a situation like this? It makes a mockery of army discipline.' The 50th Army's commander's reputation for ruthlessness had clearly been tested beyond endurance. According to Shabalin, the general dealt with the crisis by downing an entire litre of alcohol [presumably vodka] and fell into a deep sleep. 'With our commander in such a state we can expect few active measures against the enemy. Meanwhile, German tanks are racing towards Bryansk to complete the encirclement of our forces,'[23] he noted.

Yeremenko had already realized that the Bryansk front line was crumbling rapidly. With Petrov's 50th Army (along with the 3rd and 13th) in deep peril, he sought urgent permission from the Stavka to make a tactical withdrawal. He waited and waited but received no response. In the early hours of the following morning, with his own headquarters in imminent danger, he commandeered a truck for Grossmann and his colleagues and ordered them to leave forthwith. As instructed, they departed at precisely 4 a.m., laden with their mattresses, chairs and a lamp as well as their clothes and notebooks. Realizing from the map that they were almost 'caught in a sack',[24] as Grossman put it, they took the main road to Tula, which, as a major transport hub only 170 kilometres from Moscow, formed the last significant barrier protecting the capital from the south.

By this time, the evacuation of Bryansk had been underway for more than twenty-four hours. Grossman was astonished at its scale:

> I thought I'd seen retreats, but I've never seen anything like what I am seeing now . . . Exodus! Biblical exodus! Vehicles are moving in eight lanes, there's the violent roaring of dozens of trucks trying simultaneously to tear their wheels out of the mud. Huge herds of sheep and cows are driven through the fields. They are followed by trains of horse-drawn wagons . . . There are also crowds of pedestrians, with sacks, bundles, suitcases.

Many of the carts had been covered with makeshift tents, from which the faces of bearded Jewish elders with their wives, children and grandchildren peered out. 'What silence is in their eyes,' Grossman continued, 'what wise sorrow, what sensation of fate, of a universal catastrophe.'[25] Only one moment of light relief pierced the misery. Dozens of 'aerial boats', as Grossman described them, suddenly appeared over the horizon flying in the precise triangular formation of a bomber squadron. The refugees panicked and rushed into the forest to escape the expected bombardment. Then a woman's voice was heard to cut shrilly through the air: 'Cowards, cowards, they are just cranes flying over.'[26]

However, the flock was not alone in those skies. Bombs and shells were pulverizing Bryansk. Yet, despite the encroaching encirclement and the weakened and demoralized state of so many of the men under his command, Yeremenko did not yield meekly. On 6 October, soon after Grossman's departure, he glanced out of his command post to see a squadron of panzers no more than a few hundred metres from where he stood. Commandeering a scratch force of three tanks and a few trucks, he careered straight through the German unit and escaped with a handful of soldiers. Hearing only that his headquarters had been overrun, the Stavka presumed that Yeremenko, who had been seriously wounded during the Smolensk battles, had on this occasion been killed.* What remained of the front line was handed to Petrov, who – evidently recovering a modicum of sobriety – was equally determined to resist until the last.

On the same day, 6 October, at Hitler's behest, Panzer Group 2 was renamed the 2nd Panzer Army in tribute to the exploits of its dashing commander, who – largely as a result of Goebbels's assiduous propaganda – had become something of a cult hero throughout the Reich. Guderian did not lack vanity, but at this point his focus was concentrated exclusively on the need to close the Bryansk pocket. He faced greater resistance than he had expected. His 4th Panzer Division came under attack from a large tank unit south of the town of Mtsensk, fifty kilometres north-east of Oryol, and, he wrote, 'went through some bad hours'. And there was a reason for this. 'This was the first occasion on which the vast superiority of the Russian T-34 to our tanks became plainly apparent. The division suffered grievous casualties.'[27]

On 9 October, as Guderian's panzers struggled to complete the encirclement of Bryansk, Halder noted, 'Guderian is feeling the increasing pressure on his western flank',[28] and three days later, Bock wrote in frustration, 'Guderian is not moving forward . . . he is struggling with the Bryansk pockets.'[29] The 'classic' blitzkrieg of which Halder had boasted so recently was no longer as invincible as it had seemed in the heady days of victory on the Western Front in 1940 and the early days of Barbarossa.

But the end at Bryansk could not be long postponed. On 9 October Shabalin noted:

* In fact he had been severely wounded during his escape. He was evacuated to Moscow, where he was hospitalized. It took him many weeks to recover. After returning to front-line duties in January, he was wounded once more but again survived to play a leading role in the defence of Stalingrad. He was later appointed Marshal of the Soviet Union. After forty-three years of military service, he died in 1970 at the age of seventy-eight. The urn containing his ashes was buried in the walls of the Kremlin.

Our army is in a tragic situation: we no longer have any idea where the rear is, or where the front line is to be found – it is impossible to tell any more. And we have suffered such terrible losses. We are trying to salvage what we can, and our remaining vehicles are jam-packed with equipment; every soldier is carrying something, even strips of plywood. But all the time the ring around us closes.

Six days later he was in despair. 'The Germans are everywhere – incessant gunfire, mortar and machine-gun exchanges. I wandered around, seeing heaps of dead bodies and the most unspeakable horrors – ghastly evidence of the enemy's bombardment.'[30]

These hideous scenes drove him – the perfect model of a Soviet commissar – to follow his commander's example of a few days earlier:

I took a bottle of alcohol and went out into the forest. I feel our total destruction is imminent. Our army is beaten, our supply train destroyed and I am writing this by a bonfire – we have lost all our officers and I am surrounded by a mass of strangers. Our military strength has simply dissolved around us.[31]

Shabalin's last entry was on 20 October. He died soon afterwards. His diary, along with his body, was recovered by German troops, who handed it over to one of their staff officers for safe keeping.[32] The cause of his death remains unknown, though his reputation as a candid and courageous patriot was thereby preserved for posterity.

The dissolution to which Shabalin referred was hardly surprising. The 160th Rifle Division of the 24th Army had been 'reinforced' by a unit made up of teachers and students from the Institute of Transport Engineers. They not only lacked any previous experience of battle but also had been issued with Polish bullets which did not fit their elderly Soviet rifles. Overwhelmed by the speed of the German advance, they were lost, bewildered and terrified. One of their number was the now-qualified Nurse Erastova, who only a few weeks earlier had been administering sedatives in a Moscow metro station. She had graduated to the front line via Yelnya, where the line had been quiet following the German retreat and had been, she wrote, 'more like a health resort' than a warfront. This was very different:

Aircraft were 'daisy clipping', people moaning, fires, it was impossible to find our way as we had neither maps nor compasses, we lacked any military experience. In short, this was Dante's inferno. There were no longer any units, only the chaotic movement of random handfuls of completely demoralized people.[33]

As they stumbled about in no-man's land, they split up into small groups, scavenging for stale bread and drinking from puddles. Constantly harried by German tracer fire and flares, they raced from bush to bush, 'desperate like hounded hares'. Their commanding officer, whom Erastova referred to simply as Ivan, had only recently been brought out of retirement and took pity on his charges. Fearing that he would be a burden on them because of his age, he urged them to find their own ways of escape. Erastova and another student elected to stay with him as he was the only one of them with a weapon. A while later, though, they became separated. Erastova never saw him again.

The precise details of General Petrov's fate similarly remain unknown after he became trapped in the Bryansk pocket. Trying to fight his way out he was gravely wounded. The wounds became gangrenous. He was carried to a woodcutter's cottage, where he died a few days later, joining the tens of thousands of men who had served under him in the 13th, 30th and 50th armies to be mown down as they fought frenziedly but fatally to break out of the encirclement.

By the middle of October, the 2nd Panzer Army under Guderian and the 2nd Army under General Maximilian von Weichs had virtually sealed the Bryansk pocket. But their triumph was hard won. In choosing to hurl themselves at their persecutors rather than throwing down their weapons, Petrov's men exacted a heavy price from an enemy which had been told repeatedly that victory over the Russian 'beasts' was both inevitable and imminent. Will Thomas (a German, despite his Anglo-Saxon name) was in command of an infantry platoon. After ten days of severe fighting, he wrote home on 16 October, 'Where should I start to explain? Actually I can say nothing. My heart is still so full of all the horrors and difficulties of the last days and hours. Again and again comrades fall left and right, so that I often believed I was left alone on the field.'[34] The following day a twenty-two-year-old foot-soldier, Harald Henry, whose mental anguish and physical exhaustion after months of heavy fighting were obvious, wrote home:

To no avail, if one believed every time one had survived the worst. There always comes more. Since I last wrote to you I have lived through hell . . . That I survived 15 October, the most terrible day of my life, seems like a wonder. How sick my whole body is, but I will certainly not be allowed into the hospital . . . I am too miserable to write more . . . I wish everything would end. What have we been through! Oh God![35]

Many officers were similarly afflicted: 'For the first time during this exacting campaign Colonel [Heinrich] Eberbach gave the impression of being exhausted, and the exhaustion that was now noticeable was less physical than spiritual,' Guderian wrote of one of his most brilliant panzer commanders. 'It was indeed startling', he added, 'to see how deeply our best officers had been affected by the latest battles.'[36] By that point, after three weeks of battle his 2nd Panzer Army had lost 4,500 men. Altogether, since the launch of Operation Barbarossa, he had lost ten times that many, a casualty rate Guderian described as 'grave and tragic' – though his elaboration of its implications suggests that he was as concerned by the fact that their replacements 'lacked the combat experience and toughness of the older men' as he was by the loss of life per se.[37]

By the end of the third week of October, Army Group Centre had broken not only the Bryansk line but also the front at Vyazma, 140 kilometres to the north. The collapse there was even greater in scale and portent. As David Stahel has noted, Vyazma was regarded by Russians as 'one of the hallowed battlegrounds on which the country's freedom from foreign rule was won'.[38] It was there in November 1812 that – for the first time in his campaign – Napoleon's retreating forces had endured even greater casualties than their Imperial Russian opponents. If not for that reason alone, their descendants, 129 years later, fought the German invaders on the same battlefield with suicidal tenacity.

Like Yeremenko at Bryansk, Konev had warned Stalin of the threat facing his armies at Vyazma. Alerting him on 4 October to the fact that the Germans had also penetrated Budyonny's Reserve Front, he sought permission to withdraw his armies to avoid their encirclement. According to Konev's own account, 'Stalin listened to me, however [he] made no decision. Communications were disrupted and further conversation ceased.'[39]

Fearful of defying their supreme commander, both Konev and Budyonny instructed their forces to remain at their posts while Panzer

Group 3 (led by Hoth) and Panzer Group 4 (led by Erich Hoepner) closed on Vyazma, not by a head-on attack from the west, but in a joint pincer movement to the north and south of the city. It was not until late on 5 October that Moscow finally realized the scale of the crisis. At that point, Shaposhnikov contacted Konev to inform him that the Stavka 'has permitted you to begin withdrawing tonight in accordance with your request'.[40] The delay was fatal. On 6 October Vyazma fell into German hands and, as at Bryansk, hundreds of thousands of Soviet troops found themselves trapped in a vast encircling pocket from which escape was almost impossible.

Stalin had been bewildered and infuriated by the ease with which Bock's armies had punched a hole through the Red Army's defensive positions. As usual when he was at a loss, he summoned Zhukov to his presence. On 7 October, his finest general flew into Moscow from Leningrad, where his 'ring of steel' had just been completed around the besieged city. When he arrived at the airport he was taken immediately to the Kremlin. Stalin was sick with a fever and the general was taken straight to his apartment, where he found the supreme commander deep in conversation with his NKVD crony Lavrenty Beria.

'Ignoring me, or perhaps unaware of my arrival, he was telling Beria to use his agencies to sound out the possibilities for making a separate peace with Germany, given the critical situation,' Zhukov later recalled. Attributing this aberrant behaviour to the fact that Stalin was 'disorientated' – presumably either by his influenza or by the scale of the crisis or a combination of both – Zhukov did not join the discussion but waited until Stalin finally noticed his presence. After a brief greeting he told Zhukov that he had no idea what was happening at the Western and Reserve Fronts. 'He walked slowly across to a map, and moving his finger across the Vyazma district, declared angrily: "Just like Pavlov at the beginning of the war, Konev has opened up the front to the enemy here."'[41] He instructed Zhukov to find out what was happening and to report back to him.

Obtaining a map from Shaposhnikov, Zhukov drove directly to Konev's headquarters, stopping every so often to take some exercise to overcome his drowsiness. He found the Western Front commander and a number of his officers in a small room, dimly lit by candles. Discovering from them the gravity of the crisis they faced, he went on his way in search of the Reserve Front's commander, whose whereabouts were unknown to Konev. He eventually found Budyonny in a state of near-exhaustion in a deserted city. Budyonny explained that for two days he had been unable to make contact with Konev but that his predicament was equally grave. On 10 October, Zhukov returned to the headquarters of the Western Front, which had been relocated to Mozhaysk, 110 kilometres from the capital. He was soon summoned to the phone to be told by Stalin that he was to take command of a newly formed Western Army Group – an amalgamation of the Western Front and the Reserve Front – with the task of overseeing the defence of the capital.

The dictator's reflexive instinct was to hold Konev personally responsible for the collapse of the Western Front and to have him court-martialled and shot. Zhukov was not generally averse to such measures, but on this occasion he intervened to save Konev's life. 'Shooting Konev will not improve anything or encourage anyone,' he countered. 'It will only produce a bad impression in the army.' Insisting that Konev was very different from General Pavlov (who had been shot only three months earlier), he urged clemency. 'Everyone knew that Pavlov should never have been put in charge of a division . . . But Konev is not Pavlov – he is an intelligent man. He can still be serviceable.'[42] Stalin backed down. Rather than ordering Konev's execution, he agreed that he should instead serve as Zhukov's deputy. Before he rang off, though, he warned, 'If you surrender Moscow, both your heads will roll!'[43] Wisely, Zhukov chose to believe that Stalin was not joking.

Too late, the Stavka now ordered the armies entrapped at Vyazma 'to escape encirclement at all costs'.[44] It was impossible to break out of the tightening panzer ring within which they were being slowly asphyxiated. 'The situation of the encircled forces has worsened sharply,' the cool-headed commander of the 19th Army, Lieutenant General Mikhail Lukin, reported on 10 October. 'There are few shells, bullets are running out, and there is no food. They eat that which the population can provide and horseflesh. Medicines and dressing materials are used up. All tents and dwellings are overflowing with the wounded.'[45]

The beleaguered Soviet troops fought with the ferocity of the damned. Lieutnant Jaeger, serving in one of Panzer Group 3's infantry divisions, described what happened one evening when his regiment faced a large body of Soviet tanks and infantry trying to break out of the stranglehold:

> Their attacks were absolutely unbelievable. Whole columns were on the move . . . Without deviating they came directly at us. What targets they presented to our forward artillery observers! They sent salvoes of artillery, without pause, one after the other into the enemy hordes. It caused a practically unbelievable destruction.[46]

Karl Fuchs, commanding a mobile platoon of four light tanks, was among that multitude of ordinary soldiers who had been led to believe that, once the Soviet armies had been crushed at Vyazma, nothing would stop the Ostheer storming into Moscow and annihilating Jewish Bolshevism. On 12 October he wrote triumphantly to his father, 'For days now the enemy has tried to break out of our iron encirclement but their efforts have been in vain. Wherever there is a hot spot, we appear like ghosts and engage the enemy in battle.' He was especially proud of his company's performance on the previous day, when they confronted a Soviet tank unit, supported by infantry, trying to escape the ever-closing pocket under the cover of a fog bank. When the fog lifted, they had an easy target in their sights:

> We really let them have it with every barrel, tanks, anti-aircraft guns, trucks and the infantry fired on everything in sight. Once the main body of our company arrived, our comrades destroyed their remaining forces . . . You can see that we are prepared at all times to beat the enemy wherever he may appear.[47]

The hopelessness of their predicament appeared only to drive the trapped Soviet armies to ever more fanatical efforts. The German perimeter was not wholly impermeable. There were weak spots and gaps through which small units might escape. Dusk was the most favoured time to attempt a breakout. As the skies darkened, the tension in the German lines became acute as the men watched the red glow of distant villages in flames, listening for the first signs of an attempt to breach their lines – the straining of an engine, the rumble of a tank, the whinny of a horse, the jangle of a harness or the squeak of a wheel.

Serving in one of the infantry units strung out along a sparsely protected section of the pocket, H. E. Braun, an anti-tank gunner, heard the sound of approaching soldiers. He saw a Very pistol fired into the air to illuminate the night sky. What it revealed was chilling: 'Hundreds, no thousands of Russians were approaching . . . Cossack cavalry were attacking too between vehicles and columns of lorries.' The encircling Germans let fire with every weapon at their disposal – cannon, anti-tank guns, heavy and light machine guns, mortars and heavy-calibre rifles – a murderous cacophony that should have been devastating. Instead, although the Russians were 'shot to pieces' by these fusillades, they refused to fall back. Braun watched as they collected the bodies of the fallen and heaped them into quasi-burial mounds to provide cover as they advanced once more. The night battle lasted for five hours.

At dawn, Braun was astonished to see many of 'the dead' rise up and charge once again: 'a sea of Red soldiers' pressed forward breaching the German defences 'until finally the unstoppable wave flooded into the hinterland. Brave [German] infantrymen and in places even the anti-tank teams with guns were trampled into the ground by the mass of humanity driven by the certainty of death to seek an escape to the east.' Panzers were summoned. One of them let fire with its machine guns, aiming directly into the tangled horde. Even this failed to staunch the flow. Trucks and armoured vehicles, soldiers clinging to their sides, ploughed through the German defences crushing those – alive and dead, friend and foe – that lay in their path. In hand-to-hand fighting, the Germans used spades as well as pistols and grenades, their company commander alongside them, wielding a sub-machine gun. Cooks and drivers joined the fray. It took the arrival of yet another panzer unit to finish off those Red Army soldiers who preferred to die on the battlefield rather than surrender.[48]

Not every German unit displayed such resilience. Erich Krause, serving in the 35th Infantry Division, joined the front line at Vyazma on 12 October. In the middle of yet another night battle, Krause's unit broke ranks and fled as a squadron of Soviet tanks bore down on their positions:

All the swearing of the officers and NCOs availed nothing. Everybody ran away from the Russian tanks. At times we succeeded in rallying the men and making a stand, but all the same there was a whole stream of them now taking to their heels. Our killed and wounded, and our guns and other materiel we abandoned on the field. A shocking picture I should never forget as long as I live.[49]

In the ensuing confusion, the Soviet tanks punctured the 'iron encircle-ment' at that point and escaped to fight another day.

For the most part, though, the German troops fought with unswerv-ing conviction. Karl Fuchs was not untypical. His commitment to Nazism was so fervent that even as he mourned the death of a 'brave, young friend' on 15 October he did not pause to question the purpose of the Führer's enterprise but only to wonder 'Why did he have to give his life now, with the end practically in sight?'[50] On the same day he wrote to his mother, reiterating, 'Our duty has been to fight and free the world from this Communist disease. One day, many years hence, the world will thank the Germans and our beloved Führer for our vic-tories here in Russia. Those of us who took part in this liberation battle can look back on those days with pride and infinite joy.'[51]

It took several days to complete the destruction of the Vyazma pocket. The forests still concealed groups of Soviet soldiers who had become separated from their units or were still ready to ambush and shoot unwary German patrols. 'Again and again appear enemy splinter groups, which, with energetic leadership, conduct dogged resistance,'[52] the frustrated author of 46th Panzer Corps' official diary noted. The reluctance of the defeated Soviet units to concede defeat during these 'clearing operations' risked a terrible vengeance. Wolfgang Horn, serving in a panzer division at Vyazma, described how he and his men came across a group of Soviet soldiers huddling behind one of the many hundreds of vehicles destroyed in the fighting. They had lain down their weapons and were clearly unarmed. Horn went up to them and ordered them in Russian to raise their hands in the air. Paralysed by terror, they not only failed to obey but cowered closer together, covering their heads with their hands as though expecting a beating. Instead they were gunned down. As an insouciant Horn later explained, 'When they don't surrender we shoot them. It was natural for us to do so . . . They are cowards – they didn't deserve any better anyhow.'[53] As Hitler had so recently advised men like Horn, Russian soldiers were 'beasts'.

Others were less brutish. Walter Schaefer-Kehnert, an officer in the 11th Panzer Regiment, witnessed the aftermath of battle with a keen sense of the tragic. He was transfixed by the sight of a group of Russian girls walking through the killing grounds leading a horse-drawn cart, which had a barrel of water in it. 'I will never forget them – in trousers and dressed like soldiers [they] went around giving water to the dying Russian soldiers . . . They were lying there by the thousand like the battlefields of old history.'[54]

A fifteen-year-old Russian girl, who had just lost both her parents – her father shot as a partisan, her mother killed by a hand grenade tossed into the cellar where she was sheltering – emerged from that hiding place to witness the aftermath of one such bloodbath. It was a scene of such pitiful carnage as almost to defy belief:

> There were so many dead bodies all over the place. We walked on them as if it was a floor covered with bodies. They were next to each other and on top of each other. Some didn't have legs, heads or other parts. We had to walk on them because there was no other place to step . . . It's awful to remember! The river was red with blood as if there was only blood flowing there.[55]

The Third Reich's triumphalism was boundless. There was no place for doubt: in the collective mind of his fanatically loyal disciples, Hitler's exultant assertion in Berlin that 'The enemy has been broken and will never rise again' had once more proved his unique gift of foresight and leadership. German propaganda posters proclaimed 'The Outcome of the March to the East has been Decided'. And so it seemed to those senior Wehrmacht generals who were remote from the field of battle. In their purblind loyalty to the Führer, they chose to avert their gaze from the multiple hazards now confronting an Ostheer that was already severely depleted in manpower and armaments, that was running short of such basic needs as fuel and clothing, that depended on lengthening supply lines on a crumbling and overcrowded road and rail network, and that could not rely on nature to postpone the onset of the Russian winter to facilitate the surrender of Moscow in time for the Christmas celebrations. In their myopic conviction that the collapse of the Soviet Union had been preordained by the Führer, it was enough that their advance had not been unduly arrested and that the Soviet armies had yet again been broken. Choosing to interpret the bitter resistance of the enemy as evidence of a quasi-Neanderthal reaction to a superior civilization rather than evidence of an unbreakable will to defend the Motherland, they ignored any inconvenient evidence to the contrary.

It was true that a calamity of almost unimaginable proportions had befallen Stalin's armies. In addition to the three armies at Bryansk, another four – the 16th, 19th, 20th and 32nd – were lost at Vyazma. According to the best available evidence, approximately 108,000 men managed to break out from those encirclements and perhaps another 140,000 had retreated safely or escaped from other parts of the front. On the basis of these figures, the Red Army, which had fielded 1.25 million men at the start of Operation Typhoon, had lost no fewer than one million soldiers, either killed or taken captive.[56] The implications of this disaster were stark and alarming. As Zhukov advised the Stavka with his customary clarity, 'The chief danger is that almost all routes to Moscow are open and the weak protection along the Mozhaysk Line cannot guarantee against the surprise appearance of enemy forces before Moscow.'[57] Were that to happen, the Soviet capital would be in grave danger of falling to the enemy.

22. The Great Panic

'It may be unbelievable but we are getting no information from the Russians and depend entirely upon the BBC.'[1] The British military mission in Moscow was not alone in having no news from the collapsing Soviet front. The capital's citizens were equally in the dark. But the government's efforts to suppress the truth did not prevent rumours seeping through the cordon sanitaire of the official news channels.

On 7 October Dr Peter Miller, a historian working on a project at the Academy of Sciences to chart changes in Moscow's everyday life during the war, noted:

> There is a mood of catastrophe and fatalism. The shops are empty, even coffee has disappeared . . . No facts are available. Pressure is increasing to evacuate children, even though children's ration cards for milk were issued three days ago, which meant that they were assuming that the children would remain in the city. There is a feeling of approaching catastrophe in the air and endless rumours . . . The mood is particularly bad today.[2]

This mood was sharpened by letters or notes that filtered through from the front to friends and family in the city. For the most part the troops refrained from describing their own tribulations, confining themselves to expressions of love and concern for their loved ones, barely touching on the horrors they were enduring. Grigory Ufimtsev, serving in a road-maintenance regiment, wrote to his wife:

> A lovely day to you and a merry time . . . You write that life is very hard and sad, but one just has to get through it . . . The war is drawing out, becoming more and more severe and there is no end to it in sight. Valya, you wrote that you have sold the potatoes, this is good. I don't need money but do send me warm socks and mittens, and a pen knife if you manage to get one. That's it for now, warm kisses.[3]★

★ In early 1942, his family was officially notified that Ufimtsev had died of his wounds on 22 February and had been buried in a mass grave in a forest near Kalinin.

Others, though, could not restrain themselves. One wrote:

> Don't believe the papers or the radio; the things they say are lies. We've been through it all and seen it all, the way the Germans are driving us – our own people don't know where to run; we've nothing to fight with; and when the Germans catch up with us, our men have nothing to escape in. We've got no fuel, so they abandon our cars and tanks and run for it.[4]

From his vantage point as a Communist Party functionary, Victor Kravchenko witnessed the gradual disintegration of Moscow towards mass panic in the first week of October:*

> A city, like an individual, can suffer a nervous breakdown. Trams and autobuses worked in fits and starts. The shops were mostly empty, but people queued up anyhow . . . Homes and offices were unheated; water and electric service was intermittent and uncertain.† For the first time in twenty years I heard cursing of officialdom.[5]

Irina Krauze was not cursing but wondering. As a student nurse, she hoped to join the phalanx of Soviet female volunteers who wanted to be at the front. But her father was German by birth and had been interned at the start of the war and she feared this would count against her. She was relieved, therefore, when, on 6 October, she was promised her military ID and, at the same time, following a cursory medical, was passed fit for service. Her sense of duty did not blind her to the despair to which Moscow seemed to have succumbed. Disbelieving the upbeat communiqués pumped out by the state radio, she began to fear that she would soon have to fight at the very gates of the city. Cherishing her ID card 'like a favourite toy', she felt 'pain and shame about the whole course of the war'.[6]

---

* In 1943 Kravchenko was posted to the United States, where the following year he sought political asylum. His subsequent revelations about the Soviet Union made a sensational impact and have since been corroborated by numerous other witnesses. However, his story has been tainted by allegations that it was prompted and promoted by the CIA. In this book, I have only drawn on those parts of his public testimony which are consistent with other contemporary reports and reflections.
† By 29 September, Rundstedt's Army Group South had broken through the Donbass defences, seizing the mines that produced 60 per cent of the Soviet Union's coal and 75 per cent of its coking coal.

Others were rather less patriotic. Fear, deprivation and a barely suppressed loathing of the NKVD and the other instruments of a repressive state produced something of a pro-German backlash. Nazi propaganda, intimating that individual liberties and land ownership would be restored once the Jewish-Bolshevik conspiracy had been extirpated, fell on fewer deaf ears than the Politburo might have hoped. Even individuals who had been prominent and apparently loyal members of the Soviet cultural community were not immune. Alexander Osmerkin, a painter who lived in the same apartment block at the Academy of Fine Arts as Raisa Labas, the ex-wife of Robert Falk, a fellow artist, heard that she was planning to leave Moscow. Confronting her, he demanded:

Have you gone off your head? Excuse my crudeness, but who are you running from? Do you really believe our [the Communist Party's] cheap propaganda? In Kiev the Germans have set up a Social Revolutionary government. They are giving great support to the arts. They are after all the most cultured people in Europe. I'm sure they won't persecute people like you and me.

Osmerkin was so anxious to secure his future under Nazism, that he cleared out any compromising pamphlets, books and photographs from his apartment along with 'all the rest of the filthy Bolshevik rubbish'.[7]

For the most part, however, even those who were less than ardent communists, regarded the prospect of a Nazi victory with dismay. They disdained the Nazi leaflets that fluttered down over the city and its environs courtesy of the Luftwaffe. In a heavy-handed attempt to reinforce this attitude the party forbad anyone to read them. To keep one in your possession was a crime. This proved to be counterproductive as even the disinclined were tempted to pick them up, if only as a diversion from what Catherine Merridale has described as the 'stream of distortions and lies about the army's courage and the enemy's distress' that flowed incontinently from the state's propaganda outlets.[8] In the industrial centre of Bolshevo, twenty-five kilometres from the capital, Kravchenko was in charge of a unit of loyal communists ordered to pick up this Nazi litter. They were under strict orders – which they ignored – not to read a word of this polluting material. The leaflets were so written as to suggest that, under the benign oversight of the Third Reich, Russia would flow with milk and honey. Kravchenko judged their authors to be 'signally stupid':

not only was the Nazi propaganda 'arrogant' but it made the cardinal error of 'confounding love of country with love of Stalin'.[9]

During the first week of October, the Soviet media preferred to bask in the warm glow left by the Harriman–Beaverbrook visit than to report the truth from the front. But by the end of the week the tone veered dramatically away from that reassuring message. Instead of official announcements about hard-fought but inevitable victories against the Nazi hordes, the nation was suddenly warned that 'the very existence of the Soviet State was in danger'. As the Red Army newspaper *Krasnaya Zvezda* put it, every Soviet citizen was now to 'stand firm and fight to the last drop of blood' to save the nation. On 9 October *Pravda* enjoined the people of Moscow 'to mobilize all their forces to repel the enemy's offensive' and, on the following day, more darkly, it warned that the enemy was trying 'through the wide network of its agents, spies and agents-provocateurs to disorganize the rear and to create panic.'[10]

Such admonitions were not overly effective. By repeatedly telling the public that 'The Homeland is in Grave Danger' the media simply stimulated increasingly wild rumours. Irina Krauze, writing her diary, noted stories that all children were being evacuated from Moscow and that the nation's leaders had left the capital as well:

> Whether this is true or not, the government is silent, and that makes the public depressed . . . People are feeling completely lost . . . Yesterday I saw a man in the street who was carrying an empty coffin. An old lady who stopped me a few steps away from him said with conviction: 'What a lucky person he got this coffin for. He is dead and doesn't have to worry about fighting.'[11]

The first secretary of the Moscow Communist Party, Alexander Shcherbakov, whose office walls were covered with detailed maps of the city, set about the creation of resistance groups to sabotage the enemy 'if the very worst should happen'. This underground movement was to be controlled by the NKVD but operated by party cadres drawn from each district of the city. Shcherbakov took a close personal interest in the selection process. Interviewing one candidate, he informed the hapless recruit that Stalin himself had demanded this last-ditch defiance of the enemy. 'Do you realize how serious it is?' he demanded. 'Yes, I do,

Alexander Sergeevich.' 'Do you understand the danger?' 'Yes, if I get it wrong, I'll end up on a German scaffold.'[12]

There was another pressing priority: the mammoth task of dismantling score upon score of industrial plants, transporting them for hundreds of miles to the relative safety of the Urals, the Volga region, western Siberia, Kazakhstan or central Asia, to be reassembled in those remote locations with the minimum disruption to the production of critical wartime supplies. Within six weeks 498 enterprises along with 210,000 workers had been transported to one or other of those destinations by 71,000 railway wagons; by November 1941 more than 1,500 industrial enterprises – 1.5 million wagon loads – would be salvaged by this means.[13]

This achievement was possible only because a ruthless state machine commandeered huge numbers of heroically pliable patriots. They were under strict orders to erect the relocated plants rapidly enough to allow them to be in production within fourteen days. In a highly romanticized but broadly accurate account of how this was achieved, a *Pravda* reporter described how 'students, typists, accountants, shop assistants, housewives, artists, teachers' armed with 'shovels, iron bars and pickaxes' dug for industrial victory:

> The earth was like stone, frozen hard by our fierce Siberian frost. Axes and pickaxes could not break the stony soil. In the light of arc lamps people hacked at the earth all night. They blew up the stones and the frozen earth, and they laid the foundations . . . Their feet and hands were swollen with frostbite, but they did not leave work. Over the charts and blueprints, laid out on packing cases, the blizzard was raging. Hundreds of trucks kept rolling up with building materials . . . On the twelfth day, into the new buildings with their glass roofs, the machinery, covered with hoar frost, began to arrive. Braziers were kept alight to unfreeze the machines . . . And two days later, the war factory began production.[14]

Anything of material value that could not be dismantled and removed from Moscow was to be demolished. The Germans, who had already destroyed, commandeered or looted thousands of industrial plants during their rampage eastward as well as the homes and livestock of millions of peasants,★ were to be denied any further spoils. Under the chairmanship of Alexei Kosygin, the State Defence Committee (GKO) drafted orders requiring that preparations be made for the destruction of more than 1,000 factories in and around Moscow.† All defence industries were to be blown up. Engineers drawn from the Red Army and the NKVD placed explosives under these key installations and, it was presumed, under the Kremlin as well.[15] Other significant economic assets – 'bakeries, refrigerator stores, meat processing plants, stations and other railway buildings, tram and trolleybus parks, lorry parks, power stations, bridges, the Bolshoi Theatre, the Mint (Goznak), the Tass building, the Central Telegraph Office and telephone exchanges' – were to be set on fire or smashed beyond use.[16]

More extreme measures were required to prevent Bock's armies from reaching the capital. The GKO drew up plans for a new 'Moscow Defence Zone' to sheathe the city. The outer defences – tank traps, ditches and barbed-wire fences – were to be constructed along a wide arc less than a hundred kilometres from the city's perimeter. Three further concentric layers of defence were to girdle the city – one on its boundaries and two more running along the outer and inner ring roads. Within days, 600,000 Muscovites had obeyed the order to present themselves in their own districts armed with spades and, if they possessed them, axes, picks and crowbars as well. Only those who were disabled or infirm or working in the defence industries were exempt. This ramshackle army of labourers – men and women – worked at a frantic pace for little food and in deteriorating weather. Piercing winds and pouring rain intermingled with driving snow combined with a lack of heavy equipment to make their task so exhausting as to drain every last reserve of energy and morale. But they had no choice: backsliding or skiving was not permitted.

As he raced to and fro around the perimeter of the city, urging its

★ The statistics produced by Molotov at the Paris Peace Conference on 26 August 1946 claimed that the Germans had destroyed 6 million homes, slaughtered or carried off 7 million horses, 17 million head of cattle and 20 million pigs.

† During the blockade of Leningrad, Kosygin oversaw the construction of the 'ice road' across Lake Ladoga, the last lifeline to the city. He survived the Stalin era to become chairman of the Council of Ministers under Khrushchev and then Leonid Brezhnev. He resigned due to ill-health in October 1980 and died two months later on 18 December 1980 at the age of seventy-six.

defenders to ever greater effort, Zhukov was especially awed by the resolve displayed by the women labourers:

> I saw thousands and thousands of Moscow women, who were unused to heavy labour and who had left their city apartments lightly clad, work on those impassable roads, in that mud, digging anti-tank ditches and trenches, setting up anti-tank obstacles and barricades, and hauling sandbags. Mud stuck to their boots too, and to the wheelbarrows they used to haul earth, and added an incredible load to shovels that were unfamiliar in women's hands.[17]

As she waited to be summoned to the front, Irina Krauze, who had been so eager to defend the Motherland, was dogged by uncertainty and anxiety:

> It is tough. Everything is nagging inside me. Very unpleasant. There is no news . . . Everyone feels the same way: [a] realization that everything is wrecked, that the entire system and the leaders are bankrupt, that we can't believe anything any longer . . . And, at the same time, a desperate desire for a miracle . . . the leaders are so silent that no one knows if Moscow is going to fight to the end.[18]

On 13 October Shcherbakov summoned a meeting of the Moscow party hierarchy. 'Let us not shut our eyes,' he told them; 'Moscow is in danger.' Their immediate concern was that social order might collapse under the strain. For hardline communists there was only one appropriate response: 'iron discipline, emotionless struggle against even the slightest manifestation of panic, against cowards, deserters and rumour mongers'.[19] They also agreed that each Moscow district should mobilize a battalion of volunteers to help fill some of the yawning gaps at the front. Within three days 12,000 volunteers were assembled for duty. They had as yet no training, let alone experience of battle.

Nikolai Amosov and his medical team – who only six weeks earlier had been operating in their field hospital outside Roslavl, more than 350 kilometres from Moscow – were returning through the Kaluga Gate in the south-west of the city en route to a sector on the new front line when they crossed with a militia battalion heading in the opposite direction:

> a long column in rows of four, the greatcoats were new and stiff. They were middle-aged men, and some even old . . . They were not marching in step.

They had no luggage . . . They were intelligentsia or workers who had been exempt from military service because of stomach ulcers, poor eyesight, TB. Their rifles were sticking up strangely from their shoulders.[20]

Others were already in action. Kravchenko described what happened to three militia battalions, many of whom were loyal members of the Komsomol. In the early hours of 13 October, they had been taken to the front, chanting, 'For Stalin! For the Party!' Forty-eight hours later 'about one third of them straggled back, bloody, frozen, hungry and dispirited; the rest never returned'.[21] Kravchenko himself was on patrol in the forests surrounding Bolshevo. His unit's task was to watch out for German parachutists who might be dropped behind the lines. It was snowing. 'I was wearing summer underwear, light canvas boots, a summer cap, a frayed army overcoat in temperatures already far below zero. My equipment consisted of a training rifle and exactly three cartridges.'[22] Kravchenko was later to become a bitter opponent of the regime, but that complaint was echoed by many other patriots elsewhere.

By 15 October the tension in the capital was palpable. The crump of artillery could be heard clearly in the distance. Enemy aircraft droned in the sky. Rumour piled upon rumour: the Germans had reached the outskirts of the city; their spies were disguised as Soviet soldiers; paratroopers had landed in a nearby forest or in Red Square; the panzers would soon be in Gorky Street; Stalin had either been deposed or had already left the Kremlin for an unknown destination; the city was about to fall.

As it happened, the Soviet dictator had been in his Kremlin office from the early hours of that day in meetings with the most senior members of his entourage. He was unusually subdued. Aside from confirming that the capital was indeed at risk and authorizing preparations for the evacuation of the government, he held his counsel and left it to his ministers to work out the various protocols required to implement such a momentous decision. It was agreed that individual departments could be dispersed separately to various regions of the Soviet Union, but that the seat of government should be evacuated to the city of Kuybyshev, which straddled the confluence of the Volga and Samara rivers, 1,400 kilometres south-east of the capital.* According to some accounts Stalin confirmed that he would join

---

* In 1935, the city of Samara was renamed Kuybyshev in honour of a leader of the Bolshevik revolution. Its original name was restored in 1991.

the exodus, though he insisted that he merely instructed Molotov to over-see the relocation of the Supreme Praesidium and to inform the diplomatic corps to pack their bags for Kuybyshev forthwith. Molotov did not delay.

The British and American ambassadors were summoned to see the foreign minister at 12.45 p.m. Molotov looked exhausted. 'I have never seen him look so tired and ill. He obviously has been up all night, and the decision hurt him terribly as one can see,' Cripps noted.[23] He and Steinhardt were instructed to be ready to leave that evening. Members of the Western press were to depart at the same time. The Associated Press correspondent, Henry Cassidy, was called to his embassy at Spaso House, where he was told by Steinhardt to return by 5.30 p.m. carrying nothing but his hand luggage. Cassidy had just been asked by his editor to write a 'colour' piece about Lenin's tomb in Red Square. He replied succinctly, 'Tomb Closed', packed up his typewriter and prepared to leave Moscow for good.[24] Like almost everyone else, he was unaware that Lenin's embalmed corpse had already been spirited away for safe-keeping to the Siberian city of Tyumen.

Cripps – who had not stopped agitating for a recall to London despite being repeatedly rebuffed by Churchill – could not abide the idea of leav-ing the Soviet capital for a provincial city even further away from British shores. As his staff hurriedly filled cases and boxes with piles of clothes, bedding, secret documents and office equipment, he gave himself the task of finding enough lorries to ferry their luggage to the station. When these failed to materialize, he rang Molotov personally, threatening to stay in Moscow unless the transport was provided in short order. Officials just had time to light a bonfire on the embassy tennis court to incinerate those lesser files and papers for which there was no pressing need before the ambas-sadorial cavalcade set off for Kazan station. Cripps was not in a good humour. On their arrival at the station, he found 'complete chaos', which meant 'we had to wait in our car for ages [until] we were conducted through massive crowds into a restaurant which had been set aside for diplomats'.[25] He sat alone and impassive at a small table with his dog, Joe, at his feet.

The restaurant was soon filled with the diplomatic representatives of more than a dozen nations. From time to time, the *News Chronicle*'s cor-respondent, Philip Jordan, peered out into the gloom of the main hall, where, by late in the evening, 'there was no place to sit, no room to fall'.[26] The crush was so great that Henry Cassidy had the sole of a shoe ripped off. 'I had to go straight down, like a cigarette in a fresh, tight package, to retrieve it,' he recalled. At a little before midnight, Cripps and his fellow ambassadors were finally ushered to their reserved carriages on the Kuybyshev train. As he crossed the concourse, he noticed that the waiting crowds were 'as usual very patient and not at all troublesome. Just masses and masses of grey patient bundles of humanity with their white and coloured bundles of belongings. They looked as if they had been there for ever and there was a continual stream joining and swelling their ranks.'[27] The train left soon after midnight, rumbling through the night towards its destination at what Cripps estimated to be an average speed of 10 miles per hour.

Those for whom there was no room in the train went by car. British Embassy counsellor H. Lacy Baggallay was riding in a column of twelve vehicles taking wives and children to their new accommodation in Kuybyshev. He sent a report of his experience to the Foreign Office in London. His party soon joined a vast slow-moving queue of vehicles:

> private cars, lorries with soldiers, a few lorries with military equipment such as searchlights and AA guns, a great many more with miscellaneous loads such as tyres, machinery, et cetera lorries carrying civilians and every kind of bag and baggage . . . In addition to this the roads were crowded with people on the march. Some were clearly organized bodies, from factories and so on, being evacuated en masse. Others were going singly or in groups of two or three families. One large lot consisted of technical schoolboys in their uniforms. Later on, in the small hours of the morning, we passed quantities of men and women being marched under some sort of guard . . . some must have been in the last stages of fatigue as we saw many fallen or falling by the wayside . . . The stream of traffic was continuous both through the night and the next day . . . With cars hooting and chauffeurs cursing in every direction. But apart from this there was no sign of excitement, still less of panic, or indeed of any emotion at all.[28]

The diplomats were not alone in being chivvied out of the capital. Every party functionary, municipal bureaucrat or factory manager hastened to empty their premises, commandeering trucks to carry equipment and precious documents away to the east. Soon the sky was blackened by the smoke of myriad bonfires as zealous officials dutifully set alight their personnel files, party records, production quotas, payslips, inventories of alleged subversives, spies or informers and any other piece of Bolshevik detritus that might be of more than passing value to the enemy. In the confusion, some staff were told to leave and some to stay put.

Not every member of the administrative elite set the kind of example that might have been expected of a good communist. Many did not wait for permits before scrambling to escape, joining the great exodus through city streets that were soon clogged by the limousines of senior officials and their families, weaving their way through a growing stream of heavily laden horse-drawn carts, peasants herding cattle and sheep, and growing numbers of ordinary citizens who demonstrated their trust in officialdom by voting with their feet to follow their example as best they could.

Not everyone thought of fleeing. Along with a group of fellow students, the twenty-year-old Andrei Sakharov joined the throng passing through streets swirling with 'clouds of soot' to ask their local party secretary at the Moscow State University, whether they might be of use. They were given short shrift: 'When we asked whether there was anything useful we could do,' he noted, 'he stared at us wildly and blurted out "every man for himself".'[29] A little later, the future nuclear scientist and Nobel Prize-winning dissident was instructed to go by rail to Ashkhabad, the capital of Turkmenistan, where his university was to be reconstituted. As his train trundled away from the capital, he observed how rapidly the carriages seemed to become 'separate communities, as it were, with their own leaders, their talkative and silent types, their panic-mongers, go-getters, big eaters, the slothful and the hard-working. I suppose I fitted into the silent type.' He had no difficulty filling the empty hours: 'I read Yakov Frenkel's books on quantum mechanics and relativity [and] suddenly achieved new insights into those subjects.'[30]*

The already famous composer Dmitri Shostakovich did not fare quite so well. Until recently he had been living in his beloved Leningrad, where he was serving in the fire brigade after being turned down by the military on account of his poor eyesight. In his spare time he was deep

---

* Yakov Frenkel (1894–1952) was an eminent scholar who collaborated with British and American scientists to break new ground in his field, notably in relativity (which led him to meet Albert Einstein) and nuclear physics.

in writing his Seventh Symphony. In late September, however, he was told to leave the city for the comparative safety of Moscow. He had barely settled in the capital before he was once more on the move. On 16 October, along with a small army of writers, painters, musicians and artists from the Bolshoi and Vakhtangov theatres, he now found himself huddling with his baggage on the concourse of the Kazan station with his wife and children waiting for a train to Kuybyshev. When they were finally summoned to the platform, which was slippery with soft snow, he was subjected to a good deal of uncomradely pushing and shoving as Moscow's cultural elite struggled for places in their designated carriages. Standing with a child's potty in one hand and a sewing machine in the other, Shostakovich was at a loss. Eventually a place was found for the great man in the 'Bolshoi' carriage. Unhappily, a little after the train had left the station, he realized that he had left two suitcases on the platform – a predicament from which he was partially saved by the generosity of some fellow passengers who gave him socks and a spare shirt as well as other basic necessities.

Unlike Sakharov, Shostakovich was unable to work on the train. 'As soon as I got on the train, something snapped inside me . . . I can't compose just now, knowing how many people are losing their lives,' he was recorded as saying.[31] However, he managed to finish what became known as the 'Leningrad' symphony ten weeks later.*

Thursday, 16 October 1941, became known as the day of the 'Great Panic'. The early morning news bulletins advised that the 'German-fascist troops had hurled themselves against our troops using large quantities of tanks and motorized infantry, and in one section broke through our defences'. *Pravda* warned 'The Enemy is Threatening Moscow'. If further evidence were needed, the citizens could hardly fail to hear the bombs that fell on the city despite the efforts of the Red Army's fighter pilots, who, with

---

* The 'Leningrad' had its first performance in Kuybyshev. In August 1942 a copy of the score was air-dropped into the besieged city of Leningrad, where it was performed by surviving members of the city's symphony orchestra, some of whom members collapsed and died from starvation during rehearsals. In a memorable display of fortitude and defiance, the performance was relayed across and beyond the boundaries of the city with such clarity that it was said to have been heard by the Germans at the front.

suicidal courage, even rammed German aircraft in dog fights over the out-skirts of the city in desperate efforts to down the enemy planes.

At around 9 a.m., Stalin summoned his advisors to his apartment in the Kremlin. On this occasion, according to the ever-reliable Politburo member responsible for organizing the transport of food and supplies, Anastas Mikoyan, he proposed that the entire government, including the Politburo, be evacuated to Kuybyshev that day. He then added, 'I will leave tomorrow morning.' At this Mikoyan claims to have remonstrated with him, asking, 'Why do we have to leave today if you're leaving tomorrow?' Stalin backed down.[32]

Raisa Labas and her son Yury ventured out into Kirov Street to buy food. Yuri was wide-eyed:

> There was a non-stop flow of trucks and cars packed with people and stuff . . . A group of soldiers, armed with rifles, stood on the corner of Kirova and Bobrov Lane. Suddenly one of them began to swear and jerked up his rifle, taking aim at a group of officers sitting on a truck that was full of some barrels and bundles. However, no shot followed, and he quickly disappeared amidst the clamour that his comrades made.

Back at the Union of Artists, the young boy watched the 'terrible scene' as his mother fell to her knees outside their apartment block and – 'in front of all the people' – begged an administrator to allow him to join the evacuation. 'I have no right,' the embarrassed official replied, 'we are sending people away according to carefully verified lists.'[33]

Such lists had become irrelevant. Overnight social anarchy had replaced communist discipline. One shocked observer, Nikolai Verzhbitsky, a journalist who stuck rigidly to the party line when writing for his news-paper, gave vent to his dismay in the privacy of his diary: 'There are fights in the queues, people crushing old folks, there are stampedes in the queues, young people are looting, and policemen hang around sidewalks in groups . . . having a smoke, saying, "We don't have instructions".' The Entuziastov (Enthusiasts) Highway – which had first earned notoriety in the nineteenth century when felons and political dissidents were shackled together and herded to prison camps in Siberia – had become a racetrack. 'All day the vehicles of ex-"enthusiasts" rushed along it, loaded with nickel-coated beds, leather suitcases, jewellery boxes, fat wallets and fatty flesh of those that own all this stuff,'[34] the diarist noted.

It was as though a dam had suddenly been breached, releasing a resentful flood of pent-up loathing towards those bosses and party members who had left their posts without a thought for their workers. Verzhbitsky was bitter: 'Who is the author of all this mess, this general flight, this confusion in our minds?' he asked.

> The hysteria above reached down to the masses. They began to remember and count up all the insults, repression, injustices, pressure, bureaucratic machinations of officialdom, contempt and self-puffery of party members, Draconian orders, deprivations, systematic deception of the masses, the newspapers' braying self-congratulations . . . It is terrible to hear. People speak from the heart. Can a city really hold out when it's in such a mood?[35]

It looked for a while as though it would not. In their anger and resentment, usually law-abiding citizens turned to mob violence. 'People here and there are stopping automobiles heading for the highway. They pull out the riders, beat them, throw their things around, strewing them about the ground,' noted a factory worker, R. G. Reshetin. Some not only sought vengeance but found convenient scapegoats. There was an ugly outbreak of anti-Semitism – the very existence of which was vehemently denied by the party but which had long lurked beneath the surface of popular sentiment. Reshetin was horrified to hear voices cry out saying, 'Beat the Jews'. It was hard to believe. 'We had Jews at school,' he wrote, 'but I don't remember any open, clear examples of anti-Semitism. There were some quips, not malicious, more jokes than anything, nothing more. That's why these wild reprisals against the Jews . . . shook me up so much.'[36] He did not appear to realize that 'jokes' very often conceal a deep prejudice to which a name may not be given.

Anti-Semitism was not confined to the mob. From time to time, loyal communist cadres, outraged by those of their peers who had fled, succumbed to similar sentiments. As a college administrator, Mikhail Voronkov might have been presumed not to share such prejudices, yet he recorded with disdain that, on 16 October,

> a crowd of Jewish 'teachers' burst into my office in the morning, as well as graduate students, researchers, employees and librarians. Their lips were trembling, they were all white, the scoundrels. They had been

very happy to be making two thousand a month . . . They were demanding that I sign their papers for evacuation. I turned them down, I was disgusted by this herd of short, short-legged fat faces.

If there were an excuse, it was perhaps that he shared the impotent fury of his colleagues at other senior members of the staff who deserted the institution: 'The director stole the car, chairs of departments left their doors open, with all the students' papers, unfinished paperwork . . . Scoundrels, cowards . . .'[37]

Beria chose to mark the day of the Great Panic by imposing his own form of law and order on those he and Stalin regarded as miscreants. Not content with the executions of Marshal Tukhachevsky and General Ieronim Uborevich in the 1937 purges, he chose 16 October as an appropriate occasion to have their wives shot as well; soon afterwards, their corpses were thrown into the NKVD's burial pits at the Kommunarka State Farm.[38] A further group of twenty-eight 'especially dangerous state criminals' were sent to Kuybyshev, where, according to Beria's written orders, 'the highest measure of punishment' was to be inflicted on them as well. Twenty of these generals and senior officials were shot by the end of the month; the rest followed them soon after.[39]

On 17 October, at Stalin's behest, Shcherbakov took to the airwaves in an attempt to restore order to the capital. Irina Krauze, who had yet to receive her call-up papers, was not impressed: 'He said something that made little sense: "Citizens please remain calm, Moscow will be defended etc., etc." In fact, there was complete anarchy in the air.' The next day, 18 October, Vasily Pronin, the mayor of Moscow (or chairman of the Executive Committee of Moscow City Council of Labourers, as he was properly known) followed Shcherbakov with another appeal for workers to return to their factories, for merchants to provide them with plentiful supplies of food, and for the metro and the bus services to start running again. This appeared to have some effect, but Krauze was 'stunned' by his broadcast. Noting a rumour swirling around the city that Pronin had initially joined the flight from Moscow only to be caught and ordered back to his post, she wrote that it was 'as if someone was deliberately jeering at us . . . the population couldn't care less about Pronin, they hang around the streets or stand in extremely long queues trying to get their daily bread'.[40]

The journalist, Verzhbitsky, shared Krauze's dismay. He had taken to recording the time it took to buy basics like potatoes, bread and paraffin by making a note of how many were in front of him in the queue on the back of his hand in indelible ink: 31, 62, 341 and – in one case – an astonishing 5,004. Echoing Krauze, he wrote, 'Everyone is boiling with indignation, talking out loud, shouting that they have been betrayed, that "the captains have abandoned ship" and took their valuables with them into the bargain. People are saying things that would have brought them before a military tribunal.'[41]

Voronkov overheard similar sentiments and, facing comparable frustrations, shared them. On one occasion he spent an entire day in food queues, describing them to be 'as long as giant pythons and angry like a hundred hyenas'. It took him two and a half hours to buy a kilo of bagels and three hours for 800 grams of meat; then, after an even longer time queuing for butter, he was exasperated when the shop ran out while ten people were still in front of him – 'because of damned women who produced 12–15 "workers" cards and took 2–3 kilos each . . . I was ready to bite people,' he noted. Virtually the only topic of conversation was about how 'our chief, too, ran away, took the car, foodstuffs, state property and this number of thousands [of roubles] that had just been received for paying salaries to workers and employees'.[42]

Some workers were at the point of rebellion. In one factory, the manager's attempt to order his staff to return to work was met with open defiance. When he sought to persuade them to join the labour gangs constructing trenches around the city, he was similarly rebuffed. 'Don't listen to them [the party bosses], they know nothing, and they've been deceiving us for twenty-three years,' one shouted. 'They've sent their own families away, and now they're trying to send us off to dig ditches.' Another yelled out, 'Down with Soviet power! Long live good old Hitler!'[43]

The inability of the Soviet regime to manage a crisis, let alone to communicate with its subjects except in language that was bound to deepen distrust and anxiety, was cruelly exposed. When he went on a tour of his demesne, the Commissar for the Aviation Industry, Alexei Shakhurin, was astonished by the sight of so many abandoned factories, stripped bare apart from a few lathes and some part-finished aircraft. In one shell of a factory, he was taken aback to be told by a large group of workers who had stayed behind that they had been instructed to head east to work on their relocated production lines but they had neither been paid nor advised how to find homes, buy food, or educate their children so far from Moscow.

Shakhurin did his best to reassure them, but insisted that the priority was to get the new planes built. No one contradicted him, but one woman, distraught to the point of tears, came up to him saying, 'We thought everyone had left, and you'd abandoned us!' Shakhurin raised his voice above the hubbub: 'If you mean the government and the military, then no one has left. Everyone is here. Everyone is at his post, but we are sending the factories to places where they will be able to go on producing modern aeroplanes for our army.' This evidently calmed the atmosphere.[44]

Mikoyan, whose Politburo responsibilities included the strategic relocation of key industries, was another minister to brave the wrath of the workers in an attempt to quell the growing unrest. At the Stalin Car Factory he found the director and a senior trade union official berating a crowd of several thousand workers outraged to be told that their plant was to be demolished. When they saw Mikoyan, they turned on him, demanding, 'Why has the government run away?' He tried to soothe them, explaining that 'Stalin and Molotov are both here. The ministries have left because the front line has come close to Moscow. Now you must be calm. You've been given your pay, so why are you making a fuss? Please stop attacking the director and go home.' On this occasion, the workers obeyed. The crowd dispersed.[45]

In the immediate aftermath of the Great Panic, Stalin moved out of the Kremlin (much as he had done after the first shock of Barbarossa). Instead of retreating to Kuntsevo, however, he took up residence in the bomb-proof security of a metro station, where an office and living quarters had been prepared for him in a set of hastily erected cubicles sealed off from public gaze. Meanwhile, presuming that he was still intending to leave the capital, his team readied a special train to take him to Kuybyshev, where a facsimile of his Kremlin apartment had been rapidly assembled within the confines of a bunker concealed below ground close to the banks of the Volga. Four Douglas DC-3 aircraft were on standby in case he preferred to get there by air.[46] But, at some point during those critical hours, the commander-in-chief decided to remain in Moscow and made it clear that he would not be needing either the special train or the aircraft.

Beria – whose cowardice matched his cruelty – was not aware of this when, at a meeting on 18 October, he evidently told Malenkov and others, including Shcherbakov and Molotov, that Moscow was bound to fall and that 'we have to withdraw beyond the Volga'. Malenkov agreed. Shcherbakov, who was an alcoholic, evidently more or less collapsed 'into a state of terror' at the thought that Stalin might hear what had been said.[47] On the following evening, as they were on their way into a meeting with Stalin, Pronin overheard Beria talking to Molotov, insisting, 'We should abandon Moscow. Otherwise they will wring our necks like chickens.'[48]

Once they had all trooped into his presence, Stalin went round each member of the Politburo asking for his opinion: should they evacuate the capital or stay? Molotov spoke first: 'We must defend Moscow.' Taking their cue from the foreign minister, the others all nodded in agreement, including Beria, who volunteered, 'If you go, Moscow will be lost.'[49]

Immediately afterwards, after consulting Colonel General Pavel Artemeevich Artemev, the NKVD Commander-in-Chief of the Moscow Military District, Stalin ordered the capital to be placed under a 'state of siege'. The city was to be defended to the end. There was to be no mercy. On 19 October the decree was promulgated. As from the following day, the capital's troops and militia were to impose 'the most strict order': 'violators of order will be quickly brought to answer before the court of the military tribunal, and provocateurs, spies, and other enemy agents attempting to undermine order will be shot on the spot'. There was to be a curfew from midnight until 5 a.m. To be out of your home, except with a special pass, was to risk the ultimate penalty. The threat of 'on the spot' executions was not idle. The NKVD's Motorized Infantry Brigade was allotted the task of defending the city not only from the enemy but also from its citizens. One of the brigade's members, Mikhail Ivanovich, who was charged to defend the Kremlin's Spassky Gate from a perch on the second floor of the GUM department store, did not shrink from his task. 'It was necessary, absolutely necessary, to establish order,' he explained later. 'And yes, we did shoot people who refused to quit shops and offices where food and other goods were stored.'[50]

It was ruthless but it worked. 'Hooray!' Irina Krauze wrote in her diary when she heard the news of Stalin's decree. 'Authority is being re-established.' And the next day, she wrote, 'Order is being restored: enterprises are working, police are very focused on checking passports, there is a bit of food in the shops. The newspapers write about the trial of a group of panic-mongers and deserters ... According to rumours, the fugitive bosses turned up again, a lot of people have been turned back.'[51] The chaos and lawlessness which had seized Moscow did not abate overnight, but within days order was indeed restored. The city did not run out of food; shops and kiosks reopened; workers were paid; and the trams and trains began to run more or less on time. This did not mean, though, that the capital felt secure. The enemy was still closing in.

23.   General Mud

On 19 October Field Marshal Bock allowed himself a moment of unchar-acteristic and unwarranted hubris. In an Order of the Day he announced the 'collapse of the Russian Front' and congratulated his men on 'the greatest feat of arms of the campaign'.[1] If there was any basis for his tri-umphalism it lay in the long columns of starving Soviet prisoners in ragged clothes that stumbled into captivity far behind the lines. The main road to Smolensk was littered with dead and dying soldiers. 'Again and again we had to move the dying to the side of the road,' noted Josef Deck, serving in the 17th Panzer Division. 'The ever growing pile of bodies on the roadside began to form a grim embankment, rising on either side of us, veiled by the snow.' Unlike some of his peers, Deck was distressed by such degradation, noting, 'It grievously damages our cause if we do not feed the prisoners we have captured.'[2]

Bock was also disconcerted: 'The impression of tens of thousands of Russian prisoners of war who, scarcely guarded, are marching towards Smolensk is dreadful. Dead-tired and half-starved, these unfortunate people stagger along. Many have fallen dead or collapsed from exhaus-tion on the road.'[3] Though he was far too sensitive to gloat at such piteous sights, he made no effort to mitigate the suffering. Overriding all other con-siderations in his mind was the belief that the imminent fall of Moscow was a foregone conclusion.

The commander of 43rd Army Corps, the usually cautious Gotthard Heinrici, was similarly optimistic. On 8 October, before the fall of Bry-ansk and Vyazma, he had succumbed to Hitler's bombastic certainties, noting that 'by and large it must be said that the opponent is already beaten and that he will now lose the remaining core of his army, which is supposed to defend Moscow', though he added judiciously that the encircled Soviet armies would fight to escape with 'desperate courage'.[4] A week later, after what he described as 'four days of arduous battle', he was even more confident, judging that the Russians were 'crumbling' amidst 'clear signs of disintegration'. With his foremost division hardly more than seventy kilometres from the capital, there was only one lingering doubt to temper his triumphalism: 'All day long it was snowing, which turned all roads into a black, bottomless swamp . . . I could see a long line of sunken, gridlocked and broken lorries, hopelessly stuck. Almost as many dead horses lay in the mud next to the vehicles.'[5] The Rasputitsa – when roads become impassable at the onset of the autumn rains – had started to make its presence felt.

The mud was deep and glutinous. Heavy vehicles slid into shell craters concealed by pools of water. Engines roared and tyres spun as they dug themselves deeper into the mire until they were irretrievably bogged down. Only tracked vehicles were able to effect any kind of rescue, a task for which war-fighting vehicles were particularly ill suited. They not only burned greater quantities of increasingly scarce fuel in often fruitless efforts to extract the trapped machines from the morass but the wear and tear rapidly made them unfit for service. Already drained of energy, gangs of soldiers strove to recover disabled trucks, low-loaders carrying heavy artillery, boxes of ammunition and small arms. Horses floundered and fell, still trapped in the shafts, snorting in terror and kicking out in every direction in vain attempts to regain their footing. Stricken carts became entangled with one another in a confusion of ropes and chains as the rain poured down on them in an unceasing flow. Traffic was brought to a standstill as trucks, heading for the front, tried to pass one another through the widening and deepening chaos.

A surgeon commander, Peter Bamm, who was attached to a horse-drawn artillery company, described one such scene:

Everyone is infected with uncontrollable fury. Everyone shouts at everyone else. Sweating, swearing, mud-spattered men start laying into sweating, shivering mud-caked horses that are already frothing at the mouth. All at once the fury passes. Someone lights a cheroot. Someone takes the initiative. The horses are unhitched. The vehicle with the broken wheel is emptied of its load . . . The men step into the water which runs over the tops of their boots. They seize hold of the muddy wheel and shouting 'Heave! Heave!' manhandle the empty wagon off to the side . . . To the left and right the fields are strewn with a weird assortment of stoves, milking stools, bedsteads, wireless-sets, munition boxes, lamps . . .'[6]

The conditions tested even the most resolute soldiers. To ward off the worst of the cold, the men took to stuffing sheets of newspaper between their vests and shirts, around their stomachs and inside their trouser legs. This helped a little but it was not enough to prevent a chill that crept towards the marrow of the body and, in many cases, of the soul as well. Wilhelm Prüller, whose faith in the Führer was undimmed, could not help but be downcast by the rain, snow and a bitter wind, which 'whistled through every nook and cranny'. His mood was not ameliorated by the loss of a suitcase filled with fresh clothes, the lack of a greatcoat or blanket, the non-arrival of mail from home and, lurking in the back of his mind, a dawning sense that he might have to spend a long, hard winter in Russia rather than with his beloved family.[7]

Heinrici, whose men were still in their summer uniforms, was already sensitive to these privations. On the day of their wedding anniversary he told his wife:

No one can really imagine what every single man here has to endure in this weather, this terrain, the state of the country and the challenges the war forces on him . . . Only someone who has experienced this himself can understand what it means to be on watch all night long without warm clothes (for instance without gloves), with wet feet, in the forest without shelter, freezing, without a hot drink, possibly with a hungry stomach.[8]

He had already asked to be supplied with winter clothing for his men but had been sharply rebuked by Army Group Centre. Told 'categorically' that ammunition and food were greater priorities than warm clothes, he noted drily, 'In my view "categorical" decisions are mostly wrong.'[9]

Guderian had also made a formal request to provide his 2nd Panzer Army with adequate winter clothing. He fared no better, being fobbed off with the vague reassurance that the supplies were on their way and a firm instruction to make no further such requests. But the winter could not be wished away. As word reached Wolfsschanze that the performance of the Ostheer might soon be affected by a shortage of suitable clothing, even Hitler expressed concern. Summoning the army's quartermaster general, Eduard Wagner, he demanded to know whether the troops were being supplied with adequate quantities of winter clothing. Wagner was forced to acknowledge that Army Group South and Army Group North would receive only half their allotted supplies by the end of the month, while Army Group Centre would receive but a third by the same date. However, he assured the Führer that these shortfalls would soon be made good. A few days later, Wagner laid on a display of winter equipment for Hitler to inspect. The array of warm underclothes, thick shirts, woollen socks, strong leather boots, heavy lined waterproof jackets and trousers evidently impressed the Führer.[10]

A week later, on 8 November, at a speech in Munich to mark the eighteenth anniversary of the Beer Hall Putsch, the Führer became intoxicated by the power of his own rhetoric: 'Never before has a gigantic empire been shattered and defeated in a shorter time than the Soviet Union has been this time,' he told his followers, a triumph that owed much to 'the unheard-of, unique bravery and willingness to sacrifice of our German Wehrmacht'.[11] His fantasies went unchallenged by his most senior commanders, none of whom dared inject a note of reality into his musings. The Commander-in-Chief of the Army, Brauchitsch, knew that Army Group Centre had lost 300,000 men since the start of Barbarossa and that only half that number of replacements would be available but he remained convinced that Bock would take Moscow before winter set in. By the time the Führer returned to Wolfsschanze, the weather was worsening rapidly and the temperature was plummeting.[12]

The deteriorating conditions did not so much cause as magnify the difficulties that the 2nd Panzer Army was already facing as the advance on Moscow began to stutter. Guderian complained about the 'appalling mud swamps', but of far greater moment than the Rasputitsa itself was the adverse balance of firepower between his panzers and the heavier Russian tanks like the T-34 that was laid bare by such conditions. It was tempting to blame the mud, but Guderian knew that was not a good enough explanation for the increasing difficulties his panzers faced. As he complained to Army Group Centre, they were up against a superior adversary. When 'numerous T-34 tanks went in to action' they inflicted heavy losses. The shell from a Panzer IV's short-barrelled 75mm gun bounced off the hull of a T-34 like a pebble. The only way for the German crew to disable the Soviet machine was to snap one of its tracks or to destroy its power unit with a direct hit from behind. Even then a knock-out blow could be guaranteed only if the shell penetrated the grille immediately above the engine. The level of skill and daring required to accomplish such a manoeuvre was amplified by the muddy conditions.

To make matters worse, the Red Army – which, of course, had to operate in the same conditions – had adapted its battle tactics to meet the German offensive. Instead of launching their tanks in full-frontal attacks against the German positions, the Soviet generals had started to send in the infantry – at a very heavy cost in casualties – while their tanks attacked the enemy from the flanks, concealing themselves in the silver birch woodlands that girdled so much of the terrain around Moscow. To counter this, Guderian insisted that an upgraded panzer model with more effective guns was urgently needed, and also that the 2nd Panzer Army should be provided with anti-tank guns with sufficient velocity to penetrate the hull of a T-34.[13] As it was, the Soviet counterattacks combined with the weather were beginning to exact a heavy toll both on the vehicles and on the horses that pulled the German artillery. Morale plummeted.

Within days of Hitler's triumphal claims about the fall of the Soviet Union, the mood at the front altered dramatically. It was tempting for the Ostheer – officers as well as men – to blame the worsening weather for the setbacks that now started to crowd in upon them, but it was not the climate that was responsible for a rapidly worsening shortage of combat-ready troops or the critical shortfall in the supply of replacement armour, trucks, spare parts, fuel, food and suitable clothing. The conditions served merely to exacerbate a catastrophic failure of forethought, planning and logistical organization that originated with the delusions of the Wehrmacht's commander-in-chief and the supine deference of his intimidated generals.

Towards the end of October, Bock began to realize that his own recent presentiment of victory was misplaced. In an attempt to maintain the momentum of the advance, he was driven to desperate remedies. On 21 October he concluded that commanders of motorized units that had been 'paralysed' by the road conditions should be instructed to abandon their vehicles and reform themselves into ad hoc infantry regiments, which, with a modicum of artillery in support, might then go into combat 'rather than sitting about uselessly' behind the line. However, his request to Brauchitsch to approve the scheme was refused. In one of the many signs of his growing disaffection, Bock commented scathingly, 'This does not change the fact that sensible commanders take such actions on their own.'[14]

In common with most of his peers, Heinrici was prone to blame 'General Mud' rather than the failures of the OKH for the severity of the challenge now faced by his 43rd Corps:

Since the resistance of the Red Army west and south of Moscow collapsed, mother nature has taken over to defend Russia ... our potential movements are highly restricted ... a lorry took 36 hours for a distance of 35km. Everyone was thrilled that it arrived at all. Most of the convoys are stuck in deep mud, in the swamp, in deeply rutted roads with potholes half a metre deep, flooded with water. The lorries, which are already in quite a state, are now completely broken (spare parts are impossible to get). Petrol, bread, oats, nothing gets through. The horse carriages are stuck, guns are not getting through, all men, be it infantry or something else, are more pushing than fighting. The roads are covered with dead horses and broken lorries. Again and again the lamentation: it cannot go on any longer![15]

Nonetheless, he had yet to exorcize the demon of certainty. While Guderian was prone to reflect ruefully on the 'spiritual' exhaustion that had started to infect even his most senior officers, and to note the contrast between that mood and 'the high spirits in evidence at OKH and at Army Group Centre', whose generals he judged to be 'drunk with the scent of victory',[16] Heinrici did not allow himself to believe for a moment that victory was in doubt. 'Do not worry about the Christmas presents from Moscow,' he told his wife on 24 October. 'For the time being the Russian grimly defends himself. A lot of blood will flow before we get there, but definitely we will. We might go into this nest of communists or let them starve or freeze to death, instead of bothering with exhausting street fights.'[17]

Heinrici may have deluded himself, but he was not a romantic – unlike many of the rank and file whose quasi-mystical faith in Hitler had led them to accept the most extreme privations without complaint. One unnamed NCO put the point succinctly: 'for us the Führer's words are gospel'. As he battled through the worst of the weather, an infantryman, Private von Kaull, wrote:

The Führer has grown into the greatest figure of the century, in his hand lies the destiny of the world ... May his pure sword strike down the Satanic monster. Yes, the blows are still hard, but the horror will be forced into the shadows . . . through the command which derives from our National Socialist idea . . . I am glad that I can participate, even if as a tiny cog, in this war of light against darkness.[18]

The triumphs at Bryansk and Vyazma had inflicted severe wounds on the Red Army but they had not proved mortal. In fact, enough Soviet troops had survived the ordeal to offer yet more fanatical resistance as Zhukov began urgently to regroup his forces along the 220 kilometre-long Mozhaysk Line. At Borodino, scene of the famous battle between Napoleon and Kutuzov, General Hoepner's SS Reich and 10th Panzer divisions tried to force a way through the thinly held but well-echeloned Soviet defence network by driving a wedge through its very centre. On joining his men at the front, Hoepner was surprised by the stubbornness of the defenders. 'For the first time in the war, the number of Russian deaths far exceeded the prisoners we were taking,' he reflected drily.[19]

The Soviet retreat from Bryansk and Vyazma had been panicky and chaotic. 'We had been like a herd of desperate cattle,' Boris Baromykin, serving in the 32nd Rifle Brigade, recalled of their retreat to Borodino, noting that he and his fellow infantrymen had been issued with rifles, many of which were still encrusted with the blood of their comrades who had fallen. Soon after their arrival, their sinews were stiffened by an unforgettable reminder of Zhukov's iron will. An infantryman from one of the central Asian republics had been accused of dropping out of line without permission. Baromykin's unit was summoned to hear his fate. The major who had chaired the military tribunal hearing the case read out its findings to the assembled troops: 'Desertion from the front line – immediate execution.' The convicted man, who spoke very little Russian, did not understand what had been said. He was standing a couple of metres from Baromykin quietly chewing a piece of bread when the major strode up to him and shot him in the head at point blank range. 'The guy collapsed in front of me – it was horrible,' Baromykin wrote. 'Something died in me when I saw that.'[20]

Terror of such punishment, like horror at the prospect of being taken prisoner, played a significant part in driving the Soviet armies to fight with such tenacity. But the struggle at Borodino, as elsewhere, revealed the goad of patriotism to be even more potent. At Borodino, Panzer

Group 4 faced two rifle divisions, an under-strength brigade of T-34 tanks and an anti-tank regiment armed with Katyushas – newly developed multi-barrelled mobile launchers capable of firing a devastating volley of shells from all barrels at the same time. A German SS lieutenant watched the ensuing battle from the shelter of nearby woodland as the Russian tanks moved into position to confront the German infantry, which, under cover of artillery, was pushing towards the Soviet positions. As they got closer,

> a firefight began of an intensity I had never before experienced . . . I heard the characteristic sound of the Russian rocket launchers . . . I dived behind a tree, and witnessed the horrible yet strangely beautiful spectacle of the bursting rockets as they impacted . . . Suddenly all hell broke loose behind us. The ear-shattering racket had to be heard to be believed. It mixed with the crash of the incoming Russian rounds. It whistled, thundered, hissed and roared with the discharge and impact of artillery, machine guns and mortars. The effect was terrible.[21]

That evening Hoepner brought up more tanks, which, with the help of air support, pounded what remained of the Soviet defences with merciless precision. The Soviet tank commander, Major General Dmitry Lelyushenko, who was renowned for his personal courage, led his entire staff of officers, soldiers and orderlies, all armed with Molotov cocktails,* into the path of Hoepner's panzers as they sped towards his command post.[22] Lelyushenko was seriously wounded and had to be carried off the battlefield but his men still did not yield, even up to the point where they were finally overrun.

The battle lasted for several days. One of the defenders on the Borodino field, Makary Barchuk, recalled the moment when the German tanks finally came 'rolling over our trenches and their machine gunners were moving up behind them. They wanted desperately to make a final breakthrough. And they used psychological tactics – taunting us through loud-hailers and playing the sound of weapon fire all around us through their speakers.' After a while, some of his comrades could take no more.

---

* The incendiary bombs originally devised during the Spanish Civil War by General Francisco Franco's insurgent troops, and later used to devastating effect by Finnish troops in the Winter War against the Soviet invaders, when the name was coined.

Leaving their positions, they stood up and started to walk towards the enemy. Doubtless mindful of Zhukov's injunction, Barchuk did not hesitate: 'we shot them down and carried on fighting. We were not going to let the Germans through.'[23] However, according to Baromykin, he and his comrades had been inspired less by fear than by being told by their commissar that they would 'inherit the strength of those who had defeated Napoleon'. Thus, he reflected, 'We began to think about Moscow, and our responsibility to defend the Russian capital. It was our city – and we did not want the enemy to seize it. We resolved to make a stand.'[24] So dogged was this resistance that it took three more days of fierce fighting before Hoepner was finally able to drive the defenders off the Borodino salient.

The memory of their retreat was to haunt Baromykin:

> [It was] a living nightmare. Human guts hung from the trees, where soldiers' bodies had been blasted by the sheer force of the explosions. The snow around us was soaked red with blood. There was an all-pervasive, pungent smell of unwashed male bodies, hardened, encrusted blood, and burning. To slow the German advance, we set light to everything, so that the enemy would not have it. We were determined not to let them through.[25]

Hoepner was awed and chastened by such resolve. His men had been held for six days by a small number of troops – the 32nd Rifle Division – which, so far from forming part of an allegedly 'broken' army, was fresh from the Far East. Writing from his headquarters to the west of Borodino and the Mozhaysk Line, Hoepner did not dwell on how the 'terrible state' of the roads had slowed their progress but instead reported that 'the resistance from Moscow's defenders has been far stronger than I expected . . . I had a really tough fight on my hands at Mozhaysk on the main motor highway to Moscow, where the strongest defences are. The Russians here fought with remarkable courage.'[26]

The savagery of the fighting along the front also led some units to discard the last vestiges of humanity. In a remarkably candid account of one such instance, Baromykin described how

> the mood among our soldiers changed [when] at last we felt the iron determination of our commander, General Zhukov, to withstand the

enemy . . . Dull resignation was transformed into a fierce hatred of the Germans. We resolved to meet violence with violence. Once, towards the end of October, the enemy pushed us out of the village we were holding and began shooting us down. But we re-grouped – then took the village back. We seized five of the German soldiers and literally ripped them apart with our bare hands, our teeth, anything – one man was even using a table leg to smash a skull in. We killed those men in a frenzy of hatred.[27]

Retribution begat retribution. Further along the line, Robert Rupp, an officer serving in one of the 2nd Panzer Army's infantry regiments, had reached a village called Mikhailovka. The soldiers were ordered to fan out around the perimeter. Anyone acting 'suspiciously' was to be shot on the spot, civilians were to be 'strung up as a warning to others' and the village was then to be set alight. The excuse for such excesses was allegedly that Russian partisans had killed five German soldiers in nearby countryside. When Rupp asked his company commander whether the proposed response was 'an overreaction' he was firmly rebuked. 'It is a valid response. It will serve as a deterrent,' he was told. Rupp watched a group of soldiers lead away some of the cattle while others hurried into the village carrying ammunition and spades, with which, he presumed, to dig mass graves. 'Then I heard sounds of gunshot and children screaming. I realized that we were about to commit a massacre.'

One group of soldiers ran through the village hurling grenades onto the thatched roofs, which caught light almost immediately. Soon all fifty houses, in some of which entire families were huddling in terror, were ablaze. 'We heard the terrible roaring of cattle, the shrieks of women and children – and then the cries faded away . . . We drove away from the village and behind us the sky was glowing dark red.'[28]

When he took command of the Western Army Group, Zhukov, who had only recently arrived on this front, had hoped to hold the Mozhaysk Line, which ran in a 220-kilometre arc from north to south to form an outer defensive shield that bisected the main access routes to the capital. Five large rivers and a network of roads and railways to the east of this line should have made it possible to deploy troops to any point along it that was at risk of being penetrated. But, as Zhukov, always ready to blame others, was keen to point out, his predecessors had made a set of such 'serious miscalculations' that by mid October, this was no longer so. In a damning if self-serving indictment, he castigated their failure to heed intelligence warnings of an impending thrust towards Moscow, and more especially their failure to 'build defences in depth and, moreover, our backbone – the anti-tank defences – were not ready in time'.[29]

The Mozhaysk Line was now held by only forty-five battalions (rather than the 150 battalions for which it had been designed), separated from each other by an average of five kilometres and defended only by rifle and machine-gun units, supported by cadets from Moscow's Artillery and Political-Military schools. It was a very thin Red line. As Zhukov put it in his laconic fashion, 'the road to Moscow was not fully covered'.[30]

Yet, despite the fall of both Kalinin, 180 kilometres to the north-west of Moscow, on 12 October, and Kaluga, fifty kilometres to the south-west, two days later, and the encirclements at Bryansk and Vyazma, Zhukov showed no sign of panic or even alarm. Instead, on the day that Bock celebrated 'the collapse' of the Russian front and Stalin imposed a state of siege on Moscow, he presented his commander-in-chief with a plan to pull the main body of his newly formed Western Army Group back towards Moscow. The proposal was designed to thwart any further German thrust by constructing layer upon layer of heavily fortified defensive positions strategically located around the dense network of woods, rivers, railways and roads that criss-crossed the final approaches to the capital. Zhukov did not doubt that the enemy would penetrate the Mozhaysk Line, but he was confident that these in-depth defences would so disrupt, wear down, overextend and exhaust the German attackers that they would be unable to prevail. It was, in any case, the only available option. Stalin accepted it at once.

At Zhukov's instigation the Military Council of the Western Front issued a rallying call to the men under his command on the same day:

> Comrades! In this grave hour of danger for our state, the life of each soldier belongs to the Motherland. The homeland demands from each one of you the greatest effort, courage, heroism and steadfastness. The homeland calls on us to stand like an indestructible wall and to bar the Fascist hordes from our beloved Moscow. What we require now, as never before, are vigilance, iron discipline, organization, determined action, unbending will for victory and a readiness for self-sacrifice.[31]

They were not exaggerating.

In its collective contempt for the Russian people and for the leaders of the alleged Jewish-Bolshevik conspiracy based in Moscow, the Nazi High Command greatly underestimated the resolve of the Soviet people, their armies and the dictator who held sway over them. They failed to recognize that Hoepner's experiences at Borodino were not unique; that the Red Army had shown itself to be remarkably resilient; that its generals had revealed a tactical flexibility and ingenuity which had sometimes wrong-footed the Ostheer's front-line commanders; that the Red Army appeared to have a plentiful supply of armour and weaponry, the quality of which was often superior to their own; that, though they had lost more than 3 million men, the gaps had soon been filled, albeit often by ill-trained and poorly equipped replacements; that, for whatever reason, Soviet soldiers were plainly ready to die for the Motherland with every bit as much fervour as those who fought in the name of the Third Reich; that – the significance of which was hard to exaggerate – they were fighting on familiar terrain in familiar conditions to defend their homes and their families from a hated invader; and that they might have little to gain but they had everything to lose.

By the latter half of October, Hitler's strategic fantasies had started to come into direct conflict with operational realities. Sensing victory on the Central Front, he chose this moment to reassert his strategic urge to seize control of the northern and southern heartlands of the Soviet Union in parallel with the political decapitation of Moscow. Convinced that the Soviet Union had already been 'broken and would never rise again', he had given orders on 12 October that Army Group Centre should no longer seek to destroy Moscow by a frontal onslaught but encircle the capital instead, and thereby cripple the Bolshevik leadership.

Bock was ordered to divert sufficient forces from the central thrust on Moscow both to the south (to take Kursk) and to the north towards Lake Ladoga.[32] These fateful orders – echoing the Führer's preoccupations during the long August pause – paid little regard to the challenges at the front and provoked a blistering row between OKH and Army Group Centre. To deliver Hitler's new directive, the ever-pliable Brauchitsch ordered Bock to make preparations for the diversion of an entire armoured corps from Guderian's 2nd Panzer Army, which was advancing north-eastwards to Tula (170 kilometres from Moscow) to open up a route south-eastwards towards Voronezh (460 kilometres from Moscow). Bock demurred, insisting that his priority was to take Tula, and that, since 'the fighting strength of the armoured and motorized divisions were only those of regiments', he needed the entire strength of Guderian's 2nd Panzer Army to achieve that goal.[33]

Frustrated by the evidence that Operation Typhoon had lost momentum, metaphorically as well as literally, Hitler reiterated his demand for fierce and sustained attacks on Army Group Centre's northern and southern flanks. Bock was aghast:

> The splitting apart of the army group together with the frightful weather has caused us to get bogged down. As a result the Russians are gaining time to bring their shattered divisions up to strength and bolster their defence, especially as they have most of the rail lines and roads around Moscow. This is very bad.[34]

In the north the Red Army resisted the thrust towards Lake Ladoga so effectively that the assault had to be suspended before it had progressed more than a few kilometres. In the south, the plan to divert Guderian's panzers from Tula to Voronezh was stillborn amidst a confusing plethora of competing instructions. Following a message from the chief of OKH operations, Colonel Adolf Heusinger, on 26 October instructing Army Group Centre to obey Brauchitsch's orders, Bock called Halder. 'I have no idea what the objective of the 2nd Panzer Army's departure for Voronezh is,'[35] he told the chief of staff. Halder, who was similarly bemused, agreed that it would not appear to serve any useful purpose.

Brauchitsch tried to find a way out of the impasse by instructing Bock to halt Guderian's advance on Tula. Bock was incensed, responding that 'for tactical and psychological reasons' he was not willing to carry out his commander-in-chief's order. That evening, to avoid any lingering doubt, he warned Heusinger that if Brauchitsch was determined to persist, he or another senior figure in OKH would have to tell Guderian. 'The advance by the panzer army, including its infantry corps, has been started through unspeakable effort and after overcoming great difficulties. If I now order it to halt, they will think me mad,' he remonstrated.[36] But, terrified of incurring Hitler's wrath, Brauchitsch did not dare back down. That night, two further telegrams arrived from OKH, again instructing Bock to halt Guderian's advance on Tula. He ignored them both but the following morning tried to resolve the stand-off by undertaking to advise Guderian that a change of direction towards Voronezh might be required in due course.

For once, Hitler was at a loss. Unable to reconcile the differences between his generals that his ill-conceived instructions had provoked, his hand was forced by events on the ground. The assault in the north towards Lake Ladoga, which had already stalled, was to be put on hold and, as OKH instructed Bock on 28 October, Guderian's drive on Moscow was to be continued after all 'so as not to lose time'.[37] It was a bizarre but illuminating example of the Third Reich's dysfunctional leadership.

A great deal of time had already been lost. Hitler's original intention had been to launch Operation Barbarossa in May 1941. His decision to divert several divisions into the Balkans to break Yugoslavia and to occupy Greece had forced him to postpone Barbarossa by a full four weeks. A further three weeks were lost between late July and mid-August while he vacillated between competing options for the annihilation of the Soviet Union. At that point the Wehrmacht still presumed that the Red Army would collapse in weeks, and certainly well before the onset of winter. As a result, no preparations were made for the entirely predictable obstacles that would be spawned by the Rasputitsa.

In their conviction that the Third Reich was not only invincible but had an inalienable right to conquer any new horizons in the name of Nazism that the Führer might identify, the generals, both at OKH and at the front, had convinced themselves that the Soviet military colossus was at their mercy, that the huge number of prisoners taken was evidence of a breakdown in leadership and morale; and that Moscow would therefore soon be in their hands. In discounting the battlefield evidence that the Soviet military machine, though weakened, had yet to disintegrate, they chose to overlook their own glaring deficiencies. As autumn turned to winter they preferred to tell themselves that the Rasputitsa was to blame for their faltering progress – as though it represented an unforgivable violation of the rules of warfare rather than an annual phenomenon which should have been factored into the calculations many weeks earlier. Nor did it cross their minds except fleetingly that General Mud presented the Soviet armies with the same set of challenges as they themselves faced: their tanks and trucks also had to navigate atrocious roads, their horses also floundered and their supplies of fuel, spare parts, weaponry, food and clothing also had to reach their front-line troops. The Rasputitsa was not a valid excuse for the faltering progress of Operation Typhoon.

The worsening weather inevitably made an impact on Army Group Centre's ability to manoeuvre with the dexterity required to deliver that swift killer blow against Moscow which the German High Command had predicted at the start of Operation Typhoon. However, its failure to take into account the residual strength of the Red Army when set against their own diminishing resources was of significantly greater moment. By the end of October, Hitler's hubris had so infected the most senior generals in OKW and OKH as to preclude logistical forethought. As a result, Bock was perilously short of armour, weaponry, spare parts, fuel, equipment, clothing and manpower. Moreover, the Ostheer's spectacular progress had been secured at a very high price. On average, the army's infantry and armoured divisions were now between a half and two-thirds below full strength. Its panzer divisions were 65 per cent below full strength and only a third of its motor vehicles were still operational. On paper, the Wehrmacht still fielded 136 divisions on the Eastern Front, but they were equivalent to only eighty-three full-strength divisions. It had suffered 680,000 casualties (40 per cent of whom had served in Army Group Centre), which represented a full 20 per cent of the Ostheer's strength at the start of Operation Barbarossa.[38] Such levels of attrition were not sustainable.

Hitler refused to face these facts. No evidence to the contrary could dislodge his inner conviction that victory was inevitable and that Moscow would be pulverized. On 27 October he told Goebbels, 'We're waiting only for the roads to dry out or freeze. Once our tanks can start their motors again and the roads are free of mud and muck, the Soviet resistance will be broken in a relatively short period.'[39] Yet he still chafed at the delay. On 29 October, bypassing Bock, he summoned Field Marshal Günther von Kluge, commander of the 4th Army, to Wolfsschanze, not to listen but to berate. Kluge returned to his headquarters to report, 'The Führer finds it difficult to believe the written reports from Army Group Centre concerning manpower shortages, supply difficulties, and the impassable roads. He is very disturbed that Moscow has not yet fallen and is amazed that we did not foresee all the contingencies.'[40]

But for all his bullying and bluster, not even Hitler could force Bock to achieve the impossible. In every relevant respect – human and material – Army Group Centre was exhausted. No specific order to halt the advance was issued, but halt it did. Even the most diehard generals had come to realize that, without a pause to rest, recover, recuperate, regroup and rearm, 'Moscow by Christmas' would prove to be a self-deluding dream. Operation Typhoon had stalled in the mud – but not because of the mud.

24. The Jewish Question

As Typhoon stalled, the rate of killing behind the lines quickened. It also acquired a new and grotesque dimension. By October, it had become clear that the extermination of the Jewish 'bacillus' could not easily be achieved merely by lining the victims up, shooting them and throwing them into pits. There were too many Jews and too few killers. This problem became glaringly obvious when the Nazi leadership came to the decision that the Third Reich should be 'cleansed' of all its German Jews.

In the summer of 1941 Hitler came under pressure from Himmler, Heydrich and Goebbels to authorize the deportation of the Jewish populations of Berlin and other German cities to the eastern territories already conquered by the Wehrmacht. Initially, the Führer was reluctant, fearful that the dispatch of scores of thousands of German Jews to Poland, Belorussia and the Baltic States would cause more problems than it would solve. In late August, however, he apparently promised Goebbels that the trio's wishes would be granted once the Soviet Union had been defeated. By the middle of September, by which time he had concluded that victory was now inevitable, he gave Himmler the go-ahead to begin the mass deportation of Jews from the Nazi heartlands, where the Einsatzgruppen were already working to full capacity.[1]

The scale of the challenge facing Himmler was exemplified in the Lithuanian city of Kaunas, where scores of Jews had been murdered at a filling station in the opening days of Barbarossa. In the intervening weeks, Einsatzgruppe A had proved itself to be exceptionally assiduous in its task of exterminating Jews. By July, following a series of executions and pogroms, the commander of Einsatzkommando 3 (one of the three units attached to Einsatzgruppe A) was able to report that 7,800 Jews in Kaunas had been killed. Even so, this still left 29,000 to be dealt with. For the time being they were corralled behind barbed wire in an overcrowded ghetto that lacked even the most basic sanitary facilities but from where only those Jews regarded as strong enough to become slave labourers were permitted to leave.

Following his mass-killing 'triumphs' at Kamianets-Podilskyi and Babi Yar, Friedrich Jeckeln had been transferred by Himmler to become the higher SS and police leader (HSSPF) with overall responsibility for the Einsatzgruppen in what was known as the Ostland (the Baltic States and western Belorussia). Kaunas fell within his orbit, though, in practice, the Einsatzgruppen were answerable to Heydrich. On 29 October, in a further demonstration of what might be achieved in any Nazi-occupied city, 10,000 of the ghetto's inhabitants were herded into the city's nineteenth-century fortress, where Einsatzkommando 3, assisted by enthusiastic Lithuanian irregulars, corralled them into a capacious underground tunnel beneath Fort IX. There, in conformity with the practice devised by Jeckeln in Ukraine, they were stripped of their clothes and executed. The operation took most of the day. It was exceptionally bloody. By the time it was over, not one Jew was left alive. Among the dead, as well as more than 2,000 men and almost 3,000 women there were estimated to have been over 200 children (this in conformity with an instruction issued by Himmler in July that children should be regarded as no less dangerously virulent than their parents). In communication with their peers in the Wehrmacht, the leaders of the Einsatzgruppen and the Einsatzkommandos did not scruple to refer openly to their Jewish victims, irrespective of age or sex, as 'armed bandits and criminals' – a categorization that was rarely challenged by the officers and men serving in the Ostheer.

Similarly, after the Wehrmacht overran Minsk in June, the Nazis constructed a ghetto in which to incarcerate 80,000 Jews. It too was surrounded by barbed wire and overlooked by watchtowers. Ostensibly the Jews incarcerated there ran their own lives through the Judenrat (Jewish council), but these civic leaders had been powerless to protect their community from the pogroms and killings carried out by Einsatzgruppe B, under the command of Arthur Nebe, and other SS units, often supported by regular Wehrmacht troops.

By the early autumn of 1941, the Minsk ghettoes had been terrorized on an almost daily basis for more than four months. Gangs of soldiers and police would routinely break into homes at night, looting, raping and killing. Perla Aginskaya witnessed the aftermath of one such incident when she visited a house in the ghetto's Zeleny Lane. In a room containing just a bed, a lamp and a table she made a gruesome discovery: 'A girl of about eighteen was lying by the table. She was completely naked. Blood was streaming down the girl's body from deep, blackish wounds in her chest. It was quite clear that the girl had been raped and killed. There were gunshot wounds around her genitals.'[2] Near her lay a man who had been strangled. In the bed was a woman who had been stabbed. With her were two small children, both of whom had been shot.

In another home, the Kovarsky family endured a similar fate. In this incident, the SS burst in one night and pulled everyone out of bed. 'They stripped their grown-up daughter. They put her on the table and forced her to dance, then killed her. The grandfather and grandson were killed in their beds. Two children, a boy and a girl, who had been killed in their beds lay with their arms round each other.' Another child, named Malka, was badly wounded and died the next day. The father, who had hidden in the attic, and his son who hid under a bed, survived to record what had befallen them.[3]

By early November, many hundreds of Jews had been marched out of the city, lined up and shot. It was little surprise therefore to hear a rumour that ran through the ghetto warning that the Nazis were planning a pogrom to mark the twenty-fourth anniversary of the October Revolution. The rumour proved correct. On 7 November a convoy of large trucks drove into the ghetto. SS officers, armed with whips, revolvers and light machine guns, ordered the terrified population to put on their best clothes, to collect their children and infants and to form up in columns. They were taken to a nearby park, where they were mown down by a machine gun mounted on a truck.[4] This marked the start of a carnival of killing. Gallows were erected across the city in avenues, parks and bazaars. Men were hanged, their corpses garlanded with placards that read 'Partisan' or 'For collaboration with the Partisans' or 'Communist'.[5] A renowned scientist was made to crawl across Jubilee Square with a football on his back; when he reached the far side he was shot.[6]

On the same day, a cavalcade of trucks ran back and forth from the ghetto ferrying thousands of its inhabitants to a village called Tuchinki, just outside the city. When the Jews arrived they were held under armed guard, without food or water, while their captors set about their allotted task. According to testimonies provided to Vasily Grossman, one witness described seeing auxiliary police officers – mostly Lithuanians and Ukrainians but also Belorussians – snatch children from their mothers, sometimes breaking their backs or throwing them in the air, shooting them in flight and then tossing them into freshly dug trenches. The adults were forced to remove their clothes before they too were killed by machine guns and thrown into the trenches to join their children. A small fraction of the victims survived the massacre. One of these, shot only in the arm, waited until the gunfire had died down before she crawled out from beneath the heap of corpses under which she had been buried and made her way back to the ghetto to tell her story.[7] In that single pogrom, 12,000 Jews are estimated to have been murdered by the SS and its Belorussian collaborators.

As elsewhere, units of the regular army did not refrain from participating in the bloodshed. Among the more notorious of these was the 707th Infantry Division, which moved back and forth behind the Army Group Centre lines in Belorussia. Consisting largely of reservists, this 5,000-strong unit under the command of a passionate Nazi major general, Gustav von Bechtolsheim, made no distinction between Jews and partisans, as 'without a single exception Jews and partisans are an identical concept'. Each one of them had to be executed. Between 11 October and 11 November, with the help of the Order Police, the 707th executed no fewer than 10,431 prisoners.[8] But even killings on such a scale – which were replicated across the Eastern Front – were not enough to meet the growing demand.

Towards the end of September, Hitler told Goebbels that 'the first cities that have to be cleared of Jews are Berlin, Vienna, and Prague. Berlin is first in line.'[9] In the end, however, the first deportees were sent from the Austrian capital. They left Vienna by train on 15 October and were followed three days later by transports from Prague, Luxembourg and Berlin. Himmler's problem was not the departures but the arrivals. The ghettoes in Poland, Belorussia and the Baltic were already crammed to capacity. In Łódź, Minsk and Riga the Nazi administrations protested vehemently that they could not possibly accommodate any more Jews. But Himmler and Heydrich were adamant: the Führer had ordered the deportations and his will was not to be challenged.

As it happened, Minsk soon had space to spare. By dint of its murderous work on 7 November, the SS had cleared enough of the city's ghetto to allow the first trainload of deportees from the Reich, which arrived three days later, to be dumped there. They were – initially, at least – fortunate not to have been sent to Kaunas, where additional space had been similarly created. When 5,000 deportees from Germany and Austria arrived in that city a few days later, they were not taken to the ghetto but marched directly to Fort IX and, at Jeckeln's instruction, summarily executed. Jeckeln was later to claim (in a post-war attempt to escape the death penalty) that at a meeting with Himmler, he had been told by the SS Reichsführer that 'all Jews in the Ostland down to the last man must be exterminated', but no formal directive to that effect was ever found and there was no record in Himmler's appointments diary of any such meeting. The likelihood, as Christopher Browning aptly put it, was that 'confusion prevailed'.[10] In the absence of a coherent strategy, Hitler's 'Jewish question' was still being resolved in an arbitrary and haphazard fashion that did little more than consecrate hatred and sanction mass murder.

The failure to alight upon an effective 'Final Solution' for ridding the Reich of its Jews did not imply a lack of resolve. Hitler was invariably careful to avoid declaring himself overtly in favour of their physical extermination but never sought to disguise his urge to eliminate their presence from his ever-growing empire. Thus, on 25 October at Wolfs-schanze, in one of many such rambling soliloquies, he reminded his fawning dinner guests Himmler and Heydrich of his prophecy in January 1939 that, if war came, 'the Jews would disappear from Europe', adding, almost as an afterthought, 'It's not a bad idea, by the way, that public rumour attributes to us a plan to exterminate the Jews. Terror is a salutary thing.'[11] No more had to be said. Both henchmen could be relied upon to interpret his unstated will in ways that they knew would meet with his approval. All they needed was his benevolent failure to rebuke them for any decisions they might make on his behalf.

It is not credible to suppose that Himmler and Heydrich would have issued the instructions which led to the Holocaust unless they felt certain that they were carrying out Hitler's wishes. Whether he desired their physical elimination or whether his objective was merely to 'cleanse' Europe of Jews by the most efficient means available, it was his hand guiding the decisions that, in the autumn of 1941, ensured that gas chambers would become the Final Solution to his Jewish question.

By October 1941, Himmler and Heydrich faced a formidable practical task. Although many thousands of Jews had already been killed, more than 5 million remained within the Third Reich itself and in the so-called 'Occupied Eastern Territories' that had been seized during Barbarossa. Even Jeckeln, one of the most efficient killers, whose mass executions were meticulously planned and organized, struggled to dispatch more than a few thousand a day. And that was despite the help of the Ostheer.

The Einsatzgruppen did not operate in isolation. From the most senior generals to the lowliest privates, the Wehrmacht was already institutionally complicit in the Holocaust. It would have been quite impossible for the authorized killers and their collaborators to have murdered so many Jews in the first six months of the war without the knowledge, and frequently the participation, of the regular army. Some commanders, though, became troubled by the contaminating effect on the mental health of their men through their involvement in this unrelenting task. Even hardened killers were sometimes overwhelmed by the horror of the crimes for which they were individually culpable. Some collapsed with physical symptoms of severe stress. Others were tormented by guilt. Many sought to drown their nightmares in alcohol. A Jewish witness of the killings at Kamianets-Podilskyi recalled that some of Jeckeln's men 'got almost hysterical' and were clearly 'close to a nervous breakdown'.[12] One senior SS officer, Rudolf Höss, was to recall, 'Many members of the [Einsatzgruppen] unable to endure wading through blood any longer, had committed suicide. Some had even gone mad. Most . . . had to rely on alcohol when carrying out their horrible work.'[13]

Lieutenant Erwin Bingel, who was taken prisoner by Soviet forces in September 1941, told his captors what he and his men had witnessed in Ukraine when they were ordered to guard the airport on the outskirts of the town of Uman. The SS had already arrived. Tables had been set up beside a row of ditches. A large congregation of Jews had been summoned from the town. The protocols were similar to those that Jeckeln had introduced at Kamianets-Podilskyi. Once the men and women had undressed and put their valuables on the tables provided, the first row was escorted to the ditches. Armed with pistols, the Einsatzkommandos set about their business 'with such zealous intent' that, Bingel reflected, 'one could have supposed this activity to have been their life-work'. Among their victims were mothers who, before their own deaths, had to watch their infants 'being gripped by their little legs and put to death with one stroke of the pistol-butt or club, thereafter to be thrown on the heap of human bodies in the ditch, some of which were not quite dead'. Within the space of a few days, Bingel and his men were witness to two further massacres, both in the town of Vinnitsa. In the second of these they watched as 'a horde of Ukrainians' on horseback, under the command of the SS, began rounding up those Jews who had not been killed in the first massacre and had taken refuge in the town's central park. Hacking their way through the terrified crush of people, they waved their pistols and flourished their swords as they 'trampled savagely over human bodies, ruthlessly killing innocent children, mothers, and old people'.[14] Bingel recalled that as a result of their experiences 'he was compelled to send twenty per cent of [his] men on leave of absence since . . . they were quite incapable of performing any duty'.[15]

Himmler already had first-hand experience of this problem in August, while making his first tour of the killing grounds in the newly occupied Soviet territories. An entry in his appointments diary for 15 August 1941 noted his 'presence at an execution of partisans and Jews in the vicinity of Minsk'.[16] At the Reichsführer's request, the demonstration had been arranged by the leader of Einsatzgruppe B, Arthur Nebe (who only a few days earlier had reassured Army Group Centre's commander-in-chief, Bock, that only 'armed bandits and criminals' would be executed on his patch).

The hundred individuals chosen to die for Himmler's benefit were lined up by an open grave when he arrived. The SS-Reichsführer's attention was evidently caught by a youth in the middle of the group, who had 'blue eyes and blond hair'. Himmler went up to him to ask whether he was indeed a Jew, whether both his parents were Jewish, or whether he might have any non-Jewish ancestors. When the youth proved unwilling to deny his identity, Himmler allegedly said, 'Then I can't help you.'[17]

The victims were ordered to jump into the grave and lie face downwards. Himmler went to the edge of the pit for a closer look. The spectacle made him queasy. At one point, some spots of blood and a few shreds of brain tissue from one of the victims splashed up onto his coat and face. According to his adjutant, Karl Wolff, Himmler 'went very green and pale – he wasn't actually sick but he was heaving and turned around and swayed and then I had to jump forward and hold him steady and then I led him away from the grave'.[18]

32. Fires raged in towns and villages across the Barbarossa battleground. Untold millions of homes were razed under direct orders from Hitler and Stalin respectively. In this photo, German soldiers have just set fire to a building which might otherwise conceal snipers or partisans.

33. German soldiers advancing through a village set alight by Soviet troops to deny the Wehrmacht shelter, foodstuffs and clean water. Untold millions of civilians became the war's innocent victims.

34. Dmitri Shostakovich (*right, with hose*) served as a firefighter during the siege of Leningrad while also composing his Symphony No. 7, the 'Leningrad'. In September 1941, he was evacuated to Kuybyshev (Samara) where he completed the masterpiece. A copy of the score was later airlifted to Leningrad where it was performed by surviving members of the conservatoire orchestra, many of whom died from starvation during rehearsals.

35. 'General Mud' severely disrupted the German advance. The autumn rains turned roads into impassable quagmires. Many German commanders chose to blame the weather for the failure of Barbarossa. It was neither a valid excuse for poor planning nor an adequate explanation for a strategic disaster.

36. During the winter of 1941, temperatures fell as low as ⁻40 degrees centigrade. Pack horses – used for transporting supplies and men – died in huge numbers. German troops, lacking winter clothing, succumbed to frostbite. Gangrene set in. Limbs were amputated in makeshift field hospitals. Many thousands froze to death.

37. The first bombing raid on Moscow was on 21 July 1941. The British Embassy was one of more than a thousand buildings to be hit that night. Muscovites found shelter in metro stations. By comparison with London's Blitz (30,000 killed) the Moscow toll was modest (2,000 killed), though in both capitals, many more were wounded or made homeless.

38. With Moscow apparently in mortal danger, Stalin ordered the military parade marking the anniversary of the October Revolution to proceed as normal in 1941. The previous evening, from the security of a metro station, he drew a storm of applause during a broadcast speech in which he declared that a Second Front 'must come within a very short time'. As he almost certainly knew, there was little chance of that.

39. As the German armies pressed towards the capital, hundreds of thousands of civilians were recruited to shore up the city's defences against the panzers. Nonetheless the foremost units penetrated to within thirty-five kilometres of the Kremlin before they were forced to retreat on 6 December 1941.

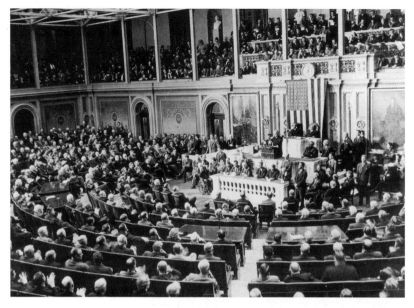

40. On 8 December 1941, the day after Pearl Harbor, Roosevelt addressed Congress to seek approval for a declaration of war against Japan. It was authorized at once. Three days later, Hitler declared war on America, thereby sealing the Third Reich's fate, already foretold in the failure of Operation Barbarossa.

41. The German retreat from Moscow was haphazard, panic-stricken, and strewn with frozen corpses. In January, Hitler reluctantly authorized a withdrawal to positions some 160 kilometres from the Soviet capital. By that time the invasion had cost more than a million casualties. Though the Red Army's losses (4.5 million) were far higher, Moscow was never threatened again.

42. SS-Obergruppenführer Friedrich Jeckeln directed the massacre at Babi Yar and other killing sites. He perfected techniques for accelerating the throughput of victims. In all, he was directly responsible for the murder of approximately 100,000 Jews.

43. At Babi Yar, on the outskirts of Kiev, in the autumn of 1941, the SS and its local collaborators murdered more than 30,000 Jews. Women and small children were stripped naked before being marched to the edge of a ravine where they were shot. The bodies were buried in layers. One small girl was heard to cry: 'Mammy, why do they pour sand in my eyes?'

44. Between them the SS and the Einsatzgruppen executed more than a million Jews in the course of Barbarossa. It was an efficient process but time-consuming. By the end of 1941, the first gas chambers were already in production and the rate of killing quickened. By the end of the war 6 million Jews had been murdered by the Nazis. A further 500,000 'undesirables' endured a similar fate.

45. A Soviet propaganda poster. Hitler – depicted as a rat – tears a hole through the Molotov–Ribbentrop Pact and suffers the consequences. The text at the top reads: 'We will mercilessly smash and destroy the enemy!'

Himmler soon recovered his composure sufficiently to address the execution squad. He said that, now he had witnessed it for himself, he realized how hard their task was, but that it was their patriotic duty to carry it out in the service of what he hoped would become the Thousand Year Reich. So saying, he drove off to inspect a nearby mental hospital, where, in a meeting with Nebe, he explored the possibility of finding more efficient and less traumatizing ways of exterminating Jews in large numbers. He had chosen the right man. As the commander of Einsatzgruppe B, Nebe had driven his men as hard as possible to eliminate the maximum number of Jews and other 'undesirables' including communists, Gypsies, the physically disabled and psychiatric patients. The addition of women and children to the official list of those Jews to be shot was threatening to overwhelm his limited resources. He had a vested interest in coming up with alternative solutions.

In his previous role as the head of the Reich's central criminal investigation department, the Reichskriminalpolizeiamt, Nebe had played a prominent role in helping to establish Hitler's euthanasia programme, Aktion T4, and he was familiar with its organization and procedures.* Aktion T4's founding mission was to purify the Aryan race by eliminating all children under the age of three who had inherited severe physical or mental disabilities. The programme was soon expanded to include adults with similar conditions as well as a wide range of other diseases, including syphilis and dementia. Those selected for treatment were transported from their various hospitals and sanatoria to T4 centres in what were known officially as 'charitable ambulances'. On arrival, they were certified as suitable candidates for treatment by teams of doctors who had volunteered for the task. They were then killed. Two main methods of euthanasia were available, though both were still at the experimental stage of development. One was by lethal injection of toxic chemicals and the other asphyxiation by carbon monoxide.

After a while some of the victims' families became suspicious about the circumstances in which their loved ones had died. Death certificates that had clearly been falsified appeared to confirm the rumours about what really happened in the T4 centres. Local protests soon led to widespread

---

* Aktion T4 was so named after the address of its headquarters in Berlin, Tiergartenstrasse 4.

revulsion, which, according to the eminent British historian Richard J. Evans, led to 'the strongest, most explicit and widespread protest movement against any policy since the beginning of the Third Reich'.[19] Its objections were certainly powerful enough for Hitler to suspend the programme. By this point, 24 August 1941, a total of more than 70,000 adults and children had been murdered by the T4 medical teams. Despite its abandonment, the project had nonetheless served a purpose, not so much by eliminating substandard Aryans but in germinating a far bigger idea.

Soon after his meeting with Himmler in the psychiatric hospital, Nebe began to explore ways in which the T4 experiments might be adapted to provide an answer to Hitler's Jewish Question. He contacted Albert Widmann, a chemist who had worked under him at the Kriminalpolizei in Berlin and had subsequently been involved in the T4 programme. Widmann arrived in Minsk with the basic equipment needed for two simple experiments. The first of these merely involved detonating explosives in a confined area. To see how effective this might be, twenty-five prisoners were taken from Minsk to a forest outside the city, where they were locked in a bunker. The experiment was not an instant success. At the first attempt, the explosions were not powerful enough to kill more than a few of the victims. A second, much larger explosion, was needed. This was too powerful. The bunker was shattered and body parts were hurled up into the air to end up hanging from trees. The idea was discarded.

The second experiment proved more promising. Nebe had once nearly died when he drove home after a bout of heavy drinking and fell asleep in his garage with the engine still running. Together, he and Widmann, who had overseen the use of bottled carbon monoxide in the T4 programme, decided to conduct a related experiment on mental patients from the local asylum at Mogilev. Twenty-five of these unfortunates were taken into a hermetically sealed room, which was connected by pipes to the exhaust systems of a car and a truck parked outside. Their engines were started up, the carbon monoxide flooded in and the results left no room for doubt: the gas was not only a fatal poison but also could be used to kill large numbers of people simultaneously.

In Berlin, under Widmann's guidance, a team of engineers was instructed to devise a container that could be used for the same purpose but mounted on a mobile platform, similar in design to the 'charity ambulances' used for the T4 programme. From the outside, the prototype was unremarkable, but the interior chamber could be linked directly to the vehicle's exhaust pipe. The design was tested at a concentration camp near Sachsenhausen, a mere fifty kilometres from Berlin. Forty Soviet prisoners of war were stripped, loaded into the van and driven to the camp crematorium where, leaving the engine running, the driver pulled a lever to divert the vehicle's exhaust fumes into the chamber. After twenty minutes the doors were opened and the corpses tumbled out. They were bright pink in colour – confirmation that it was the poison that had killed them, not asphyxiation.[20]

The first gas vans were soon in mass production for use by the SS throughout the Occupied Eastern Territories. It was hoped that this means of execution would prove less stressful for the killers than mass shootings. Such conjecture remained unproven, but since the screams of the victims as they banged frenziedly on the van's doors in their final moments were loud enough to be heard from some distance away, the psychological benefits may have been limited. Either way, the vans were soon in heavy demand.

Within weeks they were employed in the Polish village of Chełmno, north-west of Łódź. SS-Hauptsturmführer Herbert Lange, who had already proved his credentials by killing large numbers of psychiatric patients in the Warthegau,* had been selected by Himmler to find a suitable site on which to construct an extermination camp. Chełmno fitted his purpose. A group of Polish prisoners began renovating and fencing a dilapidated Schloss in the centre of the village to make it fit for that purpose. Lange's SS-Sonderkommando unit had operated a gas van during the T4 programme. On their way they evidently took time out to exercise their skills on some of the Jewish communities they encountered en route.

Chełmno would not be ready to open its doors to receive its first Jewish victims until December. In the meantime, Lange's SS killers did not pause. On 26 November they took their gas van to a Jewish labour camp at Bornhagen, some 270 kilometres south-west of Berlin. The camp's commandant, Ferdinand Göhler, summoned the ghetto's inmates to a meeting in the main square. He told them that, for their well-being, the

---

* The Warthegau (a contraction of Reichsgau Wartheland) was the name commonly given to a 45,000 square-kilometre region of Nazi-occupied Poland in the west of the country. With a population of some 4.5 million, the Warthegau had been earmarked for forcible 'Germanization'

young would be taken to a children's home and the old to a sanatorium. Names were read out and those who had been selected were taken into the synagogue. The van was backed up to the entrance of the building. Between seventy and eighty Jews were loaded into it. The doors were locked and – in a refinement of their original methodology – the killers released a canister of carbon monoxide rather than pumping the vehicle's exhaust fumes into their midst. It proved to be just as effective. The victims were carted to a nearby forest, where their corpses were hauled out and buried in hastily dug graves. These journeys continued for several days. Towards the end of the operation, the survivors, who had grown suspicious, had to be goaded into the main square to discover which of them had been selected for that day's final journey. By the time it was over, Lange's men had killed 700 Jews.[21]★

The first Jews to be exterminated at Chełmno were driven through the gates in the first week of December. When they stepped out of the transport buses they were met by reassuring officials who told them they would have to be disinfected before being sent on to labour camps in Germany. They were then taken into the main hall, where they were ordered to undress and to deposit their valuables with a team of Polish prisoners. The naked men, women and children were escorted into the cellar and thence up a ramp into the waiting gas van. The procedure was as at Bornhagen: the doors were shut, the carbon monoxide was released and the van drove the dead to a convenient forest location, where they were buried in a mass grave. As the system was perfected, groups of Jewish prisoners were formed into work teams. One of their tasks was to haul the bodies off the trucks, bury them and then clean out the vehicle in time for the next batch of victims. At least 150,000 and perhaps 180,000 Jews perished thus at Chełmno.[22]

In addition to Chełmno, three other camps were in preparation or under construction for the explicit purpose of exterminating Jews. At Bełžec, which was conveniently sited equidistant from the two large Jewish ghettoes in the Polish cities of Lublin and Lwów (Lviv), the victims arrived by train. The camp commandant, Christian Wirth (who had been prominent in the T4 programme as supervisor of six extermination hospitals), arranged for them to be told in advance that their destination

★ The bodies of these victims were exhumed after the war.

was a transit centre where they would be deloused and given clean clothes. Wirth opted for purpose-built gas chambers rather than vans, but the procedure was not dissimilar. On their arrival the unsuspecting victims were told to undress. They were then ushered down a passage towards what they presumed to be a communal shower room. As they got closer to their final destination, the guards brandished whips and yelled at them to chivvy them along. Once they had stumbled inside, the doors were closed and locked. Soon afterwards they were all dead.

By an administrative oversight, Bełżec's planners had failed to prepare adequately for the numbers of corpses that its gas chambers would produce. Within months, they were processing up to a thousand Jews a day, by which time the stench of rotting corpses was inescapable. An Austrian SS officer, Franz Stangl, arrived for a meeting with Wirth. He was directed to a hill that overlooked a large pit filled with bodies. He could not rid himself of the sight or the smell:

> I can't tell you – not hundreds, thousands, thousands of corpses . . . One of the pits had overflowed. They had put too many corpses in and putrefaction had progressed too fast so that the liquid underneath had pushed the bodies on top up and over and the corpses had rolled down the hill . . . oh God, it was awful.[23]

By the early summer of 1943, when the camp was abandoned (and then razed in a failed attempt to obliterate any evidence of its existence), upwards of 400,000 and perhaps more than 600,000 Jews had died at Bełżec.

At Sobibor, where 250,000 would perish, and at the Majdanek camp (on the outskirts of Lublin) the camp commandants also opted for gas chambers. Majdanek never reached its full potential on account of the incompetence and corruption of its first two commandants. This, along with their penchant for brutality, notorious even by the standards of the SS, led to their arrest and execution on the orders of Himmler's Reichssicherheitshauptamt or RSHA (Reich Main Security Office).[24] Nonetheless Majdanek would still carry out 78,000 killings, among whom were some 59,000 Jews, the rest being other 'undesirables'. Between them Chełmno, Bełżec, Sobibor and Majdanek would contribute more than a million deaths to the final Holocaust statistics.

Auschwitz, where an early experiment was already underway with another poison gas, would, in due course, make the largest single contribution to the Holocaust by exterminating a further million Jews. Auschwitz had previously been used principally to imprison Polish political detainees used as slave labour. In recognition of this, its commandant, Rudolf Höss, had thoughtfully erected a wrought-iron archway at the entrance which was emblazoned with the words 'Arbeit Macht Frei' – 'Work Sets You Free'.* In late 1941, Auschwitz acquired an additional role as a laboratory in which to conduct tests with a cyanide derivative which was marketed as Zyklon B, a poison in routine use as a fumigant to kill rodents and other pests. The question was whether it would be equally effective on humans.

On 3 September 1941, 600 Soviet prisoners of war were transported to Auschwitz. Along with 250 Polish prisoners who were deemed too weak to work, they were forced into a cellar under Block 11. Crystals of Zyklon-B were then released from a hole in the ceiling into this makeshift gas chamber. Within moments the victims were screaming in agony and terror, a sound that rent the air far beyond the cellar itself. In a frantic but futile effort to block the gas, some tore off pieces of clothing to stuff in their mouths. The deaths were not instantaneous, but within minutes it was clear that the experiment had shown promising results: every one of the men had died without the need to fire a single weapon.

There was, though, one problem the killers had not foreseen. As the crematorium was some distance from Block 11, the corpses had to be dragged there by other prisoners, a chore that could begin only once the cellar had been decontaminated. This took so long that by the time it was safe to enter the gas chamber, the limbs of the victims – entangled in their death throes – had stiffened and swollen to an extent that made it exceptionally difficult to separate one from another. In due course they resolved this technical issue by ensuring that new gas chambers and

---

* The slogan 'Arbeit Macht Frei' was first displayed at the entrance to Dachau concentration camp in 1933, to be followed by Theresienstadt, Flossenbürg and Sachsenhausen concentration camps, as well as Auschwitz. Dachau was intended initially to be a work camp for political prisoners. It was later expanded to imprison Jews and common criminals. Forced labour became a means of torture. Murder was commonplace. Between 1941 and 1943 some 4,000 Soviet prisoners of war were executed by firing squad on a nearby shooting range. Many more victims perished at Dachau before its liberation by US troops in April 1945.

the crematoria at the expanding Auschwitz complex – which became known as Auschwitz-Birkenau – were constructed in close proximity. It was a showpiece example of how to build an assembly line for the commission of murder on an industrial scale.

By late 1941 the Holocaust had acquired unstoppable momentum. Between them, Himmler and Heydrich had authorized the Einsatzgruppen – now reinforced with gas vans – to liquidate all and any Jews in the eastern territories conquered by the Wehrmacht. The Reichsführer-SS had also decreed that the Jewish 'bacillus' should be expelled from the territories of the Third Reich itself. As ordered by Hitler in the summer, the first mass deportations from the Reich to the Ostland were already underway. The six concentration camps in which Jews would be exterminated en masse – Chełmno, Bełžec, Majdanek, Sobibor, Treblinka and Auschwitz-Birkenau – had all been approved by Himmler and were either at the planning stage or under construction.

Hitler had willed the end; Himmler, Heydrich and tens of thousands of their loyal accomplices provided the means. When Himmler noted on 11 November 1941 that 'the destruction of the Jews is imminent', he spoke for them all. And when Alfred Rosenberg, the administrator of the Reich Ministry for the Occupied Eastern Territories, advised the German press in a background briefing that the Jewish question 'can only be solved in a biological extermination of all Jews in Europe', he did not speak merely for himself.[25] His was the collective voice of all those with the authority and power to interpret the Führer's implacable resolve to remove every single Jew from what was to become the Thousand Year Reich. Hitler's generals were in trouble on the battlefield but Operation Barbarossa had facilitated at least one part of Hitler's central objective for the campaign: behind the lines, his Jewish question was being answered with hideous clarity.

As Christopher Browning has written, 'there was not a single comprehensive killing order issued on a single date and disseminated by a single uniform method',[26] but by the late autumn of 1941 there was no longer any ambiguity about either the ends or the means. The timetable remained imprecise but the purpose and the outcome was no longer in doubt: 6 million Jews would be physically exterminated. As Himmler was to put it in a speech two years later at Posen, the Holocaust represented 'a glorious page in our history that has never been written and is never to be written'.[27]

25.   Allied Preoccupations

The picture that emerged was still murky, but evidence of Nazi atrocities on the Eastern Front was starting to trickle out to the West. From the late summer of 1941, Enigma decrypts by the code breakers at Bletchley Park offered snapshots of the mass shootings and executions reported by the perpetrators from the killing grounds to Berlin via radio telephone. These reports spoke of their victims as 'Jewish plunderers', 'Jewish Bolshevists', or simply 'Jews', along with others who were referred to simply as 'Russian soldiers'. In some of these cases, precise figures – ranging from 61 to 7,819 to 30,000 – were attached to these reports. To that limited extent, the War Cabinet in London had some awareness of the emerging Holocaust.

Throughout his political life, Churchill had been an advocate of the Jewish cause, endorsing the 1917 Balfour Declaration and subsequently arguing with passion in favour of the creation of a Jewish home in Palestine.* But in 1941 he faced a dilemma. Though he broadcast to the British people that 'scores of thousands – literally scores of thousands – of executions in cold blood are being perpetrated by the German police-troops upon the Russian patriots who defend their soil . . . there has never been methodical, merciless butchery on such a scale', he refrained from mentioning the Jews specifically. There were at least three possible reasons for this omission: (1) the risk of revealing the existence of Ultra,† (2) a reluctance to single out Jews from the millions of non-Jewish victims of the Holocaust, who included Slavs, homosexuals, dissident priests, Jehovah's Witnesses, Roma and the disabled, and (3) the fact that Britain could do nothing directly to prevent this 'crime without a name', as he called this unfolding horror.[1]

* The Balfour Declaration was a statement issued by the British government announcing its support for the creation of a 'national home for the Jewish people' in Palestine. It led directly to the establishment of the state of Israel in 1948.
† Ultra was the codename for the intelligence decrypted from German radio and teleprinter communications by the Government Code and Cypher School at Bletchley Park in Buckinghamshire.

When, however, he sent a message to the *Jewish Chronicle* to mark the newspaper's centenary on 24 November, his words were explicit: 'None has suffered more cruelly than the Jew the unspeakable evils wrought on the bodies and spirits of men by Hitler and his vile regime . . . He has borne and continues to bear a burden that might have seemed to be beyond endurance. He has not allowed it to break his spirit.'[2] It was to be one of the very few such references to the Jews in the months ahead by Western leaders. Like Roosevelt and Stalin, Churchill was careful to insist that the struggle against the Axis powers was to liberate the entire world from tyranny. The three leaders seemed to have agreed that to single out the Jews might conflict with and – given the latent anti-Semitism by which most Western nations were to a greater or lesser degree contaminated – even undermine that simple and unadorned message.

In any case, the prime minister's attention was elsewhere. On 15 November, not long before his tribute in the *Jewish Chronicle*, he had sent one of his most grandiloquent messages to General Auchinleck in Cairo, to be read out to the men of the 8th Army a few days later on the eve of a major offensive, Operation Crusader, designed to turn the tables on Rommel in the Libyan desert. 'For the first time British and Empire troops will meet the Germans with an ample equipment in modern weapons of all kinds,' Churchill declared, adding with a degree of hyperbole that few other leaders would have dared venture, 'The battle itself will affect the whole course of the war. Now is the time to strike the hardest blow yet struck for final victory, home, and freedom . . . The eyes of all nations are upon you.'[3]

Churchill's exhortation was tinged with exasperation. Increasingly anxious to rally the home front and to convince sceptics in Washington that Nazi Germany was best confronted in the Middle East, he had been flailing around for several weeks in search of an arresting military success. To this end his fertile brain threw out a range of possibilities with which he bombarded his chiefs of staff. These exuberant forays into military strategy irked his director of military operations, Major General Sir John Kennedy, who was to reflect, 'Our stable was so full of these unlikely starters that we were hard put to it to give the favourites the attention they deserved. To cope with the situation adequately, it would have been worthwhile to have had two staffs: one to deal with the prime minister, the other with the war.'[4]

Operation Crusader had emerged as the clear favourite and, for the time being, the only runner. However, to Churchill's great irritation, Auchinleck refused to be railroaded into crossing the start line prematurely. This delay served only to make a swift victory over Rommel of even greater emblematic value to the prime minister. As he had told the War Cabinet earlier in the year, 'The loss of Egypt and the Middle East would be a disaster of the greatest magnitude to Great Britain, second only to successful invasion and final conquest.' For the prime minister, the chance to crush Rommel was of surpassing importance. In a phrase that was extravagant even by his own oratorical standards, he made this abundantly clear in urging Auchinleck's men to greatness. 'The Desert Army', he declared, 'may add a page to history which will rank with Blenheim and Waterloo.'

While his attention was focused on the Middle East, the prime minister could not escape the growing pressure to give greater support to the Soviet Union. As Ivan Maisky was delighted to discover, the public chorus in favour of a second front was growing rapidly into a crusade. The Soviet ambassador found himself feted wherever he went. The mayor of Kensington organized a reception for him and his wife, Agniya, which was attended by 500 guests including, Maisky noted with satisfaction, 'many diplomats, political and public figures, the clergy, and all sorts of aristocrats'. He was elected an honorary member of two of London's stuffiest clubs, St James's and the Athenaeum. He was a guest of honour at the Livery Club – 'the City's holy of Holies' as he put it – where he was given a prolonged ovation. When he spoke to an international youth demonstration at the Albert Hall, he was given sustained applause – in contrast, he noted gleefully, to King George VI, the Archbishop of York and Churchill, all of whom, he chortled, 'were met with deathly silence'. More broadly, large crowds welcomed him at workers' rallies and in town halls across the country. 'Everything "Russian"', he noted on 12 October, 'is in vogue today: Russian songs, Russian music, Russian films, and books about the USSR.' Seventy-five thousand copies of a booklet containing the wartime speeches of Stalin and Molotov 'sold out instantly'.[5]

Churchill was also under pressure from a wide spectrum of political opinion at Westminster. The Conservative MP Robert Cary, a former

Guards officer who had served in the First World War, was not alone in demanding a 'Second Front Now!'. He was joined by Colonel Josiah Wedgwood (great-great-grandson of the famous potter) from the Independent Labour Party. The Labour MP John Tinker spoke for many of his colleagues when he said acerbically, 'I hope to goodness that we do not let it get into the minds of the Russian people that we are prepared to fight to the last Russian before risking any of our own people.'[6] No sentiment could have been better calculated to get under the prime minister's skin.

Some of his closest colleagues were also on the second-front warpath. The most vociferous and troublesome of these was Beaverbrook – 'a complete scamp', as Cadogan described him – to whom Churchill gave rare licence to defy the usual conventions of collective responsibility. He was not only free to agitate within the Cabinet for a second front but to take to the airwaves (in a coveted evening slot usually reserved for the sovereign or the prime minister) to express similar views in public. He was not rebuked for openly courting senior Conservatives to seduce them into the same cause. Nor, when his newspapers supported the quasi-communist campaign of a pro-Soviet group of Trades Unionists for a Second Front, or when one of them – the *Sunday Express* – described Soviet Russia as though it were 'a worker's paradise', was he judged to have any conflict of interest. Churchill not only admired Beaverbrook but also feared the influence of his powerful Minister of Supply should he resign and take his campaign to the country. Were he to take that step, however, as the prime minister told Eden, 'it would mean war to the knife against him'.[7]

Beaverbrook was not alone. In response to persistent demands from Stalin that the British send a substantial military force to southern Russia, his Foreign Secretary, with support from both the Chief of the Imperial General Staff, Sir John Dill, and the Chief of the Air Staff, Charles Portal, suggested that 'a token force'[8] be transferred from the Middle East to the Caucasus. This, he argued – albeit without great conviction – would be 'the best line on which to defend Russia'.[9] The Defence Committee approved this proposal. Churchill would have none of it.

Stafford Cripps, who had not only been exiled to Kuybyshev by Moscow but also, latterly, marginalized by the Foreign Office, now joined the fray to argue that a larger force than that proposed by Eden be dispatched to the Caucasus as an alternative answer to Stalin's demand for a second front. On 25 October Churchill rejected his suggestion, in terms that were bound to aggravate the already acrimonious relationship between them. 'To put two fully armed British divisions from here into the Caucasus or north of the Caspian would take at least three months,' he wrote. 'They would then only be a drop in the bucket.'[10] Cripps retorted tartly, 'A drop or two in a bucket or a tumbler may make a great deal of difference when a stimulant is urgently needed.'[11] To reinforce his case, echoing sentiments now being voiced by politicians at Westminster, he warned that the Soviet leaders were

> now obsessed with the idea that we are prepared to fight for the last drop of Russian blood as the Germans suggest in the propaganda, and they interpret every action from this point of view or else from the point of view that we are sitting back and resting while they are doing the fighting . . . if we are allies, as you have announced, surely they should not merely be told that we cannot send any troops to help them, but should also have the opportunity of discussing the matter.[12]

Moscow's 'obsession' would not have been allayed by the swashbuckling Minister of Aircraft Production, John Moore-Brabazon, who used a speech in London to declare that he 'hoped the Russians and Germans would exterminate each other'. According to Churchill's private secretary, who made a note of the minister's sentiments, such views were 'widely held'.[13] They were certainly shared in the higher reaches of the armed forces, who nurtured an abiding loathing of Bolshevism, tended to regard their Russian counterparts with fastidious disdain and certainly begrudged every weapon that left Britain for the Soviet Union that might otherwise have been sent to the Middle East or be available to protect the home front. Their attitudes were laced with an ambivalence which was summed up by Kennedy: 'The fundamental difficulty is that altho we want the Germans to be knocked out above all, most of us feel . . . that it would not be a bad thing if the Russians were to be finished as a military power too.'[14] Dill was known to share similar views while his vice-CIGS, General Henry Pownall, put it bluntly, noting, 'Would that the two loathsome monsters, Germany and Russia, drown together in the winter mud.'[15]

Churchill was no less anti-Bolshevik than they but more astute. He knew it was both diplomatically and politically impossible simply to watch the Soviet Union's agonies from the sidelines. But he was exasperated by his implacable ambassador and impatient with the Russians. In this frame of mind he wrote once again to Cripps to point out that the British had already made what he described as a significant offer of military support to the Russians only to have it turned down. From Moscow's perspective, this offer was a double-edged sword.

It originated with a joint Anglo-Soviet plan to prevent Iran falling into German hands. In August, Soviet units invaded the ostensibly neutral country from the north as British units entered from the south. It was an opportunistic venture which had oil at its heart. London wanted to prevent the fiercely nationalistic but pro-Nazi Shah Reza Pahlavi from giving the Germans access to the British-owned Anglo-Persian oil refinery at Abadan; Moscow sought to interdict the German advance towards the Caucasian oil wells at Baku. The operation was simple, swift and surgical, and led within days to the abdication of the Shah, leaving Britain and the Soviet Union in joint occupation of Teheran. In the middle of September, ostensibly to meet the Soviet demand for greater military support, Churchill proposed that the British troops now based in southern Iran (protecting Abadan) should replace the Soviet troops in the north of the country. Somewhat disingenuously, he told Cripps that this would liberate five Soviet divisions, 'to defend their own country'.[16] To the prime minister's irritation, Cripps pointed out that Britain's proposal would be regarded as an ill-disguised takeover bid for an oil-rich country of vital strategic importance to the Soviet Union. And so it was.

Churchill was unmoved. In late October, with Stalin still pressing for a second front, he chided Cripps as though picking at an itchy scab. The Russians, he wrote, 'have no right to reproach us. They brought their own fate upon themselves, when, by their pact with Ribbentrop, they let Hitler loose on Poland and so started the war . . . We were left alone for a whole year while every Communist in England, under orders from Moscow, did his best to hamper our war effort.' And he went on, 'That a government with this record should accuse us of trying to make conquests in Africa or gain advantages in Persia at their expense or being willing to "fight to the last Russian soldier" leaves me quite cold.' More generally, he wrote testily, 'We will do anything more in our power that is sensible, but it would be silly to send two or three British or

British-Indian divisions into the heart of Russia to be surrounded and cut to pieces as a symbolic sacrifice.'[17]

Cripps was infuriated. The prime minister's attitude, he noted, was 'petulant and irrelevant'.[18] In replying more formally, he modified his language but he did not retreat:

> I am afraid your telegram is no assistance to me . . . We seem to be try-
> ing to carry on two relatively unrelated wars, to the great benefit of
> Hitler, instead of a single war upon the basis of a combined plan . . . It
> appears to me that we are treating the Soviet Government without trust
> and as inferiors rather than as trusted allies.[19]

Churchill did not reply. As Eden noted with admirable understatement, the prime minister was once again 'giving very evident signs of anti-Bolshevik sentiment'.[20]

Chafing at Churchill's rebuff, Cripps once again contemplated resignation and a return to Britain to 'make a nuisance of myself about it all'.[21] Unlikely as a partnership between two such bedfellows might have seemed, the combination of Beaverbrook and Cripps campaigning together to open a second front would be a potent challenge to the prime minister's authority. Fearing Cripps above any other as a pretender to his leadership, Churchill had repeatedly blocked his requests to return to London even for the superficially innocuous purpose of briefing the War Cabinet.

The ambassador settled on a new tack, suggesting that he and Mason-MacFarlane (the head of the Moscow military mission who was similarly out of the loop) should fly back to Britain to receive a full briefing on the government's policy, the better to explain it to the Kremlin. Churchill's rebuff was unequivocal. 'I do not think it would be any use for you and MacFarlane to fly home now,' he replied. Churchill had good reason to believe that if their mutual antagonisms were to be fought out in public, he would overwhelm Cripps with the force of his personality and his rare gift for political rhetoric, but it was a disagreeable prospect. Injecting a note of self-serving menace, he added, 'I could only repeat what I have said here, and I hope I shall never be called upon to argue the case in public.'[22] He could not rid himself of his turbulent ambassador but he could effectively insist that he remained out of the way in Russia.

Nonetheless, Churchill could not entirely ignore the mounting criticism, both within Westminster and in the country. The government, he confided to Eden, was 'on thin ice . . . while we are doing so little for them [the Russians]'.[23] He settled on a smart political wheeze, a gesture to show Moscow that the will – if not the means – was there to support what the British public regarded as the heroic struggle of the Russian people. To maximize the impact, he turned to his formidable spouse, Clemmie, who shared the public mood and was given to speaking her mind with clarity and force. Well aware, as he put it, that she 'felt very deeply that our inability to give Russia any military help disturbed and dismayed the nation', he had no difficulty in recruiting her to a campaign of practical action. Telling her that 'a Second Front was out of the question', he proposed that she chair the Red Cross's Aid to Russia Fund. She was soon on the fundraising offensive. At the end of the month, in her first speech of a campaign that was to last until the end of the war, she spoke of her 'profound admiration for the valour, the tenacity, and the patriotic self-sacrifice of the Russian people. And above all, perhaps, we have been shaken with horror and pity at the vast scale of human suffering.'[24] Under her leadership, the fund would go on to raise almost £8 million (worth some £400 million in 2020 terms), largely through weekly subscriptions from the general public. This support made a notable difference to the supply of medical aid to the Soviet Union but it did little to ease the domestic pressure for a second front or to assuage the Kremlin.

For Churchill, the Soviet Union remained a tiresome distraction from what he regarded as 'the dominant theatre' of the war: Britain's imperial struggle in the Middle East.[25] But he found it impossible to disentangle himself from the diplomatic war games that had come to bedevil relations between London and Moscow, an association underpinned by mutual incomprehension and suspicion that threatened to form an insurmountable obstacle to an effective alliance, which, whether he liked it or not (and generally he did not), was crucial to the defeat of Hitler.

Thwarted in his efforts to bully the prime minister into mounting a second front, Stalin steadily increased the pressure on him to declare war on Romania, Hungary and most of all on Finland, whose armies were pressing hard on the Soviet Union's northern front in support of Hitler's siege of Leningrad. In a letter to the Soviet leader on 4 November, Churchill made it clear that he was unwilling to make such a move, which, he wrote, would only be 'a formality' because Britain had already imposed a blockade on all three countries. In addition, he informed Stalin, a British declaration of war on Finland would arouse strong opposition in the United States. Nonetheless, in a conciliatory gesture, he undertook to raise the issue again in the War Cabinet 'if you think it will be a real help to you and worthwhile'.[26]

Stalin's reply was handed to Churchill by Maisky a week later in the prime minister's room at Westminster. Churchill rose at the ambassador's entry, shook hands and, as Maisky noted, 'said with a friendly smile "Let us have a good talk." '[27] The two men and Eden (who was there at Maisky's request) sat down and Churchill began to read. Maisky watched as his face darkened at what the prime minister would describe as a 'chilling and evasive reply'.[28] In terms that were certainly as bitter in tone and brutal in content as diplomatic correspondence would allow – Cadogan, who was also present at the meeting, described him as 'cantankerous and offensive'[29] – the Soviet leader laid bare his deep grievances over Churchill's attitude and strategy. Implicitly blaming the British for failing to reach 'a definite understanding between our two countries' over 'war-aims' and 'plans for the post-war organization of peace', he also held Britain responsible for the absence of a 'mutual military assistance' deal for the defeat of Hitler. Until these questions were settled, he warned, 'there will be difficulty in securing mutual confidence'.

The immediate cause of Stalin's resentment was Churchill's refusal to declare war on Finland. This rebuff, the Soviet dictator complained, had been the more offensive because the British had created an 'intolerable situation' by allowing debate about this most delicate issue to surface in the press. 'Why is all this being done? To demonstrate the lack of unity between the USSR and Great Britain?'[30] he thundered. When Churchill had finished reading, he passed the letter to Eden without saying a word. Then he rose and paced around the room. 'His face was white as chalk and he was breathing heavily. He was obviously enraged,' Maisky noted. After a long pause, the prime minister said icily, 'Grave message,' adding a few moments later, 'I don't want to answer this message now!'[31] At that point Maisky rose to leave but Eden restrained him. After a desultory exchange about the post-war purposes of the Atlantic Charter, Churchill exploded again: 'If you want to turn England into a communist state in your post-war plans, you should know you'll never succeed.' Still pacing, he added, 'Why was it necessary for Stalin to assume such a tone in our correspondence? I am not going to stand for it. I could well say things, too! Who will profit from it? Neither we, nor you – only Hitler.'[32]

Such bitterness in Anglo-Soviet relations could not be allowed to fester. Eden – who was well aware that Stalin judged Finland to be a litmus test of Britain's commitment to the Soviet Union – sought to become an honest broker. At a meeting of the War Cabinet that evening he was unable to persuade Churchill, who was 'very sore about Russia',[33] to shift towards a declaration of war on the Finns, even though he knew it would amount to little more than a symbolic gesture. The prime minister was supported by two Labour ministers, Ernest Bevin and Anthony Greenwood, 'whose hatred of Communism', according to Eden's private secretary, Oliver Harvey, 'blinded them to any other consideration'.[34] Eventually, Beaverbrook came to the rescue, saying, 'Things are in a terrible mess. We must send Anthony [Eden] there, and he'll put it all right.'[35]

The following day the Foreign Secretary summoned Maisky to the Foreign Office, where he made a formal complaint about Stalin's letter but, according to the ambassador, he also said informally, 'Please help me patch up this unpleasant incident. I, for my part, will do all I can to achieve this.'[36] Two days later, in what his private secretary described as another 'heart-to-heart', Eden met Maisky once again to plot a means of circumventing Churchill's animosity towards Stalin. It was a fruitful conversation. Eden himself wrote, 'I told him he had better get a message from Molotov which would enable me to build a bridge again. He said that he would try.'[37]

The relationship between Roosevelt and Stalin was far more congenial than that between the Soviet leader and Churchill. Unlike the prime minister, the US president had no difficulty in acknowledging that the Soviet Union had a crucial role to play in defeating Hitler and that American largesse should be distributed accordingly. In contrast to Churchill, who acknowledged the need to sustain the Soviet war effort but could not help begrudging the competing demands of a rivalrous suppliant, Roosevelt regarded the provision of supplies to the Soviet Union as of 'paramount importance for the safety and security of the United States'.[38]

After his meeting with Stalin in Moscow, Harriman had returned to Washington to draft a report for the president detailing how the billion-dollar loan to which he and Beaverbrook had committed their respective governments should be allocated. On 30 October Harriman presented the report to Roosevelt, who not only signed it off at once but cabled Stalin two days later to tell him that the entire package would be financed under Lend Lease, that no interest charges would be levied and that the Soviets would be granted a ten-year repayment period which would not start until the end of the war. Stalin replied in terms so gracious that they would barely be recognized by Churchill as being authored by the same individual. 'Your decision', he wrote, 'is accepted with sincere gratitude by the Soviet Government as unusually substantial aid in its great struggle against our common enemy – bloodthirsty Hitlerism.'[39]

By this time Roosevelt was cautiously but cleverly nudging the United States towards a direct confrontation with Germany. On 9 October he sent a formal request to Congress – where the isolationists were still a potent force – seeking approval for a further amendment to the Neutrality Act that would allow US merchant ships to be armed and to transport supplies into war zones. It was likely to be a close call as American public opinion was still heavily opposed to taking military action against the Nazis.

Then, on 17 October, a US destroyer, the *Kearny*, was hit by a torpedo fired by a U-boat 350 miles south of Iceland. Although the vessel managed to limp back to Reykjavík, eleven of her crew were killed. For Roosevelt it was a fortuitous opportunity. Ten days later, at his annual Navy Day speech, the president used the *Kearny* affair to ramp up his rhetoric against the Nazis:

America has been attacked . . . I say that we do not propose to take this lying down . . . we Americans have cleared our decks and taken our battle stations. We stand ready in the defence of our nation and the faith of our fathers to do what God has given us the power to see as our full duty.[40]

Patriotic though they might have been, the American voters were not yet ready to follow the president where he wanted to lead them. Their reluctance to be sucked into war had been faithfully reflected in Congress two months earlier when the president's passionate plea that military service be extended from a year to eighteen months squeaked through the House of Representatives by only a single vote.★ The mood had barely changed in the interim. Even the sinking of another destroyer, the USS *Reuben James*, with the loss of 155 men, did little to sway public opinion. However, it led to just enough of a swing in Congress to carry the day, first in the Senate and then, by a margin of 212–194, in the House of Representatives to approve Roosevelt's request to amend the Neutrality Act in ways that were bound to increase sharply the risk of a confrontation in the Atlantic. This was a step forward, but it was far from providing evidence that the American people were now ready for war. Roosevelt was well aware, in the words of his speechwriter, Robert E. Sherwood, that 'as the limitless peril came closer and closer to the United States, isolationist sentiment became even more strident in expression and aggressive in action'.[41]†

The vote in Congress may have authorized him in effect to launch a war – de facto though not de jure – in the Atlantic, but that was as close to a military confrontation with the Axis powers as he could get. He had repeatedly made a public commitment to 'do everything in our power to crush Hitler and his Nazi forces',[42] but the American people were not yet willing to allow that rhetoric to be translated into practical action. It would take an open act of premeditated aggression against the United States to trigger war itself.

As it happened, that prospect was approaching rapidly over the horizon. Tensions between Washington and Tokyo had been rising sharply. Following Japan's decision to join with Germany and Italy to form the Tripartite Pact in 1940, the Japanese militarists, who were resolved on further rapid expansion of their empire, had gradually gained the upper hand. Japan's imperial aspirations had started to take tangible form with the invasion of Manchuria in 1931, an aggression that eventually led to its expulsion from an enfeebled League of Nations four years later. This had served only to accelerate the momentum of conquest. Despite desperate efforts by China, the Japanese seized (and pillaged) Nanking, Hankow and Canton in the same year. In 1940, in its next move to become the

★ The Bill passed on 12 August 1941 by 203 votes to 202.

† Robert Sherwood, who was credited with coining the phrase 'the Arsenal of Democracy', was a playwright, screenwriter and close friend of Harry Hopkins.

unchallenged suzerain of 'Greater East Asia', Japan forced the Vichy government to cede military bases in French Indo-China (Laos, Cambodia and Vietnam), which culminated in the effective occupation of the region by July 1941. This was a decisive moment. With Malaya, Singapore and the Dutch East Indies now at risk – in effect the takeover of South-East Asia – neither Britain nor the United States could stand by to see their own regional interests thus jeopardized.

Washington retaliated by imposing severe sanctions on the Japanese regime. Extending a pre-existing ban on the export of precious metals and aviation fuel, Washington froze all Japanese assets in the United States and, in conjunction with the British and Dutch, imposed a total oil embargo. As a result, Japan faced a collapse in its overseas trade and, more alarmingly, the total loss of its vital oil imports. The only way to break out of this stranglehold would be to withdraw from Indo-China or take military action to secure these resources elsewhere – from Malaya, the Philippines and, particularly for the oil, from the Dutch East Indies.

In the absence of adequate intelligence from Tokyo, it was virtually impossible to pierce the carapace of secrecy behind which Japan concealed its internal machinations. Washington therefore had no evidence on which to judge whether its punitive measures would restrain or provoke the militarists in Tokyo. Roosevelt chose to believe that the sanctions would avert, or at least postpone, the risk of a US–Japanese military confrontation in the Pacific. Fearing that Britain might be left alone to confront the powerful Japanese navy in the Far East, Churchill had urged Roosevelt at their Placentia summit to issue Japan with an ultimatum: a warning that any further military adventurism would lead to countermeasures up to and including war. Roosevelt baulked at taking this stance. Instead, Tokyo was informed that any further military action by Japan would oblige him to take any measures that might be required to ensure 'the safety and security of the United States'.[43] He still hoped that he could avert a crisis through negotiation.

All expressions of mutual regard aside, these Washington–Tokyo talks soon foundered on the rocks of the mutually incompatible ultimatums each side was to deliver to the other in the weeks ahead. In effect, Tokyo was told that sanctions would be lifted only if Japan surrendered its existing empire and abandoned its pretensions to great-power status in the

region. Japan's national pride, the militarists' sense of their intrinsic superiority and a reluctance to lose the economic gains of conquest effectively
ruled out any prospect of agreement on such terms. At its meeting on 6
September, the country's supreme governing body, the Imperial Conference, decided that unless the US sanctions were lifted without
preconditions in favour of unfettered negotiations about the empire's
legitimate role and status, an early military confrontation with the United
States and Britain would be inevitable. Since it was inconceivable that
Washington would lift the sanctions unconditionally, the chances of a
peaceful way out of the impasse had become vanishingly remote.

Blindsided by its reluctance to appreciate either the importance of
'honour' in Japanese culture or the crushing blow inflicted by its sanctions on the empire's economy, Washington lulled itself into the belief
that its severe warnings would serve to deter a Japanese attack on the
West's colonial possessions in Malaya, the Philippines and the Dutch East
Indies. Instead, Roosevelt presumed that the Soviet Union was likely to
be Tokyo's next target. On 15 October he made this explicit in a letter to
Churchill: 'The Jap situation is definitely worse and I think they are
headed north.'[44] Stalin, who was, of course, not privy to this correspondence, knew better.

26.   Mood Changes

On his long and excruciatingly slow journey from Moscow to Turk-menistan, Andrei Sakharov occasionally raised his eyes from the study of quantum physics. 'I saw a country wounded by war,' he was to recall. 'The trains moving east with us carried evacuees, damaged equipment and wounded men; those racing past us to the west carried combat troops: their faces were tense as they peered out from the train windows, and they all looked somehow alike.'[1] The soldiers that sped by day after day were being rushed from the border with Manchuria to the defence of the Soviet capital. This massive redeployment was possible only because Stalin – unlike Roosevelt – had learned that Siberia was no longer at risk from a Japanese invasion.

During the decade following Japan's invasion of Manchuria, the Russians had built up an army of 750,000 men to the east of the Urals to protect the 3,000-kilometre border with northern China, which was under the harsh military rule of the Japanese Kwantung Army. The countless border clashes between the two armies culminated in the Battles of Khalkhin-Gol in the summer of 1939. It was only after a ferocious struggle costing almost 40,000 lives that the Soviet forces, under the ruthless leadership of General Zhukov, forced the Japanese to sue for peace.

The ensuing ceasefire was fragile. The Soviet–Japanese Neutrality Pact which followed eight months later, in April 1940, was an opportunistic agreement that neither side signed with conviction. When Japan signed the Tripartite Pact less than six months later, Tokyo and Moscow were once again on a potential collision course. By the summer of 1941, to guard against this renewed threat, the Soviet Union had built up a formidable battle group of thirty infantry divisions, three cavalry brigades, sixteen tank brigades and a large fleet of warplanes in Siberia.[2] As Hitler's Ostheer threatened to pulverize the Red Army on the Motherland's Western Front, a renewal of hostilities on the Eastern Front would be calamitous.

Tokyo came under intense pressure from Berlin to seize this opportunity. Urging the German ambassador in Tokyo, Eugen Ott, to make the case forcefully, Ribbentrop wrote, 'The quicker this happens the better . . . Our goal remains to shake hands with the Japanese on the Trans-Siberian railway before the beginning of winter.'[3] From Tokyo's perspective the issue had not been so simple. For some months the regime's militarists had been torn between two competing options: invasion of the north or expansion to the south. The dilemma was resolved for them by the United States' decision to impose oil sanctions, the severity of which would rapidly strangle the empire's economy. An early attack on the Soviet Union was no longer an option.

The Kremlin was alerted to this critical development by a coded message that arrived from Tokyo on 25 August stating that Japan had 'decided not to launch the war within this year, repeat, not launch this year'.[4] Its author was Richard Sorge, the Soviet spy whose accurate warnings from the Japanese capital about the imminence of Operation Barbarossa had earlier led Stalin to denounce him as 'a little shit'. Sorge was in no doubt that an invasion of the Soviet Union by Japan was off the table. As one of his best-placed sources explained to him, 'The oil situation alone shows that Japan has two alternatives – pushing south to secure Dutch East Indies oil, or getting oil by bowing to the United States.'[5]

On 14 September Sorge confirmed his initial report by advising Moscow that Ambassador Ott had confided to him that, although 'armed forces will stay in Manchuria for a possible offensive next spring in case the USSR is defeated by that time . . . a Japanese attack is now out of the question'.[6] At the end of the month, he sent a further, definitive message, repeating, 'The Soviet Far East can be considered safe from Japanese attack.' For these revelations, he was rewarded by a rare note of gratitude from his controllers in the Soviet capital.[7]

This time, even Stalin was convinced. Any lingering doubts that he might have had were almost certainly laid to rest by corroborating evidence provided to him by the interception of Japanese diplomatic cables that were decrypted simultaneously by the NKVD's intelligence services in Moscow.[8] But Sorge's most recent message was to be his last. Two weeks later he was arrested by the Japanese security services and charged with espionage. In the absence of clear evidence against him, his interrogators subjected him to a severe bout of torture, under which he finally gave way. After a summary trial he was sentenced to death. Seeking to capitalize on their coup, Tokyo suspended his execution in the hope of securing a 'spy swop' with Moscow. When this suggestion was mooted through the Soviet Embassy, it was instantly rebuffed. Although he was well known to be one of Ott's drinking companions, Tokyo's emissaries were told on at least three occasions, 'The man called Richard Sorge is unknown to us.' He had officially ceased to exist.[9] While his master spy was awaiting execution, Stalin is reputed to have responded in similar terms, saying 'Richard Sorge? I do not know a person of this name.'[10] Sorge was hanged on 7 November 1944. True to form, Stalin was never to express any appreciation for his crucial contribution to the defence of Moscow. It was not until the Soviet dictator had been dead for thirteen years that Sorge was given the accolade 'Hero of the Soviet Union'.

In the knowledge that the Siberian border was safe from invasion, Stalin was able to withdraw 400,000 men from the Siberian front. For days at a time, a non-stop migration of trains brought them to Moscow. By the middle of November, some fifteen infantry and three cavalry divisions – along with their weaponry and at least 1,000 tanks plus many aircraft – were available to face Hitler's armies on the Western Front. The men were not only fresh but drilled, trained, armed and, in many cases, hardened by years of border confrontations with the Kwantung Army.

To conceal their existence from the Germans, a shroud of secrecy was thrown over their transit through Moscow. On occasion the message either failed to get through or was ignored. A journalist working for *Krasnaya Zvezda* was moved to an ecstasy of lyricism by the sight of one of these units heading towards the front:

> As they march their pace rings out with disciplined precision. The sun shines on their bayonets, on their helmets, on their mess cans. They march with sunburned faces, the warriors of the Red Army, and as they march they smile at Moscow, the heart of the country. Everything has stopped for them . . . Make way for the soldiers! The people of Moscow line the pavements to welcome them . . . A song rings out about our Soviet Motherland. Company after company, battalion after battalion takes up the song. And the people of the capital take up the song as well.[11]

When he read the offending article, Alexander Shcherbakov, in his role as First Secretary of the Moscow Communist Party, rang the newspaper's editor, Daniel Ortenberg, to rebuke him for this breach of security. Uncowed by Shcherbakov's authority, Ortenberg answered back, arguing that the uplifting tone of the offending article would raise public morale. Others were less Panglossian. The sculptor Daniel Mitlyansky watched one regiment heading for the front in complete silence – 'no band, no singing, gloomy faces, the faces of people who knew they would not be coming back'. When he spoke of this, many decades later, he evidently 'broke down in tears' at the memory.[12]

A boost to morale was much needed. By early November, the panicked flight from the capital of a fortnight earlier had become a more or less orderly evacuation during which hundreds of thousands of Moscow's citizens were taken by a cavalcade of trains to places of greater safety further east. Those who were left behind could rarely find jobs, and even basic foodstuffs were in short supply and exorbitantly priced. The state of siege was being aggressively policed and harshly interpreted. There was no right of appeal against the often draconian sentences imposed by the tribunals. Two officials, the head of the city council's Heating and Power Department and his deputy, made the mistake of being overheard as they criticized life in the Soviet Union and cast doubt on the prospect of victory. Each was jailed for ten years. A disabled worker called Grechichkin was unwise enough to pick up a German leaflet that had dropped near a vending machine on the corner of Dzerzhinsky Square and read it aloud; he too got a ten-year sentence. As Rodric Braithwaite has observed, he had chosen the worst place to commit this crime 'since it was opposite the Lubyanka'.[13] A shortage of buses and trams, a metro that closed at dusk, a night-time curfew and ruthlessly enforced blackout did little to lift the anxiety and gloom that permeated the capital. And in case Muscovites were still tempted to forget, the Luftwaffe bombing raids were a daily reminder that the enemy might have paused but was still alarmingly close to the gates of the city.

It was at this juncture that Stalin decided to have a celebration. On 6 November, the Soviet Union was accustomed to marking the anniversary of the October Revolution with a formal gathering of the party elite followed next day in Red Square by a spectacular parade of military might. On 30 October he asked the NKVD's Pavel Artemev how – not whether – the Red Square parade should be arranged. With the enemy dug in a mere sixty kilometres from the Kremlin, Artemev and his fellow generals were aghast. They protested that the risk of an air raid made it far too dangerous and that, in any case, the tanks were needed at the front while only a paltry handful of troops could be assembled in time for the Red Square march past. Stalin dismissed their reservations out of hand.

When he told Molotov and Beria of his decision, they thought he was joking. It was soon clear that, far from joking, he would, if necessary, supervise the arrangements himself. 'If there's an air raid during the parade and there are dead and wounded, they must be quickly removed and the parade allowed to go on,' he told them. 'A newsreel should be made and distributed throughout the country. I'll make a speech.'[14] Stalin was not a rabble-rouser or a showman but he had an uncanny instinct for the moment and he sensed that a spectacle was required to rouse the spirit of the people and to give them the confidence to believe that, rather than facing imminent defeat, victory would in due course be theirs to celebrate.

To avoid chancing fate, the ornate main hall of the Mayakovsky metro station – the deepest in Moscow – was chosen for the meeting of the party elite. Security was tight. Invitations, supervised by the NKVD, were dispatched to the party faithful only hours in advance. On the day itself, a rostrum was brought from the Bolshoi Theatre and covered with carpets. Flowers bedecked every corner. A train was drawn up on one platform, its carriages converted to buffet cars and cloakrooms.[15] But the mood was oddly subdued as Stalin and his entourage – Molotov, Mikoyan and Beria among them – mounted the platform to a round of dutiful applause. Stalin looked strained, weary and grey as he rose to speak. With microphones transmitting his words to the outside world, he spoke softly, almost flatly, without seeking to rouse his listeners with demagoguery.

Inevitably he overstated the achievements of the Red Army, but he did not gloss over the setbacks and the challenges the Soviet forces had faced. Referring warmly to the fruits of the Harriman–Beaverbrook mission, he also drew attention to the failure of the Western Allies to send troops to the European mainland, insisting that 'a Second Front . . . must come within a very short time' – a pointed rebuke that drew a spontaneous burst of stormy applause. More tellingly, despite the fact that it was the eve of the twenty-fourth anniversary of the revolution, he was canny enough to eschew Bolshevik clichés in favour – once again – of appealing to Russian nationalism. Quoting the Nazi penchant for describing his audience as belonging to a 'subhuman' species, he denounced 'these people with the morality of animals, who have the effrontery to call for the extermination of the great Russian nation'.

Invoking the names of Pushkin, Tolstoy, Gorky, Chekhov, Glinka and Tchaikovsky, among others, as well as Lenin – Trotsky, of course, was not mentioned – he roused his audience once more with a 'bring it on' challenge to the invaders. 'If they want a war of extermination, they shall have it! Our task now . . . will be to destroy every German, to the very last man, who has come to occupy our country. No mercy to the German invaders! Death to the German invaders!'[16] This time, his words were almost drowned in a barrage of sustained applause. If any of his audience were troubled by his failure to credit their revolutionary zeal they refrained from saying so. When he finished, the crowd – which included a number of uniformed soldiers who had been brought directly from the front – clambered on to their chairs for a better look at their leader. An orchestra played the 'Internationale' as a prelude to a patriotic concert that brought the evening to a triumphant close.[17]

Stalin had ordered that the precise timing of the Red Square parade should be kept secret. This instruction was so scrupulously obeyed that even he was not told until later that evening that it would start at eight the following morning. General Artemev had managed to muster some 28,000 men for the honour of parading through Red Square. To make up the numbers, this required him to withdraw the equivalent of two front-line divisions from Moscow's defensive shield; the remainder came from a pool of new recruits who had yet to experience conflict but would very soon be on their way to that front. With only a few days to drill them for an event that would normally require weeks of square-bashing, they had to march back and forth for long hours at a time until they could perform with the meticulous precision that such an event warranted. When they were issued with new greatcoats and told to polish their boots and their equipment, they guessed what was in the offing but – in the name of security – they were not officially told of their role until the evening of 6 November. Not many slept that night. By the early hours they were on their way to Red Square. It was dark, the cold was intense and the ground was icy. The Kremlin was blanketed by a snow storm. Men and tanks slipped and slithered their way up the shallow slope towards Lenin's empty mausoleum to take up their allotted positions in front of the seat of Soviet power.*

Just before the Kremlin bells chimed the hour, Stalin led the Politburo up the steps of the mausoleum. He was muffled in a plain greatcoat and wearing his emblematic flat cap, which was decorated only with the Red Star of the Revolution. In the distance it was possible to hear the boom of artillery fire from the front. With Moscow subjected to an average of six bombing raids a day, the snow storm was actually a blessing.[18] As he looked up at the darkening sky, the Soviet leader joked, 'The Bolsheviks are lucky. God is on their side.'[19]

Once all were in position, Stalin spoke, softly as always, his words reverberating – albeit indistinctly – around Red Square and from radio sets across the Soviet Union. He was in declaratory mode: succinct, direct and ostensibly indomitable. 'Comrades! We are celebrating the 24th Anniversary of the October Revolution in very hard conditions . . . The enemy is at the gates of Moscow and Leningrad . . . Yet, despite temporary failures, our army and navy are heroically repelling the enemy attacks along the whole front.' As he had done the evening before, he invoked giants from the past to underline the nation's patriotism. 'The whole world is looking upon you as their liberators,' he told the troops. 'Be worthy of this great mission! The war you are waging is a war of liberation, a just war.'[20]

At that, the bands started up and the march past began. It lasted no more than thirteen minutes but it was a potent display of defiance and it indubitably had an inspirational effect on many of those taking part. One of their number, Leonid Shevelev, reflected, 'We had heard that Stalin had left the capital. It was very important to us to see that our leader chose to stay with us . . . This made us march with the kind of determination as if we were nailing down the coffins of the advancing Nazis.'[21] Not all were as impressed, however. As he passed Lenin's tomb, Mark Ivanikin, who was marching on the outside edge of his column nearest the reviewing platform, turned his head smartly on the order

---

* Lenin's corpse was returned to the mausoleum after the end of the war to become a place of international pilgrimage.

'Eyes Right' and had a brief close-up view of the Soviet leader. He was not overawed: 'I was surprised to see Stalin looked so short in his hat and earflaps, not at all like the man we had seen in the portraits everywhere,' he recalled.[22] When he joined the ranks of those marching to the front, the phrase of Stalin's that rang loudest in his ears did not embolden him: 'At the bottom of my heart I felt a little dubious when he said that the war might be over in six months to a year.'[23] He suspected it would be much longer.

The writer and journalist Ilya Ehrenburg was shocked by another part of the speech. The implicit sneer in the phrase 'the enemy is not as strong as some frightened little intellectuals imagine' led him to retort later:

> Of course, among the intelligentsia, too, there were some who lost their bearings, but no more so than among other sections of the population. I do not know why Stalin had once again to make a scapegoat of our intelligentsia. The intellectuals were at one with the people: they fought at the front, they worked in the field-hospitals, in the factories . . . The anguish we endured was not only owing to the fact that Hitler's army was indeed strong, but also because we saw how gravely our defences had been weakened in the pre-war years: by the boasting, the bullying, the red tape, and above all, by the terrible losses inflicted on the cadres of the Red Army and on the 'little intellectuals'.[24]

For the most part, though, the speech clearly achieved its purpose. The Kremlin's commandant, Major General K. R. Sinilov, recalled that before the parade he had received sheaves of letters that betrayed 'a lack of confidence, and in some there was a palpable feeling that we could hardly hold Moscow'; a few even indicated 'that it was not right to put children and old people in danger', asking, 'wouldn't it be possible in general, not to withhold Moscow [from the enemy], not to put up resistance?'[25] Following the parade, such letters ceased: the people became 'completely different' and 'full of confidence'.[26] His anecdotal evidence was confirmed by the military censors, who dutifully opened no fewer than 2,626,507 personal letters to discover not only that the majority evinced 'positive sentiments' but also that, in 75 per cent of cases, there was a sharp spike in such feelings following Stalin's two speeches.[27]

A great many soldiers fought because they faced a Hobson's choice of appalling options: a Soviet firing squad for cowardice or a Nazi death camp. The majority, though, fought from ideological commitment to their vision of a Bolshevik paradise or from hatred for the invaders who sought to steal their birthright and their Motherland. Though all these men were under the yoke of what he described as 'the barbarous Stalin regime', the experienced and attentive British correspondent Alexander Werth was convinced from his first-hand experiences throughout this period that 'this was a genuine people's war . . . waged by a people fighting for their lives against terrible odds', and in 'the spirit of genuine patriotic devotion and self-sacrifice'. Such was the spirit that – as astute as he was ruthless – Stalin, in his quiet, flat voice, had managed to conjure up under a canopy of falling snow that morning in Red Square.

PART FOUR

Retreat

27. The Final Assault

I'm in a bad mood today because it is not going forward. One is powerless . . . Yesterday and today we finally had frost. From tomorrow the temperature should rise again. Thus the hopes of moving again are shot down. Even now I do not know how I am supposed to ensure the supply just of foodstuffs. For the new attack a preparation of at least 10 days is required.[1]

The disgruntled commander of Panzer Group 4, Erich Hoepner, waiting for the final lunge on Moscow from the north, was not alone. Guderian, impatient to reach Tula, the 'gateway' to Moscow from the south-west, was equally frustrated:

It is miserable for the troops and a great pity for our cause that the enemy should thus gain time while our plans are postponed until the winter is more and more advanced. With the best will in the world there is nothing you can do about the elements. It all makes me very sad. The unique chance to strike a single blow is fading more and more, and I do not know whether it will ever recur. How things turn out, God only knows. We can only go on hoping and keep our courage up, but this is a hard time that we are passing through.[2]

The officers and men in Army Group Centre were as dismayed as their senior commanders. An artilleryman, Franz Frisch, reflected, 'No soldier could understand the idea of a winter offensive under such miserable conditions. The spirit of the troops was also below zero. We suffered terribly . . . The wind blew almost all the time. We never officially received winter clothes and could not understand why they were not given to us.'[3] As ever, Heinrici, commanding 43rd Corps, was quick to detect this mood. He also shared it: 'The weather stays bad . . . there is snow and freezing temperatures at night, fog and rain during the day. The roads are either so slippery that our cars spin like humming tops or they turn into a deep swamp. At the moment we live in a miserable village, our quarters are horribly bug-infested.' On 8 November, the same day that Hitler, in Munich, proclaimed that the Soviet Union had been 'shattered and defeated', he noted, 'Our men keep asking me, when will this finally end? I can only shrug and answer I do not know.'[4]

During this lull, the soldiers found an outlet for their frustrations. Partisans, though not numerous, were, like hornets, able to inflict nasty surprises, by planting bombs on bridges, laying mines on roads and, most irksomely, mounting unexpected raids on the villages where the German troops had billeted themselves, setting fire to their supply dumps. Heinrici was as eager for vengeance as his men. And if they failed to distinguish between a partisan and an innocent villager, then that, he judged, was the debt owed by the latter for not revealing the whereabouts of the former. It was a frustrating task to hunt down a hidden enemy that could so easily conceal itself in deep gorges or dense forests. Tired and demoralized men were not prone to make distinctions between the 'innocent' and the 'guilty'.

Informers played a crucial role. In one incident, Heinrici was greatly assisted by an individual whom he described euphemistically as 'our interpreter'. His intelligence led to the arrest of a 'committed gang' of fifteen partisans, both men and women. Even though, Heinrici wrote, they knew that they would be 'exterminated without mercy', they refused to cooperate: 'They say nothing and claim to know nothing.' They were duly shot. On another occasion, one of his units rounded up sixty suspects. The officer in charge of these arrests detected forty Red Army soldiers among their number. Heinrici noted that 'he convicts and finishes off twenty of them', and that 'one young man was hanged in the city centre, or more precisely, he relieved the military policemen from this unpleasant work and did it himself'. These extra-judicial killings gave Heinrici considerable satisfaction. It was disagreeable, though, to see his officers execute their victims close to his sleeping quarters and he therefore instructed one of them 'not to hang partisans closer than 100m to my window. Not a pleasant view in the morning.'[5]

As commander of the Central Front, Bock faced challenges of a different order. Not only were his troops demoralized but his officers had fallen to bickering with one another about ill-judged and ill-fated skirmishes or complaining about supplies that had been promised but not delivered. A regimental commander serving in the 98th Infantry Division bemoaned the loss of 'officers, non-commissioned officers and weapons specialists', noting that 'without reordering and replacement of clothing, equipment, weapons, vehicles and horses . . . the troops have no more combat value'.[6]

Bock did not so much ignore the frustrations, resentments and grievances that permeated Army Group Centre as try to sidestep them. He had committed himself to the destruction of the main enemy force defending Moscow, presuming that the fall of the capital – a secondary objective – would follow in due course, but great logistical obstacles now stood in his path. Although the Germans had built railway lines as far as Smolensk, from there onwards the bulk of all supplies for the front had to be taken by truck along roads that were virtually impassable in many places. An acute shortage of crucial supplies, including basic foodstuffs and fuel, about which his commanders complained so volubly, was the inevitable consequence. To add to these impediments, Halder chose this point to present him with another: a grand new strategy for the next stage of the campaign.

On 7 November the army chief of staff sent him a map on which were drawn two sets of lines that depicted the 'minimum' and 'maximum' depths to which the three army groups were expected to penetrate in the weeks ahead. The 'maximum' line ran from the northern port of Murmansk via the city of Gorky (400 kilometres east of Moscow) to a point a little beyond Stalingrad (800 kilometres due south of Gorky and 900 kilometres south-east of Moscow), and ended imprecisely even further south in the depths of the Caucasus.[7] Bock ignored the 'maximum line' as too far-fetched to be worth considering, but he could not avoid responding to what he must have presumed to be Hitler's proposed 'minimum' line. This began at a point to the east of Leningrad and ran south-east to a point 250 kilometres due east of the capital before turning south to Rostov-on-Don, which was 900 kilometres south of Moscow. Bock's response was brusque. This 'minimum' line could not possibly be reached before winter; it would be hard enough as it was to encircle the capital by the end of the year as Hitler had demanded. It was quite impossible, he added in sarcastic exasperation, to transform the attack on Moscow into 'a great strategic masterpiece'.[8] Halder opted to avoid further confrontation.

The commander of Army Group South, Rundstedt, was no less aghast. As his chief of staff noted, 'It is no longer possible to mitigate the situation by saying: "It will be all right . . ." There comes a time when – physically – they [the troops] really cannot go on any longer, and having examined the situation thoroughly, I believe this point has now . . . been reached."[9] In Rundstedt's case, though, Halder insisted. General Ewald von Kleist's 1st Panzer Army (as the expanded Panzer Group 1 had been redesignated following the fall of Kiev) was ordered to drive eastwards once more. He was to make little progress. The commander of Army Group North, Leeb, also sought to advance towards his end of the 'minimum line', but he too made little headway. The burden of Hitler's deluded crusade still rested on Bock.

Hitler had ordained that the final assault on Moscow should begin at the latest by 15 November. Bock decided that the encircling operation should be spearheaded from the north by Hoth's Panzer Group 3, from the west by Hoepner's Panzer Group 4, and from the south by Guderian's 2nd Panzer Army. But he was profoundly uneasy. In conversation with his commander-in-chief, Brauchitsch, on 11 November, he refrained from mentioning Hitler's preposterously unrealistic operational ambitions – which most if not all the Führer's most senior generals still endorsed – but focused on logistics. As a result of a sharp reduction from thirty to twenty-three in the number of trains reaching his rear positions each day, Army Group Centre's stockpile of supplies was being rapidly exhausted. Unless that shortfall were made good, he warned Brauchitsch, 'I will have to give the order to dig in for the winter. It is impossible to let the units lie around for another four weeks [the time it would otherwise take to rebuild the stockpile] . . . this evening the temperature dropped ten degrees below freezing.'

Not for the first time the army's commander-in-chief temporized, but promised 'a quick review of the railroad situation'.[10] The next day Bock was told that the extra trains would be made available but almost simultaneously he was appalled to discover that several of these trains had been diverted to accelerate the expulsion of German Jews from the Reich. In a grotesque twist of irony, Hitler had elected to annihilate one 'bacillus' by depriving Army Group Centre of the essential means to annihilate another.

Field Marshal Bock was under fire from every one of his senior commanders, all demanding more rations, munitions, fuel and winter clothing. No one complained more vehemently than the head of the 2nd Panzer Army, who had a well-earned and assiduously self-promoted reputation as the most innovative and daring of all Bock's generals. On 12 November Guderian set out on a tour of his own command. Wherever he went he heard tales of woe: tanks with engines that would not start unless preheated by lighting fires under them; tanks that 'could not move up the ice-covered slopes for lack of the requisite calks [studs]'; tank brigades with only fifty operational vehicles; tanks on which the telescopic sights had frozen up and whose machine guns were similarly unusable; an entire panzer corps with only one day's supply of fuel.

And then there was the condition of the troops: infantry companies that had shrunk from upwards of 150 men to no more than fifty; officers and men who told him that 'snow shirts, boot grease, underclothes and above all woollen trousers' were unavailable and who, he noticed, were often 'still wearing denim trousers' in temperatures well below zero. In more than one regiment, he was told, 500 men had been 'lost' through frostbite.[11]

Despite these problems, Guderian's advance towards Moscow had brought his leading tanks to within four kilometres of the Tula 'gateway'. Acutely aware of the urgent need to prevent the panzers taking the city, Zhukov had already rushed reinforcements there to block Guderian's advance. They were well dug in. When Guderian tried launching a surprise frontal attack on the city he was thwarted by heavy anti-tank and anti-aircraft fire, which, he reported, cost him 'many tanks and many lives'. Heeding the advice of one of his generals, he opted instead to bypass Tula altogether with the intention of pressing on towards Moscow, a tantalizing 170 kilometres to the north.

Initially, the panzers made good progress, but – in what, from his perspective, marked an ominous shift in the military balance on this front – soon found themselves facing a series of well-organized, disciplined and ferocious counter-attacks that, despite the group's renowned speed and agility, proved exceptionally difficult to beat off. Guderian was adamant, however: there would be no pause. On 10 November he overrode Heinrici, ordering the commander of 43rd Army Corps, which was advancing from the west towards the Tula–Moscow highway, to engage the Soviet forces in open battle. To avoid heavy casualties, Heinrici did not launch his attack during daylight but waited until nightfall. Even after his infantry divisions broke through, though, they were subjected to damaging flanking attacks on both left and right. With no units from elsewhere either willing or available to provide cover, it took five days of what Heinrici described as 'violent effort' to make only modest progress. Although they took 2,000 prisoners and captured six tanks, 'the great victory we had gained', Heinrici reflected, 'was in vain in terms of operational effect'. On 15 November, as the final onslaught on Moscow began, he noted bleakly that he had already lost almost 1,000 men in four days. Of these, 790 were dead or injured while 180 had 'frozen to death'.[12] In a 'War Report' to his family, four days later, with the temperature falling to −20°C and a fierce wind that 'stings like needles in the face and blows through headgear and gloves', he wrote that his men 'had to lie on the frozen ground for hours while they were under grenade and machine-gun fire', protected only by light-weight coats and 'thin old trousers'. This was in distressing contrast to the Soviet troops, who were dressed in 'quilted uniforms, coats and trousers, which look like duvets, with round warm fur earflap caps'. His soldiers, he told his family, were required to fight in 'outrageous combat conditions'.[13]

Later on the same day, writing to his wife, his mood had darkened further:

> I doubt we will reach Moscow this winter. If it starts snowing – and it looks like it tonight – then we will be stuck here . . . Everyone is sick of this here and would love to go home on leave since there is no end in sight. It will be going on, even for next year. Russia is crumbling but not yet broken.[14]

Two days earlier, Guderian's 112th Infantry Division found itself facing the 239th Soviet Rifle Division, newly arrived from Siberia. The 112th was already battered following a bruising encounter with Zhu-kov's 50th Army to the south of Tula. Once again the 112th suffered serious damage when its 37mm anti-tank guns failed to do more than pepper the hulls of the Russian T-34s. Although the troops had finally broken through, they were exhausted and demoralized. The Siberians had already acquired mythic status in the German mind as bloodthirsty and fearless men who did not take prisoners. Forced into a firefight on open ground against the 239th, the Germans turned and fled the battlefield. 'This was the first time that such a thing had occurred during the Russian campaign,' Guderian wrote, adding with the benefit of hindsight, 'it was a warning that the combat ability of our infantry was at an end and that they should no longer be expected to perform difficult tasks'.[15]

Guderian was chastened by the novel experience of failure, unable to dispel the doubts that crowded in on him. 'We are only nearing our final objective step by step in this icy cold and with all the troops suffering from the appalling supply situation,' he wrote on 17 November, adding, 'without fuel the trucks can't move. If it had not been for this we should by now be much nearer our objectives.'[16] Four days later, on 21 November, he was even more downbeat:

> The icy cold, the lack of shelter, the shortage of clothing, the heavy losses of men and equipment, the wretched state of our fuel supplies, all this makes the duties of a commander a misery and the longer this goes on the more I am crushed by the enormous responsibilities which I have to bear, a responsibility which no one, even with the best will in the world, can share.[17]

In this catalogue of woe, it was notable that – unlike some of his peers – the adverse weather was only one of the reasons to which he attributed his multitude of problems.

Bock was still under the impression that his star commander was 'full of confidence'.[18] But the news that reached him from a number of generals on other parts of the front made it abundantly clear that the assault was already faltering. Among others, the 4th Army commander, General Günther von Kluge, leading the direct assault on the capital from the west, 'painted a black picture of the 13th Corps' situation', reporting that 'his right wing . . . is incapable of effective attacks for the foreseeable future'; General Hans Felber, commanding the 13th Division, 'made no bones about the difficulty of the struggle by his weak battalions, inadequately protected from the icy cold, against the numerically strong enemy in difficult terrain'; and the commander of the 7th Corps, General Wilhelm Fahrmbacher – who, Bock noted, 'has been visibly affected by the fighting' – described 'the pitiful state of his [four infantry] divisions, whose strength is spent'.[19]

On 23 November, Guderian decided to disabuse Bock of any

illusions he harboured about the state of the 2nd Panzer Army. His message was unadorned: his men were exhausted, they had no winter clothing, they were hungry, and they were short of tanks and guns. He no longer had the resources to fulfil his orders (to neutralize Tula before heading north-east to begin the encirclement of Moscow). For that reason, the orders should be rescinded and the 2nd Panzer Army should be permitted go on to the defensive. There and then, Bock rang Brauchitsch, with Guderian listening through an earpiece, faithfully to relay this message to the army commander-in-chief. Brauchitsch listened but refused point blank to yield. According to Guderian, 'he was, plainly, not allowed to make a decision. In his answer he ignored the actual difficulties, refused to agree to my proposals and ordered that the attack continue.'[20]

The gulf between what OKH still required of Bock's forces and what they were now capable of achieving was almost unbridgeable. Halder, who was still as obsessed as Bock had been hitherto with the need to reach Moscow by Christmas, was no more willing to absorb unwelcome facts than the malleable Brauchitsch. On 18 November, when Bock gave him a bleak appraisal of the military realities on the ground, the army chief of staff retorted, '[W]e must understand that things are going much worse for the enemy than for us and that these battles are less a question of strategic command than a question of energy'.[21] Halder was soon to be severely tested on both counts.

Soviet commanders were no less apprehensive. On 14 November Zhukov was summoned to the phone. Stalin was on the line. He asked the Western Front commander when he thought Bock's forces were likely to renew the offensive on the capital. Zhukov said he expected the attack to begin very soon from the north-west towards Klin and Istra (respectively eighty-five and fifty kilometres from Moscow) and, if Guderian were able to bypass Tula, from the south-west as well.

The ravages of the first four months of the war had cost the Red Army a horrifying total of 3 million casualties. These losses had been partially offset by a mass call-up of new recruits and reservists. But a rapid increase in the flow of reinforcements from the east of the Urals, and especially from Siberia – which was no longer threatened by the Japanese – made an even greater contribution. By the end of November, the Red Army was to number 4 million. At the start of the month, however, the 2,500-kilometre front between Leningrad and Rostov was manned by a total of 2.2 million troops. The threat still seemed potent.

As commander of the newly established Western Army Group, Zhukov was very far from complacent. With four armies (22nd, 29th, 30th and 31st) deployed at Kalinin, under General Konev's command, to protect his northern flank and two armies (3rd and 13th) under Timoshenko to secure the Southwestern Front, he had a further six armies (5th, 16th, 33rd, 43rd, 49th and 50th) to bear the brunt of the German onslaught expected from the west and the north-west. Since his appointment, he had reinforced, restructured and repositioned his forces, marshalling them at the main pressure points along this 600-kilometre front line. Under his own iron-fisted leadership, a 65,000-strong militia was now guarding the multi-tiered defensive ring around the city itself. The Stavka was hurriedly creating a further substantial reserve of nine armies (drawn from reinforcements from the Far East).

However, Zhukov still believed that his armies were not yet strong enough to guarantee that Army Group Centre's panzers could be blocked. He was dismayed, therefore, when Stalin now urged him to mount a series of major spoiling operations to disrupt Bock's imminent final thrust on the capital. 'We don't have any available troops in the Army Group,' Zhukov warned him. 'We have merely enough to hold the lines we are now occupying.' Stalin was not pleased and pressed the point. Zhukov repeated, 'We cannot do that now. We cannot send the Army Group's last reserves into uncertain counter-attacks. We won't have reinforcements for our armies when the enemy throws his strike groups into the offensive.' Stalin grew irritated: 'You have six armies in your Group. Isn't that enough?' Again, Zhukov demurred. Stalin cut the conversation short: 'Consider the question of the counter-attacks settled. Report your plan tonight.'[22]* And with that he put the phone down. Fifteen minutes later Zhukov's commissar, Nikolai Bulganin, hurried to Zhukov's office. 'Well, I really got it hard this time,' he said, explaining that Stalin had just rung him to say, 'You and Zhukov seem

---

* Zhukov's account is contested by others, notably General P. A. Belov (P. A. Belov, *Za Nami Moskva* (For Us Moscow) (Voen. izd-vo, 1963), pp. 40–43). Belov was to claim that he originated the idea, that Zhukov then approved it and persuaded Stalin to adopt it.

to be getting quite a high opinion of yourselves. But we'll find a way of dealing with you.'²³★

Zhukov could delay no longer. Within two hours he was on the phone to the commander of the 16th Army, Lieutenant General Konstantin Rokossovsky, who was one of the Red Army's most revered figures. After fighting with distinction during the Russian Civil War, Rokossovsky had been arrested during Stalin's Great Purge. Accused of being a traitor, he had been imprisoned and severely tortured but, after refusing to sign a false confession, he was reprieved. After the fiasco of the Winter War against Finland, he was soon in the front line again, serving under Marshal Timoshenko (who had replaced the disgraced Pavlov as commander of the Western Front). His courage, resolution and operational judgement led Stalin to appoint the former 'traitor' to his present senior command. Zhukov, though, was in no mood to exchange pleasantries. Even by his own standards he was aggressive, peremptorily ordering Rokossovsky to mount an immediate counter-attack against Hoepner's 4th Panzer Group, which was poised to seize the initiative once again. Rokossovsky had prepared his defences in depth with great care. Knowing that his forces were outnumbered and outgunned, he was alarmed at the prospect of mounting what he judged to be an ill-advised counter-offensive. He asked that the order should be cancelled, or at least postponed. He was overridden. The humiliation left him uncomprehendingly resentful: 'The commander [Zhukov] knew well enough what the situation was. What he was thinking of when he gave the order to attack, I do not understand.'²⁴

Rokossovsky sent his men into battle on 16 November. At great cost, they managed to advance some three kilometres before the superior might of the German forces brought them to a standstill. Forced to commit two mechanized cavalry divisions simply to hold the line, he then ordered up a mounted division – the 44th Mongolian – in the hope of forcing a way through the enemy's tanks and artillery. Like extras in a filmed re-enactment of the Crimean War, three rows of cavalry galloped

---

★ Bulganin later served as prime minister under Nikita Khrushchev. In 1956 they made a ten-day visit to Britain at the invitation of the prime minister, Anthony Eden. It was the first visit by the Soviet leadership since the revolution. Large crowds came to see them. Wags covering the visit complained it became impossible 'to see the Bulge for the Khrush'.

towards the German lines across open ground that was hard-packed with snow. The horsemen leant forward, their sabres glittering, as they rode directly into a barrage of enemy fire. An astonished German soldier, serving in the 106th Infantry Division, described the carnage that ensued:

> The first shells exploded in their midst and soon a thick black cloud hung over them. Torn scraps of men and horses flew into the air. It was difficult to distinguish one from the other. In this hell the maddened horses were running about wildly. The handful of survivors was finished off by artillery and machine-gun fire. And then out of the wood a second wave of horsemen rode to the attack. It was impossible to imagine that after the annihilation of the first squadrons the nightmare sight would be repeated. But our guns were now zeroed in on the target, and the destruction of the second wave of cavalry took place even more quickly than the first.[25]

The Germans were to claim that they killed 2,000 men without losing a single life. Zhukov, reflecting on his contretemps with Stalin but not on the fact that, to save his career (and perhaps his skin), he had caved in to the Soviet leader, merely observed in self-absolution: 'These counter-attacks, carried out mainly by cavalry, had, of course, no serious consequence because they were not strong enough to affect the enemy's shock forces. The counter-attacking forces suffered losses and, at a crucial moment, they were not where they were most needed.'[26]

As Rokossovsky had feared, the 16th Army was hounded by forward units of a reinforced Panzer Group 4 and forced to withdraw once more. 'The 16th of November was a calamity,' one Soviet soldier, Anatoly Shvebig, noted, 'Many of our forward units were surrounded by the enemy, and Rokossovsky himself was desperately trying to avoid encirclement. The Germans got on the road from Volokolamsk [130 kilometres north-west of the capital] to Moscow and we had virtually nothing left to stop them.'[27] The word 'virtually' was not without significance. Among the many units determined to defend Moscow was the 316th Rifle Division led by Major General Ivan Panfilov. A Soviet myth was to be woven around this future Hero of the Soviet Union, which, even when untangled, provides evidence of a resolve – also shown by many other units – which might fairly be described as 'heroic'.

One of Panfilov's anti-tank platoons – twenty-eight men – was dug in on the Volokolamsk Highway, a little over a hundred kilometres from the capital. On 16 November they came under a prolonged aerial bombardment. Soon afterwards a detachment of German infantry armed with sub-machine guns bore down upon their trenches. They were driven off. Shortly afterwards, the Germans tried again, this time supported by a squadron of tanks. Once again they were driven off, but soon returned with even more tanks. It was at this point that their commissar, Vasily Klochkov, already severely wounded, reportedly grabbed two or three hand grenades and threw himself under a tank, crying, 'Russia is vast, but there is nowhere to retreat – we have our backs to Moscow.' According to the myth, not only did Panfilov's men destroy a large number of tanks – the precise total was never verified – but all twenty-eight of them were killed in the battle. (This, of course, would have made it hard to confirm Klochkov's last words.)[28]

In fact some of the men survived and withdrew into the surrounding woods, perhaps to tell their tale but certainly to be reprimanded for retreating without permission. Nor had all of them died on the same day or in the same battle. Two were taken prisoner and two escaped, one of whom found his way back to Ukraine, where he lived quietly in his village under German occupation until the end of the war, when he was arrested as a 'collaborator'.[29] It is also alleged that Panfilov's own resolve to oversee a suicidal defence of this stronghold on the road to Moscow was stiffened by a phone call from Zhukov warning him 'to stand fast or face a firing squad'.[30] Panfilov's status was immortalized on 18 November when he was cut down by a shell splinter as he addressed a group of war correspondents.[31]*

Volokolamsk formed the backdrop for another legend about which there was somewhat less ambiguity. On 17 November, the Stavka issued Order No. 428, which demonstrated with brutal clarity that, in the defence of the Motherland, no measure was too extreme, even if the victims were its own children. In order to drive the advancing enemy

---

* The facts, whatever they may have been, were never allowed to get in the way of the story. Sixty-five years later, in 2016, the director of Russia's State Archive of Socio-Political History, Sergei Mironenko, made the mistake of calling the myth of the 'Panfilov 28' a deliberate falsification. He left his post soon afterwards. The Russian Culture Minister declared that, even if the story had been an invention and Panfilov had never existed, 'this is a sacred legend that shouldn't be interfered with. People who do that are filthy scum.'

out of the villages they had occupied, and to force them 'to freeze to death in the open', the army was instructed to 'burn and destroy all centres of population for a distance of 40–60 kilometres behind the German front lines and for a distance of 20–30 kilometres to the right and left of roads'.[32] This was a task, above all, for the partisans. Among these was an eighteen-year-old member of the Young Communist League called Zoya Kosmodemyanskaya, who was among the 20,000 or so who volunteered from across the Soviet Union to fight the Germans in the first days of the Great Patriotic War.

Women were not only labouring with picks and shovels to construct Moscow's defensive ring or tending the wounded at the front as nurses; as the demand for soldiers intensified, it was realized that women could play a full part on the battlefield as well. This was less from a commitment to gender equality than from desperate need. Invariably known as 'the girls', and perpetually subjected to machismo and sexist taunts by their male counterparts, they had to prove themselves in extremis. And they did. Women became fine pilots, flying long-range bombers on distant night raids; they were among the most patient and clear-sighted snipers; and as saboteurs and partisans, they showed themselves to be easily as resourceful and zealous as their male counterparts.

As a member of a sabotage unit, charged to implement Order No. 428, Kosmodemyanskaya entered the village of Petrishchevo, near Volokolamsk, armed with a pistol and petrol bombs. In her fanatical urge to destroy the enemy, she evidently gave little thought to the fact that the village had not been abandoned and that – like the further ten that her unit was ordered to raze within the week – it was still occupied by children, their mothers and the elderly as well as German soldiers. Nor did she reckon with the anger that units like hers would arouse among these unfortunate civilians, who had already lost almost all their possessions except the roof over their heads. One evening, as she prepared to set light to a barn, she was 'betrayed' and captured.

As the German soldiers began to torture Zoya, two of the peasants who had lost their homes in the arson attack joined in the beatings. One of them shouted, 'Who were you harming? You burned my house down and did nothing to the Germans.' The saboteur was then led to a scaffold, a sign hanging around her neck which read 'Arsonist of homes'. A crowd gathered at the gallows to watch her execution. According to witnesses, she shouted, 'Citizens! Do not stand there! Do not watch! You need to help us to fight! This is my death. This is my achievement!' A German officer punched her. Others took photographs as she continued her harangue. As the noose was placed around her neck, she was said to have declared, 'No matter how many of us you hang, you can't hang us all. There are 170 million of us. For me, my comrades will take revenge on you.'

Those were her last words. Her body was left to swing in the breeze for a month for German soldiers to desecrate. On New Year's Eve, a group of drunken soldiers removed her clothing and cut off her breasts.[33] Her fate soon became a major propaganda weapon after *Pravda* published a detailed account of her exploits and her execution that greatly impressed Stalin. (She had given her German persecutors a false name; it was only when the *Pravda* article appeared that her real name became known.) A little over two months after her execution – by which time Volokolamsk and the surrounding region had been liberated – Zoya Kosmodemyanskaya was duly declared a Hero of the Soviet Union.★ She was among many such women who would be given this supreme accolade.

The combination of patriotism and coercion that drove the Soviet defenders to extremes of self-sacrifice had begun to shake German morale, exacerbating their grievances at the shortage of nourishing food and – in temperatures that now routinely fell to −30°C – the continued lack of winter clothing. Helmuth Stieff, a staff officer in Kluge's 4th Army, was not ashamed to admit it:

> I am frightened by what might happen here. We have no more reserves, and fresh reinforcements will not arrive before the spring . . . We have got ourselves into a fine mess. And it is infuriating to hear the nonsense our propaganda people churn out. It is astonishing how many fairy tales they are making up. They deride the Russians, again and again. It is as if they are deliberately tempting fate.[34]

Similarly, an infantryman, Ernst Jauernick, wrote:

★ The villagers who had collaborated with the Germans were executed at much the same time.

We have now begun the last great raid on Moscow – but we lack almost everything . . . We receive little in the way of food. In the autumn it was the mud that was our enemy, but this cold may finish us off completely . . . The cold and the gruelling forced marches are pushing us to the edge of insanity . . . [we are] . . . exhausted and miserable.[35]

The temperatures had fallen so low that bread had to be sliced with a hacksaw or broken into pieces with a bayonet before a single piece could be put in a trouser pocket until it had thawed out. Bottles of hot tea froze so fast that they had to be defrosted by the same means and then drunk cold. Only the lice were unaffected. To rid themselves of this curse, the soldiers made fires with brushwood, took off their clothes and fumigated them in the smoke while they stood naked and freezing.

Along with the cold, the filthy living conditions and perpetual hunger, the lice helped spread numerous outbreaks of dysentery. These were so severe that men on the march had repeatedly to fall out of line to relieve themselves. Because of the freezing temperatures, the medical officer, Heinrich Haape, noted that, in the process, the men 'lost more body warmth than they could afford to lose'. Knowing that a combination of soiled clothing and sub-zero temperatures would exacerbate the ever-present risk of frostbite, and anxious to keep his men fit for battle, he improvised a solution:

Without regard for the niceties, therefore, we cut a slit 10–15cm long in the seats of their trousers and underpants so that they could relieve themselves without removing their garments. Stretcher bearers or their own comrades then tied up the slit for them with a string or thin wire until the operation had to be repeated. All the men had lost weight so the trousers were roomy enough to permit this solution.[36]

Never was the ancient Norwegian adage 'there is no such thing as bad weather, only bad clothes' more pertinent. Some warm clothing did make it to the front, but not nearly enough. As a surgeon, Haape had to deal with numerous cases of frostbite, some of which were terminal. He made a point of recording the cause: each company in his unit had been allocated 'four sets of winter clothing [a quota which allowed for] 'sixteen greatcoats and sixteen pairs of winter boots to be shared among a battalion of eight hundred men!'[37] It was an extraordinary oversight, a direct result of the hubris that had inspired Hitler's ill-conceived and ill-planned venture. In Berlin, the propaganda minister, Goebbels, reacted predictably. Troubled by the likely effect these tribulations could have on German civilian morale he forbade the press to carry any photos that might suggest the troops were other than well equipped, explaining, 'we do not want photos of Russian prisoners wearing coats, when their German guards have none'.[38]

Rokossovsky's left flank at Volokolamsk was starting to collapse and, sixty kilometres to the north-east, his right flank was hard pressed around Klin by Panzer Group 3. Judging that he could not hold the line much longer, Rokossovsky sought permission from Zhukov for a partial withdrawal. His intention was to retreat forty kilometres from Volokolamsk to a defensive line west of the Istra reservoir where the terrain formed the last natural barrier before Moscow on this sector. This tactical retreat, he judged, would also allow him to reinforce the Klin salient. He was confident that Zhukov would approve his proposal. Otherwise, he advised, the Germans 'would hurl back' his defending troops, 'and in close pursuit of our retreating units . . . force both the river and the reservoir'.

Zhukov not only categorically disagreed, but, according to Rokossovsky, 'ordered us to stand to the death without retreating a step'. This so horrified the 16th Army commander that he contacted Shaposhnikov, Stalin's chief of staff, and asked him to overrule Zhukov. Two hours later Shaposhnikov called him back and confirmed that he could indeed proceed with the proposal that Zhukov had so peremptorily rejected. Presuming that the Red Army's chief of staff would have discussed his decision with Stalin, Rokossovsky made urgent preparations for the withdrawal, convinced that, as a result, 'the enemy would smash his teeth on the Istra line of defence' and that the enemy's tanks would 'bog down in an impassable obstacle [while] his motorized units will be unable to make use of their mobility'. Soon afterwards, however, a furious telegram arrived from Zhukov: 'The troops of the Army Group are under *my* command! I revoke the order withdrawing forces to the Istra Reservoir and order that the defence be maintained on the present line without retreating a step backward.'[39]

Zhukov rarely conceded that he was in the wrong. He was never to make any reference to this furious row, but did later admit that 'the enemy drove head on regardless of losses in an effort to break through towards Moscow with its armoured wedges'[40] – which was precisely what Rokossovsky had foreseen.

On or around 19 November – Zhukov could not remember exactly – he was phoned by Stalin. Their exchange went like this:

> Stalin: 'Are you sure we are going to be able to hold Moscow? I am asking with an aching heart. Tell me honestly as a member of the Party.'

> Zhukov: 'There is no question we will be able to hold Moscow. But we will need at least two more armies and two hundred tanks.'

> Stalin: 'I am glad you are so sure. Call Shaposhnikov and tell him you want two reserve armies concentrated. They will be ready by the end of November. But we have no more tanks for the time being.'[41]

On 23 November, units of Panzer Group 3, under General Georg-Hans Reinhardt,* forced their way into Klin against fierce resistance from the 16th Army. His men were not only hungry but also fired by the adrenalin of battle. They scoured barns and sheds and kitchens for food. Those citizens who did not flee took refuge wherever they could find a hiding place. Valentina Ragovskaya's family hid in the cellar. When the soldiers burst into their home, one of them came down the steps holding a hand grenade. He ordered the terrified women and children to come out. When they demanded bread and sugar, Valentina handed over two loaves of bread and a couple of turnips, which was all they had in store. Outside, the soldiers had lit fires, using the furniture they had taken from the surrounding homesteads. They threw chickens into the flames without waiting to pluck them. When the birds were cooked, the ravenous men tore them apart and devoured them. They also slaughtered the family's house cow. 'It was our only cow and a young one at that, and she produced a lot of milk,' Valentina recalled. 'I cried and threw myself on the carcass.' When she remonstrated, the unit's commanding officer overseeing this desecration told her, 'German soldiers do not take foreign property.'[42]

---

* Reinhardt had replaced Hoth, who had been promoted to command the 17th Army in Ukraine early in October.

Though anguish can prompt exaggeration, there was too much widely corroborated evidence to discount these memories. 'The way they treated us!' Vera Iosefovna Makarenko recalled bitterly, adding, 'they hardly regarded us as human beings'. When the Germans arrived at Makarenko's home they stole all the family's food, burned the house down and, for good measure, hanged her husband as well. They also took away her niece for questioning. 'Where is your father?' her interrogator demanded. 'Is he defending the homeland at the front? Or is he a partisan?' In the course of the interrogation, Makarenko alleged, they sought to jog her niece's memory by cutting off one of her fingers.[43]

There was invariably a presumption that any man who hid himself from the German troops had something to hide. It only took one German to be hit by a partisan rifle for all civilians living in the surrounding area to become targets for trigger-happy soldiers: fear and vengeance numbed all other sensibilities. Wilhelm Prüller, a loving father who liked to regurgitate Hitler's views on the Slavs and Jews for the benefit of his young wife and their small son, was shameless about shooting any civilians unfortunate enough to find themselves near his line of fire: 'Armed civilians and suspicious characters on the one hand, wounded on the other – who can wonder if we mow down everything in our path?' he told his family, adding, as though it was a source of amusement, 'It was quite a difficult job to do in the case of two drunk Russians we met.'

Hoepner's Panzer Group 4 was under heavy attack – notably from bombing raids, against which the Luftwaffe's fighters provided little protection – but he sought to rally his commanders. On 19 November he instructed them, 'Russian radio transmission suggests withdrawal. Inform troops: Tireless pursuit! Saves losses, shortens the campaign.'[44] A week later – three days after Panzer Group 3 had seized Klin – Hoepner's forward units entered Istra, only fifty kilometres from the Soviet capital. The city's defenders did not readily yield. The SS Das Reich Division was forced into a sustained bout of murderous hand-to-hand combat with the 78th Rifle Division, which had arrived from Siberia a month earlier, before Rokossovsky's men finally withdrew.

'The resistance of these Soviet soldiers shows a stubbornness and fanaticism we have rarely experienced before,' Lieutenant Ernst Streng noted. 'They dig themselves into circular foxholes that we can only work around with heavy losses. They then throw their hand grenades, fire from holes in the ground and then duck back beneath their earthen shelters.'[45] According to the official diary of Streng's panzer corps, the Siberian rifle division was 'the toughest opponent we have yet met in the eastern campaign. It is well-armed and equipped – and every man is fighting to the death.'[46] More than one of the companies in the SS regiment Der Führer took so many casualties that they were left with only twenty-five men apiece.

The survivors were unforgiving. Many of Istra's inhabitants had fled into the woods, where they dug holes in the rock-hard ground to hide and shelter themselves from the worst of the weather. Others remained behind in the town. Among the latter was a sixteen-year-old girl who was with her music teacher, Mikhaylova, when they were stopped in the street by a group of soldiers. They ordered Mikhaylova to give them her winter coat. She obeyed but made the mistake of yelling at them, 'you bandits'. Her young student watched in horror as one of them shot her in the mouth.[47]

A radio operator, Wilhelm Schröder, was in the first unit to enter the defeated town. 'We did not sleep much that night,' he recalled. 'Today things look different – the town is completely in our hands . . . What we want to know is, what now? Will we continue to advance on Moscow?'[48] It was a good question. Streng had noted that the men in his platoon were 'emaciated by the constant strain, the physical and emotional exhaustion' of non-stop battle. 'Their faces are gaunt, unshaven for weeks, with dark shadows under the eyes and with a bitter turn to the mouth.'[49]

Even the hard-bitten Hoepner began to have doubts. 'We are still pushing forward . . . However my troops are suffering terrible hardships and are close to complete exhaustion,' he noted. He still appeared to believe that victory was within his grasp but – like so many of his querulous peers – he was only too ready to blame others for the increasingly effective resistance that his panzers now faced. The prime object of his censure on this occasion was Kluge. Rokossovsky's last-ditch defence of Volokolamsk had led the 4th Army commander to divert his infantry divisions away from the direct route to Moscow towards the Moskva–Volga Canal, which ran into the city's northern suburbs. But the ever-cautious Kluge doubted whether it was any longer possible to take Moscow and he was unwilling now to squander his diminishing resources on what he regarded as a precarious enterprise, if not a lost cause. Kluge's reluctance to throw all his forces into the struggle dismayed Hoepner, who observed caustically, 'We will need to play all the strings of our instrument to have a last chance of success.'[50]

With each hard-fought step towards the capital, Bock's armies were becoming weaker by the kilometre. With diminishing reserves of men, weapons and reinforcements, they were also running out of fuel, while the weather became colder than ever. The operational and psychological consequences were acute. 'Let me tell you about the recoil mechanism of the guns,' an artillery observer, Lothar Fromm, wrote. 'Minus thirty degrees was seen as the lowest temperature at which efficiency could be maintained. They were frozen up. Crews stood there and tried to make them work time and time again. It didn't happen. The barrel would not come back and the recoil mechanism was unable to move. That was really depressing.'[51] With so many of their trucks destroyed by Soviet artillery or buried under snowdrifts, Kluge's infantry slipped and slid forward through icy conditions in driving winds with barely a pause to rest. They passed captured gun emplacements, bunkers and tank traps where Soviet corpses lay frozen in the snow, blood-encrusted and half-naked, their boots, trousers and greatcoats already plundered by their comrades who had got there before them. In the worst of the weather the men huddled in the deserted enemy trenches. At night, they stumbled into empty villages and tumbled into deserted cottages or barns where they competed with each other to find space on which to lay exhausted limbs.

One of their number, Herbert Lange – who, a mere six weeks earlier, had written proudly of 'the orderly marching columns' that would soon lead on to inevitable victory – was close to despair. 'There was a lot of shoving and jostling, a clamour of angry, loud voices,' he wrote. 'Hunger, cold and fatigue welled up. Our army appeared to be on the brink of mutiny – barely retaining its former discipline and purpose.'[52]

The only escape from this ghastliness was provided by the Wehrmacht radio station: not so much Hitler's rantings or poisonous propaganda from Goebbels (though some relished these) but the music – and especially a haunting song about love and longing and romance underneath the lamplight just beyond the barrack gates. Every night, just before 10 p.m., the sweet allure of 'Lili Marlene' wafted through dugouts and shelters, prompting emotions other than fear and hatred.★ In the words of a young senior lieutenant, Johann Allmayer-Beck, ' "Lili Marlene" became a kind of evening prayer, along all the front.'[53] The prayer showed less and less sign of being answered.

Bock was well aware of the predicament. He had moved his field headquarters to an advanced forward position only a little behind the front and from there, on 23 November, he had warned both Brauchitsch and Halder that 'the eleventh hour' had arrived and that the strength of his armies should 'for heaven's sake no longer be overestimated'.[54] Six days later, on 29 November, despite the fact that his foremost forces had advanced to within forty kilometres of the capital, he was even more downbeat. In a conversation with Halder, he warned, 'if we do not succeed in bringing about the collapse of Moscow's north-western front in a few days, the attack will have to be called off; it would only lead to a soulless head-on clash with an opponent who apparently commands very large reserves of men and materiel; but I don't want to provoke a second Verdun.'[55]†

The Verdun comparison was well made. Although the capital was tantalizingly close, Bock had belatedly been forced to acknowledge that the difference between seeing ramparts and breaching them is as great as that between viewing Everest and conquering it. What had once been a panzer blitzkrieg had become a funereal slog. Since 15 November, Hoepner's and Reinhardt's panzers had only been able to advance at an average of five kilometres a day. And they were being picked off by the Soviet artillery at an unsustainable rate.

At the launch of Operation Barbarossa, Panzer Groups 3 and 4 had 1,630 tanks between them; by the end of November they could muster no more than 240. The infantry was similarly stricken: Army Group Centre's divisions were at half strength, their companies had shrunk on average to between fifty and sixty men and, according to Halder's best estimates, some had been reduced to just ten.[56] So far, Operation Barbarossa had cost the Wehrmacht almost 745,000 casualties, or 23 per cent

---

★ Although now usually associated with Marlene Dietrich's 1945 release, the song was originally recorded by Lale Andersen, whose version sold over a million copies.

† The Battle of Verdun in 1916 was one of the longest and bloodiest of the First World War. The Germans hoped to 'bleed the French to death', but, after ten months and at a cost of 350,000 casualties, their attack was repulsed.

of the original invasion force; of these, more than 250,000 had been killed in battle or died of their wounds.[57] Overall, despite replacements, the Ostheer was short of 340,000 men. Perhaps not surprisingly the army's quartermaster general, Wagner, now advised Halder, 'we are at the end of our personnel and material strength'.[58] There was no evidence that Hitler or his paladins were yet either able or willing to comprehend the implications of this dire situation.

28.   The Fateful Terminus

As the German ranks grew thinner, the Soviet armies grew stronger. Not that Zhukov drew much comfort from that. Although he did not believe that Moscow would fall, the maps he laid out in front of him appeared to offer a dismaying snapshot of the battlefield: 'It gets worse hour by hour,' the commander of the Western Front observed bleakly after the fall of Klin.[1]

The danger seemed clear: 'Our defensive line began to bend inward in an arc, some sectors became greatly weakened, and it looked as if the situation were beyond repair.'[2] There was very little margin for error. Rokossovsky's 16th Army had been forced to fall back steadily from the inner edge of that invasive arc. On 28 November, a unit of Reinhardt's Panzer Group 3 – the 7th Panzer Division – managed briefly to secure a bridgehead at Yakhroma on the Moskva–Volga canal, less than seventy kilometres from the heart of the capital. On the same day the 2nd Panzer Division, part of Hoepner's Panzer Group 4, reached Krasnaya Polyana, a mere thirty-five kilometres from the Kremlin.

Zhukov's reaction was characteristically decisive. He summoned reserves to plug the gaps and sent another peremptory order to Rokossovsky, who had retreated to a new command post a little to the south of Kryukovo, forty kilometres from the capital: 'Kryukovo is the final point of withdrawal. There can be no further falling back. There is nowhere else to fall back. . . . Each further step back by you is a breach of Moscow's defences. All commanders, from juniors to seniors, to be in their places, on the battlefield.'[3]

On 30 November, Zhukov was on the receiving end of another phone call from Stalin. The dictator was under intense strain. He had somehow got it into his head that Hoepner's panzers had taken the town of Dedovsk, which was twenty kilometres south-east of Istra and only forty kilometres from the Kremlin. He was greatly perturbed. 'Did you know that they occupied Dedovsk?' he demanded. Zhukov didn't know. This provoked Stalin to burst out, 'A commander should know what is going on at the front!' Not giving him a chance to reply, he ordered Zhukov to head towards Dedovsk and personally to organize a counter-offensive to retake the city. He then rang off.

Zhukov called Rokossovsky, wanting to know why he had not been told about the fall of such a crucial salient. Rokossovsky was at a loss. Dedovsk was still in Russian hands, he explained, wondering if there might have been some confusion with a village called Dedovo, further to the north-west, where there was indeed a heavy battle in progress. Much reassured, Zhukov at once rang Stalin to clear up the misunderstanding. The Soviet leader did not react as he expected. 'It was like trying to drive a nail into a stone,' the general recalled. 'Stalin was in a towering rage and demanded that I go immediately to Rokossovsky and do everything necessary to see that this miserable village was recovered.'[4]

As usual with Stalin, Zhukov judged in favour of discretion over valour. Rather than provoke the wrath of his mercurially merciless leader, he did as he was told. Accompanied by the commander of the 5th Army, General Leonid Govorov – whose reluctant presence was foisted on him by Stalin – he reached Rokossovsky's headquarters.★ Together, the three generals went to see the commander of the 78th Siberian Rifle Division, General Afanasy Beloborodov, whose troops were hard pressed in the midst of a raging battle near the offending village. He was not pleased to see them. Nor did he appreciate being asked to explain why the Germans had been allowed to take a few houses in a small village on the far side of a deep ravine that was of no tactical significance whatsoever. Zhukov felt unable to explain why it was so. Instead, he ordered the general to send a rifle company and two tanks to retake Dedovo. This was duly accomplished the following day.

While they were engaged on this fool's errand, Stalin, who must have forgotten his earlier order, contacted Zhukov's command headquarters demanding to know why he wasn't in his office. His chief of staff was ordered to summon him back there forthwith. Stalin asked how he proposed to arrest a breakthrough by enemy units on a part of the Central Front which hitherto had been very quiet. Zhukov took immediate steps to plug the gap and then called Stalin to update him. Only at the

---

★ Govorov had replaced General Potapov, who had been taken prisoner during the battle for Kiev in September 1941.

end of the conversation did Stalin ask, 'Well, and what about Dedovsk?' Zhukov responded evenly, merely saying that he had sent two tanks and an infantry company to oust the Germans from a village called Dedovo. Stalin said nothing.[5]

Zhukov was on edge. Soon after the fall of Krasnaya Polyana, he got in touch with Rokossovsky and raged at him, threatening to have him shot for allowing his troops to withdraw. Rokossovsky was badly shaken but Stalin, recovering his equilibrium, reassured the commander of the 16th Army that he had his personal support and that reinforcements would be sent to his front as soon as possible.[6]

On the southern end of Zhukov's front, the 2nd Panzer Army was making slow progress towards Tula, despite Guderian's own deepening doubts about the chances of success. In Moscow, the Stavka feared that Tula might fall. On 22 November – ironically, the day before Guderian was forbidden by Brauchitsch to call off the attack – Shaposhnikov summoned General Boldin to his headquarters. Boldin, who was still recuperating from the wounds he had incurred during his escape from the Vyazma encirclement, had a new assignment: he was to confront Guderian, who, Shaposhnikov told him, 'has even strengthened his onslaught'. Boldin was to take command of the 50th Army and eliminate the threat to Tula, and so seal the road to Moscow from the 2nd Panzer Army.

Crossing over to a large operations map hanging on the wall, Shaposhnikov showed him where Guderian's forces were strategically lined up for a further assault. He pinpointed Yasnaya Polyana, the former estate of the revered author of *War and Peace*, Leo Tolstoy, which lay a little over fourteen kilometres to the south of Tula and which, he fulminated, Hitler's 'vandals' had now occupied: 'Can you imagine . . . [they] have dared to defile the people's holy of holies – the grave of Leo Tolstoy. They are destroying the home where he created his work of genius . . . pillaging his museum and ravaging his estate.'[7]

Guderian's forward units had indeed set up an advance headquarters at Yasnaya Polyana, where they established a medical dressing station, but – he was later to insist – the estate was treated with respect. Apparently infuriated by Soviet allegations to the contrary, he denounced 'the grossest lies', which, he thundered, were designed only 'to prove our alleged barbarity'.[8] There was indeed no evidence that the Germans had defiled

Tolstoy's woodland grave (though a number of dead soldiers were evidently buried nearby), but it may be presumed that the new occupants did not shrink from scavenging for food and firewood from what remained of a once beautiful and bountiful demesne. As most of the great man's most precious valuables had been boxed up and carted to safety well before the arrival of the panzer army, there was little of material value left to be pillaged, though Moscow would subsequently allege that a number of precious manuscripts had been deliberately incinerated. Guderian countered that, while the museum was used to provide living quarters for Guderian's staff, he had ordered all Tolstoy's books to be locked away in two barricaded rooms.

Whatever the truth – which probably lies somewhere between the two extremes of desecration and consecration – Guderian was militarily as determined not to be expelled from Yasnaya Polyana as Boldin was to drive him out. On 28 November Guderian received a cryptic order: 'Successful completion of the battle of Tula.'[9] It was a goal as easy to set as it was hard to achieve. The 2nd Panzer Army's complement of tanks now numbered 150, or 15 per cent of the total number with which Guderian had launched Barbarossa. What was true of the tanks was true of his troops as well. Most combat units in the two infantry corps under his command were well below strength and in some case judged incapable of any offensive action at all.[10] His men were also exhausted. For these reasons, he judged that the assault should be cancelled, and that his army should withdraw to defensible lines and dig in for the winter. But he was under orders to advance.

Heinrici was similarly pessimistic. After months of heavy fighting, his 43rd Corps was close to breaking point; he had lost all but eleven pieces of his artillery and his troops were on the verge of collapse. In the absence of orders to the contrary, however, he pressed on. Unless his men advanced far and fast enough towards Tula from the east, it would be impossible to close the ring around the city which Guderian now planned to snap shut with a last-gasp surprise attack. The 43rd managed to make some progress during the last week of November but at the end of the month, after a fierce Soviet counter-attack, Heinrici was forced to call a halt:

> We are in dire straits right now. The enemy vigorously attacks our newly won positions. Our men are extremely exhausted. And we have

around minus 20C and a freezing wind from the north which blows the snow like clouds across the ground. The situation is as bad as never before and we dread the most unpleasant consequences. The situation is especially threatening because our troops are at the end of their tether . . . We know only one thing: it cannot go on like this on a permanent basis. The losses are very high; the strain on our men is beyond the power of human endurance.[11]

Guderian had repeatedly asked Bock for reinforcements that didn't exist. Though he knew that the panzer commander's demands were by no means outrageous, Bock was so wearily exasperated that, on 30 November, he sent Guderian a telex telling him that such requests were 'futile'.[12]* On the same day, he came under renewed pressure from OKH, where Brauchitsch and Halder still insisted that a mammoth encirclement of Moscow was not only possible but also essential to victory. Not for the first time, Bock told Brauchitsch that Guderian's army was 'exhausted' and that the capture of Tula was at the very limit of what it could achieve. It was to no avail. Hitler was impatient to announce publicly that Moscow had fallen. For Brauchitsch, that was enough. He clung to the Führer's manifestly absurd vision with such tenacity that Bock could only conclude that the High Command was deaf to the facts. 'Several times I had to ask if Brauchitsch was even still listening,' he noted impotently.[13]

On the following day, 1 December, still seething at Brauchitsch's obstinacy, Bock decided to confront Hitler's fantasies head-on, but without mentioning the Führer by name. In a remarkably candid appraisal of Army Group Centre's critical state, he did not hold back:

In spite of repeated inquiries and reports, sent to the Army High Command by the army group calling attention to the alarming state of its forces, it was decided that the attack should be continued, even at the risk of units being completely burned out . . . The attack will after further bloody combat, result in modest gains and will also defeat elements of the enemy forces, but it will scarcely have a strategic effect. The fighting of the last 14 days

---

* The telex was a system originally devised in Germany during the 1920s for transmitting text-written messages by shortwave radio. A precursor of the fax and e-mail, it could transmit at a rate of more than sixty words a minute. Its use was not yet widespread.

has shown that the notion that the enemy in front of the army group had 'collapsed' was a fantasy. Halting at the gates of Moscow . . . is tantamount to heavy defensive fighting against a numerically far superior foe . . . The forces of the army group are not equal to this, even for a limited time. And even if the improbable should become possible . . . my forces would not nearly be sufficient to encircle Moscow and seal it off . . . The attack thus appears to be without sense or purpose, especially since the time is approaching when the strength of the units will be exhausted.[14]

His jeremiad had no effect. Later that day the OKH forwarded to him a specific query from the Führer about the deployment of one of Kluge's divisions, which, to Bock, demonstrated yet again 'a completely false appreciation of the 4th Army's forces'. This time Bock remonstrated with Halder, complaining that 'it was astounding how little the highest levels of command were informed of my reports . . . As I have reported a hundred times, I lack the forces to encircle the enemy.'[15]

Halder's mealy-mouthed and buck-passing response was to reassure Bock that 'we, too, are concerned about the human sacrifice', but in the same breath to instruct him that 'an effort must be made to bring the enemy to his knees by applying the last ounce of strength. Once it is conclusively shown that this is impossible, we shall make new decisions.'[16] In so far as this exhortation made any operational sense at all, this was tantamount to a demand that Bock's armies should fight on until they were themselves on their knees. Tactically it was so incoherent as to be devoid of meaning; strategically it was, in effect, to play Russian roulette with a fully loaded weapon. But, on the following day, with little other choice than to resign, Bock buckled, sending a telex message to every corps under his command telling them that 'the serious moment of crisis that the Russian defenders are facing must be exploited wherever the opportunity presents itself'. In a diary note he added, 'I have my doubts whether the exhausted units are still capable of doing so.'[17]

Guderian shared those doubts with even greater intensity but he too knuckled under. After consulting his senior officers, he decided to demand one more sacrifice from the last reserves of his depleted forces for a final assault against Tula on 2 December. His plan involved two shock groups approaching from opposite directions to meet up some ten kilometres north of Tula and thus complete the encirclement.

For a brief moment, it appeared they might triumph. Spearheaded by three panzer divisions, advancing from the east, the attack took Boldin's 50th Army by surprise. Breaching the Soviet positions in two places, they fought their way through a blizzard on icy roads and on the next day managed to cut both the road and the rail link between Tula and Moscow. But their hold was fragile. Guderian knew that without greater support they would almost certainly be driven back.

None of Guderian's misgivings or Bock's forebodings were yet apparent to the Soviet High Command in Moscow. From his headquarters in central Tula, where he was in conclave with the local communist party leader, General Boldin listened to the ominous roar of not-so-distant gunfire. The official, who had overseen the formation of several workers' battalions to defend the city, was at a loss. 'What shall we do now?' he asked. Boldin, keen to stiffen morale, was robust: 'We'll just go on defending Tula as before, and go on killing Fascists.'

As soon as it became clear what was happening, Boldin called up Colonel Siyazov, the commander of the 258th rifle division, which was stationed in a village just to the north of Tula. Bellowing into a field telephone, he ordered, 'Mikhail Alexandrovich, take immediate steps to clear the Germans off the Moscow highway!' The commander, who could barely hear him against the cacophony of surrounding gunfire, asked him to repeat his message. Boldin had to spell out every word, letter by letter, before Siyazov got the message. A faint voice came back: 'Comrade General, your order will be carried out.' Boldin would later claim that he had no doubt that the counter-attack would be effective. Others were less confident.

When the inevitable call came through from Moscow, Boldin knew it would be Zhukov and that the Western Army Group commander would be in aggressive mood:

> I felt it would be an unpleasant conversation. And so it was. 'Well, Comrade Boldin,' Zhukov said in a voice heavy with sarcasm, 'this is the third time [after Białystok and Vyazma] you've managed to get yourself encircled. Isn't it rather too much? I already told you to move your headquarters ... But you were pig-headed, wouldn't carry out my order.'

Boldin, who was one of the few who was not frightened of Zhukov's wrath, retorted, 'Comrade Commander, if I and my staff had left, Guderian would already be here. The position would be much worse than it is now.'[18] Zhukov backed off, promising further tank reinforcements to ensure that the panzers could be driven off the main Moscow–Tula highway.

On the same day, 3 December, Guderian paid a visit to the headquarters of Heinrici's 43rd Corps. If the pincers were to close around Tula, it was essential for his forces to link up with the panzer units straddling the main road to Moscow. Heinrici told Guderian what he already knew: his infantry divisions had been pushed to the limits of endurance; they were half-frozen and always hungry; they slept – if they slept at all – on ground so cold that many fell sick with bladder and bowel infections; and growing numbers could no longer stomach the thought of another day of fighting and probably of dying in vain. To avoid this fate, some of his men, including those who had impeccable military records, had turned to self-mutilation. Others were on the verge of mutiny. One of Heinrici's regimental commanders, Colonel Otto Drescher, had warned him, 'Our men are in such a state that I cannot rule out that someone might point a gun against his own officer because he is truly desperate and loses his head.' A number of rank and file soldiers complained to Heinrici in person. 'Why did the 2nd Panzer Army order us to attack without being sure they could come to support us?' they asked. 'Now our blood sacrifices are in vain; why do they send us out to fight a winter war with insufficient clothing and to face challenges that are beyond human strength? Does anybody know what's going on here?'

Guderian was sympathetic, telling Heinrici that he had heard much the same from other commanders and that he was aware that 'units were depleted everywhere at a catastrophic level and the fighting morale of the divisions was lowered extremely'. However, he explained that when he had complained to Bock, 'he was not met with understanding and approval'. Similarly, he had 'failed to convince even higher authorities [Brauchitsch] to give the order to cancel the operation'.[19]

Like Bock and Guderian, Heinrici decided he had no option other than to persist with an operation that all three knew was almost certain to founder. Guderian ordered Heinrici to fight his way through the enemy forces lined up to the west of Tula and link with the 5th Panzer Brigade, which was now in tenuous occupation of the Moscow–Tula highway. If he succeeded, Tula would be encircled and the road to the capital would be open. Heinrici promised to do his best. On 4 December, forward units of 43rd Corps duly began to plod zombie-like towards the main highway north of the city. The temperature was again plummeting towards −30°C.

The 5th Panzer Brigade was a brigade in name only. With just thirty tanks at his disposal, its commander, Colonel Heinrich Eberbach, was about to face the reinforcements sent by Zhukov to support Boldin: a Soviet armoured brigade which included more than seventy of the vastly superior T-34 tanks. Without the support of 43rd Corps, these would be impossible odds. Lieutenant Hermann Hoss, who was with Eberbach as he faced this crisis, could hear the distant sound of the Soviet armour rumbling south towards their positions. 'Our line is dangerously thin. If they attack en masse they will simply roll over us . . . We are freezing in our thin uniforms – more and more of our soldiers are getting frostbite. Fresh Siberian troops are being thrown into battle against us. They are well trained – their equipment is excellent,' he noted.[20] The colonel's hope of holding his position rested on the arrival of Heinrici's infantry.

Late in the afternoon of the 4th, Boldin was at his headquarters in Tula when he received a call from the front. It was Colonel Siyazov, whom he had instructed to call him every hour to report on the course of the battle. Siyazov was exultant. After nineteen hours of sustained combat, his men had managed to make contact with Zhukov's reinforcements. The panzers had been driven off the main road. 'Traffic may be resumed along the Tula–Moscow highway,' he confirmed with understated delight.[21] It was a pivotal moment, operationally, psychologically and symbolically. The struggle for Tula was not quite over but the denouement was only hours away.

Heinrici's army corps, supported by one of Kluge's infantry divisions, made contact with elements of Boldin's 50th Army in the early hours of 5 December, but the attack petered out almost immediately. As he drove from his field headquarters towards the front, Heinrici passed his own soldiers coming the other way. They claimed to have been sent into the rear suffering from severe frostbite. He came across others huddling around small fires in a clearing. They were clearly broken men. He did his best to urge them towards the front, telling them that Guderian's panzers were only a few kilometres away and that once they made contact, Tula would be encircled. He told himself that his little homily seemed to give them cheer, but as he looked at his men – 'these frozen, poorly clothed, starved, unwashed and dirty people' – he reflected that 'if the Russian saw these people he would not have a lot of respect'.[22] Soon afterwards, he accepted the inevitable. On the afternoon of 5 December – to the relief of his exhausted troops, some of whom, of their own accord, had already started to retreat – he decided to abandon the attack.

Throughout that day, Guderian was on the receiving end of similarly bad news from every quarter. With temperatures hovering around −35°C, tank engines failed to start, oil solidified in machine guns, trucks broke down, food and other supplies did not reach the front. In short, the 2nd Panzer Army was effectively immobilized.[23] That evening the disconsolate general called Heinrici to tell him that – for the first time since the start of the Second World War – he had unilaterally decided to call off an operation. The 2nd Panzer Army was to retreat. 'The circumstances', he said, 'are stronger than the will.'[24]

Guderian, who was as willing to lay the blame on others for his own shortcomings as he was to disobey orders of which he disapproved, characteristically chose to exculpate himself from any responsibility for his failure to take Tula. Yet, aside from complaining about a shortage of supplies and the adverse weather, he had not openly challenged Bock when ordered to continue his faltering advance. Nor had he hesitated to urge his commanders to fight on despite the exhaustion of their men; and he had only called a halt to the operation when it had already been thwarted. Though he would blame those above him in the chain of command, he shared a heavy burden of responsibility for pursuing a goal long after it was clear to him that it was unachievable.

The withdrawal was not orderly. As Guderian's soldiers fell back, they came under heavy fire and, in many cases, the retreat became a rout. Men were cut down as they fled. Discipline collapsed. Several units panicked. Erich Hager, serving in the 17th Panzer Division, described a common humiliation: 'Our infantry [was] involved in lots of firing during the night. The Russians attacked twice. Infantry made a run for it, lost all vehicles. Officers all dead. Infantry could get back into the village, but not much point in that, the vehicles are all gone . . . They've had enough.'[25]

The 2nd Panzer Army was not alone. On the north-western approaches to Moscow, Reinhardt's Panzer Group 3 had fought its way slowly southwards along the Moskva–Volga Canal but, after inching forward and taking heavy casualties, Hoepner's Panzer Group 4 could make no further progress. As in the south, so in the north: the troops were almost literally on their last legs. In many cases, their morale had sunk so low that they were not only reluctant but also at the point of refusing to obey orders. Commanders in 10th Panzer Division reported that 'it was no longer possible, even with the harshest measures, to get the troops forward to attack . . . The decisive point is the complete physical and psychological exhaustion of the troops.'[26] That was not an isolated incident. On 2 December a regimental colonel serving in the 23rd Infantry Division reported, 'Two of my battalions have refused to advance any further. The losses in officers and men have simply become too high – there is hardly any ammunition left.'[27] Operation Typhoon had blown itself out.

Yet, in their purblind faith that the Führer's will would inevitably triumph over momentary adversity, the Wehrmacht's most senior commanders were still unable to contemplate the ignominy of failure. With Guderian's 2nd Panzer Army in retreat, Kluge's 4th Army on the defensive and both Panzer Groups 3 and 4 down to their last reserves, a similar hubris had seemed to infect even Bock, who had warned his superiors so often of what had now befallen his armies. As though merely to engage in battle presented a simulacrum of victory even in the midst of defeat, he refused to call off the offensive. It was to be resumed on 6 December.

For a time Hoepner continued to urge his men forward, promising that 'the goal can still be reached'.[28] On 3 December, however, he warned the commander of the 4th Army, Kluge, that unless OKH called off the attack, his panzer group would be 'bled white' and would be unable to defend itself against Soviet counter-attacks.[29] On the same day he told Bock that his 'offensive strength was largely at an end'.[30] Two days later, on 5 December, Reinhardt delivered the same bleak message about Panzer Group 3, that 'its offensive strength is gone'.[31]

Bock was now in a grave military quandary. Alarmed by Brauchitsch's failure to give Hitler 'the unvarnished truth' about the predicament facing his armies, he decided to go over his commander-in-chief's head and confront the Wehrmacht's head of operations. 'The attack is still ordered for the entire front,' he told Jodl but in the same breath he warned that 'the hour is in sight when the troops will be exhausted'. However, 'going over to the defensive' so belatedly against the rapidly growing might of Zhukov's armies now ringing Moscow would expose his forces to devastating counter-attacks. For this reason, he told Jodl, he had decided to pursue what he had once described as 'my mission' to the bitter end: the assault would not be called off.[32] What he did not tell Jodl, and apparently failed to admit to himself, was that the fate of the 'Battle for Moscow' was no longer in his hands. By not calling a halt earlier, he had handed the initiative to Stalin and the Soviet High Command.

This unpalatable truth was now evident to all three of Bock's panzer leaders. On 5 December, Reinhardt was warned by the commander of 41st Panzer Corps that a successful attack 'can no longer be expected of the corps'.[33] At this point, like Guderian in the south, Reinhardt now decided unilaterally to halt Panzer Group 3's attack. On the same day, Panzer Group 4's War Diary reported that the troops were 'lacklustre and in alarming masses indifferent'.[34] Bock, who still appeared to think that all was not lost, consulted the commander of the 4th Army to ask if Hoepner's attack, scheduled for the following day, should go ahead. Kluge's answer was blunt and brief: 'it should not'.[35] That was it. Even Bock was now obliged to concede that Operation Typhoon had run its course.

For those of his troops who still had faith, this was a crushing blow. Some may have glimpsed the Moscow skyline in the far distance though none could claim, except with the exercise of a lively imagination, that they had seen the spires of St Basil's Cathedral through their field glasses. This did not prevent the growth of a small archive of similar sightings. As David Stahel has pointed out, 'The only German soldiers who ever saw the Kremlin in the Second World War were being paraded past it as prisoners of war.'[36] Nevertheless, one or two legendary accounts fuelled the enduring Nazi myth that the Third Reich was poised for victory only to have it snatched away at the last moment. Of these, one of the most famous and least likely to be false was provided by the military surgeon Heinrich Haape, who described how he and a small group of men had reached a remote tram stop a mere sixteen kilometres from the centre of the city. 'We stopped and stared at the wooden seat on which thousands of Muscovites had sat and waited for the tram to clang down the road from Moscow,' he wrote. 'There was an old wooden bin attached to the wall. I felt inside and dragged out a handful of old tram tickets. We picked out the Cyrillic letters which by now we knew spelled "Moskva".'[37]

The truth was, the main body of Bock's troops never got closer than between twenty-five and thirty kilometres from the city. They were not even close enough to consider wasting their severely depleted supply of artillery shells by hurling them vainly at the unseen gates of Moscow. After five months, three weeks and six days, Operation Barbarossa had reached its fateful terminus. Though it might at times have seemed otherwise, the capital had never been in danger of falling. Bock seemed almost to concede this when, on 7 December, he reflected on the 'serious crisis' that now confronted him. It had been right, he concluded, to order 'the ruthless pursuit of the enemy' for so long as 'the Supreme Command believed that he was fighting for his life with the very last of his forces', but it had been a mistake to insist that 'the effort to decisively defeat him in one short push was worth "the ultimate sacrifice" . . . the army group is now forced to go over to the defensive under the most difficult conditions'.[38]

Retreat was now inevitable. The ignominy was complete. Like Bock, Halder was close to despair. Like Bock too, he was unwilling to shoulder any of the blame. Instead he passed the buck up the line. 'The occurrences of the day have again been heartbreaking and humiliating,' he wrote on 7 December, adding – with an acknowledgement of a truth he had hitherto concealed even from himself – 'ObdH [OKH] is now no more than a messenger boy. The Führer, over the heads of the ObdH, gets in direct touch with the commanders of the army groups. But worst of all, the Supreme Command does not realize the conditions our troops are in and indulges in paltry patchwork where only big decisions could help.'[39]

Almost as afterthoughts, both Bock's and Halder's diary entries for that day ended with a brief and almost identical prediction. In Halder's words, 'Japan: A conflict with the US possibly imminent.'[40]

29. A Global War

Soon after daybreak, on Sunday, 7 December 1941, the Second World War became a truly global conflict. At Chequers, Churchill was elated. Not by the fact that the Nazis had been rebuffed at the gates of Moscow, which he barely noticed, but by the news that Japan had bombed the United States naval base at Pearl Harbor. He was at dinner with the US ambassador, John Winant, and Averell Harriman, the president's special envoy, when he switched on his small wireless set and half-listened to the BBC's nine o'clock news. Fortuitously, the butler entered the dining room a moment later and confirmed, 'It's quite true. We heard it ourselves outside. The Japanese have attacked the Americans.' More than 350 Japanese dive-bombers had sunk or inflicted serious damage on nineteen US warships – including eight battleships, three cruisers and three destroyers – and 347 aircraft. During the raid, 2,403 US personnel had been killed and a further 1,178 wounded.[1]

Churchill left the table at once to put a call through to the US president. 'It's quite true. They have attacked us at Pearl Harbor. We are all in the same boat now,' Roosevelt told him.[2] This, though he would put it more decorously in public, was an answer to the prime minister's heart-felt prayers. Britain's fortunes had been transformed. Blessed by a military and industrial potential which far exceeded that of any other protagonist, the United States was no longer simply an ally but a co-belligerent bent on the same objective. For Churchill, after 'seventeen months of lonely fighting', it was a moment of 'the greatest joy' that the United States was now in the war 'up to the neck and in to the death'. There could now be no other outcome than victory. 'We had won the war,' he wrote. 'Hitler's fate was sealed. Mussolini's fate was sealed. As for the Japanese, they would be ground to powder.'[3] In that spirit, he took him-self to bed, 'saturated and satiated with emotion and sensation . . . and slept the sleep of the saved and thankful'.[4]

The following day, 8 December, Congress formally declared war on Japan. Three days later – in the belief that American support for the British and Soviet armies would be weakened thereby – Hitler declared war on the United States. It was an act of hubris: a calculated gamble that demonstrated his profound lack of strategic judgement. Churchill's cup was overflowing. The balance of war-making power had shifted dramatically away from the Axis towards the Grand Alliance of the United States, Britain and the Soviet Union, or the 'Big Three', as the principals would very soon be known.[5]

The surprise attack by the Japanese and the regime's choice of target caught the Americans off balance, but the worsening relationship between Washington and Tokyo had reached the point of no return many weeks earlier. With diplomacy between the two capitals reduced to declarations of irreconcilable ultimatums, a military conflagration had become inevitable. Churchill's priority now was to ensure that Roosevelt would not yield the 'Germany First' principle which had been painstakingly agreed earlier in the year between the British and Americans against the inevitable clamour for a 'Japan First' strategy.

The so-called ABC-1 agreement, which, after tortuous negotiation, had been signed in Washington in March 1941, contained at its core an undertaking by the American side that, even if Japan and the United States went to war, Europe and the Atlantic should remain the decisive military theatre. The ABC-1 document also implicitly endorsed Britain's imperial commitments in the Middle East, North Africa and the Mediterranean – which all formed part of the 'European' theatre – as well as in the Pacific. Churchill's self-imposed task now was to reassert these principles, knowing that they would face a strong challenge from within the divided counsels of the US administration. Powerful voices in Congress and the military believed with some passion that the White House should put the Pacific War first. With his uncanny instinct for the strategic jugular, Churchill allowed his impetuosity full rein.

On 8 December, two days after Pearl Harbor, the prime minister, discarding the usual diplomatic protocols, cabled Roosevelt, inviting himself to the White House in terms so elegantly insistent that the president, in common courtesy, could not easily rebuff him:

> Now that we are, as you say, 'in the same boat', would it not be wise for us to have another conference? We could review the whole war plan in the light of reality and new facts, as well as the problems of production and distribution. I feel that all these matters, some of which are causing me

concern, can best be settled on the highest executive level. It would also be a very great pleasure to me to meet you again, and the sooner the better.[6]

Roosevelt, who was intently focused on the implications of Pearl Harbor, tried to deter his unwanted visitor by advising Churchill that the return journey across the Atlantic (by which time German Intelligence would know about his mission) would be a dangerous undertaking. Nothing could have been better calculated to strengthen Churchill's resolve: the British bulldog was more determined than ever to charm his way into the Washington china shop.

The Foreign Secretary was on the night train to Scotland when the news of Pearl Harbor was passed to him in the late evening of 7 December. He was bound for Invergordon, from where he was to proceed to the British naval base in Scapa Flow to join HMS *Kent*, which was to take him and his entourage to the Soviet Union to meet Stalin. It was to be the first visit by a British Foreign Secretary since the Russian Revolution and he laid great store by it. Following the bitter exchange of correspondence between Stalin and Churchill in early November,* Eden – with the unlikely benefit of Beaverbrook's assistance – had managed to patch up relations with Moscow via the Soviet ambassador, Maisky. On 20 November Maisky had requested a meeting with the Foreign Secretary. He had a message from Stalin for Churchill, the gist of which was that the Soviet leader had not intended to offend Churchill but that he had been 'greatly hurt' by Britain's refusal to declare war on Finland and had been humiliated by the fact that his secret communications on this issue had been leaked to the British media. It was not quite a climb-down but – as Maisky and Eden had 'plotted' together – it was enough of an apology to mollify the prime minister.[7]

Churchill decided at once to send a personal telegram to Stalin proposing that Eden visit him in Moscow 'to discuss every question relating to the war'. Nothing, it seemed, would be off the table:

Our intention is to fight the war in alliance with you and in constant consultation with you . . . and when the war is won, as I am sure it will be, we expect that Soviet Russia, Great Britain, and the United States will meet at the council table of the victors as the three principal

* See pages 383–5.

partners and agencies by which Nazism will have been destroyed . . .
The fact that Russia is a Communist State and Britain and the United
States are not, and do not intend to be, is not any obstacle to our making
a good plan for our mutual safety and rightful interests. The Foreign
Secretary will be able to discuss the whole of this field with you.[8]

It was as generous as any message that he had ever sent the Soviet dictator and – on the face of it – laden with political and diplomatic import.
Stalin did not hesitate. Eden would be very welcome at the Kremlin.

The prospect of such a visit, originally mooted by Eden himself, had
been in discussion for at least a fortnight before Churchill proposed it
formally. It had, though, been the source of fractious debate within the
government about its purpose and timing. The issues concealed behind
the prime minister's emollient language in his message to Stalin were
complex and controversial. For some weeks, the War Cabinet had been
giddying itself with attempts to reconcile Stalin's demands with Britain's
priorities. The debate in London circled around three pressing dilemmas: should the government declare war on Finland (demanded by Stalin
but opposed by the United States); should Britain send troops as well as
armaments to support the Red Army (urged by Cripps, endorsed cautiously by Eden, but strenuously opposed by the chiefs of staff); and
should Britain discuss the post-war borders of Europe (for which Stalin
was pressing, about which Eden was open-minded and to which Churchill, in line with Roosevelt, was adamantly opposed).

The prime minister had initially been resolute in his refusal to declare
war on Finland, not only because he did not want to rile Washington but
because he had a high regard for the commander of the Finnish armed
forces, Field Marshal Baron Carl Mannerheim. The two men had forged
a bond during the Soviet revolution, when Mannerheim had led a White
Russian cavalry corps against the Bolsheviks. For Stalin, though, this was
a make-or-break diplomatic issue: the Finns were not only fighting alongside the Nazis but also helping to sustain the siege of Leningrad. Under
pressure from the War Cabinet, Churchill agreed to give Helsinki an ultimatum: either 'leave off fighting and cease military operations' or face a
British declaration of war. He loathed putting this gun to Mannerheim's
head, and in a personal plea to him wrote, 'it would be most painful to the
many friends of your country in England if Finland found herself in the

dock with the guilty and defeated Nazis'.[9] Mannerheim rejected this overture, replying that his army's 'operations' were vital for the nation's security but that he would nonetheless be 'deeply grieved if you will consider yourself forced to declare war upon Finland'.[10] The die was cast. Just before Eden's departure for Moscow, Britain issued the declaration of war and conjoined it with a similar declaration against two of Hitler's other military allies, Romania and Hungary.

The question of what kind of material support and how much of it should be offered to Stalin provoked sharper divisions. Britain's armed forces were already stretched to the limit. In addition to maintaining the country's defences on the home front against a Nazi invasion, they were charged to protect its imperial possessions in the Far East (which included Hong Kong, Borneo and Malaya, whose capital, Singapore, was Britain's main military base in the region), East Africa and the Middle East – an area that, for the prime minister, was an overriding priority. At his relentless goading, Auchinleck had finally launched Operation Crusader to drive Rommel's Afrika Korps away from the Egyptian border across the Libyan desert towards Tripoli. On the way, Churchill's 'Army of the Nile' was enjoined to retake Tobruk, which had been under siege for six months. Although this small Mediterranean port had little strategic significance, it had acquired totemic status: routing Rommel in the desert would be of surpassing psychological as well as military importance.

These immediate demands on Britain's limited military resources had to be weighed against a growing realization that Moscow would have to be provided with more material support if Stalin were to be convinced that Britain was seriously committed to the defence of the Soviet Union. On the eve of Eden's visit, the War Cabinet had yet to square this circle and the dithering chiefs of staff had proposed no way of doing so. Towards the end of November, the prime minister abruptly sacked the Chief of the Imperial Defence Staff, Sir John Dill, whom he had long unfairly judged to be pedestrian and dull-witted.* His successor

---

* Dill was reprieved to Britain's great advantage when Churchill appointed him Chief of the Joint Staff Mission to Washington, where he became the senior British representative on the Combined Chiefs of Staff. He revealed himself to be an invaluable diplomat. He formed a close friendship with the US chief of staff, General George Marshall, which in turn led to a highly productive relationship with

was Field Marshal Alan Brooke, who was a far less amenable character. Clever, abrasive and self-assured, he also had a high regard for his own talents and he did not shrink from displaying them.

Within hours of taking up his post on 1 December, he reached the conclusion that Britain was unsustainably overstretched on every front, an assessment that was brought into sharp focus on his third day in office when he was presented with a memorandum from Churchill. This missive proposed that two divisions should be dispatched to the Soviet Union forthwith to support the Russian forces defending the Caucasus. This gesture had been urged on the prime minister by Eden, who hoped to offer it to Stalin at their forthcoming meeting to demonstrate Britain's commitment to the Anglo-Soviet alliance against the Nazis.

Brooke was aghast at the prospect: 'This would probably mean closing down the Libyan offensive [Operation Crusader], whereas I am positive that our policy for the conduct of the war should be to direct both our military and political efforts towards the early conquest of North Africa.'[11] That afternoon, he argued this case so persuasively at the Cabinet Defence Committee that, as he put it, 'we succeeded in riding PM off this suggestion'.[12] His victory had a price however: an off-the-cuff suggestion from Beaverbrook that Stalin should be offered 500 tanks instead.

The next day, with Eden's departure scheduled for 7 December, Brooke was unequivocal. The army could at best afford to send only 300 tanks, and they could not be delivered before June the following year. Moreover, as he made very clear, 'I did not recommend such a gift as we should be seriously denuding this country and prematurely disclosing a new pattern of tank.' That prompted the first of many 'interminable' debates within the Cabinet, which exasperated the new CIGS. The Foreign Secretary was particularly tiresome: 'Anthony Eden [was] like a peevish child, grumbling because he was being sent off to see Uncle Stalin without suitable gifts, while Granny Churchill was comforting him and explaining to him all the pretty speeches he might make instead.'

That evening, following dinner, the chiefs of staff met again. The discussions went round in circles once more. Tanks? Aircraft? How

---

Roosevelt, who came to hold him in high regard. Dill continued to serve in Washington until his death from an auto-immune disease in November 1944 at the age of sixty-two. He was buried with full military honours in Arlington Cemetery.

many? By when? In the end, Churchill flew into a rage and started to rail at his advisors for having no ideas of their own but invariably rejecting any that he advanced. He then slammed his papers shut, closed the meeting and stalked out of the room. 'It was pathetic and entirely unnecessary,' Brooke noted. 'We were only trying to save him from making definite promises which he might find hard to keep later on. It was all the result of overworking himself and keeping too late hours. Such a pity. God knows where we would be without him; but God knows where we shall go with him.'[13] In the end, a compromise of a sort was achieved. In lieu of any troops, Eden would be authorized to offer Stalin 200 tanks and 500 aircraft – so long as the War Office could scrounge them from one or another of Brooke's reluctant legions.

The political purpose of Eden's visit was more contentious still. Even before Stalin's strangulated apology to Churchill, the Foreign Secretary had contemplated drafting an Anglo-Soviet Charter to offer Stalin as a complementary counterpart to the Atlantic Charter (which the Soviet leader had reluctantly approved in August). What this so-called 'Volga Charter' was to contain was unclear, but a fortnight earlier, from his diplomatic outpost at Kuybyshev, Cripps had sent an abrasive 'personal' message to the prime minister, urging a much bolder commitment to the Soviet Union than he had so far even begun to consider:

> Stalin is not convinced that we are in this war with the Russians whole-heartedly and without reservations . . . In spite of frequent warning His Majesty's Government have so far appeared to overlook the fundamental importance of the issues which Stalin regards as touchstones of their sincerity . . . not only during the war when the Russian army is clearly an asset of inestimable value to us, but after the war when our sympathetic collaboration with Russia may be thought by some to be more advantageous to the Soviet government than to us . . . The more this state of uncertainty continues in his mind, the more Stalin will be ready to believe . . . our only object is to keep her fighting the Germans as long as we can.[14]

The rebuke was galling but not too far from the mark. As Churchill put it when he reflected on the Wehrmacht's failure to take Moscow, 'The threat of invasion to our island was removed so long as the German armies were engaged in a life-and-death struggle in the East.'[15]

Under the influence of Cripps, Eden had come to acknowledge that some kind of shared plan for the post-war future of Europe was required; that the relationship between London and Moscow could not flourish on a thin gruel of warm words alone. Churchill was far too astute to dismiss such considerations. Despite what Eden described as 'the prime minister's reluctance to consider post-war problems at all',[16] he was persuaded by the War Cabinet that Stalin should be told that Britain would, in the words of Eden's private secretary, 'co-operate to the full with Soviet [sic] during *and* after the war'. There was, though, a carefully contrived proviso. He was to make it clear to the Soviet leader that it would not be possible at this stage 'to produce a cut and dried scheme of war aims as yet because we haven't got one'. In turn this would make it impossible to discuss in any detail what such co-operation might involve following the end of the war.[17] This was meagre negotiating fare but enough for a diplomat of Cadogan's feline skills to draft an Anglo-Soviet agreement that, with careful imprecision, indicated broadly what a post-war European settlement might look like. But even this modest ploy was too much for the prime minister. At a Cabinet meeting on 27 November he rejected the proposal out of hand, evidently 'without having read a word of it'.[18] The following day, the draft was further watered down to the point where, in Cadogan's words, it had become 'as thin as restaurant coffee'.[19] It was, though, all that Eden was going to be in a position to offer the Soviet leader. His grandiose idea for a 'Volga Charter' was dead.

On 8 December Eden was aboard HMS *Kent* at the British naval base in Scapa Flow on the eve of his departure for the Soviet Union. He was suffering from a severe dose of gastroenteritis and was confined to his bunk for most of the day. His condition was not improved by a call from the prime minister. Churchill was in ebullient mood as he told the Foreign Secretary that he too planned soon to be on the high seas on his way to the United States. According to Eden's personal secretary, Oliver Harvey, his master was 'horrified' by Churchill's plan and tried to talk him out of it. He failed. In despair, he rang the US ambassador, John Winant, who, similarly taken aback, advised that such a visit would not be appropriate until the New Year at the earliest. Harvey too was appalled, noting, 'I am aghast at the consequence of both [Churchill and Eden] being away at once. The British public will think quite rightly that they are mad.' If Eden called off his Moscow mission, however, it would send the wrong message entirely to the Kremlin, since 'it would be fatal to put off A.E.'s visit to Stalin to enable PM to visit Roosevelt. It would confirm all Stalin's worst suspicions.'[20]

Eden persisted. He phoned the deputy prime minister, Clement Attlee, who agreed with him wholeheartedly and undertook to oppose the prime minister's scheme at Cabinet. His objection had no effect: nothing would divert Churchill from his chosen course. When Cadogan spoke to him later that evening, to explain that Eden was 'distressed' at the idea of their both being out of the country at the same time, Churchill brushed him aside, saying, 'That's all right: that'll work very well: I shall have Anthony where I want him.'[21] Though he did not put it quite so bluntly when discussing this personally with Eden, Churchill left him in no doubt that 'a complete understanding between Britain and the United States outweighed all else'.[22] This conviction was reinforced by the Japanese attack on Pearl Harbor and, according to the new CIGS, Brooke, the pressing need 'to ensure that American help to this country does not dry up in consequence'.[23]

Eden's opposition to Churchill's visit had genuine diplomatic validity, but neither was he entirely disinterested, for, as Harvey put it, the prime ministerial trip would 'take all the limelight off the Moscow visit'.[24] The unfortunate Foreign Secretary was not only unwell but also disconsolate as HMS *Kent* set off into rising seas and darkening weather.

The British party of Eden, Cadogan and Harvey, accompanied by Lieutenant General Sir Archibald Nye (the newly appointed Vice Chief of the Imperial General Staff) and a phalanx of officials, set foot on Russian soil on 13 December. Their arrival gave Cadogan (who was not a seasoned traveller) an opportunity to cast his patrician eye over his strange surroundings and its even stranger inhabitants. One of these, an official from the Soviet Foreign Office, 'was alleged to speak English, but it must have been some local dialect unknown to me', he noted disparagingly; Cadogan decided to call him 'Frogface'. However, he was not entirely devoid of aesthetic sensibilities. Although he was disconcerted by 'an unknown lady swathed in fur' who leapt into their car for the trip from the port into Murmansk, saying, 'I komm with you', the view of the town from the top of a hill gave him rare satisfaction: 'The glow on the horizon, on the far side of the town, was still just sufficient to light the snow on the ignoble roofs and it looked really fairy-like.'[25] Eden was similarly and somewhat more elegantly entranced by the view of the harbour from the same vantage point: 'The colour of a pale pearl grey . . . Quite indescribable and unpaintable, the air crisp and fresh. This Arctic scenery has a beauty which is the exact antithesis of the Christmas card of tradition. Soft melting half-tones. Nothing brittle or garish.'[26]

The train journey from Murmansk to Moscow lasted forty-four hours. This afforded the British delegation more than enough time to relish the snow-covered forests and, more pertinently, to study the implications of two telegrams from Churchill that had arrived while they were still at sea and as he was preparing to board HMS *Duke of York* and embark upon a zig-zag crossing of the U-boat-infested Atlantic Ocean. In the first message, on 10 December, the prime minister advised his Foreign Secretary that the room for diplomatic manoeuvre in Moscow would be even less than Eden had hoped. Several factors – among them the decision by the US Navy to withdraw all its battleships from the Atlantic following Pearl Harbor, the prospect of heavy fighting in Libya and the urgent need to reinforce the RAF against a possible Japanese attack on Malaya – had created such uncertainty that 'you should not offer ten squadrons [as he had agreed a week earlier] at present time'.[27]

Churchill's second cable, two days later, contained dire news. The Japanese had sunk the battleship HMS *Prince of Wales* and the battle-cruiser HMS *Repulse*, 110 kilometres off the coast of Malaya, with the loss of 840 crew. This was distressing enough in itself but, more worryingly from Britain's strategic perspective, the Americans 'under [the] shock of Pacific disaster and war declarations [Germany and Italy against the United States] have embargoed everything for the present. I hope to loosen this up, but in present circumstances, with a Russian victory [the successful defence of Moscow] and our new dangers, we cannot make any promises beyond our [previously] agreed quota of supplies.'[28] Eden was to arrive in Moscow bearing no 'presents' with which to appease 'Uncle Stalin'. With his political room for manoeuvre similarly circumscribed by the prime minister, the auguries for what were supposed to be the most important high-level talks between the British and Soviet governments since the start of the war were not promising.

Much had changed in the Soviet Union while Eden had been at sea. The Red Army had not only arrested the German assault on Moscow but also forced Army Group Centre into an ignominious retreat before a full-scale counter-offensive. The speed and ferocity of the Soviet counter-attack, which began on 5 December – the same day that Bock finally conceded that Operation Typhoon had failed – took the exhausted German armies by surprise. Zhukov had presented his plan to Stalin a few days earlier, on 30 November. The Soviet leader annotated it in the margin simply, 'Agreed. J. Stalin'.[1] Reinforced by the Siberian divisions and those of the reserve armies which had not been thrown into the defence of Moscow, Zhukov had more than a million men to launch at an enemy who was demoralized and running out of armour, fuel, weapons and supplies.

His plan was to drive Panzer Groups 3 and 4 out of Istra and Klin, to evict Guderian's 2nd Panzer Army from Tula and to split Kluge's 4th Army in two to the west of the capital, with the eventual goal of opening the way for the Red Army to retake Smolensk. With the support of more than 75,000 guns and mortars, 774 tanks and, crucially, 1,370 warplanes, which, for the first time gave the Russians dominance in the air, Zhukov had marshalled an attacking force that was more than a match for Bock's armies.

Army Group Centre was drained of resolve by a toxic combination of defeat, hunger and extreme cold. Men who had lain in foxholes watching their comrades freeze to death and who themselves had lost fingers and toes to frostbite had little stomach for anything except flight. Some could barely move. Lieutenant Kurt Grumann was at his unit's field-dressing station, where he jotted in his diary, 'Eighty men were brought in here today, half of whom have second or third degree frostbite. Their swollen legs are covered in blisters, and they no longer resemble limbs but rather a formless mass. In some cases gangrene has set in.' He added, 'What is it all for?'[2] In December alone, according to the Wehrmacht's own estimates, the Ostheer suffered 90,000 casualties from causes other than enemy action.[3]

Already tested beyond endurance by their failed attempt to take Moscow, some German units stampeded. 'Out of the snowstorm soldiers were running back, scattering like a panic-stricken herd of animals,' infantryman Albrecht Linsen would recall. 'One lone officer stood against this desperate mass; he gesticulated, tried to pull out his pistol and then simply let it pass. Our platoon leader made no attempt to stop people at all.'[4] As he joined this Gadarene rush, Linsen was hit by shrapnel from a shell which crashed a few feet away from him. He felt a searing pain in his right thigh: 'I thought I am going to die here, twenty-one years old, in the snow before Moscow.' He managed to drag himself along the road watching as his fleeing comrades disappeared into a flurry of snow. He came up to a truck that had veered off the road into a ditch. The driver had fled leaving three or four men behind who were too seriously wounded to move. They waved their hands uselessly in the air as if to attract attention. Linsen limped on. As dusk fell, he stumbled past other stalled vehicles. He saw the lights of a village, which turned out to be occupied by a detachment of troops who had not yet joined the rout. One of their number tended his wound and he was handed an official form testifying that he was no longer fit for service. 'What a wonderful piece of paper! After the hell I had gone through, I felt as if I had received an absolution.'[5]

Hellish images of death and suffering on a scale that might have tested the imagination of Hieronymus Bosch horrified even those responsible for them. Two months earlier, Horst Lange's 56th Infantry Division had formed part of the encircling operation at Vyazma. He had then been contemptuous of the Red Army, and of the growing number of prisoners falling into their hands, observing that he could see 'few intelligent faces' among them. By contrast, as they advanced from Smolensk towards Moscow he had looked with pride on the 'ceaseless uninterrupted flow of our reinforcements, the orderly marching columns . . . the tangible motion and function of our machinery, organized down to the last detail'[6]. Gradually, though, after seemingly endless days on the march, his spirit, like his body, had started to flag. By the time his unit had reached the approaches to Krasnaya Polyana, he was already weary of battle and appalled by visions of the 'underworld' he witnessed in the 'charred ruins' of one victorious struggle:

> We pass Russian emplacements, bunkers, tank traps, and see the bodies of their soldiers – their grey complexions, with a greenish hue, are encrusted in dark red blood. The corpses have been plundered by our

soldiers and are without trousers or boots . . . We are seeing more and more horrendous things, glimpsing terrible images.[7]

Now, as his division retreated from Krasnaya Polyana, he became a semi-detached witness of the gratuitous destruction wrought by an army in retreat: 'We have received an order to burn everything before we leave, and buildings are going up in flames. One house is full of refugees – women and crying children, and they are all absolutely terrified.'[8] Another infantryman, Werner Host, was unnerved by the misery of the civilians whose homes and lives they had been ordered to destroy:

Red tongues of flame shot greedily upwards as if they wished to devour the heavens – the world is on fire! Stooping old men and mothers with tiny children hasten by, a small bundle on their backs, carrying their last belongings . . . Back home somewhere there is a Christmas tree, twinkling with familiar decorations. Much loved people are singing beautiful carols. It is better not to think about it.[9]

Lange noted on 6 December:

We are losing our self-confidence and self-belief. It is eroding rapidly even among our officers. The Russians have firmly grasped the battle initiative as our troops move back . . . The triumphalism with which we began our advance on Moscow has completely evaporated. Instead we are conscious of a growing fear of the Russians. And it is verging on hysteria.[10]

Barely a division across the entire front from the north to the south was spared a similar breakdown of morale in one or another unit. Panzer Group 3's official report stated:

Discipline is breaking down. More and more soldiers are heading west on foot without weapons, leading a calf on a rope or pulling a sled loaded with potatoes. The road is under constant air attack. Those killed by bombs are no longer being buried . . . A psychosis, bordering on panic, has gripped the baggage trains . . . Service troops, too, are without rations . . . They are retreating in utter confusion . . . The Panzer Group's most difficult hour has begun.[11]

To the south of Moscow, the 2nd Panzer Army began the retreat from Tula on 6 December, its temporary headquarters at Yasnaya Polyana abandoned. Heinrici's 43rd Army Corps was withdrawing southwards to Kaluga. Like many of his peers, the general was drawn irresistibly to make painful comparisons with Napoleon's decision to retreat from Moscow 129 years earlier. His gloom was profound:

> We experience the same conditions as in 1812, deep snow, almost impassable roads, drifting snow, storms and freezing temperatures. I do not know what will become of it. I can only hope that we will succeed in eventually stopping the enemy. But none of us has the slightest idea how to do it . . . Our supreme leadership thought we could ignore the circumstances, which defy human power and control. They will finally break us.[12]

Colonel Adolf Raegener noted, 'Men are in a state of shock: The sudden collapse of the offensive, followed by a disorderly retreat westwards, is difficult for our soldiers to understand. Everyone is thinking about the fate of Napoleon in 1812 – and some even say our army has been cursed.'[13] Lieutenant Hoss, retreating with Eberbach's panzer brigade, reflected on the mournful experience of defeat: 'We formed a ghostly, struggling line, a long worm winding westwards . . . A full moon hung over the winter landscape, making everything colder . . . I saw the pole star. It had marked our direction when we sped eastwards.'[14]

Like automata, the retreating forces had no choice but to adhere to one of the basic tenets of the battlefield: kill or be killed. If some still fought for Hitler's version of the Fatherland, or for Lebensraum or to destroy Bolshevism and the Jewish 'bacillus', their voices were rarely if ever heard. Heinrich Haape recalled that his comrades fought

> blindly and without asking questions, without wanting to know what lay ahead of them . . . And when the soldier's mind had become numb, when his strength, his discipline and his will had been used up, he sank into the snow. If he was noticed, he was kicked and slapped into a vague awareness that his business in the world was not finished and he staggered to his feet and groped on. But if he lay where he had collapsed until it was too late, as if forgotten, he was left lying at the side of the road and the wind blew over him and everything was levelled indistinguishably.[15]

The cold was unendurable. In Haape's makeshift sick bay, long rows of victims waited to have their boots cut off and to discover whether their frozen limbs could be massaged back into life or would require amputation. Strong boots were in such demand that when a unit stumbled across a dead Soviet soldier they amputated his legs – or rather 'hacked them off below the knees' – before putting them 'with boots still attached, into the ovens'; it was the only way to separate a pair of precious boots from a frozen corpse.[16]

The men who brought Bock's armies to this pass had themselves paid a terrible price. Between June and December, the Red Army endured more than 4.3 million casualties.[17] Yet this was barely discernible from the surviving memoirs, diaries and letters of those serving at the front, which were far fewer in number and generally thinner in content than those on the German side. The overriding task of the military censors was to prevent any inconvenient facts penetrating the carapace of the Kremlin's propaganda. The ominous oversight of the NKVD ensured that any soldier unwise enough to try circumventing these guardians of the truth would risk the ultimate sanction. Even after the war, when German veterans were free to write as they wished, their Soviet counterparts, living under the yoke of Stalinism, had no such privilege. Nonetheless, such letters as were permitted to trickle home during those blood-soaked months provide a touching and often tender insight into the preoccupations of their authors.

In July 1941, Dmitry Tkachenko, wrote to his two daughters:

My dear girls, Vita and Lyusya!

I am so far from you. Perhaps you have already started to forget your daddy?

Girls, so many children here are living in fear of air raids . . . Please, I want you to help your mummy and look after her. Don't be lazy. Anything can happen to me. Maybe I'll never see you again. Perhaps you will be left with just mummy . . .

I would love so much to be with you for just one day. To look at you and to play with you . . . Please make sure that the house is always clean, both the rooms and the kitchen . . .

Hugs and kisses,
Your Daddy

A while later he was wounded. On 28 September 1941 he wrote to his wife:

My dear, beloved Anya!

I am feeling much better, my leg is no longer in pain . . . It is autumn, I am worried about you. You often catch cold. How are the girls' studies? Why did your parents never arrive from Leningrad, what happened? Are you eating all right?

Once again thank you for the parcel. We have already received one or two collective presents for soldiers and officers. I got a handkerchief, a few sweets, socks, and a bar of chocolate. It felt great to know that people don't forget us.

A very sad thing happened today, my battle horse got killed. The first one was killed a month ago . . . They cannot hide from a shell; they are used to shelling by now. But otherwise things aren't bad with me.

Please kiss Vita and Lyusya for me.

Hugs and kisses,
Your Dmitry[18]

His wife heard no more from him. After the war she discovered that Dmitry had been killed on 30 October 1941.

In August 1941 Konstantin Titenkov, a fighter pilot, based outside Moscow, wrote to his wife and daughter, who had been evacuated to the city of Ufa, more than 1,100 kilometres east of the capital:

Hello, Galya and little Lyuda!

Please let me know whether you receive my letters. My main question is whether you have somewhere to live and enough food. Are you getting the allowance on time? If you have got quality bread, nothing bad can happen to little Lyuda.

You wrote that you would like to come back and live in Kubinka [an air force base outside the capital, where the family had presumably lived before the war]. I have to be frank with you, in no case should you do that. There are literally no families living here any more, with kids or without. You are much better off in Ufa . . .

I kiss you many many times
Kostya[19]

The family did not hear from him again. His plane was shot down on 12 October 1941. His body was never recovered. More than thirty years later, a schoolboy stumbled across a shell crater on the edge of a forest outside Moscow. He picked up a medal. It was the Order of Lenin. The serial number on it – 6776 – was traced back to Squadron Leader Titenkov.

On 12 September 1941, Lieutenant Pavel Khomyakov, serving in a tank regiment near Kalinin, wrote to his sister, Mariya:

Hello, Mura!

. . . I will tell you about my battles when I see you. And if I don't get a chance to do this, please remember that your brother Pashka did not disgrace his family . . .

Your brother Pavel.

That was the last she heard from him. Six months later she received a letter from his friend Aleksandr Yegorov:

His unit and mine were at the front line. On 15 September we were ordered to attack the enemy . . . Pavel and I crawled around the area in front of the enemy trenches studying their defence line and looking for places where tanks could pass . . . His unit was stopped before the attack began while I led my tanks to attack and was wounded. I will never forget the moment when he came to the medical truck where I was lying, and his face was very sad. He said: 'Farewell, Sasha!' He probably had a foreboding. I couldn't help crying . . .

Pavel's unit attacked on 16 September. Two enemy shells damaged his armour. His mechanic and gunner were killed and he was gravely wounded. He managed to get out of the tank and was lying on the grass for a long time. It was impossible to reach him under the fire, he was only given medical help in the evening. He was brought to a field hospital and this is all that I know . . .

A. Yegorov, 26 March 1942.[20]

On 16 September, Lieutenant-Colonel Pavel Novikov, commanding a rifle regiment in the Moscow Proletarian Rifle Division, wrote to his two sons:

> Hello, my dear sons Vitya and Gera!
>
> I send you my kisses and hugs. I am fighting so that you, my sons, don't have to suffer. Let us hope for our victory! It is a shame I cannot receive letters from you, as we keep moving . . . Winter will soon come, and you will be able to sledge. The slopes are good where you are. Mummy can order a sledge for you, or a sled. A sled you can also make your-selves: take a board, sharpen the end, pour water on it and let it freeze, do that several times.
>
> Well, that's it.
> Your Daddy[21]

Pavel Novikov was killed during the battle for Moscow, some seventy kilometres south-west of the capital.

These husbands and fathers invariably refrained from mentioning their own sufferings or the atrocities they might have experienced. Thus Edgar Birzitis: 'I am very worried about you . . .'; Grigory Ufimtsev: 'Valya, you wrote that you have sold the potatoes, that is good. I don't need money but do send me warm socks and mittens, and a penknife, if you manage to get one. That's it for now, warm kisses'; Andrei Komarov: 'Mama, if you saw me now you'd say that I look some 5 or 10 years older . . . Please write to me about everything . . . Your son who is still single, who hasn't had time to get married'; Ivan Melnikov: 'My dear son . . . You should buy a new hat . . . Don't buy one that's too small, so that you can wear it for several years, as your head is still growing . . . My son, I hope to come back to you, but the fact is that there are so many of us going to the front, and not all of us can come home, some might stay there . . . I press you to my heart.'[22]

Like all those mentioned above, and untold thousands of others who must have written no less caressingly, Ivan Melnikov did not return. None would ever know how greatly they had contributed to the arrest of the Nazi invasion. Vasily Grossman, the great chronicler of the war on the Eastern Front, understood it very well indeed: 'These are the heroes of the first period of the war. Many are nameless and received no burial. It is to them, in large part, that Russia owes her salvation.'[23]

★

The Führer's armies were on the retreat but their supreme commander was still in denial: Barbarossa was not permitted to fail. On 6 December he had insisted that, 'if we have lost 25 per cent of our fighting power, the Russians have lost far more of theirs'. So saying, he instructed Halder that Army Group South should prepare for a further offensive towards the Caucasus and that Army Group North should hold a critical salient 200 kilometres to the east of Leningrad to forestall any attempt by the Red Army to lift the siege. As for Army Group Centre, he was unequivocal: 'The Russians have not abandoned any place voluntarily; we cannot do so either. In principle no thought of shortening the line.'[24] But his field commanders knew this to be an absurd demand.

Bock's greatest fear was that Zhukov would use the superior firepower of the Soviet armour to smash a way through his disorientated forces before they could establish themselves behind secure defensive positions. Were this to happen, Army Group Centre would face a major encirclement and the prospect of a catastrophic defeat. On 8 December, with a significant proportion of his forces already in disorderly retreat, he warned Halder that 'the Army group is not anywhere in a position to check a concentrated attack'. Halder agreed, acknowledging that 'the consequences would be incalculable'.[25]

Hitler was at war with himself. On the one hand, utterly determined to advance whatever the cost, while at the same time reluctantly coming to realize that Army Group Centre could no longer do so. For a moment, what passed for common sense prevailed. Choosing to cite the adverse weather conditions – the only force which was conveniently beyond his control – he issued Directive No. 39: the Wehrmacht was 'to abandon immediately all major offensive operations and to go over to the defensive'. There was, though, rather less to this directive than met the eye. So far from resolving Bock's predicament, he compounded it by simultaneously insisting that 'areas which are of great operational or economic importance to the enemy' should be held and that, in any case, only 'lightly tenable' defensive positions should be established.[26] According to his trusted adjutant Nicolaus von Below, he repeatedly insisted, 'We have no prepared positions to the rear. The Army must stop where it is.'[27] On 9 December, Below went on a stroll with him in the evening. The Führer, he noted, was 'mentally at the front' but 'kept repeating "They must stand where they are – not a step backwards."'[28]

The next day, 10 December, Bock cabled Brauchitsch to tell him that he would not be able to hold the front without major reinforcements: 'Even if we succeeded in somehow and somewhere parrying the existing penetrations, it would mean the exhaustion of the last of my forces.'[29] Three days later, the army's supreme commander arrived at Bock's headquarters to discuss the deepening crisis. The commander of Army Group Centre was exasperated and exhausted:

> I have no more suggestions to make . . . The Führer now has to decide whether the army group has to fight where it stands, at the risk of being wrecked in the process, or whether it should withdraw, which entails the same risk. If he decides for withdrawal, he must realize it is doubtful whether sufficient forces will reach the rear to hold a new, unprepared and significantly shorter position. The few reinforcements promised to me are so slow in coming that they can play no part in this decision.[30]

Brauchitsch said that he agreed. Bock presumed that he would ensure that the burden of his report would be passed up to Hitler. It wasn't.

On 16 December, Hitler issued another directive. Army Group North was to maintain the blockade of Leningrad but two of Leeb's armies were permitted to carry out a short, tactical withdrawal to a line that had to be held 'to the last soldier'; Army Group South was to advance in Crimea and seize the Black Sea port of Sebastopol; and Army Group Centre was to hold its ground. 'Any sort of significant withdrawal is inadmissible,' Hitler instructed, adding, 'By their personal example, army commanders, formation commanders and all officers must inspire the forces with fanatical persistence to defend their occupied positions without paying attention to enemy forces penetrating along and into our forces' flanks and rear.'[31]

On the same day, with Zhukov's divisions tearing holes in weakening positions still held by the body of his forces, Bock called one of Hitler's most obsequious adjutants, Rudolf Schmundt. He demanded to know whether Brauchitsch had alerted the Führer to his earlier warning that 'the destruction of the army group cannot be ruled out if it is required to remain in its present forward position'. Schmundt replied that the Führer had received no such briefing but undertook to advise Hitler accordingly. He did so and, late that evening, Hitler himself rang Bock. He was adamant: 'There was only one decision and that was not to take a single step back, to plug the holes and hold on.'[32] At midnight Halder and Brauchitsch were summoned to see the Führer, who reiterated what he had told Bock: 'General withdrawal is out of the question. Enemy has made substantial penetration only in a few places. The idea to prepare rear positions is just drivelling nonsense.'[33] Two days later Bock received a further order from Hitler's headquarters 'calling on the troops to hold at all costs; I passed it on to the armies'.[34] Bock was a beaten man.

The mood among the troops in pursuit of Bock's forces could hardly have been in starker contrast. During their long months of retreat following the 22 June invasion, the ghastly toll in life and limb among the Soviet troops had sapped their physical and psychological resolve. Now, within the space of a few days, they had exploded the universal myth that the Wehrmacht was invincible. The threat to Moscow had been eliminated, the enemy was everywhere in retreat.

Now that they were finally on the offensive, not only was the suffering much easier to bear but also their urgency and resolve returned. Shortly after the start of the counter-offensive, a Soviet artilleryman, Pavel Osipov, detected that as soon as it had 'dawned on us that our attack was going successfully, morale among all the troops, sergeants, officers soared. From then on we pushed on to overtake the Germans before they could set villages on fire. As a rule they [the Germans] torched everything before a withdrawal.'[35]

But the Soviet forces made slow progress in severe weather and against a retreating enemy that was fighting in desperation. New recruits to Zhukov's armies, witnessing the gruesome reality of war for the first time, recoiled in horror. 'The worst thing of all were the freshly killed bodies of soldiers left steaming,' Pyotr Veselnikov recalled. 'The air was filled with the peculiar stench of flesh and blood.'[36] Doctors and nurses following the Soviet advance had no respite. Those soldiers who were close to death had very often to be left where they fell. Those who could be saved were carried to dressing stations. According to Alexander Nogaller (later to become famous as a physician and writer), 'The flow was unceasing: Our work became very intense, we treated the wounds, bandaged, and administered morphine.' The confusion of battle, the lack of vehicles, and the condition of the roads aggravated the suffering of the most seriously wounded:

'We had great problems evacuating the wounded and delivering them to the nearest field hospital.'[37]

Zhukov drove his armies with relentless energy and conviction. He spent much of his time at the front, cajoling, warning, advising – and threatening. On 9 December, frustrated by their slow rate of progress, and in some cases by the tactics adopted by his commanders, he issued a directive 'categorically' forbidding them to engage the enemy 'in frontal combat'. Instead, in a mirror image of the tactics devised by Guderian and used to such overwhelming effect earlier in the campaign, he charged them to encircle the retreating German forces and – as Bock feared – to block their escape routes. In addition, he ordered that sub-machine gunners and cavalry were to be formed into small 'shock groups' to burst through the gaps in the enemy lines and destroy their supplies in the rear areas. His message was unambiguous: 'Strike the enemy day and night.'[38]

Blessed though Zhukov was with an ox-like constitution, the strain showed. He rarely slept and when he did, it was hard to rouse him. On one occasion, according to his security chief, 'we just couldn't get him to wake up at the agreed hour. An hour passed, then two and there was no way we could get him up.' At one point when he was comatose, Stalin rang to speak to him. Zhukov's chief of staff, Sokolovsky,* explained that it had been impossible to wake him. With uncharacteristic solicitude, the imperious dictator responded, 'Don't wake him, then, let him sleep.'[39]

The Soviet forces fought from not only patriotism or fear of Zhukov's wrath but also an eager hatred. They had multiple scores to settle with an enemy that, for nearly six months, had ravaged and raped their Motherland. All about them was evidence of the ruination wrought by the invaders: the ransacked homes, razed buildings, livestock stolen and families murdered. 'We saw a lot of dead civilians, old women and children . . . It was awful,' Osipov recalled.[40] The mood of the soldiers was shockingly captured in Alexey Surkov's popular prose poem 'A Soldier's Oath':

---

* In 1943 Vasily Sokolovsky became commander of the Western Front and later of the Ukrainian Front, where he played a significant role in driving the Ostheer out of the Soviet Union. In 1945 he sat alongside Zhukov as he accepted the formal German surrender. In 1946 he was promoted to the rank of Marshal of the Soviet Union as Commander-in-Chief of the Soviet Forces in Germany and head of the Soviet administration in Berlin. In 1952 he became Chief of the General Staff. He died in 1968. His ashes were buried in the Kremlin Wall Necropolis.

Mine eyes have beheld thousands of dead bodies of women and children, lying along the railways and the highways. They were killed by German vultures . . . The tears of women and children are boiling in my heart. Hitler the murderer and his hordes shall pay for these tears with their wolfish blood; for the avenger's hatred knows no mercy.[41]

During the bitter days of the Soviet counter-offensive there was abundant evidence of that truth. In the early hours of 15 December, Dr Haape and his team were snatching some sleep when they were alerted by 'unearthly, agonized cries'. They stumbled through the dark towards the sound with loaded rifles, fearing it was a trap. They reached the edge of a wood, where they saw a man staggering towards them, crying, 'For God's sake, help me.' They grabbed his arms and shone a torch in his face. Blood was pouring down from the empty sockets where his eyes had once been. They took him back to the sick bay. He told them that his four-man squad had been surprised by a unit of Siberians. He was the only one of the four not to be killed. Instead, one of his captors brought out a knife and threw him to the ground. 'There was a terrific flash of light and a sharp pain and then the same with the other eye . . . then total darkness.' Both eyes had been gouged out. One of the men whispered in his ear, 'There, go straight forward to your brothers, the other German dogs, and tell them we'll destroy them all . . . We'll cut out their eyes and send what's left to Siberia – that will be Stalin's revenge.'[42]

Ilya Ehrenburg, whose articles in the Red Army's *Krasnaya Zvezda* attracted a huge following, did not shrink from inciting this mood. Close to what had previously been Guderian's front line north of Tula, he entered villages which had only recently been put to the torch. Near the town of Maloyaroslavets (the site of Napoleon's last battle as he began his fateful 'retreat from Moscow') he was intrigued rather than disconcerted by the sight that met him:

The bodies of dead Germans lay on the ground or here and there stood propped up against trees . . . In the frosty air the faces of the dead men were flushed and seemed alive. The officer who was with me cried in happy excitement: 'Look what a lot have been done for! *They'll* never see Moscow.' I have to confess that I shared his joy.[43]

Ehrenburg acknowledged that hate was 'an evil and heartless emotion' that 'freezes the soul' but, in one of several articles, he told his readers, 'We hate the Germans for the vile and brutal murder of our children, but we also hate them because we are obliged to kill them, because out of the whole treasury of words in man's possession we have been left with only one: "Kill".' Those words were written for public consumption but he readily acknowledged that he might as easily have written them to a friend or in his diary.

While visiting the front line, Ehrenburg was approached by numerous villagers, eager to tell him their stories. One farmer said:

> I thought the German was an educated man, that he'd leave us alone, but the parasite took my cow and fouled up our pots and pans, washing his damned feet in them. Yesterday four of them came to the house asking to be let in because they were frozen stiff. The women came rushing out and battered them to death.

The response of those who read his reports blazed with empathetic hatred. One of his correspondents was a woman who lived near Kalinin. Yelizaveta Ivanovna Semyonova's letter – which she had herself headlined 'Complaint against the wicked enemy' – took the unwitting form of a parable:

> When the enemy came to Kozitsino, they took my cow away from me before anybody else's. Then they took my geese. When I tried to prevent them, a man slapped my face. And he stamped his foot and said: 'Go away!' . . . The next day they came to take my last sheep. I cried and would not give it up. Then the German stamped his feet and shouted: 'Go away woman!' When I looked back he fired. I fell into the snow out of fright. And he took away my last sheep after all. When they were retreating from our place they burnt down my house, they burnt all my belongings, and I was left without anything, and my three children, in a stranger's house. I have two sons in the Red Army: Kruglov, Alexey Yegorich and Georgy Yegorich. Sons, if you're alive, fight the enemy without mercy.

Ehrenburg's colleague Vasily Grossman detected a similar mood: 'The population of the liberated villages burns with hatred,' he wrote in a private letter to Ehrenburg. 'I have spoken to hundreds of peasants, old men, old women, who are ready to die themselves, to burn down their own houses if that would bring destruction to the Germans. Yes, a great change has taken place; it is as if the people had woken up.'[44]

As he followed the course of the Soviet advance, Ehrenburg could not help but relish the appearance of the German prisoners of war he passed on the way: 'frozen, snivelling, they reminded one of Napoleon's soldiers in 1812, with the inevitable icicle at the tip of the nose, as depicted by our painters'.[45] In the village of Borodino he was shown the museum that celebrated General Kutuzov's heroic (though unsuccessful) stand at the famous battle on that site. On this occasion, the Germans had set the building alight before leaving. It was still ablaze when Ehrenburg arrived. Late in the day he sat with a group of officers, drinking vodka and eating sausage. As they drank and chewed, they talked themselves into believing that victory would soon be at hand. They were not alone.

Grossman identified a similar optimism among the soldiers he met. He shared it as well:

The men seem to have changed: they are animated, full of initiative, bold. The roads are littered with hundreds of abandoned guns; clouds of staff documents are blown across the steppes by the wind, German corpses lie about everywhere. This, of course, is not yet the retreat of Napoleon's army but there are indications that such a retreat is possible. It is a miracle, a marvellous miracle.

Like Ehrenburg, Grossman was not given to flights of fancy but – unwittingly foreshadowing the British prime minister's declaration following the Battle of El Alamein in November 1942 – he was tempted: 'Of course this is not the end,' he wrote, 'but it is the beginning of the end.'[46]

By the middle of December, by which time Zhukov's forces had recovered Istra, Klin, Kalinin and Tula, it was not entirely fanciful to suppose not only that the enemy was on the run but also that he would soon be expelled from the Motherland altogether.

The turnaround in the fortunes of the Soviet Union percolated through the censor's mesh to the Russian people well before it was announced officially. The capital city was still under a state of siege but Muscovites sensed that the threat had been lifted. Fear and dread gave way to relief and even jubilation.

The city had started to return to a semblance of normality soon after the 'Great Panic' was quashed. The Moscow Art Theatre was thriving: Chekhov's *The Three Sisters* and Sheridan's *The School for Scandal* proving especially popular; other venues staged a repertoire of Shakespeare plays and the Children's Theatre performed a propaganda piece called *Twenty Years On*. Tchaikovsky's comic opera *Cherevichki* was playing to enthusiastic audiences at the concert hall named after him; another comic operetta, *Les cloches de Corneville*, by the now long-forgotten French composer Robert Planquette, was in performance at the Stanislavsky Theatre. The theatres in the Hermitage Gardens provided a rich variety of plays, musicals and comedies; at the semi-open-air theatre there, the National Symphony Orchestra of the Soviet Union drew large audiences in search of grander fare from the likes of Glinka and Rimsky-Korsakov.[1]

Audiences also flocked to the cinemas, where, by late November, at least fifteen films were showing at different venues throughout the city. Even more compellingly, eight Soviet Grand Masters began the first round of a chess championship. The matches were played on Tuesdays, Thursdays and Saturdays at a variety of venues including the Central House of the Workers of Art, the Writers' Union and the House of Journalists. To begin with, play was obediently suspended when air-raid warnings drove the competitors to hurry to the nearest underground shelter. This provoked unexpected tension, however, as players feared their opponents would use the lull to plot a successful countermove and regain the initiative. After a while, though, they ignored the warnings and played on regardless. The championships were extensively covered on the radio as well as in newspapers and magazines. Rather in the manner of Bob

Hope and Bing Crosby entertaining Allied soldiers, the chess stars also played multiple games in military units or with patients in hospitals. Listeners and readers sent fan mail from all over the Soviet Union. The final was eventually won by Lieutenant Isaak Mazel, whose career was unhappily extinguished three years later when he died of typhus fever.*

On 13 December the Soviet authorities formally announced that the Germans were on the run. Newspaper headlines across the Soviet Union blazoned the news in triumph: 'The Collapse of the German Plan to Surround and Capture Moscow – Defeat of German Forces on the Approaches to Moscow'. The newspapers were instructed to pay appropriate homage to the generals responsible for this great victory. For the first time, the ubiquitous portrait of Stalin that had hitherto adorned the pages of every newspaper almost every day was joined by the unfamiliar faces of Zhukov, Rokossovsky (fully restored to favour) and seven other prominent commanders who had met the approval of the Stavka.[2] On the same day, at Stalin's command, the demolition charges that had been placed in the city's factories and public buildings and on its bridges were removed – a decision of practical as well as symbolic value.[3]†

The jubilation was restrained. There were still acute shortages of basic foodstuffs such as flour and milk. With the evacuation of at least 500 factories, jobs were hard to find. Two million Muscovites had left the capital. Families had been separated and stranded. And Moscow was not alone. The Nazi invasion had breached the Soviet border to a depth of up to 1,200 kilometres along a 1,000-kilometre front. The Nazis had corralled up to 40 per cent of the Soviet population, depriving them of some 35 per cent of the state's productive capacity. As well as losing 20,500 tanks, 101,000 guns and mortars, 17,900 aircraft and more than 6 million rifles, the Red Army had suffered between 6 and 8 million casualties.[4]

The anguish was widespread and deeply felt. In distant Ashkhabad, Andrei Sakharov, who had just restarted the studies that would lead him to become one of the world's foremost physicists, was not alone in counting the cost of the Red Army's victory:

---

* For an entertaining account of this episode, see Rodric Braithwaite's superb *Moscow 1941: A City and Its People at War* (Profile, 2007), pp. 299–300.
† Some were overlooked. During the demolition of the Hotel Moskva in 2005, the builders found a ton of TNT which had been placed there in 1941.

The news of our counteroffensive made me realize as never before the anxieties of the recent months, and, as I listened to the solemn enumeration of armies, divisions, and generals participating in the battles, I shuddered at the thought of the countless persons, dead and alive, who had been engaged in the defence of Moscow.[5]

The relief of the Soviet capital was a triumph shrouded in a tragedy.

The British Foreign Secretary arrived in Moscow late on 15 December. Cripps (who had been liberated from Kuybyshev for this visit) had joined their train earlier in the evening to brief the British party on the change in Soviet fortunes and on the worsening food shortages in the capital. At midnight they stumbled onto the platform to be greeted by bright lights, newsreel cameras, a guard of honour and Molotov. The formalities over, they drove through the blackout to the National Hotel overlooking Red Square. Harvey thought the rooms they had been allotted were 'magnificent'; Cadogan noted a grand piano but also that the tap in his bathroom 'squirts water impartially into the basin and on to the operator'; and Eden went straight to bed thinking about the challenge ahead.[6]

The following day the British delegation was preparing for Eden's first meeting with Stalin – scheduled for seven o'clock that evening – when they were interrupted at lunchtime by a sharp reminder that the war was far from over. Air-raid sirens blared a warning and they were hustled out of the hotel down to the palatial bowels of the nearby metro station. They were given the 'all clear' thirty minutes later. In his curmudgeonly way Cadogan concluded that 'the thing was a fake, just to show us what would happen if necessary'.[7]

More problematically, Eden had only the most threadbare proposals to pull out of his diplomatic bag at his meeting with Stalin. The Soviet leader had made it abundantly clear that their talks should lead to tangible results that would focus on the post-war borders of a liberated Europe as well as the supply of armaments. Cripps – who had been intensely frustrated by London's refusal to include him in the preparations for Eden's visit – was dismayed at the paucity of the British offering and made it his business to let Eden know exactly what he thought. Eden's amanuensis, Harvey, was not amused. 'Cripps [has] already weighed in with a memorandum on our proposals. He is going to be an infernal nuisance butting in everywhere,' he noted.[8] Hamstrung by Churchill, Eden had come to Moscow intending to establish no more than a broad basis on which to sign a joint declaration of Anglo-Soviet common purpose. His room for manoeuvre was further constrained by a cable that arrived in Moscow from the US Secretary of State, Cordell Hull, warning him against concluding 'any secret agreement with the Russians'.[9] Despite this, Cripps persuaded Eden to insert what even Cadogan conceded were 'certain good points' into the draft text of a 'political agreement' for a post-war settlement of Europe's boundaries.[10] Eden was clearly impressed by Cripps because, despite the Kremlin's initial reluctance, he insisted that the ambassador should join him for the meeting with Stalin. The Foreign Secretary still hoped that he might emerge from his three days of talks with a formal Anglo-Soviet agreement – though not a full-blown treaty, which he knew to be impossible without the approval of the United States, let alone the prime minister.

The first meeting with the Soviet leader lasted just under four hours and went well. 'Stalin is a quiet dictator in his manner,' Eden noted that night. 'No shouting, no gesticulation, so that it was impossible to guess his meaning, or even the subject of which he is speaking until the translation is given. Maisky [who had accompanied the delegation from London] was a good interpreter.'[11] Stalin laid out his stall with precision and clarity, handing Eden the drafts of two short treaties, one for a military alliance and the other providing for, as Eden put it, 'common action to solve post-war questions in Europe and to prevent renewed aggression by Germany'.[12] He wanted both treaties to be published but the second – in an echo of the Molotov–Ribbentrop Pact – was to contain a secret protocol, defining Europe's post-war borders. This protocol covered precisely the mine-strewn issues which Eden had intended to avoid. The plan was specific and detailed: the Soviet Union would regain its 1941 borders with Finland and Romania, 'recover' the Baltic States and establish a new border with Poland along the Curzon Line (originally proposed at the Paris Peace Conference in 1919 by the British Foreign Secretary and which, with few deviations, ran a little to the west of the line agreed in secret by Molotov and Ribbentrop in 1939). To compensate for the loss of territory to the Soviet Union, Poland would expand westwards to absorb a significant proportion of German territory. The Reich would be further punished by confiscation of the Rhineland and, very possibly, Bavaria as well. Other Nazi-occupied countries would have full sovereignty restored to them – though, in several, the Soviet Union would have the right to establish military bases while some would be partially dismembered and handed to neighbours.

It was inconceivable that the Foreign Secretary could put his name to such a document. Yet there was common ground. Eden made clear that, in defeat, Germany would come under the joint military control of the 'Big Three' – Britain, the United States and the Soviet Union. Nor was Britain opposed in principle to the partition of Germany (including the establishment of a separate Bavaria and Rhineland). The sticking point was the protocol itself. Eden tried to explain that Roosevelt had insisted, even before Barbarossa, that Churchill should refrain from entering into 'any secret arrangement as to the post-war reorganization of Europe without first consulting him'.[13] Stalin did not cavil. However, apparently unmindful or careless of the balance of power within the Anglo-American relationship, he proposed that the Anglo-Soviet agreement should at least acknowledge the Soviet Union's need to establish its western borders along the lines of his draft protocol. Again Eden demurred, explaining that he could only do this with Churchill's approval and the support of the United States. Stalin appeared to understand. To Eden's relief, the Soviet leader also seemed unconcerned when he was told that the ten air squadrons earmarked for the Soviet Union had been rushed to the defence of Singapore. 'I fully understand and I have no objection,' he replied.[14]

The meeting appeared to have gone remarkably smoothly. Cripps, who was prone to veer between extremes, emerged from the Kremlin so elated that on the following morning he noted, 'Yesterday was a most important day in the history of the world!' though he was careful to add, 'At least that is how it may turn out in the long run.'[15]

The second meeting was again scheduled to start at 7 p.m. but was delayed for five hours because Stalin was apparently locked in conclave with his Stavka commanders. At midnight Eden walked into Stalin's office with two draft agreements, one military and the other political, which he hoped would bridge the gap with Stalin. He was optimistic after Maisky (who was evidently playing the role of go-between as well as interpreter) indicated that, aside from minor alterations, the British texts would find favour with Stalin. Maisky was wrong.

Before Eden had a chance to introduce his drafts, Stalin demanded brusquely that Britain recognize the Soviet Union's western frontiers, naming the three Baltic States, Finland and Romania in particular. It was as though the previous day's meeting had not taken place. Eden reiterated that he could make no such agreement without his government's approval and after consultation with Washington. Stalin persisted. Eden said he would 'take it up when he returned to London'. Stalin retorted, 'If you say that you might as well say tomorrow that you do not recognize Ukraine as forming part of the USSR.' Eden tried to reassure him, saying that Ukraine was, of course, an integral part of the Soviet Union. The conversation went round in circles thus for ninety abrasive minutes until Stalin said he could see no point in signing any agreement that excluded guarantees about the Soviet borders: 'We are talking of common war aims, of what we are both fighting for. On one of these important aims, our western frontiers, we have no support from Great Britain.' In a passage that revealed his deep resentment and suspicion of the Western Allies, he complained, 'I thought the Atlantic Charter was directed against those people who were trying to establish world domination. It now looks as if the Charter was directed against the USSR.'[16]

Cadogan had joined Eden and Cripps for that meeting. Initially, the permanent secretary thought that Stalin was merely indulging in the diplomatic art of brinkmanship. 'With his little twinkly eyes and his stiff hair brushed back he is rather like a porcupine . . . I thought at first he was simply bluffing. I was wrong.'[17] Harvey was at the hotel to meet the gloomy negotiators on their return to the National. Like them, he was frustrated by Stalin's refusal to read between the lines of what Eden had said. Had he done so, Harvey believed, he would have drawn the implicit conclusion that 'if at the end of the war Russia is in occupation of the Baltic States no one is going to turn her out but their fate cannot be signed away by us without further thought'.[18]

Cripps was despondent but clear-sighted. Sensing the Russians 'have obviously got their tails up now' following the German retreat from Moscow, he judged that, as a result, it would be

much more difficult to arrange any compromise with them over the Baltic States than it would have been some months ago. We are already too late, I fear, to get any sort of arrangement other than that which they are demanding. This will lead to the greatest difficulties with America and with the Anti-Russian forces in England.[19]

At 7 p.m. on the 18th, Eden turned up for his third meeting with Stalin. He might as well not have bothered. Though it lasted for two hours, they made no progress. At Harvey's instigation, Eden had tried to break the deadlock by resurrecting the idea that the general principles embodied in the Atlantic Charter should be repeated in an Anglo-Soviet Charter of a similar kind, to be followed in turn by a 'tripartite conference' at which the Big Three would work out how to put those principles into practice. Stalin dismissed the proposal out of hand. The impasse appeared to be terminal. Stalin became truculent. Eden – normally urbane and suave – found it hard to contain his irritation. The atmosphere became frigid. As Harvey put it, the British negotiators 'had had a complete lemon from Stalin'.[20]

Like Cripps, Harvey also sensed that Stalin's insistence on binding Britain to a recognition of his proposed post-war borders sprang from renewed confidence about the outcome of the war. 'He feels he is strong now and can do what he likes,'[21] Eden's private secretary noted. Harvey, from whom the Foreign Secretary absorbed a great many ideas, was frustrated at Eden's inability to break through. 'We can't give any such recognition without the USA. The PM is on the high seas, the Cabinet without the PM consists of washouts.' In rejecting any agreement that excluded mention of the 1941 borders, Stalin, he noted, was missing 'a golden opportunity' to make use of the fact that Eden, more than anyone else, was able to put the Soviet case effectively to the 'anti-Russian' Churchill and his 'contemptible' Cabinet, notably its 'violently anti-Soviet' Labour members Ernest Bevin, Clement Attlee and Herbert Morrison. Only Eden had the authority to point out to his colleagues some basic truths: that 'we cannot win the war without Russia', that 'we cannot make peace without Russia' and that 'the 1941 borders (of Finland, the Baltic States and Romania) are not too bad in themselves'. Harvey was confident that if Stalin were to sign the proposed agreement without insisting on the inclusion of the 1941 clause, the Foreign Secretary would be able to talk the prime minister round, the Cabinet would then fall into line, and Churchill would 'get Roosevelt to tackle the whole question'.[22]

Cripps was even gloomier than Harvey. His elation after Eden's first meeting with Stalin had tipped to the edge of despair:

> I think the situation is little short of disastrous as I think the chances of getting HMG and the Americans to agree upon the frontiers of 1941 at this stage are not good and until that is done we shall have a worse state of affairs here than ever, if that is possible . . . all the hostile forces in England and America will be delighted at the failure and it will strengthen them and weaken those who are in favour of further collaboration . . . It is all a muddle and a tragedy of another missed opportunity.[23]

That evening in the hotel, presuming their rooms to be bugged, the British negotiators put on a pantomime for the NKGB's eavesdroppers. Eden stormed up and down his room, complaining furiously about Stalin's intransigence. Cripps and Cadogan provided a chorus of sympathetic criticism as he gave vent to keen regret at his decision ever to come to Moscow. They enjoyed the charade greatly. Whether or not their performance made any impression on the Kremlin was uncertain. 'Old Stone Arse' Molotov proved to be at his most intransigent in a meeting with Cripps the next day, telling the British ambassador in his blunt way, 'In the absence of a settlement of the frontier question, no sound basis would be created for relations between Great Britain and the Soviet Union.'[24]

Negotiations with Stalin were on hold for that day while Eden awaited a response from the War Cabinet to his account of the Soviet leader's obduracy, which he had presented to the Kremlin as 'consultation' with London. The War Cabinet – powerfully endorsed by Churchill, who had just arrived in Washington – duly approved this description of the diplomatic impasse. There would be neither an Anglo-Soviet treaty nor an agreement, nor even a declaration. All that was left was the possibility of concocting a plausible Anglo-Soviet communiqué.

On the 20th, Stalin's ability to wrong-foot his visitors was once more on display. His demeanour had changed utterly. No longer churlish and rough-tongued, he greeted Eden at their evening meeting as though they were friends and partners. Perhaps the pantomime in the hotel had proved effective after all, or perhaps Maisky had been a constructive go-between. More probably it was because the bullying dictator knew that he had achieved his primary objective. The British government could no longer be in any doubt that he would insist on securing the Soviet

Union's 1941 borders in any post-war settlement. There was no point in further damaging an uneasy, opportunistic but important alliance by allowing the talks to founder entirely. With his customary cunning, he therefore reverted to the genial 'Uncle Joe' posture with which he had so often captivated his guests in the past. Graciously acknowledging that it was not in Eden's gift to concede the border issue without further consultation, he also handed over a draft joint communiqué, which Cadogan judged to be 'much better' than the 'colourless' draft he and Cripps had cobbled together in the hotel.[25]

In the event, the agreed text was not entirely devoid of content. The communiqué confirmed the need for not only the 'utter defeat' of Germany but also 'the adoption thereafter of measures to render completely impossible any repetition of German aggression in the future'. Their 'exchange of views' about post-war 'peace and security' had made an 'important' contribution to the 'future elaboration of concrete proposals' to secure this purpose. The words were bland enough, but between the lines it was possible to detect the faint outlines of those future negotiations that were to shape the destiny of Europe.

In his meetings with Eden, Stalin had proposed a vision of a post-war settlement which, the Foreign Secretary conceded, sprang from the dictator's urge 'to secure the most tangible physical guarantees for Russia's future security'.[26] On his return to London, Eden cabled Churchill to advise him, in Harvey's summation, of 'the necessity for recognizing Soviet 1941 frontiers if we are to have any useful collaboration in future'. He also suggested that the prime minister should 'take it up with Roosevelt'.[27]

The timing was not propitious. Churchill had just been accorded the homage due to a global superstar by Congress and he was still enjoying the unstinting hospitality of the White House. More significantly, he had also secured a diplomatic triumph. Roosevelt had reaffirmed his commitment to the 'Europe First' doctrine (which for Churchill was synonymous with 'the Middle East and North Africa First'). They had also agreed to set up the Combined Chiefs of Staff, which, under their joint leadership, would be responsible for the conduct of the war against the Axis powers. The Soviet Union was not even on their agenda, let alone at the centre of their thoughts.

Eden's message was more than untimely. It was an irritant that provoked Churchill to a response that verged on the splenetic. In a point-blank refusal to countenance any such notion, he rebuked the Foreign Secretary for forgetting that the 1941 borders had been acquired 'by acts of aggression', that there could be 'no question of settling frontiers until the Peace Conference' and that Roosevelt held the same view 'as strongly as I do'. One passage was especially revealing:

> No one can foresee how the balance of power will lie or where the winning armies will stand at the end of the war. It seems probable however that the United States and the British Empire, far from being exhausted, will be the most powerfully armed and economic *bloc* the world has ever seen, and that the Soviet Union will need our aid for reconstruction far more than we shall then need theirs.[28]

On this single issue, the disagreement between the elder statesman and his protégé could hardly have been more stark. A few weeks later, in a memorandum for Cabinet, Eden was to write an implicit rejoinder:

> On the assumption that Germany is defeated and German military strength is destroyed and that France remains, for a long time at least, a weak power, there will be no counterweight to Russia in Europe . . . Russia's position on the continent will be unassailable. Russian prestige will be so great that the establishment of Communist Governments in the majority of European countries will be greatly facilitated.[29]

It was to avoid that outcome that he wanted to secure a deal with Stalin from the position of relative strength enjoyed by the Western Allies in 1941 rather than in the less favourable conditions he foresaw once the Nazis had been defeated. For the time being, however, in a coalition Cabinet dominated by Churchill and in which anti-Soviet sentiment was deeply rooted, Eden had no choice but to yield.

Before his departure, Eden comforted himself with the thought that he had established a good enough rapport with Stalin to avert a slide towards diplomatic hostilities between London and Moscow. This was confirmed when, as soon as they had put their names to the joint communiqué, Stalin spontaneously invited Eden and the rest of the British delegation to attend a banquet in the gaudy splendour of Catherine the Great's Throne Room. As Foreign Secretary, Eden was accustomed to the gastronomic extravaganzas offered to visiting dignitaries, but even he was taken aback by the 'almost embarrassingly sumptuous' feast that had been prepared for them at a time when those who lived beyond the walls of the Kremlin were enduring severe shortages of bread and milk.[30] Along with the caviar, bortsch, sturgeon and 'an unhappy little suckling pig which looked up at one from the dish with its black caper eye', there was pepper vodka, champagne (which was not to the Foreign Secretary's taste), and a variety of Russian red and white wines (one of which he greatly enjoyed).

His private secretary was entertained by the fact that in the course of the evening – which lasted for seven hours and included two films – no fewer than thirty-six toasts were proposed. A great many of the guests got drunk, though Eden, Cadogan and Harvey evidently remained sober enough for all of them to notice that Timoshenko consumed so much that he constantly rose to his feet to make a succession of disconnected speeches before marching round – more than once – to clink glasses with Stalin. Voroshilov drank so heavily that he eventually slumped into Stalin's lap, from where the former defence commissar had to be extricated and carried from the room. The British party did not leave the Kremlin until five the following morning.

On the day before the banquet, with the talks in abeyance while the British delegation awaited the War Cabinet's approval for his negotiating stance, Eden (accompanied by Maisky and Brooke's deputy, Nye) were taken on a guided tour through the recovered ruins of the warfront to the north-west of Moscow. They drove through a ravaged landscape of shell-splintered trees, past razed villages where only the brick chimneys, once attached to wooden homes, remained standing as gaunt sentinels over ruined lives. Along the roadside were burned-out tanks and, strewn in ditches, numerous German corpses swollen and frozen.

After a four-hour journey they reached Klin, from where, four days earlier, Rokossovsky's 16th Army had expelled Hoepner's Panzer Group 4. After visiting Tchaikovsky's country house, which had been ransacked by the departing enemy, the British party was treated to a late lunch that included caviar and vodka. On their way back to Moscow they were introduced to a group of German prisoners of war, who seemed to be little more than boys. They were in a wretched state, half-starved and shivering with cold. Eden felt sorry for them: 'God knows what their fate will be,' he wrote; 'Hitler's victims.'[31]

The Foreign Secretary had not seen a great deal. It was enough, however, to leave an indelible impression and to confirm his belief that the Soviet Union was a force that the Western Allies as well as the Nazi leadership would have to reckon with and – more pertinently from his perspective – that it was far from premature to discuss the implications of an eventual Allied victory in Europe for which Stalin was bound to claim the credit.

32.   The Fatal Gamble

The catastrophic failure of Operation Typhoon and the humiliation of the withdrawal from the gates of Moscow led to a collapse of morale among Hitler's generals every bit as rapid as that of the men serving under them. As they floundered into retreat, they fell to blaming one another for a disaster for which they did not dare hold their supreme commander responsible. For his part, Hitler, unable to bear the sight of his vision crumbling, thrashed around in search of scapegoats for his own maniacal errors of judgement.

The first to fall had been the commander of Army Group South. Rundstedt's ideological credentials had been impeccable, but even an ardent advocate of the Hunger Plan and the annihilation of the Jews could no more overcome the military odds against him than his fellow commanders further north. At the end of November he had made the mistake of withdrawing from Rostov without Hitler's consent, insisting that, given the forces ranged against him, he had no other option. Hitler was furious. The sixty-five-year-old commander responded by offering him a choice: 'Should confidence in my leadership no longer exist, I beg to request someone be substituted who enjoys the necessary confidence of the Supreme Command.'[1] On 1 December, Hitler duly dismissed him in favour of the commander of the 6th Army, Field Marshal Richenau, who had already proved himself to be an even more zealous Nazi than Rundstedt. However, Richenau was no more capable of holding the line than Rundstedt, a fact that, on this occasion, Hitler was grudgingly forced to acknowledge.

The Führer's deepest animosity was reserved for Brauchitsch, whom he despised and bullied to the point where the wretched OKH chief had lost all the self-confidence that must once have helped propel him to high office. As the oleaginous Goebbels was only too delighted to observe, it had become an open secret among Hitler's acolytes that the Führer had long regarded Brauchitsch as a 'vain, cowardly wretch who could not even appraise the situation, much less master it', and whose days were numbered.[2]

As he cast around for possible replacements, among them Kluge and Kesselring, it became clear to him that there was only one suitable candidate for the role. On or around 8 December, urged on by Schmundt, he realized for certain that he alone had the qualities to lead his armies to victory. The advantages were glaringly obvious. Not the least of these was that, as Supreme Commander of the Armed Forces, he could give orders to himself as the commander-in-chief of the army without fear of challenge. For a few days, though, Hitler stayed his hand. In the meantime, the head 'messenger boy' – as Halder had described Brauchitsch's status – remained in office to be sneered at for his faltering explanation for Nazism's humiliation on the battlefield.

One of Brauchitsch's last formal duties was to relieve Bock of his command. In his conversation with Schmundt on 16 December, warning that Army Group Centre was close to collapse, Bock had also advised the adjutant that his own health was 'hanging by a silk thread'. If the Führer wished to replace him, he said, he would quite understand. As though Hitler would ever indulge such feelings, he added 'under no circumstances is he to concern himself about me'.[3] The alacrity with which Hitler reacted to this opportunity took Bock by surprise. The very next day, Brauchitsch rang to inform him that he should apply forthwith for leave of absence on grounds of ill health. As Bock fully appreciated, this was tantamount to an order. Suspecting that he had lost Hitler's confidence, Bock asked whether the Führer had found cause to reproach him. The 'messenger boy' assured him this was not so.[4] Bock was not comforted. The unseemly speed with which Brauchitsch was on the phone again the following day to tell him that the Führer had approved his request for compassionate leave served only to confirm his suspicions. To eliminate any doubt, the commander of the 4th Army, Kluge, arrived at Bock's headquarters to replace him that very day.★

★ Bock was soon restored to health. In late January 1942, after Richenau died following a stroke, Hitler assigned him to command Army Group South. That summer he enjoyed notable success at the battles of Kharkov and Kursk. But Hitler sacked him in July, when he resisted his plans for a premature assault on Stalingrad. Bock survived in relative obscurity until, just before the end of the war, his car was strafed by a British fighter aircraft. His wife and stepdaughter were killed outright. He died of his wounds the following day, 4 May 1945.

Within hours, it was also announced that the Führer had appointed himself as the new OKH commander-in-chief in place of Brauchitsch, who was dispatched to the military graveyard of the Officer Reserve. In his new operational role, Hitler did not allow military realities to challenge his ideological fantasies or to qualify his fury at the sight of the men under his command retreating before the Bolshevik armies. His first action on taking command was to issue a furious injunction to Kluge at Army Group Centre. His 'Stand Fast' order insisted:

> The fanatical will to defend the ground on which the troops are standing must be injected into the troops with every possible means, even the toughest . . . When this is not fully present the front will begin to crumble without any prospect of stabilizing it . . . Talk of Napoleon's retreat is threatening to become reality.[5]

The troops were to hold the line 'down to the last man'.[6]

The ruthlessly ambitious Kluge immediately aligned himself with this draconian diktat. 'Our soldiers must realize that beginning a large-scale retreat is a certain death sentence – the Russians will harry our forces mercilessly, and will not allow them any breathing space to regroup,'[7] he told his senior commanders – including the two panzer leaders, Guderian and Hoepner, neither of whom trusted or respected him. During his recent incarnation at the 4th Army, they had come to regard Kluge with disdain as an over-cautious commander who put his own narrow interests above their need for support from his infantry. The animosity was mutual.

A few days earlier, Guderian's retreating forces had come under severe pressure from units of Boldin's 50th Army and the recently formed 10th Army. In a series of flanking operations – which bore a notable resemblance to the heyday of the panzer blitzkrieg – these two armies were threatening to break through the gaps between the 2nd Panzer Army's widely scattered divisions; some units had already been encircled. Kluge had been asked to send a full infantry division to Guderian's support as a matter of urgency to shore up his left flank. Only four battalions had arrived. The situation was so perilous that Guderian, in his headstrong way, drove along snow-covered roads through a blizzard to Roslavl for a meeting with Brauchitsch (who was at that point still in post) at which Kluge (still commanding the 4th Army) was also present. Guderian arrived on 14 December. It had taken him twenty-two hours to drive some 250 kilometres, which may have helped to explain why he was at his least tactful. Seeing that Kluge was there, he went on the offensive at once. Protesting that the 4th Army commander had sent him 'a totally inadequate force', he demanded that the other half of the division be sent at once.[8] Kluge listened but gave no such undertaking. Brauchitsch failed to resolve that issue but offered Guderian some compensation by placing the 2nd Army under his command to ease the threat to his right flank. He also appeared to approve Guderian's plan for both armies to retreat to a defensible line in front of Kursk along an axis from Aleksin (seventy kilometres north-west of Tula) towards Oryol (170 kilometres south-west of Tula). Guderian reflected ruefully that he presumed this 'order' would be passed on to Hitler.[9]

That evening Guderian met Schmundt at Oryol airport to report on the crisis facing his forces in what he described as 'the gravest terms'. He was exhausted and demoralized. 'I frequently cannot sleep at night and my brain goes round and round while I try to think what more I can do to help my poor soldiers who are out there without shelter in this abominable cold,' he wrote later that night. 'It is frightful, unimaginable. The people at OKH and OKW, who have never seen the front, have no idea what conditions here are like. They keep on sending us orders which we cannot possibly carry out and they ignore all our requests and suggestions.'[10]

A while later, as he had half-expected, he received a call from Hitler, who had finally been briefed by Schmundt. Over a line so static-filled that he had to repeat his words, Hitler reiterated that further withdrawals were forbidden; that his men should hold their ground. As one of the very few commanders willing to stand up to Hitler, Guderian asked for a face-to-face meeting. This was agreed. He duly presented himself at Wolfsschanze on 20 December.

The auguries were not good. Hitler was impatient. When Guderian started to explain that his two armies were withdrawing to defensive positions that had been fortified in the autumn, Hitler interrupted, shouting, 'No! I forbid that!' Guderian replied that it was too late to halt the withdrawal (which had been authorized by Brauchitsch six days earlier) as otherwise his men would be left dangerously exposed on open ground. Hitler retorted that they should dig in where they were. Guderian remonstrated that the ground was frozen to a depth of five feet and their picks could not break it open. Hitler told him that howitzers should be used to blast craters. Guderian tried to explain that to adopt such 'positional' tactics would lead to 'a useless and irreplaceable' loss of precious lives. Hitler reiterated that they should hold their ground. In an increasingly abrasive exchange, in which no other general would have dared to engage, the two men were soon trading historical analogies featuring the First World War and Frederick the Great to no discernible purpose.

Guderian then complained that his soldiers had yet to receive adequate winter clothing and that frostbite was cutting a swathe through their numbers. The greater part of the infantry, he told Hitler, was still dressed in denim, while their boots, vests, gloves and woollen helmets were 'either non-existent or worn out'. At this Hitler burst out again, 'That is not true. The Quartermaster General informed me that the winter clothing had been issued.' Guderian did not back off. Wagner was summoned and, when asked, he apparently confirmed that Guderian was right – the supplies had been held up in Warsaw.

Including a break for dinner, the meeting lasted for five truculent hours. As he looked at the Führer's acolytes, Keitel and Schmundt among them, sitting stony-faced around the table, it became clear to Guderian that, like the Führer, they thought he was exaggerating when he described the unspeakable conditions facing his men at the front. None of them gave any indication that within hours Goebbels – who only a month earlier had forbidden the press to print photos of German soldiers without winter clothing – would be instructed to launch a nationwide plea for families to ransack their wardrobes for

> overshoes, if possible lined ones, or fur-lined ones; warm woollen clothing, socks, stockings, heavy underwear, vests, or pullovers; warm, especially woollen, underclothing, undershirts, chest and lung protectors; any kind of headgear protection, ear muffs, wristlets, ear protectors, woollen helmets; furs in all senses of the word, fur jackets and fur waistcoats, fur boots of every kind, and every size; blankets, especially fur covers, thick warm gloves, again especially fur-lined leather ones, or knitted gloves, and wool mittens; altogether everything of wool is needed urgently on the front and will be doubly welcome.[11]

By the end of a bruising evening they had found virtually no common ground. On the most critical issue of all, Hitler remained adamant:

there was to be no further retreat. Guderian judged the meeting to have been 'a complete failure'.[12] Halder was well aware that Guderian's case for withdrawal made military sense but he had never forgiven him for failing to stand up to Hitler in August and he clearly relished his fall from grace, noting disdainfully, 'Guderian seems to have lost his nerve completely.'[13]

Halder was himself trapped in the vortex of confusion and disarray into which the most senior officers in the armed forces had fallen. In the absence of a coherent strategy they thrashed around in search of a way through a crisis their leader, whom some revered and all feared, attributed to their pusillanimity and lack of Prussian backbone. The void was rapidly filled with a resurgence of old rivalries and jealousies as individual commanders sought to protect themselves from the ire of the Führer without leading their men towards mass military suicide. Halder thus found himself trying to prevail on the Führer to permit a 'long-range withdrawal' while at the same time seeking 'to steel' Kluge against succumbing to the pressure from his field commanders to allow just such a retreat.[14]

Kluge, who had so recently nailed his colours to the 'Stand Fast' mast, soon found an opportunity to demonstrate that he was more than willing to resist 'the pressure from below', albeit for reasons bearing little relationship to operational necessities but a great deal to a clash of egos. In the days following his appointment to Bock's old post, Guderian had authorized a number of tactical withdrawals, for which the army's telephone log evidently showed that he had 'meticulously sought Kluge's permission'. Kluge had consented, but so superciliously as to suggest that if Guderian had been a better commander such withdrawals would not have been required.[15] On 24 December, four days after Guderian's abortive meeting with Hitler, his 10th (Motorized) Infantry Division found itself all but surrounded at a town called Chern and withdrew. Seizing his chance, Kluge upbraided Guderian for authorizing an unwarranted retreat. Guderian hotly repudiated the allegation. Later that day, their row flared up once more during a phone conversation in which Kluge accused his rival of filing an 'incorrect' report about the incident. 'I shall inform the Führer,' he warned. Guderian lost his temper and threatened to resign. Kluge got there first. On 26 December Guderian was informed that he had been dismissed by Hitler and that his punishment would be to join Brauchitsch in the dustbin of the Officers Reserve. His career as a front-line commander was over.

Guderian's arrogance, his self-serving demands, his readiness to ignore or flout orders – not to mention his astonishing triumphs and his star status – had provoked deep resentment. For the most part, his peers, whom he tended to treat as inferiors, were not unhappy to see his downfall. But those who served under him felt very differently. 'It was an absolute disaster – our soldiers found Hitler's action incomprehensible,' one of his officers, Joachim von Lehsten, recalled. According to Colonel General August Schmidt, whose unit had been involved in the withdrawal from Chern, 'It was a catastrophe. Guderian was dismissed because he had the courage to stand up to Hitler and challenge his misguided halt order, an order which threatened to destroy our entire army.'[16]

Guderian was only the first of Hitler's senior commanders to fall foul of his decision to use his newfound role as its commander-in-chief to seize day-to-day control of the army. Front-line commanders were arbitrarily summoned to his presence at Wolfsschanze to be given instructions that bore little or no relationship to tactical coherence. It was also made very clear to them that to exercise any independent initiative was tantamount to a breach of discipline. According to the head of the army's Operations Section, Colonel Adolf Heusinger, the Führer used his briefing conferences to issue stern reminders of this: 'Generals must obey orders just like any private soldier. I am in command and everybody must obey me without question. I carry the responsibility! I and no one else! Any idea other than this I shall eradicate root and branch.'[17]*

The virus of Hitler's contempt for the generals spread rapidly through his entourage. As Goebbels relished putting it, the Führer had come to judge that his senior commanders were 'incapable of withstanding severe strain and major tests of character'.[18] After a conversation with Goering – whose own prowess as Supreme Commander of the Luftwaffe was to prove lamentably inadequate – Goebbels was pleased to discover that they

---

* Heusinger rose to become Chief of the Army General Staff in 1944. Captured in May 1945 by the Western Allies, he was interned until 1947. With the establishment of West Germany's armed forces, the Bundeswehr, in 1955, he rejoined the army. Appointed a general two years later, he became chairman of the NATO Military Committee in Washington DC. He retired in 1964 and died at the age of eighty-five in 1982.

shared an identity of view: 'We are in complete agreement about the Wehrmacht. Goering has the most abysmal contempt for the cowardly generals.' Schmundt similarly met with the approval of Goebbels when he complained about 'the indolence of a number of senior officers who either do not want, or in some cases, are unable to understand the Führer' and who were 'thereby robbing themselves . . . of the greatest happiness any of our contemporaries can experience – that of serving a genius'.[19]

The 'genius' had now rid himself of Rundstedt, Bock, Brauchitsch and Guderian. He was not yet finished. In the fortnight following Guderian's dismissal, some forty other senior officers were summarily banished, either for failing to stem the retreat or for withdrawing without permission. Most prominent among these was the commander of Panzer Group 4. In the past Hoepner had not shrunk from expressing his disdain for Kluge, and the vindictive new commander of Army Group Centre had not forgotten or forgiven. With Kluge rather than Bock as his commander-in-chief, Hoepner rubbed salt into this wound by insisting he should be allowed to exercise his own initiative and to withdraw as he judged fit rather than at Hitler's whim. 'Our High Command is making a series of fundamental errors and I am putting my head on the line by continuing to complain about them,' he noted angrily, ten days after the Führer's 'astonishing' decision to sack Guderian: 'There is a serious cost to one's nerves fighting against the enemy and one's own supreme commander at the same time.'[20]

A few days later, without first consulting Kluge, Hoepner authorized one of his units to withdraw from a salient where they risked encirclement by units of Rokossovsky's 16th Army. Sensing another opportunity to settle an old score, Kluge immediately told Hitler about the panzer leader's temerity. The Führer was moved to a terrible rage. In an act of what the Wehrmacht's deputy chief of operations, Walter Warlimont, described later as 'little short of unbridled tyranny',[21] he declared, 'Generaloberst Hoepner has endangered my authority as Commander-in-Chief of the Wehrmacht and as Head of State of the Greater German Reich. Generaloberst Hoepner is dismissed from the Wehrmacht with all the consequences that implies.'[22]

Hoepner, who had been one of the most zealous advocates of a 'merciless' war to exterminate 'Jewish Bolshevism', was not only deprived of his right to wear his uniform but also, at Hitler's insistence, barred from receiving his pension. By a quirk of the Nazi constitution, however, he was able to file a lawsuit to reclaim his pension rights – a case that, to the Führer's further fury, he won. It was a brief reprieve. Two and a half years later he was implicated in the 20 July Plot to assassinate Hitler. In the rabid atmosphere of a show trial at the Court of Military Honour – during which the judge repeatedly screamed his loathing at the defendants – he was found guilty and sentenced to death. At his Führer's specific instruction, he was hanged from a meat hook in a whitewashed cell alongside his fellow conspirators while Goebbels's cameras whirled for posterity and as a warning to anyone else who might contemplate ridding the Third Reich of its Supreme Commander.★

Following Rundstedt, Bock, Brauchitsch, Guderian and Hoepner, the commander of Army Group North was the next on Hitler's list. Leeb, who had authorized a number of his units to make tactical withdrawals to avoid encirclement, had become so frustrated by the 'Stand Fast' order that he was emboldened to offer Hitler a 'back me or sack me' choice: either he should be permitted to exercise his own judgement or he should be relieved of his command. For Hitler, the decision was simple. Leeb forthwith joined Brauchitsch and Guderian in the swelling ranks of the Officer Reserve, where he languished until the end of the war. In Leeb's case, though, there was significant compensation. In the arbitrary way of dictators, the Führer decided to reward the sixty-five-year-old general for his long years of military service by giving him a large country estate to add to the one he already owned.

In addition to those who were sacked or cashiered by Hitler, many other commanders, veterans of the First World War, men who were now in their late fifties and sixties, were broken by what Richard J. Evans has described as 'the severe mental and physical strain' of a campaign that even its most zealous advocates agreed had reached the point of no return – quite literally when the retreat failed.[23] A litter of nervous breakdowns, strokes, heart attacks and other ailments provided symbolic as well as tangible evidence that Hitler's fantastical project was disintegrating.

★ Kluge, who replaced Bock as commander of Army Group Centre was also implicated in the 20 July Plot, albeit on thin evidence. He chose to commit suicide on 4 August 1944 rather than face trial.

As commanders along the crumbling front sought frantically to plug the ever widening gaps between their units, Hitler issued a further directive that uncannily echoed Stalin's Order No. 428 of two months earlier:* 'Every piece of territory which is forced to be left to the enemy must be made unusable to him as far as possible. Every place of inhabitation must be burnt down and destroyed without consideration for the population, to deprive the enemy of all possibility of shelter.'[24] Nothing was to be spared: no village, no hut, and no barn; all wells and feedstuffs were to be destroyed. Though it gave him no pleasure whatsoever, Haape recorded that his battalion did not hesitate to follow these instructions: 'The night shone red,' the surgeon wrote. 'We marched with the flames licking our footsteps, marched day and night, with only short halts, for we well knew that we were the rearguard of the army that had fallen back from Kalinin; there were no troops between us and the pursuing Russians.'[25]

Hitler's 'scorched earth' directive added greatly to the suffering of the civilians who found themselves once more trapped between two armies but was of negligible tactical advantage as division after division fell back before the Soviet counter-attack. Haape's unit – with which he had reached a tram stop only sixteen kilometres from the capital a mere three weeks earlier – fell steadily back, town by town, village by village, street by street, until it reached Staritsa, some fifty kilometres from Kalinin and 150 kilometres north-west of Moscow.

It was not permitted to voice such heresies, but General Heinrici was aghast at the Führer's obstinacy. Repeatedly forbidden to withdraw his 43rd Corps, despite the sustained ferocity of the Soviet onslaught, on 22 December, he noted:

> The consequences for the future will be much worse than withdrawing 200km now ... Sleeping, eating, drinking, everything is over. Only our whipped-up nerves keep us awake. But this is beyond our strength, to run for our lives day after day and no hope of a turn-around.

And, two days later:

> We are going to our doom. And the highest authorities in Berlin do not want to see it. Whom the Gods want to ruin they strike with blindness ...

* See pages 412–13.

in their blindness they tumble into the abyss. They do not want to admit failure. And this will end with the loss of their army . . . and afterwards with the loss of the war. Day after day we feel the noose around our neck is tightening . . . The Führer does not want to believe it. For us who see the situation, it is gruelling to have been slaughtered piece by piece.[26]

Had those words been spoken in public he would have been fortunate to have been consigned to the Officers Reserve rather than facing a firing squad. As it was, they were written for his wife's eyes only and, since he was a senior officer, his diaries and letters were not subject to censorship.

Halder's bewildered dismay at the Führer's obduracy grew in parallel with the worsening situation. His diary entries for the closing days of the year charted the crisis facing the entire Ostheer. On 29 December: 'A very bad day!'; 30 December: 'Again a very bad day!'; 31 December: 'Again an arduous day!'[27] The army chief of staff was at a loss. By this time, so too was Kluge. Within three weeks of declaring his unwavering commitment to Hitler's 'Stand Fast' order (ridding himself of both Guderian and Hoepner in the process), Kluge found himself forced to execute a sharp U-turn by seeking the Führer's approval for a strategic withdrawal along Army Group Centre's entire front to secure defensive lines. Hitler was enraged. After enduring what Halder described as 'very stormy discussions' with the Führer, in the course of which the new supreme commander indulged in 'mad outbursts . . . ravings interspersed with utterly baseless accusations' against his most senior commanders, Kluge appeared to be 'at the end of his wits and talks of utter loss of confidence'.[28] As Heusinger noted, 'The chaos at the head of affairs is becoming greater every moment.'[29]

By New Year's Eve, Staritsa was already ablaze as the retreating Germans hurriedly prepared to move out before the Russians arrived. Haape's unit had to commandeer trucks, sledges and gun carriages from panicked units at pistol point so that hundreds of wounded men might be evacuated even as 'they felt the breath of the Red Army on their backs'.[30] As they waited for midnight to chime, Haape and his team uncorked a bottle of champagne in the smouldering ruins of the town. None of them said a word. There was nothing to say: 'We were sadly mindful of the missing faces and 1942 did not strike us as having entered on a particularly well-omened note.'[31] Up and down the line, the bewildered and exhausted instruments of Hitler's malign but implacable will huddled in forlorn silence to mark the passing of a terrible year. Few of them had any expectation that the next one would be better.

On the same evening, Hitler, who was still at Wolfsschanze, invited his staff to join him to celebrate the New Year. They drank beer and listened to the intoxicating strains of Strauss and Wagner, which emanated from a newly acquired gramophone. In another room, Hitler spent three hours on the phone to Kluge, insisting yet again that the front should be held at all costs. Well after midnight, when he had finished his harangue, he summoned them to join him for a late-night cup of tea and promptly fell asleep. The celebrations came to an abrupt halt. The smiles disappeared.[32] There was, as they all knew, very little to smile about.

By the end of December 1941, according to OKH's own statistics, the German armies on the Eastern Front had lost a total of 804,148 men killed, wounded, or missing in action in the six months since the launch of Barbarossa.[33] Later estimates would put the total number of German casualties at over a million.[34] In the same period Soviet casualties numbered at least 4.5 million, and very possibly much higher than that. At a casual glance, the imbalance of losses in this ghastly tabulation might have suggested – as it did to Hitler – that the Soviet Union was getting weaker by the month. In fact, the reverse was true. By the end of the year, the Wehrmacht was facing an acute manpower shortage while the Red Army was expanding. Despite its huge losses, the number of Soviet divisions rose from 360 in June 1941 to 600 by December.[35] In the short term, the Wehrmacht could just about fill the places of the fallen with teenagers, fresh from college but with virtually no military training, and middle-aged workers recruited from the armaments factories. This could only be achieved by press-ganging slave labour from other parts of the Third Reich's new empire to replace that civilian workforce. And even these extreme measures could not for long offset a sustained haemorrhage of battlefield casualties.

As telling as the shifting balance of manpower was the balance of mechanized power. By the end of 1941 Operation Barbarossa had cost the Wehrmacht an estimated 2,700 tanks, 41,000 trucks, 13,600 artillery pieces, 4,900 aircraft and more than 200,000 horses. In the same period the Red Army's losses – 20,500 tanks, 17,900 aircraft and 101,000 pieces of artillery and mortars[36] – were far higher but had relatively less impact. In the first half of 1941 – when the Soviet Union was not yet on a war footing – its factories turned out 1,800 modern tanks, 3,950 aircraft and 15,600 pieces of artillery and mortars. In the second half of the year, despite the massive disruption caused by Barbarossa – the destruction of 35 per cent of its productive capacity[37] and the relocation of entire industries – they managed to produce 4,740 tanks, 8,000 aircraft and 55,500 artillery pieces and mortars.[38] This astonishing surge meant that even in the first year of the Great Patriotic War, the Soviet Union produced more military hardware – 6,540 tanks, 11,950 aircraft and 70,600 artillery pieces – than the Third Reich, which in the same period produced just 5,200 new tanks, 11,776 aircraft and 7,000 artillery pieces.[39]

These growing imbalances were significant but they did not alone explain the course of the campaign or its outcome. The collapse of Barbarossa owed more, far more, to a catalogue of self-delusions, false assumptions and miscalculations that flowed directly from the arrogance of the German High Command and the folly of its supreme commander, the Führer. Lulled into complacency by the lamentable performance of the Red Army in the Winter War against Finland, the Nazi generals allowed themselves to believe that the Bolshevik enemy would crumble within a few weeks before 'the shock and awe' of the initial blitzkrieg. They were taken aback by the ferocity with which day after day – even when they were in the direst straits and taking huge casualties – the Soviet troops fought back against apparently overwhelming odds. In their contempt for the '*Untermenschen*'* against whom they were fighting, they also discounted the will of the Russian people to defend the Motherland and, as diehard patriots rather than zealous communists, to support a repressive regime by which they were routinely terrorized. In every relevant respect the Nazis underestimated the strength and resolve of the Soviet Union.

Paradoxically, it was the lightning successes in the early weeks of the invasion that began to lay bare the folly of Barbarossa. By high summer, a chronic shortage of crucial supplies, replacements and reserves had

---

* An inferior, sub-human species which included Slavs (Poles and Russians) and Roma as well as Jews.

already become apparent; likewise, the enervating effect on the troops of gruelling marches interspersed with vicious battles. By early August Hitler's commanders in the field were already having doubts. Bock had fallen to worrying about 'the slowly sinking fighting strength of our constantly attacking forces' as they faced the savagery of the Soviet counter-attacks at Smolensk.[40] 'If the Russians do not collapse somewhere soon, then it will be very difficult to hit them so hard as to eliminate them before winter sets in,' he noted.[41] It was in those dog days too that Halder noted, 'it is becoming ever more apparent that the Russian colossus . . . has been underestimated by us'.[42]

Operation Barbarossa did not go to plan. A vainglorious strategy based on the assumption of a rapid victory slowly gave way to a myopic imperative which insisted that advancing was synonymous with winning. Blinded by Hitler's insistence that the Soviet Union had to be destroyed by the end of the year, the Wehrmacht's most senior generals came to regard the Ostheer as a zombie army, capable of perpetual motion in any direction under any conditions, marching and fighting like automata until the Führer's will had been realized.

If the writing was already on the wall in August, by October it was flashing in neon lights. The Wehrmacht's original hubris was now compounded by a series of disastrous oversights and errors which flowed directly from the reckless presumption of an easy victory. In a devastating indictment of German 'negligence and omission', the commander of 43rd Corps, General Heinrici – who was to become a renowned defence analyst – identified numerous ways in which the German High Command sealed Barbarossa's fate. Tellingly, he did not mention the growing imbalance of military power between the Ostheer and the Red Army. Nor did he identify 'General Winter' as a principal source of the collapse at Moscow. Instead he focused on the failure to provide the front-line armies with the resources to fight a sustained campaign, from the lack of 'motorized units and air transport formations' to the absence of the 'required fuel reserves' for such an operation 'in the depths of Russia'. He cited too the 'complete dependence on the railroads for supply' and the inevitable delays caused thereby to the delivery of vital provisions, delays aggravated by the 'few good roads', 'the wide unregulated river courses' and the 'wide marshes and impassable regions, the great primeval-like forests'. In the latter stages of the campaign he had complained bitterly about the appalling weather conditions that his men had to endure, but in retrospect he judged that the 'climate and terrain' had merely 'complicated matters'. Rather than blaming either the natural topography or meteorological conditions – both of which were predictable and beyond human control – he observed tartly that 'the coming of the Russian winter did not correspond with German expectations'. Against the background of a deteriorating economy, falling output, a shortage of manpower and weaponry, and a host of insuperable logistical challenges, this was tantamount to charging the High Command with a fatal lack of judgement, foresight and planning.[43]

Operation Barbarossa had been a massive gamble. Until August, it looked as though it might just succeed. But there could be only one surprise attack and only one blitzkrieg. Hitler had sown the wind and by October he had started to reap the whirlwind; the odds against taking Moscow by Christmas were shortening rapidly. By November, it was clear the gamble would fail. By December it had failed utterly. The invaders were on the run, never again to threaten Moscow.

Whichever month might be picked out as the date at which it became clear that Barbarossa was doomed – as early as August or as late as December – it was clear, or should have been, that by the end of 1941 the Wehrmacht would never again acquire the means to inflict a final defeat against the Red Army on its own soil. In manpower and weaponry, in industrial output and economic resilience, in logistical support, in proximity to supply lines, in the capacity to cope with the climate, and in the readiness to fight to the bitter end, Stalin's armies had already shown themselves superior to those marshalled by Hitler on 22 June 1941. The Ostheer's astounding successes of 1942, which took Hitler's armies to the edge of the Volga and the Caucasus, may have provided the diehards with a glimmer of hope, but the crushing defeats at Stalingrad and Kursk the following year, after the invaders had deployed every resource at their disposal, served merely to illustrate that 1941 was the decisive year of the war.

Operation Barbarossa marked the zenith and the nadir of Hitler's attempt to destroy Bolshevism, the beginning and the end of his psychotic fantasy that the Thousand Year Reich's Lebensraum could be established on the soil of the Soviet Union. On the basis of the available evidence, he should have withdrawn forthwith to a much diminished

Third Reich. But he was not endowed with a scintilla of Napoleonic wisdom. To the great torment of humankind, his megalomania was boundless.

In the months and years ahead, the Soviet Union would be drenched with yet more human blood. The savagery of the war on the Eastern Front – which became as pointless and as terrible as any war of attrition could ever be – would result in the deaths of tens of millions of soldiers and civilians and the wanton destruction of countless thousands of human habitations. Although Hitler would survive until his suicide in the Führerbunker on the last day of April 1945, it was on the killing grounds of the Eastern Front between June and December 1941 that the fate of Nazi Germany was sealed.

Epilogue

On 1 January 1942, Hitler released two New Year proclamations, one to the party faithful and the other to the Wehrmacht. Even by his own standards they were egregious in content and sentiment. They bear repeating only because they illuminate his tenuous grasp of reality.

The year which had just passed, he informed his 'National Socialists and Party Comrades' was 'the year of the greatest victories in the history of man. The accomplishments of the German soldiers and the soldiers of the allied nations are unique and immortal. The millennia to come will speak of these battles and victories. They will admire them as the greatest self-preserving acts ever undertaken by honourable nations.' To the Wehrmacht he marginally recalibrated his bombast to concede that 1941 had been 'a year of the most difficult decisions and extremely bloody battles . . . the scope and harshness of which taxed you severely, but which, in their successes, are the most glorious military feats in history'. In 1942, the Ostheer would, he said, 'engage this enemy of mankind anew and do battle with him for as long as it takes to break the destructive will of the Jewish-capitalist and Bolshevik world'.[1]

Hitler was not alone in believing that the Third Reich would emerge triumphant from that struggle. There were those in the Wehrmacht who shared his delight at Japan's attack on Pearl Harbor. 'The entire headquarters', according to the deputy chief of operations, Warlimont, 'seemed to be caught up in an ecstasy of rejoicing.'[2] Hitler's reaction to Pearl Harbor was immediate, unplanned and reckless. He hastened from Wolfsschanze to Berlin, where he formally declared war on the United States on 11 December 1941. By 3 January 1942, he appeared to have discovered a rationale for this bizarre gambit. At a meeting with the Japanese ambassador, General Hiroshi Ōshima, he confided that, 'provided we co-ordinate our military operations in detail', the two Axis powers could disrupt any effort by the United States and Britain to defeat either of them. His implicit assumption that the two powers might combine effectively to defeat their common enemy was out of character. Hitler had never trusted the Japanese, whose non-white ethnicity was distasteful to his Aryan sensibilities; moreover, he believed them to be inherently duplicitous. There was no basis for any significant tactical or operational co-ordination. Moreover, he entirely underestimated the strategic response of the Anglo-American alliance.

In Washington for the Anglo-US summit – codenamed Arcadia – which he had initiated a month earlier, Churchill had a paramount objective: to convince the Americans 'that the defeat of Japan would not spell the defeat of Hitler, but that the defeat of Hitler made the finishing of Japan merely a matter of time and trouble'. He was well aware that the Japanese were bound to inflict 'a lot of punishment' on British and American interests in the Pacific, but he believed that to be a price worth paying to secure the 'Europe First' doctrine that had been agreed with the United States in the spring of 1941.

In the aftermath of Pearl Harbor, American public opinion, thirsting for revenge, was overwhelmingly in favour of treating Japan as the 'prime and major foe', an attitude that also prevailed in Congress. Roosevelt's military advisors were divided. With Japan launching attacks on Guam, Midway and the Philippines, some of his most senior military advisors, notably the abrasive Chief of the US Navy, Admiral King, argued strongly for a 'Pacific First' strategy that made 'crushing Japan'[3] the 'major priority'. Conversely – to Churchill's relief – it was clear, in the prime minister's words, that 'the president and General Marshall,* rising superior to powerful tides of public opinion, saw in Hitler the prime and major foe'.[4] But this fundamental clash of judgement within the Joint Chiefs could not easily be sidestepped. As the following months were to demonstrate, it was one thing for the president to assert a priority but quite another to realize it. Nor would it be possible for the British to escape the backwash.

At Arcadia, though, Churchill seized the moment to advance a project

---

* George C. Marshall, the army chief of staff, wielded great influence. He oversaw the dramatic expansion of the US Army in 1942. Generals Eisenhower, Bradley and Patton owed their rapid rise to him. He was to be instrumental in planning Operation Overlord – the invasion of Europe – in 1944. In 1947, as Secretary of State under President Truman, he was the principal advocate and agent of the Marshall Plan for the reconstruction of western Europe. He later became Secretary of Defense. He retired in 1951 and died at the age of seventy-eight in 1959.

that was bound to provoke even greater internecine dissent. Reassured by the president's support for the 'Europe First' policy, he made the bombshell proposal that this should not entail an early second front in Europe itself but in North Africa instead. Victory against the Axis forces in the Libyan desert, the prime minister argued, would secure the Mediterranean for the Allies and open the way to an Anglo-US invasion of Sicily and Italy (which, in a later unhappy phrase, he would describe as the 'soft underbelly' of Europe).

This suggestion horrified not only the 'Pacific First' adherents like King but also those who saw Churchill's proposal as an attempt to steamroller the Americans into sending 'Our Boys' into a war to salvage the British Empire rather than to destroy the Nazis on their own territories. In turn, this aggravated the latent but widespread Anglophobia with which many Americans were infected; even Roosevelt thought fit to remind Churchill at a formal dinner party in the White House that Britain's empire still inspired 'dislike, even hatred' in many American hearts.[5] Among the most prominent of these was the influential General Joseph 'Vinegar Joe' Stilwell, who wore his Anglophobia as a badge of honour, complaining, 'The Limeys have his [Roosevelt's] ear, while we have the hind tit.'[6] More importantly, it set the British Joint Chiefs against the majority of their US counterparts, who supported 'Europe First' but – like Marshall – believed that it should mean what it said: an early invasion of Europe rather than landings on the continent of Africa.

These differences and animosities were subsequently played out in a sustained and often acrimonious debate in the meetings of the Combined Chiefs of Staff.* There were to be several showdowns. The first of these was prefaced in a personal letter from Roosevelt to the exiled Queen Wilhelmina of the Netherlands on 6 April 1942. It summarized his views with rare brevity and precision:

I think we realize that the principal danger in the next six months is German success against Russia – for if Russia is driven to her knees this Summer Germany will be able to release very large forces against the Near East and the Middle East and seek to join hands with Japan . . . our major strategy must be the defeat of Germany . . . in her Russian effort,

* Established in February 1942 to provide a forum for the British and American military chiefs to thrash out a strategy for the defeat of the Axis powers.

for the very simple fact that if this can be accomplished the probability is that Germany cannot survive another year.[7]

On 1 June 1942, after three days of talks at the White House with Molotov, Roosevelt committed the United States to 'the urgent tasks of creating a second front in Europe in 1942'.[8] A few days later in London, the prime minister had little choice but to give Molotov the same undertaking in the same words. However, he added an escape clause in the form of an aide-memoire advising the Soviet foreign minister that it was 'impossible to say in advance whether the situation will be such as to make this operation feasible when the time comes. We can therefore give no promise in the matter.'[9]

Pressure in favour of a second front was growing on both sides of the Atlantic. In New York, Beaverbrook – who had recently resigned from the government – was so carried away by his own rhetoric that, before an audience of his fellow publishers in New York, he declaimed, 'Strike out to help Russia! Strike out violently! Strike out even recklessly.'[10] There were campaigns and demonstrations to the same end. Churchill was unmoved. His 'second front' was to be in North Africa.

The denouement came in late July 1942, when Hopkins, Marshall and King flew to London. The two chiefs argued forcefully for the invasion of Europe and, simultaneously, that victory against Japan should precede any military landings in North Africa. Quite why they were so insistent remains unclear: the French coast was well defended, the Luftwaffe was still powerful and victory over the U-boats in the Atlantic – without which no seaborne landings would be sustainable – had yet to be achieved. As it was, after three days of acrimonious discussion, Churchill intervened decisively. He told Marshall bluntly that there were no circumstances in which the British would land troops on European soil in 1942. The US Secretary of War, Henry L. Stimson, had been an advocate of Sledgehammer, as this operation had been codenamed, and he was furious. Britain, he fumed, was led by 'a defeatist government which had lost its initiative, blocking the help of a young and vigorous nation whose strength had not yet been tapped'.[11]

The president, however, was unruffled. His overriding concern was to have American troops fighting Germans somewhere, and as soon as possible, if only for the somewhat venal reason that he wanted to demonstrate

American resolve before the Senate elections due in November 1942. In an emollient note to Churchill, he affirmed his support for the prime minister's favoured option, the Allied invasion of Axis-occupied North Africa. With a chutzpah few of his peers would have essayed, the grateful prime minister responded by reassuring Roosevelt not only that his plan offered 'the best chance for effecting relief to the Russian front' but also that it should therefore be seen as 'the true Second Front of 1942'.[12] That settled the matter. Although there would be many more harsh disagreements between London and Washington, and even greater public pressure, Roosevelt was unwavering. The Allied campaign against the Axis powers in Europe would be fought initially in North Africa and then, via the Mediterranean, in Sicily and Italy.

In an unusually prolix and tortuous telegram to Stalin, Churchill sought to soften the blow but, inevitably, the Soviet leader saw only the salient fact that there would be no second front in Europe in 1942.[13] He reacted with barely controlled fury at what he regarded as an act of bad faith. Complaining that the Allies had not treated the issue 'with the seriousness it deserved', he protested 'in the most emphatic manner that the Soviet Government cannot acquiesce in the postponement of a second front until 1943'.[14]

In truth, Stalin could do little more than protest. Relations between London and Moscow reached a new low. On 12 August 1942 Churchill flew into Moscow for the first time in an attempt to reassure the Soviet leader that the invasion of North Africa would be no less effective than a cross-Channel invasion of France. Stalin's response was icy as he accused the prime minister openly of a breach of faith. Churchill could not stomach this rebuke, and for a while it looked as if the talks would founder in the quicksands of mutual recrimination. But, just before the prime minister's departure on 16 August, the combination of a fine suckling pig and copious quantities of wine helped to restore a degree of personal amity. On his return to London, Churchill told Maisky that, during his late-night session with the dictator, 'I saw Stalin's soul'[15] – by which he presumably meant the brighter side of a very dark spirit.

It is probable that Stalin's anger was synthetic and that Moscow never really expected a second front in 1942, and certainly not until the Germans were on the run from the Red Army, when – as Maisky pointed out at the time – there would be 'a scramble to get to Berlin'. Many years later, in 1976, as David Reynolds and Vladimir Pechatnov have noted, 'Molotov asserted bluntly that neither he nor Stalin believed in such a possibility, and said that they had pressurized the Anglo-Americans on the matter only to gain moral advantage and obtain concessions on other issues.'[16]

In the meantime the only direct military assistance that the Soviet Union received from its Western Allies took the form of materiel delivered initially by the Arctic convoys and latterly overland via Persia as well. The provision of these supplies was to prove no less contentious than the second front. Moscow was to be persistently aggrieved by the failure of London and Washington to meet its aggressively insistent demands for planes, tanks, trucks, jeeps and ammunition as well as communications equipment, clothing and more. And though Churchill knew he could not escape this commitment, he greatly resented the diversion to the Soviet Union of precious armour and weaponry that could otherwise be used by Britain's hard-pressed forces in the Middle East and beyond. Britain and the Soviet Union thus found themselves in fierce competition for the limited supplies that could be released to them from Roosevelt's 'Arsenal of Democracy', which also had to supply the US navy, army and air force. As the American service chiefs were also scrambling competitively for the same weapons, the tensions within the US-Anglo-Soviet alliance were persistent and acute.

American largesse, through the Lend Lease scheme, was constrained not only by the size of the arsenal but also by an acute shortage of merchant shipping to convey US supplies across the Atlantic and through the equally perilous Arctic Ocean to the Soviet ports of Murmansk and Archangel. Britain's very survival as a functioning modern state – let alone its ability to wage war – depended on American supplies of oil, raw materials and food. For this reason, Churchill was haunted by the threat of the German U-boats, which consistently appeared to be on the verge of severing Britain's Atlantic lifeline. In early 1942, when a posse of German U-boats began to wreak havoc along America's Atlantic seaboard, he became so alarmed by the rate at which they were sinking Britain-bound oil tankers that he was moved to write an urgent note to Hopkins demanding 'drastic action' to prevent Britain running out of this crucial resource.[17] A year later, the British Admiralty came close to panic, fearing that the U-boats were very close to 'disrupting communications between the New World and the Old'.[18] The Russians would never understand how critical this was from London's perspective. As Rodric Braithwaite has pointed out, 'the U-boats posed an existential threat to Britain, as great in its own way as the Ostheer posed to the Soviet Union'.[19]

By May 1943, though, in an abrupt change of fortune, the Royal Navy and the RAF contrived to scatter the U-boat 'packs' away from the transatlantic sea-lanes which opened the way not only to Britain but to Russia as well. Until that point the U-boats had been sinking merchant ships more rapidly than they could be replaced. Victory in what Churchill called the 'Battle of the Atlantic' coincided fortuitously with the arrival of the 10,000-ton Liberty ships,* which had started to come off the American production lines at the rate of three every two days. With an abundance of freighters and the shipping lanes virtually free of U-boats, Washington and London could finally start planning the invasion of Nazi-occupied France in earnest, secure in the knowledge that the armadas of men and materiel required to sustain the second front would not face any significant threat on their transatlantic crossings.

By this point the Red Army's ascendancy over the Wehrmacht was beyond question. In the middle of January 1942, even Hitler was forced to acknowledge reality. Kluge was at last authorized to withdraw the body of Army Group Centre to defensive lines up to 150 kilometres west of Moscow. On 17 January a Luftwaffe pilot, Paul Stahl, observed the full-scale retreat from his aerial vantage point:

> We are offered a sorrowful view: long columns of our own soldiers strenuously stumbling back. Everywhere one can see abandoned vehicles, some half covered with snow, and others just recently abandoned. As we fly past the columns and small groups of soldiers at low altitude, it is evident that they are half unconscious out of fatigue. They pay no attention to us. We pass by burning villages . . . The entire horizon is filled with columns of black smoke. It is a merciless war.[20]

---

* The Liberty ships were cargo vessels that were mass produced on production lines according to principles adapted from the motor industry. Between 1941 and 1945, more than 2,700 were built in eighteen US shipyards. Dubbed 'Ugly Ducklings', they were cheap to build and played a crucial role ferrying men and supplies across the Atlantic.

Harried by Zhukov's advancing forces, the retreat from Moscow, which had cost some 90,000 casualties by the end of January, was an expensive illustration of the Führer's winter folly. But those who believed that Hitler's defeat at the gates of Moscow would force him – like Napoleon – to retreat from the Soviet Union altogether were horribly mistaken. Indifferent to the Ostheer's enormous casualty rate – which, by March 1942, the Wehrmacht itself estimated at 1.6 million men – Hitler continued to defy the odds in the apparent belief that his invincible will would lead on to victory.

The Red Army's initial success in forcing the Germans to call off the attack on Moscow provoked Stalin to similar hubris. In January 1942 he issued a directive instructing the Red Army to mount a full-scale offensive along the 1,500-kilometre front from the far north to the far south of the Soviet Union. Zhukov protested, arguing that a narrowly targeted attack against the main body of Kluge's Army Group Centre would be the most effective way of shattering the enemy and thereby forcing the Ostheer into a retreat of Napoleonic proportions. He was overruled. As a result there was no Soviet breakthrough while key salients at Kursk, Oryol, Bryansk, Vyazma and Smolensk remained in German hands. Moreover, Army Group Centre was given respite, a chance to dig in, refresh, rebuild, reorganize and redeploy behind the so-called Königsberg Line.★ The campaign on the Eastern Front turned into a war of attrition that would cost tens of millions more lives and provoke an untold number of further atrocities.

In June 1942, while holding the line in the north and the centre, Hitler was emboldened to mount a 'summer offensive' – codenamed Case Blue – in southern Russia. It was to be a two-pronged assault, one against the Caucasus (to seize the Baku oil wells) and the other to reach the Volga at Stalingrad. The attack was launched in late June. The Red Army, which had expected a renewed offensive against Moscow, was ill prepared for the speed of the assault and its response was leaden footed, poorly organized and incompetently directed from the Kremlin.

At first both thrusts displayed the characteristics of the original Barbarossa blitzkrieg twelve months earlier. However, in both cases the German onslaught could not be sustained for long enough to avoid defeat, let alone

★ See map on p. xxx.

secure victory. The disparities in military power and resources were becoming glaringly obvious. In every relevant respect the Red Army was getting stronger as the Ostheer became weaker. The number of German divisions capable of sustaining an offensive had fallen from more than 180 in June 1941 to sixty by the early summer of 1942 (though the addition of fifty divisions of uneven quality from other Axis powers took the overall total to over a hundred). By this time, however, the Red Army was able to mount more than 300 operational divisions. The Stavka could not only deploy many more men and better weaponry but were also fielding more of both at an increasing rate while the Germans were fielding fewer of both at a slowing rate. The trends that had become discernible in 1941 began to accelerate rapidly. In 1942 the Russian armaments industry turned out 24,000 tanks while Germany's could produce no more than 9,200, a little under 40 per cent of the Soviet output. Similarly, in the same year, the Russians produced three aircraft for every two that left German factories.[21] In every key area of output – albeit in differing proportions – the disparities would persist. Despite the strenuous efforts of Hitler's newly appointed armaments minister, Albert Speer, who exploited the Reich's contracting economy to the full, the gap would never be narrowed.

It was not only a matter of armaments. Although the Ostheer commanders often deployed their forces with greater flair and speed than their Soviet counterparts, their troops were no longer fuelled by Hitler's certainties. They fought because they had no alternative. In contrast, the Soviet troops, who had fought for survival in the early months of Operation Barbarossa, had acquired a new confidence after the German reverses before Moscow. They sensed that their enemy was vulnerable, that the Nazis could and would be vanquished. The 'shock and awe' that had wrought such havoc in June 1941 was no longer a war-winning tactic a year later.

Although Army Group A seized the Crimean city of Sebastopol in July 1942, and swept on into the Caucasus, its offensive was soon blunted. With its supply lines impossibly extended, it was clear by late August that the Baku oilfields would remain in Soviet hands. The Red Army's losses were greater, but the operation cost 100,000 German casualties that OKH could ill afford. The second thrust, led by Army Group B, enjoyed greater initial success. After a rapid advance towards the Volga, the 6th Army, under the command of General Friedrich Paulus, supported by the 4th

Panzer Army (as Panzer Group 4 had been redesignated in January 1942), entered Stalingrad in force on 12 September. By that time the city was in ruins, carpet-bombed into smithereens by the Luftwaffe. But the defenders resisted with desperation, street by street, house by house and hand to hand, to prevent the Germans getting a permanent foothold.

Zhukov's men fought as though their lives depended on it. And they did. Any doubts they may have had about sacrificing themselves for the Motherland were offset by the brutality of a Soviet regime that executed 13,500 Red Army soldiers for cowardice, incompetence, self-mutilation, 'anti-Soviet agitation' and even drunkenness.[22] These coercive measures allied to genuine patriotism made it impossible for Paulus's troops to dislodge the Soviets from their troglodyte strongholds in the heart of the city.

In November, Red Army units, under Zhukov's overall direction, launched a surprise counter-attack, moving at speed to encircle the German troops to the west of the city and trapping the 6th Army inside it. On this occasion, the Germans were suitably dressed for the Arctic conditions, so they did not freeze to death as their fellows had during the previous winter. Instead, they died of starvation. Hitler was unmoved. On 23 January 1943 he not only ordered that the sick and wounded should be left to die but also refused to allow Paulus to accept the Soviet offer of surrender, although by this time 100,000 German soldiers had already been killed in the impossible attempt to hold the occupied city. A week later though, on 31 January, Paulus bowed to the inevitable and, in defiance of Hitler's orders, formally capitulated.*

It was a catastrophe for the Third Reich, a shattering blow to its already shaken morale. If, as Antony Beevor has written in his peerless account of the battle, 'the balance of power – geographical, industrial, economic and demographic – swung decisively against the Axis in December 1941', it was the battle for the city of Stalingrad that marked the Second World War's 'psychological turning point'.[23]

Yet Hitler still refused to concede. At Kursk in July and August 1943,

---

* Ironically, it was on this day that Paulus was promoted by Hitler to the rank of field marshal. The Führer was enraged by his surrender, insisting that he should have chosen suicide. Once in captivity, Paulus urged the Nazis to surrender. After the war he settled in the East German city of Dresden, where he died in 1957 at the age of sixty-six.

Army Group Centre, supported by Army Group South, made one last lunge at Zhukov's massed armies along a salient running north to south for a length of 250 kilometres and heavily fortified to a depth of up to 300 kilometres. Involving 3,000 tanks and 780,000 men, the Kursk offensive was the last throw of Hitler's dice – and it proved catastrophic. After only a week, Kluge's forces were halted by the superior might of the Red Army's 5,000 tanks and 2 million men. After five further weeks of combat, in which hundreds of thousands of men from both sides were killed, wounded or listed as missing in action, the Germans were forced once again to retreat. In the following weeks, the Soviet Union recovered a vast swathe of territory, including Bryansk, Oryol and, by late September, Smolensk as well.

Following the success of the Kursk battles, the focus of the Red Army's offensive operations shifted back to the south. Kharkov was retaken in late August. In November, the Stavka launched an offensive to retake Kiev and to drive Army Group South back across the River Dnieper. By 3 January 1944 the Germans had retreated behind the Polish border (as defined in the 1939 Molotov–Ribbentrop Pact). Three months later, in April, the Red Army launched an offensive to drive the Germans out of Crimea, which culminated in the liberation of Sebastopol four months later.

In June 1944 the Stavka launched another massive offensive further north. Codenamed Operation Bagration, the campaign lasted from 23 June to 19 August, by which time the Red Army had retaken Minsk, Kaunas and Brest-Litovsk, which Guderian's forces had seized in the opening days of Operation Barbarossa. In the course of eight weeks, the Red Army destroyed twenty-eight of Army Group Centre's thirty-four divisions, a coup de grâce during which both sides endured hundreds of thousands more casualties and from which the Wehrmacht had no hope of making even a partial recovery.

The price in blood was almost beyond the capacity of the human mind to absorb. The sentiment that 'one death is a tragedy, a million deaths is a statistic' – attributed to Stalin, among others – contains the kernel of a cruel truth. It is certainly simpler and no less painful to contemplate a single death than the deaths of tens of millions. The mind and the heart can wrestle with the meaning of a particular loss, but to weigh the deaths of 15 million soldiers on the front lines between June

1941 and May 1945 is to be simultaneously shocked and numbed. It is the individual mortalities – human heads severed by a shell, human skin hanging in trees, human guts smeared on the windscreen of an aircraft – that lead us to recoil in enduring horror. But, of course, when it comes to war, the quantity, however difficult for the mind to encompass, matters every bit as much as the quality.

The suffering of those who died on the battlefield was indiscriminately endured but the allocation of death was not in balance. Some 5 million Axis soldiers – 4 million of whom were German – were killed or listed as missing in action. Soviet battlefield deaths numbered perhaps 10 million. Of the 5.7 million Soviet soldiers taken into captivity, 3.3 million died from starvation, disease, or, in the case of at least 140,000 individuals, at the point of an executioner's gun. Behind the lines, a further 700,000 civilians were murdered in reprisal for the acts of sabotage by the partisans.

Altogether 15 million Soviet civilians died as a direct result of Hitler's attempt to obliterate the Soviet Union. Of these, a million were deliberately starved to death in Leningrad until, after a siege lasting 872 days, the city was liberated on 27 January 1944. These deaths were not a side-effect of war but deliberate acts of mass homicide. To a regime that had predicted the deaths of 30 million Soviet citizens in the course of accomplishing the Führer's Hunger Plan, the erasure of this 'subhuman species' was not only desirable but necessary. Their lives were of no value.

Barbarism was not confined to the Nazis. Stalin's inhumanity had been attested well before the start of the Soviet Union's Great Patriotic War. During the Great Famine of 1932–33, in which 5 million peasants died, the NKVD executed upwards of 680,000 kulaks. In 1937–38 a similar number of individuals, labelled as 'enemies of the state', were liquidated in the Great Terror. Whatever the precise figure may be – Timothy Snyder's analysis of the available evidence suggests that some 6 million civilians were killed under Stalin's dictatorship – it far exceeded the numbers killed by the Nazi regime before Hitler launched Operation Barbarossa.★

★ Timothy Snyder, 'Hitler vs. Stalin: Who Killed More?', *New York Review of Books*, 10 March 2011. All statistics are subject to revision and challenge, and this is particularly true of those to which I have drawn attention. Both in the source cited here and in his brilliant and excoriating *Bloodlands*, Snyder has sought to distinguish between demonstrable fact and plausible conjecture.

However, following the invasion, that balance was dramatically reversed. Although the Red Army took some 3 million prisoners altogether – of whom up to a million and perhaps even more died either on their way to or in the Soviet camps – they were, for the most part, victims of chaos and neglect rather than revenge or racial hatred. There was, though, a closer parallel in the case of 'reprisals', when the NKVD executed tens of thousands of civilians in the Baltic States, Belorussia and Ukraine after the end of the war for their alleged collaboration with the Nazis.

Stalin's tyranny was animated by a malign combination of ideology and paranoia, which, following the Nazi incursion, was intensified by a ruthless determination to drive the invaders out of the Soviet Union regardless of the human price. Hitler's tyranny was also underpinned by ideology, though not by paranoia. Rather, he was animated by a deranged belief in the sacred supremacy of the Aryan people, the right to give them living space wherever he chose and, worst of all, a deep hatred for individuals based solely on their race or creed, which led to the most unspeakable of all the horrors perpetrated in his name.

By the end of 1941 the SS and the Einsatzgruppen had exterminated around a million Jews in the Soviet Union. These executions generally took the form of mass shootings in front of open pits, but towards the end of the year the first gas chambers entered production. Thereafter, the industrialization of murder accelerated sharply as Himmler's interim solution for Hitler's Jewish Question gradually mutated into the Final Solution. On 30 January 1942 the Führer addressed a rally of the party faithful in the Berlin Sportpalast. In the midst of a lengthy ramble, he reminded them that three years earlier he had prophesied that the only way to avoid the extermination of the European-Aryan peoples would be 'the annihilation of Jewry'. On this occasion he made it clear that his war was the means to that end: 'For the first time the old Jewish law will now be applied: an eye for an eye, a tooth for a tooth . . . And the hour will come when the most evil world-enemy of all time will have played out its role, at least for a thousand years.'[24]

His followers did not need further instruction. They read between Hitler's quasi-mystical lines and – as Heydrich's secret police reported – they drew the conclusion that 'the Führer's battle against the Jews would be followed through to the end with merciless consistency, and that very soon the last Jew would disappear from European soil'.[25]

Ten days earlier, on 20 January, in the Berlin suburb of Wannsee, Heydrich had told delegates to his 'Final Solution' conference that up to 11 million Jews would have to be annihilated by one means or another across the continent and – once they had been occupied – in Britain and Ireland as well. In March, Goebbels, after several conversations with the Führer, came to the conclusion that around 40 per cent of European Jewry could be worked to death but that 60 per cent would have to be 'liquidated'. There was no doubt in the minds of all those who were assiduously 'working towards the Führer' what this would entail, or that, in the words of the propaganda minister, 'the Führer is the unswerving champion and spokesman of a radical solution'.[26]

By the end of the first six months of the Eastern Campaign, the Nazis had killed more than a million Jews. By that point – hideous as the thought may be – Himmler and Heydrich could claim that at least one part of Barbarossa's mission was already proving to be a spectacular success. The invasion had provided them with the Lebensraum in which, by trial and error, they were able to establish an extermination programme which soon accelerated sharply. Before long, the output of corpses from the death factories at Chełmno, Bełżec, Sobibor and Auschwitz-Birkenau began to surpass the numbers executed in mass shootings by the Einsatzgruppen.

By the end of the war the Nazis had murdered 2.8 million Jews with gas and 2.6 million with guns: altogether 5.4 million men, women and children. Several hundred thousand more – the precise figure is unlikely ever to be known – died from hunger and disease either in the ghettoes or on their way to them. A further 300,000 or so were slaughtered by Germany's close ally, Romania, working in collaboration with the Nazis.*

Such statistics are too horrifying for the imagination to absorb, but a simple epitaph for the horror of the Final Solution may perhaps be found in the anguished words of twelve-year-old Yunita Vishnyatskaya as she waited her turn to die when the SS ran amok in the small town of Byten, near Białystok, on 31 July 1942. In a note to her father she wrote: 'I'm saying goodbye to you before I die. I'm so afraid of this death

---

* These figures exclude a further 500,000 'Undesirables' – Slavs, Gypsies, homosexuals and the mentally handicapped – who suffered similar fates.

because they throw small children into the mass graves alive. Farewell for ever. I kiss you. I kiss you.'[27]★

By the spring of 1943, Hitler's armies were not only on the retreat from the Soviet Union but had been comprehensively defeated in North Africa. At the battle of El Alamein in November 1942, Rommel's forces had been routed by the British 8th Army under General Bernard Montgomery.† Rommel was forced to retreat to Tripoli pursued, more tentatively than necessary, by the British. A few days later the first wave of 100,000 Allied troops under the overall command of General Dwight D. Eisenhower landed on the shores of Morocco and Algeria to launch Operation Torch – Churchill's 'true Second Front'. The US troops met much stiffer resistance than they might have expected from the Vichy French and it was not until early December that the Allies were able to consolidate their hold on both Morocco and Algeria.

Realizing the threat to the Axis presence in the region, Hitler dispatched an entire panzer army across the Mediterranean to Tunisia to shore up Rommel's forces, which had withdrawn from Libya into the mountainous terrain in the west of the country. For the Americans it was a baptism of fire for which they were ill prepared. On more than one occasion, a number of US units retreated in disarray, and at the Battle of Kasserine Pass they were comprehensively defeated by Rommel's reinforced panzer divisions. The arrival of General George Patton to take command of the US troops in the field shored up their resolve and in March the Anglo-American pincers began to close around the Axis forces. Rommel advised further retreat but was overruled by Hitler. Apparently on the grounds of sickness, he then flew back to Germany.

★ The letter was found by Major Vladimir Demodov two years later in Byten following the liberation of Białystok by the Red Army in August 1944.
† In August 1942 Churchill flew to Cairo on his way to Moscow for his summit with Stalin. Frustrated by General Auchinleck's wise decision not to launch a premature counter-attack against the Axis forces, he sacked him. He had hoped to replace him with General Gott, who was killed a few days later when his plane was shot down in the desert. Montgomery was summoned from Britain to take command of the 8th Army. He proved to be even more cautious than Auchinleck, which was why, to Churchill's further frustration, the battle of El Alamein did not begin until the end of October.

On 13 May 1943 the Axis forces surrendered, handing over 270,000 prisoners to Patton and Montgomery. The Allies now were not only unassailably in control of North Africa but had eliminated the Axis threat to the Middle East and thus put themselves in a position to dominate the seaways across the Mediterranean. This opened the way – in line with Churchill's original proposal to Roosevelt – for a full-scale invasion of Sicily and Italy. The landings in Sicily on 10 July 1943 were accomplished so easily that the Axis forces were driven off the island in less than ten days. With the overthrow of Mussolini a fortnight later, the Italian armies were in a state of shock and disarray. In September the Allies came ashore at the Italian port of Salerno, forcing Hitler once again to withdraw units from other fronts, including Kursk, to shore up the Third Reich's 'soft underbelly'. For the Anglo-US armies, it was the start of what would be a long, hard-fought slog to the north. This attritional battle became a major distraction for the Wehrmacht and was therefore of significant if indirect benefit to the Soviet Union.

As the Allies began to close in on the weakening Third Reich, the flow of aid to the Soviet Union surged. This was due to several factors. First, victory in the Mediterranean allowed merchant ships to reach Egypt and so (via the Suez Canal) to access the Red Sea and the Persian Gulf directly rather than making the twelve-week voyage around the Cape of Good Hope. That, in turn, made it possible to open the overland route from Basra and other ports to southern Russia. Added to these were successes against the U-boat menace in the Atlantic, a sharply reduced Luftwaffe threat over the Arctic passage to Murmansk and Archangel and the soaring output of US armaments from Roosevelt's 'Arsenal of Democracy'. As a result, Anglo-US supplies to the Soviet Union more than doubled (from 2.74 million tons to 6.96 million tons) between 1942 and 1944.[28]

Competing estimates of the impact of this aid – which by 1945 would amount to more than $11 billion ($160 billion in 2020 figures) – on the Red Army's war-fighting capacity were to range from 4 per cent (Soviet figures) to 11 per cent (US figures). Whichever figure is nearer to the truth (a continuing source of friction, recrimination and dispute between the Soviet Union and the Western Allies), the supply of tanks, aircraft, motor vehicles, communications equipment, high-octane fuel and much, much more made a greater contribution to the performance of the Soviet armies than Moscow would ever concede, though significantly less than some in the West were wont to believe.* While Zhukov was to concede grudgingly that Lend Lease was 'of certain help', while claiming that it was 'insignificant against the overall requirements of our country',[29] General Marshall was, preposterously, to claim, as late as 1944 – by which time Hitler's armies were stumbling back to Berlin – 'If Russia suddenly lost Lend Lease, the Nazis could still probably defeat her.'[30] Perhaps the most balanced assessment came from the secret conclusions of the Joint Chiefs of Staff, who judged that it was the mobilization of Soviet industry, 'aided by the critical marginal imports under Lend Lease', that allowed the Soviet Union to maintain its fighting strength.[31]

Western aid undoubtedly facilitated and perhaps accelerated the Red Army's successes in 1943 and thereafter, but Hitler's fate had already been sealed in 1941, at a point when, even though the Wehrmacht was at its strongest and the Red Army at its weakest, Hitler's armies proved themselves incapable of defeating the Soviet Union. By the end of that year, aid from the West had barely made any impact on the outcome for both genuine reasons (scarce shipping, a shortage of supplies, competing priorities) and less sound ones (the widespread belief that the Soviet Union was doomed). Britain had managed to deliver a total of only 676 aircraft, 446 tanks and 867 other vehicles, while the United States contributed a mere 29 aircraft, 35 armoured vehicles and 1,506 other vehicles.

It is not to dismiss the fortitude of those who offered – and gave – their lives to deliver that aid across enemy-infested oceans to point out that the main motive behind the delivery of Western aid to the Soviet Union was not altruistic but the unwarranted fear that, in the absence of such commitment, Stalin might have been tempted to sue for peace with Hitler. As both Washington and London recognized, defeat for the Soviet Union on the Eastern Front would have been catastrophic for the Allies. In effect, as they were well aware, the Red Army was fighting Britain's and America's wars as well as its own. Churchill's combustible relationship with Stalin was frequently ignited by the Soviet dictator's churlish insistence that Western aid was an 'obligation', but the prime minister never shied away from acknowledging the fact that – greatly to the advantage of the West – the Russians 'had broken the German Army as no other nation would have done'.[32]

---

* The dispute did not end with the collapse of the Soviet Union in 1991 but continues to this day.

In 1941, as Army Group Centre began the retreat from Moscow, Churchill and Roosevelt had forbidden the Foreign Secretary to discuss the future shape of Europe at his meetings with Stalin except in the vaguest terms. When Eden argued that a Soviet victory over Hitler's armies would make Russia's position in Europe 'unassailable',[33] and that serious talks should begin before that point, Churchill had slapped him down, insisting that 'the United States and the British Empire' would emerge from the war so militarily and economically powerful that the Soviet Union would have no choice but to become a supplicant for Western largesse; only then would it become necessary to discuss the future contours of the map of Europe.[34] By 1943 – by which time it was abundantly clear even to the Jeremiahs in London and Washington that the Soviet Union would prevail on the Eastern Front – the prime minister's stance had ceased to be tenable, and he knew it.

On the back of the Red Army's victories at Stalingrad and Kursk, Stalin was in an immeasurably stronger position to set his own terms, and he did so. Thus, at the Teheran Conference in November 1943, the Big Three agreed – as Stalin had demanded during his discussions with Eden a little under two years earlier – that the Curzon Line should become the post-war border between Poland and the Soviet Union. They further agreed – as Stalin had also demanded – that the Baltic States should be reincorporated into the Soviet Union, though they added a codicil to the effect that this assimilation should be subject to referenda in all three countries. In the harsh world of Europe's emerging realpolitik, this was tantamount to acknowledging that Stalin had the right – from might – to establish a Soviet 'sphere of influence' in Eastern Europe.

It was during the Teheran Conference that Churchill and Roosevelt alerted Stalin to their decision that the long-postponed European second front was to be opened in the late spring of the following year. Operation Overlord, launched on 6 June 1944 – D-Day – was the greatest amphibious invasion in history. Its military purpose was clear – to destroy Hitler's armies in the west and (via the liberation of Paris) to join up with Stalin's armies in Berlin. It was more than 1,000 kilometres from the Normandy beaches to the German capital, a long and arduous struggle against skilled, experienced and latterly fanatical resistance.

It was an expensive campaign. In September, Operation Market

Garden, the poorly conceived brainchild of General Montgomery, cost almost 17,000 Allied casualties. Nonetheless, though the Wehrmacht won that battle, it was a pyrrhic victory. Even so, it was not until January 1945, after a five-week battle that cost some 89,000 US and 1,400 British casualties, that the Allies could claim with confidence that at the Battle of the Ardennes they had well and truly broken Hitler's stranglehold on western Europe.

If there was no doubt about the eventual outcome of Operation Overlord, there was likewise none about its strategic purpose. Knowing that the fate of the continent would be decided on the battlefield as much as in the conference chamber, the Allies were resolved not only to play their part in the final overthrow of the Third Reich but also to ensure that in the process they would secure their share of what was bound to be a broken and divided Europe. Although Operation Overlord was not exclusively designed to prevent the Soviet Union from bestriding too much of the European continent in addition to completing the downfall of a murderous dictator, it had that purpose as well. In either case, it was deemed important to reach Berlin at much the same time as the Russians, warm words on typed pages being no substitute for tough boots on firm ground.

In October 1944, as the Allies closed on the German capital, the prime minister flew to the Soviet Union for his second Moscow Conference, accompanied by the Foreign Secretary, Eden. The CIGS, Sir Alan Brooke and Averell Harriman (appointed US ambassador to Moscow a year earlier) were in attendance as observers. However, it was a private session between the prime minister and Stalin that was later to garner the most attention. In the midst of discussing the contours of post-war Europe, Churchill seized a scrap of paper and jotted down a list of East European nations, each with a percentage allocation as though to confirm that the Big Three should carve up the continent between them. It was a dramatic gesture but far less significant than Churchill would choose to believe. Stalin only gave the proposal cursory attention while Roosevelt – who had not been consulted beforehand – refused to endorse it. It therefore merely confirmed Britain's status as the junior partner in their alliance while reinforcing the unpalatable fact that virtually nothing could prevent Stalin from calling the political as well as the military shots in the territories soon to be liberated by the Red Army.

At the Yalta Conference in February 1945, just before the final collapse of the Third Reich, the Big Three appeared to circumvent the formal division of the continent into 'spheres of influence' mooted at Teheran by making an agreement allowing the people of every country of liberated Europe to hold free elections that would 'create democratic institutions of their own choice'. If this was an attempt to stymie the creation of a Soviet-dominated eastern bloc, it could hardly have served Stalin's purpose better. He happily agreed, in the full knowledge that the repressive power of the Soviet Union could be deployed to bluff and bully the nations of eastern Europe into succumbing to Moscow's menacing embrace.

As the Foreign Secretary had forewarned more than three years earlier – when he advised negotiating the borders of Europe well before Stalin was in a position to dictate terms – 'the establishment of Communist Governments in the majority of European countries' was indeed 'greatly facilitated' at Yalta.[35] As the world would soon discover, Stalin had no qualms about violating either the spirit or the letter of the 'Declaration of Liberated Europe', as the Yalta accords were grandiosely entitled, and he would do so with impunity while the West watched on with frustration but without the means – military or diplomatic – to prevent it.

By the time of the Potsdam Conference five months later, when the European war was over, the Soviet Union, which had by then retaken Ukraine, was in occupation of the Baltic States, Poland, Czechoslovakia, Hungary, Bulgaria and Romania. Eastern Europe was at that point not only within Moscow's sphere of influence but was trapped behind what became known as the Iron Curtain.

As Stalin would never refrain from pointing out, it was to the Soviet Union, far more than to the other anti-Nazi belligerents, that the peoples of Europe owed the destruction of the Third Reich. And he was determined to exact his due in full measure. To protect his regime from any external threat to its ruthless internal hegemony, he required these satellite states to endure what became almost half a century of coercive rule by stooges who willingly sold their souls to an over-mighty Moscow. The principles of freedom and democracy, which were supposed to have been restored to those benighted nations following the defeat of Nazism, were stifled in the name of a 'socialist solidarity' that became indistinguishable from tyranny.

None of that would have happened had Europe not been cursed by the emergence of Adolf Hitler from the convulsive miseries of the continent following the First World War. What might have transpired if the Führer's world view had been bounded by a modicum of reason or humanity, or if Britain and the Soviet Union had found common cause before Ribbentrop and Molotov put their names to that eponymous pact in August 1939, leads to fruitless speculation.

It is similarly futile to wonder what might have happened once the Red Army had the Wehrmacht on the run if Britain and the United States had failed either to take up arms against the Third Reich or had launched the second front before June 1944. As it was, their intervention on the ground at that point was crucial to the restoration of freedom and democracy in western Europe. For the most part, those tender plants were to survive, if not always flourish, during the decades in the second half of the twentieth century when the peoples of all Europe – east and west – shivered under the nuclear umbrella that the architects of the Cold War had erected to protect themselves from each other.

That virus was incubated in the European conflagration of 1939–45, during which tens of millions of soldiers and tens of millions of civilians of many nationalities died in hideous circumstances. The ultimate responsibility for that carnage lay with Adolf Hitler. If there is any small comfort to be drawn from the cataclysm that engulfed the continent in those years, it is that his decision to invade the Soviet Union on 22 June 1941 led directly to the annihilation of the Third Reich and the demise of both Nazism and, by his own hand, the Führer himself. The German invasion of the Soviet Union was strategically ill conceived, tactically ill planned and operationally incoherent. The criminal venture of a monster, Operation Barbarossa was indeed how Hitler lost the war.

Acknowledgements

My bookshelves groan under the weight of the books, essays, research papers and official documents I have consulted in my search better to understand Operation Barbarossa. Although most of these are listed in the Select Bibliography, I also owe their authors a debt of gratitude – sometimes through gritted teeth – for the knowledge I have acquired from them. They have been my principal sources as I explored the origins and the global context of the conflict as well as the character and scale of the titanic struggle itself.

I have drawn heavily from a voluminous archive of memoirs, diaries and reports written by those who fought in the front line, who had command over those who did, or who found themselves for one reason or another caught up in a genocidal struggle. Among these are several that are so gruesome in detail or horrifying in outlook that I would never have read them for pleasure. Others are implausible attempts at self-exculpation which deserve at best our contempt. All of them, however, contain vivid and telling insights into the horror of total war.

I have also been fortunate to learn from some brilliant works of British, American, Russian and German scholarship that are both illuminating and easily accessible to the lay reader. Of particular value among these have been the books (all cited in the Select Bibliography) written by Anne Applebaum, Tim Bouverie, Antony Beevor, Christopher Browning, Alan Bullock, John Erickson, Richard J. Evans, Jürgen Förster, David Glantz, Vasily Grossman, Gabriel Gorodetsky, Max Hastings, Waldo Heinrichs, Gerhard Hirschfeld, Michael Jones, Ian Kershaw, Robert Kershaw, Catherine Merridale, Richard Overy, Laurence Rees, Andrew Roberts, Simon Sebag Montefiore, Timothy Snyder, David Stahel, Adam Tooze and Alexander Werth.

I am indebted to seven leading historians of the period covered by this book who read parts or all of the manuscript with the care and perception of specialists: Tim Bouverie, Sir Rodric Braithwaite, Professor Sir Richard J. Evans, Professor Gerhard Hirschfeld, Robert Kershaw,

Roger Moorhouse and Dr Lyuba Vinogradova added immeasurably to such quality as the book may have. They were sometimes trenchant but always constructive in criticism. Between them, they saved me from egregious errors and offered wise suggestions, many of which I have incorporated. Needless to say, they bear no responsibility for any errors of fact or judgement that the reader may nonetheless identify.

I am especially grateful to Sir Rodric Braithwaite, who – along with Sir Antony Beevor and Sir Max Hastings – gave me encouragement and advice as I embarked on this daunting project. Like Sir Rodric, Professor Gerhard Hirschfeld, who encouraged me to persist with my initial approach, has from the start added fruitful insights drawn from his own pioneering work while guiding me to fellow German historians such as Dr Christian Streit, to whom I am also grateful.

Not for the first time, I am indebted to the Russian historian and my researcher, Lyuba Vinogradova. She has pioneered the study of Soviet women on the battlefield and is the author of two excellent books on the subject. I benefited from these and especially, for this book, from letters and diaries that she retrieved and translated from various Russian archives. She also corrected my lamentable spelling of Russian proper names.

Kate Patten undertook the massive task of sifting through Foreign Office and Cabinet papers to select relevant documents and memoranda which she organized into a coherent set of files. Her speed and diligence have been invaluable. She was also given access to the Liddell Hart Centre for Military Archives and King's College London Archives, to whose staff I am grateful.

Veronique Baxter, my agent at David Higham Associates, has yet again demonstrated why she is so highly regarded by her peers. Her judgement is invariably astute and her support has been unwavering.

The production of a book is a complex team effort. The Viking team who have worked on *Barbarossa* have once again been peerless. I am grateful to them all, and notably to Jess Barnfield (audio editor), Emma Brown (managing editor), Bela Cunha (proofreader), Charlotte Daniels (cover designer), Charlotte Faber (producer), Amelia Fairney (communications director), Sam Fanaken (sales director), Anthony Hippisley (proofreader), Olivia Mead (campaign manager), Ben Murphy (indexer), Poppy North (publicist) and Caroline Wood (picture researcher). I worked particularly closely with Con Brown and Alpana Sajip (editorial assistants), to whom I am indebted for their patience as well as their expertise.

Trevor Horwood, my copy editor, has yet again demonstrated his unique talent in this most testing of responsibilities. He is meticulous about detail of every kind. He points out repetitions of words and phrases and suggests better alternatives; remarkably, he notes self-contradictions – often separated by hundreds of pages – and suggests politely but firmly that I resolve them. I owe him a great debt.

My editor, Daniel Crewe, not only suggested that I should write about Barbarossa (as he had done with *Destiny in the Desert* and *The Battle of the Atlantic*) but also gave unstintingly of his rare editorial gifts. His quiet wisdom, guidance, judgement and humour have been of incalculable value. My debt to him goes far beyond what one might expect; I treasure his friendship.

Stella Keeley, my PA, has the patience of many saints. As well as imposing order on my office (which has proved even more challenging than usual during lockdown) she typed up hundreds of pages of dictated notes, made sense of my filing system and, more generally, saved me from being overwhelmed by a surfeit of email correspondence while gently reminding me of what I have forgotten, overlooked, or assiduously ignored. She is unfailingly and reassuringly calm in any tempest.

I am indebted to Daniel Flowerday, a professional librarian, who, with skill and patience, put my books in a coherent order, thereby saving me hours of fruitless searching.

I am grateful too for the support of family, friends and colleagues, too many of whom have had to endure my incontinent urge to tell them more than they need or may wish to know about the importance of Operation Barbarossa. But none of these had to endure as much as my wife, Jessica, and our daughters, Daisy and Gwendolen. I am ashamed to think of the number of times that one or other of the children has burst into my study to tell me the latest news from school only to be dismissed with the words, 'Later, later, I'm writing.' I hope they forgive me. Their adult siblings, Dan and Kitty, who have been through it all before, would sympathize with them.

It is Jessica, though, who has had to bear much the heaviest burden.

As well as running our home life, she has her own demanding career as a teacher of troubled teenagers. I sometimes think that I have been more trouble than all her students put together, yet she has never complained or protested. She has tolerated the fact that for much of the time I have been semi-detached – or, as she puts it, 'in the zone' – while absorbing my sudden bursts of enthusiasm or bouts of gloom with a quite extraordinary generosity of spirit. Without her at my side, I would be quite lost.

Notes

1. Paving the Way

1 House of Commons, 3 April 1922, Hansard, vol. 152, cols. 1886–7.

2 66th Congress, 1st session, Senate Documents: Addresses of President Wilson, May–November, vol. II, no. 120, p. 206.

3 Edward H. Carr, *German–Soviet Relations: Between the Two World Wars, 1919–1939* (Johns Hopkins University Press, 1954), p. 10.

4 Quoted in Margaret MacMillan, *Peacemakers: The Paris Conference of 1919 and Its Attempt to End War* (John Murray, 2002), p. 76.

5 Quoted ibid., p. 75.

6 Quoted ibid.

7 Edwin L. James, 'Russians Put in Big War Bill to Allies; Lloyd George Responds with Warning They Must First Accept Allied Claims', *New York Times*, 16 April 1922, cited in 'Extra! Extra! Read All About It: The British and American Press Coverage of German-Soviet Collaboration, 1917–1928', MA thesis, Harvey Daniel Munshaw, University of Michigan, 2013.

8 Arthur Ransome, 'Russians Prepare for Genoa Session, Plan to Live 30 Miles Out of City Irks Bolshevist', *Manchester Guardian*, 31 March 1922, cited in Munshaw, 'Extra! Extra!'.

9 Carr, *German–Soviet Relations*, p. 17.

10 Roy Hattersley, *David Lloyd George: The Great Outsider* (Abacus, 2012), p. 55.

11 Carr, *German–Soviet Relations*, p. 9.

12 Note by Cabinet Secretary Maurice Hankey to Austen Chamberlain, 18 April 1922, cited in Carole Fink, *The Genoa Conference: European Diplomacy, 1921–1922* (Syracuse University Press, 1994), p. 179.

13 Curzon minute, 29 April 1922, FO 371/8188/N 3869 – cited in Stephanie C. Salzmann, *Great Britain, Germany and the Soviet Union: Rapallo and After, 1922–1934* (Royal Historical Society, 2013), p. 19.

14 'Placing the Blame', *New York Times*, 9 May 1922, cited in Munshaw, 'Extra! Extra!', p. 28.

15 Sir William Tyrrell to Curzon, 27 April 1922, Curzon papers, MSS Eur F 1.2/227. Quoted in Salzmann, *Great Britain, Germany and the Soviet Union*, p. 26.

16 Heinz Guderian, *Panzer Leader*, trans. Constantine Fitzgibbon (Penguin, 2009), p. 26.

17 Chamberlain minute, 4 January 1925, *Documents on British Foreign Policy* (hereafter *DBFP*), cited in Salzmann, *Great Britain, Germany and the Soviet Union*, p. 56.

18 Harold Nicolson memo, 20 February 1925, PRO FO 371/10727/C2, cited in Salzmann, *Great Britain, Germany and the Soviet Union*, p. 57. Nicolson was later to achieve renown both as a diarist and as the wayward husband of the equally wayward Vita Sackville-West.

19 Chamberlain to D'Abernon, 26 April 1926, PRO, FO 371/113245/N19564.

20 Chamberlain to Sir R. M. Hodgson, British chargé d'affaires in Moscow, 26 April 1926, *DBFP*, cited in Salzmann, *Great Britain, Germany and the Soviet Union*, p. 79.

21 Conversation between Chamberlain and the French prime minister, Aristide Briand (who was leading his seventh administration in twenty years), 18 May 1927, *DBFP*, cited in Salzmann, *Great Britain, Germany and the Soviet Union*, p. 86.

22 Adolf Hitler, *Mein Kampf*, 2 vols., trans. Ralph Manheim (Pimlico, 1992), vol. I, pp. 272–98 passim.

23 Ibid., vol. II, p. 577.

24 Ibid., pp. 597–8.

25 Ian Kershaw, *Hitler, 1889–1936: Hubris* (Penguin, 2001), p. 440.

26 Quoted in Adam Tooze, *The Wages of Destruction: The Making and Breaking of the Nazi Economy* (Penguin, 2007), p. 100.

2. Dictators and Democrats

1 Quoted in *Russia Beyond*, 26 July 2016, www.rbth.com/arts/literature/2016/07/26/bernard-shaw-i-cant-die-without-having-seen-the-ussr_615147.

2 Quoted in Anna Reid, *Borderlands: A Journey Through the History of Ukraine* (Westview Press, 1999).

3 *Manchester Guardian*, 25, 27 and 28 March 1933.

4 Minutes of 7th Plenum of the Central Black Earth Regional Committee, quoted in Jonathan Dimbleby, *Russia: A Journey to the Heart of a Land and Its People* (BBC Books, 2008), p. 155.

5 Official documents cited ibid., p. 156.

6 Lev Kopelev, *No Jail for Thought* (Penguin, 1979), p. 33.

7 Quoted in Sheila Fitzpatrick, *Everyday Stalinism: Ordinary Life in Extraordinary Times: Soviet Russia in the 1930s* (Oxford University Press, 1999), p. 18, cited in Catherine Merridale, *Ivan's War: The Red Army 1939–1945* (Faber & Faber, 2005), p. 30.

8 Kopelev, *No Jail for Thought*, p. 33.

9 Quoted in Timothy Snyder, *Bloodlands: Europe Between Hitler and Stalin* (Vintage, 2001), p. 48.

10 Letters to the Editor, 'Social Conditions in Russia', *Manchester Guardian*, 2 March 1933.

11 Arthur Koestler, *The Yogi and the Commissar and Other Essays* (Cape, 1945), p. 142.

12 Arthur Koestler in Richard Crossman (ed.), *The God That Failed* (Hamish Hamilton, 1950), cited in Snyder, *Bloodlands*, p. 54.

13 *New York Evening Post*, 30 March 1933; London *Evening Standard*, 31 March 1933.

14 *New York Times*, 31 March 1933.

15 *New York Times*, 20 August 1933.

16 [Malcolm Muggeridge], 'The Soviet and the Peasantry, an Observer's Notes 1. Famine in North Caucasus (from a Correspondent in Russia)', *Manchester Guardian*, 25 March 1933.

17 [Malcolm Muggeridge], 'The Soviet and the Peasantry, an Observer's Notes 2. Hunger in the Ukraine (from a Correspondent in Russia)', *Manchester Guardian*, 27 March 1933.

18 *The Diaries of Beatrice Webb*, ed. Norman and Jeanne MacKenzie (Virago, 2000), p. 514.

19 Anne Applebaum, *Red Famine: Stalin's War on Ukraine* (Penguin, 2018), p. 324.

20 Quoted in Sally J. Taylor, 'A Blanket of Silence: The Response of the Western Press Corps in Moscow to the Ukraine Famine of 1932–1933', in Wsevolod Isajiw (ed.), *Famine-Genocide in Ukraine, 1932–1933* (Toronto: Ukrainian Canadian Research and Documentation Centre, 2003), pp. 77–95, cited in Snyder, *Bloodlands*, p. 55.

21 *New York Times*, 30 March 1933.

22 Quoted in Robert Dallek, *Franklin D. Roosevelt and American Foreign Policy, 1932–45* (Oxford University Press, 1995), p. 36.

23 Cited ibid.

24 Douglas MacArthur, *Reminiscences* (New York, 1964), p. 101, quoted ibid.

25 *The Roosevelt Letters, 1928–1945*, vol. I, pp. 449–52, cited ibid., p. 97.

26 Quoted in Dallek, *Franklin D. Roosevelt and American Foreign Policy*, p. 80.

27 Duranty writing in the *New York Times*, 3 February 1931, cited in Tim Tzouliadis, *The Forsaken: An American Tragedy in Stalin's Russia* (Penguin, 2009), p. 27.

28 See ibid., passim.

29 Will Brownell and Richard N. Billings, *So Close to Greatness: A Biography of William C. Bullitt* (Macmillan, 1987), passim.

30 Shaw quoted in the *Daily Telegraph*, 18 June 2003.

31 Osip Mandelstam, *Selected Poems*, trans. Clarence Brown and W. S. Merwin (New York Review Books, 2004), p. 69. I am grateful to Rodric Braithwaite for drawing my attention to this poem.

32 Joseph E. Davies, *Mission to Moscow* (Victor Gollancz, 1944), pp. 34–5.

33 Memo to the Honourable Secretary of State, Moscow, 17 February 1937, quoted ibid., pp. 31–41.

34 Peter Whitewood, 'The Purge of the Red Army and the Soviet Mass Operations, 1937–1938', *Slavonic and East European Review*, 93(2), pp. 286–314.

35 Simon Sebag Montefiore, *Stalin: The Court of the Red Tsar* (Weidenfeld and Nicolson, 2003) p. 219.

36 Ibid., p. 206.

37 Ibid.

38 Stalin in conversation with Beria in November 1938, quoted ibid., pp. 216, 217.

3. Shuttle Diplomacy

1 Gabriel Gorodetsky (ed.), *The Maisky Diaries: Red Ambassador to the Court of St James's, 1932–1943*, trans. Tatiana Sorokina and Oliver Ready (Yale University Press, 2015), p. 103.

2 Chamberlain, quoted ibid., p. 82.

3 House of Commons, 13 July 1934, Hansard, vol. 292, cols. 732–5.

4 Hitler, *Mein Kampf*, pp. 116–43 passim; *Mein Kampf*, vol. II, *The National Socialist Movement*, 70th impression, (JAICO Publishing, 2001), pp. 563–4.

5 Quoted in Tooze, *The Wages of Destruction*.

6 Gerhard Weinberg, *Hitler's Foreign Policy, 1933–1939: The Road to World War II* (Enigma, 2004), p. 258.

7 Harold Nicolson, *The Harold Nicolson Diaries, 1919–1964* (Weidenfeld and Nicolson, 2004), p. 139.

8 A. J. P. Taylor, *The Origins of the Second World War* (Penguin, 1991), p. 132.

9 'Record of a Discussion Which Took Place Between the Prime Minister and a Deputation from Both Houses of Parliament on 28 July 1936', PRO PREM1/193, cited in Michael J. Carley, *1939: The Alliance That Never Was and the Coming of World War II* (Ivan R. Dee, 1999), p. 33.

10 House of Commons, 12 November 1936, Hansard, vol. 317, col. 1107.

11 Ian Kershaw, *Hitler, 1936–1945: Nemesis* (Penguin, 2001), p. 61.

12 Victor Klemperer, *I Shall Bear Witness: The Diaries of Victor Klemperer, 1933–41*, trans. Martin Chalmers (Weidenfeld and Nicolson, 1998), p. 268.

13 Ibid., p. 280.

14 William L. Shirer, *Berlin Diary: The Journal of a Foreign Correspondent, 1934–1941* (Knopf, 1941), p. 142.

4. Self-Delusion and Bad Faith

1 Letter of 2 October 1938, quoted in Tim Bouverie, *Appeasing Hitler: Chamberlain, Churchill and the Road to War* (Bodley Head, 2019), p. 305.

2 For a full account, see ibid., pp. 301–2.

3 Letter of 9 October 1938, quoted in Bouverie, *Appeasing Hitler*, p. 306.

4 David Dilks (ed.), *The Diaries of Sir Alexander Cadogan, 1938–45* (Faber & Faber, 2010), p. 127.

5 Quoted in Kershaw, *Hitler, 1936–1945*, p. 167.

6 Quoted in Tooze, *The Wages of Destruction*, p. 284.

7 Quoted in Kershaw, *Hitler, 1936–1945*, p. 168.

8 Paul Schmidt, *Hitler's Interpreter: The Memoirs of Paul Schmidt* (The History Press, 2016).

9 Kershaw, *Hitler, 1936–1945*, p. 171.

10 Memorandum by Jebb, 19 January 1939, CAB27/627, quoted in Dilks, *Cadogan Diaries*, p. 130.

11 Speech at Nuremberg rally, 2 September 1936, quoted in Kershaw, *Hitler, 1936–1945*, p. 17.

12 Quoted ibid.

13 Quoted in Roger Moorhouse, *The Devil's Alliance: Hitler's Pact with Stalin, 1939–1941* (Vintage, 2016), p. 15.

14 Quoted in Tooze, *The Wages of Destruction*, p. 307.

15 Kershaw, *Hitler, 1936–1945*, pp. 190–93.

16 Christopher Andrew and Oleg Gordievsky, *KGB: The Inside Story of its Foreign Operations from Lenin to Gorbachev* (Hodder and Stoughton, 1990), p. 187.

17 House of Commons, Foreign Affairs and Rearmament Debate, 24 March 1938, Hansard, vol. 333, cols. 1399–514.

18 Gorodetsky, *Maisky Diaries*, 8 March 1938.

19 Letter of 20 March 1938, quoted in Bouverie, *Appeasing Hitler*, p. 199.

20 Dilks, *Cadogan Diaries*, 17 February 1939.

21 Memo of 19 April, CAB, quoted in Anthony Read and David Fisher, *The Deadly Embrace: Hitler, Stalin and the Nazi-Soviet Pact, 1939–1941* (W. W. Norton, 1988), p. 72.

22 Collier to Strang, 28 April 1939, C6206/3356/18, PRO FO 371 23064, quoted in Carley, *1939*, p. 131.

23 Gorodetsky, *Maisky Diaries*, 18 May 1939.

24 House of Commons, 19 May 1939, Hansard, vol. 345, cols. 2475–588.

25 Dilks, *Cadogan Diaries*, 16 May 1939.

26 Ibid., 20 May 1939.

27 Letter to Ida, 21 May 1939, quoted in Bouverie, *Appeasing Hitler*, p. 337.

28 Halifax (in Geneva) to Cadogan, 22 May 1939, *DBFP*, quoted in Carley, *1939*, p. 150.

29 Dilks, *Cadogan Diaries*, 20 June 1939.

30 Winston S. Churchill, *The Second World War*, vol. I: *The Gathering Storm* (Cassell, 1948), p. 303.

31 Lord Strang, *The Moscow Negotiations, 1939* (Leeds University Press, 1968), quoted in Read and Fisher, *The Deadly Embrace*, p. 100.

32 Dilks, *Cadogan Diaries*, 20 June 1939.

33 Molotov to Maisky and Surits, 17 July 1939, *Dokumenty vneshnei politiki*, vol. XXII: *1939* (Moscow, 1992), bk. 1, pp. 535–7.

34 Strang to Sir Orme Sargent, 20 July 1939, *DBFP*, quoted in Bouverie, *Appeasing Hitler*, p. 354.

35 Quoted in Read and Fisher, *The Deadly Embrace*, p. 110.

36 Loraine to Halifax, 24 July 1939, *DBFP*, quoted in Bouverie, *Appeasing Hitler*, p. 345.

37 John Harvey (ed.), *The Diplomatic Diaries of Oliver Harvey, 1937–1940* (Collins, 1970), p. 303.

38 Chamberlain to Ida, 23 July 1939, NC18/1/1108, Chamberlain Papers, quoted in Carley, *1939*, p. 180.

39 Chamberlain to Hilda, 30 July 1939, NC18/1/1110, Chamberlain Papers, quoted ibid., p. 173.

40 Quoted in Laurence Rees, *The Nazis: A Warning from History* (New Press, 1997), p. 93.

41 Dilks, *Cadogan Diaries*, p. 193.

42 Seeds, no. 172, 23 July 1939, C10325/3356/18, PRO FO 371, quoted in Carley, *1939*, p. 183.

43 Drax, 'Mission to Moscow, August 1939', Churchill Archives, Drax Papers, 6/5, f. 6., quoted in Carley, *1939*, p. 185.

44 House of Commons, 2 August 1939, Hansard, vol. 350, cols. 2425–525.

45 Quoted in Read and Fisher, *The Deadly Embrace*, p. 137.

46 Speech at the 18th Communist Party Congress, 10 March 1939 (Soviet Documents on Foreign Policy, vol. III), quoted in Moorhouse, *The Devil's Alliance*, p. 24.

47 Committee on Imperial Defence, Deputy Chief of Staffs Sub-Committee, 16 August 1939, C11506/335/18, PRO FO 371 23072, cited in Carley, *1939*, p. 199.

48 Dilks, *Cadogan Diaries*, 18 August 1939.

49 Quoted ibid., p. 235.

50 Moorhouse, *The Devil's Alliance*, p. 35.

51 Charles Burdick and Hans-Adolf Jacobsen (eds.), *The Halder War Diary, 1939–1942* (Presidio, 1988), 28 August 1939.

52 The League of Nations Commissioner in Danzig, *Documents on German Foreign Policy* (hereafter *DGFP*), Series D, vol. II, no. 175, quoted in Alan Bullock, *Hitler and Stalin: Parallel Lives* (HarperCollins, 1991), p. 708.

53 Albert Speer, *Inside the Third Reich: Memoirs by Albert Speer*, trans. Richard and Clara Winston (Weidenfeld and Nicolson, 1970), p. 161.

54 Cited in Carley, *1939*, p. 205.

5. A Pact with Satan

1 Quoted in Sebag Montefiore, *Stalin*, p. 276.

2 Victor Kravchenko, *I Chose Freedom: The Personal and Political Life of a Soviet Official* (Robert Hale, 1947), p. 332.

3 Klemperer, *I Shall Bear Witness*, 29 August 1939.

4 Burdick and Jacobsen, *Halder War Diary*, 28 August 1939.

5 Quoted in Kershaw, *Hitler, 1936–1945*, pp. 207–8.

6 Churchill, *The Gathering Storm*, p. 307.

7 Guderian, *Panzer Leader*, pp. 82–3.

8 Quoted in Moorhouse, *The Devil's Alliance*, p. 50.

9 Quoted in Kershaw, *Hitler, 1936–1945*, p. 243.

10 Quoted in Snyder, *Bloodlands*, p. 126.

11 Quoted in Kershaw, *Hitler, 1936–1945*, p. 242.

12 Quoted in Snyder, *Bloodlands*, p. 131.

13 Blaskowitz to Wehrmacht High Command, 27 November 1939, cited in Gerhard Hirschfeld, *The Policies of Genocide: Jews and Soviet Prisoners of War in Nazi Germany* (Allen & Unwin, 1986).

14 Richard Giziowski, *The Enigma of General Blaskowitz* (Hippocrene, 1997), pp. 172–3.

15 Kershaw, *Hitler, 1936–1945*, p. 248.

16 Sebag Montefiore, *Stalin*, p. 297; Snyder, *Bloodlands*, pp. 136–7.

17 See Snyder, *Bloodlands*, pp. 125–6.

18 Ibid., pp. 129–30.

19 Ibid., p. 151.

20 Memo, Cadogan to Halifax, December 1939, FO371/23678 N7198/57/38.

21 War Cabinet Joint Planning Sub-Committee, 19 February, CAB 84/2 JP (40) 10.

22 Dilks, *Cadogan Diaries*, 13 March 1940.

23 These are approximate and disputed totals drawn from a variety of sources, including Sami H. E. Korohonen, The Battles of the Winter War, www.winterwar.com, and https://en.wikipedia.org/wiki/winter_war.

24 Sebag Montefiore, *Stalin*, pp. 292–3.

25 Harold Shukman (ed.), *Stalin's Generals* (Phoenix, 2001), p. 317.

26 Nikita Khrushchev, *Khrushchev Remembers: The Last Testament*, ed. and trans. Strobe Talbott (Little, Brown, 1970), p. 154.

27 FO 371/23678 NS240/57/38, quoted in Gabriel Gorodetsky (ed.), *Stafford Cripps' Mission to Moscow, 1940–42* (Cambridge University Press, 1984), p. 17.

28 CAB 80/8 COS(40)227, 31 January 1940; COS(40)24, 6 February 1940; CAB 84/2 JP(40)10, JP(40)12, 19 February and 19 March 1940, cited in Gorodetsky, *Mission to Moscow*, p. 18.

29 FO 371 24846 N3698/40/38, 23 and 25 March, cited in Gorodetsky, *Mission to Moscow*, p. 24.

30 Gorodetsky, *Maisky Diaries*, 13 March 1940.

31 FO 371 24846 N3698/40/38, 18 and 29 March, cited in Gorodetsky, *Mission to Moscow*, p. 24.

32 House of Commons, 13 May 1940, Hansard, vol. 360, cols. 1501–3.

6. Thieves Fall Out

1 Fred Taylor (ed.), *The Goebbels Diaries, 1939–1941: The Historic Journal of a Nazi War Leader* (Sphere, 1983), 12 and 13 November 1940.

2 Sebag Montefiore, *Stalin*, p. 299.

3 Ibid.

4 FO 371 24582N6029/243/38, memorandum by Sargent, 17 July 1940.

5 *DGFP*, Series D, vol. IX, cited in Moorhouse, *The Devil's Alliance*, p. 198.

6 BBC broadcast, 1 October 1939.

7 Meeting between Molotov and Ambassador Augusto Rosso, 27 June 1940, cited in Gabriel Gorodetsky, *Grand Delusion: Stalin and the German Invasion of Russia* (Yale University Press, 1999), p. 29.

8 Max Hastings, *The Secret War: Spies, Codes and Guerrillas, 1939–1945* (William Collins, 2015), p. 104.

9 'The Situation in Germany After a Year of War', 4 November 1940, report by first secretary of the Berlin Embassy, cited in Gorodetsky, *Grand Delusion*, p. 56.

10 Special report by Filipp Golikov, cited ibid.

11 Schmidt, *Hitler's Interpreter*, p. 205.

12 Ibid.

13 Valentin Berezhkov, *History in the Making: Memoirs of World War Two Diplomacy* (Moscow, 1983), p. 23, quoted in Moorhouse, *The Devil's Alliance*, p. 207.

14 Schmidt, *Hitler's Interpreter*, p. 208.

15 Ibid., p. 209.

16 World War II Database, https://ww2db.com/doc.php?q=31.

17 Sebag Montefiore, *Stalin*, p. 300.

18 *DGFP* Series D, vol. X (London, 1957), no. 13, p. 554, quoted in Moorhouse, *The Devil's Alliance*, p. 211.

19 Schmidt, *Hitler's Interpreter*, p. 210.

20 *DGFP* Series D, vol. X, no. 13, quoted in Moorhouse, *The Devil's Alliance*, p. 212.

21 Ibid.

22 In correspondence with the author.

23 Fireside Chat, 29 December 1940, The American Presidency Project, University of California, Santa Barbara.

24 Burdick and Jacobsen, *Halder War Diary*, 5 December 1940.

25 Adolf Hitler's War Directives, http://der-fuehrer.org/reden/english/war-directives/directives.html.

26 Hastings, *The Secret War*, p. 105.

27 David E. Murphy, *What Stalin Knew: The Enigma of Barbarossa* (Yale University Press, 2005), p. 65.

28 Ibid.

29 Quoted in Gorodetsky, *Grand Delusion*, p. 53.

30 See ibid., pp. 126–7.

31 Georgi Dimitrov, *The Diary of Georgi Dimitrov, 1933–1949*, ed. Ivo Banac, trans. Jane T. Hedges, Timothy D. Sergay and Irina Faion (Yale University Press, 2003), 21 January 1941.

32 Rodric Braithwaite, *Moscow 1941: A City and Its People at War* (Profile, 2007), p. 146.

33 Quoted in Merridale, *Ivan's War*, p. 62.

34 Ibid., p. 63.

35 Alexander Solzhenitsyn, *The First Circle* (Collins, 1970), pp. 132–3, cited in Uri Bar-Joseph and Rose McDermott, *Success and Failure: The Human Factor* (Oxford University Press, 2017), p. 90.

36 General Field Marshal Fedor von Bock, *The War Diary, 1939–1945*, ed. Klaus Gerbet, trans. David Johnston (Schiffer, 1996), 1 February 1941.

37 Burdick and Jacobsen, *Halder War Diary*, 17 March 1941.

38 General Walter Warlimont, *Inside Hitler's Headquarters, 1939–45*, trans. R. H. Barry (Presidio, 1964), p. 161.

39 Burdick and Jacobsen, *Halder War Diary*, 30 March 1941.

40 Warlimont, *Inside Hitler's Headquarters*, p. 162.

41 'General Instructions for Dealing with Political Leaders and for the Co-Ordinated Execution of the Task Allotted on 31 March 1941', quoted ibid., p. 163.

42 'Guidelines for the Behaviour of the Fighting Forces in Russia', 19 May 1941, cited in Horst Boog et al., *Germany and the Second World War*, vol. IV: *The Attack on the Soviet Union*, trans. Dean McMurry, Ewald Osers and Louise Willmot (Clarendon, 1998) pp. 514–15.

43 Burdick and Jacobsen, *Halder War Diary*, 28 January 1941.

44 Leaflet on the peculiarity of Russian warfare, quoted by Jürgen Förster, 'Hitler's Decision in Favour of War Against the Soviet Union', in Boog et al., *Germany and the Second World War*, vol. IV, p. 237.

45 See Jonathan Dimbleby, *Destiny in the Desert: The Road to El Alamein – The Battle that Turned the Tide* (Profile, 2013), pp. 58–82.

46 Douglas Porch, *Hitler's Mediterranean Gamble: The North American and Mediterranean Campaigns in World War II* (Cassell, 2004), p. 28 and Dimbleby, *Destiny in the Desert*, pp. 59ff.

47 John Kennedy, *The Business of War: The War Narrative of Major General Sir John Kennedy* (Hutchinson, 1957), p. 72.

48 Ibid., pp. 75–6.

49 Winston S. Churchill, *The Second World War*, vol. III: *The Grand Alliance* (Cassell, 1950), pp. 143–4.

50 Quoted ibid., p. 146.

51 Hitler Directive No. 25, 27 March 1941, http://der-fuehrer.org/reden/english/wardirectives/directives.html.

52 See Andrew Roberts, *Masters and Commanders: How Roosevelt, Churchill, Marshall and Alanbrooke Won the War in the West* (Allen Lane, 2008), p. 124.

7. Stalin Ignores the Warnings

1 Peter Clarke, *The Cripps Version: The Life of Sir Stafford Cripps, 1889–1952* (Allen Lane, 2002), p. 365.

2 Quoted in Gabriel Gorodetsky, *Stafford Cripps in Moscow, 1940–1942: Diaries and Papers* (Vallentine Mitchell, 2007), p. 7.

3 Quoted in Gorodetsky, *Mission to Moscow*, p. 17.

4 Ibid.

5 FO 371 29475 N941/40/38, cited in Gorodetsky, *Mission to Moscow*, p. 37.

6 Quoted ibid., p. 23.

7 Sir Robert Rhodes James (ed.), *'Chips': The Diaries of Sir Henry Channon* (Phoenix, 1996), 21 July 1940.

8 Gorodetsky, *Maisky Diaries*, 5 June 1940.

9 Gorodetsky, *Stafford Cripps in Moscow*, 13 June 1940.

10 Winston S. Churchill, *The Second World War*, vol. II: *Their Finest Hour* (Cassell, 1949), pp. 119–20.

11 Quoted in Gorodetsky, *Mission to Moscow*, p. 52.

12 Letter to Sir Tobias Weaver (Cripps's foster son), 25 August 1940, quoted in Gorodetsky, *Mission to Moscow*, p. 67.

13 Gorodetsky, *Stafford Cripps in Moscow*, 10 October 1940.

14 CAB 65/9245 (40) 5, cited in Gorodetsky, *Mission to Moscow*, p. 71.

15 Dilks, *Cadogan Diaries*, 6 January 1941.

16 Ibid., 17 August 1940.

17 Gorodetsky, *Maisky Diaries*, 2 March 1941.

18 Churchill to Field Marshal Smuts, 27 June 1940, Churchill, *Their Finest Hour*, p. 200.

19 CAB 69/8 DO(40), 39th Meeting SSF of 31 October, cited in F. H. Hinsley et al., *British Intelligence in the Second World War: Its Influence on Strategy and Operations*, 4 vols. (HMSO, 1979–90), vol. I, p. 432.

20 Churchill to Stalin, 3 April 1941, Churchill, *The Grand Alliance*, p. 320.

21 Cripps to Eden, 12 April 1941, ibid., p. 321.

22 Foreign Secretary to Churchill, 3 April 1941, ibid., p. 320.

23 Ibid., p. 321.

24 Prime Minister to Foreign Secretary, 18 April 1941, ibid., p. 322.

25 House of Commons, 9 April 1941, Hansard, vol. 370, cols. 1587–605.

26 Gorodetsky, *Maisky Diaries*, 30 April 1941.

27 Quoted in Gorodetsky, *Grand Delusion*, p. 170.

28 Alexander Werth, *Russia at War, 1941–1945* (Pan, 1964), p. 264.

29 FO 371 29465 N1828/3/38, quoted in Gorodetsky, *Mission to Moscow*, pp. 126–7.

30 Quoted in Braithwaite, *Moscow 1941*, p. 55.

31 Quoted in Murphy, *What Stalin Knew*, p. 131.

32 Quoted ibid., p. 132.

33 Quoted in Werth, *Russia at War*, p. 132.

34 Quoted in Murphy, *What Stalin Knew*, p. 87.

35 Taylor, *The Goebbels Diaries*, 14 May 1941.

36 Dilks, *Cadogan Diaries*, 12 May 1941.

37 Ibid., 15 May 1941.

38 Ibid., 19 May 1941.

39 JIC (41) 218, PRO WO208/1761, quoted in Braithwaite, *Moscow 1941*, p. 56.

40 Dilks, *Cadogan Diaries*, 9 May 1941.

41 Hinsley et al., *British Intelligence in the Second World War*, vol. I, p. 481.

42 Ibid., p. 482.

43 US Department of State, *Foreign Relations of the United States, Diplomatic Papers, 1941*, vol. I, Document 151.

44 Taylor, *The Goebbels Diaries*, 14 June 1941.

45 Nicolaus von Below, *At Hitler's Side: The Memoirs of Hitler's Luftwaffe Adjutant, 1937–1945*, trans. Geoffrey Brooks (Frontline, 2012), p. 102.

46 Taylor, *The Goebbels Diaries*, 15 June 1941.

47 Ibid., 16 June 1941.

48 Quoted in Murphy, *What Stalin Knew*, p. 87.

49 Quoted ibid., p. 16.

50 Quoted in Braithwaite, *Moscow 1941*, p. 58.

51 Gorodetsky, *Grand Delusion*, p. 299.

52 Braithwaite, *Moscow 1941*, p. 58.

53 Timoshenko volunteered this recollection to General N. Liashchenko. Quoted in Gorodetsky, *Grand Delusion*, p. 299.

54 Shukman, *Stalin's Generals*, pp. 347–8.

55 Quoted in Murphy, *What Stalin Knew*, p. 69.

8. The Blitzkrieg

1 Quoted in Robert Kershaw, *War Without Garlands: Operation Barbarossa, 1941–1942* (Ian Allen, 2000), p. 62.

2 Guderian, *Panzer Leader*, p. 152.

3 Quoted in Kershaw, *War Without Garlands*, p. 66.

4 Taylor, *The Goebbels Diaries*, 21 June 1941.

5 The Wehrmacht propaganda department, quoted in Boog et al., *Germany and the Second World War*, vol. IV, p. 516.

6 Wilhelm Prüller, *Diary of a German Soldier*, ed. H. C. Robbins Landon and Sebastian Leitner (Coward-McCann, 1963), 21 June 1941.

7 Horst Fuchs Richardson (ed.), *Sieg Heil! War Letters of Tank Gunner Karl Fuchs, 1937–1941* (Archon, 1987), 1 June 1941.

8 Ibid., 3 June 1941.

9 Quoted in John Christopher Hibbert, *Mussolini: The Rise and Fall of Il Duce* (Macmillan, 2008), p. 124.

10 Hitler to Mussolini, 21 June 1941, Nazi–Soviet Relations, German Foreign Office Files, quoted in William L. Shirer, *The Rise and Fall of the Third Reich* (Pan, 1968), pp. 1016–17.

11 John Erickson, *The Road to Stalingrad: Stalin's War with Germany,* vol. 1 (Cassell, 2003), p. 102.

12 John Erickson, *The Soviet High Command* (St Martin's Press, 1962), cited in Seweryn Bialer (ed.), *Stalin & His Generals: Soviet Military Memoirs of World War II* (Souvenir Press, 1970).

13 Ibid., p. 202.

14 Quoted in Erickson, *The Road to Stalingrad*, p. 110.

15 Werth, *Russia at War*, p. 154; Erickson, *The Road to Stalingrad*, p. 104.

16 Merridale, *Ivan's War*, p. 73.

17 Ibid.

18 Erickson, *The Road to Stalingrad*, p. 106.

19 Sebag Montefiore, *Stalin*, p. 365.

20 Quoted ibid.

21 Pavlov's testimony at his interrogation, 7 July 1941, quoted in Merridale, *Ivan's War*, p. 74.

22 Erickson, *The Road to Stalingrad*, p. 109.

23 Ibid., p. 111.

24 Ibid., p. 112.

25 David M. Glantz, *Before Stalingrad: Barbarossa – Hitler's Invasion of Russia, 1941* (Tempus, 2003), p. 30.

26 Taylor, *The Goebbels Diaries*, 21, 22 June 1941.

27 Below, *At Hitler's Side*, p. 102.

28 Quoted in Kershaw, *Hitler, 1936–1945*, p. 387.

29 Antony Beevor, *Stalingrad* (Penguin, 1999), p. 6.

30 Ibid., p. 4.

31 Quoted ibid., p. 7.

32 Quoted ibid., p. 8.

33 Quoted ibid.

34 Quoted in Sebag Montefiore, *Stalin*, p. 323.

35 Boldin quoted in Bialer, *Stalin & His Generals*, p. 229.

36 Braithwaite, *Moscow 1941*, p. 69.

37 Sebag Montefiore, *Stalin*, p. 323.

38 Shukman, *Stalin's Generals*, p. 348.

39 Quoted in Sebag Montefiore, *Stalin*, p. 324.

40 Werth, *Russia at War*, p. 160.

9. Hatreds and Horrors

1 Quoted in Kershaw, *War Without Garlands*, p. 102.

2 Quoted ibid., pp. 106–7.

3 Russian police officer Nikolai Yangchuk, quoted ibid., p. 107.

4 Starinov quoted in Bialer, *Stalin & His Generals*, pp. 224–7.

5 Ibid.

6 Hans-Ulrich Rudel, *Stuka Pilot* (Black House, 2012, p. 13).

7 Quoted in Kershaw, *War Without Garlands*, p. 120.

8 Rudel, *Stuka Pilot*, p. 16.

9 Ibid., p. 13.

10 Quoted in Kershaw, *War Without Garlands*, p. 121.

11 Sebag Montefiore, *Stalin*, p. 315.

12 Braithwaite, *Moscow 1941*, p. 61.

13 Quoted in Merridale, *Ivan's War*, pp. 77–8; Braithwaite, *Moscow 1941*, pp. 74–5.

14 Sebag Montefiore, *Stalin*, p. 325.

15 Braithwaite, *Moscow 1941*, p. 77.

16 Quoted ibid.

17 Quoted ibid., p. 79.

18 Quoted in Merridale, *Ivan's War*, p. 79.

19 Kravchenko, *I Chose Freedom*, pp. 358–9.

20 Nikolai Amosov, *Notes of a Military Surgeon* (Algoritm, 2016), trans. Lyuba Vinogradova.

21 Quoted in Werth, *Russia at War*, p. 156.

22 Boldin quoted in Bialer, *Stalin & His Generals*, pp. 230–31.

23 Quoted in Erickson, *The Road to Stalingrad*, p. 134.

24 Merridale, *Ivan's War*, pp. 81–2.

10. Watching On

1 Quoted in Dimbleby, *Destiny in the Desert*, p. 99.

2 Churchill, *The Grand Alliance*, pp. 307–8.

3 Martin Kitchen, *Rommel's Desert War: Waging World War II in North Africa, 1941–1943* (Cambridge University Press, 2009), p. 120.

4 Churchill, *The Grand Alliance*, p. 308.

5 Lord Ismay, *The Memoirs of General the Lord Ismay* (Heinemann, 1960), p. 225.

6 Anthony Eden (Earl of Avon), *The Eden Memoirs: The Reckoning* (Cassell, 1965), p. 269.

7 Hinsley et al., *British Intelligence in the Second World War*, vol. I, p. 482.

8 Eden, *Eden Memoirs: The Reckoning*, p. 269.

9 John Colville, *The Fringes of Power: Downing Street Diaries 1939–1955* (Weidenfeld and Nicolson, 2004), 22 June 1941.

10 Ibid.

11 Quoted in Gorodetsky, *Maisky Diaries*, 22 June 1941.

12 Eden, *Eden Memoirs: The Reckoning*, p. 270.

13 Churchill, *The Grand Alliance*, pp. 331–2.

14 Gorodetsky, *Maisky Diaries*, 22 June 1941.

15 Dilks, *Cadogan Diaries*, 22 June 1941.

16 See Kitchen, *Rommel's Desert War*, pp. 120–21.

17 Churchill, Mansion House Speech, 9 November 1942.

18 Nigel Nicolson (ed.), *Harold Nicolson Diaries and Letters,* vol. II: *1939–45* (Collins, 1967), 24 June 1941.

19 Ibid., 26 June 1941.

20 Kennedy, *The Business of War*, p. 148.

21 Gorodetsky, *Mission to Moscow*, p. 178.

22 General Major Fritz Schlieper, report to OKW, quoted at War History Online: www.warhistoryonline.com/world-war-ii/defense-brest-fortress-in-wwii.html.

23 Erickson, *The Road to Stalingrad*, p. 120.

24 Quoted in Kershaw, *War Without Garlands*, p. 205.

25 Guderian, *Panzer Leader*, p. 154.

26 Burdick and Jacobsen, *Halder War Diary*, 22 June 1941.

27 *The War Years 1939–45, Eyewitness Accounts* (Marshall Cavendish, 1994), Dealerfield limited edition, p. 91.

28 Quoted in Kershaw, *War Without Garlands*, pp. 296–7.

29 Quoted ibid., p. 298.

30 For a full account of this incident see ibid., pp. 297–9.

31 Communication from Central Office for Political Propaganda of Soviet 5th Army signed by Major General Potapov, C-in-C for 5th Army, cited ibid., p. 300.

32 Quoted ibid.

33 Quoted ibid., p. 195.

34 Quoted ibid., p. 196.

35 Quoted in Omer Bartov, *Hitler's Army: Soldiers, Nazis, and War in the Third Reich* (Oxford University Press, 1992), p. 26.

36 Johannes Hürter (ed.), *A German General on the Eastern Front: The Letters and Diaries of Gotthard Heinrici, 1941–1942*, trans. Christine Brocks (Pen and Sword, 2014), 25 April 1941, p. 61.

37 Ibid., 23, 24 June, 4, 6 July 1941, pp. 66–8.

38 Quoted in Bartov, *Hitler's Army*, p. 85.

39 Quoted in Kershaw, *War Without Garlands*, p. 311.

40 Quoted in Kershaw, *Hitler, 1936–1945*, pp. 357–8.

41 Bock, *War Diary*, 4 June 1941.

42 Kershaw, *Hitler, 1936–1945*, p. 359.

43 Guderian, *Panzer Leader*, p. 152.

44 Bartov, *Hitler's Army*, p. 86.

45 Ibid., pp. 86–7.

46 Communication from Central Office for Political Propaganda of Soviet 5th Army, cited in Kershaw, *War Without Garlands*, p. 300.

11. *Stalin's Rallying Cry*

1 Guderian, *Panzer Leader*, p. 156.

2 Ibid. for this and the following quote.

3 Burdick and Jacobsen, *Halder War Diary*, 24 June 1941.

4 Quoted in Kershaw, *War Without Garlands*, pp. 184–5.

5 Quoted ibid., pp. 185–7.

6 Bock, *War Diary*, 25, 26 June 1941.

7 In correspondence with the author.

8 Werth, *Russia at War*, p. 158.

9 Ibid., p. 159.

10 Quoted in Glantz, *Before Stalingrad*, p. 34.

11 See Braithwaite, *Moscow 1941*, p. 89.

12 Quoted in Bialer, *Stalin & His Generals*, p. 233.

13 Sebag Montefiore, *Stalin*, p. 326.

14 Quoted in Braithwaite, *Moscow 1941*, p. 90.

15 Ibid., p. 91; Sebag Montefiore, *Stalin*, pp. 332–3.

16 Quoted in Braithwaite, *Moscow 1941*, p. 92.

17 Werth, *Russia at War*, p. 168.

18 Quoted ibid., pp. 164–9.

19 Quoted in Braithwaite, *Moscow 1941*, p. 97.

20 Quoted in Robert W. Thurston and Bernd Bonwetsch (eds.), *The People's War: Response to World War II in the Soviet Union* (University of Illinois Press, 2000), p. 121.

21 Alexander Werth, *Moscow '41* (Hamish Hamilton, 1942), p. 32.

22 Quoted in Merridale, *Ivan's War*, p. 77.

23 Bock, *War Diary*, 28 June 1941.

24 Quoted in Kershaw, *War Without Garlands*, p. 188.

25 Siegfried Knappe with Ted Brusaw, *Soldat: Reflections of a German Soldier, 1936–1949* (Orion, 1992), p. 187.

26 Ibid., pp. 187–8.

27 Ibid., p. 187.

28 Heinrich Haape, *Moscow Tram Stop: A Doctor's Experiences with the German Spearhead in Russia* (Collins, 1957), quoted in Kershaw, *War Without Garlands*, p. 210.

29 Knappe, *Soldat*, p. 186.

30 Glantz, *Before Stalingrad*, pp. 36–9.

31 Ibid., p. 46.

32 Burdick and Jacobsen, *Halder War Diary*, 3 July 1941.

33 Glantz, *Before Stalingrad*, p. 46.

12. A Shaky Alliance

1 Gorodetsky, *Stafford Cripps in Moscow*, 28 June 1941.

2 Gorodetsky, *Mission to Moscow*, p. 181.

3 Gorodetsky, *Stafford Cripps in Moscow*, 9 July 1941.

4 Churchill to Stalin, 7 July 1941, Churchill, *The Grand Alliance*, p. 340.

5 Cripps to Churchill, Personal, Gorodetsky, *Stafford Cripps in Moscow*, 6 July 1941.

6 Ibid., 14 July 1941.

7 House of Commons, 15 July 1941, Hansard, vol. 373, cols. 463–7.

8 Prime minister to First Lord and First Sea Lord, 10 July 1941, Churchill, *The Grand Alliance*, p. 341.

9 Quoted in Dallek, *Franklin D. Roosevelt*, p. 278.

10 Quoted ibid., p. 279.

11 Roosevelt to Leahy (in Vichy), 26 June 1941, in Elliott Roosevelt (ed.), *The Roosevelt Letters*, vol. III: *1928–1945* (Harrap, 1952), p. 377.

12 Quoted in Dallek, *Franklin D. Roosevelt*, p. 279.

13 Churchill, *The Grand Alliance*, p. 338.

14 Gorodetsky, *Maisky Diaries*, 13 July 1941.

15 Stalin to Churchill, 18 July 1941, Churchill, *The Grand Alliance*, p. 343.

16 Ibid., pp. 344–5.

17 Ibid., pp. 346–7.

18 Merridale, *Ivan's War*, p. 86.

19 Ibid., p. 87.

20 Ibid.

21 Quoted in Werth, *Russia at War*, p. 152.

22 Ibid., p. 153.

23 Quoted in Merridale, *Ivan's War*, p. 88.

24 Gabriel Temkin, *My Just War: The Memoir of a Jewish Red Army Soldier in World War II* (Presidio, 1998), pp. 36–40, for this and following quotes.

25 See Braithwaite, *Moscow 1941*, p. 117.

26 Quoted ibid., p. 119.

27 Ibid., p. 121.

28 Konstantin Simonov, *Sto Sutok Voiny* (One Hundred Days of War) (Smolensk, 1999), p. 131, cited in Braithwaite, *Moscow 1941*, p. 122.

13. Hideous Realities

1 Prüller, *Diary of a German Soldier*, 3 July 1941.

2 Ibid., 7 July 1941.

3 Knappe, *Soldat*, pp. 192–3.

4 Ibid., pp. 193–4.

5 Benno Zieser, *The Road to Stalingrad*, trans. Alec Brown (Ballantine, 1957), p. 13.

6 Ibid., p. 14.

7 Edwin Erich Dwinger, cited in James Lucas, *War on the Eastern Front: The German Soldier in Russia, 1941–1945* (Greenhill, 1998), p. 51.

8 Ibid.

9 Richardson, *Sieg Heil!*, letter of 3 August 1941, p. 122.

10 Warlimont, *Inside Hitler's Headquarters*, p. 172.

11 Adolf Hitler, *Hitler's Table Talk, 1941–1944*, trans. Norman Cameron and R. H. Stevens (Oxford University Press, 1988), Introduction by Hugh Trevor-Roper, pp. xxiii and xxiv.

12 Ibid., night of 5–6 July 1941, p. 5.

13 Burdick and Jacobsen, *Halder War Diary*, 8 July 1941.

14 Quoted in Tooze, *The Wages of Destruction*, p. 478.

15 See Snyder, *Bloodlands*, pp. 162–3; Tooze, *The Wages of Destruction*, pp. 478–82.

16 Hitler, *Hitler's Table Talk*, 27 July 1941, p. 16.

17 Prüller, *Diary of a German Soldier*, 21 July 1941.

18 Ibid.

19 Warlimont, *Inside Hitler's Headquarters*, pp. 178–9.

20 Hürter, *Letters and Diaries of Gotthard Heinrici*, letters of 11 and 13 July 1941, pp. 70–71.

21 Burdick and Jacobsen, *Halder War Diary*, 15 July 1941.

22 Ibid.

23 Bock, *War Diary*, 13 July 1941.

24 Burdick and Jacobsen, *Halder War Diary*, 13 July 1941.

25 Quoted in Warlimont, *Inside Hitler's Headquarters, 1939–45*, p. 183.

26 Bock, *War Diary*, 15 July 1941.

27 Hitler Directives No. 33 and 33a, Hugh Trevor-Roper, *Hitler's War Directives, 1939–1945* (Birlinn, 2004), pp. 139–45.

28 Warlimont, *Inside Hitler's Headquarters*, p. 184.

29 Bock, *War Diary*, 24 July 1941.

30 Burdick and Jacobsen, *Halder War Diary*, 26 July 1941.

31 Hürter, *Letters and Diaries of Gotthard Heinrici*, 22 July 1941, p. 72.

32 Quoted in Bartov, *Hitler's Army*, p. 21.

33 Bock, *War Diary*, 26 July 1941.

34 Ibid., 31 July 1941.

35 Hürter, *Letters and Diaries of Gotthard Heinrici*, 30 July 1941, p. 73.

36 Ibid., 1 August 1941, p. 73.

37 Warlimont, *Inside Hitler's Headquarters*, p. 180.

38 Gerhard Engel, *At the Heart of the Reich: The Secret Diary of Hitler's Army Adjutant*, trans. Geoffrey Brooks (Frontline, 2017), pp. 114–16.

14. America Makes a Move

1 Quoted in Dallek, *Franklin D. Roosevelt*, p. 280.

2 Robert E. Sherwood, *The White House Papers of Harry L. Hopkins*, vol. I: *September 1939 – January 1942* (Eyre and Spottiswoode, 1948), p. 120.

3 Ibid., p. 5.

4 Ibid., p. 245.

5 Francis L. Lowenheim, Harold D. Langley and Manfred Jonas (eds.), *Roosevelt and Churchill: Their Secret Wartime Correspondence* (Barrie and Jenkins, 1975), 3 May 1941, p. 141.

6 Sherwood, *Papers of Harry L. Hopkins*, vol. I, p. 317.

7 Berle to Hopkins, 30 July 1941, Box 305, Harry L. Hopkins Files, bk 4, FDR Library, Hyde Park, NY.

8 Gorodetsky, *Maisky Diaries*, 29 July 1941.

9 Telegram, 25 July 1942, 'For the President Only', quoted in Sherwood, *Papers of Harry L. Hopkins*, vol. I, pp. 327–8.

10 William Averell Harriman and Elie Abel, *Special Envoy to Churchill and Stalin, 1941–1946* (Random House, 1975), p. 73.

11 Davies, *Mission to Moscow*, pp. 315–17.

12 Gorodetsky, *Stafford Cripps in Moscow*, pp. 136–7.

13 Ibid.

14 Sherwood, *Papers of Harry L. Hopkins*, vol. I, pp. 331–2.

15 Werth, *Moscow '41*, pp. 76–8.

16 Henry C. Cassidy, *Moscow Dateline, 1941–1943* (Cassell, 1943), pp. 69–70.

17 Gorodetsky, *Stafford Cripps in Moscow*, 22 July 1941.

18 Werth, *Moscow '41*, p. 79.

19 Ibid., p. 80.

20 See ibid., p. 100.

21 A. G. Dreitser in Mikhail M. Gorinov, 'Muscovites' Moods, 22 June 1941 to May 1942', chapter 6 in Thurston and Bonwetsch, *The People's War*, p. 114.

22 Archive of the Solzhenitsyn Center (Dom Russkogo Zarubezhya), R-384, unpublished memoirs by N. Erastova, trans. Lyuba Vinogradova.

23 Sherwood, *Papers of Harry L. Hopkins*, vol. I, p. 6.

24 Article in *The American Magazine,* quoted ibid., p. 344.

25 Ibid., pp. 328–30.

26 Steinhardt to Secretary of State Cordell Hull, 1 August 1941, US Department of State, *Foreign Relations of the United States, Diplomatic Papers, 1941*, vol. I, p. 814, quoted in Sherwood, *Papers of Harry L. Hopkins*, vol. I, p. 347.

27 Hopkins Papers, Box 306, quoted in Gorodetsky, *Mission to Moscow*, p. 202.

28 Hopkins Memorandum of 31 July Conference, quoted in Theodore A. Wilson, *The First Summit: Roosevelt and Churchill at Placentia Bay, 1941* (Macdonald, 1969), pp. 50–51.

29 Article in *The American Magazine*, quoted in Sherwood, *Papers of Harry L. Hopkins*, vol. I, pp. 344–5.

30 Quoted in Gorodetsky, *Mission to Moscow*, p. 202.

31 Quoted ibid., p. 202.

32 Roosevelt Papers, Box, 2987, Cripps to Roosevelt, 1 August, cited ibid., pp. 202–3.

33 Quoted in Dallek, *Franklin D. Roosevelt*, p. 280.

34 Quoted ibid., p. 281.

35 Sherwood, *Papers of Harry L. Hopkins*, vol. I, p. 350.

36 Churchill, *The Grand Alliance*, p. 381.

37 Wilson, *The First Summit*, p. v.

38 Colville, *The Fringes of Power*, 2 August 1941.

39 Sherwood, *Papers of Harry L. Hopkins*, vol. I, p. 351.

40 Quoted in Wilson, *The First Summit*, p. 103.

41 Quoted in Dallek, *Franklin D. Roosevelt*, p. 285.

42 Ibid.

43 See Churchill, *The Grand Alliance*, p. 394.

44 John Harvey (ed.), *The War Diaries of Oliver Harvey, 1941–1945* (Collins, 1978), 12 August 1941.

45 Nicolson, *Diaries and Letters*, 17 August 1941, p. 183.

46 Churchill broadcast, 24 August 1941, http://www.ibiblio.org/pha/policy/1941/410824a.html.

47 'Shoot on Sight', Harry L. Hopkins Files, bk 4, FDR Library, Hyde Park, NY.

48 Ibid.

49 CAB, 65/84 (41), 19 August 1941, cited in Dallek, *Franklin D. Roosevelt*, pp. 485–6.

50 Franklin D. Roosevelt, Fireside Chat, 11 September 1941, The American Presidency Project, University of California, Santa Barbara.

51 Prime minister to Lord Privy Seal, 12 August 1941, Churchill, *The Grand Alliance*, p. 397.

52 Roosevelt and Churchill to Stalin, sent 14 August 1941, David Reynolds and Vladimir Pechatnov (eds.), *The Kremlin Letters: Stalin's Wartime Correspondence with Churchill and Roosevelt* (Yale University Press, 2018).

53 Quoted in Harriman and Abel, *Special Envoy*, p. 77.

15. Disarray on the Soviet Front

1 Sebag Montefiore, *Stalin*, pp. 336–7; Geoffrey Roberts, *Stalin's General: The Life of Georgy Zhukov* (Icon, 2013), pp. 111–12.

2 Antony Beevor and Luba [sic] Vinogradova (ed. and trans.), *A Writer at War: Vasily Grossman with the Red Army, 1941–1945* (Pimlico, 2006), p. 7.

3 Ibid., p. 8.

4 Ibid., p. 11.

5 Ibid., pp. 11–12.

6 Ibid., p. 14.

7 Ibid., pp. 15–16.

8 Ibid., p. 16.

9 Ibid., p. 17.

10 Ibid.

11 Amosov, *Notes of a Military Surgeon*.

12 Ibid.

13 Quoted in Merridale, *Ivan's War*, p. 99.

14 Alexey Isaev, *From Dubno to Rostov* (Moscow, 2004), pp. 418–19, cited in https://en.wikipedia.org/wiki/Battle_of_Uman.

15 Merridale, *Ivan's War*, p. 98.

16 Order No. 270, Government Documents of the Soviet Union, http:/en. wikipedia.org/wiki/Order_No_270.

17 Quoted in Merridale, *Ivan's War*, p. 99.

18 Quoted ibid., p. 122.

19 See Snyder, *Bloodlands*, p. 176.

20 Benno Zieser, *In Their Shallow Graves*, trans. Alec Brown (World Distributors, 1957), p. 59.

21 See Kershaw, *War Without Garlands*, p. 312.

22 Hans Becker, *Devil on My Shoulder*, trans. Kennedy McWhirter and Jeremy Potter (Jarrold, 1955), pp. 23–4.

16. Hitler's Hiatus

1 Prüller, *Diary of a German Soldier*, 4 August 1941.

2 Ibid., 6 August 1941.

3 Ibid., 12 August 1941.

4 10 August 1941, quoted in Kershaw, *War Without Garlands*, pp. 254–5.

5 11 August 1941, quoted ibid., p. 255.

6 10 August 1941, quoted ibid.

7 Hürter, *Letters and Diaries of Gotthard Heinrici*, 3 August 1941, p. 74.

8 Quoted in Kenneth Macksey, *Guderian: Panzer General* (Greenhill, 1992), p. 142.

9 Quoted ibid., p. 140.

10 Quoted ibid.

11 Quoted ibid., p. 141.

12 BA-MA, RH27-189/4, 19 June 1941, cited in Bartov, *Hitler's Army*, p. 96.

13 Bartov, *Hitler's Army*, pp. 96–7.

14 BA-MA, RH27-28, 18 August 1941, cited ibid., p. 97.

15 Burdick and Jacobsen, *Halder War Diary*, 2 August 1941.

16 Below, *At Hitler's Side*, p. 109.

17 Bock, *War Diary*, 4 August 1941.

18 Burdick and Jacobsen, *Halder War Diary*, 4 August 1941.

19 Ibid., 5 August 1941.

20 Ibid., 6 August 1941.

21 Ibid., 7 August 1941.

22 Engel, *At the Heart of the Reich*, 8 August 1941.

23 Bock, *War Diary*, 12 August 1941.

24 Burdick and Jacobsen, *Halder War Diary*, 10 August 1941.

25 Ibid., 11 August 1941.

26 Warlimont, *Inside Hitler's Headquarters*, p. 187.

27 Quoted ibid.

28 Bock, *War Diary*, 14 August 1941.

29 Ibid., 15 August 1941.

30 Army Group Centre War Diary, 15 August 1941, quoted in David Stahel, *Operation Barbarossa and Germany's Defeat in the East* (Cambridge University Press, 2014), p. 395.

31 Burdick and Jacobsen, *Halder War Diary*, 15 August 1941.

32 Bock, *War Diary*, 15 August 1941.

33 Ibid.

34 Burdick and Jacobsen, *Halder War Diary*, 15 August 1941.

35 12 August 1941, quoted in Macksey, *Guderian*, p. 144.

36 Guderian, *Panzer Leader*, p. 195.

37 Quoted in Macksey, *Guderian*, p. 144.

38 Franz Halder, *Hitler as War Lord*, trans. Paul Findlay (Putnam, 1950), bk III, 15 August 1941, p. 180, cited in Stahel, *Operation Barbarossa*, p. 396.

39 Below, *At Hitler's Side*, p. 110.

40 *Die Tagebücher von Joseph Goebbels*, ed. Elke Fröhlich, Teil II, *Diktate 1941–1945*, Band 1, Juli–September 1941 (Munich, 1998), 19 August 1941, quoted in Stahel, *Operation Barbarossa*, p. 402.

41 Tooze, *The Wages of Destruction*, p. 489.

42 Engel, *At the Heart of the Reich*, 8 August 1941.

43 Burdick and Jacobsen, *Halder War Diary*, 22 August 1941.

44 Ibid.

45 Ibid.

46 Bock, *War Diary*, 22 August 1941.

47 BA-MA, RH 1911/386, quoted in Stahel, *Operation Barbarossa*, p. 429.

48 Bock, *War Diary*, 22 August 1941.

49 Guderian, *Panzer Leader*, p. 199.

50 Colonel Rudolf-Christoph Freiherr von Gersdorff, *Soldat im Untergang* (Soldier During the Downfall) (Ullstein Taschenbuchverlag, 1982), p. 65, quoted in Stahel, *Operation Barbarossa*, p. 432.

51 Guderian, *Panzer Leader*, pp. 199–200.

52 Ibid.

53 Ibid.

54 Burdick and Jacobsen, *Halder War Diary*, 24 August 1941.

55 Guderian, *Panzer Leader*, p. 202.

56 Army Group Centre, War Diary, 22 August 1941, quoted in Stahel, *Operation Barbarossa*, p. 419; for more details, see ibid., pp. 417–22.

17. Between the Lines

1 See Christopher Browning, *Ordinary Men: Reserve Police Battalion 101 and the Final Solution in Poland* (Penguin, 2001), pp. 9–11.

2 Quoted in Peter Longerich, 'From Mass Murder to the "Final Solution" ', in Bernd Wegner (ed.), *From Peace to War: Germany, Soviet Russia, and the World, 1939–1941* (Berghahn, 1997), p. 262.

3 Quoted in Jürgen Förster, 'The German Army and the Ideological War Against the Soviet Union', in Hirschfeld, *The Policies of Genocide*, p. 24.

4 Quoted in Christopher Browning, *The Origins of the Final Solution: The Evolution of Nazi Jewish Policy, 1939–1942* (Arrow, 2005), p. 281.

5 Quoted ibid.

6 See ibid., p. 282.

7 Browning, *Ordinary Men*, pp. 11–12.

8 Ibid.

9 Ibid., p. 15.

10 Quoted ibid., pp. 13–14.

11 Quoted ibid., p. 16.

12 Peter Longerich, *The Unwritten Order: Hitler's Role in the Final Solution* (The History Press, 2016), p. 13.

13 Quoted in Richard J. Evans, *The Third Reich at War: How the Nazis Led Germany from Conquest to Disaster* (Penguin, 2009), p. 217.

14 'Einsatzgruppen A, The Massacres in Kovno, Reports and Eyewitness Accounts', Education and Archive Research Team, www.holocaustresearchproject.org/einsatz/kovnomassacres.html.

15 'Findings of Investigation S1/00/Zn into the Murder of Polish Citizens of Jewish Origin in the Town of Jedwabne on 10 July 1941, Pursuant to Article 1 Point 1 of the Decree of 31 August 1944', in Antony Polonsky and Joanna B. Michlic (eds.), *The Neighbors Respond: The Controversy over the Jedwabne Massacre in Poland* (Princeton University Press, 2004), pp. 133–6.

16 In correspondence with the author.

17 Quoted in 'The Nazi Invasion of Kamenets', https://kehilalinks.jewishgen.org/Kamyanets-Podilskyy/Kamianets-Podilskyi%20%201939-1945.htm.

18 Ibid.

19 Quoted in Peter Hayes, *Why? Explaining the Holocaust* (W. W. Norton, 2017), p. 100.

20 Extracts from *Mein Kampf*, collated by Lothar Kettenacker, 'Hitler's Final Solution and Its Rationalization', and quoted in Hirschfeld, *The Policies of Genocide*, p. 75.

21 Otto Kulka, '"Public Opinion" in Nazi Germany and the "Jewish Question"', cited in Browning, *Origins of the Final Solution*, p. 389.

22 Ian Kershaw, *Popular Opinion and Political Dissent in The Third Reich: Bavaria 1933–1945* (Oxford: Clarendon Press, 1983), p. 277, cited ibid.

23 *Mitteilungen für die Truppe*, No. 16, cited in Manfred Messerschmidt, *Die Wehrmachtjustiz, 1933–1945* (Schoeningh Ferdinand, 2005), pp. 326–7, quoted in Bartov, *Hitler's Army*, p. 126.

24 Quoted in Browning, *Ordinary Men*, p. 293.

25 See Bartov, *Hitler's Army*, pp. 129–30.

26 Bock, *War Diary*, 4 August 1941.

18. The Carnage of Kiev

1 Irina Krauze Diary, Memorial Society, Moscow, published online by Irina Ostrovskaya at Voenno-Istoricheskaya Biblioteka, trans. Lyuba Vinogradova.

2 Bock, *War Diary*, 2 September 1941.

3 Franz Halder, *Kriegstagebuch: Tägliche Aufzeichnungen des Chefs des Generalstabes des Heeres, 1939–1942*, Band III: *Der Russlandfeldzug bis zum Marsch auf Stalingrad (22.6.1941 – 24.9.1942)*, ed. Hans-Adolf Jacobsen and Alfred Philippi (Arbeitskreis für Wehrforschung, 1964), p. 182 (16 August 1941), quoted in Stahel, *Operation Barbarossa*, p. 411.

4 Burdick and Jacobsen, *Halder War Diary*, 28 August 1941.

5 Stahel, *Operation Barbarossa*, pp. 411–12.

6 Bock, *War Diary*, 2 September 1941.

7 Quoted in Stahel, *Operation Barbarossa*, p. 412.

8 Werth, *Russia at War*, p. 188.

9 Werth, *Moscow '41*, p. 183.

10 Ibid., p. 185.

11 Ibid., pp. 188–9.

12 Ibid., p. 192.

13 Ibid., p. 203.

14 Ibid., p. 204.

15 Ibid., p. 205.

16 Ibid., p. 210.

17 Ibid., pp. 213–14.

18 Quoted in Macksey, *Guderian*, p. 151.

19 Burdick and Jacobsen, *Halder War Diary*, 31 August 1941.

20 Ibid., 2 September 1941.

21 Bock, *War Diary*, 4 September 1941.

22 Ibid., 5 September 1941.

23 Guderian, *Panzer Leader*, p. 216.

24 Message to Yeremenko and [Major General Mikhail] Petrov [commander of the 50th Army], 2 September 1941, quoted in Erickson, *The Road to Stalingrad*, p. 202.

25 Quoted ibid., p. 208.

26 Quoted in Sebag Montefiore, *Stalin*, p. 337.

27 Quoted in Glantz, *Before Stalingrad*, p. 127.

28 Quoted in Erickson, *The Road to Stalingrad*, p. 208.

29 Glantz, *Before Stalingrad*, p. 127.

30 Quoted in Kershaw, *War Without Garlands*, p. 347.

31 Quoted ibid., p. 348.

32 Max Kuhnert, *Will We See Tomorrow? A German Cavalryman at War, 1939–42* (Leo Cooper, 1993), pp. 96–7.

33 Joshua Rubenstein and Ilya Altman (eds.), *The Unknown Black Book: The Holocaust in the German-Occupied Soviet Territories*, trans. Christopher Morris and Joshua Rubenstein (Indiana University Press, 2008), p. 72.

34 Quoted in Martin Gilbert, *The Holocaust: The Jewish Tragedy* (Collins, 1986), p. 202.

35 Ibid., p. 203.

36 Statement of truck driver Hofer, cited in Michael Berenbaum, *Witness to the Holocaust* (HarperCollins, 1997), pp. 138–9.

37 Testimony of the Lukianov Cemetery Watchman: Babi Yar Memorial Volume, Tel Aviv, 1978, cited in Gilbert, *The Holocaust*, p. 203.

38 Quoted in Michael Berenbaum, *The World Must Know: The History of the Holocaust as Told in the United States Holocaust Memorial Museum* (Johns Hopkins University Press, 2006), pp. 97–8.

39 Testimony of the Lukianov Cemetery watchman: Babi Yar Memorial Volume, cited in Gilbert, *The Holocaust*, p. 203.

40 Ilya Ehrenburg and Vasily Grossman (eds.), *The Black Book: The Ruthless Murder of Jews by German-Fascist Invaders Throughout the Temporarily Occupied Regions of the Soviet Union and in the Death Camps of Poland During the War of 1941–1945*, trans. John Glad and James S. Levine (Holocaust Library, 1981), pp. 9–10.

41 Gilbert, *The Holocaust*, pp. 204–5.

42 Quoted in Kershaw, *Hitler, 1936–1945*, p. 468.

19. Leningrad

1 Amosov, *Notes of a Military Surgeon*.

2 Beevor and Vinogradova, *A Writer at War*, p. 23.

3 Ibid., pp. 28–9.

4 Ibid., p. 33.

5 Ibid.

6 Ibid., p. xiii.

7 Ibid., pp. 36–7.

8 Ibid., p. 38.

9 Interview, *Der Verdammte Krieg*, ZDF German TV, 1991, cited in Kershaw, *War Without Garlands*, p. 272.

10 Ibid.

11 Quoted in Sebag Montefiore, *Stalin*, p. 342.

12 Quoted ibid.

13 Quoted in Shukman, *Stalin's Generals*, p. 350.

14 Quoted in Richard Overy, *Russia's War* (Penguin, 2010), p. 105.

15 Quoted in Kershaw, *War Without Garlands*, p. 276.

16 Interview, *Der Verdammte Krieg*, ZDF German TV, 1991, cited ibid.

17 Sebag Montefiore, *Stalin*, p. 338.

18 Quoted in Braithwaite, *Moscow 1941*, p. 153.

19 Ibid., p. 150.

20 Cited in A. A. Maslov, 'How Were Soviet Blocking Detachments Employed?', *Journal of Slavic Military Studies*, 9(2) (1996), pp. 427–35.

21 Quoted ibid.

22 Beevor and Vinogradova, *A Writer at War*, p. 269.

20. Wars of Words

1 Mary Soames (ed.), *Speaking for Themselves: The Personal Letters of Winston and Clementine Churchill* (Black Swan, 1999), p. 464.

2 Letter to Stalin, 21 September 1941, Churchill, *The Grand Alliance*, p. 414.

3 Quoted in Reynolds and Pechatnov, *The Kremlin Letters*, pp. 38–9.

4 Ibid.

5 Stalin to Churchill, sent 3 September, received 4 September 1941, ibid., pp. 40–41.

6 Roberts, *Masters and Commanders*, p. 220.

7 Stalin to Churchill, sent 3 September, received 4 September 1941, Reynolds and Pechatnov, *The Kremlin Letters*, pp. 40–41.

8 Churchill, *The Grand Alliance*, 4 September 1941, p. 407.

9 Gorodetsky, *Maisky Diaries*, 4 September 1941.

10 Churchill, *The Grand Alliance*, pp. 406–7.

11 Former Naval Person [Churchill] to President Roosevelt, 5 September 1941, ibid., p. 409.

12 Cripps to Foreign Office, quoted in Gorodetsky, *Stafford Cripps in Moscow*, 4 September 1941.

13 Prime minister to Sir Stafford Cripps, 5 September 1941, Churchill, *The Grand Alliance*, p. 410.

14 Quoted in Dallek, *Franklin D. Roosevelt*, p. 295.

15 Harriman and Abel, *Special Envoy*, p. 78.

16 Ibid., pp. 78–9.

17 Letter, Kathleen Harriman to Frances Poniatowski, quoted ibid., p. 79.

18 Ibid., p. 83.

19 Ibid., p. 87.

20 Ibid., pp. 87–8.

21 Ibid., p. 88.

22 Ibid., p. 91.

23 Gorodetsky, *Mission to Moscow*, p. 234.

24 Gorodetsky, *Stafford Cripps in Moscow*, 29 September 1941.

25 Harriman and Abel, *Special Envoy*, p. 89.

26 Ibid., p. 90.

27 Ibid.

28 Cassidy, *Moscow Dateline*, p. 99.

29 Werth, *Moscow '41*, p. 227.

30 Churchill, *The Grand Alliance*, 3 and 4 October 1941, p. 418.

31 Ibid., pp. 415–16.

32 Harriman and Abel, *Special Envoy*, pp. 98–9.

33 Gorodetsky, *Stafford Cripps in Moscow*, 2 October 1941.

34 Ibid., 2 October 1941, p. 176.

35 Quoted ibid., p. 171.

36 Ben Pimlott (ed.), *The Second World War Diary of Hugh Dalton* (Cape, 1986), 29 January 1942.

37 Gorodetsky, *Stafford Cripps in Moscow*, 4 October 1941.

38 Ibid.

39 Ibid.

40 Harriman and Abel, *Special Envoy*, p. 91.

41 Quoted in Cassidy, *Moscow Dateline*, p. 100.

21. Operation Typhoon

1 Hitler's Order of the Day to the German Troops on the Eastern Front, 2 October, 1941, quoted in the *New York Times*, 10 October 1941.

2 Quoted in Kershaw, *Hitler, 1936–1945*, p. 433.

3 David Stahel, *Operation Typhoon: Hitler's March on Moscow, October 1941* (Cambridge University Press, 2015).

4 See Glantz, *Before Stalingrad*, p. 136.

5 Helmut Pabst, *The Outermost Frontier: A German Soldier in the Russian Campaign* (William Kimber, 1957), 1986 edn, pp. 30–32.

6 Burdick and Jacobsen, *Halder War Diary*, 2 October 1941.

7 Bock, *War Diary*, 2 October 1941.

8 Prüller, *Diary of a German Soldier*, 3 October 1941.

9 Hans Jürgen Hartmann, quoted in Michael Jones, *The Retreat: Hitler's First Defeat* (John Murray, 2009), p. 33, and Stahel, *Operation Typhoon*, p. 58.

10 Quoted in Kershaw, *Hitler, 1936–1945*, p. 431.

11 Quoted in Jones, *The Retreat*, pp. 37–8.

12 Quoted in Glantz, *Before Stalingrad*, p. 138.

13 Quoted ibid.

14 For details, see ibid., pp. 126–39.

15 Beevor and Vinogradova, *A Writer at War*, p. 46.

16 Bock, *War Diary*, 3 October 1941.

17 Guderian, *Panzer Leader*, p. 230.

18 Quoted in Stahel, *Operation Typhoon*, p. 59.

19 Burdick and Jacobsen, *Halder War Diary*, 5 October 1941.

20 Quoted in Kershaw, *Hitler, 1936–1945*, p. 433.

21 Quoted in Jones, *The Retreat*, pp. 38–9.

22 Quoted ibid., p. 39.

23 Quoted ibid., p. 40.

24 Beevor and Vinogradova, *A Writer at War*, p. 47.

25 Ibid., p. 48.

26 Ibid.

27 Guderian, *Panzer Leader*, p. 233.

28 Burdick and Jacobsen, *Halder War Diary*, 9 October 1941.

29 Bock, *War Diary*, 12 October 1941.

30 Quoted in Stahel, *Operation Typhoon*, p. 115.

31 Quoted in Jones, *The Retreat*, p. 60.

32 See Kershaw, *War Without Garlands*, p. 446.

33 Archive of the Solzhenitsyn Center (Dom Russkogo Zarubezhya), R-384, unpublished memoirs by N. Erastova, for this and the following.

34 Quoted in Stahel, *Operation Typhoon*, p. 159.

35 Quoted ibid., pp. 159–60.

36 Guderian, *Panzer Leader*, p. 235.

37 Ibid., p. 230.

38 Stahel, *Operation Typhoon*, p. 142.

39 Quoted in Glantz, *Before Stalingrad*, p. 142.

40 Quoted ibid., p. 143.

41 Quoted in Shukman, *Stalin's Generals*, p. 351.

42 Quoted in Braithwaite, *Moscow 1941*, p. 225.

43 Shukman, *Stalin's Generals*, p. 351.

44 Quoted in Glantz, *Before Stalingrad*, p. 145.

45 Quoted ibid.

46 Quoted in Kershaw, *War Without Garlands*, p. 413.

47 Richardson, *Sieg Heil!*, 12 October 1941.

48 Kershaw, *War Without Garlands*, pp. 415–16.

49 Quoted in Stahel, *Operation Typhoon*, p. 146.

50 Richardson, *Sieg Heil!*, 15 October 1941.

51 Ibid.

52 Quoted in Stahel, *Operation Typhoon*, p. 148.

53 Quoted ibid., pp. 149–50.

54 Quoted ibid., p. 148.

55 Quoted ibid., p. 149.

56 For details, see ibid., p. 161.

57 Quoted in Glantz, *Before Stalingrad*, p. 144.

22. *The Great Panic*

1 British Military Mission War Diary, 8 October 1941, PRO WO178/25 – cited in Braithwaite, *Moscow 1941*, p. 224.

2 Quoted ibid.

3 Collection, *Poslednie pisma s fronta* (Last Letters from the Front) (Molodaya gvardiya, 1983), vol. I: *1941*.

4 Merridale, *Ivan's War*, p. 109.

5 Kravchenko, *I Chose Freedom*, p. 374.

6 Irina Krauze Diary, 9 October 1941.

7 Quoted in Braithwaite, *Moscow 1941*, pp. 237–8.

8 Merridale, *Ivan's War*, p. 109.

9 Kravchenko, *I Chose Freedom*, p. 374.

10 Werth, *Russia at War*, p. 226.

11 Irina Krauze Diary, 11 October 1941.

12 Quoted in Braithwaite, *Moscow 1941*, p. 241.

13 Werth, *Russia at War*, pp. 210–11.

14 *Pravda*, 18 September 1942, cited in Werth, *Russia at War*, p. 213.

15 Kravchenko, *I Chose Freedom*, p. 375.

16 Braithwaite, *Moscow 1941*, pp. 240–41.

17 Georgi K. Zhukov, *Marshal Zhukov's Greatest Battles*, ed. Harrison E. Salisbury, trans. Theodore Shabad (Macdonald, 1969), p. 60.

18 Irina Krauze Diary, 12 October 1941.

19 Werth, *Russia at War*, p. 227.

20 Amosov, *Notes of a Military Surgeon*.

21 Kravchenko, *I Chose Freedom*, p. 374.

22 Ibid., pp. 374–5.

23 Gorodetsky, *Stafford Cripps in Moscow*, p. 184.

24 Cassidy, *Moscow Dateline*, p. 111.

25 Gorodetsky, *Stafford Cripps in Moscow*, 16 October 1941.

26 Philip Jordan, *Russian Glory* (Cresset Press, 1942), p. 98.

27 Gorodetsky, *Stafford Cripps in Moscow*, 16 October 1941.

28 PRO FCO371/29558, BP 46-55, cited in Braithwaite, *Moscow 1941*, p. 267.

29 Andrei Sakharov, *Memoirs*, trans. Richard Lourie (Hutchinson, 1990), p. 43.

30 Ibid., pp. 43–4.

31 Quoted in Braithwaite, *Moscow 1941*, pp. 272–3.

32 Sebag Montefiore, *Stalin*, pp. 350–51.

33 Yuri Labas, *Kogda ya byl Bolshoi* (When I Was Big) (Novy khronograf, 2016).

34 N. Verzhbitsky, *Dnevnik 1941 goda* (1941 Diary), quoted in Thurston and Bonwetsch, *The People's War*, p. 124.

35 Ibid.

36 Quoted ibid., p. 123.

37 M. I. Voronkov, *Intelligent i epokha: Dnevniki, vospominaniya i stat'i (1911–1941)* (The Intellectual and His Historical Period: Diaries, Memoirs and Articles (1911–1941)) (Ryazan, 2013), pp. 7–82, trans. Lyuba Vinogradova.

38 Braithwaite, *Moscow 1941*, p. 258.

39 See ibid., pp. 258–9.

40 Irina Krauze Diary, 18 October 1941.

41 Quoted in Braithwaite, *Moscow 1941*, p. 250.

42 Voronkov, *Intelligent i epokha*, pp. 7–82.

43 Braithwaite, *Moscow 1941*, p. 252.

44 Ibid., p. 253.

45 Ibid., pp. 252–3.

46 Sebag Montefiore, *Stalin*, p. 352.

47 Ibid., p. 354.

48 Quoted in Braithwaite, *Moscow 1941*, p. 254.

49 Sebag Montefiore, *Stalin*, p. 354.

50 Quoted in Merridale, *Ivan's War*, p. 104.

51 Irina Krauze Diary, 20 October 1941.

23. General Mud

1 Bock, *War Diary*, 19 October 1941.

2 Quoted in Jones, *The Retreat*, p. 68.

3 Bock, *War Diary*, 20 October 1941.

4 Hürter, *Letters and Diaries of Gotthard Heinrici*, 8 October 1941, p. 90.

5 Ibid., 16 October 1941, pp. 91–2.

6 Peter Bamm, *The Invisible Flag: A Report by Peter Bamm*, trans. Frank Herrmann (Penguin, 1962), pp. 69–70.

7 Prüller, *Diary of a German Soldier*, various entries between 8 and 29 October 1941.

8 Hürter, *Letters and Diaries of Gotthard Heinrici*, 16 October 1941, p. 92.

9 Ibid., 10 October 1941, p. 91.

10 See Kershaw, *Hitler, 1936–1945*, p. 435.

11 Adolf Hitler, speech in the Löwenbräukeller, Munich, 8 November 1941, www.der-fuehrer.org/reden/english/41-11-08.htm.

12 See Kershaw, *Hitler, 1936–1945*, p. 437.

13 Guderian, *Panzer Leader*, pp. 234–7.

14 Bock, *War Diary*, 21 October 1941.

15 Hürter, *Letters and Diaries of Gotthard Heinrici*, 23 October 1941, p. 93.

16 Guderian, *Panzer Leader*, p. 235.

17 Hürter, *Letters and Diaries of Gotthard Heinrici*, 24 October 1941, p. 96.

18 *Deutsche Soldaten sehen die Sowjetunion: Feldpostbriefe aus dem Osten* (Berlin: Wilhelm Limpert Verlag, 1941), quoted in Bartov, *Hitler's Army*, p. 166.

19 Jones, *The Retreat*, p. 62.

20 Ibid., p. 61.

21 Quoted ibid., p. 64.

22 Quoted ibid.

23 Quoted ibid.

24 Quoted ibid., p. 65.

25 Quoted ibid., p. 67.

26 Quoted ibid., p. 69.

27 Quoted ibid., p. 74.

28 See ibid., pp. 72–3.

29 Zhukov quoted in Bialer, *Stalin & His Generals*, p. 282.

30 Zhukov, *Greatest Battles*, p. 47.

31 Quoted ibid., p. 55.

32 See Boog et al., *Germany and the Second World War*, vol. IV, p. 676.

33 Bock, *War Diary*, 22 October 1941.

34 Ibid., 25 October 1941.

35 Ibid., 26 October 1941.

36 Ibid., 27 October 1941.

37 Ibid., 28 October 1941.

38 See David M. Glantz and Jonathan House, *When Titans Clashed: How the Red Army Stopped Hitler* (University Press of Kansas, 1995), p, 82; Glantz, *Before Stalingrad*, pp. 156–7.

39 Quoted in Ralf Georg Reuth, *Goebbels: The Life of Joseph Goebbels, the Mephistophelean Genius of Nazi Propaganda*, trans. Krishna Winston (Constable, 1995), 28 October 1941, p. 297.

40 Quoted in Jones, *The Retreat*, p. 73.

24. The Jewish Question

1 Quoted in Browning, *Origins of the Final Solution*, p. 327.

2 Testimony recorded by Major A. Krasov, 1944, cited in Rubenstein and Altman, *The Unknown Black Book*, p. 244.

3 Ibid.

4 See Ehrenburg and Grossman, *The Black Book*, pp. 151–2.

5 See ibid.

6 Snyder, *Bloodlands*, p. 250.

7 See Ehrenburg and Grossman, *The Black Book*, pp. 151–2.

8 Monthly report, 11.10–10.11.1941, BA-MA RH 26–707/v.1, cited by Jürgen Förster, 'The German Army and the Ideological War against the Soviet Union', in Hirschfeld, *The Policies of Genocide*, p. 26.

9 Quoted in Browning, *Origins of the Final Solution*, p. 327.

10 Ibid., p. 305.

11 Hitler, *Hitler's Table Talk*, 25 October 1941, p. 87.

12 Quoted in Gilbert, *The Holocaust*, p. 188.

13 Quoted in Evans, *The Third Reich at War*, p. 256.

14 See Gilbert, *The Holocaust*, pp. 197–9, and www.holocaustresearchproject. org/einsatz/bingel.html.

15 Quoted in Gerhard Schoenberner, *The Yellow Star* (Bantam, 1973), cited in Rubenstein and Altman, *The Unknown Black Book*, p. 3.

16 Browning, *Origins of the Final Solution*, p. 283.

17 Testimony by HSSPF Erich von dem Bach-Zelewski at the Nuremberg Military Tribunal, cited in Raul Hilberg, *The Destruction of the European Jews* (Holmes and Meier, 1985), p. 136.

18 Recollection of former SS General Karl Wolff, *The World at War*, Thames Television, 27 March 1974, quoted in Gilbert, *The Holocaust*, p. 191.

19 Evans, *The Third Reich at War*, p. 98.

20 See Browning, *Origins of the Final Solution*, p. 356.

21 See ibid., p. 417.

22 Ibid., pp. 416–19.

23 Gitta Sereny, *Into That Darkness: An Examination of Conscience* (Pan, 1977), pp. 111–12, quoted in Evans, *The Third Reich at War*, p. 286.

24 Evans, *The Third Reich at War*, p. 296; Browning, *Origins of the Final Solution*, pp. 419–20.

25 Quoted in Christopher R. Browning, *Fateful Months: Essays on the Emergence of the Final Solution* (Holmes and Meier, 1991), p. 33.

26 Browning, *Origins of the Final Solution*, p. 313.

27 Quoted in Kershaw, *Hitler, 1936–1945*, p. 487.

25. Allied Preoccupations

1 BBC broadcast, 14 August 1941, quoted in Gilbert, *The Holocaust*, p. 186.

2 Quoted ibid., p. 232.

3 Churchill, *The Grand Alliance*, p. 493.

4 Kennedy, *The Business of War*, p. 173.

5 Gorodetsky, *Maisky Diaries*, 12 October 1941.

6 Quoted in Roberts, *Masters and Commanders*, p. 55.

7 Harvey, *War Diaries*, 21 October 1941.

8 Eden, *Eden Memoirs: The Reckoning*, p. 279.

9 Gorodetsky, *Mission to Moscow*, p. 260.

10 Churchill, *The Grand Alliance*, 25 October 1941, p. 413.

11 Gorodetsky, *Stafford Cripps in Moscow*, 26 October 1941.

12 Ibid.

13 Colville, *The Fringes of Power*, 1 September 1941.

14 Sir John Kennedy, diary manuscript, 7 September 1941, quoted in Max Hastings, *Finest Years: Churchill as Warlord, 1940–45* (Harper, 2009), p. 168.

15 Henry Pownall, *Chief of Staff: The Diaries of Lieutenant General Sir Henry Pownall*, ed. Brian Bond, 2 vols. (Leo Cooper, 1972/1974), quoted in Hastings, *Finest Years*, p. 168.

16 Churchill, *The Grand Alliance*, 25 October 1941, p. 413.

17 Prime minister to Sir Stafford Cripps, 28 October 1941, ibid., p. 420.

18 Gorodetsky, *Stafford Cripps in Moscow*, 30 October 1941.

19 Ibid.

20 Harvey, *War Diaries*, 27 October 1941.

21 Gorodetsky, *Stafford Cripps in Moscow*, 27 October 1941.

22 Churchill, *The Grand Alliance*, 28 October 1941, p. 421.

23 FO 371 29469 N5585/3/38; CAB 120/683, quoted in Gorodetsky, *Mission to Moscow*, p. 257.

24 Churchill, *The Grand Alliance*, p. 421.

25 Ibid., p. 432.

26 Churchill to Stalin, 4 November 1941, ibid., p. 468.

27 Gorodetsky, *Maisky Diaries*, 11 November 1941.

28 Churchill, *The Grand Alliance*, p. 469.

29 Dilks, *Cadogan Diaries*, 11 November 1941.

30 Stalin to Churchill, 7 November 1941, in Reynolds and Pechatnov, *The Kremlin Letters*, p. 67.

31 Gorodetsky, *Maisky Diaries*, 11 November 1941.

32 Ibid.

33 Harvey, *War Diaries*, 11 November 1941.

34 Ibid.

35 Ibid.

36 Gorodetsky, *Maisky Diaries*, 12 November 1941.

37 Eden, *Eden Memoirs: The Reckoning*, p. 282.

38 Note to US Secretary of War, Henry Stimson, 30 September 1941, quoted in Dallek, *Franklin D. Roosevelt*, p. 293.

39 Stalin to Roosevelt, Ministry of Foreign Affairs of the USSR (comp.), *Correspondence Between Stalin, Roosevelt, Truman, Churchill and Attlee During WWII* (University Press of the Pacific, 2001).

40 Franklin D. Roosevelt's Navy Day address on the attack on the destroyer *Kearny*, www.ibiblio.org/pha/policy/1941/411027a.html.

41 Sherwood, *Papers of Harry L. Hopkins*, vol. I.

42 1 September 1941, Labor Day remembrance address, Franklin D. Roosevelt Presidential Library and Museum, https://fdr.blogs.archives.gov/2015/09/01/a-labor-day-remembrance.

43 Quoted in Dallek, *Franklin D. Roosevelt*, p. 300.

44 Roosevelt to Churchill, 15 October 1941, Lowenheim et al., *Roosevelt and Churchill*, p. 162.

26. Mood Changes

1 Sakharov, *Memoirs*, p. 44.

2 See Erickson, *The Road to Stalingrad*, pp. 237–8.

3 Andrew and Gordievsky, *KGB: The Inside Story*, p. 218.

4 Robert Whymant, *Stalin's Spy: Richard Sorge and the Tokyo Espionage Ring* (I. B. Tauris, 2013), p. 234.

5 Ibid., p. 240.

6 Ibid., p. 244.

7 Andrew and Gordievsky, *KGB: The Inside Story*, p. 218.

8 See ibid., p. 219.

9 Whymant, *Stalin's Spy*, p. 316.

10 Murphy, *What Stalin Knew*, p. 90.

11 Quoted in Braithwaite, *Moscow 1941*, p. 228.

12 Ibid., p. 229.

13 Ibid., p. 256.

14 Sebag Montefiore, *Stalin*, p. 357.

15 See Braithwaite, *Moscow 1941*, pp. 279–80.

16 Werth, *Russia at War*, p. 236.

17 Ibid., p. 238; Braithwaite, *Moscow 1941*, p. 280.

18 Gorinov, 'Muscovites' Moods', in Thurston and Bonwetsch, *The People's War*, p. 114.

19 Braithwaite, *Moscow 1941*, pp. 284–7; Cassidy, *Moscow Dateline*, p. 125; Werth, *Russia at War*, p. 238.

20 Werth, *Russia at War*, pp. 238–9.

21 Quoted in David Stahel, *The Battle for Moscow* (Cambridge University Press, 2015), p. 83.

22 Quoted in Kershaw, *War Without Garlands*, p. 455.

23 Quoted ibid.

24 Ilya Ehrenburg, *The War, 1941–45*, trans. Tatiana Shebunina (MacGibbon and Kee, 1964).

25 Quoted in Thurston and Bonwetsch, *The People's War*, p. 126.

26 Quoted in Gorinov, 'Muscovites' Moods', in Thurston and Bonwetsch, *The People's War*, p. 126.

27 Ibid.

27. The Final Assault

1 Quoted in Stahel, *The Battle for Moscow*, p. 71.

2 Guderian, *Panzer Leader*, p. 246.

3 Franz A. P. Frisch and Wilbur D. Jones Jr, *Condemned to Live: A Panzer Artilleryman's Five-Front War* (Burd Street, 2000), p. 85.

4 Hürter, *Letters and Diaries of Gotthard Heinrici*, 8 November 1941, p. 102.

5 Ibid., 5–7 November 1941, p. 102.

6 Quoted in Stahel, *The Battle for Moscow*, p. 75.

7 For further details, see ibid., pp. 75–6.

8 Bock, *War Diary*, 11 November 1941.

9 Quoted in Stahel, *The Battle for Moscow*, p. 78.

10 Bock, *War Diary*, 11 November 1941.

11 Guderian, *Panzer Leader*, pp. 247–8.

12 Hürter, *Letters and Diaries of Gotthard Heinrici*, 15 November 1941, pp. 103–4.

13 Ibid.

14 Ibid., 19 November 1941, p. 107.

15 Guderian, *Panzer Leader*, p. 249.

16 Private letter, 17 November, quoted ibid.

17 Ibid., p. 251.

18 Bock, *War Diary*, 16 November 1941.

19 Ibid., 14, 15, 16 November 1941.

20 Guderian, *Panzer Leader*, p. 252.

21 Bock, *War Diary*, 18 November 1941.

22 Zhukov, *Greatest Battles*, pp. 64–5.

23 Sebag Montefiore, *Stalin*, p. 359; Zhukov, *Greatest Battles*, pp. 66–7.

24 Quoted in Braithwaite, *Moscow 1941*, p. 291.

25 Captured German Report, cited ibid.

26 Zhukov, *Greatest Battles*, p. 67.

27 Jones, *The Retreat*, p. 92.

28 Ibid., p. 93; Braithwaite, *Moscow 1941*, p. 295; Stahel, *The Battle for Moscow*, p. 144.

29 See Braithwaite, *Moscow 1941*, p. 296.

30 Overy, *Russia's War*, p. 117.

31 'Putin Backs WW2 Myth in New Russian Film', BBC News, 11 October 2016, www.bbc.co.uk/news/world-europe-37595972.

32 Order No. 428, quoted in Lyuba Vinogradova, *Avenging Angels: Soviet Women Snipers on the Eastern Front (1941–45)*, trans. Arch Tait (MacLehose, 2017), p. 96.

33 Ibid., pp. 96–8.

34 Quoted in Jones, *The Retreat*, p. 95.

35 Quoted ibid., pp. 95–6.

36 Haape, *Moscow Tram Stop*, quoted in Kershaw, *War Without Garlands*, p. 498.

37 Haape, *Moscow Tram Stop*, quoted in Stahel, *The Battle for Moscow*, p. 132.

38 Quoted in Jones, *The Retreat*, p. 79.

39 Rokossovsky quoted in Bialer, *Stalin & His Generals*, p. 296.

40 Zhukov, *Greatest Battles*, p. 69.

41 Ibid., p. 70.

42 Cited in Kershaw, *War Without Garlands*, p. 503.

43 Ibid., pp. 503–4.

44 Quoted in Stahel, *The Battle for Moscow*, p. 151.

45 Quoted in Jones, *The Retreat*, p. 123.

46 Quoted ibid.

47 Quoted in Kershaw, *War Without Garlands*, p. 504.

48 Quoted in Jones, *The Retreat*, p. 104.

49 Quoted ibid., p. 123.

50 Quoted ibid., p. 103.

51 Quoted in Kershaw, *War Without Garlands*, p. 522.

52 Quoted in Jones, *The Retreat*, p. 112.

53 Quoted in Stahel, *The Battle for Moscow*, p. 201.

54 Bock, *War Diary*, 23 November 1941.

55 Ibid., 29 November 1941.

56 Burdick and Jacobsen, *Halder War Diary*, 30 November 1941.

57 Stahel, *The Battle for Moscow*, p. 258.

58 Wagner to Halder, 27 November 1941, cited ibid., p. 227.

28. The Fateful Terminus

1 Quoted in Erickson, *The Road to Stalingrad*, p. 258.

2 Zhukov, *Greatest Battles*, p. 72.

3 Quoted in Erickson, *The Road to Stalingrad*, p. 258.

4 Zhukov, *Greatest Battles*, p. 86.

5 Ibid., pp. 86–8.

6 See Jones, *The Retreat*, p. 122.

7 Quoted in Shukman, *Stalin's Generals*, p. 50.

8 Guderian, *Panzer Leader*, p. 257.

9 Ibid., p. 255.

10 See Stahel, *The Battle for Moscow*, p. 158.

11 Hürter, *Letters and Diaries of Gotthard Heinrici*, 1 December 1941, pp. 109–10.

12 Bock, *War Diary*, 30 November 1941.

13 Ibid.

14 Ibid., 1 December 1941.

15 Ibid.

16 Burdick and Jacobsen, *Halder War Diary*, 1 December 1941.

17 Bock, *War Diary*, 2 December 1941.

18 General I. V. Boldin, *Stranitsy zhizni* (Pages of Life) (Voyenizdat, 1961), cited in Werth, *Russia at War*, p. 246.

19 Hürter, *Letters and Diaries of Gotthard Heinrici*, 4 December 1941, pp. 110–12.

20 Quoted in Jones, *The Retreat*, p. 134.

21 Boldin, *Stranitsy zhizni*, cited in Werth, *Russia at War*, p. 246.

22 Hürter, *Letters and Diaries of Gotthard Heinrici*, 5 December 1941, p. 113.

23 See Stahel, *The Battle for Moscow*, pp. 281–2.

24 Hürter, *Letters and Diaries of Gotthard Heinrici*, 5 December 1941, p. 113.

25 Kenneth Andrew and David Garden (eds.), *The War Diaries of a Panzer Soldier: Erich Hager with the 17th Panzer Division on the Russian Front 1941–1945* (Schiffer, 2010), p. 60, cited in Stahel, *The Battle for Moscow*, p. 294.

26 Panzer Corps War Diary, cited ibid.

27 Quoted ibid.

28 Quoted ibid., p. 295.

29 Ibid.

30 Bock, *War Diary*, 3 December 1941.

31 Ibid., 5 December 1941.

32 Ibid., 3 December 1941.

33 Quoted in Stahel, *The Battle for Moscow*, p. 307.

34 Quoted ibid., p. 307.

35 Bock, *War Diary*, 5 December 1941.

36 Stahel, *The Battle for Moscow*, pp. 296–7.

37 Haape, *Moscow Tram Stop*, p. 206.

38 Bock, *War Diary*, 7 December 1941.

39 Burdick and Jacobsen, *Halder War Diary*, 7 December 1941.

40 Ibid.

29. A Global War

1 The National WWII Museum, New Orleans, 'A Pearl Harbor Fact Sheet', www.census.gov/history/pdf/pearl-harbor-fact-sheet-1.pdf.

2 Churchill, *The Grand Alliance*, pp. 537–8.

3 Ibid., p. 539.

4 Ibid., pp. 540.

5 Harvey, *War Diaries*, 18 November 1941.

6 Churchill, *The Grand Alliance*, p. 541.

7 Eden, *Eden Memoirs: The Reckoning*, p. 283; Harvey, *War Diaries*, p. 65; Churchill, *The Grand Alliance*, p. 470.

8 Churchill to Stalin, 21 November 1941, Churchill, *The Grand Alliance*, p. 472.

9 Prime minister to Field Marshal Mannerheim, 29 November 1941, ibid., p. 474.

10 Field Marshal Mannerheim to prime minister, 2 December 1941, ibid.

11 Field Marshal Lord Alanbrooke, *War Diaries, 1939–1945*, ed. Alex Danchev and Daniel Todman (Phoenix Press, 2002), 3 December 1941.

12 Ibid.

13 Ibid., 4 December 1941, p. 207.

14 Cripps to Churchill, Personal and Secret, Gorodetsky, *Stafford Cripps in Moscow*, 15 November 1941.

15 Churchill, *The Grand Alliance*, p. 477.

16 Eden, *Eden Memoirs: The Reckoning*, p. 282.

17 Harvey, *War Diaries*, 17 November 1941.

18 Dilks, *Cadogan Diaries*, 27 November 1941.

19 Ibid., 28 November 1941.

20 Harvey, *War Diaries*, 8 December 1941.

21 Dilks, *Cadogan Diaries*, 8 December 1941.

22 Churchill, *The Grand Alliance*, p. 555.

23 Alanbrooke, *War Diaries*, 8 December 1941.

24 Harvey, *War Diaries*, 8 December 1941.

25 Dilks, *Cadogan Diaries*, 13 December 1941.

26 Ibid.; Eden, *Eden Memoirs: The Reckoning*, p. 289.

27 Prime minister to Mr Eden (at sea), 10 December 1941, Churchill, *The Grand Alliance*, p. 554.

28 Prime minister to Mr Eden (at sea), 12 December 1941, ibid., p. 554.

30. The Retreat

1 Quoted in Roberts, *Stalin's General*, p. 143.

2 Quoted in Jones, *The Retreat*, p. 140.

3 Quoted in Stahel, *The Battle for Moscow*, p. 255.

4 Quoted in Jones, *The Retreat*, p. 141.

5 See ibid., pp. 141–2.

6 Quoted ibid., pp. 54–5.

7 Quoted ibid., p. 111.

8 Quoted ibid., p. 144.

9 Letter home of 19 December 1941, quoted in Kershaw, *War Without Garlands*, p. 546.

10 Quoted in Jones, *The Retreat*, p. 144.

11 Quoted in Tooze, *The Wages of Destruction*, p. 500; Kershaw, *War Without Garlands*, p. 541.

12 Hürter, *Letters and Diaries of Gotthard Heinrici*, 16 December 1941, p. 120.

13 Quoted in Jones, *The Retreat*, p. 143.

14 Quoted ibid.

15 Haape, *Moscow Tram Stop*, p. 172.

16 Ibid., p. 163.

17 Glantz and House, *When Titans Clashed*, p. 292

18 Collection, *Poslednie pisma s fronta* (Last Letters from the Front), vol. I (Molodaya gvardiya, 1983), trans. Lyuba Vinogradova (unpaginated).

19 Ibid.

20 Ibid.

21 Ibid.

22 Ibid.

23 Vasily Grossman, *Stalingrad, A Novel*, trans. Robert and Elizabeth Chandler (Harvill Secker, 2019), pp. 278–9.

24 Burdick and Jacobsen, *Halder War Diary*, 6 December 1941.

25 Ibid., 9 December 1941.

26 Directive No. 39, 8 December 1941, Trevor-Roper, *Hitler's War Directives*.

27 Below, *At Hitler's Side*, p. 118.

28 Ibid., p. 119.

29 Bock, *War Diary*, 10 December 1941.

30 Ibid., 13 December 1941.

31 OKW Order, Führer Headquarters, 16 December 1941, quoted in Glantz, *Before Stalingrad*, p. 286.

32 Bock, *War Diary*, 16 December 1941.

33 Burdick and Jacobsen, *Halder War Diary*, 16 December 1941.

34 Bock, *War Diary*, 18 December 1941.

35 Interview in Kershaw, *War Without Garlands*, pp. 532–3.

36 Quoted ibid., p. 528.

37 Alexander Nogaller, 'Memoirs, December 1941–February 1942', www.uvarovka.ru, translated for the author by Lyuba Vinogradova.

38 Glantz, *Before Stalingrad*, p. 183.

39 Quoted in Shukman, *Stalin's Generals*, p. 352.

40 Interview in Kershaw, *War Without Garlands*, p. 530.

41 Quoted in Werth, *Russia at War*, pp. 261–2.

42 Haape, *Moscow Tram Stop*, pp. 167–8.

43 Ehrenburg, *The War, 1941–45*, p. 34, for this and what follows.

44 Quoted ibid., p. 38.

45 Ibid., p. 36.

46 Quoted ibid., p. 38.

31. Eden Meets Stalin

1 Werth, *Moscow '41*, pp. 121–3.

2 Cited in Braithwaite, *Moscow 1941*, p. 309.

3 See ibid., p. 318.

4 See Glantz, *Before Stalingrad*, p. 200.

5 Sakharov, *Memoirs*, p. 45.

6 Harvey, *War Diaries*, 15 December 1941; Dilks, *Cadogan Diaries*, 15 December 1941; Eden, *Eden Memoirs: The Reckoning*, pp. 288–9.

7 Dilks, *Cadogan Diaries*, 16 December 1941.

8 Harvey, *War Diaries*, 16 December 1941.

9 Dilks, *Cadogan Diaries*, editor's note, p. 420.

10 Ibid., 16 December 1941.

11 Eden, *Eden Memoirs: The Reckoning*, diary entry of 16 December 1941, p. 289.

12 Ibid.

13 Ibid., p. 290.

14 Verbatim extract, ibid., p. 293.

15 Gorodetsky, *Stafford Cripps in Moscow*, 17 December 1941.

16 Verbatim extracts, *Eden Memoirs: The Reckoning*, diary entry of 17 December 1941; Dilks, *Cadogan Diaries*, 17 December 1941; Gorodetsky, *Stafford Cripps in Moscow*, 18 December 1941; Harvey, *War Diaries*, 18 December 1941.

17 Dilks, *Cadogan Diaries*, 17 December 1941.

18 Harvey, *War Diaries*, 18 December 1941.

19 Gorodetsky, *Stafford Cripps in Moscow*, 18 December 1941.

20 Harvey, *War Diaries*, 18 December 1941.

21 Ibid.

22 Ibid.

23 Gorodetsky, *Stafford Cripps in Moscow*, 18 December 1941.

24 Eden, *Eden Memoirs: The Reckoning*, p. 299.

25 Dilks, *Cadogan Diaries*, 20 December 1941.

26 Eden, *Eden Memoirs: The Reckoning*, p. 289.

27 Harvey, *War Diaries*, 6 January 1942.

28 Prime minister to Foreign Secretary, 8 January 1942, Churchill, *The Grand Alliance*, pp. 615–16.

29 Memorandum, 28 January 1942, quoted in Eden, *Eden Memoirs: The Reckoning*, p. 318.

30 Ibid., p. 302.

31 Ibid., pp. 298–9.

32. The Fatal Gamble

1 Charles Messenger, *The Last Prussian: A Biography of Field Marshal Gerd von Rundstedt, 1875–1953* (Pen & Sword, 2018), p. 155.

2 Taylor, *The Goebbels Diaries*, 20 March 1942.

3 Bock, *War Diary*, 16 December 1941.

4 Ibid.

5 Quoted in Kershaw, *Hitler, 1936–1945*, p. 453.

6 Quoted in Jones, *The Retreat*, pp. 186–7.

7 Quoted ibid., pp. 187–8.

8 Guderian, *Panzer Leader*, p. 262.

9 See ibid.

10 Ibid., p. 263.

11 www.jewishvirtuallibrary.org/joseph-goebbels-plea-for-clothing-for-troops-on-the-russian-front-and-hitler-s-proclamation.

12 Guderian, *Panzer Leader*, pp. 265–8.

13 Burdick and Jacobsen, *Halder War Diary*, 21 December 1941.

14 Ibid., 21, 22 December 1941.

15 Macksey, *Guderian*, p. 159.

16 Quoted in Jones, *The Retreat*, p. 234.

17 Colonel Adolf Heusinger, quoted in Warlimont, *Inside Hitler's Headquarters*, p. 222.

18 Quoted in Macksey, *Guderian*, p. 160.

19 Quoted in Warlimont, *Inside Hitler's Headquarters*, pp. 213–14.

20 Quoted in Jones, *The Retreat*, p. 235.

21 Warlimont, *Inside Hitler's Headquarters*, p. 223.

22 Quoted in Below, *At Hitler's Side*, p. 126.

23 Evans, *The Third Reich at War*, pp. 210–12.

24 Quoted in Kershaw, *Hitler, 1936–1945*, p. 453.

25 Haape, *Moscow Tram Stop*, p. 215.

26 Hürter, *Letters and Diaries of Gotthard Heinrici*, 22, 24 December 1941, pp. 123–4.

27 Burdick and Jacobsen, *Halder War Diary*, 29, 30, 31 December 1941.

28 Ibid., 2 January 1942.

29 Quoted in Warlimont, *Inside Hitler's Headquarters*, p. 215.

30 Haape, *Moscow Tram Stop*, p. 217.

31 Ibid., p. 218.

32 See Kershaw, *Hitler, 1936–1945*, p. 455.

33 Burdick and Jacobsen, *Halder War Diary*, 5 January 1942.

34 Glantz, *Before Stalingrad*, p. 200.

35 Tooze, *The Wages of Destruction*, p. 488.

36 Glantz, *Before Stalingrad*, p. 200.

37 Ibid.

38 Stahel, *Operation Barbarossa*, p. 442.

39 Richard Overy, 'Statistics', in Ian Dear and M. R. D. Foot (eds.), *The Oxford Companion to the Second World War* (Oxford University Press, 1995), table 2: Military Production, p. 1060, cited in Stahel, *Operation Barbarossa*, p. 441.

40 Bock, *War Diary*, 7 August 1941.

41 Quoted in Tooze, *The Wages of Destruction*, p. 488.

42 Burdick and Jacobsen, *Halder War Diary*, 11 August 1941.

43 Gotthard Heinrici, 'The Campaign in Russia', vol. I, Washington DC, United States Army G-2, 1954, unpublished National Archives manuscript report translated by Joseph Welsh, p. 190, cited in Glantz, *Before Stalingrad*, pp. 202–3.

Epilogue

1 Neues Europa, Adolf Hitler – New Year's Proclamation, 1 January 1942, der-fuehrer.org/reden/English/42-01-01.htm.

2 Warlimont, *Inside Hitler's Headquarters*, pp. 207–8.

3 Winston Churchill, *The Second World War*, vol. IV: *The Hinge of Fate* (Cassell, 1951), p. 290.

4 Ibid.

5 Dallek, *Franklin D. Roosevelt*, p. 324.

6 Ibid., p. 322.

7 Roosevelt, *Roosevelt Letters*, vol. III, p. 423.

8 Quoted in Dallek, *Franklin D. Roosevelt*, p. 344.

9 Churchill, *The Hinge of Fate*, p. 305.

10 Quoted in Hastings, *Finest Years*, p. 424.

11 Quoted in Roberts, *Masters and Commanders*, p. 251.

12 Churchill to Roosevelt, Churchill, *The Hinge of Fate*, 8 July 1942, p. 392.

13 Churchill to Stalin, 17 July 1942, in Reynolds and Pechatnov, *The Kremlin Letters*, pp. 124–7.

14 Ibid., p. 129.

15 Quoted ibid., p. 148.

16 Ibid., p. 143.

17 Churchill to Hopkins, Churchill, *The Hinge of Fate*, p. 103.

18 Captain S. W. Roskill, *The War at Sea 1939–1945*, vol. II: *The Period of Balance* (Naval and Military Press, 2009), p. 15.

19 In correspondence with the author.

20 Quoted in David Stahel, *Retreat from Moscow: A New History of Germany's Winter Campaign, 1941–1942* (Farrar, Straus and Giroux, 2019), p. 373.

21 Overy, 'Statistics', table 2, cited in Stahel, *Operation Barbarossa*, p. 442.

22 Beevor, *Stalingrad*, pp. xiii–xiv.

23 Ibid., p. 48.

24 Adolf Hitler Speech at the Berlin Sportpalast, 30 January 1942, quoted in Kershaw, *Hitler, 1936–1945*, p. 494.

25 Quoted ibid.

26 Quoted ibid., p. 495.

27 Rubenstein and Altman, *The Unknown Black Book*, p. 246.

28 Hubert P. van Tuyll, *Feeding the Bear: American Aid to the Soviet Union, 1941–1945* (Greenwood Press, 1989), table 16, Shipments from the Western Hemisphere to the USSR, p. 164.

29 Quoted ibid., p. 73.

30 Quoted ibid., p. 139.

31 Quoted ibid., p. 73.

32 Quoted ibid., p. 138.

33 Memorandum, 28 January 1941, quoted in Eden, *Eden Memoirs: The Reckoning*, p. 318.

34 Churchill to Eden, 8 January 1941, Churchill, *The Grand Alliance*, pp. 615–16.

35 Memorandum, 28 January 1941, quoted in Eden, *Eden Memoirs: The Reckoning*, p. 318.

Select Bibliography

Alanbrooke, Field Marshal Lord, *War Diaries, 1939–1945*, ed. Alex Danchev and Daniel Todman (Phoenix Press, 2002)

Andrew, Christopher and Oleg Gordievsky, *KGB: The Inside Story of its Foreign Operations from Lenin to Gorbachev* (Hodder and Stoughton, 1990)

Applebaum, Anne, *Gulag: A History of the Soviet Camps* (Penguin, 2004)

———, *Red Famine: Stalin's War on Ukraine* (Penguin, 2018)

Axell, Albert, *Russia's Heroes, 1941–1945: True Stories of the Soviet Patriots Who Defied Hitler* (Magpie, 2010)

Bailey, Thomas A. and Paul B. Ryan, *Hitler vs. Roosevelt: The Undeclared Naval War* (The Free Press, 1979)

Bamm, Peter, *The Invisible Flag: A Report by Peter Bamm*, trans. Frank Herrmann (Penguin, 1962)

Barber, John and Mark Harrison, *The Soviet Home Front, 1941–1945: A Social and Economic History of the USSR in World War II* (Longman, 1991)

Bartov, Omer, *Hitler's Army: Soldiers, Nazis, and War in the Third Reich* (Oxford University Press, 1992)

Battistelli, Pier P., *Heinz Guderian: Leadership, Strategy, Conflict* (Osprey, 2011)

Becker, Hans, *Devil on My Shoulder*, trans. Kennedy McWhirter and Jeremy Potter (Jarrold, 1955)

Beevor, Antony, *Stalingrad* (Penguin, 1999)

———, *The Second World War* (Weidenfeld and Nicolson, 2012)

Beevor, Antony and Luba [sic] Vinogradova (ed. and trans.), *A Writer at War: Vasily Grossman with the Red Army, 1941–1945* (Pimlico, 2006)

Bellamy, Chris, *Absolute War: Soviet Russia in the Second World War* (Macmillan, 2007)

Beloff, Max, *The Foreign Policy of Soviet Russia, 1929–1941*, vol. I: *1929–1936* (Oxford University Press, 1949)

———, *The Foreign Policy of Soviet Russia, 1929–1941*, vol. II: *1936–1941* (Oxford University Press, 1952)

Below, Nicolaus von, *At Hitler's Side: The Memoirs of Hitler's Luftwaffe Adjutant, 1937–1945*, trans. Geoffrey Brooks (Frontline, 2012)

Berezhkov, Valentin M., *At Stalin's Side: His Interpreter's Memoirs from the Octo-
    ber Revolution to the Fall of the Dictator's Empire*, trans. Sergei V. Mikheyev
    (Birch Lane, 1994)

Berkhoff, Karel C., *Harvest of Despair: Life and Death in Ukraine under Nazi Rule*
    (Harvard University Press, 2004)

Bialer, Seweryn (ed.), *Stalin & His Generals: Soviet Military Memoirs of World
    War II* (Souvenir Press, 1970)

Bock, General Field Marshal Fedor von, *The War Diary, 1939–1945*, ed. Klaus
    Gerbet, trans. David Johnston (Schiffer, 1996)

Boog, Horst, Jürgen Förster, Joachim Hoffman, Ernst Klink, Rolf-Dieter
    Müller and Gerd R. Ueberschär, *Germany and the Second World War*, vol. IV:
    The Attack on the Soviet Union, trans. Dean McMurry, Ewald Osers and Lou-
    ise Willmot (Clarendon, 1998)

Bornstein, Ernst Israel, *The Long Night: A True Story* (Toby, 2015)

Bouverie, Tim, *Appeasing Hitler: Chamberlain, Churchill and the Road to War*
    (Bodley Head, 2019)

Braithwaite, Rodric, *Moscow 1941: A City and Its People at War* (Profile, 2007)

Brownell, Will and Richard N. Billings, *So Close to Greatness: A Biography of
    William C. Bullitt* (Macmillan, 1987)

Browning, Christopher R., *Fateful Months: Essays on the Emergence of the Final
    Solution* (Holmes and Meier, 1991)

———, *Ordinary Men: Reserve Police Battalion 101 and the Final Solution in Poland*
    (Penguin, 2001)

———, *The Origins of the Final Solution: The Evolution of Nazi Jewish Policy,
    1939–1942* (Arrow, 2005)

Bryant, Arthur, *The Turn of the Tide, 1939–1943: A Study Based on the Diaries and
    Autobiographical Notes of Field Marshal the Viscount Alanbrooke* (Collins, 1957)

———, *Triumph in the West: Completing the War Diaries of Field Marshal Viscount
    Alanbrooke* (Collins, 1959)

Bullock, Alan, *Hitler: A Study in Tyranny* (Penguin, 1986)

———, *Hitler and Stalin: Parallel Lives* (HarperCollins, 1991)

Burdick, Charles and Hans-Adolf Jacobsen (eds.), *The Halder War Diary,
    1939–1942* (Presidio, 1988)

Burleigh, Michael, *The Third Reich: A New History* (Pan, 2001)

Caddick-Adams, Peter, *Snow and Steel: The Battle of the Bulge, 1944–45* (Arrow,
    2014)

Calder, Angus, *The People's War: Britain 1939–1945* (Granada, 1982)

Carley, Michael J., *1939: The Alliance That Never Was and the Coming of World War II* (Ivan R. Dee, 1999)

Carr, Edward H., *German–Soviet Relations: Between the Two World Wars, 1919–1939* (Johns Hopkins University Press, 1954)

Cassidy, Henry C., *Moscow Dateline, 1941–1943* (Cassell, 1943)

Cesarani, David, *Final Solution: The Fate of the Jews 1933–49* (Macmillan, 2016)

Churchill, Winston S., *Secret Session Speeches* (Cassell, 1946)

———, *The Second World War*, vol. I: *The Gathering Storm* (Cassell, 1948)

———, *The Second World War*, vol. II: *Their Finest Hour* (Cassell, 1949)

———, *The Second World War*, vol. III: *The Grand Alliance* (Cassell, 1950)

———, *The Second World War*, vol. IV: *The Hinge of Fate* (Cassell, 1951)

———, *The Second World War*, vol. V: *Closing the Ring* (Cassell, 1952)

———, *The Second World War*, vol. VI: *Triumph and Tragedy* (Cassell, 1954)

Clark, Alan, *Barbarossa: The Russian-German Conflict, 1941–45* (Cassell, 2012)

Clarke, Peter, *The Cripps Version: The Life of Sir Stafford Cripps, 1889–1952* (Allen Lane, 2002)

Colville, John, *The Fringes of Power: Downing Street Diaries, 1939–1955* (Weidenfeld and Nicolson, 2004)

Conquest, Robert, *The Harvest of Sorrow: Soviet Collectivization and the Terror-Famine* (Pimlico, 2002)

Craig, Gordon A., *Germany, 1866–1945* (Oxford University Press, 1984)

Dallek, Robert, *Franklin D. Roosevelt and American Foreign Policy, 1932–1945* (Oxford University Press, 1995)

Davies, Joseph E., *Mission to Moscow* (Victor Gollancz, 1944)

Dawson, Raymond H., *The Decision to Aid Russia, 1941: Foreign Policy and Domestic Politics* (University of North Carolina Press, 1959)

Deane, John R., *The Strange Alliance: The Story of American Efforts at Wartime Co-operation with Russia* (John Murray, 1947)

Dilks, David (ed.), *The Diaries of Sir Alexander Cadogan, 1938–1945* (Faber & Faber, 2010)

Dimbleby, Jonathan, *Destiny in the Desert: The Road to El Alamein – The Battle that Turned the Tide* (Profile, 2013)

———, *The Battle of the Atlantic: How the Allies Won the War* (Penguin, 2016)

Dimitrov, Georgi, *The Diary of Georgi Dimitrov, 1933–1949*, ed. Ivo Banac, trans. Jane T. Hedges, Timothy D. Sergay and Irina Faion (Yale University Press, 2003)

Eden, Anthony (Earl of Avon), *The Eden Memoirs: The Reckoning* (Cassell, 1965)

Ehrenburg, Ilya, *The War, 1941–45*, trans. Tatiana Shebunina (MacGibbon and Kee, 1964)

Ehrenburg, Ilya and Vasily Grossman (eds.), *The Black Book: The Ruthless Murder of Jews by German-Fascist Invaders Throughout the Temporarily Occupied Regions of the Soviet Union and in the Death Camps of Poland During the War of 1941–1945*, trans. John Glad and James S. Levine (Holocaust Library, 1981)

Eisenhower, Dwight D., *The Eisenhower Diaries*, ed. Robert H. Ferrell (W. W. Norton, 1981)

Engel, Gerhard, *At the Heart of the Reich: The Secret Diary of Hitler's Army Adjutant*, trans. Geoffrey Brooks (Frontline, 2017)

Erickson, John, *The Road to Stalingrad: Stalin's War with Germany*, vol. I (Cassell, 2003)

Evans, Richard J., *The Third Reich in Power: How the Nazis Won Over the Hearts and Minds of a Nation* (Penguin, 2006)

———, *The Third Reich at War: How the Nazis Led Germany from Conquest to Disaster* (Penguin, 2009)

Fallada, Hans, *Alone in Berlin*, trans. Michael Hofmann (Penguin, 2009)

Frisch, Franz A. P. and Wilbur D. Jones, Jr, *Condemned to Live: A Panzer Artilleryman's Five-Front War* (Burd Street, 2000)

Gamache, Ray, *Gareth Jones: Eyewitness to the Holodomor* (Welsh Academic Press, 2016)

Garrard, John and Carol Garrard, *The Bones of Berdichev: The Life and Fate of Vasily Grossman* (The Free Press, 1996)

Gibson, Hugh (ed.), *The Ciano Diaries, 1939–1943: The Complete Unabridged Diaries of Count Galeazzo Ciano, Italian Minister for Foreign Affairs* (Simon Publications, 2001)

Gilbert, Martin, *The Holocaust: The Jewish Tragedy* (Collins, 1986)

Glantz, David M., *Before Stalingrad: Barbarossa – Hitler's Invasion of Russia, 1941* (Tempus, 2003; repr. as *Operation Barbarossa: Hitler's Invasion of Russia, 1941*, The History Press, 2011)

———, *The Siege of Leningrad, 1941–1944: 900 Days of Terror* (Cassell, 2004)

Glantz, David M. and Jonathan House, *When Titans Clashed: How the Red Army Stopped Hitler* (University Press of Kansas, 1995)

Gorodetsky, Gabriel, *Grand Delusion: Stalin and the German Invasion of Russia* (Yale University Press, 1999)

Gorodetsky, Gabriel (ed.), *Stafford Cripps in Moscow, 1940–1942: Diaries and Papers* (Vallentine Mitchell, 2007)

———, *Stafford Cripps' Mission to Moscow, 1940–42* (Cambridge University Press, 1984)

———, *The Maisky Diaries: Red Ambassador to the Court of St James's, 1932–1943*, trans. Tatiana Sorokina and Oliver Ready (Yale University Press, 2015)

Gregory, James S., *Land of the Soviets* (Pelican, 1946)

Grossman, Vasily, *Everything Flows*, trans. Robert and Elizabeth Chandler (Harvill Secker, 2010)

Guderian, Heinz, *Panzer Leader*, trans. Constantine Fitzgibbon (Penguin, 2009)

Haape, Heinrich, *Moscow Tram Stop: A Doctor's Experiences with the German Spearhead in Russia* (Collins, 1957; repr. Stackpole, 2020)

Halder, Franz, *Hitler as War Lord*, trans. Paul Findlay (Putnam, 1950)

Harriman, William Averell and Elie Abel, *Special Envoy to Churchill and Stalin, 1941–1946* (Random House, 1975)

Harvey, John (ed.), *The Diplomatic Diaries of Oliver Harvey, 1937–1940* (Collins, 1970)

———, *The War Diaries of Oliver Harvey, 1941–1945* (Collins, 1978)

Hastings, Max, *Nemesis: The Battle for Japan, 1944–45* (Harper, 2007)

———, *Finest Years: Churchill as Warlord, 1940–45* (Harper, 2009)

———, *All Hell Let Loose: The World at War, 1939–1945* (Harper, 2011)

———, *Overlord: D-Day and the Battle for Normandy, 1944* (Pan, 2015)

———, *The Secret War: Spies, Codes and Guerrillas, 1939–1945* (William Collins, 2015)

Hattersley, Roy, *David Lloyd George: The Great Outsider* (Abacus, 2012)

Heinrichs, Waldo, *Threshold of War: Franklin D. Roosevelt and American Entry into World War II*, eds. Mac Gallichio and Jonathan Utley (Oxford University Press, 1989)

———, *Diplomacy and Force: America's Road to War, 1931–1941*, eds. Marc Gallichio and Jonathan Utley (Imprint, 1996)

Herf, Jeffrey, *The Jewish Enemy: Nazi Propaganda During World War II and the Holocaust* (Harvard University Press, 2008)

Herman, Arthur, *Freedom's Forge: How American Business Produced Victory in World War II* (Random House, 2012)

Hilberg, Raul, *The Destruction of the European Jews* (Holmes and Meier, 1985)

Hinsley, Francis H. with E. E. Thomas, C. F. G. Ransom and R. C. Knight, *British Intelligence in the Second World War: Its Influence on Strategy and Operations*, 4 vols. (HMSO, 1979–90)

Hirschfeld, Gerhard, *The Policies of Genocide: Jews and Soviet Prisoners of War in Nazi Germany* (Allen & Unwin, 1986)

Hitler, Adolf, *Hitler's Table Talk, 1941–1944*, trans. Norman Cameron and R. H. Stevens (Oxford University Press, 1988)

———, *Mein Kampf*, 2 vols., trans. Ralph Manheim (Pimlico, 1992)

Hoth, Hermann, *Panzer Operations: Germany's Panzer Group 3 during the Invasion of Russia, 1941*, trans. Linden Lyons (Casemate, 2015)

Hürter, Johannes (ed.), *A German General on the Eastern Front: The Letters and Diaries of Gotthard Heinrici, 1941–1942*, trans. Christine Brocks (Pen and Sword, 2014)

Ismay, Lord, *The Memoirs of General the Lord Ismay* (Heinemann, 1960)

James, Sir Robert Rhodes (ed.), *'Chips': The Diaries of Sir Henry Channon* (Phoenix, 1996)

Jarausch, Konrad H. (ed.), *Reluctant Accomplice: A Wehrmacht Soldier's Letters from the Eastern Front* (Princeton, 2011)

Jones, Michael, *The Retreat: Hitler's First Defeat* (John Murray, 2009)

Jordan, Philip, *Russian Glory* (Cresset Press, 1942)

Kay, Alex J., Jeff Rutherford and David Stahel (eds.), *Nazi Policy on the Eastern Front, 1941: Total War, Genocide, and Radicalization* (University of Rochester Press, 2012)

Keitel, Wilhelm, *In the Service of the Reich*, ed. Walter Gorlitz, trans. David Irving (Stein and Day, 1979)

Kennan, George F., *Memoirs, 1925–1950* (Pantheon, 1967)

Kennedy, John, *The Business of War: The War Narrative of Major General Sir John Kennedy* (Hutchinson, 1957)

Kershaw, Ian, *Hitler, 1889–1936: Hubris* (Penguin, 2001)

———, *Hitler, 1936–1945: Nemesis* (Penguin, 2001)

———, *To Hell and Back: Europe 1914–1949* (Penguin, 2016)

Kershaw, Robert, *War Without Garlands: Operation Barbarossa, 1941–1942* (Ian Allen, 2000)

Khrushchev, Nikita, *Khrushchev Remembers The Last Testament*, ed. and trans. Strobe Talbott (Little, Brown and Company, 1970)

Klemperer, Victor, *I Shall Bear Witness: The Diaries of Victor Klemperer, 1933–41*, trans. Martin Chalmers (Weidenfeld and Nicolson, 1998)

Knappe, Siegfried with Ted Brusaw, *Soldat: Reflections of a German Soldier, 1936–1949* (Orion, 1992)

Koestler, Arthur, *The Yogi and the Commissar and Other Essays* (Cape, 1945)

———, *The Invisible Writing: The Second Volume of an Autobiography: 1932–40* (Hutchinson, 1979)

———, *Scum of the Earth* (Eland, 1991)

———, *Darkness at Noon*, trans. Daphne Hardy (Vintage, 1994)

Kopelev, Lev, *No Jail for Thought*, trans. Anthony Austin (Penguin, 1979)

———, *The Education of a True Believer*, trans. Gary Kern (Harper, 1978)

Kravchenko, Victor, *I Chose Freedom: The Personal and Political Life of a Soviet Official* (Robert Hale, 1947)

Littell, Robert, *The Stalin Epigram: A Novel* (Duckworth Overlook, 2010)

Lloyd George, David, *War Memoirs of David Lloyd George*, 2 vols. (Odhams, 1938)

Longerich, Peter, *The Unwritten Order: Hitler's Role in the Final Solution* (The History Press, 2016)

Lowenheim, Francis L., Harold D. Langley and Manfred Jonas (eds.), *Roosevelt and Churchill: Their Secret Wartime Correspondence* (Barrie and Jenkins, 1975)

Lucas, James, *War on the Eastern Front: The German Soldier in Russia, 1941–1945* (Greenhill, 1998)

Lukacs, John, *June 1941: Hitler and Stalin* (Yale University Press, 2006)

Macksey, Kenneth, *Guderian: Panzer General* (Greenhill, 1992)

MacMillan, Margaret, *Peacemakers: The Paris Peace Conference of 1919 and Its Attempt to End War* (John Murray, 2002)

Mandelstam, Osip, *Selected Poems*, trans. Clarence Brown and W. S. Merwin (New York Review Books, 2004)

Matthews, Owen, *An Impeccable Spy: Richard Sorge, Stalin's Master Agent* (Bloomsbury, 2019)

Medvedev, Roy and Zhores Medvedev, *The Unknown Stalin: His Life, Death and Legacy*, trans. Ellen Dahrendorf (Overlook, 2004)

Merridale, Catherine, *Ivan's War: The Red Army, 1939–45* (Faber & Faber, 2005)

Ministry of Foreign Affairs of the USSR (comp.), *Correspondence Between Stalin, Roosevelt, Truman, Churchill and Attlee During WWII* (University Press of the Pacific, 2001)

Moorhouse, Roger, *The Devil's Alliance: Hitler's Pact with Stalin, 1939–1941* (Vintage, 2016)

Mosley, Leonard, *Marshall: Hero for Our Times* (Hearst, 1982)

Murphy, David E., *What Stalin Knew: The Enigma of Barbarossa* (Yale University Press, 2005)

Neumann, Peter, *The Black March: The Personal Story of an SS Man*, trans. Constantine Fitzgibbon (Bantam, 1985)

Nicolson, Nigel (ed.), *Harold Nicolson: Diaries and Letters*, vol. II: *1939–45* (Collins, 1967)

Overy, Richard, *Why the Allies Won* (Pimlico, 2006)

———, *Russia's War* (Penguin, 2010)

Pabst, Helmut, *The Outermost Frontier: A German Soldier in the Russian Campaign* (William Kimber, 1957)

Padfield, Peter, *Dönitz: The Last Führer: Portrait of a Nazi War Leader* (Victor Gollancz, 1993)

Pimlott, Ben, *Hugh Dalton: A Life* (Harper, 1995)

Platonov, Andrey, *The Foundation Pit*, trans. Robert Chandler and Geoffrey Smith (Harvill, 1996)

Pritt, D. N., *Light on Moscow: Soviet Policy Analysed* (Penguin, 1939)

Prüller, Wilhelm, *Diary of a German Soldier*, ed. H. C. Robbins Landon and Sebastian Leitner (Coward-McCann, 1963)

Read, Anthony and David Fisher, *The Deadly Embrace: Hitler, Stalin and the Nazi–Soviet Pact, 1939–1941* (W. W. Norton, 1988)

Rees, Laurence, *World War II: Behind Closed Doors: Stalin, the Nazis and the West* (BBC Books, 2008)

———, *The Holocaust: A New History* (Viking, 2017)

———, *Hitler and Stalin: The Tyrants and the Second World War* (Penguin, 2020)

Reese, Roger R., *Stalin's Reluctant Soldiers: A Social History of the Red Army, 1925–1941* (University Press of Kansas, 1996)

———, *Why Stalin's Soldiers Fought: The Red Army's Military Effectiveness in World War II* (University Press of Kansas, 2011)

Reese, Willy P., *A Stranger to Myself: The Inhumanity of War: Russia, 1941–1944* (Farrar, Straus and Giroux, 2005)

Reuth, Ralf Georg, *Goebbels: The Life of Joseph Goebbels, the Mephistophelean Genius of Nazi Propaganda*, trans. Krishna Winston (Constable, 1995)

Reynolds, David, *From Munich to Pearl Harbor: Roosevelt's America and the Origins of the Second World War* (Ivan R. Dee, 2001)

Reynolds, David and Vladimir Pechatnov (eds.), *The Kremlin Letters: Stalin's Wartime Correspondence with Churchill and Roosevelt* (Yale University Press, 2018)

Richardson, Horst Fuchs (ed.), *Sieg Heil! War Letters of Tank Gunner Karl Fuchs, 1937–1941* (Archon, 1987)

Roberts, Andrew, *Masters and Commanders: How Roosevelt, Churchill, Marshall and Alanbrooke Won the War in the West* (Allen Lane, 2008)

———, *The Storm of War: A New History of the Second World War* (Penguin, 2010)

Roberts, Geoffrey, *Stalin's General: The Life of Georgy Zhukov* (Icon, 2013)

Roosevelt, Elliott (ed.), *The Roosevelt Letters*, vol. III: *1928–1945* (Harrap, 1952)

Rubenstein, Joshua and Ilya Altman (eds.), *The Unknown Black Book: The Holocaust in the German-Occupied Soviet Territories*, trans. Christopher Morris and Joshua Rubenstein (Indiana University Press, 2008)

Rudel, Hans Ulrich, *Stuka Pilot* (Black House, 2012)

Sajer, Guy, *The Forgotten Soldier: War on the Russian Front – A True Story* (Weidenfeld and Nicolson, 1999)

Sakharov, Andrei, *Memoirs*, trans. Richard Lourie (Hutchinson, 1990)

Salzmann, Stephanie C., *Great Britain, Germany and the Soviet Union: Rapallo and After, 1922–1934* (Royal Historical Society, 2013)

Schmidt, Paul, *Hitler's Interpreter: The Memoirs of Paul Schmidt* (The History Press, 2016)

Sebag Montefiore, Simon, *Stalin: The Court of the Red Tsar* (Weidenfeld and Nicolson, 2003)

———, *Enigma: The Battle for the Code* (Cassell, 2004)

Service, Robert, *Stalin: A Biography* (Pan, 2010)

Shalamov, Varlam, *Kolyma Tales*, trans. John Glad (Penguin, 1994)

Sherwood, Robert E., *The White House Papers of Harry L. Hopkins*, vol. I: *September 1939 – January 1942*; vol. II: *January 1942 – July 1945* (Eyre and Spottiswoode, 1948/1949)

Shirer, William L., *Berlin Diary: The Journal of a Foreign Correspondent, 1934–1941* (Knopf, 1941)

———, *The Rise and Fall of the Third Reich* (Pan, 1968)

Shukman, Harold (ed.), *Stalin's Generals* (Phoenix, 2001)

Snyder, Timothy, *Bloodlands: Europe Between Hitler and Stalin* (Vintage, 2011)

Soames, Mary (ed.), *Speaking for Themselves: The Personal Letters of Winston and Clementine Churchill* (Black Swan, 1999)

Spahr, William J., *Zhukov: The Rise and Fall of a Great Captain* (Presidio, 1995)

Speer, Albert, *Inside the Third Reich: Memoirs by Albert Speer*, trans. Richard and Clara Winston (Weidenfeld and Nicolson, 1970)

Stahel, David, *Operation Barbarossa and Germany's Defeat in the East* (Cambridge University Press, 2014)

————, *The Battle for Moscow* (Cambridge University Press, 2015)

————, *Operation Typhoon: Hitler's March on Moscow, October 1941* (Cambridge University Press, 2015)

————, *Retreat from Moscow: A New History of Germany's Winter Campaign, 1941–1942* (Farrar, Straus and Giroux, 2019)

Starinov, Colonel Ilya G., *Over the Abyss: My Life in Soviet Special Operations*, trans. Robert Suggs (Ivy Books, 1995)

Steinhoff, Johannes, Peter Pechel and Dennis Showalter, *Voices from the Third Reich: An Oral History* (Da Capo, 1994)

Taylor, A. J. P., *The Origins of the Second World War* (Penguin, 1991)

Taylor, Fred (ed.), *The Goebbels Diaries, 1939–1941: The Historic Journal of a Nazi War Leader* (Sphere, 1983)

Temkin, Gabriel, *My Just War: The Memoir of a Jewish Red Army Soldier in World War II* (Presidio, 1998)

Thurston, Robert W. and Bernd Bonwetsch (eds.), *The People's War: Response to World War II in the Soviet Union* (University of Illinois Press, 2000)

Tooze, Adam, *The Wages of Destruction: The Making and Breaking of the Nazi Economy* (Penguin, 2007)

Trevor-Roper, Hugh, *Hitler's War Directives, 1939–1945* (Birlinn, 2004)

Tzouliadis, Tim, *The Forsaken: An American Tragedy in Stalin's Russia* (Penguin, 2009)

van Tuyll, Hubert P., *Feeding the Bear: American Aid to the Soviet Union, 1941–1945* (Greenwood Press, 1989)

Vinogradova, Lyuba, *Defending the Motherland: The Soviet Women Who Fought Hitler's Aces*, trans. Arch Tait (MacLehose, 2015)

————, *Avenging Angels: Soviet Women Snipers on the Eastern Front (1941–45)*, trans. Arch Tait (MacLehose, 2017)

Volkogonov, Dmitri, *Stalin: Triumph and Tragedy*, ed. Harold Shukman (Forum, 1996)

Warlimont, Walter, *Inside Hitler's Headquarters, 1939–45*, trans. R. H. Barry (Presidio, 1964)

Webb, Beatrice, *The Diaries of Beatrice Webb*, ed. Norman and Jeanne MacKenzie (Virago, 2000)

Werth, Alexander, *Moscow '41* (Hamish Hamilton, 1942)

————, *Russia at War, 1941–1945* (Pan, 1964)

Wette, Wolfram, *The Wehrmacht: History, Myth, Reality*, trans. Deborah L. Schneider (Harvard University Press, 2006)

Whymant, Robert, *Stalin's Spy: Richard Sorge and the Tokyo Espionage Ring* (I. B. Tauris, 2013)

Wilson, Charles, *Churchill at War, 1940–45* (Robinson, 2002)

Wilson, Theodore A., *The First Summit: Roosevelt and Churchill at Placentia Bay, 1941* (Macdonald, 1969)

Yakovlev, Alexander N., *A Century of Violence in Soviet Russia*, trans. Anthony Austin (Yale University Press, 2002)

Zhukov, Georgi K., *Marshal Zhukov's Greatest Battles*, ed. Harrison E. Salisbury, trans. Theodore Shabad (Macdonald, 1969)

Zieser, Benno, *In Their Shallow Graves*, trans. Alec Brown (World Distributors, 1957)

———, *The Road to Stalingrad*, trans. Alec Brown (Ballantine, 1957)

Index

He just wanted a decent book to read ...

Not too much to ask, is it? It was in 1935 when Allen Lane, Managing Director of Bodley Head Publishers, stood on a platform at Exeter railway station looking for something good to read on his journey back to London. His choice was limited to popular magazines and poor-quality paperbacks – the same choice faced every day by the vast majority of readers, few of whom could afford hardbacks. Lane's disappointment and subsequent anger at the range of books generally available led him to found a company – and change the world.

'We believed in the existence in this country of a vast reading public for intelligent books at a low price, and staked everything on it'
Sir Allen Lane, 1902–1970, founder of Penguin Books

The quality paperback had arrived – and not just in bookshops. Lane was adamant that his Penguins should appear in chain stores and tobacconists, and should cost no more than a packet of cigarettes.

Reading habits (and cigarette prices) have changed since 1935, but Penguin still believes in publishing the best books for everybody to enjoy. We still believe that good design costs no more than bad design, and we still believe that quality books published passionately and responsibly make the world a better place.

So wherever you see the little bird – whether it's on a piece of prize-winning literary fiction or a celebrity autobiography, political tour de force or historical masterpiece, a serial-killer thriller, reference book, world classic or a piece of pure escapism – you can bet that it represents the very best that the genre has to offer.

Whatever you like to read – trust Penguin.